In the Seat of Moses

Westar Studies

The Westar Studies series offers distinctive scholarly publications on topics related to the field of Religious Studies. The studies seek to be multi-dimensional both in terms of the subject matter addressed and the perspective of the author. Westar Studies are not related to Westar seminars but offer scholars a deliberate space of free inquiry to engage both scholarly peers and the public.

In the Seat of Moses

*An Introductory Guide to Early Rabbinic
Legal Rhetoric and Literary Conventions*

Jack N. Lightstone

CASCADE *Books* • Eugene, Oregon

IN THE SEAT OF MOSES
An Introductory Guide to Early Rabbinic Legal Rhetoric and Literary Conventions

Westar Studies

Copyright © 2020 Jack N. Lightstone. All rights reserved. Except for brief quotations in critical publications or reviews, no part of this book may be reproduced in any manner without prior written permission from the publisher. Write: Permissions, Wipf and Stock Publishers, 199 W. 8th Ave., Suite 3, Eugene, OR 97401.

Cascade Books
An Imprint of Wipf and Stock Publishers
199 W. 8th Ave., Suite 3
Eugene, OR 97401

www.wipfandstock.com

PAPERBACK ISBN: 978-1-5326-5901-0
HARDCOVER ISBN: 978-1-5326-5902-7
EBOOK ISBN: 978-1-5326-5903-4

Cataloguing-in-Publication data:

Names: Lightstone, Jack N., author.

Title: In the seat of Moses : an introductory guide to early rabbinic legal rhetoric and literary conventions / Jack N. Lightstone.

Description: Eugene, OR: Cascade Books, 2020. | Westar Studies. | Includes bibliographical references and index.

Identifiers: ISBN 978-1-5326-5901-0 (paperback). | ISBN 978-1-5326-5902-7 (hardcover). | ISBN 978-1-5326-5903-4 (ebook).

Subjects: LCSH: Mishnah | Tosefta. | Halakhic Midrashim. | Talmud Yerushalmi. | Rabbinical literature—History and criticism. | Talmud. | Judaism—History—Talmudic period, 10–425.

Classification: BM496.5 L54. 2020 (print). | BM496.5 (ebook).

Manufactured in the U.S.A.   AUGUST 13, 2020

Scripture quotations are from the Revised Standard Version of the Bible, copyright © 1946, 1952, and 1971 National Council of the Churches of Christ in the United States of America. Used by permission. All rights reserved worldwide.

Contents

Preface | vii

1. Introduction | 1
2. Historical Contexts: Whence and Whither the Rabbis and Their Movement in Roman Palestine and Persian Babylonia? | 19
3. Early Rabbinic Legal Literature: A Brief Survey | 58
4. Mishnah | 109
5. Tosefta | 166
6. Halakhic Midrash | 230
7. The Two Talmuds: The Jerusalem Talmud | 284
8. The Two Talmuds: The Babylonian Talmud | 338
9. Final Thoughts: You and Early Rabbinic *Paideia* | 425

Bibliography | 455

Preface

The historical era commencing with Jesus' birth and ending with Muhammad's death was one of major political, cultural, and religious change and development in middle eastern and Mediterranean lands. Religious currents saw the Jesus movement emerge within Judaism and after a time, as "Christianity," displace paganism in Roman-ruled territory. Simultaneously, Jews experienced in 70 CE the loss of their Temple in Jerusalem in the Judean homeland, and with it the Temple-centered religious, civil, and administrative institutions. Much of the religious life enjoined in the Hebrew Scriptures thereby became defunct, and forms of Judah-ist cultural, civil, and religious practice that had begun to develop in the Diaspora even before the Temple's destruction by the Romans in 70 CE provided a template for Jews and early Christian communities alike in a formative and still-intertwined period of development for both.

So, what do we know from Jewish sources about Jews and Judaism in this formative era of late Roman imperial and early Roman-Byzantine times? By far the most significant and voluminous body of literature *about* Jews and Judaism *from* Jews was authored by the early rabbinic movement between c. 200 and 600 CE, first in the Land of Israel and second in Babylonia-Mesopotamia. These early rabbis produced a substantial body of homiletic and legal literature in which they articulated their understanding of Jewish life and ethos in accordance with God's will as revealed in Torah. Early rabbinic legal literature, in particular, expressed a life lived in accordance with Torah, and within several centuries of the rise of Islam, the rabbis and their rabbinic legal literature (authored between 200 and 600 CE) defined normative Jewish civil and religious practice for the vast majority of Jews in the middle east and Mediterranean worlds. Concomitantly, the early rabbis self-defined as the heirs of Moses, "restyled" Moses as a rabbi,

Preface

and declared rabbinic legal pronouncements, interpretations, and literature to be rooted in Mosaic revelation (his Oral Torah).

Yet early rabbinic legal literature is almost impenetrable, even in translation from the original Hebrew and Aramaic, for the reader not knowledgeable in this literature's core rhetorical and literary conventions and constructs. As explained more fully in chapter 1, this volume aims to make the principal documents of this early-rabbinic, legal corpus more accessible to the novice and nonspecialist reader by providing an introduction to these basic rhetorical and literary conventions and constructs. These are the keys and the code to deciphering this voluminous and important library of Judaic texts from late antiquity.

Given its aims, I have written this volume in a decidedly pedagogical and instructional style. Throughout I address the reader more directly and informally than one normally would in academic pose. The volume is composed in a manner meant to engage the reader. In fact, critical to getting the most out of this book is reader engagement in its pedagogy.

While this volume is founded on a great deal of academic research by specialists, including my own research, the book does not have the accoutrements of an academic specialist's research monograph. It is, by comparison to a research monograph, more lightly footnoted, and specialized academic debates about literary-historical issues related to these early rabbinic legal texts are often sidestepped. Only in chapters 2 and 9 do more "classic" footnotes appear abundantly because of the more directly historical nature of the arguments of these two chapters. Instead of an abundant use of academic-scholarly footnotes, the book provides at the ends of chapters 1 through 8 lists of recommended books and articles for the reader who wishes to delve more deeply into the related scholarship.

As I composed early drafts in this volume's chapters, I consulted a number of academic colleagues about many topics. I am grateful for the time they gave me and am humbled by their knowledge. I consulted William Scott Green, Meir Bar-Ilan, Nissan Rubin, and Lee I. Levine about the plan for this volume as a whole and/or about its first three chapters. In fact, Lee Levine graciously read and commented upon the first draft of chapter 2. Before writing chapters 7 and 8, I sat down to chat with Daniel Boyarin. His answers to my pointed questions helped me conceptualize a number of key issues at the heart of these chapters. Chapter 9, which attempts to demonstrate the social-historical meaning and significance of what readers acquired in working through chapters 4 through 8, brings

Preface

together the findings of three research papers (now published, soon to be in print, or under consideration for publication) that I initially wrote over the course of 2016 to 2019 and presented at the European Association of Biblical Studies. These papers benefited from the constructive comments and questions of Simcha Fishbane, Calvin Goldscheider, Shaye Cohen, Harry Fox, Tirzah Meacham, and Michael Satlow. Cassandra Farrin read the first draft of chapters 2 through 4 and provided valuable suggestions to improve the reader experience. David Galston, Arthur Dewey, and Barbara Hampson, all associated with the Westar Institute, encouraged my work on this volume and greatly contributed to its improvement along the way. I am grateful too for the invaluable work of the editors at Cascade Books in the preparation of the final version of this volume. To paraphrase an old aphorism: success has many parents, but failure is an orphan. This book benefited from all of these colleagues' work and sage advice, but this volume's failings are entirely attributable to me.

As already stated, not only others' scholarship underpins this book, but many of my own previously published research monographs and articles do as well. Since the early 1990s, I have been researching and writing about the rhetorical and literary conventions and constructs of early rabbinic legal literature and have argued that they are valuable social-historical evidence to be used in understanding the developing social identity of the early rabbinic movement. Five of my scholarly works in particular inform this book and are repeatedly referenced in its notes. Among my reliance on them are the original translations by me of a number of early rabbinic legal passages and compositions, which have either been reused in this volume or which informed revised versions of these translations in this volume. In these regards, I acknowledge the Canadian Corporation for Studies in Religion and Wilfrid Laurier University Press, the joint publishers of two of my earlier-published books: *The Rhetoric of the Babylonian Talmud: Its Social Meaning and Context* (Waterloo: Wilfrid Laurier University Press, 1994); and *Mishnah and the Social Formation of the Early Rabbinic Guild: A Socio-Rhetorical Study* (Waterloo: Wilfrid Laurier University Press, 2002). As already noted, chapter 9 (and to some lesser degree chapters 7 and 8) draw liberally upon three of my recently written scholarly papers, some of which are in print or will soon be in print. These papers are "Study as a Socially Formative Activity: The Case of Mishnah Study in the Early Rabbinic Group," in *Exploring Mishnah's World(s): Social Scientific Approaches*, edited by Simcha Fishbane, Calvin Goldscheider and myself (forthcoming from

Preface

Palgrave-Macmillan); this essay is a slightly revised version of my journal article "Textual Study and Social Formation: The Case of Mishnah," *Studies in Judaism, Humanities and the Social Sciences* 1/1 (2017) 23–44; "When Tosefta was Read in Service of Mishnah-Study: What Pervasive Literary-Rhetorical Traits of Toseftan Materials Divulge about the Evolution of Early Rabbinic Group Identity on the Heels of Mishnah's Promulgation," also in *Exploring Mishnah's World(s)*, a lightly revised version of my "Textual Study and Social Formation, Part II: Does the Evidence of Tosefta Confirm that of Mishnah?" *Studies in Judaism, Humanities and the Social Sciences* (publication pending); and "Studying Mishnah 'Talmudic-ly': What the Basic Literary-Rhetorical Features of the Talmuds' Legal Compositions and Composite 'essays' Tell Us about Mishnah Study as an Identity-Informing Activity within Rabbinic Groups at the End of Late Antiquity," again in *Exploring Mishnah's World(s)*. I am grateful to these publishers for my drawing on these essays in this volume.

This book was largely written while on leave from Brock University in the academic years 2016–17 and 2017–18. The work was also supported by grants from Brock, and the underlying research for chapter 9 was made possible from funds provided by the Social Sciences and Humanities Research Council of Canada. I am grateful for their aid.

No support of my work by anyone else matches that of my wife and very best friend, Dorothy (Dora Devorah) Markiewicz. It is but a small and inadequate gesture to dedicate this book to her. But with love and gratitude I do so.

> For Dorothy (Dora Devorah)

I

Introduction

This introduction is the first of three chapters that serve to orient the reader. It (a) introduces the principal objectives of the book, (b) explains for which audiences the volume is intended, and (c) articulates how and why this intended readership might benefit.

The Introduction is followed by two chapters that provide background and context for tackling the remainder of the book. They are written with an eye to the book's intended audience, about which more will be said later. At this point I will say merely that the intended readership are in the main not specialists in, or regular students of, early rabbinic legal literature. To these ends, chapter 2 surveys the formation and development of the early rabbinic movement from sometime in the second century CE (AD in Christian parlance) to the rise of Islam in the seventh century. The survey locates these developments within the context of the dominant political, cultural, and religious currents that impacted Jews and Judaism generally, and the trajectory of the early rabbinic group(s) specifically. These currents have much to do with (1) Roman imperial history and policy in the western part of the Middle East and in the lands of the Mediterranean basin; (2) the rise of Christianity (or Christianities) within Judaism (or Judaisms), their separation, and both communities' continued movement to self-define or redefine, while Christianity spread, ultimately achieving dominance in the Roman Empire; (3) Persian Imperial policy regarding delimited autonomy and self-administration for many Jews living (primarily) in the Mesopotamian-Babylonian Plain; and (4) the early Islamic Caliphate's policies regarding the authority of the rabbis over Judaic life and institutions in the rapidly expanding Muslim-ruled territories of the seventh century.

Again because of this book's intended readership, chapter 3 continues the orientation by providing an overview of the principal documents of the early rabbinic legal corpus of literature dealt with in this volume. These are Mishnah (produced c. 200 CE), Tosefta (c. 250–425 CE), the several compositions of Halakhic Midrash (c. 250–425 CE), the Jerusalem Talmud (c. 400–450 CE), and the Babylonian Talmud (c. 600 CE).[1] Finally, this book's focus on *rhetorical* and literary conventions of early rabbinic legal literature begs the question: What do I mean by "rhetoric" when specifically seeking to use it as an analytic tool for shedding light on early rabbinic literature and those that produced it? The concluding section of chapter 3 addresses this question, bringing our orientation to its end.

PRINCIPAL OBJECTIVES AND INTENDED READERSHIP: WHO SHOULD CARE, HOW AND WHY MIGHT THEY BENEFIT?

Principal Objectives

The volume's principal objective is to make early rabbinic legal literature more accessible, in the specific sense of rendering it more "intelligible," to those who are not regular or seasoned students of these works, but for whom the ability to make better sense of passages of this literature (even in translation) would significantly round out their understanding of religious and cultural developments in Mediterranean and Middle Eastern worlds in the Roman period. Who among a modern readership should want this literature to be more intelligible to them? What are the principal barriers for the nonspecialist to making sense of early rabbinic legal literature (even

---

1. The time frames given for these documents' production and promulgation by and within the early rabbinic movement are my own best estimates. But they have been and to some degree remain also a matter of scholarly discussion and disagreement. An account and assessment of that discussion is outside of the scope of this book. Most of the debate now focusses on the dates for the production of Tosefta and of the texts of Halakhic Midrash, particularly of Tosefta (see chapter 5, of this volume, notes 4, 14, 16, and 21. The reader of this volume, however, can take confidence that all of these documents were produced between 180 CE and 630 CE, and that the range of likely dates for the production of Tosefta (more or less in its current form) and of the Halakhic-Midrashic documents overlap and likely precede the production of the Jerusalem Talmud.

Introduction

in translation)? How does this book help remove a swath of these barriers? These are questions with which this part of the introduction deals.

It is a basic premise of this volume that one of the major reasons that the principal literary productions of the early rabbis are difficult to make sense of, even in translation, is because the dominant rhetorical and literary conventions that drive this literature are alien to those who are not well schooled in it. That is why the central, major parts of this book (chapters 4 through 8) provide an introduction to a number of core, dominant literary and rhetorical conventions and constructs of early rabbinic legal literature and show how they function in exemplary passages. Familiarity with these conventions and with their use are necessary keys unlocking this literature's intelligibility.

The second objective of this book is covered in chapters 2 and 3. As stated earlier, they survey what I believe can be known about the formation and development of the early rabbinic movement, and they introduce the early rabbis' principal legal literary compositions.

Finally, this volume seeks to unpack (at the end of chapter 3 and in chapter 9) what I mean by rhetorical and literary conventions in reference to early rabbinic legal literature, and what may be said of the social meaning and significance of these rhetorical and literary conventions for understanding the social formation and development of the early rabbinic movement (perhaps "guild," "occupational class," or "specialist class" is a more appropriate designation) within Judaic, Middle Eastern and Mediterranean society.

The Intended Audience(s)

Who are the intended readers of this book? I have already stated that they are *not* specialists or specialists-in-training in the study of early rabbinic Judaism or its literature, whether in the university, the seminary, or the rabbinic academy. To the latter, years of studying these documents will have made their rhetorical and literary conventions normal and commonplace. To them, this literature is already accessible and intelligible, even if it is at times still difficult because of its content. For them, rhetorical and literary conventions experienced as normal and commonplace do not beg serious questions or demand scrutiny (even if they should, because what is commonplace is usually not examined with a critical eye).

Rather, the value of gaining increased accessibility to this literature by reason of an account of its principal rhetorical and literary conventions accrues to a range of readers for whom such access is of important *cognate* interest. That is to say, the book serves those whose principal foci and interests have been "outside" of early rabbinic literature and the early rabbinic movement per se, but who are very much focused on the development of early Christianities, or of Judaisms, or of other cultural and religious currents in the Roman world and in immediately adjacent Persian-controlled territory of the Middle East. For them, a better grasp of what is going on in this literature supplements and complements their capacities to understand these other phenomena that are centrally of interest to them. The book will help them better contextualize their understanding of cultural, religious, or social developments of the Middle Eastern and Mediterranean lands during the Roman imperial and late Persian imperial eras.

Whom do I have in mind specifically? Readers may include academics, students, and an educated general readership whose major interests lie in a range of topics, including: the emergence of Christian communities, Christian institutions, and early Christianities in context; developments within Judaism(s) and Jewish societies in the aftermath of the destruction of the Jerusalem Temple in 70 CE and the failure in 135 CE of the Bar Kokhba rebellion (named for its leader, Simeon Bar Kokhba, aka Simeon Bar Kuziba) to restore Jewish self-rule and the Jerusalem Temple cult in the Land of Israel; the evolution of intellectual, civil, and religious elites in late antiquity; law, jurists, legal thinking, and legal literature in late antiquity; rhetoric in the ancient world; or institutionalized forms of education in the Roman period. For all of these topics, a better grasp of what is going on in early rabbinic literature provides opportunities to glimpse important contemporary cultural and religious comparisons or contrasts. The opportunity to compare contemporary phenomena within the same broad cultural and historical milieu places our principal objects of interest in higher relief. We see them more clearly as one social or cultural option among other possibilities.

Moreover, since rabbinic literature is also an important antecedent to early Islam, the proposed book is of value to those interested in intellectual, religious, and legal currents that got pulled into nascent Islam in the seventh and eighth centuries. And the book is, of course, of interest to nonspecialists and a general readership interested in the history of Judaism *after* the rise of Islam and the Christianization of much of Europe, since

Introduction

early rabbinic literature and its purveyors, the rabbis (together with the Hebrew Bible, of course), became authoritative for the vast majority of Jews in the medieval and into the modern periods. Most Jewish communities from at least the ninth century onward accepted the authority of early rabbinic literature and of the rabbis. What remained, or arose, as detractors of the authority of the rabbis within Jewish society had to muster their arguments in opposition to this literature. And medieval rabbinic apologists had to defend their rabbinic authority by specifically defending rabbinic literature's pedigree.

If, then, you are an upper-year undergraduate university student studying any of the foregoing topics, a student in a Christian seminary, or count yourself to be among an informed and interested general readership for whom *accessible* scholarship about ancient Judaism and early Christianity is of interest, you may find this book of value.

Making the Case for Increasing Accessibility to Early Rabbinic Legal Literature

This chapter has already made a number of blanket claims, without much justification or elaboration. Two of them are paramount, namely (i) the importance of making early rabbinic (legal) literature more accessible and intelligible to a range of nonspecialists; and (ii) the centrality of a grasp of this literature's principal rhetorical and literary conventions, the specific focus of this book, to making such texts accessible to a general readership. Consequently, these claims warrant some discussion and substantiation.

The importance of making early rabbinic (legal) literature more accessible to a range of nonspecialists

The first through seventh centuries CE saw developments in the Middle East and Mediterranean lands that became pivotal for so-called Western society, civilization, and culture. The Roman Empire expanded and then contracted (as did the Persian Empire several times and then disappeared with the early Islamic Caliphate). Both the expansion and the contraction of these two empires had profound social and cultural effects across broad territories. During the period in question, multiple Christianities emerged within a contemporary pool of multiple Judaisms, or as some would rather characterize matters "*complex* [my italics] common Judaism."[2] At stake in the terminological use of the plurals versus the singulars is one's best judgment about how much was shared over against how much divergence may be observed within Christian and Judaic circles respectively. But no historian of religion today doubts that both Christian and Judaic circles each displayed considerable diversity and divergence in the first half of the first millennium CE.

These two groups of religious communities, Christian and Judaic, developed in intertwined ways before, and in the aftermath of, the demise in 70 CE of the Jerusalem Temple cult and its associated institutions. And these communities slowly and unevenly separated over the course of the second and subsequent centuries.[3] So-called pagan religion and culture—the worship of household gods (*lares*) or Olympian gods, the worship of the Invincible Sun, the "mystery" religions, the Romanized cults of the east, such as the worship of Mithra and of Isis, and finally the imperial cult of the emperor itself—all waned within the Roman world as a result of Christianity's expansion and successes, ending in the Christianization of the Roman Empire during the fourth through mid-sixth centuries. Islam, with its roots in both contemporary Christianity and Judaism, arose in the mid-seventh-century Arabian Peninsula. Islam rapidly spread across the Middle East and Eastern Mediterranean, North Africa, and the Iberian Peninsula. Only Christian and Jewish groups were tolerated religious minorities in the "house of Islam." To so much of this the Judaisms of the Roman period were integral in one way or another: first, they served as a "parent" and authoritative source of teachings and practice to an "offspring" religious culture, and then they served as a rival or a foil (and the closest "other") over against which early Christianities and subsequently Islam felt compelled to legitimate and define themselves.

As the Christianities of the first through sixth (or seventh) centuries developed and coalesced, first as a persecuted minority and later as a dominant force within the Roman world, the Judaisms of the first through seventh centuries were undergoing a parallel, but—not entirely—unrelated

2. Miller, "Stepped Pools"; he also uses the term in Miller, *Sages and Commoners*.

3. Debates over the choice of appropriate terms to describe the divergence of Judaism and Christianity between c. 100 CE and c. 450 CE has been a subject of much scholarship over the last decade or two. Above all, the readers of this volume should keep in mind that that divergence was neither "neat" nor "quick." I say more about this later in this chapter, and several of the suggested further readings appearing at the end of this chapter deal with this critical historical issue.

process. For both Judaic groups and Christian groups, the destruction of the Jerusalem Temple in 70 CE and the failure in 135 CE of the Bar Kokhba rebellion in the Land of Israel were important. (And one could add to the list the failed "Diaspora" Jewish revolts in what is today Libya, Egypt, and Syria around 112–115 CE, which caused a century or more of social and cultural decline among Jewish Diaspora communities in Egypt and Libya specifically.) The political, social, and economic repercussions of these events affected both Jewish and early Christian communities. They were historical shocks that redefined the trajectory of, and the relationship between, still inchoate Christian groups and a now-reeling range of Jewish groups and classes. Among the latter one might reasonably include Jewish Christians, that is, people comprising Jewish communities that still self-defined as Jews and loyal adherents of Judaism, but who accepted and revered Jesus and what they understood to be his teachings.

One of the repercussions of these calamities has to do with the body of sacred texts that both early Christians and contemporary Jews shared. These were the Judaic biblical Scriptures and related works. Over the first several centuries of the development of early Christianities, what Christians understood to be the body of Jewish Scriptures constituted their Scriptures as well. Early Christians had as yet no other official scriptures than these. Only later did these books become the Church's "Old Testament" in an expanded scriptural canon that also included the books of the "New Testament."

Yet in the first century, when the Jesus movement began, the collection(s) of Hebrew Scriptures, and especially its first five books, which Jews referred to as the Torah of Moses, were inextricably linked to the institutions, officials, and religious cult of the central Temple in Jerusalem. So dissident or outright sectarian Jewish groups had to defend their legitimacy both in terms of their stance toward the Temple *as well as* in terms of their understanding of the Jewish biblical Scriptures. An example of this is the Dead Sea "sect" at Qumran, which in the first century sequestered their library—what we now call the Dead Sea Scrolls—in nearby caves. With respect to the Temple, disputes might revolve around (im)proper ritual, purity practices, or the lineage of the officiating priestly class and of the high priest in particular. To control the Temple was largely tantamount to controlling Jewish society in Jerusalem and the adjacent region and to exercising significant moral authority and influence in more distant Jewish communities. The establishment of the Hasmonean monarchy in the second century BCE was just an overlay over the institutions of the Temple, for example. The Hasmoneans were a priestly family, not one of the Davidic line; they married the kingship to the office of the high priest. The injunctions of the Torah of Moses and the teachings of the biblical prophetic literature, and their interpretation, often composed the playing field upon which these confrontations were played out. The authoritative place of the Torah of Moses had already become unassailable in Jewish society by Hasmonean times.

No doubt, the very earliest Christian groups had to enter this fray. They had to define their stance with respect to the Temple, its cult, and its leadership. And they had to stake out their positions in light of an interpretation of the Torah, the Prophets, and other Judaic sacred writings. The echoes of this register in the Gospels, in Acts, and in the genuine Pauline epistles.

One can, therefore, readily see how the events of 70 CE and of 135 CE in particular would be a turning point for Jews and for early Christians; many of the most important aspects of the religious cult and associated institutions enjoined in the Torah of Moses were wiped away, with little expectation or hope of their imminent restoration. After 70 CE, of course, the Temple cult of the God of Israel ceased, and it was deeply symbolic that the annual levy paid by all Jewish communities in both the Mediterranean Lands and the Middle East to support the Temple was converted after 70 to the *fiscus iudaius*, a head tax paid by all Jews in the Roman Empire to the imperial treasury. The failed Bar Kokhba rebellion was perhaps particularly critical, because it indicated that a historic, now mythologized, paradigm would likely *not* be repeated. That is to say, Jews would not reexperience what happened about half a millennium earlier, as recounted in the books of Ezra and Nehemiah, when in the latter decades of the sixth century BCE King Cyrus and his immediate successors of the Persian Empire permitted the reestablishment of Jerusalem and of its Temple cult to YHWH that had been destroyed by the Babylonian Imperial armies early in the sixth century BCE. In sharp contrast to Persian policy of the late sixth century BCE, after 135, Rome rebuilt Jerusalem as a typical Roman garrison town, renamed the city Aelia Capitolina, and built temples to the Roman gods in the city.[4] Moreover, as a result of the Bar Kokhba defeat, militant-political

---

4. While the establishment of Aelia Capitolina as a Roman military garrison city and the building of temples to Roman gods in Aelia took place *after* the defeat of Bar Kokhba, some sources claim that Hadrian's plans to do just this sparked the rebellion in the first place. See, for example, Eisenstadt, "Aelia Capitolina"; Eshel, "Bar Kochba"; Goodman, "Trajan"; Eliav, "Urban Layout."

Introduction

messianism—that is, the attempt to reestablish by militancy an autonomous Jewish commonwealth centered on Jerusalem and its (reestablished) Temple cult—was largely discredited as having brought disaster, not national salvation and restoration.

As noted, for some early Christians, the events of 70 CE and 135 CE were also existentially challenging. On the other hand, for other early Christians, these same events could be interpreted to speak to the validity of their (new) covenant with God, making them in their own eyes the legitimate heirs of the Judaic scriptural tradition. For Jews in the Land of Israel these calamities made observance of some Torah law and much of Torah-enjoined cultic practices impossible to implement in the manner set forth in Scripture. For all Jews, whether resident in the Land of Israel or outside of it in the Diaspora Jewish communities in the Mediterranean lands and the Middle East, it removed authoritative symbols and institutionalized authority structures from the scene. Up until 70 CE, Jews resident both inside and outside the Land of Israel sent their Temple head-tax to Jerusalem, paid for offerings to be made at the Temple on their behalf, aspired to be among the many pilgrims that went to Jerusalem for the cycle of pilgrimage festivals (much as Muslims aspire to undertake to Mecca), and received periodic festal and other instructions from the Jerusalem priestly authorities and their associated administrative retainers. Indeed, the book of Acts appears to place Paul among the latter, before his "conversion on the road to Damascus." In Acts' portrayal of matters (partially corroborated in Paul's genuine epistles), before his "conversion," Paul was an agent and emissary of the Jerusalem Temple's priestly administration charged with suppressing the early Jesus movement and conveying instructions to Jewish communities in the larger region (for example, Damascus) to act similarly.

So, in the second century CE, after the destruction of the Temple in 70 CE and the defeat of Bar Kokhba in 135 CE, the intricate, still intertwined dance of Christianities and contemporary Judaisms inexorably changed. And it inevitably changed again in the early fourth century for both

---

It is difficult probatively to establish what caused which, since Hadrian's construction of Aelia Capitolina undoubtedly commenced *after* the revolt, not before. But the claim that Hadrian's plans preceded and provoked the rebellion have the apologetic merit of 'excusing' the rebellion and condemning the pagan Roman emperors of the early second century, who were perceived by both Jews and early Christians as hostile to both Judaism and Christianity respectively. Precisely because this depiction so aptly serves these interests, it should be at the very least suspect. Rome was generally not in the business of unnecessarily provoking war. But it was in the business of punishing populations who rebelled.

partners, when the Roman emperor Constantine bestowed preferred status on "Christianity" and lent his support to a process of defining a Christian "orthodoxy." My pivot here to the use of "Christianity" in the singular is significant, even if not strictly speaking historically warranted. Christian unity and consistency across Constantine's empire was an as yet unrealized aspiration of the new imperial dynasty and of some among the Church leadership. Constantine expressly desired Christianity to be a unifying force across the Roman Empire, achieving what, in his mind, the imperial cult (the worship of the Roman emperor or of the "genius" of the emperor) had not successfully attained. In any case, from Constantine on, the rebellious but compelling "offspring" of Judaic groups, namely, early Christian communities, became the overlords of their "parent" religion in Roman-ruled lands. In the fourth and fifth centuries, Christian authorities, now backed by Roman authorities, were in an increased position to act toward Judaism in accordance with anti-Judaic polemics that had become part and parcel of dominant forms of Christian self-legitimation and self-definition during the second and third centuries.

Before Constantine, Jewish communities had what Christian communities desperately sought: legitimacy within the Roman legal and political system. Roman authorities were not enamored of Judaism, but felt compelled to recognize its legitimacy because of its antiquity. Jews were, consequently, excused from participating in the imperial cult, among other dispensations. Christianity, on the other hand, was an upstart development, and therefore was neither liked nor tolerated by Roman authorities. Christians were viewed as following a seditious "superstition"—seditious because they, like Jews, refused to participate in the imperial cult, and a superstition because they were newfangled. Unlike Jews, Christians were not afforded a dispensation from that participation. All the while, much of what would only later be retroactively deemed the "orthodox" leadership of early Christian groups (e.g., figures like Justin Martyr, Irenaeus, Ignatius of Antioch, Eusebius) sought to appropriate—and adapt—Judaic teachings, Scriptures, liturgy, practice and institutions, as they simultaneously sought to construct a distinctively Christian self-definition, to separate Jews from Christians, and to claim Judaism's legitimacy for themselves.

Undeniable facts, however, demonstrate that the disentanglement of Judaisms from Christianities was, as I have now twice stated, a longer, slower moving process than often depicted by early Church leaders. Consider that about fifty years *after* Constantine had issued the Edict of Toleration

Introduction

early in the fourth century, thereby commencing the era of state *sponsorship* of Christianity, a presbyter in Antioch named John Chrysostom felt compelled to deliver a series of anti-Judaic sermons to his (certainly Gentile) Christian community. Why? He railed against his congregants' attendance year after year at the local synagogue for prayers on the Jewish High Holy Days, their visits to Jewish holy men for health remedies, exorcisms and amulets, and their voluntary recourse to Jewish tribunals, also located in the synagogue, to adjudicate disputes. Clearly the intertwined relationship of Jews and Christians, and the allure for Christians of Jewish/Judaic institutions persisted some 330 years after Jesus' execution, 290 years after the destruction of the Jerusalem Temple and its institutions, and about 230 years after the failure of the Bar Kokhba rebellion.

In light of the foregoing, it should not surprise anyone, nor is it a coincidence, that *ecclesia* and *synagogue* are approximate synonyms indicating "assembly" or "place of assembly." Likewise, the councils of presbyters ("elders") that ruled early local churches resemble the council (*gerousia*) of elders that held authority over contemporary synagogues. The "presidents" (*archontes*) of these synagogue councils resemble in role the earliest functions of the "overseers" (*episcopoi*) of the early Christian "elders." Why would one be taken aback that St. Jerome felt compelled to learn Hebrew to go back to the sources, rather than rely on the several Greek translations of the Judaic biblical Scriptures in wide use among the early churches and among Greek-speaking Jews, in order to create the Vulgate (Latin) version of the "Old Testament" to serve the Latin Church?

Brief as this explanation may be, I hope that it makes clear the value for the intended readership of familiarity with states of affairs in contemporary Judaisms and Judaic communities to any attempt to frame developments in early Christian circles in roughly the first half of the first Christian millennium—all within the context of Roman-era society, culture, and policy. Now, why attach value to increasing that readership's capacity to access early rabbinic legal literature specifically?

The answer lies in a few glaring facts. First, *early rabbinic literature (legal and homiletic) is the only surviving, substantial body of Judaic literature authored between 135 CE and the rise of Islam*. Second, *early rabbinic literature is voluminous*. Permit me to elaborate.

Aside from early rabbinic literature, almost no Judaic literature authored and preserved by Jews living after the Bar Kokhba rebellion exists (or has survived). The very few, often fragmentary, exceptions do not belie this blanket claim, important though they may be to historians of late Antique Judaisms. Indeed, much of Jewish-authored/Judaic literature *outside* of the rabbinic collection of biblical Scriptures and of the corpus of early rabbinic literature *transmitted* to us from the ancient period—as opposed to dug up in some archaeological discovery—was passed down to us by *Christians, not Jews*. And almost all of what has been so transmitted, such as the works of Philo and Josephus, and the so-called Apocrypha and Pseudepigrapha of the "Old Testament," date from before 135 CE.

This state of affairs arises from two likely factors. First, after the Bar Kokhba rebellion, the relationship between Judaisms and Christianities—or perhaps more properly stated, between Judah-ists who did not revere Jesus and Judah-ists who did revere him—may have begun to change. And perhaps as a result, Jewish-authored works were less likely to be absorbed into what ultimately and later became "orthodox" Christian collections, *if* they had not already secured an established place there.

Second, around the time of the rise of Islam in the seventh century and over the several centuries following Islam's advent, the leadership of the rabbinic movement (about which I shall say more in chapter 2) solidified their authority over Jewish life, and more or less eliminated their Judaic competition. The rabbis tended to preserve their own early literature, not that of their Judaic detractors and competitors. This should not surprise anyone. It is common in the history of religions generally. The Church leaders of the emerging Christian "orthodoxy" of the fourth and subsequent centuries did much the same as regards Christian writings from earlier centuries. They preserved earlier writings that agreed with, could be (re)interpreted to accord with, or which foreshadowed their own. The writings of others they did not transmit. We know of the writings of Christian teachers whose Christian teachings did not accord with the emerging, ultimately deemed orthodox strain only because of the episodic and partial representations of their "heretical" views in the "orthodox" texts that fulminated against them. Would you trust your adversary to portray your views accurately, let alone expect them to preserve your literature? (Only rarely have we been so extraordinarily lucky as to rediscover in modern archaeological finds writings previously lost or suppressed, such as the Nag Hammadi documents.) This tendency to preserve only one's own literature, when coupled with an historical dynamic whereby one group emerges as dominant and over time eliminates all or most of the competition, is of course a major limitation for

Introduction

those who wish to better understand the Judaisms and Christianities of this formative period of the second through sixth or seventh centuries.

So, in combination and independently of one another, the emergence of a Christian "orthodoxy" and Christianities' increased distancing from contemporary Judaisms, on the one hand, and, on the other hand, the ultimate triumph within Jewish society of rabbinic authority, largely wiped out the active transmission to us of nonrabbinic Judaic literatures dating from the mid-second century on. The few exceptions to the rule only serve to emphasize that rabbinic literature from late antiquity is pretty much what we have to work with in seeking out writings by Jews authored between the mid-second century and the rise of Islam in the seventh century. But "so it goes," to use Kurt Vonnegut's turn of phrase from *Slaughterhouse Five*. If one wishes to consult Judaic literature *written by Jews after the Bar Kokhba revolt*, for the most part early rabbinic literature is overwhelmingly what survives.

Second, as stated, early rabbinic literature is a voluminous, substantial, and rich body of documentary evidence. Chapter 3 will provide a survey of early rabbinic "legal" literature. But at this juncture I should like to stress that like the patristic literature of the early Church, early rabbinic literature, particularly legal literature dealing with the praxes of life and ritual as a Torah-true Jew, is voluminous and topically wide-ranging. Mishnah comprises sixty-three thematic tractates, grouped as six major topical collections. Tosefta uses Mishnah's tractates as its organizing principle, and is even longer than Mishnah because the Tosefta supplements that work.[5] The volumes of the standard printed editions of the Jerusalem Talmud and the Babylonian Talmud (which include the main text and the most often used medieval commentaries on it) occupy about six linear feet on my bookshelf. Although composed in Hebrew, or in the case of the Talmuds, in Hebrew and Aramaic, English translations exist for almost all of these documents. So, language itself is not a serious barrier to accessing these documents for the English-language reader.

5. There has been much scholarly debate about the precise literary-historical relationships that entail between Mishnah passages and Tosefta passages (see chapter 5 of this volume, notes 4, 14, 16 and 21). As I shall remark many times in this book, this volume is not particularly concerned with literary-historical issues in the academic study of early rabbinic legal literature. That said, my own views on some of these questions do creep into the pages of this volume from time to time. A good serviceable summary of the issues and debates pertaining specifically to the literary-historical relationship of Mishnah passages to Tosefta passages may be gleaned from two places: Fox, "Introducing Tosefta"; and Brody, *Mishnah*.

In sum, the content of early rabbinic literature proffers a voluminous and important body of Jewish/Judaic literary evidence for the development of the rabbinic movement and of its formulation of Judaism after 135 CE. Early rabbinic literature also represents the only substantial, *contemporary and comparative* body of Judaic literature for Christianity's development during the second and several subsequent centuries when Christianity was solidifying its own self-definitions, to a certain degree within Judah-ist circles and to a degree over against Judaism. Yet who regularly consults this voluminous literature other than rabbis, dedicated students of it, or professional academic specialists in rabbinic literature? Few, and for reasons to which I now turn.

The centrality of a grasp of this literature's principal rhetorical and literary conventions to making these documents more accessible and intelligible

Let us try a thought experiment. Imagine that you have had a head injury. As a result, temporarily you retain your entire capacity to understand the English language except one, your grasp of English language syntax—the way words are supposed to be ordered in a sentence to create the desired meaning. Someone would speak to you. You would understand every word and recognize every grammatical inflection and verb tense. But until your temporary condition resolved itself, the meaning of the sentences would be difficult to grasp. In intelligible language, there is a normative, conventional order of things (syntax), and all those who understand the language have come to grasp that normative order, to the point that we seem to know where each sentence is going, even while the speaker is still articulating it. This sense of "knowing where things are headed" is vital to understanding language. Otherwise parsing out the meaning of someone's discourse would be a slow and laborious task, and we would likely fall behind the speaker unless he or she were talking very, very slowly. The classic late-1940s-to-1980s comedy team, Bob and Ray, cleverly used this aspect of language in their famous routine, "Slow Talkers of America." The "interviewer" converses with the head of the fictional Slow Talkers of America Association, who, yes, talks very slowly. The interviewer grows increasingly impatient and begins finishing the interviewee's sentences for him. Our intuitive grasp of a shared syntax is in part what makes this possible, once the context is known.

Introduction

There are uses of language where knowledge of *other* normative conventions *beyond* syntax (and beyond other points of grammar) are vital to making sense of it. These tend to be highly specialized uses of language used by experts. In some such uses of language, important structures exist beyond mere syntax. But the analogy to syntax holds true; if you do not know these other normative structures and conventions, you do not know where things are headed and to what meaningful end even when you reach the end of the literary unit, whether that is a sentence or a paragraph or a chapter. This is the case where a body of literature adheres to strict literary and rhetorical conventions that are rule-like, in addition to the common use of vocabulary, grammar and syntax. But once you become familiar with these literary and rhetorical conventions, and you know where things have been heading in the sentence, paragraph or chapter, a whole level of difficulty falls away. Remaining problems are likely restricted to attaining background knowledge of one sort of another that the specialist has acquired in his or her training.

Early rabbinic legal literature is a body of writings that uses very pronounced literary and rhetorical conventions. It was authored in Hebrew—the case, for example, for Mishnah, Tosefta and the compositions of Halakhic Midrash. Or it was authored in Aramaic alternating with Hebrew—the case for both Talmuds. The literature was produced by a type of ancient specialist for other specialists of the same type, namely, members of the early rabbinic class. That is why, even in English translation, this literature is still difficult to read and understand, unless the English translator has largely "undone" for the reader those conventions and structures, in which case one is really reading a combination of paraphrase and commentary, not an actual translation. Herbert Danby's masterful English translation of the Mishnah, first published in the 1933, is an example of the latter. In such renderings of rabbinic literature, the cadence and character of the original is often largely lost. In other instances, especially when the translator attempts very closely to represent the original Hebrew or Aramaic, the reader's lack of familiarity with the normative rhetorical and formal patterns of expression makes it difficult to comprehend the logic or reasoning of the passage. Such is the case with significant parts of the Halakhic Midrash and the Talmuds. What is "lost even in translation" is not only the capacity to comprehend the text. One also has lost the opportunity to understand who and what the early rabbis were, and what they were all about. (It is akin, perhaps, to taking all the specifically "lawyerly" and "legal" language out of briefs and contracts, but still wanting to grasp what the "lawyering" and the judicial world is all about.)

It is worth illustrating the foregoing with a *simple*, quite straightforward example (to be discussed more fully in chapters 3 and 4). A very literal, almost word for word, translation of the opening passage of the first chapter of the Mishnah Tractate on the theme of the priestly offering of the firstling would read as follows.

> He who purchases the foetus of an ass of a Gentile, and he who sells to him, even though it is not permitted, and he who forms a partnership with him, and he who receives from him, and he who gives to him in trust is exempt from the law of the firstling, as it is said, "Of an Israelite" (Numbers 3:13), but not of others (m. Bekhorot 1:1a, translation my own).

Whether one reads this in this English translation or in the original Hebrew, the language seems quite simple and straightforward. But if asked to recount or explain what the passage means, the uninitiated reader is quickly overwhelmed by a sense of being lost, of not being able even to articulate the specific conditions of the cases to which the ruling at the end applies. Why? Because a lot seems to be missing that would make it more intelligible. Obviously, what is missing has nothing to do with what precedes it in the tractate, because this is how the tractate begins—chapter 1, section 1a of Mishnah Tractate Bekhorot. What is *not* there, but which needs to be in order to make sense of the passage, has to do with literary and rhetorical norms of Mishnah.

Let me spell this out a little further. There is nothing inevitable, let alone "natural," about this passage missing the information that would make its meaning entirely transparent. That information could just as easily have been provided in Hebrew by the Mishnah's authors, inserted before and in between the bits that we do have. I shall do just that for this very passage in chapter 4, so that readers can see the difference. The supplementary information that would render this passage more intelligible is *not* there because of rhetorical and literary conventions that appear to be normative for Mishnah. These norms can be described, as I will do in chapter 4, and they are generalizable to other Mishnah passages across Mishnah's tractates. Moreover, it is a by-product of these norms that even the most experienced and well-schooled reader of Mishnah must mentally supply the antecedent and missing information in order to grasp the meaning of Mishnah passages like the one presented above. Having to learn to do this

Introduction

is part and parcel of being a devoted student of Mishnah, which is what the ancient rabbis were. And since no one is born with the capacity to do this, there have to have been (or there are likely to have been), as there are today, social institutions and structured social relations of some sort that inculcate that capacity in the next generation of experts. Consequently, by looking at what the rhetorical and literary conventions of Mishnah demand of the ancient reader, one may infer the existence of certain types of social settings and institutions that were likely to have existed or arisen within the early rabbinic group. And historians may then look for other evidence of their existence and make-up. In short, one will have gleaned much about what it meant to be, or become, a rabbi in the ancient world, and what social contexts supported this. As a historian of religion and society, that seems to me to be a worthwhile potential payoff for the effort of becoming more aware of the early rabbinic legal literature's rhetorical and literary conventions.

Awareness results from questioning both the unfamiliar and especially the familiar, which we tend to take for granted. Those of us who have read early rabbinic literature daily for many years, first as students and later as specialists, by now experience its literary and rhetorical structures and conventions as commonplace. We tend not to think about them, and I suspect many of us do not even recognize them for what they are, just as all of us proceed daily to understand our native language without thinking about, or even being aware of, its rules of syntax. We are modern specialists, immersed in the writings of ancient specialists, whose writings few people outside these modern or ancient circles understood or understand—except that, as explained, this literature is an important body of evidence for early Judaism(s) and Jews living at a compelling period for the development of both Christian and of Judaic groups, and of the Roman world generally.

In sum, by providing (in English) an accessible introduction to the more pervasive and important formal rhetorical and literary structures and conventions of early rabbinic legal literature, this book offers the reader something analogous to his or her intuitive grasp of language syntax.

What would count as success for this volume? It will have succeeded: (1) if it will have made this literature's content more accessible in translation—or for that matter, in the original Hebrew/Aramaic, if known—for readers; and (2) if it will have provided a unique window into the nature of what it was to be a member of the rabbinic group in the Roman period devoted to studying these texts. But additionally, the book may even have helped those who regularly study these texts today become more aware of this literature's specialized, formal literary/rhetorical traits.

Now the work for you, the reader, really begins, as this volume turns (in chapter 2) to a whirlwind introduction to the formation and development of the early rabbinic movement in context, subsequently (in chapter 3) to a primer on the principal compositions of early rabbinic legal literature, namely, Mishnah, Tosefta, the compositions of Halakhic Midrash, and Jerusalem and Babylonian Talmuds, and finally (at the end of chapter 3), to what, for the purposes of this book, is the nature and significance of rhetorical and literary conventions when looking specifically at early rabbinic legal literature.

SUGGESTIONS FOR FURTHER READING

Boyarin, *Border Lines: The Partition of Judaeo-Christianity.*

Goldenberg, *The Origins of Judaism.*

Goldenberg, "The Destruction of the Jerusalem Temple," 191–205.

Harland, *Dynamics of Identity in the World of the Early Christians.*

Schaefer, "Bar Kokhba and the Rabbis," 1–22.

Schwartz and Weiss, eds. *Was 70 CE a Watershed in Jewish History?*

Schwartz, *Imperialism and Jewish Society.*

Schwartz, *Ancient Jews.*

Wilson, *Related Strangers.*

2

Historical Contexts
Whence and Whither the Rabbis and Their Movement in Roman Palestine and Persian Babylonia?

To begin to appreciate why one would wish more easily to access early rabbinic legal literature, it is germane to understand who the early rabbis were, and how their network, association, group, movement, guild or class—all of these designations having been considered by various scholars[1]—developed over approximately half a millennium and in two neighboring social and historical contexts. An account of that development constitutes a bit of a "shaggy dog story." That is, it has many twists and turns before reaching its conclusion around the period of Islam's advent and early expansion.

My shaggy-dog story begins, appropriately, with a paraphrase of one of "Murphy's Laws": to do anything, you must do something first. In this case, I must first explain how difficult it is to describe in detail the development of the early rabbinic movement. The movement's origins are especially hard to glimpse. Then you, the reader, can follow what I have to say in the rest of this section of the chapter with the requisite degree of cautious skepticism.

Unlike early Christian literature, indeed unlike *earlier* Judaic literature, early rabbinic literature of the late second century through to the

---

1. As remarked upon in Miller, *Sages and Commoners*, 1–30.

dawn of the seventh century eschewed sustained history-like narratives about anything and everything. There are no "biographies" of the great rabbis of antiquity; there are no rabbinic-authored histories of the Jews or of the rabbinic group during this period. There is nothing similar to any one of the Gospels, or the Acts of the Apostles, or Eusebius' *Church History*. And no one *outside* the rabbinic movement in antiquity, whether Jew, Christian, or pagan, has incorporated any extended account of the early rabbinic movement or its main luminaries into their narratives. For example, elements of the history of the Jewish people in the first through early fourth centuries are found in Eusebius' *Church History*. But Eusebius, living in the Land of Israel, writes nothing about the rabbinic movement, its makeup, organization or place within Jewish polity in the Land of Israel. Yet by Eusebius' time, the Mishnah and probably some version(s) of the Tosefta and the Halakhic Midrashim had already been produced and were studied by rabbis. Libanius, a pagan teacher living in Antioch in the latter half of the fourth century, has provided posterity with his active correspondence with the Jewish Patriarch of the Land of Israel of his day. Later in this chapter I shall say something of the relationship of the Patriarch's administration to the early rabbinic movement. But nothing in Libanius' letters to the Patriarch touches upon the early rabbis. Were it not for the voluminous literature that the rabbis themselves composed in antiquity, and, as I argue at several junctures in this chapter, were it not for the rabbis' ultimate success in the seventh through eleventh centuries in establishing their authority over the vast majority of Jewish communities, we might not have even known of the rabbinic movement's existence or the production of their literature from the late second to the dawn of the seventh century. Perhaps a few inscriptions might have aroused speculation—like the one dated to the fourth century CE from a site on today's Golan Heights that reads, "this is the study house of Rabbi Eliezer Ha-Qappar," or another from the ancient Rehov synagogue from the sixth century CE in the Land of Israel that looks like it reflects the substance of several passages in early rabbinic legal texts[2]—but that is all.

In fact, it is not until the tenth century CE that *anyone* attempts to produce an extended "history" of the rabbinic movement and of its principal literature. Rabbi Sherira Gaon, the head of a major rabbinic academy in Pumbeditha in the Muslim-ruled Babylonian Plain, writes such a work.

---

2. Specifically, texts found in Tosefta Shevi'it 4:8–11, Sifre Deuteronomy 51, and Jerusalem Talmud Demai 2:1, 22c–d and Shevi'it 6:1, 36c.

He does so in an epistle (*Iggeret Rav Sherira Gaon*) responding to questions posed by the leaders of the Jewish community of Kairouan in North Africa. Someone or some group in Kairouan has challenged the authority of the rabbis and of their literature. These (certainly Jewish) detractors of the rabbis appear to have been articulating historical criticisms that undermine what by the tenth century are the standard claims rabbis make in support of their literature's and their movement's authenticity. Consequently, the leaders of the Jewish community ask Sherira to give them an account of the history of rabbinic authorities and of the principal texts of rabbinic literature. In effect, the elders of Kairouan have requested a pedigree for both.

But what are we modern students of religion and society to make of Sherira's work? Certainly, we have to read it as an apology for, and as a defense of, rabbinic authority. It cannot be taken to be an evenhanded assessment of the past. Additionally, Sherira is writing many centuries after the events about which his epistle deals, especially when providing an account of the earlier phases of the rabbinic movement. But he does not seem to have access to any additional sources than one has in hand today for the period much before the fifth or early sixth centuries CE. For example, Sherira possesses no elaborated histories covering these early centuries of the rabbinic group's development that have subsequently been lost to modern historians.

To get a sense of how problematic this is for the modern historian of religion, let me paint a fictional scenario. Imagine that the author of Acts had written not in the latter part of the first century about the earliest developments of the Jesus movement, but in the tenth century, with no other earlier elaborated historical narrative available to us (or perhaps even to the author of Acts). Historians of Christianity would be working with such a tenth-century Acts with great caution and reserve in terms of assessing what conclusions one could draw on its basis about the development of Christian communities in the first century. As it is, working with a late first-century Acts is not without its historiographical challenges because of the religious-ideological purposes for which the author writes. This is the situation one faces in using Sherira's history of the rabbinic movement and its literature. He seems to have some sources that have not independently survived and been transmitted to modern scholars. But these appear to be chronicles in his academy covering just the several centuries immediately preceding his own era, from the sixth or seventh centuries to the tenth. As stated, and worth repeating, the earlier the period about which he speaks, the more he seems to have no sources that modern scholars do not already have. And these sources are thin gruel of problematic ingredients.

What are these sources which he and modern scholars both possess, because they are already embedded in the early rabbinic literature transmitted to us? They are mainly episodic, very short, often homiletically oriented or legal-precedent-purposed stories about this or that rabbi or this or that event. These scattered stories were not composed to give an account of the rabbinic movement's history, organization, economic base, or an account of some of its more seminal figures. They usually serve to convey some moral lesson or to establish the authenticity of some legal ruling. That is all. Sherira reads and repurposes such stories as part of a history, as have many early modern and modern scholars, often influenced by Sherira's particular reconstruction. But frankly, many scholars, myself included, recognize how difficult the methodological path is for such an exercise of historical and social reconstruction, and how speculative, qualified, and incomplete is the resulting picture.

Consequently, I look to other types of evidence in order to characterize the early rabbis and their movement, class, network, guild, or whatever one decides is the more appropriate label. As I stated earlier, pervasive rhetorical and literary trends in rabbinic literature and other *indirect* attestations in early rabbinic literature to the social and historical realities of the rabbinic movement during the second through the dawn of the seventh centuries are reliable attestations to some historical realities. And this is the case, even if the results are more difficult to come by and render descriptions that are necessarily lacking the level of detail and narrative flow one would ideally want in an historical account. Why? Precisely because they are pervasive traits of a literature both produced and relentlessly studied by the members of the group we seek to understand in the period in question. What, however, one ends up with, which I will more fully spell out in the concluding chapter of this book, speaks more to early rabbinic culture and its development in "snapshots" than to a narrative history of the early rabbinic movement in "video" format, which is the fraught and more speculative task of this chapter. But "so it goes."

I have done what I first had to do in deference to Murphy's law. Now, I present my best estimate (some may rightly say, "guestimate") of the development of the early rabbinic movement in its historical contexts. As one might predict from what I have said in the preceding paragraphs, I will frequently be "hedging" my remarks, where I feel it inappropriate to firmly come down on one side or another of an issue.

I divide my account into two parts or periods, (a) from the mid to late second century CE on, and (b) before the mid- to late second century. I do this for a very specific reason. As far as I am concerned, we have no literary works produced by the rabbis before the end of the second century or so, and lots from that period forward. Some *sources* of the Mishnah and the Tosefta are likely earlier, but we do not possess these sources as documents transmitted independently to us. And what antecedent sources or traditions that may be found in Mishnah and Tosefta have been for the most part (re)cast in the idiomatic language and literary forms that characterize Mishnah and Tosefta as a whole.

What do I mean by these statements? If Mishnah (or Tosefta) were compared to the Gospel of Matthew (or Luke), one has for Mishnah (or Tosefta) nothing like a "Gospel of Mark" that (in some earlier version, 'proto-Mark') provided the basis for a "Gospel of Matthew" (or a "Gospel of Luke").[3] Moreover, what early rabbinic literature has to say or implies about the rabbinic movement *before* the end of the second century is even likelier to be tendentious mythmaking than what it has to say for the period contemporaneous with these texts' authors, all of which date from c. 200 CE and later. After all, the texts can be said to reflect the rabbinic culture of those who produced and studied them; one cannot say whether they reflect the culture of the rabbinic movement much before the production of Mishnah, the earliest rabbinic composition, at the end of the second century. So, an account of the earlier period is, admittedly, even more speculative.

It is worth noting that the distinction this chapter makes between rendering an account of the rabbinic movement (a) from the latter second century on *versus* (b) before and up to the latter second century has an important analog in what early fifth century and turn of the seventh

---

3. Whether some "core-Tosefta" is actually earlier than and formed the basis of or model for some proto-Mishnah has been debated regularly over the past twenty years. I do not subscribe to this view for reasons that I have reviewed in passing in chapter 9 of this book and have articulated in chapter 5, notes 4, 14, 16 and 21. Since generally, this book is not concerned with literary-historical issues, unless absolutely germane to its primary purpose, I do not in this volume take up the issue of the literary history (or prehistory) of Tosefta (or of any other early rabbinic legal text). Harry Fox at the end of the 1990s ably summarized the positions on the nature and origins of Tosefta and puts forward his own quite thorough assessment in Fox, "Introducing Tosefta." More recently, scholarly positions of Tosefta's literary-historical relationship with Mishnah have been critically assessed by Brody in *Mishnah*.

century rabbinic documents (the two Talmuds) posit about the generations of rabbis that preceded them. These rabbinic texts draw a line in the historical sand not in the latter second century (as I have done) but in the early third century, just *after* Mishnah was produced and promulgated. Rabbis whom these documents' authors believed lived before and up to the time of the production of Mishnah were called *tanna'im* ("the teachers," in Aramaic with a Hebrew plural ending); their authority is superior to those that followed them as are all traditions attributed to *tanna'im* or to their era. Rabbinic figures who lived afterward, in the Land of Israel up to the c. 400 CE or in the Mesopotamian-Babylonian Plain until c. 500 CE, were called *amora'im* (the "sayers," in Aramaic, again with a Hebrew plural ending). The designation *amora'im* served to differentiate them and teachings from their era from "tannaitic" sources that allegedly preceded them, and from materials that postdated "amoraic" traditions. This late antique or early medieval distinction between "tannaitic" and "amoraic" traditions plays out in how rabbinic legal literature produced c. 400 or in the first decades of the fifth century (in the case of the Jerusalem Talmud) and c. 600 (in the case of the Babylonian Talmud) treat the sources and traditions with which they work. So, I will return to these distinctions in the next chapter, my background survey of early rabbinic legal literature.

At this juncture, then, I must make confession, if you, the reader, have not already surmised it. Despite having devoted more than forty-five years to the study of the early movement and its literature, there are many historical issues with which I still struggle. I might as well alert you to them in advance. For most of the period of the second to the dawn of the seventh century, I have difficulty offering sound historical judgments about the size of the rabbinic movement,[4] about its level of social importance and authority in Jewish society, about its economic base, and about its forms of organization and institutionalization. I am prepared to say this: they were likely more numerous toward the end of that period, carried more authority within Jewish society in the Land of Israel and in Persian-rule Babylonia

---

4. For example, Mishnah and Tosefta attribute legal positions to about 120 named rabbis. About twenty of these are unique to Tosefta, and many seem to be rabbis from the very end of the second century or the first decade or two of the third. Does this represent the sum total of all members of rabbinic movement for the 150 years or so up to about 220 CE? Or are these the VIPs among the membership of the rabbinic movement over that 150-year period, those whose careers where particularly valued by their more numerous rabbinic disciples? One could legitimately go in either direction, in the absence of probative, explicit evidence.

nearer the end of that period, and had larger, more formally organized institutions of rabbinic learning for the training and continuing education of rabbis by the dawn of the seventh century. But by the end of that period, they likely still did not enjoy a monopoly, or near monopoly, as purveyors of norms and laws about living a Jewish life in a community of other Jews, within a larger host society of non-Jews. That achievement had likely to wait another several centuries.

The reason I feel compelled to get this off my chest at the outset of my account is simple. Rabbinic literature has a tendency to portray directly and indirectly rabbis as authoritative, and to have *always been* authoritative since the advent of the group, which rabbis of the fourth or fifth century (and later centuries) portray as having happened in the immediate aftermath of the destruction of the Temple in the first century (if not in the several decades before 70 CE). Even the terms and titles used to refer to rabbis by the *earliest* rabbinic document, the Mishnah (c. 200 CE), convey this assumption (or more accurately, pretense and perhaps conceit). *Rabbi* literally means "my master." This is the honorific that precedes almost every named authority in Mishnah. This is the same honorific used in the Gospel of Mark (9:5; 14:45) and the Gospel of John (1:38) to refer to Jesus. And when Mishnah refers to rabbis *collectively*, they refer to them as "the sages" (*hakham* (sing.)/*hakhamim* (pl.). "Sage" is a positively loaded term in ancient Judaic culture. All of the biblical wisdom literature extols the virtue and talents of "the sage." Could one think of a more socially self-promoting term in ancient Judaic culture, if one is referring to someone who is *not* claiming authority and respect by reason of their Levitical-priestly lineage (as did the High Priest and the Hasmonean kings) or monarchic lineage (as Matthew does for Jesus based on a genealogy linking him to the biblical King David)? That the rabbis from the outset offered themselves as the obvious and "natural" alternative authority figures to priests and Jewish nobility in a world changed by the destruction of the Jerusalem Temple in 70 CE and the defeat of Bar Kokhba in 135 CE is not surprising. We just do not know how and when many others accepted the offer. Nor do we know who made competing offers and with how much success. It is unlikely that those with priestly lineage just packed up and ceded authority and influence to others, rabbis perhaps among them, the day after the Temple was destroyed.[5]

5. Based on inscriptions from Caesarea, there is evidence of the existence of "priestly courses" in late Roman Israel well after the destruction of the Temple. This was or may

So, the account that follows may refer to a relatively small group, loosely organized, and with limited power and authority until nearer the fifth or sixth century CE (or later). Or rabbinic ranks and prestige may have swelled earlier (as their literature often seems self-servingly to portray). I have canvassed and read the writings of a number of trusted academic colleagues on these points, and I am less prepared today to defend a particular position on many of these matters than I was ten or twenty years ago. Such are my caveats to what now follows.

FROM THE SECOND CENTURY FORWARD, THE DEVELOPMENT OF THE EARLY RABBINIC MOVEMENT

The legal literature of the early rabbinic movement, the Mishnah, Tosefta, Halakhic Midrash, and Jerusalem and Babylonian Talmuds, was produced, in my view, probably in that very order,[6] by a group of self-regarded, self-declared, intellectual elites who, as I have stated, addressed one another, and *eventually* were addressed by almost all Jews, as *rabbi* (meaning "my master") and as *hakham* (meaning "wise one" or "sage"), with all the deference and authority that those titles claimed. The historical processes that led eventually to the general recognition within almost all Jewish communities (first largely concentrated in the Middle East and Mediterranean lands, and by the time of the Crusades also in the Rhine valley of central Europe and in England) that the teachings and rulings of the rabbis—referred to generically as *Halakha*, "the way" (that is, the way one comports oneself in religious practice and in civil, economic, and social relations to reflect a life of Torah)—were authoritative for all aspects of Jewish life was a long one.

That process started with the earliest formation of the rabbinic movement in the Land of Israel, most likely sometime in the second century CE, and progressed over the subsequent seven or so centuries. The rabbis' aspirations to rise to such levels of authority had much to do with the political, social, and cultural dynamics of the Land of Israel (under Roman

---

have been a system of twenty-four divisions of the ranks of the priests, each stationed at a different town in the Land of Israel, and in turn still performing some vestigial functions related to their priestly authority. See Avi-Yonah, "List."

6. To remember the order of these rabbinic compilations, I offer this very mnemonic ditty: "My Toast with Home-Made Jam and Butter" (Mishnah, Tosefta, Halakhic Midrash, Jerusalem, Babylonian).

and Byzantine rule) and of the Mesopotamian-Babylonian Plain (what the rabbis called simply, "Babylonia," under Persian rule). A definite spur to that progress happened at the time, and perhaps as a result, of the early spread of Islamic rule in the seventh and early eighth centuries, first across the Middle East, and thereafter westward across North Africa and into the Iberian Peninsula to the very southwestern boundaries of France.

The ups and downs of the fortunes of the rabbis and of their authority within Jewish circles over those seven centuries were likely many. Sometimes members of the rabbinic class ended up filling power vacuums in Jewish community institutions, vacuums largely created by outside forces. Or they competed with other nonrabbinic "sages" for such positions with, at first, episodic success. When individual rabbis did succeed, they filled bureaucratic-administrative functions in Jewish communities by reason of their high level of Judaic literacy, including their command of Jewish law and practice—of course, as *they*, the rabbis, defined that law and practice.

As I have implied, it is unlikely that they were the only pretenders. Nor can one say whether they comprised even a significant proportion of these functionaries—indeed they likely did not—before the latter part of this four-hundred-year period. Much has to do, on the one hand, with the policies of the Roman Empire, of the late Persian Empire, and of the early Islamic Caliphate toward Jews and the Jewish communities in their respective territories. And it has to do, on the other, with the presence of other, nonrabbinic, highly Judaicly literate administrative and legal experts, the extent of which is now obscured because of the rabbinic movement's ultimate success in the seventh and subsequent centuries.

Under Roman Imperial rule, several developments were key. Some I have already mentioned in the Introduction of this book. In 70 CE, the Jewish Temple in Jerusalem was destroyed over the course of the Roman defeat of a rebellion by Jewish groups against Roman rule in the Land of Israel. Until 70 CE, the Temple, its functionaries, and its bureaus were the central institutions of Jewish religious and civil life, even under Roman hegemony in the Land of Israel. The events of 70 CE largely wiped that away. A second rebellion, associated with the leadership of Simeon bar Kuziba, who took on a messianic *nom de guerre* Bar Kokhba ("Son of the Star"), and who appears to have been viewed by a number of his contemporaries as the messiah, ended in 135 CE in the Roman defeat of those rebels as well as in the imposition of harsh (in the main, temporary) punitive measures

In the Seat of Moses

against Jews in the Land of Israel, especially in Judea, the southern portion of the Land.

One measure was not intended to be temporary. Jerusalem, which had already seen destruction in 70 CE, was now rebuilt as a Roman garrison city, was renamed Aelia Capitolina, and a Temple to Jupiter was built either near the current site of the Church of the Holy Sepulchre (the more current scholarly view) or in the Mount Moriah area of the Roman city (a once accepted but now questionable view) at, even if not directly overtop, the very site where the Temple—three successive Temples, in reality—to the Israelite god, YHWH, had stood for about a millennium since the time of David and Solomon.[7] In short, all forms of Judaic religious and civil leadership, and all religious and cultic practices associated with, and dependent upon the functioning of, the Jerusalem Temple and its institutions appeared irrevocably gone, or if not entirely expunged, lacking their former, formal-institutionalized basis and setting. Many of these were enjoined in the Jewish biblical Scriptures, especially in the first five books of those Scriptures (the Pentateuch), which since the fifth century BCE bore the moniker "the Torah of Moses." Consequently, the understanding and use of these Scriptures also became a matter of uncertainty, although sacred Scriptures they continued to be. Moreover, militant Jewish political and national messianism, the attempt to bring about by civil disobedience and military action the era of the messiah in this world and renewed Davidic monarchic rule over the Land of Israel, will have received a very black eye indeed. Jews and Judaism in the Land of Israel, and to some extent in the

---

7. The current Mount Moriah compound in Jerusalem, where the Dome of the Rock and the Al-Aqsa Mosque now stand, derives from the Roman reconstruction of the site after 135 CE during Hadrian's time. This "more or less" coincides with the compound created by Herod's reconstruction of the Temple Mount. As to the exact location of pre-Islamic structures—such as Solomon's Temple, the reconstructed Temple of YHWH in the fifth and subsequent centuries BCE, and Herod's reconstruction of the Jewish Temple—within the Temple Mount or Mount Moriah compound, there is active debate among archaeologists. The compound itself is of substantial size, and, moreover, was increased in size in Herod's major reconstruction of the site, making it one of the largest such sites in the Roman world. In the religiously charged politics of the region today, whether this or that Temple was twenty or fifty meters this way or that within the compound takes on more significance than historians and archeologists would normally assign it. For example, does the Dome of the Rock sit on the site of the Holy of Holies of Herod's Temple to Yahweh? Or is YHWH's Temple's Holy of Holies a little to the south within the same compound, between what is today the Al-Aqsa Mosque and the Dome of the Rock? See Eliav, "Urban Layout."

Historical Contexts

Diaspora too,[8] had experienced severe civil, cultural, and religious shocks to the system. And early Christian communities—*especially* those still largely comprised of Jews who were followers of Jesus and his teachings and whose self-definition blended their Judaic and Christian identities, lives, and practices—likely experienced an equal shock.

The (temporary) retaliatory and punitive measures the Romans imposed in Land of Israel after 135 CE were brought to an end sometime in the mid-second century. Later in that century Rome seems[9] formally to have recognized some forms of Jewish communal self-rule and organization in the Land of Israel. Its details are sketchy. But two trends seem to be in force in the latter decades of the second century in areas of substantial Jewish settlement. These were along the coastal plain of the Land of Israel

---

8. Of course, the modalities of Diaspora Jewry's experiences of the events of 70 and 135 CE were greatly conditioned by the fact that the Temple ceased well before its destruction in 70 CE to be an active reality in their social and religious lives as Jews. Jerusalem was simply too far away. Theirs was a reconstruction of Jewish life *on the foundations of* a biblical tradition that placed the Temple at its center, but that is hardly the same.

9. The state after 70 CE and 135 CE of formalized leadership and authority over Palestinian Jewish society, whether endowed with Roman authority or not, after 70 is a much-debated issue. The debate revolves explicitly or implicitly around a series of interrelated questions, answers to which can be given with too little certainty. My take, as expressed in this chapter, is just one navigation through this minefield among other possible ones, and I can only say that I prefer it marginally to others based on the evidence. I do not capture the scholarly debate in the body of the text of this chapter, because it is an introductory, orienting chapter for a volume the purpose of which is quite other than the discussion of these historical question, just as the volume's aim is not to systematically address literary-historical questions. Let me, however, spell out, at the very least, what some of the major, still-burning questions are: (1) When exactly did the rabbinic movement coalesce into some institutionalized entity or group in Roman Palestine? (2) When did the Jewish Patriarchate arise as a formally or informally recognized institution of Jewish leadership in Roman Palestine? (3) Whence did the power and authority of the Patriarchate derive—from the Roman state, by prestige (only) within the Jewish communities of Roman Palestine—over whom and what? (4) What is the relationship of the rabbis and/or the Patriarch to other forms of Jewish communal leadership in Roman Palestine—city and town elders, city and town councils, city magistrates/magistracies? What were the powers and authority of the rabbis in Roman Palestine—formally or informally—over whom and what? Does the evidence evoke different answers to some of these questions depending upon the time period examined—in Palestine, between 70 CE and 135 CE, or 135 CE to c. 200 CE, or c. 200 CE to 400 CE, or after c. 400 CE (all of which time frames correspond to known changes in Roman Palestine)? Moreover, a similar set of questions may be articulated, *mutandis mutandis*, for the rabbinic movement and the Exilarchate (the office of the Resh Galuta) in the Mesopotamian-Babylonian Plain under Persian rule. And, as intimated, specific answers to all of these questions have been vigorously debated by modern scholars.

and in the lower and upper Galilee into what today is known as the Golan Heights. The aftermath of the Bar Kokhba rebellion resulted in major migration of Jewish survivors from the territory around Jerusalem (in Judea) to these other regions of the Land of Israel long inhabited by Jews.

One form of Jewish self-administration was at the local level and may have already existed for some time. The Jews of local towns and cities with substantial Jewish populations seem to have been in the charge of councils of elders, on which sat local gentry. Synagogues, whatever, wherever, and whenever their origins,[10] came in a number of locales to function as the seat of these governing councils and related institutions, not just as gathering places for prayers or the reading of Scriptures (as attested in the Gospels and in Acts). So, in a gradual transformation that in time frame paralleled rabbinism's early development in the Land of Israel from the late second to the fifth and into the sixth centuries, the synagogue came to be the seat of both communal religious practice and local Jewish civil administration (just as they were in this time frame outside of the Land of Israel in the Graeco-Roman Jewish Diaspora). In Roman terms, synagogues over this period came to house under one roof the functions that in a typical Roman city would be handled by the council building (*hostilia* or *bouleterion*), the temple(s), and the facility for public civic and judicial proceedings (the *basilica*).

As noted, the emergence in the Land of Israel over these centuries of such a form of Jewish communal organization was not a newfangled or unique development. It is attested in evidence concerning Jewish communities outside the Land of Israel in Roman-ruled lands dating at least as far back as the mid-first century CE. And it is well attested in these "diaspora" Jewish communities thereafter. For example, in the first century, the aristocratic Alexandrian Jewish philosopher Philo (in *Legatio* and *Flaccum*) remarks upon the centrality of such councils and their presidents or "rulers" for the Jews in Alexandria. Alexandrian Jews boasted a number of synagogues with their respective councils and council presidents, and the Jewish population of the city as a whole also seems to have had a super-council and president (comprised of representatives from individual synagogue councils). Alleged Roman edicts of the early Caesars (mentioned in Josephus' *Antiquities of the Jews* (Book XIV,183–267), subsequent Roman edicts dating from the fourth, fifth, and sixth centuries and preserved in Roman legal texts, inscriptional evidence from Jewish communities around

---

10. See Levine, *Ancient Synagogue*.

the Mediterranean basin, and references in early Christian literature (such as John Chrysostom's fourth-century sermons, *Against the Jews*) all corroborate this depiction of local Jewish communal organization and governance in the Roman Mediterranean lands. And as regards the land of Israel, such forms of local communal organization are consistent with passages in early rabbinic literature itself. As I shall discuss shortly, the members of the nascent rabbinic movement or class or guild (whatever the appropriate designation) in the Land of Israel would have had to find their way within, between, on top of, or around such established forms of communal governance to exercise any authority.

The second form of Jewish self-rule in the Land of Israel was the Jewish Patriarchate. Its precise origins are obscure, and there is some dispute about the full range of its civil and religious authority and powers, especially over matters beyond Jewish ritual observance and its coordination within the Land. But the Patriarchate's established presence near the end of the second century, headquartered in the lower Galilee, is clear.

It is uncertain to what degree the Jewish Patriarchate in the Land of Israel operated under some form of official *license* from the Roman Imperial government at the end of the second and during the first decades of the third century. But the Patriarch certainly operated with Roman acquiescence and recognition, as well as by some form of broad acceptance on the part of Jews in the Land. Indeed, it seems that by the fourth century CE (and probably somewhat earlier as well), the Jewish Patriarch was formally addressed using titles and honorifics generally reserved for Roman senators and imperial officials. He was, it seems, properly addressed as "the illustrious Patriarch" or "most illustrious Patriarch." For example, in his correspondence with the Patriarch, the fourth-century Antiochene pagan educator and orator Libanius uses such titles in addressing him. Rome at some point permitted the monies raised annually in Jewish communities in the Land of Israel and the Diaspora to be sent in whole or in part to support the Jewish Patriarch's administration. And when in the early fifth century the powers and privileges of the Patriarch were revoked by imperial decree, one of the privileges that was removed was the Patriarch's status as honorary prefect of Rome, as was the power to levy or collect funds from Jewish communities in the Land and abroad to support the Patriarchate.

The Patriarch's administration seems to have had some pan-communal responsibilities and authority over a number of defined Jewish religious and distinctively Jewish civil matters and perhaps over other matters devolved to it (officially or by benign neglect) by the Roman-imperial provincial administration. The third-century Caesarean Christian writer Origen (who refers to the Patriarch by the term "ethnarch") complains that the powers routinely exercised by the Patriarch in the Land of Israel are extensive and exceed his formal authority. The Patriarchate's relationship to local Jewish community elites and their local councils seems to have operated on the basis of some agreed-upon division of powers and responsibilities, the details of which, and the official basis for which, one cannot today completely reconstruct. Perhaps the division of responsibilities that was *de rigueur* in the empire between the Roman imperial provincial administration and local city and town government was a justificatory parallel for the division between the Patriarchate's roles and those of the local Jewish council.

The Jewish Patriarchs constituted a dynasty. Son succeeded father until the Patriarchate's authority was whittled down and ultimately revoked in the first half of the fifth century CE by the now well Christianized Roman imperial government. The Patriarch's family were likely Jewish aristocrats of some renown. Early rabbinic literature attributes to the Patriarch's dynasty a pedigree going back to King David, just as the Gospel of Matthew does for Jesus or as monarchists in Canada did for Queen Elizabeth II in the 1960s during the debates in Canada that resulted in jettisoning the British Navy's "Red Ensign" as Canada's national flag. In so doing, rabbinic literature likely reflects the Patriarchal family's own genealogical claim for itself. The Hebrew and Aramaic titles for the Patriarch, *nasi* and *nesia* respectively, mean literally "the Prince."

Early rabbinic literature, however, also and always refers to the Patriarch using the honorific "rabbi," the same honorific by which the early rabbis addressed one another. Moreover, at some point in the third or fourth century, the early rabbis attributed the production of the first rabbinic *magnum opus*—the Mishnah, composed near the turn of the third century—to one of the Patriarchs, "Rabbi" Judah "the Prince." Rabbi Judah the Prince (or simply, *Rebbi*, as rabbinic literature starting with Tosefta often refers to him) held office during the last decades of the second century CE and the first several of the third century. It is unlikely that Judah wrote the Mishnah, or indeed that Mishnah was the work of any single author. But *attributing* the composition of Mishnah to a Patriarch, "Rabbi" Judah, is a significant statement about what the early rabbinic movement wished the relationship to be between themselves and the Patriarchate. Moreover, it constitutes a statement that the rabbinic movement saw the Patriarchs as fully rabbinized, in my view an overstatement.

The rabbinic attempt, from the early or mid-third century on, to portray the Patriarchs as their "brothers" in the rabbinic movement is indeed extensive. Like other major rabbinic figures, Judah the Patriarch is depicted as teaching illustrious students who thereafter themselves become renowned rabbinic masters. And Judah's (alleged?) immediate ancestors—such as Gamaliel the Elder (known to us from New Testament literature as well), Simeon ben Gamaliel I, Gamaliel II, Simeon ben Gamaliel II—all appear in Mishnah and Tosefta as typical renowned rabbinic figures to whom legal positions are attributed, just as these texts do with other named rabbinic figures. It is all the more curious, then (and perhaps significant), that Judah's immediate descendants and successors in the Patriarch's office nowhere figure in rabbinic literature as prominently as Judah, at least not as "rabbis" fully engaged in typically rabbinic teaching and learning.

That said, the relationship between the rise of the early rabbinic movement in the Land of Israel sometime in the second century CE and the establishment of the Patriarchate also in the (late?) second century is unclear. What is likely is that they are in some sense codevelopments that somehow became intertwined (at the very least for the rabbis)—the rabbis as a "wannabe" professional-like, social formation, the Patriarchate as an institution of administration with some (and growing) *de facto* powers recognized by Rome. The rabbis, initially, seemed to desire a close relationship with the Patriarch, and by reason of it some sought or expected appointments of various sorts. The members of the early rabbinic movement promoted their candidacy for professional posts in the Patriarch's administration and for those appointments in local Jewish communities in the Land of Israel over which rabbinic literature assumes the Patriarchate had sway. To what degree were the rabbinic sentiment and ambitions equally reciprocated and satisfied by successive Patriarchs from the end of the second century CE to the early fifth century, when Rome abrogated the powers of the Patriarch? That is difficult to surmise. Did the rabbis define or seek to define the Patriarch as their "patron" and themselves as his "clients" in the Roman sense of these terms? Perhaps so. In any case, it is reasonably certain that the early rabbinic group tried to hitch its wagon in some fashion to the Patriarchate, on the one hand, and sought to either "rabbinize" the Patriarch or claimed to have "rabbinized" the Patriarch, on the other. Why, otherwise, would the rabbis not only have called the Patriarch rabbi but also have attributed the composition of *their* Mishnah to an illustrious member of the Patriarchal dynasty, "Rabbi" Judah? In any case, by the mid-fourth century, the rabbis seemed to have soured somewhat on the Patriarchs, whom they portrayed, among other things, as highly hellenized and romanized.[11] Is this souring a result of sour grapes? Perhaps.

What was the urban and rural social topography in which the early rabbinic movement in the Land of Israel developed? As I have stated, after the failure of the Bar Kokhba rebellion, many Jews in the region of Judea migrated to join brethren in communities in the coastal plain and in lower and upper Galilee (which then seems to have included at least part of the Golan, the high plain east and northeast of the Sea of Galilee). Local Jewish governance, the Patriarchate, along with an aspiring rabbinic class seeking to find its place in the former two spheres, all inhabited a social-geographical landscape that was anything but uniformly Jewish.

In Hellenistic and early Roman times, a number of "Greek cities" were founded in the Land of Israel; non-Jews from adjacent territories migrated into the Land, increasingly so after the Bar Kokhba rebellion, attracted to the more highly Hellenized-Romanized urban centers. Rabbinic literature knows of "(primarily?) Jewish towns," "(primarily?) Gentile towns" and towns with both substantial Jewish and non-Jewish populations.[12] The Land of Israel in the late second and early third centuries might well be described as follows: larger urban centers with mixed populations displaying the cultural, economic, and organizational traits of other major cities in the eastern end of the Roman Empire; smaller cities and towns, whether primarily Gentile, or Jewish, or Samaritan (in the case of the territory between Judea and Galilee and east of the coastal plain); a substantial agricultural hinterland around larger and smaller urban centers, comprising smaller freehold farms, tenant farmers, and wealthy landed gentry with substantial agricultural lands as well as (second) dwellings in a nearby urban center.

While urbanization in the Land of Israel had been a steady ongoing process from Hellenistic times, it seems, then, to have accelerated in the late second and early third centuries, as attested by the archaeological remains

---

11. A point emphasized by Lee I. Levine in conversation with me in the fall of 2017.

12. It is important to take cognizance of the fact that the Roman-ruled Land of Israel in the aftermath of the Bar Kokhba rebellion (if not before) had a remarkably robust pagan culture intermingled with the "native" Jewish one. Evidence for this comes from the many pagan cults and cultic sites in the Land of Israel from c. 200 CE to 400 CE (when, of course, the Christianization of the Roman Empire begins to reshape and curtail pagan culture throughout the empire). See Belayche, *Iudaea-Palaestina*.

of substantial urban building projects and urban infrastructure, including monumental structures dating from this period. This appears to have been a period of "investment" by Roman authorities in the region's development, further bolstered by Rome's granting in 212 CE by the edict of Caracalla of Roman citizenship to all free inhabitants of the empire.[13]

The latter third and especially fourth centuries may well have been a period of economic (and, therefore, of cultural) decline in the Galilee, the very center of Jewish settlement (and of rabbinic activity) in Land of Israel. A major earthquake and the revolt of Gallus, both mid-fourth-century occurrences in the region, will only have made matters worse. It appears, many settlements in the region between Sepphoris and Tiberius seem to have lost substantial population. And some scholars posit that the intellectual rigor of the rabbinic movement in the Land of Israel was dealt a serious blow in this period, while, in parallel, the Roman support for the stature and authority of the Patriarchate diminished near the end of the fourth century, culminating in Rome's abrogation of many/most of the Patriarch's formal, legal powers in the early fifth century. Some attribute to the conditions of this fourth century "crisis"-period the impetus to commence work on producing the Jerusalem Talmud (or Yerushalmi), which work is generally thought to have been completed (or abandoned in its more or less current state) by the beginning of the fifth or so century.

Yet, by the fifth and sixth centuries we encounter the expansion, renewal, or building of many synagogues in the Galilee and the beginning of a renewed period of homeland-based, Jewish literary activity, the editing of major Haggadic-Midrashic collections of earlier rabbinic homiletic (as opposed to legal) materials,[14] and the beginning of the production of liturgical poetry (the *piyyutim*). None of this is to say that agriculture ceased to be the backbone of the economy, even during the posited decline of the fourth

---

13. In conversation with me in the fall of 2017, Lee I. Levine emphasized these developments as pivotal contextual elements for the development of the rabbinic movement and of the Patriarchate. Think for a moment what bestowing Roman citizenship on all Jews in the Land of Israel (and beyond) would have meant in terms of the legal jurisdictions and processes under which the Jews now fell! Ironically, in the fifth and sixth centuries now-Christian Roman emperors sought to reverse the process in a manner of speaking; Imperial edicts order that disputes among Jews be arbitrated in Jewish communal tribunals. This was part of an emerging Roman policy increasingly to separate the Jewish and Christian populations of the Roman Empire, so that Jews would not influence Christians.

14. A distinction discussed further in chapters 3 and 6.

century. Local, translocal, and transregional trade seems still to have dealt largely in agriculture-based products.

Forms of Jewish governance and formal Jewish communal organization, as well as the nascent and aspiring early rabbinic movement, had to find their places in this diverse, evolving landscape. We do not really know when the Patriarchate began. In my opinion, early rabbinic literature quite anachronistically assigns its origins in the first century (or earlier). But something seems to have given it considerable impetus in the last decades of the second century, during the Patriarchate of Judah the Prince, even if some may assign its origins to an earlier date. And these are precisely the decades that the nascent rabbinic movement is sufficiently institutionalized to produce their first literary oeuvre, the Mishnah. In the social topography of the Land of Israel just described, both the rabbinic movement and the Patriarchate are both situated in tier 2 and tier 3 urban settings, like Usha and Beit Shearim (both in the Galilee), or, in the case of many rabbis, in still smaller towns. In the early third century the Patriarchate (perhaps under an aged Judah the Patriarch, perhaps under his successor) moves to Sepphoris, a tier 1, highly Hellenized and Romanized city. Later in the third century, the Patriarch's court moves to another tier 1 urban center, Tiberius.

It is evident too that over this time frame some prominent members of the early rabbinic movement situate themselves in the largest urban centers as well, in Caesarea, Sepphoris and Tiberius. The work on the "Jerusalem" Talmud (composed c. 400 or in the several subsequent decades) was likely completed in Tiberius.[15] But it seems that many rabbis did not migrate to these larger centers, continuing rather to live in the smaller cities and towns of the coastal plain, of the lower and upper Galilee, and of the Golan, surrounded by and serving a still largely agrarian economy. Certainly, when Mishnah, Tosefta and later rabbinic literature name the centers of gravity of the nascent rabbinic group, they repeatedly mention Yavneh and Lod on the coastal plain (when speaking of the decades before Bar Kokhba) and Usha and Beit Shearim (after Bar Kokhba).

---

15. The hypothesis that some of the civil-tort sections of the Jerusalem Talmud were drafted earlier in Caesarea was put forward and defended by Saul Lieberman. Jacob Neusner has forcefully challenged Lieberman's conclusions on the grounds that those characteristics that are alleged to set these sections of the Jerusalem Talmud apart from the whole, also set these same tractates of the Babylonian Talmud apart from the rest of the BT. Consequently, in Neusner's view, these sections' distinguishing characteristics, in so far as they are significant at all, must be attributed to some other factors, not to their origins in Caesarea.

Thus, the early rabbis and even Judah the Patriarch were by Roman standards Roman provincials and townsfolk within a larger, encompassing, rural-agricultural milieu.[16] To Roman officials, the Patriarchs of the end of the second century and the beginning of the third would have looked like prestigious, wealthy country/provincial gentry. As the Patriarchate became more closely associated in the third century with the major urban centers of Sepphoris and, later, Tiberius, and as their privileges and rank, like honorary prefect, came to be defined in typically Roman terms, it is understandable that many members of the rabbinic movement, whose literature often displays overt aversion to Hellenization and Romanization, would have viewed the later Patriarchs with more jaundiced eyes.

Within the general "landscape" in the Land of Israel in which the early rabbinic group coalesced and operated, what precisely did rabbis do, for whom, for what recompense (if any), by reason of what (claimed) expertise, and on what authority? And where did they seek to fit or position themselves, likely in competition with others (whose identity and affiliations are now obscured), within the well-established systems for local governance by local gentry ("elders") and within the panlocal institution of the Patriarchate?

Whatever the origins of the rabbinic movement in the second century CE in the Land of Israel, over the course of the next 200 years, the rabbis in part seem increasingly to have promoted themselves as a possessing professional-like qualifications by reason of their learning. That learning they characterized particularly as "torah" (singular, indefinite in English grammar), which in biblical terminology means revelatory or divine teaching. The rabbis claimed knowledge of torah extends well beyond expertise in the Judaic Scriptures and their interpretation. It encompasses all aspects of Halakha, the "way" one lives a Judaic life with others in accordance with God's will. Halakha was wide-ranging in is scope. It concerned religious rites and purity law; civil, criminal, and family law; judicial and administrative process. The rabbis' "torah" knowledge also provided the basis for many

---

16. Hayim Lapin makes the point that emerging or aspirational rabbinic power and authority in Roman Palestine is best understood within the context of typical eastern Roman-Imperial social and political order, in which wealthy landowners take up their duties in the councils and magistracies of their towns and cities, served by (what Lee Levine would call) a "retainer class" of administrative-legal experts and what others might call a class of "scribes." See, for example, Lapin, "Hegemony and Its Discontents." See also Levine, *Rabbinic Class*, 38–42, 167–75. On where rabbis fit, and do not fit, within the Roman social and cultural world, see Schwartz, *Were the Jews*, 110–64.

other activities, including teaching, preaching, medical practices, methods of demon-avoidance and exorcism, incantations, and dream interpretation.

The relationship (portrayed, sought, or fantasized) with the Patriarchate appears to support the aspirations of the rabbis to act as a profession-like cadre to implement their Halakha within organized and institutionalized community settings. Moreover, contemporary developments in Roman provincial governance paralleled and perhaps provided a model for such aspirations. During the latter part of the second century CE and the third, Roman imperial provinces were in the process of "professionalizing" the ranks of its civil, provincial administrations rather than continuing to rely on the appointment of Italian and provincial gentry, who were at best skilled amateurs. To the degree that the Patriarch in the Land of Israel may at times have responded to the aspirations of the members of the rabbinic movement by placing some of them, rather than their competitors, in various positions, he may have been imitating a contemporary trend in Roman imperial provincial governance.

Moreover, historically speaking, it is hard to know what to make of occasional third-, fourth-, and fifth-century references in early rabbinic literature to a supposedly late first-, second-, or early third-century institution of the Patriarch's "Court" or "Council" (*beit din*), the sitting members of which were said to be, in whole or in part, rabbis. Are these few references an anachronistic retrojection into earlier times of a state of affairs in the third, fourth or early fifth centuries? Are they merely self-serving fictions about the late first, second, and early third centuries? If they are the latter, which I suspect, then such portrayals of an early period of Patriarchal and rabbinic codependency may nevertheless still reflect something of closer relationships between the rabbis and the Patriarchate that entailed at the turn of the third century but had largely fractured by the fourth century.

While the early rabbinic movement sought relations with, and appointments from, the Patriarch, and from local Jewish administrations, as judges, agents of the courts, civil administrators, teachers, and sometimes preachers, this, as I have already implied, was not their only means, and maybe not their principal means, of exercising their expertise and authority, let alone of earning a living. Core steady income for rabbis likely did not come from any of these activities, any more than it did for community leaders and authorities generally in the cities and towns of the Roman Empire. According to early rabbinic literature, rabbis seem to have had businesses and enterprises unrelated to their activities as rabbis. Some were very wealthy as a result; others were not. What is probable is that the time and dedication involved in becoming a rabbi, and mastering the requisite body of knowledge, is likely to have been something that mostly those of sufficient independent economic means could pursue. The rabbinic mythology about Rabbi Aqiva starting out his life in poverty (and therefore ignorance) works to aggrandize Aqiva's rabbinic stature only if Aqiva is understood to be the exception, not the rule.

Additionally, rabbis offered services based on their rabbinic skills and knowledge as independent operators and contractors to the Jewish population at large. As I already stated, rabbis seem to have promoted themselves as service providers and arbiters in all sorts of matters in which they could render opinions or reconcile conflicts in light of their Torah learning and teachings. The Talmuds show that the range of what rabbis subsumed under their Torah-based learning was wide indeed. I have already mentioned that that range includes claimed expertise about potions, amulets, dream interpretation, demon avoidance and exorcism, and incantations. It is likely that no late antique "sage" was worth his salt without claimed prowess in these domains. (Indeed, Acts depicts Paul as possessing such gifts, and implies that these gifts corroborate his authority to preach the gospel.)

Such services included mystical and gnostic praxa undertaken by some rabbis.[17] These rabbis practiced techniques for entering trances and made claims of out-of-body journeys through the heavenly spheres, there to learn esoteric knowledge about God, the angels, and the underlying workings of the world. Mere echoes only of these pursuits are contained in the Talmuds. But they are certainly there. No doubt early rabbinic literature exhibits a reticence openly to teach and to compose elaborated textual traditions about esoteric matters. But some such elaborated texts with an undeniably "rabbinized" literary layer, found in the cache of medieval manuscripts in a medieval synagogue repository in Egypt (the "Cairo Geniza"), arguably reflect these esoteric teachings, practices, and arts from the period before the seventh century CE. Again, the practice by some rabbis of trance-inducing techniques to effect heavenly journeys and visions, and to garner, thereby, special knowledge, is neither new in Judaic circles nor unique to rabbis. Jewish Apocalyptic literature such as 4 Ezra and the Book of Enoch, and the nonrabbinic, late-antique Jewish text referred to as Sefer Ha-Razim (the Book of Mysteries) demonstrate this. And again Paul, this time in his own

---

17. See, e.g., these classic and accessible works: Scholem, *Jewish Gnosticism*, and Blumenthal, *Understanding Jewish Mysticism*, vol. 1.

writings, seems to make similar claims when he states in 2 Corinthians 12:2 that he was "... in Christ ... caught up to the third heaven ..." A late antique holy man is a late antique holy man, whether a rabbi or not. To act or claim otherwise is to cede ground to the competition, as Acts portrays Paul refusing to do to the sons of Sceva, a Jewish "priest" (Acts 19:13–14).

Of course, rabbis also taught disciple-students, who would constitute the next generation of rabbis. The institutional arrangements for rabbinic education range from circles comprising a single master and his students—much like Libanius' arrangement with his students of rhetoric in Antioch—to the development by the sixth century of larger rabbinic academies with an institutional head and organized faculty—much like the last major academies of pagan learning in the eastern Roman Empire, some of which in the sixth century were transplanted into Persian imperial territory at the invitation of the emperor, Kushro Noshirwan. Earlier evidence for such organized rabbinic academies is largely absent. Third- and fourth-century rabbinic documents refer to rabbinic "Houses of Study" (*beit midrash* in the singular). How much more structured and "permanent" a House of Study was than a master-disciple circle is difficult to say. On the Golan Heights at Kfar Dvora, just east of the Galilee, archeologists discovered a likely fourth-century inscription on what had probably been the stone lintel of a doorway; the inscription reads, "This is the house of study of Rabbi Eliezer Ha-Qappar." A Bar-Qappara is known to us from early rabbinic literature as an important rabbi in the Galilee in the early third century. Whether or not the Eliezer of the fourth-century inscription is the Bar-Qappara otherwise known to us from the early third, the inscription has some significance as an attestation to the formalization and institutionalization of rabbinic learning in the Land of Israel by the fourth century. It implies the existence of something more highly institutionalized, with some institutional longevity, than what is usually imagined when one refers to master-disciple circles.

What does any of the foregoing say or imply about the material and economic basis for the rabbinic movement or of its individual members? I have noted that the mythology about Rabbi Aqiva implies that rarely could someone from humble economic origins aspire to become a rabbi. And the third-century addition to the Mishnah, Tractate Avot (3:21) provides an aphorism, "If there is no [economic basis for purchasing] flour [to make bread], there [can be] no torah [learning]." It is entirely consistent with my depiction thus far of rabbinic activities and roles that many (perhaps most) rabbis seemed to have had other, nonrabbinic-related forms of principal employment and income, and offered their services as rabbinic arbiters, service providers, and teachers "on the side," as it were. Some were skilled artisans; some were landholders; others were merchants and traders. (Again, the case of Paul offers an apt parallel. Paul was a skilled artisan and practiced his skills to support himself while teaching and preaching. But before his conversion, he was for a time in the "employ" of the Jerusalem Temple authorities as their agent.) A number of rabbis were simply wealthy in their own right. In all, rabbis' economic security achieved in conventional pursuits allowed them to provide services as rabbis and to engage in teaching and study.

Certain rabbis became more renowned than others in offering opinions, rendering judgments, and arbitrating disputes for those who voluntarily sought them out, rather than seeking recourse at the formal courts. For this to work, not only those who voluntarily sought their services, but others, would have had to come to recognize the legitimacy of the rabbis' decisions. If this were not the case, the value to the clients would have been much diminished. Such "independent operations" were often done for a fee or honorarium paid to literati, teachers, scribes, sages, and other holy men in the Levant, Egypt, and the Middle East, and had been so for centuries. It is likely that rabbis, too, accepted and expected such payment.

Thus far, I have primarily framed my account within the social, economic, and historical context of the Land of Israel in the late Roman period. The rabbinic movement first developed in the Land of Israel, and to some degree was, as already stated, a codevelopment of the Jewish Patriarchate there. But sometime in the third century, some members of the rabbinic movement began operating in the Jewish communities of the Persian-ruled, Mesopotamian-Babylonian Plain. If it is accurate to call the rabbis' relationship with and their attempt to "rabbinize" the Patriarch's dynasty in the Land of Israel a deliberate strategy that by the fourth century had failed, then it would be accurate to assert that they used a similar strategy, perhaps with more success by the sixth century, in insinuating themselves into the operations of the Jewish Exilarch (in Aramaic, the *Resh Galuta*, "head of the community in Exile") in Persian-ruled Babylonia. The Babylonian-Jewish Exilarchate was probably an older institution than the Jewish Patriarchate in the Land of Israel. Persian imperial rule over its domains was by policy less centralized than Roman imperial rule, and part of Persian policy was to grant ethnic-religious groups in its domains some fair degree of autonomy and self-rule, by appointment of, and with reporting lines to, the imperial throne. Rabbis in Babylonia began training their own cadre of rabbinic recruits, imported traditions and knowledge over the course of the third into the fifth centuries from their counterparts in the Land of Israel, and over some unspecifiable period of time seemed to have ultimately rabbinized the Exilarch's dynasty. If early medieval rabbinic sources are to be believed, by the time of the Islamic conquest of the Persian Empire in the seventh century, the norm was that the Exilarch's successor had to have acquired a complete rabbinic education before assuming the office of his father, and the heads of the larger rabbinic academies in Babylonia-Mesopotamia claimed the authority to exercise some sort of veto power over the Persian emperor's choice of Exilarch from among members of the dynastic family.

The parallels between rabbinic attempts in the period before the Muslim conquest at co-opting of the Exilarchate in Persian Babylonia and their *ultimately* less successful attempts to co-opt the later Patriarchs in the Roman-ruled Land of Israel, whom they began to criticize in the fourth century as overly Romanized, also extends to the demise of both the Patriarchate and the Exilarchate. In the fifth century, the Roman imperial government, with a century of Christianization under its belt, begins to rescind the powers of the Patriarchate in the Land of Israel, eventually eliminating the office altogether. Although we have too little information about the development, stature, and roles of members of the rabbinic class in a post-Patriarchate era in the Land of Israel, the composition of the Jerusalem Talmud took place sometime near the end of the Patriarchate. Additionally, anti-Judaic Roman imperial policy increased over the course of the fifth century and into the sixth from the reigns of Theodosius II to Justinian and his successors, negatively affecting the vitality of the rabbinic group and its institutions in the Land of Israel.

In Mesopotamia-Babylonia the powers of the Exilarchate fell victim to something else entirely. In the sixth and into the seventh centuries, the Persian emperor revised models of imperial government. Persian governance became more centralized based upon Roman-Byzantine models of administration. As a result, the position of Exilarch, while not eliminated, became more of an honorific and ceremonial one, and power and authority over matters of Jewish life to some large extent seems to have passed to the heads of the several large rabbinic academies that had (recently?) developed, likely in the sixth century. Unlike developments in the Land of Israel under Roman rule in the fifth century, these changes in Persian ruled Babylonia seem not to be part of any specifically anti-Judaic policy. The advancement of rabbinic institutions and learning continued unabated in Babylonia (unlike the situation in the Land of Israel) with the Babylonian Talmud being composed sometime near the turn of the seventh century.

Thus far, I have said little about the ideology that buttressed the early rabbinic group and its claims to authority, other than to say they laid claim to "torah" learning. How, then, did the rabbis in the Land of Israel and Babylonia justify and legitimate their authority, that of their teachings, and the legitimacy of their emerging literature in the face of whatever resistance or competition they faced? After all, for many centuries the Torah of Moses, identified as the first five books of the Judaic Bible, the biblical books of the Prophets, and other writings widely recognized in Judaic communities as scriptural were the basis of authority. Even the writings of the early Church acknowledge this state of affairs. The earliest rabbinic group may not have had any formally accepted, well-articulated ideology grounding their own sense of authority, or that of their traditions or of their first literary compositions. Perhaps it sufficed within their own circles to be conscious of being dedicated to honing their skills to apply Torah-based law to the array of activities and the many real and hypothetical exigencies that might arise and constitute the everyday business of living a life as a Jew among Jews and Gentiles. (This is certainly one way to describe what is going on in Mishnah and the Tosefta.) But at some point, there seemed to be felt the need to say more about the basis of their enterprise and the authority of the traditions and teachings that they articulated and contemplated. What they came to say about that authority seems to have developed in stages.

The earliest articulation of a "myth" about themselves and their authority is likely the one found in Tractate Avot, which is probably a mid- to late third-century addition to the Mishnah. Avot articulates an ethos of earnest and dedicated discipleship and master-disciple relations. Avot makes the first master God, and the first disciple Moses, followed by Joshua, and so on down through a chain of generations of masters and disciples to the very rabbis whose names appear in the Mishnah (and the Tosefta). What is passed from master to disciple is "Torah" (divine-based teaching in a more generic sense) not simply "*the* Torah (of Moses)," that is, the first five books of the Judaic Scriptures specifically. In the fourth, fifth and sixth centuries, this emerging myth further develops to become the ideology of the Oral Torah. In this more elaborated form, God on Sinai revealed to Moses two Torahs, one to be written down by Moses as "Written Torah," that is the Torah of Moses in the Judaic Scriptures. The other is transmitted orally as

"Oral Torah" from master to faithful and diligent disciple through the ages to the rabbis at the latter end of the chain. Together, the Oral and the Written Torah constitute the "Whole Torah." In the later articulations of this emergent mythology or ideology it is made clear that the "Oral Torah" is in dynamic evolution; it does not seem to be something that is fixed. Thus, the substance of debates and discussions among rabbinic students and between students and teachers was also part and parcel of "Oral Torah" that Moses received on Sinai. It is as if acts of authentic rabbinic learning and study taking place in the Roman era generate content that automatically and retroactively becomes part of what God revealed to Moses. Think of it as a kind of rabbinic version of quantum entanglement in quantum physics, according to which two widely separated atomic particles effect changes in one another; what is generated in rabbinic study sessions in the third century immediately transforms what was supposedly revealed by God to Moses many centuries earlier.

The notion of Oral Torah in its full-blown version is a justificatory mythology and religious ideology that ought not to surprise any historian of religion. In the history of religions novelty is not valued. Quite the opposite. Antiquity is the basis for legitimacy. Yet novel developments happen all the time in religions. Consequently, one often finds mythologies and ideologies in religions that articulate how the newfangled is actually ancient.

Even in the history of early Judaism the rabbinic myth or ideology of the dual, Oral and Written, Torah has precursors. In 4 Ezra (chapter 14), a first-century Jewish text preserved and only lightly supplemented by early second-century Christians, the biblical figure Ezra receives *again*, through divine revelation, God's revelation to Moses from centuries before. So far so good; this is an emerging myth of how Ezra is a kind of second Moses, restoring matters after the catastrophe of the Babylonian conquest of Judah and the exile of Jerusalem's upper classes. But the story in 4 Ezra takes an interesting turn: what is said to be revealed (again) to Ezra are ninety-four books. Twenty-four of the ninety-four are said to be the "standard" Judaic Scriptures; an additional seventy are to be secreted away to be given only to the wise, the "sages." All ninety-four books are said by 4 Ezra to be written down by scribes transcribing Ezra's revelation, even if seventy of them were to remain secret, but for their communication to limited circles. So, we are not dealing here with a contrast between written and oral transmission of revelation. But we are dealing with a notion of a *dual* revelation, part of which is reserved for a restrained group who on that basis have greater knowledge of God's teachings and greater authority.

Some notion of this dual revelation claimed by some Jews to be their unique heritage seems to register, too, in a number of early Christian documents, particularly those registering anti-Judaic polemics. These second- to fourth-century Christian writings refer to a "second" body of divine teachings (*deuterosis*) claimed to be possessed by Jews. The fourth century Christian author of the *Didaschalia Apostolorum* is particularly concerned with this Jewish claim about a "second" revelation and stands at the tail end of an established patristic tradition about the Jews' alleged *deuterosis*. The implication is that the Jews' claim to possess this second body of divine teaching makes them, not Christians, the true heirs of God's revelation. Patristic writers disabuse their readers of such notions.

For modern scholars of early rabbinism and its literature, the emerging mythology of dual Torah, the "Written Torah" and "Oral Torah," is confounded with a vexatious historical-literary debate, about which I have, after forty-five years in the academic trenches, still not fully made up my mind. A number of modern academics claim that some rabbinic literature, most notably the Mishnah, once composed in writing, was transmitted and studied orally, that is, without a written text in front of the student. Others have concluded that Mishnah was *both* written *and* promulgated in written form, but was studied and cited largely from memory by reason of ideology. Some pretty good evidence suggests this may well have been the case. But there are also scholars who maintain that the text or texts were originally *composed* orally (like Homer's *Iliad*), and only perhaps half a century or more after its/their oral composition were "fixed" in writing. About this I am much less certain. I lean toward the hypothesis, written composition, and written *cum* oral transmission—that is, written texts serving as an authenticating base as needed—coupled with a strong tradition of memorization, oral use and citation in the context of the early study of Mishnah in the third and perhaps part of the fourth century. After that, my best judgment is that Mishnah both circulated and was used in written form, although rabbis still knew much of it by heart and often quoted it by heart. Did the mythology of Oral Torah spur this tradition of memorization and oral-use in study (or spur oral composition, for those scholars who see matters that way), or vice versa? To this question I can offer no definitive answer.

What happens to the rabbinic movement immediately *after* the era of central concern to us, that is, after the turn of the seventh century?

In the middle of the seventh century, the Persian Empire fell to the armies of Islam. The early Islamic Caliphate presented both a challenge and an opportunity for the rabbis. Islam inherited from Christianity much of the latter's supercessionist attitudes to Jews and Judaisms, and the early Caliphate adopted, but often tempered, some late Roman anti-Jewish/anti-Judaic policies, applying them first to Christians in the House of Islam and then to Jews. As a result, neither Jews nor the rabbis in the lands ruled by the Caliphate experienced anything close to the active suppression of Jewish culture and learning that had taken hold in the Christian-ruled territories of the early medieval period.

In fact, the Caliphate needed to consider who would exercise authority over proper Judaic practice, and ultimately, they seem to have supported the rabbis over against the rabbis' competition among Jewish literati, sages or scribes. In so doing, the Caliphate effectively made the heads of the large rabbinic academies in Babylonia, who already may have exercised considerable moral authority over the rabbis of Babylonian-Mesopotamia, into the *de facto* arbiters over disputes and questions about Judaic practice in Jewish communities across the rapidly expanding Muslim-ruled territory. With that, the die was cast. Within several centuries of the rise of Islam, virtually all Jewish communities, even those in Christian lands, recognized the authority of the rabbis in the domains of life over which they claimed expertise as arbiters of a life lived in accordance with Torah-teachings. Under Torah-teachings was now subsumed not only the teachings of the Hebrew biblical Scriptures but also all rabbinic instruction, interpretation, and literature, understood as well to be part and parcel of the Torah of Moses revealed on Sinai. Only early modernity, the enlightenment, secularism, and eighteenth-century pietism in the form of the early Hasidic movement, all nearly a millennium later, presented truly serious challenges to rabbinic authority.

FROM THE SECOND CENTURY CE BACKWARD, THE HISTORICAL AND CULTURAL ORIGINS OF THE EARLY RABBINIC MOVEMENT

Having concluded one "shaggy dog" story about the development of the early rabbinic movement, guild, or class from the latter second century to the dawn of the seventh, I will now begin another. Let us consider the origins of the rabbinic group in the decades, century, or centuries leading up to the latter second century.

To this juncture, I have intimated that the rabbinic movement coalesced sometime in the second century. I have pointed to the aftermath of the failure of the Bar Kokhba rebellion in 135 CE as a pivotal point of some sort in that development. However, it is improbable that the rabbinic movement appeared out of nowhere and spontaneously on the social stage of the Land of Israel at that moment. After all, by the end of the second century the rabbinic movement had coalesced sufficiently to produce a magnum opus, the Mishnah, which they immediately promulgated as the most important focus of rabbinic study, and the mastery of which was quintessential to membership in the rabbinic movement. These developments in and of themselves bespeak a certain level of institutionalization and organization that could not have happened overnight. Moreover, such newly formed organized groups within any social setting arise out of a social and cultural background that would have rendered the nature, identity, preoccupations, and activities and aspirations of the group plausible and appropriate, at least in the eyes of its members and arguably in the eyes of some (significant) others. Much in the Land of Israel's culture and society in the early Roman period would have made the early rabbis in the second century culturally and socially believable figures, or it is unlikely that the early rabbis would have exhibited the traits and preoccupations that mark them as a distinctive (quasi-occupational) group.

The foregoing may seem like an odd, convoluted, and rather indirect way to formulate the issue of the origins of the early rabbinic group. Admittedly, it is. But I have resorted to it for a reason. Simply put, we lack evidence that is both explicit and reliable about the historical and social origins of the early rabbinic movement much earlier than several decades prior to the authorship and promulgation of the Mishnah. However, that does not prevent us from attempting to surmise what the most plausible cultural and historical "soil" was from which the early rabbinic group germinated and sprouted.

Let me begin with describing the problems ahead of us. Addressing the early rabbinic group's origins and development in the years preceding the latter part of the second century CE, we find ourselves once again in difficult historiographical straits. On the one hand, if we take at face value what the rabbis' documents purport to tell us, we are often confronted with vexatious issues about the historicity of the evidence. At the risk of repeating myself, so much of what rabbinic literature says about its origins, which is not all that very much, comes from documents that are several and more centuries later than the events and personages about which the documents speak. How much did the authors of these documents really know about these earliest stages of the rabbinic movement's development? In addition, much of what these documents do say about the earliest rabbis' activities is obviously stylized, the result of mythologizing, and self-servingly tendentious—or all three at once. Origin stories in these texts are bent upon inculcating a certain perspective in service of bolstering the image and authority of the rabbis. Consequently, these sources tell us a lot about the culture and ideology of the documents' authors, *their* time, and *their* intended audience, but have much less to tell us that is valid about those who preceded by several centuries these authors and their readers.

On the other hand, we know a fair bit about the culture, religion, society, and history of the Jewish community of the Land of Israel in the last two centuries BCE and the first century CE from documents actually authored *during that period*. Many documents collected in what we call the Apocrypha and Pseudepigrapha of the Judaic Bible, the Dead Sea Scrolls, other texts found in the Judean desert, some New Testament literature and other early Christian writings, and the writings of Flavius Josephus all fall into this category. Yes, these documents' authors also have their particular ideological bents. They too are tendentious. They too will often engage in mythologizing. But they inevitably reflect the views of some group, persons, or person contemporaneous with *their* authorship (just as the rabbinic documents represent the views of their authors). That contemporary scene is the immediate antecedent of the decades in which the nascent rabbinic group appeared. And, additionally, they are at least not offering tendentious and mythologized depictions of the early rabbis, because they are not talking about, let alone for, rabbis at all. We also have archaeological evidence for this period in the Land of Israel. And we know what was going on in the territories adjacent to, and culturally linked with, the Land of Israel in the last several centuries BCE and the first two centuries CE.

Consequently, these roughly contemporary bodies of evidence for the period leading up to the mid- to late second century CE, while telling us little or nothing explicitly about the first rabbis, tell us much about the cultural, social, and historical landscape from which and in which the earliest rabbinic movement emerged. As a result, we can perform a kind of triangulation using the very earliest rabbinic documents we have, that is, the Mishnah (c. 200 CE) and the Tosefta (c. 250–425 CE), together with these other, earlier, nonrabbinic bodies of evidence. We may triangulate by asking, first: what do these earliest rabbinic documents *implicitly* reflect about the culture and sociology of the documents' authors and intended readers? And we can, second, try to correlate the answers to these questions with cultural and social parallels or likely cultural and social antecedents attested in these other, earlier bodies of evidence from the centuries immediately preceding the authorship of the Mishnah and the Tosefta.

But let me begin by somewhat deviating from the approach that I have just advocated. What, at least, do Mishnah and Tosefta tell us *explicitly* about the rabbinic movement and rabbis that they allege commenced the rabbinic movement?

Mishnah, the earliest rabbinic document, refers to the legal opinions of rabbis and protorabbis which Mishnah's authors place in (a) the mid- to late second century after Bar Kokhba, (b) the early second century before Bar Kokhba and the late first century following the Temple's destruction in 70 CE, and (c) in the generation or generations immediately preceding the destruction of the Temple. Among these pre-70 figures are Hillel and Shammai and their "Houses" (disciples), and Gamaliel (the Elder), mentioned also in early Christian literature as a prominent Pharisee, the teacher of Paul (himself a self-declared Pharisee), and, in Acts, as a moderate voice among Jewish authorities dealing with the followers of the Jesus movement.

Mishnah and Tosefta also attribute legal rulings to a Rabbi Yohanan ben Zakkai, whom Mishnah and Tosefta understand to be a figure straddling the decades before and after the destruction of the Temple in 70 CE. In several of these Mishnah passages (in Tractate Yadayim), Yohanan is portrayed as articulating *specifically labeled* Pharisaic legal positions over against contrary "Sadducean" positions. One such dispute concerns an issue of purity law that also registers in one of the Dead Sea Scrolls (4QMMT). It is later rabbinic texts (in succession Avot, Avot de Rabbi Nathan, the Talmuds, and Lamentations Rabbah) that progressively fashion or refashion a narrative that makes Yohanan ben Zakkai into the founder of the organized rabbinic group in the coastal town of Yavneh during the last phases of, and immediately following, the Roman siege of Jerusalem in 70 CE. Based on such accounts of Yohanan's activity and what is alleged to have occurred at Yavneh, several generations of nineteenth- and twentieth-century historians of Judaism elaborated a picture of a great, ongoing Council of Yavneh (akin to the major Church Councils of the fourth and fifth centuries), where major decisions were made about Judaism's practice after the Temple's destruction and concerning the stabilization of the list of books comprising Hebrew Scriptures. Avot (c. 250), moreover, provides lists of rabbinic figures, organized as successive generations of masters and their disciples, from pre-70-CE rabbinic or protorabbinic authorities to rabbis of the time of Judah the Prince.

As stated—and worth repeating—any attempt to reconstruct the history of the early rabbinic movement much before the middle of the second century CE from such rabbinic sources is difficult because of the nature of the evidence. After all, Mishnah is composed around 200 CE, attributes rulings to these early figures, but otherwise tells us virtually nothing about them. Later rabbinic texts from the third century into the seventh offer short vignettes about some of them, but clearly a fair degree of mythologizing is going on. Moreover, given the dates of these texts, several or more centuries after these early rabbinic and protorabbinic authorities were said to have lived, one may well be circumspect in thinking that these texts' authors had any historical basis at all for their stories and mythologizing. And few academic scholars today support the notion of a Council of Yavneh that looked like or did anything like what nineteenth- and early twentieth-century scholars depicted. Indeed, few would today maintain that a "Council of Yavneh" likely took place at all, even if places like Yavneh and Lod on the coastal plain were centers of activity of the early rabbis sometime between 70 CE and 135 CE. However, to return to the method I have advocated, we may ask what may we glean from Mishnah and Tosefta, the earliest rabbinic documents, that does not succumb to later rabbinic texts' mythologizing or these documents' own speculation about rabbinic origins?

First and foremost, Mishnah and Tosefta reflect a group and group-culture that sees its members and, therefore, its founders as the go-to experts in, and students of, how to live a Jewish life in accordance with the "way" (the Halakha) consistent with Torah teaching. As I have stated in earlier parts of this introduction, that "way" encompasses in theory a broad spectrum of individual, group, and societal behavior: prayer, Sabbath and festival practice, cultic sacrifices, agricultural tithes in support of the Levitical-priestly classes and the Jerusalem Temple, and purity law to guard the Temple against the powers of uncleanness. But it also includes family law and laws concerning damages, injury, theft, judicial practice, and legislative processes.

On face value, there are some curious aspects to Mishnah and Tosefta's treatment of agricultural tithes, purity, and sacerdotal law. In the Hebrew Bible, these laws have to do with support of the central Temple cult and its officiating castes, the priests and Levites, and guarding that Temple cult and all who participate in it from the powers of uncleanness. Mishnah and Tosefta were, respectively, composed roughly 130 and 180 or more years after the destruction of the Temple and the cessation of the cult. Yet, about half of Mishnah and Tosefta are dedicated to these topics. The framers of Mishnah and Tosefta, and those assiduously studying these texts and traditions in the early rabbinic group to some significant extent, are imaginatively living in the Land of Israel as it was before 70 CE (or as it might be in some future age in which the Temple and its cult are restored). And yet, neither Mishnah nor Tosefta imagines rabbis to be remnants of the priestly caste, nor do Mishnah and Tosefta appear to be addressing priests. They do portray rabbis as possessing the expertise, and therefore the authority, to direct members of the priestly caste in their functions.

There is another trait of Mishnah's and Tosefta's treatment of purity law (and to some extent of agricultural tithes) that may be relevant to our attempt to triangulate to their social and cultural origins and antecedents. Documents representing Jewish culture and society in the first centuries BCE and CE, including early Christian literature, seem to agree that one must be in a state of purity to participate as a priest, Levite, or lay Israelite/Jew in the Temple cult. If one is a priest, Levite, or lay Jew eating tithed produce, one must also be free from uncleanness. The laws of Mishnah and Tosefta square with this as well. But the laws of both Mishnah and Tosefta exhort Jews to do more than this. They exhort them, within limits that they consider 'reasonable', to eat all meals in a state of cleanness, as if one were eating holy foodstuffs, and they demand that all produce be tithed, that is, the sanctified portion be separated, *before* the produce is consumed as regular daily food. Mishnah and Tosefta, however, assume that many or most Jews neither practice purity rites when they eat regular meals and go about their daily business, nor tithe their produce before using any of it. So, Mishnah and Tosefta must also articulate procedures for dealing with the uncertainties that result from these assumptions.

Finally, while neither Mishnah nor Tosefta spills much ink on what a Jew or a rabbi is to believe, they do insist (in Tractate Sanhedrin) that a life after death in "the world to come" is a basic tenet of Judaism, and that denial of this is tantamount to heresy, bordering on apostasy.

In the Seat of Moses

When one compounds (1) these characteristics of Mishnah's and Tosefta's treatment of purity law and tithing with (2) their depiction of Rabbi Yohanan ben Zakkai as the defender of Pharisaic legal positions against those of the Sadducees, (3) these documents' identification of Gamaliel the Elder, a known Pharisee, as one of the early illustrious rabbinic figures, and (4) the insistence on some future postmortem life, one cannot escape seriously considering that based upon what Josephus and early Christian literature have to say about Pharisees (as tendentious as those depictions might be) some strong Pharisaic element is part and parcel of the early development of the rabbinic group. Further than this I do not believe we can responsibly go; we cannot simply identify the early rabbis as remnants of the Pharisees.

Earlier in this section, I stated that Mishnah and Tosefta reflect a group and group-culture which sees its members as the go-to experts on how to live a Jewish life in accordance with the "way" (the Halakha) consistent with Torah teaching down to the most highly differentiated situational circumstances. Exactly *how* Mishnah and Tosefta reflect, model, and inculcate this expertise is precisely what will emerge from other chapters in this book. These are matters tied to Mishnah and Tosefta's pervasive rhetorical and formal literary traits. So, I put this issue aside in this chapter. What I will say now is that a group dedicated to perpetuating and inculcating such expertise expects to be (or dreams of being) in charge of Judaic life and society and regularly consulted by those who are; or they expect to serve or dream of serving those in charge. Since Mishnah's passages make reference to priests, Levites, judges, courts, legislative bodies, and so on, and since Mishnah clearly implies that those who hold such offices for whatever reason are not necessarily or even usually rabbis, then I would suggest that the Mishnah and the Tosefta largely imagine rabbis to be *a group of specifically schooled individuals regarded as authoritative consultants to, and agents of, the ruling civil, administrative, judicial, and sacerdotal authorities*. In our social-historical exercise in triangulation, we may now proceed to ask, are there any groups operating within the social and institutional landscape of the Land of Israel in the period immediately preceding the appearance of the rabbinic group that fit such a description? These would be the most likely candidates as cultural, social, and historical antecedents of the earliest rabbinic movement. And identifying them, if we are able, will help us place the rabbis' very earliest compositions, Mishnah and Tosefta, and the early rabbinic group itself, into a meaningful context (even if we cannot go so far as to say that these groups actually formed the earliest rabbinic circles).

In response to the task at hand, I offer two assertions, for which I think there is more than ample warrant. First, the rabbinic movement was decidedly a "lay" movement. Second, I believe the most probable antecedents to the earliest rabbinic movement lie in several occupational or quasi-occupational classes the members of which were known or addressed as "Scribes" (*soferim*) and/or "sages" (*hakhamim*). "Scribes" or "sages" were a normative part of structures of authority, administration, and governance in Judaic society in Land of Israel in the period before 70 CE. They were likely either subordinate to, or sometimes a subset of, the members of Levitical-Priestly classes that occupied the very apex of Judaic society and polity in the period immediately preceding the destruction of the Temple in Jerusalem. Therefore, someone could be both a priest and a scribe, or a priest and a "sage." It seems that being the former, a priest, was not a necessary prerequisite for being the latter. Rather, being a member of an elite class by genealogy, as in the case of priests and Levites, likely made it easier to perform elite roles in other senses and to get the education to do so. Putting these two assertions together leads me to a third, somewhat speculative, claim. The earliest rabbinic movement finds its likely social and historical antecedents and origins in the classes of scribes/sages operating within Jewish society in the Land of Israel in the period before the Temple's destruction. But what the early rabbinic movement did was to decouple the pretension or aspiration to proffer and exercise this expertise, and to acquire the requisite training, from traditional Levitical and priestly status, prerogatives, and authority.

Let me now unpack these assertions a bit.

What I mean by "lay" must be viewed against the context of Judaic society and culture in the Land of Israel over the course of the centuries leading up to the demise of the Temple. The evidence of the Hebrew Bible, as well as that of the Apocrypha, Pseudepigrapha, the Dead Sea Scrolls, and Josephus for ancient Israelite society from the thirteenth century BCE to the early sixth century BCE presents us with a highly stratified society, with elements of a caste-like system based on birth, kinship, and heredity. Clan "princes," supported by clan elders, ruled clan lands and their inhabitants. And local altars where officiated at by members of the Levitical-priestly caste associated with and in service to the members of the clan. Only some types of mendicant groups of ecstatic seers and healers, which the Hebrew

In the Seat of Moses

Bible refers to as bands of prophets or "sons of the prophets," seem to have been able socially to locate themselves outside, or in the interstices, of this differentiated social hierarchy.

When in the tenth century BCE, the Israelite monarchy overlaid the older clan/tribal system of social organization, kings assumed social and political positions above clan/tribal chieftains (with the obvious frictions that would ensue). Central royal temples and their Levitical-priestly officiants claimed greater importance than local altars and their clan-based Levites. And both royal courts and central temples assumed "national" administrative and organizational roles that required an increasingly professional group of administrators, record keepers, and judicial-legal experts. These cadres of experts seem to have been largely drawn from the upper echelons of society and were educated for their elite roles in a central sacerdotal and civil administration.

Centralization before the Babylonian conquest seems to have reached its ultimate expression in the reforms of King Josiah in the late seventh century CE, but still faced serious resistance from local clan/tribal leaders and local religious functionaries. With the Persian rule of the Land of Judah (Yahud) and the Persian imperial sponsorship of a faction, which the Hebrew Bible closely associates with the careers of Ezra and Nehemiah in the fifth century BCE, centralists triumphed, albeit initially in a much-reduced territory. The monarchy disappears, and Judean life and society come to be governed by a central Temple administration at the apex of which is the High Priest. Even when the Hasmoneans establish a monarchy in the Land of Israel that lasted about one hundred years (from the mid-second century BCE to the mid-first century BCE) and for a time expanded the territory of the Jewish-ruled Levant to an area that likely rivaled or exceeded the territory once ruled by David and Solomon, they claimed their crowns as priests and High Priests, not as descendants of the Davidic kings.

Throughout this period, from the Persian (so-called) restoration to the fall of the Temple in Jerusalem, a profession-like cadre or guild of "Scribes"—I will use a capital S here—served as agents of and retainers to institutionalized governance, both sacerdotal and civil, in the Land of Israel. The books of Ezra and Nehemiah designate Ezra as a "Scribe" and a "Priest," as well as one who is "expert" in the Torah of Moses. It is on the basis of this triple designation that his authority over the community derives, according the books of Ezra and Nehemiah. Such "Scribes" are to be distinguished from persons with the same moniker providing basic services to a nonliterate or quasi-literate public, when the latter needed agreements cast in writing, or letters and other documents written, or even needed scrolls with Hebrew scriptural passages inscribed upon them. Rather, Scribes (with a capital S) were the Scribes of the Temple and its administration and were assigned positions throughout the Land of Israel to operate as the agents of the central Temple and of its administrative, judicial, and legislative functions.

It is probably these Scribes that are referenced in the Gospels as the "Scribes of the Pharisees" and the "Scribes of the Priests," who are portrayed as confronting Jesus and his disciples because of the latter's "off-side" behavior by accepted standards of practice under Torah law. In the Gospels, they are the "doctors of the (Torah) law." Indeed, sometimes in the Gospels one gets the impression that "Scribes" (of the Pharisees) and "Pharisees" are interchangeable equivalents, who "sit on the seat of Moses." Additionally, underlying these portrayals in the Gospels and in Acts is the assumption that factions among the elite of Judean society did not agree on a number of specifics regarding living a life in accordance with Torah teachings. Even if it is generally accepted that a "common Judaism" may have existed in the Land of Israel in the first century BCE and the first century CE, it was undoubtedly a "complex common Judaism" (the term Stuart Miller[18] prefers to the plural "Judaisms"), exhibiting factionalism and even sectarianism. The Gospel writers and Acts make hay with, and rhetorically exploit, this factionalism and complexity, in which the Scribal authorities of the competing groups are portrayed as playing a role. As we have already seen, such factionalism is reflected in the few disputes in Mishnah in which Yohanan ben Zakkai is pitted against "the Sadducees."

The literature of the Hebrew Bible, Apocrypha, and Peudepigrapha associate Scribes with another designation, "sage" (*hakham*) and with Wisdom literature, a body of texts proffering wise aphorisms that reflect the proper attitudes and appropriate comportment of the "sage." There is an established tradition both in Judean society and adjacent Middle Eastern society that links this type of literature to an elevated class of government and temple administrators, agents, and retainers. The author of the Wisdom of Ben Sira, writing in the second century BCE, aptly reflects these associations, and he adds to the mix the operations of organized schools to educate future members of this professional class. In fact, the author promotes his own school.

---

18. Miller, *Sages and Commoners*, 23–28.

In the Seat of Moses

Finally, and most probative, a class of Scribal administrators, produced by scribal schools where students, among other things, practiced literacy skills by copying documents akin in context to Judaic Wisdom literature, was a principal element in the ancient Middle East and of governance in the Ptolemaic Empire in Egypt. The Land of Israel was ruled by the Ptolemies during the first one hundred years or so of the empire's existence. This is significant, because the districts and the "super"-districts of the Ptolemaic Empire were each headed by an official duo, an *archon* (Ruler) and a *grammateus* (Scribe). The system was, in the main, retained in the Land of Israel after Ptolemaic rule, during the periods of Seleucid, Hasmonean, and early Roman hegemony. These "Scribes" were obviously not posted to write contracts, loan agreements, and letters, or to write mezuzah and phylactery scrolls for the general population. Rather they supported the need to interpret, explicate, ramify, implement, and administer the normative legal framework as enjoined by the Temple authorities. And in so far as "the Torah of Moses" was the constitution of the Land (even if it did not exhaust the sum total of the law of the Land), that support entailed application of rulings deemed consistent with Torah in their domains of responsibility.

The most probable historical, cultural, and social antecedents to the type of rabbinic expertise reflected, as we shall see in this book, in the dominant traits of Mishnah and Tosefta, lie in the class of Temple/government administrators, agents, and retainers that operated in the Land of Israel in the several centuries immediately preceding the Temple's destruction in 70 CE. Of these, the professional class of Scribes, who styled themselves as "sages," offers the most germane model. Just as we cannot say that the early rabbis were the Pharisees, it would be a bridge too far to say that the early rabbis were simply, or were trained by, the last generation of Scribes who operated on the eve of the Temple's demise, much as this is a distinct possibility. But that Scribes were a relevant social, cultural, and historical antecedent to, and partially a model for, the rabbinic movement is more than a possibility. The alignment of traits makes it reasonably plausible.

SUGGESTIONS FOR FURTHER READING

Boyarin, *A Traveling Homeland: The Babylonian Talmud as Diaspora*.

Hezser, *Oxford Handbook of Jewish Daily Life in Roman Palestine*.

Hezser, *The Social Structure of the Rabbinic Movement in Roman Palestine*.

Kalman in *Jewish Babylonia between Persia and Roman Palestine*.

Lapin, "The Origins and Development of the Rabbinic Movement in the Land of Israel," 206–29.

Lapin, *Rabbis as Romans*.

Levine, *The Rabbinic Class of Roman Palestine in Late Antiquity*.

Levine, *The Ancient Synagogue*.

Rubenstein, "Social and Institutional Settings of Rabbinic Literature," 58–74.

Schwartz, *Imperialism and Jewish Society*.

Schwartz, *The Ancient Jews*.

3

Early Rabbinic Legal Literature
A Brief Survey

MISHNAH, TOSEFTA, COMPOSITIONS OF HALAKHIC MIDRASH, AND THE JERUSALEM AND BABYLONIAN TALMUDS

As stated in the Introduction, this book aims to introduce the reader to the more dominant rhetorical and literary conventions of the most important works of early rabbinic *legal* literature. That objective is founded on the assertion that a basic grasp of these conventions makes this literature more intelligible, and therefore more accessible, to those who have not dedicated years to reading it. Chapters 4 through 8 of this volume deal in turn with Mishnah (c. 200), Tosefta (sometime between c. 250 and 425), the Halakhic Midrashim (sometime between c. 250 and 425,[1] with one, Mekhilta de Rabbi Ishmael, perhaps later still), the Jerusalem Talmud (sometime between c. 400 and 450, also called the Palestinian Talmud), and the Babylonian Talmud (c. 600).[2] In this chapter, I endeavor to describe

---

1. At least one prominent modern scholar of the twentieth century dates one of the Halakhic Midrashim, the Mekhilta deR. Ishmael, to the early medieval period; few subscribe to this view today. More on this issue, and on the dating of the Halakhic Midrashim generally, is provided in chapter 6.

2. Recall from earlier my mnemonic for remembering their order: My Toast with Home-Made Jam and Butter.

these works more generally. By way of orientation, I shall say something of each's overall agenda, provenance, date of composition, and place within the larger set of texts that comprise early rabbinic literature.

Types of early rabbinic literature: Halakha (i.e., legal), (h)aggada(h) (i.e., homiletic-narrative), midrash (i.e., biblical-exegetical)

As my use of the adjective *legal* suggests, there are types of early rabbinic literature other than these. They are primarily nonlegal in substance. In rabbinic Judaism, primarily *non*legal documents are collectively referred to as *Aggada* (or *Haggadah*) and as *midrash aggada*.

Midrash is the term used to describe rabbinic texts that take biblical scriptural verses as their base texts and proceed to link rabbinic teachings to those verses and support these teachings through analogy and the adducing of additional scriptural proof-texts. For example, the rabbinic text Lamentations Rabbah takes the biblical book of Lamentations as its base text and proceeds to "attach" to the verses of Lamentations rabbinic reflections on sin, destruction, redemption, and restoration, liberally citing verses from elsewhere in the Hebrew Bible to prove and bolster its reflections. *Aggada* (or *Haggadah*) refers to the "telling" of a story, parable, or aphorism, as opposed to *Halakha*, the "way" one acts in accordance with rabbinic legal dicta and principles. The elements of an aggadic work are not woven together into a coherent, extended narrative that would look like a biography or history, as the Gospels do for stories about Jesus and the parables and aphorisms attributed to him. Lamentations Rabbah's reflections, stories, and parables are *Aggada*. For example, the elaborated, mythologized story of Rabbi Yohanan ben Zakkai's escape from still-besieged Jerusalem to request permission from Vespasian to gather "the sages" of (or at) Yavneh appears in Lamentations Rabbah. *Midrash Halakha* (or Halakhic Midrash), by contrast, proceeds through the verses of a given biblical text, such as Leviticus, as a base text and links rabbinic legal dicta to scriptural phrases (in ways that we will see later in this book).[3] Finally, not all *Aggada*

---

3. To every generalization there are exceptions that, nonetheless, prove the rule. Two works of midrash Halakha, the Mekhilta de Rabbi Ishmael and the Mekhilta de Rabbi Simeon Bar Yohai, have substantial aggadic materials, but are otherwise primarily legal/ Halakhic in substance. The two 'Mekhiltas' simply could not ignore some of the narrative of the book of Exodus, their base text, despite their principal focus on the legal dicta of

is cast in the forms of *midrash*, that is, organized with a biblical scripture as the document's base text. Avot, a late aggadic addition to Mishnah, which (without Avot) is Halakhic, is not a midrashic text. How so? Avot offers aphorisms and sayings on the ethos of rabbinic study, of discipleship, and of comporting oneself as a rabbinic sage, but Avot is not organized as a series of explications of a biblical book. Similarly, Avot deRabbi Nathan, which takes Avot as its base text, is not a *midrash*.

Literary works of *aggada* generally have a diminished status in rabbinic Judaism and the classical rabbinic curriculum of study. It is considered edifying and instructive to study aggada. By contrast, Halakha is normative and authoritative. That is why it is often said that theology and ideology tend to take a back seat to appropriate action and practice in rabbinic Judaism, even if this is sometimes an overplayed and overstated generalization. What is not an overstatement is that the importance in rabbinic circles of the study of the principal *Halakhic/legal texts* of the early rabbinic movement tended to overshadow the study of other types of rabbinic literature. And this remained the case from late antiquity to the early modern period. When, for example, Maimonides (twelfth century), himself a formidable scholar and author of Halakhic texts, recommended that one should master the Halakhic tradition of the rabbis so that one might then move on to the higher calling of studying philosophy, he was roundly criticized by his peers, and triggered the "Maimonidean controversy." Maimonides' detractors viewed the study of rabbinic texts, and particularly of legal texts, as a lifeong pursuit of the highest order. They rejected Maimonides' implication that the mastery of Halakha and Halakhic documents like the Babylonian Talmud was (merely?) a stage in the intellectual development of the rabbi on the way to the study of philosophy or of anything else. Over the course of the century following Maimonides' death near the turn of the thirteenth century, his status was rehabilitated within rabbinic circles, but on the basis of his legal writings, his magisterial Code of Jewish Law (the Mishneh Torah) and his commentary on Mishnah.

In short, throughout the medieval period and into the modern era, to be a rabbi required one to have mastered the early rabbinic Halakhic/legal classics, especially (after c. 600 CE) the Babylonian Talmud, the principal commentaries on these classics, and the medieval legal codes, like Maimonides', based upon them. This is an apt segue to our immediate task, to

---

Exodus. As one might predict, there is no Halakhic-Midrashic composition that takes Genesis as its base text.

provide a general introductory orientation in context to the major compositions of early rabbinic legal literature:

Mishnah (M/m.);

Tosefta (T/t.);

the Halakhic Midrashim (in the plural, HM);

the Jerusalem and Babylonian Talmuds (JT/y. and BT/b.).

Survey of the Principal Legal Compositions of the Early Rabbinic Movement

Mishnah and Tosefta were composed in the Land of Israel in the Galilee. The Jerusalem Talmud too was produced in the Land of Israel, its moniker notwithstanding, largely in the Galilee, and was completed in Tiberias. And the Babylonian Talmud was composed in Babylonia-Mesopotamia near the end of the Persian period. There has been much scholarly ink used in writing about the provenance of the Halakhic Midrashim. I am of the view that they are the products of rabbinic circles in the Land of Israel. All of these texts, whether their provenance is in the Land of Israel or Babylonia, have been passed down to subsequent generations via, and by reason of the success of, the rabbinic movement in Babylonia-Mesopotamia in the sixth, seventh, and subsequent centuries.

I begin my account of these principal, early-rabbinic, legal documents with what I believe to be a fairly well founded and important historical claim about the inner-group life of the early rabbinic movement. Before the composition and promulgation of the Babylonian Talmud (c. 600), and other than the mastery of the Hebrew Bible itself, the study, mastery, explication, and the critical analysis of Mishnah seems to have been the principal qualification for being a bona fide member of the rabbinic group. This was so from the moment of Mishnah's promulgation within rabbinic circles near the turn of the third century on. Indeed, that a single document almost immediately upon its production and promulgation could attain such a status says much indirectly about either the level of institutionalization of the early rabbinic group, or its restrained size, or both at the end of the second century.

Tosefta and both Talmuds are composed and compiled (whatever is the more appropriate term) as commentaries and supplements to Mishnah tractates. That is to say these documents' tractates treat the corresponding Mishnah tractates as their base texts. Each in their own manner adduces materials from the rabbinic traditions they have in hand to (nominally, at least) explicate Mishnah. In the case of the two Talmuds, they pose stock critical and analytic questions about the base Mishnah text, which they proceed to answer in formalized ways. My phrase, "each in their own manner" is critical here, because the rhetorical and literary conventions of each document in turn—Tosefta, the Jerusalem Talmud, and the Babylonian Talmud—affect significantly what each does with Mishnah. When I examine in the subsequent chapters a number of the more dominant rhetorical and literary conventions of these documents, how Tosefta's and each Talmud's approaches to the explication of Mishnah differ will become evident. Suffice it to say here that the nature and range of what counts as appropriate ways of elucidating Mishnah changes and expands over time, as one progresses from Tosefta through the Babylonian Talmud.

Tosefta's explication of Mishnah treats all but three of Mishnah's sixty-two tractates, Avot excepted in the count;[4] Tosefta is roughly three and a half to four times the length of Mishnah. Neither the Jerusalem nor the Babylonian Talmud deals with all of Mishnah's tractates. Rather, each of the Talmuds covers about 60 percent of the tractates in Mishnah; thirty-eight in the case the Jerusalem Talmud, thirty-six in the case of the Babylonian. Since the Babylonian Talmud's compositions explicating Mishnah passages tend to be longer and more elaborate than the Jerusalem Talmud's, the Babylonian Talmud is more than two-and a half times the length of the Jerusalem Talmud. The Jerusalem Talmud retains greater focus on Mishnah's agricultural laws, and less of a focus on Mishnah's tractates on sacrificial practice, than the Babylonian Talmud. For the Babylonian Talmud the case is the reverse; Mishnah tractates on sacrificial rites remain a preoccupation and those on tithing and agricultural gifts are not. Attempts to explain

---

4. Mishnah Tractates Tamid, Middot and Kinnin (in addition to Avot) have no corresponding Tosefta tractates. That Avot has no associated Tosefta tractate may be further indication that Avot was originally not considered part of Mishnah, if further indication is needed. I know of no compelling explanation as to why there are no Tractates Tamid, Middot, or Kinnim in Tosefta. Their absence in Tosefta is briefly discussed in Brody, *Mishna and Tosefta Studies*, 132. Brody's book is a thoughtful and carefully argued work on modern Tosefta scholarship, with the exception of the work of Jacob Neusner, whose well-known studies on Tosefta are left unconsidered by Brody.

these mirror-image preoccupations of the two Talmuds amount to mere speculation.[5]

The early Halakhic/legal Midrashim are a different kettle of fish. The extant Halakhic Midrashim are organized with respect to base texts of the Hebrew Bible: the two Mekhiltas to Exodus, Sifra to Leviticus, and the three Sifres to Numbers and Deuteronomy (excuse the English plurals attached to Hebrew/Aramaic nouns). As the term "midrash" implies, they cannot take Mishnah as their base text and proceed to explicate Mishnah. But these Halakhic Midrashim do attempt systematically to link Mishnah's dicta and associated legal traditions to Scripture, as we shall see in a subsequent chapter.

When describing, even in a cursory manner, the focus on Mishnah's substance in the other major documents of the early rabbinic legal corpus, I repeatedly have referred to the practice of adducing other or associated rabbinic legal traditions to explicate Mishnah. There was undoubtedly a substantial pool of rabbinic legal tradition that continued to accumulate and expand from the second through roughly the sixth century. This pool was drawn upon first by Mishnah and subsequently by Tosefta, the Halakhic Midrashim and the two Talmuds. The two Talmuds cite traditions also found in Tosefta and the Halakhic Midrashim, as well as other traditions that in literary form look very much like them. And both Talmuds quote rabbinic traditions that are patently later than those found in Mishnah, Tosefta and Halakhic Midrashim. Furthermore, those who composed the Babylonian Talmud seems to have had ample access to rabbinic traditions from the Land of Israel up to the mid-fourth century, to which the authors of Jerusalem Talmud also had access. The inverse seems less the case; beyond the first or second generation of named post-Mishnaic rabbis, Babylonian rabbinic traditions are somewhat less prominent in the Jerusalem Talmud. West to East flow of traditions and teachings attributed to named rabbinic

---

5. Sometimes offered as an explanation is that the laws pertaining to agricultural gifts do not apply to produce and livestock outside of the Land of Israel, an assumption that underlies Mishnah's treatment of the theme of agricultural gifts. The biblical phrase, "When you shall come into the Land . . ." (e.g., Leviticus 19:23–25; 25:1–7) and other biblical references to "your Land" that are juxtaposed with biblical injunctions regarding agricultural gifts and the sabbatical year (when fields are left fallow) are the often adduced rationale for Mishnah's premise. But Mishnah, following the Deuteronomic trend in the Hebrew Bible, also assumes that sacrifice to YHWH takes place in one place, in Jerusalem, and nowhere else. Yet the Babylonian Talmud chooses to retain Mishnah's utopian interest in Temple sacrifices, while no tractates about such matters appear in the Jerusalem Talmud.

masters in the Land of Israel ends near the mid-to late fourth century, after which, for another century, the completed rabbinic compilations of several generations of Palestinian authors and editors find their way to rabbis in Babylonia. One is tempted to conclude that as long as the Patriarchate functioned in the Land of Israel, the prestige of rabbinic circles in the Land of Israel was significant, perhaps in part because of their location in the "homeland." Over the following two centuries, Babylonian rabbinic circles and the Exilarch increasingly attempted to assert their preeminence.[6]

As it will prove relevant to understanding the rhetorical and literary conventions of the two Talmuds in particular, permit me to recall from chapter 2 the distinction made in late antique and early medieval rabbinic traditions between *tanna'im* and *amora'im*. You will remember that this distinction involved drawing a "line in the chronological sand" sometime in the early third century. For the sake of simplicity, I picked c. 220 CE, an approximate date for the end of the career of the Patriarch, Judah. A sharp distinction was drawn between rabbinic traditions *believed to be* from the era of "Rabbi" Judah the Prince and earlier, on the one hand, and rabbinic traditions stemming from the generations thereafter. Rabbis understood to have lived and worked before c. 220 are, in later rabbinic works, referred to as *tanna'im* (*tanna*, sing.). Those from c. 220 until the chronologically-latest-named rabbinic authorities in the Babylonian Talmud (who lived and taught up to c. 500) bear the collective moniker *amora'im* (*amora*, sing.). Both terms are Aramaic, and both convey the notion of someone who passes on traditions by "repeating" them. Since in the rabbinic ethos, all rabbinic traditions are transmitted by people, that is, by rabbis and their disciples, including anonymous materials that bear no attributions to any named figure, rabbinic literature treats rabbinic traditions as "tannaitic" or "amoraic" and all rabbinic documents as either tannaitic or amoraic in origin. Moreover, because in rabbinic ethos someone chronologically closer to the source is more authoritative than someone temporally more distant from it, tannaitic traditions trump amoraic traditions in early rabbinic literature. Ideologically, the ultimate source is, of course, Moses, as is articulated in the rabbinic ideology of the dual (Written and Oral) Torah that was articulated in rabbinic circles in the late third and fourth centuries

6. The attempt of Babylonian rabbinic circles to assert their preeminence over their counterparts in the Land of Israel is poignantly expressed in the former's appropriation of the moniker "Zion" to refer to the Babylonian Plain and its rabbinic circles. They were the "new" Zion from which the law would "come forth." Daniel Boyarin describes this well in his book, *Traveling Homeland*.

CE. Mishnah is, then, the quintessential tannaitic document, and its constituent passages are the most authoritative tannaitic traditions. Next in significance are the passages in Tosefta and the Halakhic Midrashim, as well as other traditions understood to be contemporary with them. These too are tannaitic, but to distinguish them from Mishnah's passages, later rabbinic texts designate them as *beraitot*, the term for all tannaitic rabbinic traditions that do *not* appear in the Mishnah.

Given the chronological classifications devised by late antique rabbinic circles to differentiate rabbinic traditions, it follows that for these circles, *tanna'im* lived and worked in the Land of Israel; the provenance of *amora'im* could be either the Land of Israel or Babylonia-Mesopotamia. The differentiation of tannaitic from amoraic rabbinic traditions also plays out linguistically in early rabbinic literature. Almost invariably tannaitic rabbinic traditions are cited in Hebrew, while some amoraic traditions are cast in Aramaic and some in Hebrew. Moreover, the overarching "voices" of the editors/authors of tannaitic literature, which includes Mishnah, Tosefta and the Halakhic Midrashim, "speak" in Hebrew, while the editorial/authorial voices of the two Talmuds proceed mostly in Aramaic and sometimes in Hebrew. Use of language (Hebrew vs. Aramaic) becomes, then, one marker of the pecking order of rabbinic teachings adduced in early rabbinic documents.

Mishnah, the foundational document of early rabbinic legal literature

From everything that I have said to this point, it is an inescapable conclusion that Mishnah study was a formative activity within the early rabbinic movement, and that the other principal legal works of the early rabbinic movement in some fashion reflect and serve the study of Mishnah. Whatever the eventual resolution of the modern scholarly debate about whether Mishnah was initially composed and promulgated in writing or composed and first transmitted orally, like Homer's great epic sagas, there was undoubtedly a strong tendency to memorize Mishnah, and to cite it from memory.[7] The memorized Mishnah, no doubt, reinforced its status as "Oral

---

7. There has been of late much scholarly debate about the role "orality" may have played in the composition and promulgation of Mishnah. One exemplary voice of the "oral-composition" advocates is Elizabeth Shanks Alexander, in *Transmitting Mishnah*, and "Fixing"; she argues that both Tosefta and Mishnah were composed and initially promulgated via a process of oral performance. I am far from convinced that the evidence bears out the hypothesis that both Mishnah and Tosefta were composed via oral

Torah," in line with the emerging third and fourth century rabbinic mythology about the divine origins of the rabbis' teaching.

The authority of the content of Mishnah's passages was exceeded only by the laws contained in the Hebrew Bible itself (albeit understood through the rabbinic lens). Thus, the late third or fourth century text Avot deRabbi Nathan (AVRNa) 8:1, explicating its base text, Avot, provides this thumbnail list in priority order of the core rabbinic curriculum.

AVRNa 8:1 (AVRNa's citation of Avot in **boldface**)

A. **Joshua b. Perahiah and Nithai the Arbelite received** [the transmitted Torah] **from them.**
B. **Joshua b. Perahiah says,**
   1. **"Appoint for yourself a rabbinic master [as a teacher]** (*rav*);
   2. **"and acquire for yourself an associate [with whom to study];**
   3. **"and judge every person as meritorious [on balance, that is, give everyone the benefit of the doubt]."**
C. **"Appoint for yourself a rabbinic master."** How so?
D. This teaches that one should appoint for oneself a rabbinic master [that is, one should not flit from one rabbinic master to another] [with whom to study on a] regular basis.
E. And one should learn from him scripture, and mishnah, and legal midrash, and aggadot . . . .[8]

Only biblical Scripture itself outranks Mishnah, and Halakhic/legal Midrashim outrank Aggada (or Aggadic Midrashim). A tradition preserved in the Babylonian Talmud (b. Baba Mesia 33a) relays a similar sentiment about Mishnah study.

b. Baba Mesia 33a,

> Our Rabbis taught: Those that occupy themselves [just] with [the study of] scripture are of limited value; with [the study of] Mishnah [but not of subsequent rabbinic teachings] are certainly of

---

performative acts, as she spells out. To argue the point more fully is beyond the ken of this book's "introductory" purposes. It suffices that this volume's readers are aware of these debates.

8. The translation is my own and is taken from Lightstone, "Textual Study and Social Formation." Note 29 of the latter discusses the dating of AVRNa.

value and will be recompensed [for their study]; with [the study of] Talmud, nothing is of greater value. But always pursue the [study of the] Mishnah more than the [study of the] Talmud.[9]

To me it is historically ironic that this passage extolling Mishnah study appears in the only rabbinic text, the Babylonian Talmud, that sometime subsequent to its composition in the sixth century CE came to supplant Mishnah as the principal object of rabbinic study. Until that time, Mishnah study was of preeminent importance in the inner-group life of the rabbinic group.

Let me say more about Mishnah. I have already stated that Mishnah is organized in sixty-three thematically based compositions in the Hebrew language,[10] each referred to as a "tractate" (*masekhet* [sing.], *masekhtot* [pl.])—62 tractates when one removes Avot, which many scholars consider a later, perhaps-mid-third-century addition. Mishnah's tractates are gathered in the extant (medieval) manuscripts under six grand topical collections; these are Mishnah's "orders" (*seder* [sing.], *sedarim* [pl.]). The division of "tractates" may well stem from the time of Mishnah's composition (although in a few instances, a few of "today's" tractates may be subdivided parts of what had been longer ones). The distribution of tractates within the six orders may well be later, as the evidence of the earliest manuscripts (all of which are medieval) seems to imply. The extant manuscripts of Mishnah further subdivide Mishnah's tractates into chapters and individual Mishnah passages. Chapter numbers and their internal subdivisions are likely the innovation of medieval scribes seeking to systematize and facilitate references to Mishnah passages, as was done in the early medieval period for the books of the Hebrew Bible. Before that innovation, chapters of Mishnah were usually referred to by one or more distinctive words in the chapter's opening passage.[11]

---

9. Again, my translation of this passage is from Lightstone, "Textual Study and Social Formation," and my translation was, in turn, influenced by that previously done in Zaiman, "Traditional Study," 3.

10. Only a few scattered phrases in Mishnah are in Aramaic.

11. The Babylonian Talmud (like the Jerusalem Talmud) is organized in accordance with Mishnah's tractates and chapters (but not its "orders"). When, however, the Babylonian Talmud needs to refer to a particular Mishnah chapter, it does so by naming it after the chapter's opening word or words, not by referencing a chapter number. Immediately post-Talmudic rabbinic writings do the same. The boundaries of the medieval chapter divisions may not have always been identical to earlier views of where a "chapter" began and ended. This is not dissimilar to the case of subdivisions in the Hebrew Bible.

Medieval rabbinic authorities state that the sixty-two Mishnah tractates, and therefore the thirty-eight or thirty-six corresponding Talmud tractates too, may be studied in any order. Remember, each of the Jerusalem and Babylonian Talmuds treats only about 60 percent of Mishnah's tractates. But the chapters of a Mishnah (or Talmud) tractate should be studied in their proper sequence. So, early medieval rabbis treated Mishnah (and consequently the Talmuds as well) as a *collection* of carefully composed tractates; they saw no such deliberation or significance in the ordering of tractates.[12] Tractate *y*, in their view, did not logically follow tractate *x*. But chapter *b* of tractate *x*, did in some real and important sense follow chapter *a* as an act of deliberate literary composition, and should be treated as such. Medieval rabbis never imagined one studying Tosefta's tractates for their own sake and as objects of study in their own right, notwithstanding the fact that there are corresponding Tosefta tractates for almost all of the sixty-two Mishnah tractates. Tosefta remained a "reference work" only, as it were. One would no more study its tractates on their own (that is, without Mishnah) than one would study an encyclopedia or a dictionary. Indeed, as will be evident later in this volume, significant swaths of Tosefta are not fully intelligible on their own; one *must* have the corresponding Mishnah text in hand to make complete sense of a significant proportion of the Tosefta.

What types of topics do Mishnah's tractates, Avot aside, cover? While Mishnah's six "Orders" may be a *later* attempt to group tractates topically, they do help one grasp the topical range of Mishnah:

Order 1: Agricultural Law and Tithing

Order 2: Sabbath and Festival Law

Order 3: Family Law

Order 4: Torts, Damages, and Judicial Law

Order 5: Sacrificial Offerings

Order 6: Purity Law

Some tractates' themes did not neatly fall into these topical categories. The tractate on the laws of the firstling (Bekhorot) is found in Order 5; it could just as well have been located in Order 1. Order 1 opens with a tractate on prayers and benedictions (Berakhot). Topically, it really does not fit there, and some manuscript traditions place it elsewhere. A tractate

---

12. Except in those instances where contemporary division of tractates may have subdivided what may have been a single larger tractate.

on the slaughter and handling of meat for *daily consumption* (Tractate Hullin, from the same root as the Arabic term *hallal*) is in Order 5, which deals with Temple *sacrifices*. But since sacrificial animals had to be properly slaughtered too, no better place for Hullin likely seemed appropriate.

Several things may be said about this topical range of Mishnah's tractates. First, the entire range covers both Judaic practices that are relevant to a context *after* the Temple's destruction as well as rites that can only be carried out *with* a functioning Temple. Obviously, the latter could not be implemented at the end of the second century CE, when Mishnah was composed. Mishnah's authors seem unconcerned about this; the Judaic "world" they are defining in law is an ideal or utopian one. Why do this? In my view, because the Hebrew Bible describes such a world in biblical law, the framers of Mishnah deemed it necessary to do so too; it is, simply, the "world of the Torah," period.[13] *How* Mishnah goes about doing this is significant; but that is a matter best discussed after we have looked at Mishnah's rhetorical and literary conventions. At this juncture, I may provide two illustrative "morsels" of Mishnah to offer a "taste" of how a Mishnah passage typically goes about its business. The first is the same passage cited without explanatory interpolations in chapter 1, m. Bekhorot 1:1a.

> He[14] who purchases the foetus of an ass of a Gentile, and he who sells to him, even though it is not permitted, and he who forms a partnership with him, and he who receives from him, and he who gives to him in trust is exempt from the law of the firstling, as it is said, "Of an Israelite" (Numbers 3:13), but not of others (translation my own[15]).

---

13. This belies that often-made statement that the earliest rabbis are to be credited with inventing a Judaism without a Temple, a Judaism centred in the synagogue, home, and street and in which prayer, the reading of the Torah, and other rituals supplanted animal sacrifices and other priestly gifts. If anything, Mishnah ignores the fact that the Temple is gone, and the reason Mishnah has something to say at all about synagogue life and prayer likely stems from the fact that these were assumed by Mishnah's authorship to (already) be part of the Judaic landscape of life in accordance with Torah.

14. Throughout this book, I endeavour to use gender-neutral pronouns wherever I feel I can legitimately do so. The notable exceptions will be in translations of ancient texts, in which I try to reflect their use of language as faithfully as I can. They did not use gender-neutral language, and that, like it or not, often (but not always) reflects the cultural norms of the times and community of these texts' authors. I would be doing the readers of this book a disservice were I to mask their cultural predilections by masking their use of gendered pronouns.

15. Adapted from Lightstone, *Rhetoric*, 79.

In the Seat of Moses

As I wrote in chapter 1, to a novice reader of this typical Mishnah passage (whether in English translation or in the original Hebrew) the overwhelming first impression is one of being somewhat lost, of not fully knowing what is being talked about or what the legal ruling actually means. This first impression is completely understandable and justified. One should not be either dismayed or put off by it. Indeed, it is an important first lesson about Mishnah's defining literary and rhetorical conventions. How so? Several things stand out at first glance about this text, which is the *opening* passage of the Mishnah tractate from which it is cited.

First, it is bereft of meaningful context. A whole set of laws about the holy status of the firstling, some of which are found in the Hebrew Bible[16] and some of which are not, is assumed to be known to the reader, but is not articulated or even referred to in this passage. For example, Scripture explicitly states that *all* firstborn, male offspring of humankind and of (domestic) mammalian, animalkind, whether of clean or unclean species, are holy. Scripture then proceeds to enjoin how that holiness is to be dealt with (in the case of animals fit for the sacrificial altar) or "deactivated" (in the case of humans or of animals that are not fit for the altar). These scriptures underlie m. Bekhorot 1:1a and the tractate as a whole. But the relevant content of these scriptures is not rehearsed by Mishnah as a preface to its treatment of the law of the firstling, and these biblical verses are rarely referenced or explicated in the body of the tractate. In addition, m. Bekhorot 1:1a (as well as the rest of the tractate) assumes that notwithstanding what Scripture explicitly says, it is the first-born male offspring of donkeys alone of all unclean animal species that are subject to the laws of the firstling. Without knowledge of these logically antecedent rules, many in Scripture and some not, m. Bekhorot 1:1a is quite unintelligible. This says something about Mishnah's intended readership and about the social setting in which Mishnah-study took place, a matter to which we will return at the end of this book.

Second, m. Bekhorot 1:1a's lengthy compound sentence—with four "ands" joining its clauses—is so sparsely worded that one has great difficulty even articulating the precise "circumstances" that make up the cases to which the ruling applies. The passage evinces a very tight, almost lyrical-like repetition and "spinning out" of language that may give m. Bekhorot 1:1a a sense of "flow," but leaves no room for elaboration. To make Mishnah

---

16. See, for example, Exodus chapters 13, 22 and 34, Leviticus chapters 27, Numbers chapters 3 and 18, Deuteronomy chapter 15.

Behkorot 1:1a's compound sentence fully intelligible, the reader must be capable of interpolating into the sentence a lot of *relevant* content that is not explicitly there, as I show in chapter 4. Again, something is assumed about the role and capacity of the experienced intended-reader or about the novice's recourse to a setting in which one is mentored to become an autonomous reader of the Mishnah. Welcome to the social world of Mishnah's first intended audience!

The second "morsel" from Mishnah helps consolidate and broaden the initial impressions gained from the first. Following is the opening passage of Mishnah Tractate Gittin[17] (m. Gittin 1:1–3), which deals with matters of divorce, again without explanatory interpolations. By the way, in this and in all subsequent citations from early rabbinic literature, I will begin to use the abbreviation R. for the titles Rabbi ("my master"), Rav ("master"), and Rabban ("our master"), as well as the abbreviation b. for *ben* ("son").

> 1:1 He who brings a writ from a Mediterranean province—it is required that he say: In my presence it was written, and in my presence it was signed. R. Gamaliel says: Even so he who brings from Reqem[18] and from Heger.[19] R. Eliezer says: Even so, from Kefar Ludim to Lod. And the sages say: It is not required that he say, In my presence it was written, and in my presence it was signed, except he who brings from a Mediterranean province and he who takes.
>
> And he who brings from province to province in a Mediterranean province—it is required that he say: In my presence it was written, and in my presence it was signed. R. Simeon b. Gamaliel says: Even from hegemony to hegemony.
>
> 1:2 R. Judah says: From Reqem to the East, and Reqem is like the East; from Ashqalon to the South and Ashqalon is like the South; from Acco to the North, and Acco is like the North. R. Meir says: Acco is like the Land of Israel for writs.
>
> 1:3 He who brings a writ within the Land of Israel—it is not required that he say: In my presence it was written, and in my

---

17. *Get* (sg.)/*gittin* (pl.) is the Mishnaic Hebrew word for "writ," any writ; it is roughly a synonym for the Hebrew word *shtar* (sg.)/*shtarot* (pl.), which in Mishnah seems to have the more general sense of any legally enacted document.

18. The Roman-period, Nabatean metropolis, Raqim/Reqmu = Petra, today in Jordan south and slightly east of the Dead Sea.

19. Another major Roman-period, Nabatean city, Hegra, south and east of Petra in what is today northwestern Saudi Arabia.

presence it was signed. If there are regarding it challengers, it shall be made to stand on its signatures.

He who brings a writ from a Mediterranean province, and he cannot say, In my presence it was written, and in my presence it was signed—if there are on it witnesses, it shall be made to stand on its signatures.

(m. Gittin 1:1–3, translation my own[20])

Again, one's initial reaction to reading this text might well be that one has been dropped into the middle of the topic, and not commenced at the beginning. But, as with m. Bekhorot 1:1a, this passage opens the Mishnah tractate on writs of divorce. And as was the case with m. Bekhorot 1:1a, a great deal of context is missing that would make m. Gittin 1:1–3 fully intelligible to the "uninformed" reader. Even the fact that we are dealing with writs of divorce, rather than writs in general, is not made explicit in this opening passage of the entire tractate. Indeed, the reader is left to surmise the circumstances with which the passage concerns itself. A husband is abroad. His wife, whom he wishes to divorce, is in the Land of Israel. He must send her a valid writ of divorce to be legally received by her at some distance. Nowhere are we informed that "divorce at a distance" is allowed or under what circumstances. The Hebrew Bible says that if a man wishes to divorce his wife he must "write her a scroll of severance," "place it in her hand," "send her from his home," after which "she goes out from his home," and "may go and be another man's [wife]" (Deuteronomy 24:1–2). That is all the Hebrew Bible has to say about the process of divorce. There is a lot of content "daylight" separating that biblical injunction from this *opening passage* of the tractate, which deals with a man *at a distance* divorcing his wife. A lot of germane information is assumed. This requirement to have so much contextual content filled in for the reader of Mishnah should now seem familiar, having looked briefly at the opening passage of m. Bekhorot 1:1a, cited above.

Another feature of m. Gittin 1:1–3 is the repeated use of identically phrased, tightly cast, and laconically formulated language to spin out a mini-composition. We saw this, too, with m. Bekhorot 1:1a. It gives the whole an almost lyrical or poetic quality, but it does not make it easier to understand for the novice Mishnah reader. Just as context must be provided the novice, this lyrical-like use of highly compact language requires

20. Adapted from Lightstone, *Mishnah*, 35.

a great deal of supplementary information to be "filled in" by or for the reader. Furthermore, nowhere are we given reasons for the rulings so that we may discern the logic of Mishnah's content. In this regard, readers of Mishnah are again left to their own devices, either to bootstrap themselves if they have the requisite expertise, or to turn to a mentor who can guide them through the passage making its content and modes of legal thought more transparent.

We see in this passage some rulings attributed to named rabbis. Often, these rabbis' stated views dissent from the anonymous ruling, as in the case of the view attributed to Simeon b. Gamaliel in 1:1. Or named rabbis are portrayed as disputing one another, as in what is attributed to Judah and Meir in 1:2. Does it not seem odd for a law code to have diametrically opposed views registered? And why do the disputants disagree in the first place? Mishnah does not enlighten us on either of these queries. Finally, the language in "sayings" attributed to disputing named rabbis is phrased in the exact same language as the phrasing of the extended composition as a whole. So, what is attributed to any one rabbi cannot be taken to be a quotation in his very words. Patently, the language of the attributed "citations" comes from the authors of the mini-composition, not from the rabbi to whom the view is attributed. What is the significance of this blatant fact? These are all quite legitimate questions that stem from Mishnah's pervasive literary and rhetorical conventions, so aptly represented in this "sample morsel."

The foregoing provides a "taste" of the "flavor" of Mishnah's typical, dominant literary and rhetorical traits. And the latter are central for you, this book's readers, because Mishnah, as will be clear, is the "jumping off point" for how other early rabbinic legal literature goes about its business. We are entering a world of ancient rabbinic legal literature and of early rabbinic learning to which Mishnah, together with the Hebrew Scriptures of course, is central, and in which the relationship of other early rabbinic legal texts to Mishnah is of paramount importance to understanding what these texts are and how they reflect a developing early rabbinic social identity.

In the Seat of Moses

Establishing the literary-historical relationships among Mishnah, the foundational rabbinic composition, and Tosefta, the Halakhic Midrashim and the two Talmuds: the challenges of collectively authored documents, each produced over some extended time-period.

Turning now to the Tosefta, the Halakhic Midrashim, and the two Talmuds—we have already said much about their focus on the explication of Mishnah, and in the case of the Halakhic Midrashim, the attempt systematically to link Mishnah and other associated tannaitic-legal substance to biblical Scripture. Earlier in this chapter I made some general remarks about the literary relationship entailing among these documents and of their additional dependence upon a "pool" of the tannaitic and amoraic rabbinic traditions that they use, each in their own way, in accordance with distinctive rhetorical and literary conventions that help frame how each document goes about its business. But beyond these very general statements, I have said relatively little that is specific about each type of composition. What, then, can be reliably said of the dating, authorship, and provenance of Mishnah, Tosefta, the Halakhic Midrashim, the Jerusalem Talmud, and the Babylonian Talmud? With this question, we enter a realm of considerable scholarly debate, the texture of which is important, even if the results are often inconclusive or unspecific.

Let us start with dating. Throughout this chapter and the two that precede it, I have frequently used "c.," standing for "circa" (meaning "around" or "approximately"). Almost all modern scholars do the same when trying to assign dates to the authorship of these early rabbinic texts. Earlier I mentioned the Epistle of Sherira Gaon, a tenth-century document that attempts to compose the first history of the principal rabbinic texts and of the dominant rabbinic figures that preceded him. Few scholars take Sherira's work at face value for the period of interest to us, the second to early seventh centuries CE. It is not that Sherira is simply making things up; he is trying to draw conclusions from the very meagre evidence he possesses for this earlier period as well as from his own sense of how these rabbinic documents relate to one another (just as we are trying to do). But his work is based on certain assumptions that many modern scholars do not share.

Here are some of those assumptions. One, these books have authors, in the sense that Sherira is an author of his Epistle and that I am the author of this book. Two, the anecdotes that he finds in early rabbinic literature, some of which talk about (or speculate about) who wrote what, are historically reliable. Three, what early rabbinic literature depicts as the ordered chronology of rabbinic masters through the centuries and says about who was the disciple of whom is historically accurate. On this basis, for example, Sherira accepts: that Rabbi Judah the Prince composed Mishnah; that Rabbi Hiyya, a disciple of Rabbi Judah the Prince, composed the Tosefta; and that Rav Ashi began and Ravina II concluded the composition of the Babylonian Talmud, since Ravina II and his contemporaries are, chronologically speaking, the latest named, prominent (amoraic) rabbis whose views are cited in the Babylonian Talmud. Sherira also works with a well-defined chronology of the named rabbinic sages, divided into "tannaim," who in his view flourished up to and during the career of Judah the Prince, and "amoraim," rabbinic masters in the Land of Israel and in Babylonia whose careers postdated Judah the Prince and predated or were contemporary with Ravina II. Sherira uses references to historical events in early rabbinic literature to peg certain figures to precise dates, and therefore can peg the entire ordered chronology to calendar dates (using the Seleucid system for counting years since the founding of the Seleucid dynasty in the Middle East after the death of Alexander the Great).

Sherira's epistle is a brilliant work of attempted historical reconstruction, if one accepts assumptions such as these, which one cannot. Perhaps the most significant problem with Sherira's work stems from the fact that none of the major texts of early rabbinic literature is the work of a single author. They are collectively authored works completed over time, each within some literary and rhetorical framework that at some point in the process of composition became normative and was imposed on all of the materials. So Mishnah, or the Tosefta, or the Halakhic Midrashim, or the Talmuds may have each been composed over years or decades by many people before each reached some more-or-less stable form with a normative conventional literary framework. When we ask, for example, *When was Mishnah or Tosefta composed?* we are in effect asking, *When did it reach a fairly stable state exhibiting the literary traits and conventions it now possesses?* And all that we can do is "approximate" when that happened for each. Hence the "circa" before all dates. All this makes questions about who authored Mishnah or Tosefta somewhat moot. Additionally, it makes queries such as, *What was the state of Mishnah or Tosefta before it stabilized?* quite challenging, often without probative answers, or any answer at all.

The current scholarly views about the collective authorship of these documents, each over some period of time that is difficult to specify, makes discerning the literary-historical relationship among these texts a difficult matter of considerable, legitimate debate as well. For example, the *extant* Tosefta is certainly organized as a kind of commentary and supplement to the *extant* Mishnah. But *if* their periods of composition before stabilization considerably overlapped, then the relationship of Tosefta to Mishnah *might* be very complex. Passages *found* in Tosefta and passages *found* in the Halakhic-Midrashic texts are cited in the Palestinian Talmud. But did the latter periods of composition of Tosefta and the Halakhic-Midrashim overlap with the earliest periods of the formulation of some extended compositions that found their place in the Palestinian Talmud? Can we say that the rhetorical and literary conventions that came to *govern* the formulation of passages in the Halakhic Midrashim had stabilized before they were cited in compositions that found their place in the Jerusalem/Palestinian Talmud?

Modern scholars have felt compelled to pose these questions, not because they are just logical possibilities, but because the literary evidence at hand requires us to at least consider a series of more or less probable "what ifs" and their implications. So, what if the principal documents of this literature are (1) the product of collective authorships working over extended periods of time? What if (2) each text's normative characteristics also emerged and became fixed over some period? What if, additionally, there is a likelihood that (3) some of these time frames overlapped and were not simply sequential? What if, as is probable, (4) a number of these authorships had access to common pools of accumulating rabbinic traditions? What if (5) the current versions of the "final" texts we have in hand also include some significant layer(s) of later additions that postdate other rabbinic compilations that seem to cite these texts? The upshot of the "what ifs" generates a Rubik's Cube of possibilities and probabilities concerning when these documents were "completed" and how precisely they relate to one another. Perhaps the only near certainty is the dependence of all of them on Mishnah, or on some protoversion of Mishnah that significantly resembles the one currently extant. This book is obviously not the place to unravel and reconstruct claims about these complex matters. But I will venture some claims that can act as stakes in the ground for this book's intended readers.

The Tosefta, serving Mishnah study by completing and supplementing Mishnah

The extant Tosefta (which means "the Supplement") is organized and composed as a kind of commentary and "supplement" to Mishnah ("[the] Teaching").[21] Tosefta is *largely* organized in accordance with Mishnah's tractates and tractates' constituent "chapters." And as Jacob Neusner has demonstrated,[22] notwithstanding the notable exceptions that other scholars have uncovered, the dominant *tendency* in a Tosefta "chapter" is to explicate more or less in order the passages of the correlative chapter of Mishnah with three types of material in sequence:

(1) by citing and glossing the correlative Mishnah passage;

(2) by presenting materials that complement the Mishnah passage in some fashion, where the complementary material relies on the Mishnah passage for an intelligible context, even if it does not cite the Mishnah; finally,

(3) by appending supplementary material that is topically related to the Mishnah passage, but does not depend upon Mishnah for a meaningful context.[23]

As one might expect, and as Neusner states, a *tendency* is not a hard-and-fast rule, but a tendency does show a more or less stable compositional framework and consistent authorship that comes later than and is decidedly dependent upon Mishnah's.[24] Moreover, as we shall see, many, indeed most,

---

21. Just this simple statement, which I stand by, runs helter-skelter over considerable scholarly debate about how Tosefta came to be and what Tosefta's literary-historical relationship with Mishnah is. I will make some further reference to this debate in chapter 5 (see especially notes 4, 14, 16 and 21), which deals with Tosefta at length, and in chapter 9.

22. Neusner has written much about Tosefta and its relationship to Mishnah. Perhaps the most concise formulation of his findings is "Describing Tosefta," 39–72; See also Neusner, *Tosefta, An Introduction*.

23. Most scholars of Tosefta, even those who do not agree with Neusner's conclusions about Tosefta's literary-historical relationship to Mishnah, point to some version of these different ways in which Toseftan materials relate to Mishnaic materials. See, for example, Kulp, "Organizational Patterns"; see also Fox, "Introducing Tosefta."

24. As is hinted at in the preceding footnotes, the literary-historical relationship between the substance and constituent sources of Mishnah and Tosefta is a matter of considerable debate. They both draw from a common pool of earlier rabbinic traditions, some of which may have circulated in written form and some of which circulated in oral

rhetorical and literary conventions that characterize Mishnah are present in Tosefta, although sometimes modified and extended in interesting ways. Yet all this being said, Tosefta has a proclivity to draw upon preexistent traditions likely circulating before not only Tosefta's composition but also Mishnah's. And in some instances, Tosefta seems to have recourse to rabbinic traditions the origins of which are just barely post-Mishnaic, that is, from c. 200 to 230 CE. It follows from this that the extant Tosefta has no overarching topical agendas of its own; its topical agenda is Mishnah's—no more, no less. And it should not surprise one that given its compositional tendencies, Tosefta is, relative to Mishnah's size, an enormous document. As already stated, Tosefta is about three and a half to four times Mishnah's length. Finally, despite Tosefta being topically tied to Mishnah's apronstrings, Tosefta sometimes exhibits its own distinct legal positions on topics it shares with Mishnah. Still awaiting sufficient academic study, in fact, is whether there is some overarching coherence and tendency to Tosefta's *legal* positions that may be contrasted to Mishnah's.

What does a typical passage of Tosefta look like? Again, as a foretaste of chapter 5 of this volume, I present a "snippet" of a Tosefta passage, t. Bekhorot 1:1a, the correlate of m. Bekhorot 1:1a, cited earlier. Represented here (and elsewhere in this book) is the Hebrew text of Tosefta bound together with the standard printed (i.e., Vilna) edition of the Babylonian Talmud.[25] Where Tosefta's language exactly parallels Mishnah's, I have used boldface.

---

form. None of the items of this pool have survived independently of Mishnah, Tosefta, and of other later rabbinic legal compositions. So, to maintain that some Tosefta passages reflect something of this common pool that is older than the formulation in the related passage in Mishnah is certainly reasonable and at times demonstrable. But I am ever more convinced that Tosefta *as a whole* is post-Mishnaic both as regards time of composition as well as substantive agenda. Moreover, I am convinced that the major constituent bodies of material in Tosefta that either cite and gloss Mishnah or, to use Neusner's term, complement Mishnah are post-Mishnaic in formulation, even if they draw on older content. I am unconvinced of the validity of an hypothesis articulated by Judith Hauptman that the "core" of Tosefta *is* the *first* Mishnah, and that our extant Mishnah is a development of it. One of the reasons for my stance is that even if the substance of a number of Tosefta passages can be argued to be pre-Mishnaic and underlying a Mishnah passage, the rhetorical and literary traits—the way things are formulated in language—show over and over again Tosefta's dependence on language that was formulated by our extant Mishnah's authorship. See Hauptman, "Does the Tosefta"; and Hauptman, *Rereading Mishnah*. Robert Brody offers a parallel argument in his book, *Mishnah*, to my own in which he asserts that scholars who share Hauptman's perspective (including Albertina Houtman, Shamma Friedman, and Joshua Kulp) cannot draw from the evidence they adduce the conclusions that they have articulated.

25. The text of the Tosefta printed in the Vilna edition of the Babylonian Talmud

> **He who purchases the foetus of an ass of** an idol worshipper, **and he who sells to him, even though it is not permitted, and he who forms a partnership with him**—he who gives to him in partnership—**and he who receives from him, and he who gives to him in trust is exempt from the law of the firstling, as it is said, "Of an Israelite"** (Numbers 3:13), **but not of others.**
>
> (t. Bekhorot 1:1a, translation mine.[26])

Here is Tosefta at its most simple. It cites Mishnah word for word and inserts one explanatory gloss ("—he who gives to him in partnership—") into the Mishnah text. The use of the term "idol worshipper" in Tosefta instead of "Gentile" (as found in the Mishnah passage), is insignificant. The variant probably results from the differing terminological preferences of different medieval scribes who have copied manuscripts of Mishnah and Tosefta.[27] What is striking is how Mishnah-like Tosefta seems in its literary style. Just as Tosefta is largely dependent upon Mishnah for its agenda,[28] so too it largely reflects most of Mishnah's literary and rhetorical conventions. More so, this Tosefta passage is completely dependent upon its correlative

---

is universally understood *not* to be the best text of the Tosefta for scholarly purposes. And I too generally eschew this version for my own scholarly work. However, given this book's purpose, as an introduction to the literary-rhetorical forms of early rabbinic literature, I decided to use a version of the Hebrew text of Tosefta that is most widely available. Any library or reading room that has any early rabbinic texts in their original languages on their shelves will have a set of the reprinted volumes of the Vilna edition of the Babylonian Talmud, and, therefore, a text of the Tosefta printed therein. By contrast the (scholarly) Zuckermandel or Lieberman editions of the Tosefta may not be there. Furthermore, it is increasingly the case that online editions of the Vilna edition of the Babylonian Talmud are available, and with them, in some instances, online reproductions of the Tosefta text within Vilna edition. For example, the online Hebrew text of the Tosefta made available by Mehon Mamre (mehon-mamre.org) reproduces that bound with the Vilna edition of the Babylonian Talmud.

26. Adapted from Lightstone, *Rhetoric*, 190.

27. Such terminological differences in medieval manuscript copies of early rabbinic literature reflect the religious politics and theological thinking of the time of the copiests. "Idol worshippers" was sometimes used so that Christian (or Muslim) readers of these texts—yes, there were some—would not see these passages as reflecting disparaging teachings about Christians (or Muslims), but rather about "pagans," whose religious beliefs and practices Jews, Christians, and Muslims disdained. Attention to such terminological usages were particularly germane in periods and places where the Church assigned persons to read Jewish texts to ascertain whether they should be censored, confiscated, or destroyed.

28. At least, for those of us who see Tosefta as largely a post-Mishnaic composition that may frequently have recourse to pre-Mishnaic rabbinic traditions.

Mishnah passage for its very language; that is why so much boldface type appears in my translation of t. Bekhorot 1:1a. Indeed, to have mastered the passage in Mishnah is to have acquired all that one needs to understand fully this passage in Tosefta.

If t. Bekhorot 1:1a represents Tosefta in its most simple mode (that is, citing Mishnah and inserting a single, explanatory gloss), it is worth also seeing Tosefta in a different, more elaborated mode vis-à-vis Mishnah. Let us look at a Tosefta passage that cites, comments upon, and complements Mishnah. Tosefta Gittin 1:1–7 does just this for m. Gittin 1:1–3, presented earlier. Go back and reread m. Gittin 1:1–3 one more time, and then turn to t. Gittin 1:1–7, which follows. (Again, I am translating the text of the Tosefta published with the Vilna edition of the Talmud, and, again, language in Mishnah that also appears verbatim in the Tosefta passage is in boldface.)

> 1:1 **He who brings a writ from** Syria **is like** him who brings a writ from outside the Land; **it is required that he say: In my presence it was written, and in my presence it was signed.**
>
> From trans-Jordan—**is like he who brings from the Land of Israel,** and **it is not required that he say; In my presence it was written, and in my presence it was signed.**
>
> 1:2 **He who brings a writ from a Mediterranean province, and cannot say: In my presence it was written, and in my presence it was signed**—if it is possible to **make it stand on its signatures,** it is fit; and if not, it is unfit.
>
> They used to say, They did not say that **he should say: In my presence it was written, and in my presence it was signed,** in order to be stringent, rather to be lenient upon him.
>
> 1:3 **He who brings a writ from a Mediterranean province,** and it was not **written in his presence,** and it was not **signed in his presence**—Lo, this person returns it to its locale, and he convenes a court, and it **makes it stand upon its signatures,** and **he brings** it and says: An agent of the court am I.
>
> In **the Land of Israel,** an agent appoints an agent. R. Simeon b. Gamaliel says: An agent does not appoint an agent as regards writs.
>
> 1:4 In the beginning, they used to say: **From province to province.** They revisited to say: From neighborhood to neighborhood. **R. Simeon b. Gamaliel says: Also from hegemony to hegemony.**

1:5 There is a stringency as regards **the Mediterranean province** that is not so as regards **the Land of Israel**, and with regards **the Land of Israel** that is not so as regards **the Mediterranean province**.

Since **he who brings a writ from a Mediterranean province—it is required that he say: In my presence it was written, and in my presence it was signed; if there are regarding it challengers, it shall be made to stand on its signatures.** He who brings a writ from the Land of Israel cannot say: **In my presence it was written, and in my presence it was signed**; if there are on it [the signatures of] witnesses, **it shall be made to stand on its signatures.**

1:6 How [do they proceed when] they said, **it shall be made to stand on its signatures?** When they said: This is our handwriting—it is fit. But we do not recognize either the man or the woman—it is fit. This is not our handwriting, but others testify that it is their handwriting, or their handwriting was adduced from another place—it is fit.

1:7 **R. Meir says, Acco** and its hinterland **are like the Land of Israel as regards writs**. And the sages say, **Acco** and its hinterland are like outside the Land as regards writs.

It once happened concerning someone from Kefar Sissi, who brought before R. Ishmael a writ of divorce. He said to him: Even so, you are required **to say, In my presence it was written and in my presence it was signed**, and it does not require witnesses. After he left, said before him R. Illai: Rabbi, Kefar Sissi is the territory of **the Land of Israel**, closer to Sepphoris than to **Acco**. He said to him, Since the matter is settled with a leniency, it is settled.

(t. Gittin 1:1–7, translation my own[29])

What is notable at first glance about this Tosefta passage, and how does it relate to the corresponding text in m. Gittin 1:1–3? First, we see once again that a great deal of Tosefta's language exactly parallels Mishnah's. As any professor suspecting plagiarism in a student's work would recognize in an instant, someone has copied from someone, verbatim—directly or indirectly. Second, Tosefta is not *fully* intelligible on its own. Or perhaps it is more apt to say that Tosefta is much less intelligible on its own, and much more intelligible when one has m. Gittin 1:1–3 in hand. Why? At a minimum, m. Gittin 1:1 together with the first statement of 1:2 serve to provide a meaningful context for t. Gittin 1:1. Else, why should Tosefta launch its

---

29. Adapted from Lightstone, *Mishnah*, 82–83.

passage with a statement telling us that Syria is considered outside the Land of Israel and trans-Jordan is considered inside the Land as regards procedures for executing writs of divorce at a distance? A similar relationship between the Tosefta passage and the Mishnah passage entails throughout t. Gittin 1:1–7 and m. Gittin 1:1–3. Tosefta in some manner or another "adds to" the treatment of the matter in Mishnah, and Tosefta is *more* intelligible when read with Mishnah in hand, and *less* intelligible when it is not. And all the while, much language in both passages is identical, word for word. For example:

> t. Gittin 1:1 adds more geographical pin-points to Mishnah's map defining what is inside and outside the Land of Israel;

> t. Gittin 1:2 starts by providing an explanatory gloss to Mishnah's treatment, making explicit what is only implicit in the Mishnah text; it then goes on to remark that Mishnah's requirements are intended to make things easier on the parties involved, not more difficult—a commentary of sorts;

> t. Gittin 1:3 completes Mishnah by specifying procedures for validating the writ when the emissary cannot vouch for having seen the writ prepared and witnessed;

> t. Gittin 1:4 offers some legal historical background for Mishnah's ruling, indicating the supposed evolution of Mishnah's requirements;

> t. Gittin 1:5–6 return to the themes of what is stringent and what is lenient about Mishnah's requirements and further "fills in" procedural matters to illustrate the point;

> t. Gittin 1:7 returns to the theme of m. Gittin 1:1, pinpointing the boundaries of the Land of Israel for the purposes of transmitting writs of divorce; adding that the surrounding hinterland of a city shares the status of the city at its center as regards executing writs of divorce "at a distance." The typically formulated precedent story at t. Gittin 1:7 adds to Mishnah's treatment of the matter by indicating that in Ishmael's view, if one makes an inappropriate judgment in this matter that is a "leniency," one "lets it ride" and does not overturn the decision.

As stated, Tosefta in many respects looks very Mishnah-like. That is why you will find reading and understanding Tosefta that much easier, once you have gained more comfort with Mishnah's dominant rhetorical and literary conventions. But it should already be evident from the two sample snippets presented in this chapter that Tosefta also differs in quite discernible ways from Mishnah. And how can it not, in literary and rhetorical terms, when Tosefta's intelligibility depends in passage after passage upon the correlative Mishnah passages that Tosefta serves to illuminate and complement? To read Tosefta without Mishnah in hand is a struggle, in a way somewhat similar to reading any "commentary" without the text being commented upon open before one. But we are getting ahead of ourselves. At this point, you can be assured that learning to read Mishnah, by acquiring familiarity with its dominant literary and rhetorical conventions, will engender skills that may be transferred entirely to reading Tosefta.

Halakhic Midrashim: "Reasoning" from Scripture to articulate the Halakha

The Halakhic Midrashim (HM) are organized as sustained exegetical commentaries (of a sort) on extended sections of the last four books of the Pentateuch (that is, Exodus, Leviticus, Numbers, and Deuteronomy), focusing primarily on the major *legal* collections within these biblical books.[30] The extant texts of Halakhic Midrashim are all considered and treated by later rabbinic documents as "tannaitic" in origin. The extant principal Halakhic-Midrashic texts are

- **—on Exodus,**
    Mekhilta deRabbi Ishmael, and
    Mekhilta deRabbi Simeon bar Yohai;

- **—on Leviticus,**
    Sifra deBe Rav;

- **—on Numbers,**
    Sifre on Numbers (Bamidbar), and
    Sifre Zutta (on Numbers);

---

30. The use of "primarily" in the sentence betrays the existence of exceptions to the rule. For example, the authorship of the HM compositions on Exodus could not resist treating some of the narrative components of Exodus, and so have included compositions of Aggadic Midrash in what is otherwise an Halakhic text.

—on Deuteronomy,

Sifre on Deuteronomy (Devarim).

The biblical Scriptures function as the base text for each of the books of HM. That is, in order, each verse of the (selected) salient sections of Scripture, sometimes phrase by phrase, is cited and commented upon before preceding to the next. Each passage of HM then references the authoritative rabbinic legal dictum/dicta derived from the "base" verse, or derived from the base verse read in combination with other Scripture. Passages of HM then proceed to demonstrate how this rabbinic legal position is so derived from Scripture, without being grossly misconstrued by faulty reasoning left to its own devices without the benefit of Scripture. As you shall see in chapter 6 of this volume, the dominant outcome of patterns of formalized rhetoric in HM is to show the necessity of appealing to scriptural grounds and the insufficiency of legal reasoning alone in deriving the Halakha. This is a decided ideological bent of HM, to recontextualize Mishnah, Mishnah-study, and other associated early rabbinic legal teachings, within the frame of Scripture.

Passages of HM at times cite Mishnah verbatim, or reflect legal positions articulated in Mishnah, or attempt to ground in Scripture rules logically antecedent to, and assumed by, Mishnah. Similarly, legal teachings (also) found in Tosefta are sometimes referred to in HM's passages. It is not always possible to determine whether HM's dependence on content found in Tosefta indicates a reliance on the Tosefta as we have it, or upon a pool of accumulated traditions circulating to edify Mishnah that were also available to Tosefta's authors. Some of the rhetorical and literary forms that are characteristic and formative of the HM as a distinct rabbinic literary genre—and we shall study them in chapter 6—are in a few instances also found in Tosefta passages. By contrast, I have never encountered these HM-like forms anywhere in Mishnah. One is faced, then, with a choice. Either HM's dominant and formative rhetorical and literary conventions are decidedly post-Mishnaic and later than the materials drawn upon by the authorship of Tosefta, or the framers of Mishnah and of Tosefta's materials knew of traditions like those that characterize HM and assiduously avoided using them or imitating their characteristic rhetorical and literary conventions. In my judgment, the former is the more likely, although some scholars propound the latter view.[31]

---

31. These scholars depict HM as a revival or adaptation of an early rhetorical and

As I did above for Mishnah and Tosefta, I present two short passages of HM to give a foretaste of things to come in this book. Let me begin, as I did with Mishnah and Tosefta, with the "raw" text of a passage, without explanatory interpolations. This first passage of HM is taken from Sifre on Numbers, Korah 118 (edition Horovitz, p. 138, lines 16ff, translation my own[32]). I have chosen it because the theme, the redemption of the firstborn, male offspring of a donkey, will already be familiar to you from our earlier presentation of m. Bekhorot 1:1a.

Sifre on Numbers, Korah 118:

> "But, you shall surely redeem" (Numbers 18:15). I understand that also any other unclean beast is meant!? Scripture says, "But the firstborn of a donkey you shall redeem with a lamb" (Exodus 13:13). The firstborn of a donkey you redeem, and you do not redeem the firstborn of any other unclean beast.
>
> Or "the firstborn of a donkey you shall redeem with a lamb" (Exodus 13:13), and any other unclean beast with clothing and utensils!? Scripture says additionally in another place, "But the firstborn of a donkey you shall redeem with a lamb" (Exodus 34:20). With a lamb you redeem, and you do not redeem with clothing and utensils.
>
> If so, why does Scripture say, "But you shall surely redeem" (Numbers 18:15)? If it does not relate to the matter that they redeem an unclean beast, apply it to the matter that they sanctify an unclean beast for the upkeep of the Temple, and they return and redeem it from among the sanctified things for the upkeep of the Temple.

As you read this passage and strive to make sense of it, I have no doubt that this particular formalized manner of argument from Scripture appears alien and obtuse. I assure you that it will not appear to be either, when in

---

literary genre that Mishnah's authorship and the framers of most of the passages found in Tosefta knew but suppressed. The most prominent proponent of the "suppression and revival" hypothesis is David Weiss Halivni in his book, *Midrash, Mishnah and Gemara*, 1986. Except for the suppression-and-revival hypothesis which he advocates for the genre of Halakhic Midrash, Halivni's is an otherwise brilliant book. His support for the hypothesis is based, in my opinion, on an untenable "argument from silence," one based on a quasi-ideological stance on the origins of rabbinic law in the processes of scriptural exegesis. As we shall see when in subsequent chapters we look carefully at the dominant rhetorical and literary conventions of HM, seeing them as acts of, or the results of, scriptural exegeses is not apt.

32. And influenced by my prior translation in Lightstone, *Rhetoric*, 216–22.

chapter 6 I present the recurrent rhetorical traits of HM and how they are used. The force of HM's dominant rhetorical and literary conventions, as you shall see later in this book, is to anchor legal teachings from Mishnah and related rabbinic traditions in Scripture. The method of doing so and its results often seem highly contrived and *a priori*; in passage after passage of HM, the conclusion is assumed at the outset. Without that prior knowledge of the legal outcome, it is difficult to move logically from the biblical verse or verses to the rabbinic legal position(s) said to flow from them. As such, one rarely sees in HM a genuine exercise to understand the discursive meaning of Scripture in context or to clarify Scripture's meaning where it begs for clarification. Rather bits and pieces of Scripture, often taken out of context, are treated as a code that is *said to* justify the Mishnaic or related rabbinic law in question. As you shall see in chapter 6, what the code conveys, first and foremost, in instance after instance of its use in HM is a message about the relative roles of Scripture and of legal reasoning without Scripture in the determination of the Halakha. Second, the resulting passages convey that no "bit, jot or tittle" of Scripture is superfluous. What appears to be superfluous or redundant is there to anchor a legal teaching that we might otherwise get wrong. "The firstborn of a donkey you shall redeem with a lamb" appears word for word in two places in Exodus, once in chapter 13 and again in chapter 34. If one instance of the biblical phrase grounds one teaching, then the other must be there to ground some other teaching, even if *in context* in Exodus that does not seem its intent. So, for HM, legal reasoning without Scripture is dangerous, nothing in Scripture is superfluous, and scriptural phrases, even taken out of context, encode meaning other than, or in addition to, what they mean in context. More on this later in the volume.

The second sample snippet of HM presented in this chapter deals with what by now is another familiar theme, the proper execution of writs of divorce. The base text in Scripture is Deuteronomy 24:1–2. These verses are the central injunctions in Scripture dealing with divorce proceedings. The HM passage is from Sifre Deuteronomy, Ki Tetzeh, Pisqa 269 (edition L. Finkelstein, pp. 288, translation my own), and language in this passage that parallels verbatim language in Mishnah is in boldface type.
Sifre Deuteronomy, Ki Tetzeh, Pisqa 269 :

> "And he shall write for her" (Deuteronomy 24:1)—in her name. On the basis of this they said: **Any writ that is not written in the name of the wife is unfit. How so? He was walking in the**

marketplace (=m. Gittin 3:1)—the remainder of the Mishnah follows.

"And he shall write" (Deuteronomy 24:1)—I [might] conclude that only [if] he has written **in ink** (=m. Gittin 2:3) [the writ is valid]. **In arsenic, in red chalk, and in resin, in copper sulfate**[33] (=m. Gittin 2:3)—whence [do we learn that these too are permitted]? Scripture says, "he shall write" (Deuteronomy 24:1)—from whatever.

There is little doubt that this passage in HM directly cites Mishnah, from m. Gittin 3:1 and 2:3. The statement "the remainder of the Mishnah follows" references Mishnah explicitly, and may come from some scribe copying Sifre Deuteronomy who simply did not wish to copy the entirety of m. Gittin 3:1. The copyist made the quite reasonable assumption that the reader of his manuscript of Sifre Deuteronomy had a copy of Mishnah at hand (or knew Mishnah by heart), just as the reader was assumed to have a copy of the Scriptures. At this juncture in our rapid introductory "fly-by" survey of early rabbinic legal literature, I wish to highlight two standard rhetorical formulae in this passage of HM. "On the basis of this they said" is typical formulaic joining language; it is used to ascribe the basis of a rabbinic legal tradition to a scriptural verse or phrase. The second rhetorical formula I wish bring to your attention is a "triple-header": (1) "I [might] conclude that . . . ; (2) ". . . whence . . ."; (3) "Scripture says . . ." The formula itself conveys a message, however contrived its use may seem here. Without careful attention to Scripture's precise phrasing, one might reason to an erroneous conclusion, in this case, that only standard inks may be used to write a writ of divorce. Again, Mishnah is cited verbatim, but HM's "argument" is that Mishnah would have stopped at specifying the use of ink (alone) and would not have proceeded to list other media for writing were it not for a careful reading of Scripture. Of course, there is *no* indication in Mishnah that anything like this reading of Scripture is the ground for m. Gittin 2:3's list of pigments. Nor does it seem logically necessary to have such "extra" scriptural ground to justify the teaching that pigments other than ink may also be used. But such is the ideology-driven "program" of HM, as conveyed by its formalized rhetorical conventions. And this is a harbinger of things to come in chapters 4 through 8 of this volume: namely,

---

33. I am indebted to the notes to m. Gittin 2:3 in H. Albeck's edition of the Mishnah for the identification of these compounds.

the lesson that *recurrent rhetorical patterns can in and of themselves reflect and reinforce ideologies.*

Again, Mishnah, Tosefta, and the Halakhic Midrashim are all viewed by late antique and medieval rabbinic literature as *tannaitic* productions, deriving from rabbinic authorities who lived prior to c. 220 CE. For example, both Talmuds cite Tosefta (or Tosefta-like passages) as well as HM (or HM-like passages) in a manner that clearly indicates that the Talmuds' authorships view them as tannaitic and wish to signal this to the reader. It is (of course) highly unlikely that the actual composition of Tosefta or of the literary works of HM date from the period before 220. Tosefta as a whole is clearly post-Mishnaic. Moreover, the literary formulation of a significant portion of Tosefta's constituent passages—that is, those Toseftan passages that cite the extant Mishnah or rely upon Mishnah for their intelligibility—likely date from a time after Mishnah's completion or stabilization. Much the same may be said for the literary oeuvres of HM. HM seems post-Mishnaic; it periodically cites Mishnah. And HM's compositions appear to be later than much of the materials in Tosefta, even if the period of Tosefta's composition may significantly overlap that of HM's composition. If Mishnah was composed near the turn of the third century, the composition of Tosefta may span the mid-third century to the turn of the fourth (or as some maintain, to the early fifth) and the span of HM's composition may similarly range from the mid-third to the mid-fourth century (or, again as some would argue, to the early fifth). These "tannaitic" materials are liberally used in the extended compositions that comprise the Jerusalem Talmud, the authorship of which is often specified as c. 400, as well as in the Babylonian Talmud (c. 600).

Let us now turn to the two Talmuds (*Gemarot*, pl., in Aramaic).

The Jerusalem Talmud: from Tosefta-like complement to fundamental analysis of Mishnah

The Jerusalem Talmud's (JT or y.) tractates, as previously noted, are organized as systematic explication of thirty-eight of Mishnah's sixty-two tractates (Avot excepted). In elucidating in sequence Mishnah passage after Mishnah passage, each "mini-essay" of JT often makes extensive use of Tosefta (or of materials also reflected in Tosefta) and of other Tosefta-like materials. JT's use of passages of HM or HM-like passages is comparable. Additionally, JT regularly cites amoriac traditions, that is, sources and rabbinic authorities which the authorship of JT dates to the period after c. 220 CE. The substantial portion of these amoraic materials are attributed to named rabbinic figures living in the Land of Israel. This contrasts passages in Mishnah and Tosefta, where anonymous, unattributed rulings tend to prevail. In JT, amoraic traditions may appear in Aramaic or in Hebrew, in contrast to tannaitic ones which, like Mishnah, Tosefta, and HM themselves, are cast almost exclusively in Hebrew. Whether cast in Aramaic or Hebrew, some amoraic sources cited in JT exhibit formal rhetorical and literary traits that strongly resemble, indeed imitate, tannaitic ones that dominate in Mishnah, in Toseftan and Tosefta-like passages, and in HM or HM-like materials. Other amoraic traditions in JT are quite different, in that they are deliberatively "argumentative" and "analytic" in a manner or to a degree that one does not find in Mishnah and Tosefta, where straightforward declarations of legal positions prevail. The editorial language of the JT, that weaves together tannaitic and amoraic sources to form a critical/analytic mini-essay elucidating the Mishnah passage at hand, is mostly in Aramaic. And, as we shall see in a subsequent chapter, it is the editorial language of JT's extended mini-essays, plus those amoraic traditions that are deliberatively analytic and argumentative, which give the Jerusalem Talmud its distinct rhetoric and formal literary character. Otherwise, JT would be another Tosefta of sorts, merely presenting materials that shed light on or supplement Mishnah.

What do such mini-essays in JT *do with* the Mishnah passages that they serve to elucidate? The more complete answer to this question must wait for this volume's presentation in chapter 7 of major features of JT's distinctive rhetorical and literary conventions. But what follows (JT Gittin 1:1a) is *part* of such a mini-essay from JT, by way of a sample. The opening of m. Gittin 1:1 (which you will have read earlier in this chapter) is the explicitly designated background and context for the passage from JT. I have tried to minimize the use of explanatory interpolations in square brackets in my translation of JT, but I have not been able to eliminate them entirely and still produce a readable text. Language that exactly parallels Mishnah's is once more in boldface, and language that reflects Tosefta's wording is underscored. Translated Aramaic is in italics.

JT Gittin 1:1a (*italics* = language in Aramaic, **boldface** = Mishnah's language, underscore = Tosefta's language, translation my own):

In the Seat of Moses

And [they raised an] objection [about] whether **he who brings** a writ of gift **from a Mediterranean province**—troubles to say: **In my presence it was written, and in my presence it was signed**!?

R. Joshua b. Levi said: *It is different,* as they are not expert in the details of writs [of divorce].

Said R. Yohanan: They dealt leniently with her, that she should not remain an abandoned wife.

But is this <u>leniency</u>, not a <u>stringency (see t. Gittin 1:2,5)</u>!? Since if he did not say to her: **In my presence it was written, and in my presence it was signed**, even so, you do not permit her to be married [again].

Said R. Yose: The <u>stringency</u> that you have imposed upon her at the outset, that **he is required** to say: **In my presence it was written, and in my presence it was signed,** you have made a <u>leniency</u> for her in the end. Since if one came and challenged (see m. Gittin 1:3) [the writ's validity], his challenge is null and void.

R. Mana *is of the view: Say,* when he challenged [a matter] extraneous to the body [of the writ's text]; rather when he challenged [a matter] intrinsic to the body [of the writ's text]!? When he challenged [a matter] that is not material. Even when he challenged a matter that is material!?

Said R. Yose b.R. Bun: Because *you say that the reason [is],* the <u>stringency</u> that you have imposed upon her at the outset, that **he is required** to say: **In my presence it was written, and in my presence it was signed,** you have made a <u>leniency</u> for her in the end, since if one came and challenged [the writ's validity], his challenge is null and void, *[then] it is [established] that there is no difference,* [whether] he challenged [a matter] extraneous to the body [of the writ's text]; [or] he challenged [a matter] intrinsic to the body [of the writ's text], [or] he challenged [a matter] that is not material, [or] he challenged a matter that is material.

And trouble [him] to say[, In my presence it was written, and in my presence it was signed], lest they signed [it] with unfit witnesses!?

Said R. Abun: Is it suspect of having an error by the hand of heaven [i.e., do such things just happen by chance]!? [No!] In a court it is suspect of having an error, such that because it [the court] knows that if someone comes and challenges it, his challenge [must be] null and void, it has it signed by fit witnesses.

The passage in JT begins by ostensibly questioning Mishnah's requirement that one who brings a writ of divorce from abroad must be able to declare that he saw the divorce document written and signed by witnesses. But it does so by posing a counterfactual question: 'Do we make such demands of one bringing a deed of gift from abroad? No we do not!' This allows JT's authorship to cite the tradition attributed to Joshua b. Levi that articulates why writs of divorce are treated differently than other legal documents prepared outside the Land of Israel and brought to the Land for enactment. Simply put, JT (in Joshua b. Levi's name) states why the two cases differ. They are not analogous, even if at first glance they seem to be. JT has, in effect, posed and answered an *analytic-critical question* of Mishnah in order to probe the rationale for Mishnah's legal position.

The remainder of this passage of JT takes up a matter first introduced in the Tosefta passage presented earlier in this chapter. Tosefta, as we have already seen, proffers that Mishnah's requirement that the bearer of a writ of divorce from outside the Land of Israel attest to having seen the document written and signed is a "lenient" legal position; the procedural requirement is meant to decrease rather than increase potential demands on the parties. JT critically probes this point, starting the analysis by citing Yohanan's position that Mishnah's lenient stance is meant to reduce the incidents of "abandoned wives." This refers to women who are abandoned by their husbands, but who cannot remarry, because they are not formally divorced. The anonymous voice of JT's authorship then questions whether this is in fact a leniency or its opposite, seeing that Mishnah is "piling on" additional procedural requirements that Mishnah seemingly does not demand when other types of writs are brought from outside the Land of Israel. JT's authorship then cites a tradition attributed to R. Yose to "neutralize" the force of the question.

The JT then uses the position of R. Yose as a springboard for further analytical-critical positions, appealing to positions attributed to Mana and Yose b. Bun. Maybe the declaration by the bearer that he saw the writ of divorce written and signed obviates some types of challenges but not others. This brief analytical-critical foray ends by taking Yose's position as normative. If Yose's view is normative, it is inappropriate to make distinctions between various types of challenges.

The sample "snippet" from JT ends with the return to a fundamental, critical question about m. Gittin 1:1. What (else?) might Mishnah be worried about in having articulated its requirement? A hypothetical answer is provided, and then argued against.

At this juncture, what may be said is that JT (like the later, Babylonian Talmud) tends to approach a Mishnah passage by choosing from a set of stock analytical-critical questions, stated or implied. Our sample text primarily focuses on why Mishnah has ruled as it has. Who benefits? Under what circumstances? Is there a reason for not parsing circumstances more precisely, such that the declaration made by the bearer of the writ of divorce suffices in some instances to validate the process, but not in other instances? In addition to the types of questions raised in our sample snippet, JT may also inquire what named authority's position underlies Mishnah's anonymous ruling. Or JT may ask whence Mishnah's legal position is derived. And in search for an answer to these and other stock questions, JT might cite other passages, from elsewhere in Mishnah, or JT might turn to other tannaitic or amoraic traditions that can be brought to bear.

As we shall see, the effect of posing and answering these queries about a given Mishnah passage is to produce what, in my view, looks like a very *new* type of Tosefta on our Mishnah. This new type of Tosefta does several things. First, like Tosefta, JT compiles Tosefta(-like) materials, or HM(-like) traditions, and amoraic ones that upon inspection help us better understand Mishnah's treatment of a matter. But, second, in so doing JT extends the "range" of sources used to do this. Within that extended range are included traditions attributed to rabbinic authorities in the Land of Israel living after c. 220, that is to amoraim, who are reported to have ruled on matters of Halakha, or to have acted and practiced in accordance with the Halakha. These traditions too elucidate Mishnah's meaning and the significance of other tannaitic materials brought to bear to understand Mishnah. This contrasts with Mishnah's more utopian bent and focus on an "ideal" Judaic world. The challenges of society and life of the Jews in the Land of Israel sometimes show through the lines of JT's materials in a manner that they do not in Mishnah.[34] Finally, third, with JT we will see the introduction into Mishnah study of a decidedly analytic and text-critical agenda. Whose position is this anonymous Mishnah-passage? What is the warrant for this position? Does it apply in all circumstances? And one will see other stock questions and ways to address them. This reflects something of *how* Mishnah was coming to be studied critically and analytically in the Late-Roman/Byzantine period in the Land of Israel.

---

34. This is one of the conclusions of Jacob Neusner in his scholarship on the JT. See Neusner, *Judaism in Society*.

The Babylonian Talmud: From analysis of Mishnah in the service of understanding Mishnah, to critical analysis commencing in analysis of Mishnah in service of critical analysis of all things that are Torah

JT is not a polished document, at least in comparison with the Babylonian Talmud (BT or b.), the composition of which is now conventionally given as c. 600 CE, or roughly two centuries after JT's. Viewed against the BT's standard, the text of JT can be confused and corrupted, and relatively few medieval commentaries come to our aid. The BT was more studied. More commentaries were written on the BT, and compendia of BT's positions on matters were composed quite early on. These provided readings of BT passages that scribes could use to correct texts they believed to be corrupt. BT's text continued to be polished for several centuries after its composition and after the BT's characteristic rhetorical and literary traits achieved a fairly final and stable state c. 600.

Few modern scholars would assert that the collective authorship of BT modeled their work upon or extensively used the JT.[35] True, much of the amoraic and most, if not all, of the tannaitic materials available to the authorship of JT were indeed also in the hands of those who formulated the extended passages of the BT. But if one places side by side JT's mini-essay on a particular Mishnah passage and BT's essay on the same Mishnah passage it is apparent that far more often than not BT's essay did not use (or know?) JT's, even though many of the same tannaitic and amoraic traditions will appear somewhere in both.

That said, BT like JT elucidates Mishnah by application of a range of analytical-critical questions to a Mishnah passage, proceeding from Mishnah passage to Mishnah passage through the "chapters" of a complete Mishnah tractate. For each Mishnah passage BT, like JT, composes an extended composition or mini-essay, using its own (much more extensive) suite of stock queries and equally stock methods of analysis to address them, while adducing tannaitic and amoraic traditions to do so. Of course, BT's amoraic materials encompass rabbinic sources from both the Land of Israel and Babylonia-Mesopotamia, and include Babylonian-Mesopotamian materials attributed to rabbinic authorities who flourished as late as c. 500, such as Ravina II and his contemporaries.

---

35. It may go too far too say that the authorship of BT did not know the JT, but to the degree they did, BT's authorship did not significantly build upon JT's compositions of mini-essays in formulating their own.

In the Seat of Moses

As has already been done for Mishnah, Tosefta, HM, and JT, permit me to provide a typical BT passage as a "sampler" to give you the "flavor" of BT. BT Gittin 2a–4a takes the first sentence of m. Gittin 1:1 as its point of departure and base text. As you will see, this "sampler" is longer than those that have already been presented in this chapter, much longer. But it is, after all, BT's mini-essay on just one sentence of Mishnah, and so I have chosen not to truncate it. To do so would have not given a fair first impression of BT. You will also note that I have included many more interpolations (in square brackets) in my translation of BT Gittin 2a–4a. Why? For two reasons. First, because without these interpolations on my part, the ebb and flow, and coherence of the passage is not apparent to the novice reader of BT, and reading a BT composition or mini-essay is about discerning and getting into the structure and flow of the passage—of anticipating. Creating that structure and flow is a stock set of structural-rhetorical terms; each such term is a "code" of sorts for what happens next in the passage. Once you know these "coded" terms, as I hope you will by the end of the book, many of the interpolations I provide in this sample will be unnecessary. I have also done one more thing, also in service of helping you discern the structure of the sample composition; I have subdivided the passage using Roman numerals and numbered the paragraphs in each subdivision. As you read this sample text of BT, first read it through to discern its structure and flow; then reread it for its content. Again, I have rendered Aramaic in italics. Mishnah citations are in boldface; language paralleling Tosefta, if any, is underscored.

BT Gittin 2a–4a (i.e., BT to m. Gittin 1:1–3, Aramaic in *italics*, Hebrew in standard font, **boldfaced** = Mishnah, underscored = Tosefta), translation my own):

I

> 1. *What is the reason?* Rabbah said: Because they are not expert [in the Mediterranean provinces] with regard to [executing the writ of divorce] in her name [see m. Gittin 3:1]. Rava said: Because witnesses are not present to make it stand [see m. Gittin 1:3 and t. Gittin 1:3,5–6].

II

1. *What differentiates them [i.e., Rabbah's and Rava's answers, in practical terms]? What differentiates them is:*

   −*[a state of affairs in] which two [emissaries together] have brought it,* [in which case Rabbah only would require the declaration, as two witnesses are present];

   −*if so, [also] from province to province in the Land of Israel* [in which case Rava only would require the declaration, as within the Land of Israel those who execute such writs know and observe the requirement to execute it in the wife's name];

   −*If so, [also] within the same province in a Mediterranean province* [in which case Rabbah only would require the declaration, since the witnesses are nearby if the writ's witnesses must be authenticated].

III

1. *And as regards* Rabbah, *who said*: Because they are not expert with regard to [executing the writ of divorce] in her name, *let him [ie., why does he too not] require [that] two [bring the writ], so that it accords with all [cases requiring] witnesses in [the laws of] the Torah!?*

2. [Perhaps, Rabbah is of the view that] one witness is trustworthy regarding prohibitions. [Well, one might counter such a position hypothetically attributed to Rabbah on these grounds:] *let us say that we say* [that] one witness is trustworthy, when [we are dealing with a case] such as, [when] we do not know whether [at hand is] a piece of fat [forbidden for consumption] or fat [permitted for consumption], *in which instance it is not known* [for certain whether one is dealing with a matter that is] *a prohibition. But here* [in the case at hand] *in which it is known* [for certain that one deals with a potential instance of] *the prohibition* of adultery, *it is a matter of forbidden sexual relations, and a matter of forbidden sexual relations is not* [dealt with by] *less than two* [witnesses].

3. Most [in fact] are expert [with regard to executing the writ of divorce in her name]. *And even as regards R. Meir, who is concerned about exceptions,* [nonetheless] *the ordinary judicial scribe* [who would be preparing the document] *has learned the teaching* [that the writ of divorce must be executed in her name]. *And it is the rabbis who have required* [the declaration

by the bearer of the writ coming from the Mediterranean provinces]. *And in this* [case], *on account of* [their concern that the woman not become] *an abandoned wife, our rabbis dealt leniently with her* [by allowing a single emissary bringing a writ of divorce from a Mediterranean province to the Land of Israel to validate the document by testifying that the writ was written and signed in his presence].

4. *This is a leniency [for her]!? It is a stringency [for her]! Since if you required two* [emissaries], *the husband* [can]*not come and challenge* [the writ's validity] *and invalidate it.* [But if] *one* [brings the writ], *the husband* [can] *come and challenge* [the writ's validity] *and invalidate it.*

5. [Not at all!] *Because of what Mar has said*: Before how many [witnesses] do they give it [the writ of divorce] to her? R. Yohanan [is of one view], and R. Hanina [is of another view]. *One said*: Before two [witnesses]. *And one* [i.e., the other] *said*: Before three [witnesses]. [Therefore,] *ab initio*, [the emissary, knowing that the writ must be presented before witnesses] *is scrupulous* [about the process and all requisites], *and he will not come* [bearing an invalid writ], *and* [allow] *himself to be denigrated* [before two or three witnesses].

6. *And as regards* Rava, *who said*: Because witnesses are not present to make it stand, *let him [ie., why does he too not] require [that] two [bring the writ], so that it accords with all [cases requiring] deeds?*

7. [Perhaps, Rava is of the view that] one witness is trustworthy regarding prohibitions. [Well, one might counter such a position hypothetically attributed to Rava on these grounds:] *let us say that we say* [that] one witness is trustworthy, when [we are dealing with a case] such as, [when] we do not know whether [at hand is] a piece of fat [forbidden for consumption] or fat [permitted for consumption], *in which instance it is not known* [for certain whether one is dealing with a matter that is] *a prohibition. But here* [in the case at hand] *in which it is known* [for certain that one deals with a potential instance of] *the prohibition* of adultery, *it is* a matter of forbidden sexual relations, and a matter of forbidden sexual relations is not [dealt with by] less than two [witnesses].

8. In truth, [it is the case] *that in the execution of deeds we do not even need* [witnesses' signatures]—[this] *in accordance with* [the view of] Resh Laqish, *as said* Resh Laqish: the [legal force of

names of] witnesses inscribed on the deed are like those whose testimonies are examined by a court. [That is, the witnesses' signatures have true value only on appeal, but ab initio are not needed to execute the deed]. *And it is the rabbis who have required* [the declaration by the bearer of the writ coming from the Mediterranean provinces]. *And in this* [case], *on account of* [their concern that the woman not become] *an abandoned wife, our rabbis dealt leniently with her* [by allowing a single emissary bringing a writ of divorce from a Mediterranean province to the Land of Israel to validate the document by testifying that the writ was written and signed in his presence].

9. *This is a leniency [for her]!? It is a stringency [for her]! Since if you required two* [emissaries], *the husband* [can]*not come and challenge* [the writ's validity] *and invalidate it.* [But if] *one* [brings the writ], *the husband* [can] *come and challenge* [the writ's validity] *and invalidate it.*

10. [Not at all!] *Because of what Mar has said*: Before how many [witnesses] do they give it [the writ of divorce] to her? R. Yohanan [is of one view], and R. Hanina [is of another view]. *One said*: Before two [witnesses]. *And one* [i.e., the other] *said*: Before three [witnesses]. [Therefore,] ab initio, [the emissary, knowing that the writ must be presented before witnesses] *is scrupulous* [about the process and all requisites], *and he will not come* [bearing an invalid writ], *and* [allow] *himself to be denigrated* [before two or three witnesses].

IV

1. *And* [as regards] *Rava, what is the reason he did not say as Rabbah did?*

2. [Rava would say:] *Who has learned* [in Mishnah that the bearer of the writ of divorce must say:] **In my presence it was written** in her name, **and in my presence it was signed** in her name!?

3. *And Rabba* [would respond to this argument how]? *In truth, let* [Mishnah] *teach thusly. But if you increase what one* [must] *say, he will truncate* [what he must say]. *Here too, he will come and truncate one [word] in three; one in two he will not truncate.*

4. *And* [as regards] *Rabbah, what is the reason he did not say as Rava did* [i.e., share Rava's view]?

5. *He* [Rabbah] *would say to you*: If so, *let the Mishnah teach,* **In my presence it was signed**, *and no more.* **In my presence it was**

written—Why do I require it [be taught by Mishnah]? *Learn from this, that it concerns the matter* [of writing the writ of divorce] *in her name* [see m. Gittin 3:1].

6. *And* [as regards] *Rava,* [how would he respond to this argument]? *In truth, let the Mishnah teach thusly.* But if so, *he will come and substitute* [this process for the one that] *validates ordinary deeds,* [namely] with one witness.

7. *And* [how would] *Rabbah* [retort]? [Rabbah would say:] *How are* [the cases] *similar!? There* [as regards ordinary deeds], [the bearer must declare], "*We know . . .*" *Here* [as regards writs of divorce], [the bearer must declare], "*In my presence . . .*" *There a woman is not* [considered a] *trustworthy* [witness]. *Here a woman is* [considered a] *trustworthy* [witness]. *There the person directly concerned in the matter is not* [considered a] *trustworthy* [witness]. *Here the person directly concerned is* [considered a] *trustworthy* [witness].

8. *And* [how would] *Rava* [retort]? *He would say to you: It is because here* [too, in the case of the bearer of writs of divorce]*, if they should say,* "*I know . . .*" [rather than, "In my presence . . ."], *who will not deem* [the bearer] *trustworthy? And since should he say,* "*I know . . . ,*" *they deem* [him] *trustworthy, he will come and substitute* [this process for the one that] *validates ordinary deeds,* [namely] with one witness.

V

1. *And* [as regards] *Rabbah, who said, Because they are not expert* [in the Mediterranean provinces] *with regard to* [executing the writ of divorce] *in her name* [see m. Gittin 3:1]*, who is the tannaitic authority who requires that* [the writ of divorce] *be written in her name, and requires that* [the writ] *be signed in her name?*

2. *If* [one hypothesizes that] *it is* R. Meir [who is the tannaitic authority], [then] *signing* [a writ of divorce]—*he requires* [being in her name], [but] *writing* [a writ of divorce]—*he does not require* [being in her name]. [So, one cannot adduce R. Meir as the tannaitic authority for these requirements.] As we have taught [in m. Gittin 2:4]: **They do not write [a writ of divorce] on something affixed to the ground. If they wrote it on something affixed to the ground, and uprooted it, and gave it to her—it [the writ] is fit.** [And the BT assumes that anonymous legal views in Mishnah follow R. Meir's views.]

3. *If* [one hypothesizes that] *it is* R. Eleazar [who is the tannaitic authority], [then] writing [a writ of divorce]—*he requires* [being in her name], [but] signing [a writ of divorce]—*he does not require* [being in her name]. [So, one cannot adduce R. Eleazar as the tannaitic authority for these requirements.] *And if you should say* [that nonetheless] *it is invariably* R. Eleazar [who is the tannaitic authority], *since* R. Eleazar *does not require* signing [the writ in her name, by reason of an injunction] *from the Torah,* [but] *does require* [signing the writ in her name, by reason of an injunction] from the rabbis—*but lo,* three [types of] writs are declared invalid by [decree of] the rabbis, *and* R. Eleazar [in contrast] *does not require* signing [the writ] in her name [for the writ to be valid].

4. *As we have taught* [in Mishnah 9:3]:

   Three [types of] **writs** [of divorce] **are unfit, and if** [the wife re]**married** [on the assumption that the writ was indeed valid], **the offspring** [resulting from the remarriage] **is fit:** [i] **He** [the husband] **wrote** [the writ] **in his handwriting, and there are no witnesses[' signatures] on it; [ii] there are witnesses[' signatures] on it, and there is no date [specified] in it; [iii] there is a date [specified] in it, and there is only one witness['s name specified] in it—lo, these three** [types of] **writs** [of divorce] **are unfit, and if** [the wife re]**married** [on the assumption that the writ was indeed valid], **the offspring** [resulting from the remarriage] **is fit. R. Eleazar says: Even if there are no witnesses'** [names or signatures] **on it, but it** [the writ of divorce] **was given to her before witnesses,** [the writ] **is fit, and she claims** [the settlement specified in her marriage contract even] **from mortgaged assets** [of her former husband]**, since witnesses sign the** [writ of divorce] **only due to** [the aspiration to effect] **social justice in the world** (*tiqun 'olam*) [that is, by further protecting the woman].

5. But [rather] it is [indeed] R. Meir [who is the tannaitic authority], *since* R. Meir *does not require* signing [the writ in her name, by reason of an injunction] *from the Torah,* [but] *does require* [signing the writ in her name, by reason of an injunction] from the rabbis—*and lo, said* R. Nahman: R. Meir used to say: Even if he found it [a writ of divorce] in the garbage, and he signed it, and he gave it to her—[the writ] is fit.

6. *And if you should say: We teach thusly* [namely, that in R. Meir's view, such a writ is valid by reason of the requirements] *from the Torah* [only, but we do not teach that the writ is valid when

In the Seat of Moses

the further requirements set by the rabbis are taken into account]—*if so, he* [R. Nahman] *would have to* [have said that] R. Meir used to say: [the writ is fit by reason of] a dictum of the Torah.

7. *Rather, invariably it is* R. Eleazar [who is the tannaitic authority], *since* R. Eleazar *does not require* signing [the writ in her name]. [But perhaps this is Eleazar's view] *when there are no witnesses*[' signatures on the writ of divorce] *at all,* [but] *when there are witnesses*[' signatures on the writ of divorce], [perhaps] *he* [Eleazar] does *require* [that the writ be signed in her name], *as* R. Abba *said:* R. Eleazar acknowledges that in the case of [a writ of divorce with] an error in [the body of] it[s text], it [the writ] is unfit.

8. R. Ashi *said: Who is this* [who is the tannaitic authority]? *It is* R. Judah. *As we have taught* [in m. Gittin 2:4]: (**They do not write [a writ of divorce] on something affixed to the ground. If they wrote it on something affixed to the ground, and uprooted it, and gave it to her—it [the writ] is fit.**) **R. Judah declares [it] unfit, until its writing and its signing is on something uprooted.**

9. *And ab initio, what is the reason that we have not established* [at the outset that] *R. Judah* [is the tannaitic authority]? *We* [first] *have* [attempted] *to return to* R. Meir [as the possible tannaitic authority], *since anonymous Mishnah* [law] *is* [generally based on the views of] *R. Meir. We* [then] *returned to* [consider] *R. Eleazar* [as the possible tannaitic authority], *since we have established* [that generally] *the Halakha accords with him in cases of writs* [of divorce].

I fully realize that your head may be spinning after having read this passage of BT. But let us stand back from the detail and look at it from the fifty-thousand-foot level, and bracket the arcane substance for the purposes of this chapter's "fly-by" overview.

The BT passage opens at section I with a stock question, "What is the reason" for m. Gittin 1:1a's ruling that the bearer of a writ of divorce from outside the Land of Israel to the Land must declare that he was present when the writ was written and signed? Two different answers are given, each attributed to a different amoriac authority, Rabbah and Rava. The remainder of the mini-essay is less about m. Gittin 1:1, and predominately about the critical examination of the views attributed to Rabbah and Rava. That is the first thing to note. Second, the ensuing analysis in parts II, III, and IV of Rabbah and Rava's stated reasons for Mishnah's ruling is entirely hypothetical.

–In section II: In what specific *hypothetical* cases *would* Rabbah and Rava rule differently, given their differing reasons in section I for Mishnah's law?

–In section III: Given their differing stated reasons in section I, why *would* Rabbah or Rava not require that two persons bear such a writ of divorce and make the required declaration, since two persons would constitute a valid pair of witnesses?

–In section III: Why *would* Rabbah reject Rava's stated reasons for Mishnah's ruling, and why would Rava reject Rabbah's?

These three hypothetical questions (about the initial differing rationales attributed to two rabbinic authorities) are among the repertoire of the critical-analytical agenda of BT. And each of the three stock hypothetical questions is posed via standard formulaic language that repeats throughout the entirety of the BT. All of the rest of the critical analysis *within* sections II, III and IV, is *drawn in the wake* of the questions posed at the sections' beginning. They are the *standard spinning out* of these matters; and they may be spun out more or less in any particular composition. This is an important point, to which we will return later in this volume, because it has to do with the function of BT to *model* types of standard analysis of rabbinic teachings. When one models something, one can do more or less of it.

The final part of this mini-essay, section V, commences with another standard critical-analytic question. Who is the tannaitic authority who stands behind Mishnah's anonymous teaching—here not m. Gittin 1:1a, the base text of this mini-essay, but m. Gittin 3:1, the Mishnah passage which is ostensibly at the heart of Rabbah's stated rationale in section I? In the preceding paragraph, I remarked about the rhetorical-literary tendency to spin out the consideration of hypothetical possibilities in order to critically examine each. Section V does just that, going several rounds at exploring whether Meir or Eleazar is the underlying tannaitic authority, before introducing and examining the proposition that the source is Judah. If the authorship of this composition knew from the outset that Judah was the best candidate, why indeed exhaustively explore several times over that it might have been Meir or Eleazar? Posing and addressing such questions about the BT's (typical) *modus operandi* opens the door to exploring the intended purpose and readership of BT, and to discussing what the BT's role was in shaping the ethos and "professional" identity of the cadre of rabbis near the turn of the seventh century, when BT was composed.

When, in chapter 8, this volume examines extensively the BT's use of characteristic rhetorical and literary conventions, it will be apparent that BT's analytic agenda and interests far exceed those of JT, if that is not already evident from the sample texts presented. Yes, BT is interested in many of the same issues as JT—the more obvious critical ones, such as: Who is the authority for this anonymous ruling in Mishnah? What are the underlying reasons for this legal position? What is the basis (in Scripture) for it? Whose view do we in fact implement as Halakha? But BT shows far greater interest than does JT in text-critical and content-analytical questions. BT might ask of a list of cases in Mishnah: Why do we need all the items on the list? Is something missing that should also be on the list? Or BT will sometimes ask speculative questions: How would (or did) Rabbi x, who rules in such and such a manner in this case in Mishnah, rule in this other case found elsewhere in Mishnah or Tosefta, or in some case the circumstances of which are simply posited by the BT? Would Rabbi y, who disagrees with Rabbi x in this case, also disagree with him in that case, and for what reasons? Such questions and their responses framed within a single extended composition/mini-essay that began as an exercise to elucidate the Mishnah passages at hand can stray quite far from its initial focus. As we shall see, and to a degree have already seen in the sample passage, elucidating Mishnah is thereby seen to be only *one* of BT's objectives, even though commenting on Mishnah is the overarching organizing principle of BT's authorship's compositions. There seems in BT to be a broader objective at work as well: the practice of critical-analytics for its own sake, using rabbinic sources. Consequently, as I began already to intimate above, a new, extended set of elaborated rabbinic-analytic skills is modeled in the BT, ones that differ from those implicit, as we shall see, in Mishnah. Furthermore, BT shows more interest in weaving Aggada and Aggadic Midrash into its extended mini-essays, although Halakhic interests and traditions still overwhelmingly dominate. There is, then, an almost encyclopedic interest that one can discern at times in BT, in the sense of the "Encyclopedists" of eighteenth-century Europe.

With BT's characteristic rhetoric it is evident that the art of being a rabbi has shifted significantly from the way of being a "Mishnaic" rabbi, and with that shift the shared normative identity of the rabbinic movement will have changed as well. But this is a discussion that will occupy us at length in the last chapter of this book.

The Babylonian Talmud is not only the final document the rhetorical and literary conventions of which will occupy us in this book, BT was promoted and accepted within medieval rabbinic circles as the movement's crowning, most significant intellectual achievement. For the first time since the production and promulgation of Mishnah some four hundred years earlier in the Land of Israel, another rabbinic literary work, the Babylonian Talmud, displaced Mishnah as the principal object of study by rabbis and rabbinic novices. The Babylonian Talmud's mastery, not Mishnah's mastery, became a hallmark, a marker of rabbinic status. The great rabbis of the medieval and early modern periods were renowned because of their commentaries on the BT, and to a lesser extent for their commentaries on Mishnah. After Maimonides, the major rabbinic codes and legal responsa-epistolary literature looked increasingly to the Talmud's legal discussions for legal sources and for legitimation of positions and rulings. Even today, in the traditional rabbinic academies (the *yeshiva* [sing.]/*yeshivot* [pl.]), study of the Babylonian Talmud claims a preeminence above all else.

In the section just concluded of this chapter, you have had to deal with a number of sample texts of a type likely alien to most of you. By the end of this volume, they will not seem alien at all, but familiar. Moreover, the effort you have expended in getting an intellectual toe-hold on these sample texts will pay dividends; we will return to these very texts, among others, throughout the book.

The Study of Rhetorical and Literary Conventions in the Context of Early Rabbinic Legal Literature

You will have just completed in chapter 2 a whirlwind tour of the history of the early rabbinic movement and, thus far in chapter 3, of its principal legal works from c. 200 to c. 600 CE. Like all whirlwind tours of a country or continent, one sees only a sampling of the sites and gains a general, exterior view—and still it is hard to remember and grasp it all. When in the next five chapters we turn to introducing a critical mass of the dominant rhetorical and literary conventions that "drive" the compositions of Mishnah, Tosefta, the Halakhic Midrashim, and the Jerusalem and Babylonian Talmuds, we will begin to "get inside" these edifices, begin to understand better their "architecture" and "engineering." But before proceeding to do so, I feel a mild case of Murphy's Law coming on again: "To do anything, one must do something else first." I must say something about what I mean by "rhetoric," when applying this as an analytic descriptor to literary conventions of early rabbinic literature. And I will also say something more of the gains to be made by considering dominant literary conventions of early rabbinic legal literature as rhetoric, beyond simply making these documents more intelligible to those not experts in them.

In our modern world, the term "rhetoric" has come to have a pejorative meaning. "He is just spouting rhetoric." "Are you being rhetorical?" "Is that a rhetorical question?" In these contemporary, common uses of the term, one is implying that the speaker is somehow not genuine or not serious. But before modernity, and especially in the ancient and late antique worlds, "rhetoric" was viewed as an important skill, the possession of which was viewed as essential for leaders of society. Rhetoric was the art of mustering evidence in an argument that would be seen as persuasive within a given context: in the court of justice; in the legislative council; in the public assembly; in the ecclesiastical council. The upper crust of society and of the Church studied rhetoric formally. Consequently, rhetoric became formalized. This is *how* one structures an argument for this; this is *how* one structures an argument for that. Great handbooks of rhetoric were composed in the ancient/late antique world that conveyed these formalized conventions, which further institutionalized them. As a result, if one did not follow the "formula" for arguing in a given context, one ran the real risk of one's argument not being viewed as persuasive, no matter how good the evidence or the manner in which the evidence was adduced to support a conclusion. Better, then, to stick to the formulas for argument, to follow the norms of rhetoric as laid down. In chapter 2 I mentioned that a renowned fourth-century teacher of rhetoric living in Antioch corresponded with the Jewish Patriarch in the Land of Israel. By the fourth century, some rabbis were openly criticizing the Patriarchs, whom they had early on sought as patrons, as overly Hellenized and Romanized. A major literary work of exercises in classical rhetoric is attributed to a Libanius, likely to "our" Libanius, *Libanius' Progymnasmata*.

In the late 1980s and early 1990s some scholars, most notably Vernon K. Robbins and Burton Mack,[36] began to consider whether early Christian writers were to a significant degree abiding by established Greco-Roman rhetorical "rules." Their work started an entire new subdiscipline in the

---

36. Robbins and Mack, *Patterns*.

study of early Christian literature, sociorhetorical analysis. For almost three decades now the study of the rhetoric of the New Testament has been one of the major pathways to shed light not only on the meaning and methods of the New Testament texts, but also on the social formations out of which these texts emerged, and in which they were revered as authoritative. But with such a plethora of work now done has come a *richèsse* of approaches. Underlying these is a range of analytic definitions of what one means by "rhetoric."

For this reason alone, it would be worthwhile for me to say something of my own conceptual framework in studying rhetoric in early rabbinic literature. However, there is yet another, even more compelling reason. I have offered to provide readers with a basic catalogue of, a primer, on, early rabbinic legal rhetoric. In form and substantive agenda early rabbinic legal texts differ considerably from the New Testament and other early Christian literature. And so do their predominant rhetorical traits. So, it appears even more judicious to say something more about my own use of the term "rhetoric" as an analytic category.

In my conceptual and methodological frame, "rhetoric" entails communicating *authoritatively*, whether orally or in writing, in accordance with implicitly or explicitly understood rules and norms for such expression. All rules and shared norms bespeak relatively sustained social formations and their established institutions, for only established groups can have rules and shared norms. And if among these shared rules and norms are rhetorical conventions, then rhetoric provides one more link to those social settings, and gives us evidence about them.

So whether an act of expression, oral or written, counts as an act of rhetoric, in my sense, depends upon our capacity to show that the expression accords with rules and norms—rules that then link to some institutional or social context. Earlier in this book, I made reference to how lawyers write or argue cases in court. I stated that I may read a modern legal contract and find it to be gobbledygook, or nearly so. When the contract is explained to me—that is, translated into "plain, everyday" English—I can grasp its meaning and its importance. For me, the legal contract thereby gains in intelligibility. But the actual language of the contract is as it is *supposed* to be for legal circles, if it is to be assessed by *those circles* as clear, authoritative expression. For the circle of lawyers, the translation made for me actually loses precision and therefore substance. Lawyers have created this language in order to say things to one another, and in order to have their documents have *standing* in courts of law. And as I implied earlier, learning to use language in this way is part of the process of being recognized as part of the guild of legal experts. So the guild of lawyers created a professional ingot (a "rhetoric"), and learning to read and compose it properly helps sustain the guild of lawyers as a specific social formation within society, although the law profession may demur at this interpretation of matters. For them, their rhetorical ingot is a requisite for clarity.

I keep harping on the notion of authority when speaking of rhetoric. All language accords with rules (of grammar, syntax, etc.) that are socially determined. These rules, again, may be explicit or implicit. They are the rules one must abide by if one is to be *intelligible* within the community of speakers of the language. In dealing with modes of expression that count as rhetoric, we are not talking about intelligibility only, but *authority*. And our legal example is apt; most speakers of the English language might well conclude that lawyers' use of legal rhetoric is at the expense of general intelligibility, but this is in order to attain *authoritative* legal precision.

The upshot of this contemporary example is this: assuming a common language, there are many different ways in which one may communicate given content with equal clarity and intelligibility using the vocabulary, grammar, syntax and elements of style of the language. But the use of established rhetorical modes *narrows* that range in accordance with explicit or implicit rules from, and for, a special social context (e.g., courts) or group (e.g., members of the bar). The use of such established modes of rhetoric, moreover, serves to *uphold* that social context, and it imbues its users, and what they have to say, with an air of *prima facie* authority and legitimacy within the community of those who recognize the rhetorical patterns and its circle of users for what they are intended to be.

For those of us who make use of ancient religious literature to shed light on social formations for which we have little detailed, *independent* evidence, identifying and analyzing rhetoric becomes yet another tool in a social-historical exercise that is inherently fraught with methodological circularities: we seek to understand a text in its social context, the evidence for which comes from the text that we seek to understand. When, however, we discern rhetorical patterns, in my definitional sense, we may ask, *Who benefits? Over whom? At whose expense?* and *What social formations would result from the inculcation and sustained use of such a rhetoric?* We thereby gain some purchase on matters of social formation that we might not otherwise have, just as the rhetoric of lawyers' legal documents tells us something about what is involved in being a member of the bar. And this is the type of purchase we may gain as a "value-added" component of this book; in addition to learning something about early rabbinic rhetorical and literary conventions, and thereby gaining some accessibility to early rabbinic legal literature, we will also learn more about what it was *to be* a rabbi in late antiquity, to be a member of the rabbinic social formation over a four-hundred-year span of that group's development. We will tease out some of this added value in the last chapter of this book.

In sum, rhetoric, in this sense, serves us in this manner, because matters could have been expressed in a different way, indeed most often in many different ways. Such is the richness of "ordinary" language—any "ordinary" language. But where identifiable rhetorical norms are at work, this inherent richness is *highly restricted*, and always *in the same way and direction*. That is to say, such language is rigorously formalized. This restriction appears to us as the repetition of patterns where, otherwise, a "normal" range and richness of discourse would be found and expected. The *relevant* social formation imparts an especial importance and authority *in context* to that which is expressed in this rigorously formalized way, and recognizes the document or speaker as *ab initio* authoritative, because the rhetorical patterns are perceived as the hallmark of that authority.

You will notice that I have not used the words "argument" or "persuasion" as of yet. This would seem odd to any scholar of New Testament rhetoric or to any student of *Libanius' Progymnasmata*. I have held off doing so for a reason. As we shall see below, not all early rabbinic rhetoric, by my definition, especially in Mishnah and Tosefta, is expressly argumentative or an obvious attempt to persuade—even though it is intended to be perceived by the intended reader or listener as particularly authoritative. That being said, "argument" does appear in early rabbinic literature—relatively sparingly in Mishnah, somewhat more so in Tosefta, and significantly in the Halakhic Midrashim and the two Talmuds. Moreover, the constitutive rhetorical patterns of early rabbinic legal literature, from Mishnah to the Babylonian Talmud, appear intended for a highly restricted readership or audience. They are handbooks or study books for the members themselves of the rabbinic guild. As I have said, the documents represent the focus of inner-guild professional life, and their study and analysis help constitute that inner-guild life and, therefore, the guild itself. They do not represent an attempt on the part of the early rabbis to inform, teach, or preach to the Jewish communities in the Land of Israel and Mesopotamian-Babylonian

Plain. In this too, early rabbinic legal texts, with their characteristic rhetoric, would seem to differ from the types of documents that came to be included in the New Testament and from patristic literature. *If* the rabbis or rabbinic novices regularly taught in the Jewish communities at large, something for which we have only the sparsest evidence, the way they did so seems not to be reflected in their earliest documents, Mishnah and Tosefta.[37] In the chapters that follow, we are entering the life of the early rabbi-disciple circles, the third- or fourth-century rabbinic "houses of study" (*beit midrash*), and, finally, the major rabbinic academies, the *yeshivot*, of Babylonia just before the dawn of Islam. Look around as we go; be prepared for a social world with intellectual pursuits that differ greatly from our own, or even from others in late Roman antiquity with which you are familiar. It is from what first seems alien that we learn most about what it is to be human with others in a social setting.

SUGGESTIONS FOR FURTHER READING

Akenson, *Surpassing Wonder*.

Neusner, *Introduction* to *Rabbinic Literature*.

Samely, *Forms of Rabbinic Literature and Thought*.

Strack et al., *Introduction to the Tamud and Midrash*.

---

37. Given our focus on the rhetoric of early rabbinic legal literature specifically, and not on Aggadic or Midrash Aggadic works, it is worth providing the reader with references for some more recent works on rabbinic/Talmudic rhetoric or modes of argument in general. Excluding my own work on the topic, two of which are frequently referenced in this book, see Moscovitz, *Talmudic Reasoning*; Samely, *Forms*; Hidary, "Classical Rhetorical," 33–6; Dolgopolski, *What Is Talmud?*; Greenbaum, "Talmudic Rhetoric." With regard to works from the 1980s and 1990s, much of Jacob Neusner's corpus applies, of which corpus some only are referenced in this book. From these decades see Kraemer, *Mind of the Talmud*; Jacobs, *Talmudic Argument*; Halivni, *Midrash*.

4

Mishnah

From the three preceding chapters it will have become apparent that Mishnah (M/m.) is both the core of, and the entry point for gaining familiarity with, early rabbinic literature. Moreover, Mishnah (produced c. 200) ought to be the starting point for any attempt to discern the mutually upholding, historical relations that entailed between the production and study of that literature, on the one hand, and the development of the early rabbinic group, first in the Land of Israel and a little later in the Mesopotamian-Babylonian Plain in the Late Roman and Late Persian imperial eras.

In chapter 3, I provided a brief survey of early rabbinic legal literature, Mishnah included. As stated, Mishnah was the first document promulgated by and among the early rabbis, and the first to become authoritative within that emerging group. In that chapter, I offered a few remarks about how Mishnah came to be produced, by whom, and from what sources. You may wish to know more about such matters. But that is not the purpose of this volume. Besides, questions about Mishnah's origins, authors, and sources are still unresolved matters of scholarly debate.

There is, however, a firm scholarly consensus that, once it was produced and promulgated in the early third century CE, Mishnah study was a formative activity for the early rabbis. In addition, early rabbinic legal literature was subsequently produced to serve (or was pressed into the service of) Mishnah study, analysis, and critique in one fashion or another. That "fashion" is largely reflected and modeled in the distinctive, normative conventions that characterized each of the principal documents of this corpus of literature. This is so because normative intellectual modes of engagement, analysis, and critique are demanded of these documents' engaged students and "encoded" in these texts' literary and rhetorical conventions. This volume, as already stated, aims to make this literature more accessible by familiarizing readers with these dominant literary and rhetorical conventions. But there is a bonus that accrues to gaining this familiarity; this volume also will provide a window into the intellectual life that characterized being a member of the early rabbinic social formation.

So, Mishnah is key. It all starts with Mishnah, composed as sixty-two topically based tractates (if Avot, the sixty-third, is a slightly later addition), themselves organized in the extant medieval manuscripts under six grand, thematic groupings called "orders," outlined in the previous chapter.

Let us proceed, then, to explore Mishnah's dominant literary and rhetorical patterns and conventions, beginning with how Mishnah formulates a "declarative sentence," since it is not how you or I would normally do so. We shall see how sequences of typically Mishnaic declarative sentences are spun out to create Mishnah passages and mini compositions comprising several (or more) passages. Additionally, we shall look at "attributed saying," "disputes," "debates," "precedent stories," and "scriptural prooftexting."[1] I shall define and explain each of these designations when dealing with them in the subsections of this chapter.

Perhaps this sounds like a lot of ground to cover. Perhaps it is. But when you have completed his chapter, you will have almost all of the tools you need to read not only Mishnah, but also Tosefta and a good deal of the other legal "tannaitic" traditions that are liberally cited in the constituent compositions of both the Jerusalem and Babylonian Talmuds.

---

1. These designations for Mishnah's formalized rhetorical patterns are largely adopted from the late Jacob Neusner. Neusner, who was my teacher when I pursued graduate studies in the early and mid-1970s, was a monumental figure in the modern academic study of early rabbinic literature. He was a remarkably productive scholar, and a controversial one, too. He vociferously challenged the views of others in the field, and his views, in turn, were aggressively critiqued by others. But the detailed work that he has done on the analysis of early rabbinic literature, particularly legal literature, is unparalleled in its scope. His identification of repeatedly used literary forms in Mishnah, Tosefta, and tannaitic traditions in later rabbinic compositions began with Neusner, *Rabbinic Traditions*, and a more complete statement of the same appeared in his *History of the Mishnaic Law*. My designations for formal literary patterns in Mishnah, Tosefta, and in tannaitic traditions that resemble Tosefta derive from Neusner's nomenclature. Jacob Neusner died in 2016.

Mishnah

MISHNAH'S "DECLARATIVE SENTENCES," THE FOUNDATION OF "SPUN-OUT" MISHNAIC PASSAGES

Mishnah's content is overwhelmingly legal. Therefore, Mishnah's sentences start by defining a set of circumstances that comprise a case (usually a hypothetical one) and conclude with a ruling on that case. Since all of the other formalized rhetorical conventions and literary constructs of Mishnah (and of Tosefta) build on Mishnah's "declarative sentences," looking at these statements is the best place to begin.

First off, how would you or I typically formulate such rule-statements in standard, fully intelligible, colloquial English? Let me try to articulate such a statement, so that we may then compare and contrast it with how Mishnah does such things.

Imagine that we are articulating "rulings" about legally mandated behavior at city intersections, and we are dealing (hypothetically) with pedestrians, cyclists, and motor vehicles that must all pass through an intersection where there is a four-way stop. I might say:

> **If two motor vehicles, or two cyclists, or a motor vehicle and a cyclist, approach an intersection with a four-way stop from directions that are at right angles to one another, and no pedestrians are attempting to cross, such that the pedestrians would cross in front of the approaching vehicles or cyclists,** *then the vehicle or cyclist* **that reaches the intersection first** *and first comes to a full stop,* *proceeds first through the intersection, and the other vehicle or cyclist, after also coming to a full stop, proceeds through the intersection only after the first vehicle or cyclist has cleared the intersection.*

This is a long sentence, with a lot of information in it. That information is of two types, represented respectively by boldface and italics print. The parts in boldface define the circumstances that together make up the case for which a ruling is given. Henceforth, we will call this part of a rule-giving sentence the "protasis" (pl. protases). The sections of the statement that are in italics form the ruling, the declaration of what the "actors" must do. An "apodasis" (pl. apodases) is the part of a rule-statement that conveys the judgment or ruling.[2] There is a bit in the middle of our particular sentence

---

2. From the term "apodasis" one derives the literary designation for such legal statements, "apodictic law." The Hebrew Scriptures, particularly the books of the Pentateuch, are filled with apodictic law. Halivni, *Midrash*, sees apodictic law as a pervasive feature of

In the Seat of Moses

that does double duty as both an articulation of a circumstance and a ruling at the same time; it appears in both boldface and italics. What is clear from this English sentence is that all the information required to make sense of it is contained somewhere in the sentence. One just has to take note of all of its details. We are told the relative positions of all of the motor vehicles, cyclists, or pedestrians involved, in so far as it impacts the ruling about their legally mandated actions. We are told that one vehicle (or cyclist) has arrived at the intersection first and is the first to come to a full stop, a legal requirement before proceeding.

Missing is a highway statute that would underlie this rule-statement, as well as a number of other possible scenarios to which the statute would apply. Such a statute might read something like this:

> All vehicles, motorized or not, and pedestrians come to a full stop at intersections with stop signs facing them; the order of priority in which vehicles and/or pedestrians proceed is: vehicles that do not have a stop sign facing them as they approach the intersection, followed by pedestrians, followed by the vehicles in the order that they first came to a full stop, or if two stopped simultaneously, the vehicle that is to the right hand of the driver of the other.

That is it. You now have it all. And in any case, the articulation of the case and ruling in boldface and in italics provided above is so complete and comprehensive that you could easily have surmised the *relevant* content contained in the statute that applies to our particular hypothetical case, even if you did not have the highway code in your glove compartment for reference purposes. After all, who does?

There is something else that I wish to point out about our hypothetical ruling and my made-up statute that underlies it. The former, the rule-statement, *tests* the application of the latter for a particular set of circumstances. The statute is general in nature; it is intended to serve as a legally binding guide for many different types of particular circumstances. The hypothetical ruling is one such set of possible circumstances comprising one hypothetical case among many possible ones to which the statute would apply or would have to be made to apply. What do I mean by "tests," and why do I use the term at all? A series of hypothetical cases, whether they would (or have) come to pass in reality or not, tests how the world of human activity, which can often be a complex and messy affair, can be ordered by the statute, which is pretty cut and dry, and general. Think of how many different

---

how Jews in Antiquity articulated their religious culture.

hypothetical situations one could define in which various combinations of motor vehicles, cyclists, and pedestrians could in different sequences and from varying directions approach an intersection that has either a two-way or four-way stop.

Before turning to how Mishnah articulates rulings in its declarative sentence, I want you to consider something additional. I want you to imagine that all statutes of the highway codes of each state or province, including our made-up statute, were adopted because of a Supreme Court ruling that stated:

> It is unconstitutional to not have a highway code, lest the constitutional right to have one's life reasonably protected by government be abrogated by any level of government—federal, state/provincial, or municipal.

I have no idea whether the Supreme Court of the United States or of Canada has ever issued such a ruling. But Supreme Courts have ruled that it is unconstitutional not to have, and sometimes to have, legislation of one type or another, without specifying the details of such legislation. Legislation is the business of other authoritative bodies.

If the foregoing is something like the articulation of rules in a world ordered by law as we might experience it in Canada, the United States, or elsewhere in the modern world, how do Mishnah's typically formulated declarative sentences compare? Let us first look at a Mishnah passage, m. Bekhorot 1:1a, with which you are already familiar, because it has been cited twice already, in both chapter 1 and chapter 2. My translation, as before, is as "literal" as I can make it, and I am going to use boldface type and italics, as I did above, to distinguish the articulation of circumstances that define a case or cases (the protasis) from language that conveys the ruling (the apodasis).

> **He who purchases the foetus of an ass of a Gentile, and he who sells to him,** *even though it is not permitted,* **and he who forms a partnership with him, and he who receives from him, and he who gives to him in trust** *is exempt from the law of the firstling,* as it is said, "Of an Israelite" (Numbers 3:13), but not of others.
>
> (m. Bekhorot 1:1a, translation my own[3])

---

3. This translation is based on that in Lightstone, *Rhetoric*, 78.

In the Seat of Moses

Let us compare the nature of m. Bekhorot 1:1a to our ruling about a case concerning a four-way stop, as such a comparison will highlight a number of typical features of a Mishnaic-declarative sentence.

Mishnaic Sentences, and the Mishnah Passages They Constitute, Frequently Require Antecedent Information as Context to Be Fully Intelligible

I begin with the need for contextual information, that is, knowledge of things that are the necessary logical antecedent to begin to make sense of a legal rule-statement. In our four-way-stop rule-statement, no antecedent contextual knowledge is necessary to make sense of the statement. Yes, the statute of the highway code is the basis for the ruling, but lack of knowledge of the statute does not make the rule-statement less intelligible.

Matters seem quite different in m. Bekhorot 1:1a. As I have previously pointed out, m. Bekhorot 1:1a seems to be an odd statement with which to *open* the Mishnah tractate on the laws of the firstling. After all, we have here the first passage of the first chapter of the tractate. There is no context provided. There is nothing that would resemble a statute or statutes to underlie this opening legal statement. And we have no articulation of what one might liken to a legal mandate from a Supreme Court for the articulation of such a ruling. We do have an allusion to a biblical verse added at the end of the sentence. But the verse is not cited in its entirety.

In other words, whatever context is required, or would be helpful, fully to make sense of or even to begin to read the ruling with a fulsome level of comprehension is entirely absent. And I challenge any novice or experienced reader of Mishnah to tell us what this Mishnah passage "means" without, in the process, introducing these missing elements of context in order to do so.

Lesson number one about the literary-rhetorical conventions governing typically Mishnaic, legal declarative sentences is, then, this: often the reader must supply, or be supplied with, necessary contextual information to render the statements intelligible. Here that context includes the biblical laws pertaining to the sanctity of the firstling, understood to be the first offspring of its mother, if the offspring is male. Taken together, the biblical verses about the sanctity and disposition of firstlings are the statutes underlying m. Bekhorot. The reader of m. Bekhorot 1:1a must previously have learned the biblical injunctions concerning the disposition of the firstling born to domestic animals and to Israelite human mothers: if it is the offspring of a "clean" species, "fit"—the literal translation of *kasher*—for the sacrificial altar or for consumption by an Israelite, the firstling is given to a priest for his use; if the firstling is an animal of an "unclean" species, it is redeemed with a lamb, which is a "clean" species, and the lamb is given to the priest. If the firstling is a human baby, the baby is redeemed by a fixed amount of redemption money being given to the priest. These are the biblical "statutes," if you will. And unlike our four-way-stop rule-statement, the parts of the biblical injunctions that pertain to making sense of m. Bekhorot 1:1a are not rehearsed or summarized within the Mishnah statement at all, even though they are critical to its intelligibility. Nor can all the relevant parts of the statutes be arrived at inductively from a close reading of the cases and the ruling at m. Bekhorot 1:1a.

Permit me to provide another demonstration of lesson number one, by citing a Mishnah sentence that, again, you will recognize from the discussion in chapter 2.

> He who brings a writ from a Mediterranean province—it is required that he say: In my presence it was written, and in my presence it was signed.
>
> (m. Gittin 1:1a, translation my own[4])

This opening sentence of m. Gittin 1:1 not only commences the Mishnah passage in question. Like m. Bekhorot 1:1a, the first declarative sentence of m. Gittin 1:1 commences the opening chapter of the tractate Gittin on writs, primarily writs of divorce. A significant amount of antecedent, contextual information is, once again, missing to begin to make sense of the content of this declarative sentence. As I wrote in chapter 2, we seem to have been dropped into the middle of the treatment of a topic, not to have entered at its commencement. Biblical law/statute concerning divorce proceedings is thin, but specific. The husband who wishes to divorce his wife, "because he sees in her something untoward," must "write her a scroll of severance," "place it in her hand," "send her from his home," after which "she goes out from his home," and "may go and be another man's [wife]" (Deuteronomy 24:1–2).[5] Even knowledge of this biblical law only brings us part way to

---

4. Adapted from Lightstone, *Mishnah*, 35.

5. Yes, this biblical statute is patriarchal, and the wife seemingly has no say in the matter. By early rabbinic times, the wives had considerably more rights, including, according to some early rabbinic authorities, the right not to receive the "scroll of severance." All early rabbinic authorities agreed that a husband divorcing his wife had to pay

grasping the antecedent information that would provide a logically necessary context for grasping the meaning of the first declarative sentence of m. Gittin 1:1. After all, it is obviously not the case that the husband imagined in m. Gittin 1:1 is in the presence of his soon-to-be-divorced wife. He cannot give her anything. And he is not personally there to "send her out." Where are the statements of law that permit such a process in absentia? They are not in Scripture, and they are not in Mishnah either. Yet without them, and without knowledge of them, the reader of m. Gittin 1:1 cannot make sense of this passage. So, the reader must command this knowledge in advance, or have access to a mentor who may supply it.

The Often Highly Laconic Nature of Mishnah's Declarative Sentences and Their Sometimes-Apocopated Structure

A "lacuna" (adjective: "laconic") refers to something that is missing but needs to be present in a statement for it to be complete. *Apocopation* is the term that describes a "sentence" in which the grammatical subject of the sentence keeps changing before the reader encounters the main verb of the sentence's predicate. Take this "sentence," for example, "Mary, who confronted John, because, went to calm down in the men's locker room." One would think that Mary ought to be the grammatical subject of the verb, "went." But unless we are to understand that Mary went to the men's locker room, which is certainly possible, we would more likely surmise that John went to the men's locker room as a result of his need to calm down after being confronted by Mary. This sentence is "apocopated," and as a result, the reader of the sentence must figure out whether Mary or John is, reasonably, the more likely subject of the verb, "went."

There is also a major lacuna in the sentence; there is nothing following "because" to inform us about the basis for Mary's upset with John. And filling in the lacuna would tell us why John felt the need to go to the men's locker room to calm down, if indeed John is the likely subject of the verb, "went." Clearly, what is missing after "because" is germane to understanding what is going on and why. If I were to write a paper for a course, and the

---

her a considerable amount of money, as specified in the marriage contract (*ketubbah*) that in a rabbinic marriage was a required part of the marriage procedures. What the wife did not have was the right to initiate a divorce under biblical or rabbinic law, although in modern times there are provisions in certain rabbinic circles to compel a husband to grant his wife a dully executed, rabbinically valid divorce.

paper's sentences routinely were missing important, necessary bits, and if, in addition, it was often difficult to figure out what the grammatical subject was of the main predicate of many of my paper's sentences, then the grader of my paper would be justifiably frustrated.

What makes for poor English grammar and style remains well within the bounds of propriety for elegant Mishnaic declarative sentences in accordance with Mishnah's normative literary-rhetorical conventions. That is not to say, that a "good" Mishnaic sentence *must* have lacunae and show apocopation. Rather, they often do display one or the other, or both, and this is, seemingly, well within the bounds of what is normal.

To illustrate these points and their significance, let us return to our four-way-stop statement and to m. Bekhorot 1:1a. A comparison of the nature of this Mishnaic declarative sentence to our rule-statement of a hypothetical case concerning vehicles approaching an intersection with a four-way stop highlights the degree to which necessary elements are conspicuously absent in m. Bekhorot 1:1a. Not all the language is present in the protasis of the Mishnaic declarative sentence that is required to define factors that constitute the case to be ruled upon. Nor is the behavior enjoined of the "actors" fully specified in the apodosis. By contrast, in our four-way-stop ruling, *all* of the information is present that fully defines the case in the protasis and expected behavior in the apodosis. Indeed, so much so that a thoughtful reader of the four-way-stop ruling could easily surmise the principal elements of the statute that underlies it, even if the highway code were unavailable or unknown to the reader of the apodictic legal statement. So, to emphasize the point, not only is no *contextual* information needed to fully understand the four-way-stop rule-sentence, no additional information is required to understand *all the relevant factors that together constitute the hypothetical case* for which the ruling is given. Moreover, the ruling is *explicit about what the hypothetical actors are to do* in order to comply with the law.

What would it take for m. Bekhorot 1:1a to be as fully articulated as our four-way-stop rule-sentence? Such a rule-sentence would need to introduce all the factors that comprise the cases of the protases for the reader, and, in the apodosis, what the actor is to do or refrain from doing. M. Bekhorot 1:1a would have to look something like this (with additional language interpolated as indicated in square brackets):

1. He [an Israelite] who purchases the [unborn] foetus of an ass [but not the ass itself] of a Gentile[, and the foetus, when born,

In the Seat of Moses

if it turns out to be male, will be both a firstborn of the ass still owned by the Gentile and a male offspring, since the ass has never before given birth to either a male or female offspring],

2. And he [an Israelite] who sells to him[, the Gentile, the unborn foetus of an ass, but not the ass itself, and the foetus, when born, if it turns out to be male, will be both the firstborn and a male offspring of the ass still owned by the Israelite, since the ass has never before given birth to either a male or female offspring],

3. Even though it is not permitted [for an Israelite to contract such a sale to a Gentile].

4. And he [an Israelite] who forms a partnership with him [the Gentile, so that they co-own the foetus of an ass owned by either the Gentile or the Israelite, and, subsequently, when the foetus is born, it is both male and a firstborn of the ass, since the ass has never before given birth to either a male or female offspring],

5. And he [an Israelite] who receives [in order to care for, but has not acquired ownership of, a pregnant ass] from him [a Gentile, and, subsequently, when the foetus is born, it is both male and a firstborn of the ass, since the ass has never before given birth to either a male or female offspring],

6. And he [an Israelite] who gives [a pregnant ass] to him [a Gentile, so the Gentile may care for the pregnant ass] in trust, [but has not ceded ownership of the ass to the Gentile, and, subsequently, when the foetus is born, it is both male and a firstborn of the ass, since the ass has never before given birth to either a male or female offspring]—

7. [in all of the foregoing cases, the foetus, when born] is exempt from the law of the firstling [of unclean species as enjoined in the biblical Scriptures, which specifies that if the firstborn of an unclean domesticated species is male, the newborn is redeemed with a lamb, which in turn is given to an Israelite priest for his consumption or use—with the added, nonbiblical, provisio understood that the only unclean species to which the biblical law applies is the ass].

8. as it is said, "Of an Israelite" (Numbers 3:13),

9. but not of others, [that is, Scripture talks of the firstlings born to domestic animals of Israelites].

(m. Bekhorot 1:1a, translation my own[6])

---

6. Based on Lightstone, *Rhetoric*, 78. The interpolations are based on a similar but less

Mishnah

What is demonstrated by these extensive interpolations? It shows how much additional information the reader must supply on his/her own, or be supplied with by a mentor or tutor, to fully articulate or grasp what the passage is talking about—both to fully spell out the circumstances of what are actually five more or less—closely related hypothetical cases, and to understand in the ruling what actions are to be taken or, in this case, not taken. The intelligibility of the appeal to a scriptural proof-text also benefits from interpolation, although please note that Mishnah usually does *not* justify its rulings by explicit appeal to Scripture, even when scriptural law underlies the Mishnah's ruling, which is very often the case. This *typical* paucity of the required information to make a Mishnaic sentence or passage fully intelligible highlights the frequently highly *laconic* nature of Mishnaic declarative sentences.

From this comparison of m. Bekhorot 1:1a to our rule-statement about two cars approaching a four-way stop at an intersection, one may articulate lesson number two about typical declarative sentences in Mishnah: they often are bereft, sometimes severely so, of the information that would permit the reader fully to articulate the cases upon which the declarative sentences rule and, sometimes, to completely specify the normative behavior demanded by the ruling. It is assumed that the reader can, on the spot, supply that information for himself or herself, or that the reader will, again on the spot, be supplied with it by someone else, namely, a tutor or teacher (or later, in the medieval and subsequent periods, by an accompanying written commentary).[7] So, reading typically Mishnaic declarative sentences

---

fully articulated exercise to do the same to this Mishnah passage in Lightstone, "Textual Study and Social Formation."

7. It would be an interesting scholarly exercise to compare Mishnah commentaries authored over the course of medieval through modern eras. That of Maimonides (Rabbi Moses ben Maimon, twelfth century) is perhaps the best-known early systematic commentary on the Mishnah. (Rabbi Shlemo Yitzhaqi, aka Rashi, who preceded Maimonides, wrote such a commentary on the Babylonian Talmud, and as a consequence also on the Mishnah passages that the Babylonian Talmud analyzes. But as noted in chapter 3, the Babylonian Talmud deals with only roughly 60 percent of Mishnah's tractates (thirty-six tractates of a total of sixty-two, Avot excepted). Maimonides' Mishnah commentary is interesting, given what I have said both about the need for antecedent knowledge and about the need to fill in missing content of Mishnah's declarative sentences. Maimonides' commentary routinely does the latter, but he also periodically in his opus provides extensive introductions to the legal topic, including an extensive introduction to the Mishnah itself. In these introductions, he, among other things, supplies antecedent information required to begin to read the tractate(s). A well-known mid-twentieth-century Mishnah commentary, that of Albeck, *Shishah*, engages in a similar exercise. But Albeck provides

assumes a social context and social institutions. How so? The ancient Mishnah reader was part of an institutionalized social setting in which the requisite background knowledge—to recall lesson number one—was taught and—with respect to lesson number two—the reader was tutored to fill in the information that fully articulated the cases for which the Mishnah supplied rulings. Ancient Mishnah readers had to be part of a *community* of Mishnah readers that included experts of a particular sort, with particular knowledge and skills that the novice had eventually to master to become a fully autonomous reader of Mishnah. We shall return in the last chapter of this book to such issues of social context and characteristic expertise within the early rabbinic movement.

To summarize matters thus far, Mishnaic declarative sentences often lack key background information that is contextual and are in many instances so laconic in formulation as to have not fully articulated the cases upon which they rule or the behavior expected of the actors under these circumstances.

There are still other features of the Mishnaic declarative sentences that are germane to understanding Mishnah's literary and rhetorical features and to making Mishnah more accessible to a novice reader. To some extent these features are either correlates of their laconic nature or perhaps drivers of their tendency to be laconic. Earlier, I introduced the notion of apocopated sentences. Mishnah often, but certainly not always, displays apocopation. Predicates, verbs, and objects of the sentence will sometimes not align grammatically with the subject. The sentence may start with one subject (stated or implied) of the verb that commences the predicate, but by the time one actually gets to the predicate, the now implied subject of the verb has changed, and nothing in the sentence has explicitly alerted us to this. Since the main predicate of a Mishnaic declarative sentence is most often its apodasis, the part of the sentence that expresses the ruling for the case, then the "lost" grammatical subject is the one to whom the rule applies. Let me provide a very simple, made-up example, with explanatory interpolations.

> A cow which gives birth to a male [and the cow has never before borne young], [the owner] gives [the offspring] to a priest.

---

complete introductions for each and every Mishnah tractate, in addition to commenting in turn on each Mishnah passage. How a Maimonides or an Albeck chose to define their tasks as Mishnah commentators lends weight to my observations about the nature of Mishnah's declarative sentences.

Without the interpolations, the English sentence says that the cow gives the firstborn offspring to the priest. Patently, this is not the intended meaning. The sentence, therefore, is apocopated. Of course, in Hebrew the cow is a feminine noun, and the verb, "gives," would be in the masculine form in our made-up sentence. So, no reader of the Hebrew would for a second read "cow" as the subject of the verb. But in very many cases the mix of feminine nouns with verbs in the masculine would not be present to alert the reader that the subject has changed. And in any case, Hebrew verb morphology aside, it remains the case that the actual subject of the verb that begins the predicate is nowhere specified in our made-up example. Interpolations made by the reader "on the fly" supply the additional content that would identify the proper subject of the predicate. Furthermore, our made-up example highlights another claim that I feel justified in making about Mishnah's declarative sentences: apocopation is sometimes exhibited precisely because Mishnah's declarative sentences typically are laconic. Why do I say this? If all the necessary bits were there, as I have done in my made-up example by supplying interpolated language in square brackets, the grammatical subject of the main verb and the apodasis would be clearly specified, although the sentence structure would still be apocopated, and we would rightly deem it a poor or outright improper English sentence.

So, apocopation is generally not a desired feature of good English sentences. But lesson number three about Mishnaic declarative sentences is that they often display "apocopation"[8]—a change in the subject of the sentence (at times specified and in other instances not identified at all) somewhere between the sentence's start and the main verb of the predicate. In fact, sometimes the subject can change more than once in a Mishnaic sentence. Fully articulated sentences, by contrast, would have straightened all this out for the reader. Instead, and perhaps because of Mishnaic declarative sentences' typically laconic nature, the reader is often "finding Waldo" or supplying Waldo—finding or supplying the subject of the verbs. In fact, for a real, rather than made-up, example of apocopation in a Mishnah passage, one need go no further than our now familiar m. Bekhorot 1:1a.

> He who purchases the foetus of an ass of a Gentile, and he who sells to him, even though it is not permitted, and he who forms a partnership with him, and he who receives from him, and he who

---

8. Again, Jacob Neusner extensively documented the presence of apocopation in Mishnah's and Tosefta's declarative sentences. See Neusner, *History of the Mishnaic Law*.

> gives to him in trust is exempt from the law of the firstling, as it is said, "Of an Israelite" (Numbers 3:13), but not of others.

By Mishnaic standards, this statement is mildly apocopated. Until one gets to the ruling, "he who" looks like it must grammatically be the subject of the verb and predicate, "is exempt..." But before we get to that main predicate, the ownership of the ass and/or of its unborn, soon-to-be-firstling offspring changes several times. In the final analysis, the logical, but not grammatical, subject of the verb and predicate that comprises the apodasis (the ruling) is the soon-to-be-born foetus; *it* is exempt from the law of the firstling, not the Israelite or Gentile who are hypothetically contracting different sorts of arrangements about the foetus and the dame-donkey that will give birth. Together with the penchant for highly laconic language, this form of apocopation, it seems, permits multiple, complex variations of hypothetical circumstances, generating a series of cases, governed by a single apodasis/ruling. And this is exactly what we see in m. Bekhorot 1:1a.

From Generating a Case from the Juxtaposition of Bits of Phrases to the Concatenation and Permutation of Phrases in Order to Spin Out a Series of Hypothetical Cases for Which One or More Rulings Are Given

As is evident from m. Bekhorot 1:1a, a Mishnah passage will often generate not one hypothetical case upon which to rule, but a series of related cases, for which one common ruling or several rulings are given. Our opening passage of Mishnah Tractate Bekhorot articulates five such cases. By what literary-rhetorical devices does it do so? Let us look at my translation yet again, without explanatory interpolations.

> He who purchases the foetus of an ass of a Gentile, and he who sells to him, even though it is not permitted, and he who forms a partnership with him, and he who receives from him, and he who gives to him in trust is exempt from the law of the firstling, as it is said, "Of an Israelite" (Numbers 3:13), but not of others.

At the simplest level, the coordinating conjunction, "and" serves to join or concatenate the last four cases with the first. I am here translating the Hebrew letter *vav* (ו), which is a prefix and in Mishnah can mean either "and" or "but," depending upon the implied intent. The prefix *vav* is routinely used to string together a series of cases, or to string together a series of circumstances that comprise a single complex case. Less frequently two cases will be concatenated with the conjunction "or" (Hebrew, או). As we shall see a bit later, another prefix, *sh* (ש, vocalized as *she*, with a short *e*, as in "shed"), which may be translated as the English relative pronouns, "which" or "that," often serves with "and" to concatenate bits and pieces of language in order to define a case with more than one defining element. *Vav* ("and" or "but") and *she* ("which" or "that") are major and ubiquitous features of the typical Mishnaic declarative sentence and of the passages that these sentences help form. Their repetition, over and over again, in clause after clause, phrase after phrase, and sentence after sentence is a major feature of Mishnah, joining together the highly laconic bits and pieces that define individual, highly differentiated hypothetical cases.

M. Bekhorot 1:2b offers a good example of the use of *vav* and *she* to join short phrases or terms in order to define, concatenate, and spin out a series of hypothetical cases. Be warned, despite this passage's location in the opening chapter of tractate Bekhorot, m. Bekhorot 1:2b does not concern itself with the firstling, but with fish that are fit (*kasher*) for consumption.

1. An unclean fish **which** swallowed a clean fish—[the clean fish] is permitted as to eating.

2. **And** a clean fish **which** swallowed an unclean fish—[the unclean fish] is prohibited as to eating,

3. for it is not its product

(m. Bekhorot 1:2b translation my own[9])

In this passage, two contrasting hypothetical cases have been concatenated in two well-coordinated, matching declarative sentences. "And" (*vav*) joins the two cases, and in each case "which" (*she*) joins the two circumstances that serve to define each case. An explanatory gloss concludes the passage; such glosses are *not* a regular feature of a Mishnaic declarative sentence but do appear from time to time (just as is the case of appeals to scriptural proof-texts). One could well imagine a series of "and"s joining many more than two contrastive, hypothetical cases together in an extended passage. Similarly, "which" may be used to join together not two, but three or four circumstances that define a single case. I may add, that both declarative sentences in m. Bekhorot 1:2b are mildly apocopated. In both instances, the grammatical subject of the sentence at its commencement is not the

---

9. Based on Lightstone, *Rhetoric*, 176.

grammatical subject of the apodasis/predicate. My interpolated language (in square brackets) had to designate the subject of the latter.

In typically Mishnaic declarative sentences it is not only *vav* and *she* that serve to join bits and pieces to spin out several or more contrastive or differentiated cases. Let us return to what will be the now-familiar passage at m. Bekhorot 1:1a. In my translation of m. Bekhorot 1:1a, the lion's share of the work that serves to differentiate each of the five sets of circumstances or cases is done by the following:

"he who"

plus a different verb in the present tense,

plus "to him" or "with him."

In the fifth case of the series, "in trust" is added to modify the verb in the English translation. The English translation, however, does a disservice in representing the literary-rhetorical character of the Hebrew original. In Hebrew one can form a word that is both a noun and a verb at the same time, sometimes referred to by grammarians as a "substantive." Please excuse this short excursus into Hebrew grammar. I shall not do this often in this volume. But here it will pay off in spades, as you shall see.

Nouns in Hebrew appear in one of three forms; let us take the word for "house." "A house has a roof" speaks of no particular house. In English, we use the indefinite article, *a*, to indicate this generality. "The house at the end of this street has a red roof" refers to a particular house. We use the definite article, *the*, to convey this particularity. "The house of Jack" uses the possessive preposition, *of*, to denote belonging. In Hebrew there is strictly speaking no definite or indefinite article, and while there is a possessive preposition, *shel* (pronounce like "sea*shell*"), it is not usually necessary to resort to its use. Indefinite, definite, and possessive states of nouns are denoted in Hebrew by the morphology of the noun itself. "House" in Hebrew is *bayit*. "The house" in Hebrew is *ha-bayit*. Jack's/Jacob's house is *bayt Yaaqov*.

The prefix *ha-* attached to a noun, therefore, denotes specificity or particularity. But it can also be attached to a Hebrew verb that is in the present participle form. (Hebrew has no real present tense and uses the present participles of verbs instead.) The resulting word then does the job of both a noun and a verb at the same time; this is the substantive. The Hebrew verb "to give" in the present-participle, masculine form is *notein*. The substantive is *ha-notein*. The easiest way to render this in colloquial English is "he who gives." But in the Hebrew *ha-notein* there is no pronoun "he," and no relative pronoun "who," but just one word, a verbal substantive. So, nearly the entirety of the each of the five protases (cases) of m. Bekhorot 1:1a, for which a single ruling is given near the end of the passage is comprised of one word, a verbal substantive. "Listen" to how the five sound in sequence:

> ha-loqe'ah ha-mokher ha-mishtatef ha-meqabel ha-notein

Five hypothetical cases are spun out and concatenated in m. Bekhorot 1:1a by using the exact same Hebrew grammatical form five times over with each of five verbal roots: *lqh, mkhr, shtf, qbl,* and *ntn*. If one could think of several more verbs that might possibly define a business relationship between our hypothetical Israelite and Gentile, one could continue to spin out the chain further in exactly the same manner. Switching out the verbal roots, but using the same repeated grammatical-morphological form of the verb, is one more Mishnaic technique of permuting hypothetical circumstances to generate a series of potentially related cases, upon which to rule. And the whole passage at hand would display a type of unity and coherence that, in part, derives not only from its substance and content, but also from the sound, rhythm, and cadence of the same morphological form of the verb being repeatedly used.

A little later we shall make further observations about rhythm, cadence, and other poetic or lyrical-like features of Mishnah's sentences and passages, because they are a blatant feature of Mishnah's pervasive literary-rhetorical conventions and give Mishnah texts an aural character that we do not usually associate with normal speech or declarative sentences. But before doing so, I want to give you an example of how far joining and concatenation techniques can take one in Mishnah in spinning out a series of hypothetical cases. An apt example of such an extended, spun-out passage is found a little further on in the first chapter of tractate Bekhorot, at m. Bekhorot 1:3–4a. I shall present two versions of my translation. The first contains the explanatory interpolations required to make the passage more easily intelligible. The second removes the interpolations, allowing one to see (and hear) more clearly what is going on in this extended passage that concatenates a number of related cases. In the second go-through, I have placed "and," "or," and "which/that" in boldface. First, then, with interpolations:

1:3

In the Seat of Moses

1. An ass which had not given birth and [which] bore two males [and it is not known which of them came out first]—

2. one gives a single lamb to the priest.

3. [If it bore] male and female [and it is not known which of them came out first]—

4. one separates a single lamb for himself.

5. Two asses which had not given birth and [which] bore two males—

6. one gives two lambs to the priest.

7. [If they bore] a male and a female or two males and a female,

8. One gives a single lamb to the priest.

9. [If they bore] two females and one male, or two males and two females,

10. there is nothing here for the priest.

1:4a

11. One [of which] gave birth, and one which had not given birth, and they bore two males—

12. one gives a single lamb to the priest.

13. [If they produced] a male and female,

14. one separates a single lamb for himself.

Now without interpolations, but with joining terms highlighted in boldface:

1:3

1. An ass **which** had not given birth **and** bore two males—

2. one gives a single lamb to the priest.

3. Male **and** female—

4. one separates a single lamb for himself.

5. Two asses **which** had not given birth **and** bore two males—

6. one gives two lambs to the priest.

7. A male **and** a female **or** two males **and** a female—

8. one gives a single lamb to the priest.

9. Two females **and** one male, **or** two males **and** two females—

10. there is nothing here for the priest.

126

1:4a

> 11. One gave birth, **and** one **which** had not given birth, **and** they bore two males—
>
> 12. one gives a single lamb to the priest.
>
> 13. A male **and** female—
>
> 14. one separates a single lamb for himself.
>
> (m. Bekhorot 1:3–4a, translation my own[10])

It is clear from this second rendering of the Mishnah passage how Mishnah's very limited number of stock joining terms function to knit together a series of related cases (protases) for which a number of parallel rulings (apodases) are provided. But it is also apparent that what is being joined are not otherwise independently articulated "cases." Rather, as one proceeds through m. Bekhorot 1:3–4a, the very same bits and pieces of language are repeatedly joined in different combinations in order to define an ever more complex set of hypothetical circumstances. We are first asked to consider one dame-ass that has never before given birth; then later in the passage Mishnah deals with two dame-asses that have not previously given birth. And finally, the passage considers two dame-asses, only one of which has never given birth. For these three groups of soon-to-be mothers, Mishnah considers various combinations of offspring, male and/or female. These include:

–two males;

–male and female;

–male and a female, or two males and a female;

–two females and one male, or two males and two females

The underlying premise is that all this has happened in a field or stable without humans to witness the births. Consequently, one does not know birth orders, or which dame gave birth to which offspring. However, as complicated as the cases become in the progression of the passage, the use of language to "generate" these hypothetical cases is remarkably simple. In fact, I challenge you to continue to spin out this passage's consideration of additional hypothetical cases by permuting and recombining the very same language. But this would also require one to think about the additional rulings such cases would generate. What would those rulings be in light of

---

10. Based on Lightstone, *Rhetoric*, 177–78.

the implicit but unstated principles underlying the cases and rulings that m. Bekhorot 1:3–4a has already articulated?

My challenging you to undertake such an exercise says something important about the reader engagement made possible, even demanded, by ancient (or modern) Mishnah students, a matter to which I will return in the last chapter of this book. At this juncture, however, I wish to articulate the lesson about Mishnah's rhetorical conventions indicated by what we have just seen in m. Bekhorot 1:3–4a. Mishnah passages often spin out a series of hypothetical cases by simple permutation and recombination of a few phrases and terms—this in addition to joining these permuted and recombined bits and pieces of language with "and/but," "or," and "which/that."

This use and reuse, permutation and recombination of the same bits and/or the repetition of the same grammatical-morphological form, as was highlighted with the series of identically formulated verbal substantives in m. Bekhorot 1:1a, produces more than sets of related hypothetical cases upon which to rule. It also makes Mishnah "sound" distinctively "Mishnaic." This sound is, in my view, an integral aspect of Mishnah's literary-rhetorical character, the topic of this chapter's next subsection on Mishnah's declarative sentences and their use to construct typically Mishnaic passages.

Balance, Assonance, Alliteration, Meter, and Repeated Phraseology in Declarative Sentences and in the Mishnah Passages They Serve to Constitute

Although Mishnaic declarative sentences are laconic and frequently show apocopation as well (perhaps, in part, because of their laconic nature), Mishnah statements often have a highly lyrical (even poetic] quality to them. What do I mean? Poetic or lyrical language in English is often characterized by repeated use of assonance, alliteration, rhyme, rhythm, balance and repeated meter. Mishnah is not Hebrew poetry or Hebrew lyrical language. In classical and middle Hebrew, poetry was primarily based upon the repetition of the same *thought* in *different language*; permit me to concoct in English something that has the qualities of classical Hebrew poetry:

> The Lord is my rock;
> and He is my fortress.
> I trust in Him for protection;
> He will shield me.

The biblical Psalms and the compositions attributed to the "literary" prophets, like the biblical books of Isaiah and Jeremiah, are replete with such classical Hebraic poetic forms, as are the great Hebrew liturgical poems of the Middle Ages. The artistry in Hebrew poetry is grounded on the poet's ability to keep saying the same thing twice, using different language each time.

In contrast, the lyrical-like quality of a Mishnah sentence or Mishnah passage derives from (a) repetition, (b) the permutation of the *same* bits of language; (c) the repeated use of the *same* grammatical morphological form (like the same verb tense or verbal substantive form) as well as from (d) the *alternation of opposing terms*. All of this combines with the laconic nature of declarative sentences, allowing the framer of a Mishnah passage to eschew any additional language, even language that is, strictly speaking, required to make sense of the passage, in order to repeat or permute the bare-bones phrases that permit the framer to define a case or a series of more or less subtly different cases.

The resulting effect, articulated in modern literary terms, is that the Mishnah student, consequently, often encounters rhyme, rhythm and meter, balance, assonance, and alliteration. Whether the framers of Mishnah would have used comparable literary descriptors to denote what they achieved I do not know, and, frankly, I doubt. That these features are intentional, I do not doubt. The intent, likely deliberate, is to present the Mishnah student with passages that display a sort of "singsong" quality. To be jocular and irreverent about it, what is displayed in, for example, m. Bekhorot 1:3–4a, which takes us through various combinations of male and female births to one and then two dame-asses, is a serious legal composition more akin in *sound* to "Ninety-Nine Bottles of Beer on the Wall" or to "I Know an Old Lady Who Swallowed a Fly" than to Psalm 24 or 150. Those who composed Mishnah were, therefore, not trying to be poetic; they would have been quite familiar with the qualities of Hebrew poetics. But they were trying to do something in composing passages with such *sound* qualities. Whether or not Mishnah was first composed in written form or composed orally (as Homer did in creating the *Iliad*) is a matter of considerable scholarly debate. But it is not disputed that Mishnah was cited from memory in early rabbinic circles, and that Mishnah students and masters alike were served by resource persons who had memorized the entire Mishnah. The "singsong" nature of so many of Mishnah's declarative sentences and passages would have served this ethos to recite Mishnah passages from memory. And in the modern rabbinic academy or rabbinic study circle, when Mishnah passages are studied (usually in the process of studying a portion of the Babylonian Talmud), one reads Mishnah passages softly, but aloud, to oneself in a kind of singsong voice. It is as if the rhythm and rhyme of the singsong helps the student perceive the logical flow of the Mishnah passage, as indeed it probably does.

Almost all of these lyrical-like qualities are so evident in the sample Mishnah passages already cited in this chapter and in chapter 3 that I will not trouble you with more exemplary texts in order to demonstrate my claims. However, one such literary-rhetorical technique, the use of balanced lexical opposites in the language of the rulings (the apodases), is worth some additional attention, since the discussion thus far in this chapter has, perhaps, focused attention principally on the spinning out of prodases, that is, on the differentiated, hypothetical cases, rather than on the rulings that follow them. We may look no further than the balanced, repeated terms of m. Bekhorot 1:2b, with which you are already familiar. Below in **boldface** are simply the balanced, opposing bits of both the protases and the apodases of the passage, with most everything else excised:

–**unclean** fish, swallowed, **clean** fish—**permitted** as to eating;

–**clean** fish, swallowed, **unclean** fish—**prohibited** as to eating.

Both the protases *and* the apodases are composed as two balanced pairs in which lexical opposites are juxtaposed: unclean+clean+permitted juxtaposed with clean+unclean+forbidden. How simple and elegant! And how lyrical! And because it is so important to understanding what to make of other aspects of Mishnah's conventional literary-rhetorical traits—how deliberately contrived! No one could, or should, mistake this for some version of case law, as some nineteenth- and early to mid-twentieth-century historians of early rabbinic Judaism seem at times to have done. While not quite as simple and bare-bones as m. Bekhorot 1:2a, the longer composition at m. Bekhorot 1:3–4a, which *permutes* the number and gender of dame-asses and offspring, also displays a series of opposing apodases (rulings), in order. Again, please attend to the boldfaced words in the following:

–**gives** a **single** lamb to the **priest**.

–**separates** a **single** lamb for **himself**.

–**gives two** lambs to the **priest**.

–**gives** a **single** lamb to the **priest**.

–**there is nothing** here for the **priest**.
–**gives** a **single** lamb to the **priest**.
–**separates** a **single** lamb for **himself**.

These verbs are juxtaposed throughout: "gives," "separates," "there is nothing." The indirect object of the verbs contrasts two terms: "priest" and "himself." Otherwise we have the distinction established by the use of "single" (lit. "one") versus "two." In truth, this is not that much more complicated than opposing "permitted" and "forbidden."

ATTRIBUTIONS TO NAMED AUTHORITIES, DISPUTES, DEBATES, AND PRECEDENT STORIES

The Mishnah is replete with names of persons whom, as remarked in chapters 2 and 3, Mishnah designates with the honorific *rabbi* ("my master") or *rabban* ("our master"). Collectively, "the rabbis" refer to themselves as "sages," again discussed in chapters 2 and 3. Only in a few instances, does Mishnah proffer names *without* the honorific titles, *rabbi* or *rabban*, as in the case of (protorabbinic?) authorities whom Mishnah places in the Land of Israel in the early first century CE and the first two centuries BCE—all well before the destruction of the Jerusalem Temple in 70 CE. About ten dozen "rabbis" and "protorabbinic" personages are named in Mishnah, of whom less than 20 appear with any frequency.

Historians of Early Judaism struggle with serious historiographical questions when using what Mishnah and other early rabbinic texts say about, or attribute to, these named early rabbinic authorities. How do we know these named authorities really said what is attributed to them? Is it the substance of the historical person's views that is preserved? Is it their actual language? Is it conjecture about what they *would* have ruled based on other knowledge about them (about which we no longer have any evidence)? Did the historical person actually render an opinion on this exact case, or on something that approximates it? The ensuing historiographical problems resemble the challenges faced by scholars of the history of early Christianity when they struggle with what is said about, or attributed to, Jesus in the Gospels, who at times is also addressed as *rabbi* ("my master") in early Christian documents. Although this type of reconstruction of the history of the early rabbinic movement and of the lives of its grandees is not the purpose of this book, understanding Mishnah's rhetorical and literary conventions that govern these rabbis' "sayings" *is* highly germane to assessing their historical value. What is of principal interest for this volume's purposes is the nature and place of attributions of teachings to named rabbinic authorities within the normative literary-rhetorical structures of early rabbinic legal texts, starting in this chapter with Mishnah. In the last chapter of this volume we will more explicitly venture a cautious return into the historical arena, which was also the topic of chapter 2. But the last chapter will have a different focus than chapter 2. The last chapter of this book will consider what the characteristic literary-rhetorical features of early rabbinic legal texts may tell us about the nature, development, and identity structure of the early rabbinic group. We shall certainly *not* entertain questions about whether sayings attributed to rabbi x or rabbi y tell us about the historical x or y.[11]

By way of history, all that need be said for now is to rehearse briefly my remarks in chapter 1. The "rabbis" clearly were not the only elements of society in the Roman-ruled Land of Israel addressed with this honorific title.[12] Rabbinic texts use this title when mentioning rabbinic authorities and their alleged teachings *precisely because* it is a common way of addressing a Jewish grandee of a certain ilk in the Roman-ruled Land of Israel. Were it not, the honorific would not serve to claim similar social standing for "rabbis," along with the honorific designation by which rabbis refer to themselves as a group, *hahkamim*, "sages." "Sages" (in the plural), like *rabbi* and *rabban*, has a literary-rhetorical function in Mishnah in accordance with decided conventions, as we shall see.

In spite of the fact that much of what has been written about early rabbinic Judaism focuses on the named figures, by far the lion's share of declarative sentences in Mishnah bears *no* attributions to individual rabbis or to a collective referred to as "[the] sages." Most declarative sentences are anonymous,[13] jokingly said to be the most prolific author of Mishnah teachings. That said, it is *not uncommon* in Mishnah to come across attributions to named rabbinic authorities. Sometimes a rabbinic rule-statement—that

---

11. For a brief account of why it is difficult to ascertain whether a particular rabbi actually said what in language or substance is attributed to him in Mishnah, see Lightstone, "Naming Names."

12. The use of the term "rabbi" as an honorific title for all sorts of social "grandees" in Roman-ruled Palestine was established years ago in Cohen, "Epigraphical Rabbis."

13. A fact documented in Neusner, *History of the Mishnaic Law*.

is, both the protasis (the "case") and the apodasis (the "rulings")—is entirely attributed to a named rabbi. At other times, only the apodasis is attributed.

"Independent" Attributed Sayings

When these attributed rule-statements are *not* juxtaposed with another, opposing ruling, Jacob Neusner used the term "independent sayings" as a literary-rhetorical designator for rule statements bearing attributions to named rabbis. I shall do the same, although "independent" claims too much, since it is not always (and perhaps, usually not) the case that such attributed sayings have been formulated "independently" of the declarative sentences that precede or follow them.[14] It may be more accurate to call them "unopposed, attributed sayings." Why "sayings"? Because the attribution is usually conveyed by the use of the verb "says" (in the present participial form) or "said" (in the past perfect form) to rhetorically link the declarative sentence or its apodasis to a named authority, such as Rabbi Judah or Rabbi Meir. Another standard literary-rhetorical, attributional formula is "the words of."

Using (and recognizing) this standard attributional language is easy, and easily demonstrated with our earlier, made-up, mildly apocopated sentence:

> A cow which gives birth to a male [and the cow has never before borne young], [the owner] gives [the offspring] to a priest.

Such a declarative sentence may be *attributed* to a named rabbinic authority in few standardized ways. Below three of the most common forms of attribution (in boldface) are used in turn with our made-up declarative sentence.

> **Rabbi Judah says:** A cow which gives birth to a male [and the cow has never before borne young], [the owner] gives [the offspring] to a priest.
>
> Or
>
> A cow which gives birth to a male [and the cow has never before borne young], **Rabbi Judah says:** [the owner] gives [the offspring] to a priest.
>
> Or

---

14. Again, see Neusner, *History of Mishnaic Law*.

> A cow which gives birth to a male [and the cow has never before borne young], [the owner] gives [the offspring] to a priest, **the words of Rabbi Judah.**

Notice that attributions may be positioned at the beginning of the sentence, between the protasis (the statement of case) and the apodasis (the ruling), or at the end of the sentence. "The words of . . ." may only be placed at the end.

Disputes

While independent sayings appear in Mishnah, by far most attributions of rulings to named authorities appear in the context of "disputes." In fact, after anonymous declarative sentences, disputes are the most frequently encountered literary-rhetorical, standard formulation in Mishnah.

In a dispute, one of three things takes place:

a. An anonymous declarative rule sentence is followed by a diametrically opposing ruling attributed to a named rabbi for the same hypothetical circumstance(s);

b. One encounters, in immediate succession, two diametrically opposed rulings, each attributed to a different named rabbi, concerning the same hypothetical circumstance(s);

c. A ruling attributed to a named rabbi is followed by an opposing ruling on the same hypothetical circumstance(s) attributed to the "sages."

Let me provide three made-up examples to illustrate each of these three modes of Mishnaic dispute.

> a   A cow which gives birth to a male, and they do not know if she has [previously] borne [offspring], [the owner] gives nothing to a priest.
>
> **Rabbi Judah says:** [The owner] gives [the offspring] to a priest.
>
> a' A cow which gives birth to a male, and they do not know if she has [previously] borne [offspring]—
>
> **Rabbi Judah says:** [The owner] gives [the offspring] to a priest.
>
> **And [the] sages say:** [The owner] gives nothing to a priest.

b   A cow which gives birth to a male, and they do not know if she has [previously] borne [offspring],

Rabbi Yose says, [The owner] gives nothing to a priest.

Rabbi Judah says: [The owner] gives [the offspring] to a priest.

b' A cow which gives birth to a male, and they do not know if she has [previously] borne [offspring], [the owner] gives nothing to a priest, **the words of Rabbi Yose**.

Rabbi Judah says: [The owner] gives [the offspring] to a priest.

In the foregoing ersatz examples, I have distinguished the first two from last two formulations by designating the former *a* and *a'*, and the latter *b* and *b'*. In the first pair, a ruling attributed to a single named authority, Rabbi Judah, is juxtaposed with the opposite ruling attributed to a *collective voice*. In effect, an unattributed, anonymous ruling in Mishnah represents the opinion of the collective that is Mishnah's authorship. And the attribution of a ruling to "[the] sages" conveys exactly the same message; there is a collective view on the matter, opposed by an individual's view, albeit a very important individual's view, since it warrants statement in Mishnah. In contrast, the second pair of made-up disputes, *b* and *b'*, juxtaposes the opposite rulings of two individual, named rabbinic authorities, Yose and Judah, for the same circumstances.

Now before I present some "real" examples of Mishnah's disputes, I would like to explore with you some literary-critical issues using my ersatz ones. First, in all four made-up examples the language of the rulings, the apodases, is identical. More to the point, the language of the apodasis attributed to one of the disputing authorities is *in each case* the mirror image of the language attributed to the other disputant. Thus:

[The owner] gives nothing to a priest,

versus

[the owner] gives [the offspring] to a priest.

This is typical of "well-formulated" disputes in Mishnah. Frankly, when it is not the case, we literary-historical analysts of Mishnah look for some distinctively unusual literary-historical explanation for the "glitch." But this proves my point about what is overwhelmingly the norm in Mishnah, does it not? What this shows is that the language attributed to the named rabbis is not their language (*ipsissima verba*) at all—even if the content may

In the Seat of Moses

somehow be based in their teachings. Rather, the language put in their mouths is that of the authorship of the Mishnah.

What now may be said of the language of the protasis (the statement of circumstances ruled upon) in each case? In the last example, *b'*, one might surmise that the protasis is part and parcel of what is attributed to Rabbi Yose, and that Rabbi Judah is providing an opposing ruling for a case the language of which is Yose's. But *b'* is just an alternative way of formulating *b*. That is, they display alternative standard ways of formulating disputes in accordance with the literary-rhetorical conventions of Mishnah. So, *b'* should not be read as attributing the protasis to Yose any more than the formulation of *b* does. Indeed, it is more likely the case that protases in all four examples will have come from the authorship of the Mishnah passage or the larger mini-composition in which such disputes appear. In other words, whether in Mishnah we are confronted with disputes or unattributed declarative sentences, the language in front of us is more often that of the passages' or extended passages' authorship, formulated in accordance with rather specific, tightly defined literary rhetorical conventions shared by the parties that collectively are at work in creating Mishnah. Moreover, this explains how (and why) the balance, repetition, assonance, alliteration, and permutative and "singsong" qualities that often run through Mishnah passages and extended mini-compositions in Mishnah frequently run through both unattributed and attributed materials alike in these passages and mini-compositions, as we shall see nearer the end of this chapter.

Now let us move from "made-up" examples to some "real ones."

Mishnah Tractate Ketubbot concerns the marriage contract that the rabbis demanded be established between couples to increase a wife's rights both in marriage and if divorced—this over against the rather flimsy rights women are accorded in biblical law. In m. Ketubbot 3:3, two opposing rulings (apodases) are provided for one and the same "case" (protasis).

- a. [Concerning] a girl who was betrothed and divorced [and subsequently raped]—
- b. Rabbi Yose the Galilean says: She has no fine [that is, the rapist is not fined],
- c. Rabbi Aqiva says: She has a fine, and her fine is hers.

[m. Ket. 3:3, translation my own]

In biblical law, if a man rapes a virgin, since virginity was highly prized in a female marriage partner, her rapist must pay a fine to the woman's father

Mishnah

as a bride price, and the rapist must marry her, since it is presumed that her eligibility for marriage to another prospective husband is significantly impaired. If the father is unwilling to give his sexually violated daughter to her rapist as a wife, the father nonetheless receives the fine/bride price. This is hardly a moral code that we would countenance today. In its day, when these biblical laws were promulgated in ancient Israelite society, this was progress!? The Mishnah passage considers a hypothetical case in which a woman who was betrothed but not yet married—so she is possibly still a virgin—is divorced and subsequently raped, a matter about which the biblical law is silent. Here one sees Mishnah's all-too-frequently-displayed literary tendency to define hypothetical, "in-between" cases for consideration. Is a fine imposed on the rapist or not? Two diametrically opposed rulings attributed to Yose the Galilean and to Aqiva follow.

Even in the English translation, the penchant for repetition of exact language in the sayings attributed to Yose and Aqiva is evident. Only the shift from the negative particle to the positive—"has not" (*ayn*/ אין) vs. "has" (*yesh*/יש)—carries the weight of the dispute. In the "purest" formulations of a dispute, the second clause of the saying attributed to Aqiva ("and her fine is hers") would not appear, since it addresses an issue not raised in the protasis at all. That being said, one finds assonance and alliteration between the second clause of Aqiva's saying and the protasis, (*she-nitarsah ve-nitgarshah*/שנתארסה ונתגרשה vs. *ve-qansah shel atzmah*/וקנסה של עצמה). Perhaps the last clause is a later gloss; perhaps not. Who can say? By the way, look at the features of the protasis. It is highly laconic, as demonstrated by my explanatory interpolations in square brackets. And "and" (*ve-*) and "which/that" (*she-*) join two verbs that together comprise the laconically stated hypothetical case—just as in unattributed, declarative sentences in Mishnah.

Let us look at another dispute passage in Mishnah, this time from m. Berakhot 2:3, which provides a pair of disputes. Mishnah Tractate Berakhot concerns recited blessings and prayers, although its treatment of this larger topic is quite episodic and incomplete. (By the way, do not expect from Mishnah Berakhot anything like the elaboration of a standard liturgy. The earliest rabbinic documents to do so are early medieval in origin.) That said, the topic of m. Berakhot 2:3, the recitation of the *shema*, that is, the recitation in the morning and evening prayer services of Deuteronomy 6:4–9, 11:13–21 and Numbers 15:37–41, is one cornerstone of the standard

In the Seat of Moses

rabbinic liturgy, and still is today both in private prayer and communal prayer in the synagogue.

> a One who recites the *shema,* and does not [do so loud enough] to cause oneself to hear [one's own words]—
>
> b has fulfilled [one's obligation to recite the *shema*].
>
> c Rabbi Yose says: One has not fulfilled [one's obligation to recite the *shema*].
>
> d One recited [the *shema*], and did not precisely enunciate its letters—
>
> e Rabbis Yose says: [Such a one] has fulfilled [one's obligation to recite the *shema*];
>
> f Rabbi Judah says: [Such a one] has not fulfilled [one's obligation to recite the *shema*].
>
> [m. Berakhot 2:3, translation my own]

Here we have two variations of the dispute form. If one looks back to our four made-up, typically formulated disputes presented earlier, we have in m. Berakhot 2:3 examples of version *a* and version *b*. To jog your memory (and to cement matters further), let me schematically represent each of those two variations here, before turning to remarks about m. Berakhot 2:3. Version *a* was structured as follows:

> circumstance + ruling,
>
> Rabbi x says + opposing ruling.

Version *b* took the following form:

> circumstance,
>
> Rabbi x says + ruling,
>
> Rabbi y says + opposing ruling.

Version *a* essentially opens with a complete, unattributed, declarative rule-sentence. In version *b*, the dispute begins with an articulation of the circumstances of the case only, followed by two attributed, opposing rulings.

The first dispute of m. Berakhot 2:3, at "a–c," is an example of version *a*. The second dispute at "d–f" displays the patterning of version *b* (indeed, just as the previous "real" example at m. Ketubbot 3:3 does). The highly laconic, repetitive, and balanced language of the apodases, or rulings, is evident. All comprise one verb in the perfect, third-person singular form—with or without the negative, "not." The two protases (at "a" and "d") also exhibit balance and repetition. Both open with a form of the verb "recite" (albeit the first in the substantive participial form, the other in the perfect tense) followed by the negative, "and did not." The balance and assonance within "a" itself (שמע vs. השמיע, shema vs. hishmy'a) simply cannot be rendered into the English language.

You, the reader, have now seen two "real" examples of the standardized dispute-pattern that I have called version *b*, and one example of version *a*. We could go on and look at exemplars of patterned disputes that look like versions *a'* and *b'*, but the value added for you would not be substantial. If we were to do so, all that we would see are variations of the same; whether a dispute displays the formal patterning of version *a*, *a'*, *b*, or *b'*, all versions of the formal dispute provide the same potential for achieving, and display the same penchant for, laconic, balanced phrases showing alliteration, assonance, and rhythm. More often than not, they display the same basic literary-rhetorical features one sees in Mishnah's unattributed, anonymous declarative sentences. While we have still to look at Mishnaic "debates" and "precedent stories," it is important to know that with an understanding of the normative literary-rhetorical traits of Mishnah's declarative sentences and disputes, one has mastered what characterizes easily 90 percent or more of Mishnah's content.

Debates

Disputes are commonly found in Mishnah, "debates" far less so. In a Mishnaic dispute, usually nothing is explicitly communicated about why the rabbinic authorities in question (would) hold their respective views, or why one disputant might reject the other's opinion. Of course, when a disputant's ruling differs from that conveyed in an unattributed declarative sentence—version *a* of the standard dispute pattern—one is invited to draw the conclusion that Mishnah is representing a majority versus a minority opinion (here a minority of one). The same may be said of version *a'* of the dispute, in which one named authority's "saying" is juxtaposed with an opposing "saying" attributed to "[the] sages." In both cases, Mishnah's literary-rhetorical patterning may imply something about which view is normative; but even here the dispute pattern does not imply that the minority-of-one opinion is illegitimate.

Mishnaic "debates," by contrast, proffer *alleged* reasoning (or perhaps more accurately stated, counterreasoning) for disputants' views. Consequently, Mishnaic "debates" follow upon disputes, which provide these "debates" with a necessary antecedent context. Below is a made-up debate joined to version *b* of our earlier forged dispute.

1. A cow which gives birth to a male, and they do not know if she has [previously] borne [offspring]—
2. **Rabbi Yose says**, He [the owner] gives nothing to a priest.
3. **Rabbi Judah says**, He [the owner] gives [the offspring] to a priest.
4. **Said he** [Judah] **to him** [Yose], Shall the priest be deprived of what may belong to him!?
5. **Said he** [Yose] **to him** [Judah], Shall he [the owner] be deprived of what may belong to him!?

Parts 1 to 3 of this ersatz passage form our now-familiar dispute. The two opposing, balanced, and matched rulings attributed to Yose and Judah respectively are introduced as usual with the verb "says," in present participial form in Hebrew—present participles are used for the present tense in Hebrew. Parts 4 and 5 constitute the debate, a *one-round* contest of very sparsely articulated reasoning in which an argument or counterargument is attributed to each of the two disputants in turn using the verb "said," in the perfect tense in Hebrew. That is it! That can constitute a Mishnaic debate! In some, the counterreasoning is a little more elaborate; just as often it is not. Whether more or less elaborately articulated, the "reasoning" attributed to each of the disputants is often closely matched, as we have done in our made-up example. In a "properly" patterned Mishnaic debate, disputants usually do not get a second kick at the can, and no disputant will get more kicks than his fellow debater. There is no sense or indication that someone has "won" the debate.[15]

---

15. Later rabbinic literature, particularly in the early medieval period, had to distill normative rabbinic law from Mishnah's and other tannaitic passages. Disputes and debates posed a problem. Consequently, these later legal texts developed rules of thumb for declaring which of the disputant's/debater's views was the law, the Halakha. We must be wary about reading these rules of thumb back into the earlier rabbinic sources, in which, from a literary-rhetorical perspective, no one has "won." The only implication of normativity is that a ruling that is anonymous or is attributed to the "sages" is conveyed as the view of the many over against the position of the few or of an individual.

Mishnah

Just as there were various but limited versions of the standardized dispute pattern, so too there are some variations of the standard debate pattern. But these variations only have to do with alternative formulations of the language used to attribute reasons/reasoning to the debaters. *Invariably*, "said" (in the perfect tense) is used, and "to him" is either stated or implied. The most common variations are

Said he to him;

Said to him Rabbi x;

Said Rabbi x.

As to the order in which debaters are made to articulate their reason/reasoning, often it is in the reverse order in which their names appear in the dispute that precedes the debate. Consequently, we frequently see the following sequence in Mishnaic dispute-debates.

Case;

Rabbi x says + ruling;

Rabbi y says + ruling;

Said [to him, i.e., x,] Rabbi y + reason/reasoning;

Said [to him, i.e., y,] Rabbi x + reason/reasoning.

Before proceeding to look at "real" examples of Mishnaic debates, I wish to broach one more matter, using our contrived debate about our now-familiar hypothetical cow to make the point. When this chapter discussed disputes, I stated that the language that was attributed to the disputants, usually matched and balanced apodases, is most likely the contrived language of the Mishnah passage's authorship, even if some living historical memory of the named disputants' legal traditions are somehow reflected in the dispute. And we added that the language of the protases (the hypothetical cases) to which the disputants' "sayings" are attached is most likely the work of the passage's authorship as well. The whole dispute is basically a typical Mishnaic sentence, but with two opposing apodases for a single protasis. What now of the language attributed to the named authorities of a Mishnaic debate? Is it likely that these authorities actually "said" what is attributed to them as reasoning? Likely not, and for much the same rationale as I earlier articulated for the attributed "sayings" in disputes. Whatever historical legal traditions lurk behind what is "said" in debates, the language Mishnah attributes to the debaters is that of Mishnah's framers, framed

In the Seat of Moses

(again) in balanced, matched sets in accordance with Mishnah's norms for "speaking," which, as we have seen, are very particular indeed, unlikely to represent how anyone would speak in "real life."

So, what does a "real" Mishnaic debate look like? By way of example, I have chosen a passage from Mishnah Tractate Negaʿim, which deals with the topic of skin diseases that render one unclean, a major preoccupation of the laws of the biblical book of Leviticus. Following is m. Negaʿim 10:1-2, which presents two disputes cum debates. As you read the passage, please note the boldfaced attributions to named authorities.

10:1

A. The balding spots [of the head and beard] are rendered unclean over a two-week period,

B. 1. and with [the appearance of] two symptoms:

    2. [viz.,] with [the appearance of] thin yellow hairs [within the circumference of the spot]

    3. and with [the appearance of] spreading [of the area affected].

C. "'With [the appearance of] thin yellow hairs' [means] afflicted [with] short [yellow hairs]," **the words of Rabbi Aqiva.**

D. **Rabbi Yohanan ben Nuri says,** "Even long [yellow hairs suffices]."

E. **Said Rabbi Yohanan ben Nuri,**

    1. "What [is the meaning of what] they commonly say: This staff is thin; this reed is thin?

    2. [It signifies that] thin [means either] afflicted [with] short [yellow hairs],

    3. or thin [means] afflicted [with] long [yellow hairs]."

F. **Said to him Rabbi Aqiva,**

    1. "Before we learn [i.e., draw conclusions] from the reed, let us learn from hair [itself],

    2. [about which they commonly say:] So-and-so's hair is thin—

    3. [signifying that] thin [means] afflicted [with] short [yellow hairs],

    4. and thin [does] not [also mean] afflicted [with] long [yellow hairs]."

10:2

A. 1. "Thin yellow hair [in the circumference of the bald spot] renders unclean,

2. [whether the thin yellow hairs] are gathered [together within the spot],

3. or spread [throughout],

4. [whether] forming a circle [within in the spot],

5. or not forming a circle,

6. [whether] preceding [the bald spot's appearance],

7. or not preceding [the bald spot's appearance],"

the words of Rabbi Judah.

B. **Rabbi Simeon says**, "[The thin yellow hair] render unclean only [when] preceding [the bald spot's appearance]."

C. **Said Rabbi Simeon**,

1. "And [lo] it is reasonable [from an argument *a fortiori*];

2. if [in the case of the appearance of] white hairs, [with respect to] which [the presence in the affected spot of] other [normal-colored] hair does not forefend from its [ie., the white hair's] power [to render one unclean], [nonetheless, the white hair] renders [one] unclean only [when the bald spot's appearance] has changed,

3. [then in the case of the appearance of] thin yellow hair, [with respect to] which [the presence in the affected spot of] other [normal-colored] hair does forefend from its [i.e., the thin yellow hair's] power [to render one unclean], is it [then] not [all the more so] reasonable that [thin yellow hair] renders [one] unclean only [when the bald spot's appearance] has changed?"

D. **Said [to him] Rabbi Judah**,

1. "[In] every case where one is required to say [i.e, rule, that abnormally colored hair renders one unclean only when the bald spot's appearance] has changed, it [Scripture explicitly] stated [that the appearance] changed (see Leviticus 13:3).

2. But [concerning] the bald spot—as it is said [in Scripture] concerning it, 'and there not be in it yellow hair' (Leviticus 13:32)—

3. [the appearance therein of yellow hair] renders unclean [whether the bald spot's appearance] changed,

4. or has not changed."

(m. Nega'im 10:1–2, translation my own)

These two disputes-plus-debates are, admittedly, far more elaborate than the made-up example presented earlier. But take heart. First, once we take a closer look at it, using our knowledge of the standard literary-rhetorical conventions for patterning disputes-plus-debates, each of 10:1 and 10:2 will break down easily into recognizable and digestible chunks. After all, that is the purpose of becoming familiar with Mishnah's standard ways of patterning language—and the purpose of this book. Second, I doubt that in reading Mishnah, Tosefta, or other Tosefta-like, tannaitic traditions embedded in either of the two Talmuds, you will likely encounter a dispute-plus-debate more elaborate than these. So, if you can render m. Nega'im 10:1–2 intelligible, you are on firm ground indeed to confront many other rabbinic legal passages.

Let us begin by simply isolating the language that attributes content to named authorities. I placed this language in boldface type in my translation.

10:1

C. ... **the words of Rabbi Aqiva.**

D. **Rabbi Yohanan ben Nuri says,** ... ,

E. **Said Rabbi Yohanan ben Nuri,** ....

F. **Said to him Rabbi Aqiva,** ....

10:2

F. ... **the words of Rabbi Judah.**

G. **Rabbi Simeon says,** ....

H. **Said Rabbi Simeon,** ....

I. **Said [to him] Rabbi Judah,** ...

Mishnah

If one attends to the standard attributional language in m. Negaʿim 10:1–2—"the words of," "says," "said to him," "said [to him]"—the overall patterned structure of m. Negaʿim 10:1–2 now looks both simple and familiar, even if the content still seems arcane and complex. In each of the passages 10:1 and 10:2, we find a dispute followed by a debate. Each dispute has two opposing rulings, and no more. Each of the two debates goes "one round" only, just as we would expect. We could argue until the cows come home—sorry for the cow references—whether all of section A of 10:2 is attributed by the passage's author(s) to Judah, or just the last bits of A, since Judah and Simeon are portrayed as disagreeing about the last bits only. (No such argument could be had about 10:1.) Does the authorship of 10:2 intend only the last bit of section A to be attributed to Rabbi Judah, since only the last bit is represented as "disputed" by Simeon? This is the stuff that literary scholars of the Mishnah and even traditional rabbinic students of the Mishnah will argue about. It is difficult to come to any probative opinion. But you, the reader of this volume, already possess the literary-rhetorical tools to offer an opinion. How so? Disputes in Mishnah normally attribute matched, opposing views to each of the two named authorities. If that is the *usual* literary-rhetorical convention for disputes in Mishnah, then for that which is attributed to Juduh and Simeon to be "matched" in 10:2, what is attributed to Judah ought only to be the last bits of section A. You see! Recognizing Mishnah's literary-rhetorical conventions makes digesting what is going on easier.

Let me now say more about the internal structure of the debate portions of m. Negaʿim 10:1 and 10:2, because they provide a good example of how early rabbinic legal texts "reason out" matters. Mishnah has relatively few debates, as I have mentioned. So, we do not get many examples of early rabbinic legal reasoning *explicitly* spelled out in Mishnah. Reasoning remains mostly *implicit* in Mishnah, and a matter that the engaged ancient student of Mishnah had to infer from the text. But where we do have debates, these modes of reasoning are transparent. Moreover, they carry over to other early rabbinic texts, where they appear to be *normative* forms of reasoning and of proffering rationales.

When *explicitly* expressed, as in debates, early rabbinic "reasoning" tends to be limited to a restrained number of modes. Two of the most common are represented in our sample texts. They are:

> 1) arguments from analogy, of which arguments *a fortiori*, (i.e., from the "weaker" to the "stronger" analogue, and *a miniori*, (i.e,

In the Seat of Moses

from the "stronger" to the "weaker" analogue) are mere subcategories; and

2) arguments from Scripture.

An argument from analogy generally uses some version of the following form:

If with respect to case *a*, which has characteristic *b*, the law is *c*,

then with respect to case *a'*, which has characteristic *b'*, the law should also/should not be *c*.

Anyone who has taken SATs and GREs on applying to colleges and universities will be familiar with standardized texts of analogical reasoning. Arguments from Scripture simply adduce proof texts, with or without some interpretive gloss.

Since so much of explicitly articulated early rabbinic legal argument displays these standard forms and modes of reasoning, starting with Mishnah's debates (few as they are) permit me to elaborate, using a relatively simple, made-up example. We shall together look at an argument that is an argument from analogy, *a fortiori* (that is, from a weaker to a stronger analogous circumstance). Let us imagine that the highway code of your state or province reads as follows:

Exceeding the posted speed limit by ten miles an hour shall result in no less than ten demerit points being applied, at the officer's discretion, to the speeder's driver's permit; the accumulation of thirty demerit points shall result in the suspension of the permit for a period of two years.

Now imagine a driver stopped and ticketed for exceeding the limit by 20 miles an hour. The ticket indicates that the officer has made the discretionary judgment to assign twenty demerit points against the driver's license. The driver decides to challenge this in traffic court, and tries to argue that the *literal* meaning of the highway code is that demerit points are assigned for exceeding the posted speed limit by 10 miles an hour, and only by 10 miles an hour. How deluded is the driver!? The legal counsel for the town states that the highway code cannot have been intended by its framers to be limited to the meaning that the driver says is its literal meaning. Rather, counsel for the municipality argues as follows:

> *If* one loses points on one's driving license for exceeding the speed limit by ten miles an hour,
>
> *then* one should certainly lose points on one's driving license for exceeding the speed limit by twenty miles an hour.

The analogous circumstances compared here are driving ten miles an hour over the limit *versus* driving twenty miles an hour over the limit. If one were foolish enough to maintain that one should only get demerit points for exceeding the limit by ten miles an hour, but not for speeding by twenty miles an hour, then the argument from analogy *a fortiori*, from the weaker to the stronger analogous condition, should set one straight. Characteristic *b*, driving ten miles an hour over the limit, is being compared to analogous characteristic *b'*, exceeding the speed limit by twenty miles per hour. As we can readily see, whether an argument from analogy lends itself to being cast as an argument *a fortiori* (or *a miniori*) depends upon the relative "strengths" of characteristics *b* and *b'*.

The two principal forms of normative argument found in "debates," from analogy and from Scripture, are not mutually exclusive, since arguments from analogy may also appeal to scriptural data, as when characteristics *b* and *b'* are replaced with scriptural verses:

> *If* with respect to case *a*, *regarding which Scripture says b*, the law is *c*,
>
> *then* with respect to case *a'*, *regarding which Scripture says b'*, the law should also be/should not be *c*.

In the debates formulated in m. Negaʿim 10:1 and 10:2 we see three arguments from analogy, at E and F of 10:1 and at C of 10:2. C of 10:2 is also an argument *a fortiori*, and explicitly says so. D of 10:2 is an argument from analogy in which what is compared is what Scripture *says* in *other* analogous cases of skin abnormalities, on the one hand, with what Scripture *does not say* as regards *this* case, the case at hand in 10:2, on the other. There, in the former instances, Scripture explicitly states something that it expressly does *not* state here in the case at hand. This absence, therefore, is deliberate, indicative, and consequently probative for "Simeon."

Why did I just place Simeon's name in quotation marks? Again, to reinforce a point made earlier: With the Mishnaic debate, we are dealing with something that is highly stylized. The broader range and richness of how real or fictionalized people would *really* converse or argue their points is reduced to a limited number of formulaic possibilities. As with disputes, the language of debates is highly laconic—generally, not a feature of living prose. The use of "said" in these stylized debates, may sound like a historical report, perhaps more so than "says" used in disputes. But this is, in my view, a false road.

In the end, therefore, much of what we have said of the significance of the Mishnaic dispute holds as well for the Mishnaic debate. This with one important addition—*the debate models authoritative forms of reasoning for (or against) a legal position*, although it does so in a very stylized and highly laconic fashion. The authority for these stylized and formalized modes of reasoning derives from the attribution of these arguments to named rabbinic masters. This is important, because as in the case of Mishnaic disputes, it need not have been this way. Arguments for or against a legal position could just as easily have been presented anonymously, in the same fashion as most of Mishnah's rulings bear no attribution at all to named rabbis. Again, we return to the question, Why should Mishnah (or Tosefta, or other early rabbinic texts) attribute anything to named rabbinic authorities? We shall venture some hypotheses about this matter in the last chapter of this book.

Precedent "Stories"

I have just remarked that the use of the verb "said" with attributions of arguments to named rabbis in debates should not be taken as a literary-rhetorical marker of Mishnah's framers' intent to reflect some historical encounter between the debaters, any more than does the use of "says" in disputes. But there is one standardized literary-rhetorical structure in Mishnah that certainly does explicitly denote that a historical reminiscence of what a named rabbinic figure did or said is being presented to legitimate a ruling. These are Mishnah's precedent stories, which invariably take the form:

–**an incident** [once happened] (ma'aseh/ מעשה):

–**concerning**(*be-*/ ב) and/or **that/which/who** (*she-*/ ש) + connoting or denoting, as appropriate, the actors, the time, and/or the place;

–**and** (*ve*/ ו) used one or more times to conjoin elements of circumstance in order to define a "case" that requires a ruling;

–**and** (*vel* ו) used once more to join to the foregoing some alleged authoritative action or ruling by a named rabbinic sage.

That is it: "an incident" (once happened) + *dramatis personae* and/or place + circumstances of case + ruling or act indicative of a ruling by a named rabbinic authority.

The legal precedent "stories" structured in this formalized manner with these standardized literary markers are barely stories at all, and are usually very short. Let us go back to our speeder behind the wheel of an automobile (formulaic language in boldface):

> **an incident** [once happened] **concerning** a man **who** drove twenty miles an hour over the speed limit on Bloor Street in Toronto, **and Rabbi** Judah stopped him **and** issued him a ticket **and** the ticket assigned twenty demerit points.

Bingo! We have created a well-formulated and fully articulated Mishnaic precedent story using the required literary-rhetorical markers. Any more detail or greater elaboration is unnecessary and would be decidedly un-Mishnaic.

Of course, to call some class of literary formulations in Mishnah a "precedent" story already indicates that they are used to legitimate some antecedent ruling(s) proffered in the Mishnah passage(s) of which the story is a part. In other words, Mishnaic precedent stories are made to gloss, and thereby to support, some antecedent ruling. That antecedent ruling may be conveyed an anonymous (that is, unattributed) declarative rule-sentence, or it may be an attributed ruling conveyed in an independent saying or by one of the rulings in a dispute. Finally, the precedent story itself may be attributed to a named rabbinic authority, implying that it is that authority's reminiscence that is conveyed in the precedent story. When precedent stories are attributed, the attributional formula "said rabbi x" is invariably used. Why "said" (in the perfect tense), just as in the case of the language of debates? Because just as in the case of debates, the attribution "said rabbi x" is meant to support an opinion or ruling that immediately precedes it.

How might all this work together? Let me, first, present another made-up example, and then provide a real Mishnah passage in which a precedent story is used.

> A. He who exceeds the posted speed limit by ten miles an hour—
>
> B. ten demerit points are applied.

In the Seat of Moses

C. He who exceeds the posted speed limit by twenty miles an hour—

D. Rabbi Yose says, ten demerit points are applied.

E. Rabbi Meir says, twenty demerit points are applied.

F. Said Rabbi Judah,

   1. **an incident** [once happened]

   2. **concerning** a man **who** drove twenty miles an hour over the speed limit on Bloor Street in Toronto,

   3. **and Rabbi** Aqiva stopped him **and** issued him a ticket **and** the ticket assigned twenty demerit points.

In our ersatz Mishnah passage, section A–B is an anonymous (unattributed) declarative rule-sentence; section C–E is a dispute on a related case (at C) with different circumstances than A; and F is a typically formulated precedent story, attributed to Judah as a "reminiscence" supporting Meir's view at E. Once one knows the literary-rhetorical rules for constructing such a passage, it is all very straightforward, is it not?

Now let us look at a real precedent story used in the context of an elaborated Mishnah passage, m. Gittin 4:7:

A. One who sends forth [i.e., divorces] his wife, on account of [her having gained] a bad reputation

B. may not bring [her] back [in order to remarry her].

C. On account of a vow [Bertinoro: made by his wife that he will not tolerate]—

D. [he] may not bring [her] back.

E. Rabbi Judah says: [On account of] any vow that many know [about],

F. [he] may not bring [her] back,

G. and [on account of any vow] that many did not know [about],

H. [he] may bring [her] back.

I. Rabbi Meir says: [On account of] any vow that requires examination by a sage [i.e., only a sage, upon examination, may annul her vow],

J. [he] may not bring [her] back,

K. and [on account of any vow] that does not require examination by a sage [i.e., her husband may himself annul her vow, because it does not please him],

L. [he] may bring [her] back.

M. Said Rabbi Eleazar: They forbade [him taking her back] only on account of this [i.e., the case of a vow that would require a sage to annul it, as specified by Rabbi Meir, and not upon the other grounds mentioned earlier].

N. 1. Said Rabbi Yose the son of Rabbi Judah: An incident once happened (*ma'seh*)

2. in (*be-*) Sidon

3. concerning (*be-*) one

4. who (*she-*) said to his wife: I swear that I shall divorce you—

5. and (*ve-*) he divorced her [and subsequently repented of his decision],

6. and (*ve-*) the sages permitted him to take her back [in marriage],

7. by reason [of the merit to contribute to] the mending of the world.

(m. Gittin 4:7, translation my own)

The last section of this passage (at N) is a well-formulated Mishnaic precedent story, attributed (using the attributional formula "said," in the perfect tense) as a reminiscence of Yose b. R. Judah. But let us consider it in context, that is, as the concluding part of the entire passage.

I cannot decide whether the formulation of the whole of m. Gittin 4:7 is elegant or somewhat "mongrel" by the literary-rhetorical conventions of Mishnah. You should by now know enough about how Mishnah normally formulates matters to pick out what may appear to be either literary-rhetorical anomalies or standard formulations pushed elegantly a little beyond their normal boundaries. The passage begins with a double-barreled anonymous ruling (A–B and C–D), exhibiting what one would expect from two such matched and balanced Mishnaic declarative sentences. The second ruling (C–D) also forms the first part of a Mishaic dispute (C–D and E–H), of the type I have called version *a*:

Circumstance + ruling

Rabbi x says + opposing ruling.

However, the opposing ruling (E–H), which is attributed to Rabbi Judah, is itself double-barreled, achieving this by further refining the circumstances so as to define two subspecies of the case. Then the opposing ruling attributed to Judah (E–H), is opposed by yet another double-barreled ruling attributed to Rabbi Meir (I–L). What is attributed to Meir is a different refinement of the circumstances than the one conveyed in the ruling attributed to Judah. So, taken on their own, what is attributed to Judah (E–H), juxtaposed with what is attributed to Meir (I–L), forms a second dispute of the type we have called version *b*:

> Rabbi x says + ruling
>
> Rabbi y says + ruling

In sum, the double anonymous ruling with which the passage begins provides the starting point for two alternative disputes, both generated by providing alternative refinements of the circumstances to which the rulings apply.

The two disputes are then glossed by language attributed in turn to Eleazar (at M) and to Yose b. R. Judah (at N). That they are intended to be read as glosses or comments on the foregoing is indicated by the use of "said" in the perfect tense, just as one would find in a good Mishnaic debate. But this is obviously not a debate. What Eleazar "said" is simply that the ruling attributed to Meir is correct. Admittedly, one does not see a great deal of this in Mishnah. However, the language attributed to Yose b. R. Judah is, finally, our typically formulated precedent story. *In situ*, the precedent story functions to counter what Eleazar "said" about the validity of Meir's position. The alleged actions of the "sages" in the precedent story appear to be more lenient than the position attributed to Meir. But clearly this "precedent" story purports to tell us about a case that is unrelated to the disputes of the rest of this passage. The latter concern vows made by the wife; the precedent story concerns a vow made by the husband. Well, the authors/editors of Mishnah passages do not always get it right, and in these instances the literary-critical historian may make considerable hay in proposing how this passage came to be—which is not our purpose in this volume.

But enough about the vagrancies of this perhaps peculiarly formulated Mishnah passage, m. Gittin 4:7. What is important to take away from this brief discussion is this:

1) you now know enough about "conventional" disputes and debates to follow an account of what is going on, and (perhaps) not going on as it *should*, in this Mishnah passage; and

2) you should also recognize a typically formulated precedent story, as found here—except that here it simply is not a precedent story that legitimates anything that precedes it in the passage.

Before leaving our account of the Mishnaic precedent stories for our next (and final) literary-rhetorical form in Mishnah, I wish to use the final section (N) of m. Gittin 4:7 to make another point about such typical "stories." If one removes the thin veneer of standard literary markers that make it a precedent story, there is almost nothing left that is story-like about this (or most other) precedent stories. In fact, what remains after such surgery is not that far from a standard, concisely formulated Mishnaic declarative sentence. Let me show you:

> One who says (the perfect tense has been changed to *ha*+present participle) to his wife:
> I swear that I shall divorce you,
> and he divorced her,
> is permitted to take her back,
> by reason of the mending of the world.

I needed to make one modification only, beyond excising the literary-rhetorical formularies that made it a precedent story: I changed "one who said" to "one who says" (the perfect tense has been changed to *ha*+present participle). That is all! The precedent story is gone, and instead we have a declarative rule-sentence. What has just been demonstrated? One can easily form a declarative rule sentence from a precedent story, and vice versa. Perhaps, then, one may legitimately say that typical precedent-story literary-rhetorical markers serve to "narratize" typically formulated Mishnaic declarative sentences.

Scriptural Proof-texting in Mishnah

As I have stated, at the foundation of much Mishnaic law is scriptural law. So, one might have expected citations of Scripture to appear as a dominant literary feature of Mishnah. But as you now know, such is not the case. The novice reader of Mishnah will at frequent junctures be searching through the Pentateuch for the relevant background required to understand

In the Seat of Moses

Mishnaic passages, because one of the pervasive literary-rhetorical features of Mishnah passage after Mishnah passage is the absence in the text of the information and background that makes the passage fully intelligible. And this is the case even if that background is in Scripture. Scripture's explicit "absence" in Mishnah is part and parcel of the highly "laconic" nature of typical Mishnah compositions. Relevant Scripture is often in the background and rarely referenced or cited explicitly. That said, citation of Scripture is not entirely absent in Mishnah. Indeed, in some of the sample passages that have already been presented in this chapter and in chapter 3, citations of Scripture appear. When they do appear, they are used in one of two ways, and you will have seen examples of both:

(1) as a part of a gloss that supports an attributed or anonymous ruling that immediately precedes the citation of Scripture, and

(2) as part of the data of an argument from analogy within a debate.

Whether it is for one or the other purpose, the entire, relevant scriptural verse or verses need not be cited, and hardly ever are. It is sufficient to cite just a phrase or a few words of the relevant biblical verse. Mishnaic style is extremely economical even when citing Scripture. At times the phrase cited is that part of the verse that the editor/author of the passage wishes to highlight in order to justify the antecedent ruling in the Mishnah passage. At other times, what is cited is intended to be sufficient for the Mishnah student to identify or recall the entire relevant biblical verse or biblical passage. This, again, says something of the institutional context in which Mishnah was studied in the ancient world. Because unlike printed editions of the Mishnah from early modern and modern times, ancient manuscripts of the Mishnah did not indicate the biblical book, chapter, and verse from which the snippet of biblical text cited was taken. (In fact, the books of the Hebrew scriptural canon were not themselves divided into chapters and verses until the medieval period, as indicated by the manuscript evidence.) And in so far as ancient Mishnah students were expected to have memorized significant portions of the Mishnah—and some specialists were expected to have memorized the entire Mishnah—all the more so, these snippets of biblical text cited came with no references to chapter and verse in the Hebrew Bible. All such references relied on recall on the part of the ancient student of Mishnah, and the novice student needed to be mentored to the point that one commanded such recall. But more on this will follow in the last chapter of this book.

Just as attributions to named authorities are almost invariably signaled in Mishnah by strictly prescribed forms of the verb "to say," so too are citations of Scripture in Mishnah. Rabbi *x* "says" (in the present participial form) attributes a ruling or entire declarative rule-sentence to an authority, whether as an independent saying or, far more frequently, within a dispute. "Said rabbi x to him" or "Said rabbi x [to him]" (in the perfect form) attributed arguments to a sage in the context of a dispute. And "said rabbi x" also introduced attributed glosses of an antecedent ruling, including, at times, glosses that contained precedent stories. The verb "to say" in the passive form of the perfect, "it is said" (*ne'emar*), invariably introduces a biblical citation in Mishnah, often with the prefix *she-* (ש), giving us the scriptural citation formulary, "as it is said" (*she-ne'emar*) followed by the citation of a scriptural phrase.

Permit me to demonstrate this scriptural citation formulary's use in a made-up example. Our topic will again be highway rules. But, remember my fabricated Supreme Court ruling?

> It is unconstitutional to not have a highway code, lest the constitutional right to have one's life reasonably protected by government be abrogated by any level of government, federal, state/provincial, or municipal.

Let us treat this imaginary Supreme Court ruling as if it were Scripture. An ersatz Mishnah-like passage that cites this "Scripture" might look like this.

> A. He who exceeds the posted speed limit by 10 miles an hour—
>
> B. ten demerit points are applied,
>
> C. as it is said, "To have one's life reasonably protected."

In such a passage, an appeal is made to the authority of one phrase of the Supreme Court's full statement. The implication is that applying demerit points to driver's permits, potentially leading to the permit's revocation, affords reasonable protection to others, who may be harmed by a habitually speeding driver.

We have already seen several "real" Mishnah passages that present scriptural citations in one of the two manners outlined above: (1) as a supporting gloss; and (2) as an authoritative datum in an argument from analogy within a dispute. For convenience's sake, let me reproduce them here. Note the language in boldface. An example of the first type of usage is m. Bekhorot 1:1a.

> A. He who purchases the foetus of an ass of a Gentile [and the ass had never before borne offspring],
>
> B. and he who sells to him, even though it is not permitted,
>
> C. and he who forms a partnership with him,
>
> D. and he who receives from him,
>
> E. and he who gives to him in trust—
>
> F. [the newborn, if male,] is exempt from the law of the firstling,
>
> **G. as it is said, "Of an Israelite" (Numbers 3:13),**
>
> **H. but not of others.**
>
> (m. Bek. 1:1a, translation my own[16])

A through E is a list of five different but related protases, cases. F is an apodasis, a ruling, serving them all. G glosses the entirety with a supporting scriptural citation from Numbers 3:13. H is a further very short gloss that makes more explicit the relevance of the scriptural citation to the ruling. What is cited at G is just a snippet of the biblical verse, which in its entirety reads.

> For Mine are all firstborn [males]; from the day [that] I smote all firstborn in the land of Egypt, I sanctified for Myself all firstborn of an[y] Israelite; from among humankind to [any] beast—they shall be Mine; I am YHWH.
>
> (Numbers 3:13, trans. my own)

When one peruses the entirety of Numbers 3:13, it is clear that, on the one hand, the entirety of the verse is *generally speaking* relevant background to m. Bekhorot 1:1a, the opening passage of the first chapter of the Mishnah tractate on the law of the firstling. That said, the snippet, "of an[y] Israelite," cited at G, is especially relevant to Mishnah's ruling at F for the list of cases at A through E. The ancient reader of Mishnah needed to recognize the snippet, identify where in Scripture it appears in a verse relevant to the topic at hand, and, finally, must recall the entire verse to provide relevant context. That is not an insignificant demand on the Mishnah student, made much easier for the modern readers of Mishnah, since modern editions of Mishnah in Hebrew or in English translation routinely supply the scriptural references when Scripture is cited.

---

16. Based on Lightstone, *Rhetoric*, 79.

As to a scriptural citation used in a Mishnaic debate as a datum in an argument from analogy—I turn to m. Negaʿim 10:1–2, also cited earlier in this chapter. I shall reproduce only the section at the very end of the passage that uses Scripture in this manner. Again, note the language in boldface.

> D. Said [to him] Rabbi Judah,
>
> 1. "[In] every case where one is required to say [i.e, rule, that abnormally colored hair renders one unclean only when the bald spot's appearance] has changed, it [Scripture explicitly] stated [that the appearance] changed (see Leviticus 13:3)
>
> 2. But [concerning] the bald spot—**as it is said** (*she-neʾemar*) [in Scripture] concerning it, **'and there not be in it yellow hair'** (Leviticus 13:32)—
>
> 3. [the appearance therein of yellow hair] renders unclean [whether the bald spot's appearance] changed,
>
> 4. or has not changed."
>
> (m. Negaʿim 10:1–2, translation my own)

The argument from analogy in what is attributed to Rabbi Judah is based on the comparison of two analogous pieces of data in Scripture. One is alluded to only, but not cited; that is Leviticus 13:3. The other is explicitly cited verbatim; that is, Leviticus 13:32. The topic, as you may recall, concerns skin diseases that render one unclean. Permit me to cite Leviticus 13:3 and Leviticus 13:32 in their entirety. First, Leviticus 13:3; note the boldface language:

> And the priest shall inspect the disease[d area] in the skin of the flesh, and [if] the hair on the disease[d area] **has changed** [to] white, and the appearance of the disease[d area] is deeper than the [surface] skin of his flesh, [then] it is a leprous disease[d area], and the priest shall inspect him and shall declare him unclean.
>
> (Leviticus 13:3, translation my own)

Now Leviticus 13:32:

> And the priest shall inspect the disease[d area] on the seventh day [after the initial inspection], and, lo, [if] the balding spot has not spread, and[/or] there is not within it yellow hair, and[/or] the appearance of the balding spot is not deeper than the [surface] skin—
>
> (Leviticus 13:32, translation my own)

Verse 13:3, which deals with leprous diseased areas of the skin, has the priest specifically look for changes over time. On the other hand, verse 13:32, which concerns a different skin affliction characterized by bald spots with a few abnormally colored hairs, says nothing about changes over time. Scripture appears to treat the cases differently. The argument from analogy attributed to Rabbi Judah in the dispute makes hay from this difference, by contrasting the two analogous dicta in Scripture.

With this discussion of the literary-rhetorical conventions of the use of scriptural proof-texting in Mishnah, this chapter has concluded its survey of all of the major literary-rhetorical conventions of Mishnah. Our survey is not exhaustively comprehensive. But I do not want it to be. What you have now seen is enough to recognize easily what Mishnah does throughout its tractates in terms of its formalized modes of speech. This is not to master its legal content; but it is the necessary requisite for doing so.

This is not yet the place to end this chapter, however. It is instructive to see how Mishnah uses many of these literary-rhetorical conventions over the course of an entire Mishnah "chapter," that is, over an extended topical mini-essay in Mishnah. And it is to that, that this chapter turns in its concluding section.

A MISHNAH "CHAPTER": FROM EXTENDED COMPOSITE MISHNAH PASSAGES TO TOPICAL MINI-ESSAYS IN MISHNAH

Many of the same literary-rhetorical conventions and techniques described to this point come into play to "frame" a number of topically related Mishnah passages so that they constitute a mini-essay on more or less closely related matters. A bit of history of scholarship will help here. In the late 1970s, Jacob Neusner used the term Mishnah "chapters"—in quotation marks—to designate these topical mini-essays, because they approximately, but often not exactly, corresponded to how the extant medieval manuscripts formalized the chapter divisions within Mishnah tractates.[17] And it was Neusner who pointed out that these chapters' *topical* unity and coherence were often *additionally* paralleled by literary-rhetorical techniques. These techniques do not differ from those already examined in this volume. Rather the same ones in evidence in Mishnah passages, particularly longer, extended

---

17. Neusner, *History of Mishnaic Law*.

passages, are often at work over the course of an entire "chapter," or the "shank" of a Mishnah "chapter," which may be its opening passage, a middle passage, and its concluding one—a sort of literary-rhetorical skeleton, if you will. You will now easily recognize them.

Following is an entire Mishnah "chapter," m. Gittin 1:1 to 2:2, some parts of which you have already seen. Read through it quickly just to get a sense of its literary flow—its repetitions, rhythm, rhyme, assonance and alliteration. Do not fret about its legal substance. But do try to spot the use of the literary-rhetorical conventions presented in the preceding sections.

1:1

    a. One who brings a writ from a Mediterranean province—

    b. it is required that he should say: In my presence it was written and in my presence it was signed [by the witnesses].

    c. R. Gamaliel says: Also one who brings [a writ] from Reqem and from Heger [must be able to so declare].

    d. R. Eliezer says: Even [one who brings a writ] from Kefar Luddim to Lud [must be able to so declare].

    e. And sages say: It is not required that he should say: In my presence it was written, and in my presence it was signed [by the witnesses]—except one who brings [a writ] from a Mediterranean province and one who takes [a writ to a Mediterranean province].

    f. And one who brings [a writ] from province to province in the Mediterranean provinces—

    g. it is required that he should say: In my presence it was written and in my presence it was signed [by the witnesses].

    h. R. Simeon b. Gamaliel says: Even from district to district [within a single Mediterranean province must make such a declaration].

1:2

    a. Rabbi Judah says: [One must make the declaration if taking a writ]:

    b. from Reqem to the East, and Reqem is like the East;

    c. from Ashqalon to the South, and Ashqalon is like the South;

    d. from Akko to the North, and Akko is like the North.

In the Seat of Moses

e. R. Meir says: Akko is like the Land of Israel with respect to writs.

1:3

a. One who brings a writ within the Land of Israel—

b. it is not required that he should say: In my presence it was written and in my presence it was signed [by the witnesses].

c. If there are challengers to it[s validity], it[s validity] shall stand upon [the authentication of] it[s witnesses'] signatures.

d. One who brings a writ from a Mediterranean province,

e. and cannot say: In my presence it was written, and in my presence it was signed [by witnesses]—

f. if there are upon it [the signatures of] witnesses, it[s validity] shall stand upon [the authentication of] it[s witnesses'] signatures.

1:4

a. One [and] the same are writs [of divorce] of women and manumission papers of slaves;

b. they equated [them] with regard to one who takes [them to a Mediterranean province] and with regard to one who brings [them from a Mediterranean province].

c. And this is one of the ways [only] that they equated writs [of divorce] of women with manumission papers of slaves.

1:5

a. Any writ that has upon it [the signature of] a Samaritan witness

b. is unfit,

c. except for writs [of divorce] of women and manumission papers of slaves.

d. It once happened that they brought before R. Gamaliel in Kefar Otnai a writ [of divorce] of a woman,

e. and its witnesses were Samaritan witnesses,

f. and he declared [it] fit.

g. Any bonds issuing from [court] bureaus of the Gentiles—

h. even though their signatories are Gentiles—

i. are fit,

Mishnah

j. except for writs [of divorce] of women and manumission papers of slaves.

k. R. Simeon says: Also these are fit.

l. They specified [that the latter were unfit] only when they were done in a nonprofessional tribunal.

1:6

a. One who says: Give this writ [of divorce] to my wife and this manumission bond to my slave—

b. if he desired to retract with respect to both of them, he may retract, the words of R. Meir.

c. But sages say: With respect to writs [of divorce] of women, [he may retract]; however not with respect to manumission papers of slaves,

d. because they benefit one when not in his [or her] presence, but they obligate him [or her] only in his [or her] presence;

e. since if he should desire not to feed his slave, he is allowed, but not to feed his wife, he is not allowed.

f. He said to them: But lo he renders unfit his slave for the [eating of] heave offering [if the owner is a priest], just as he renders unfit his wife.

g. They said to him: Because he is his property [and she is not].

h. One who says: Give this writ [of divorce] to my wife and this manumission bond to my slave,

i. and he died—

j. they may not give [either] after [the person's] death.

k. [One who says:] Give [an amount equal to the measure of] a *maneh* to such-and-such person,

l. and he died—

m. they may give [the *maneh*] after [the person's] death.

2:1

a. One who brings a writ from a Mediterranean province,

b. and one said: In my presence it was written, however not in my presence was it signed [by the witnesses];

c. in my presence it was signed [by the witnesses], however not in my presence was it written;

In the Seat of Moses

    d. in my presence it was written in its entirety, and in my presence it was signed in part;

    e. in my presence it was written in part, and in my presence it was signed in its entirety—

    f. [the writ] is unfit.

    g. One says: In my presence it was written, and one [i.e., another] says: In my presence it was signed—

    h. [the writ] is unfit.

    i. Two [bring a writ and] say: In our presence it was written, and one says: In my presence it was signed—

    j. [the writ] is unfit.

    k. And R. Judah declares fit.

    l. One says: In my presence it was written, and two [i.e., both] say: In our presence it was signed—

    m. [the writ] is fit.

2:2

    a. It [the writ] was written in the daytime and was signed in the daytime,

    b. [or was written] in the nighttime and was signed in the nighttime,

    c. [or was written] in the nighttime and was signed in the daytime—

    d. [the writ] is fit.

    e. [The writ was written] in the daytime and was signed in the nighttime—

    f. [the writ] is unfit.

    g. R. Simeon declares [such a writ] fit,

    h. for R. Simeon used to say: All writs that were written in the daytime and were signed in the night time

    i. are unfit,

    j. except for writs [of divorce] of women.

                      (m. Git. 1:1–2:2, translation my own[18])

It is not difficult to identify the repeated phrases, repeated verb tenses (i.e., verb morphology), balance, and balanced opposites that recur

---

18. Lightstone, *Mishnah*, 35–37.

throughout the Mishnah "chapter." Beyond the topical unity of this Mishnaic mini-essay, these other literary techniques help frame and unify this rather elegant composition. Based on the appearance of these repeated, contrasted, and balanced phrases, one can easily spot the "shank" of this mini-essay. They are passages 1:1, 1:3, 2:1 and 2:2. Passages 1:2 and 1:4–6 are slotted in between, with 1:4–6 looking like a mini-essay within the larger whole comparing writs of divorce and manumission papers of slaves—hardly a comparison that would ethically sit well with us today. Some of these dominant, recurring, and contrasting phrases that help set off the shank are

- –one who brings a writ; one who takes; two who bring a writ
- –from Mediterranean province(s); from province to province in the Mediterranean provinces;
- –it is required that he say; cannot say;
- –one says; [the other] one says; two say;
- –in my presence it was written; in my presence it was signed; in my presence it was not written; in my presence it was not signed;
- –signed in the daytime; signed in the night time; daytime; night time;
- –fit; unfit.

Based on the occurrence and recurrence of this repeated, balanced phraseology, can anyone deny that the editors/authors who, whether in writing or orally, composed this Mishnaic mini-essay, this "chapter," did not at least reshape and rephrase the language of whatever sources they had in hand to give the whole a greater sense of unity and flow?! But that is a literary-historical matter that is beyond the focus of this volume.

It remains only to challenge you to recognize among the constituent passages of this Mishnah "chapter" some of those conventional literary-rhetorical structures that were discussed earlier. We certainly see unattributed (anonymous) rulings. The passage at 1:1 has a multibarreled dispute; the view presented anonymously at the beginning is attributed to "the sages" at the end—this in order to round out the dispute form in this multi-barreled affair. The text at 1:2 presents a dispute between Judah and Meir; in it, Meir disputes only one of the items in the ruling attributed to Judah. Passage 1:3 provides two well-matched anonymous declarative rule-sentences. Passage 1:5 contains a precedent story supporting the preceding anonymous declarative rule-sentence. It also contains a dispute in which a "saying" attributed to Simeon disputes the antecedent anonymous ruling. Judah "disputes" one of the anonymous declarative rule-sentences in 2:1. Similarly, a ruling attributed to Simeon disputes one of the anonymous rulings of 2:2; Simeon's opinion is then followed by a commentary-gloss, not an often-observed phenomenon in Mishnah, even if not unheard of.

In all, most of the conventional Mishnaic literary-rhetorical structures covered in this chapter are used, and easily identified, in this mini-essay in Mishnah. We do not see a debate, which, in any case, is used much less frequently than disputes in Mishnah. And this Mishnah "chapter" does not use any scriptural proof-texting, even though a biblical law underlies it, as discussed in chapter 3.

We have come to the conclusion of this chapter and its introduction to the core, basic rhetorical and literary conventions of Mishnah. Are there no other such conventions in Mishnah than those we have covered and that the chapter should cover? The answer to this question is threefold. One, those that have been described are dominant in Mishnah; they are the conventions that are "conventional." Here and there in Mishnah others are evident. For example, in Mishnah Tractate Yoma, which deals with the Temple's rituals on the Day of Atonement, Mishnah's authorship slips in and out of a literary style that is meant to "feel" like a historical reminiscence: He [the High Priest] would do this; he would [then] do that. Two, what has been described in this chapter are not only the more dominant rhetorical and literary conventions in Mishnah, they are the ones familiarity with which most facilitates the reading of Mishnah. And, three, it is these conventions, more than others, that form the firmest stepping-stone to accessing the other documents of early rabbinic legal literature, as you will see in the next and subsequent chapters, commencing with the treatment of Tosefta in chapter 5.

Tosefta uses every one of the literary-rhetorical structures that we have discussed in this chapter about Mishnah, although the frequency with which Tosefta uses some of these structures is one of the features that differentiates Mishnah and Tosefta. And Tosefta uses a few literary-rhetorical structures that are not used at all, or are very uncommonly used, in Mishnah. The upshot, however, is that you have now covered 90 percent of the conventional literary-rhetorical structures that are evident, not only in Mishnah, but also in all other "tannaitic" passages, whether they appear in Tosefta or in the *beraitot* cited in the Jerusalem and Babylonian Talmuds.

Mishnah, as I stated at the outsets of chapters 3 and 4, is the foundation for everything else in early rabbinic legal literature, and so are its conventional literary-rhetorical forms. You are well underway to their mastery, as we now turn in chapter 5 to Tosefta.

SUGGESTIONS FOR FURTHER READING

Kraemer, "The Mishnah," 299–315.

Neusner, *Mishnah: Introduction and Reader*.

5

Tosefta

FAMILIARITY WITH MISHNAH IS THE FIRMEST FOUNDATION FOR READING TOSEFTA, SAVE FOR THE "DIFFERENCES THAT MAKE A DIFFERENCE"

As intimated in chapters 2 and 3, Tosefta (T/t.) is an early rabbinic Halakhic (i.e., legal) document produced c. 250–425 CE. Its materials are organized in tractates that parallel Mishnah's. Fifty-nine of Mishnah's sixty-three tractates—sixty-two tractates if one is of the view that "Mishnah" Tractate Avot was not originally part of Mishnah—have corresponding Tosefta tractates,[1] with the passages within each (roughly speaking) following the order of, and topically relating to, those of their parallel Mishnah "chapters."

Moreover, as will soon be evident, Tosefta's passages (together with Tosefta-*like* passages found in the Talmuds) are the most Mishnah-*like* passages of the early rabbinic legal literature discussed in this volume. So much

---

1. Mishnah Tractates Tamid, Middot and Kinnin (in addition to Avot) have no corresponding Tosefta tractates. That Avot has no associated Tosefta tractate may be further indication that Avot was originally not considered part of Mishnah, if further indication is needed. I know of no compelling explanation as to why there are no Tractates Tamid, Middot or Kinnim in Tosefta. Their absence in Tosefta is briefly discussed in Brody, *Mishnah*, 132.

the better for you! How so? Because familiarity with the dominant literary-rhetorical conventions of Mishnah is the best foundation for mastery of those in Tosefta—so much so that one might be tempted to say "nothing new to see here; move on please." That was the reassurance given at the conclusion of chapter 4. But on what grounds? Because the formalized literary and rhetorical traits characteristic of Mishnah, all now familiar to you—

(a) the laconic Mishnaic declarative sentence,

(b) the repetition, permutation, and concatenation of similar (usually short) phrases in ways that exhibit balance, cadence, assonance, and alliteration to generate hypothetical cases (protases),

(c) the provision of equally laconic, economically worded and balanced rulings (apodases) for these cases,

(d) the attribution of some these legal rulings (as "sayings") to named rabbinic masters, most frequently in

(e) "disputes," and sometimes as

(f) "independent sayings" that are not part of a dispute structure, the periodic use of the

(g) "debate" structure and the

(h) "precedent story," and, now and again, the

(i) citation of a supporting proof text from the Hebrew Scriptures—

are all found in Tosefta. And while this is certainly so, it is my impression that these traits' and constructs' frequency of use in Tosefta is different than Mishnah.[2] Moreover, and even more significant, when one compares passages in Tosefta with their (largely) parallel sections in Mishnah—and between 66 percent to 80 percent of Tosefta has directly parallel texts in Mishnah[3]—it is undoubtedly the case that for each set of parallel passages taken on its own, these formalized literary-rhetorical traits are used in the Tosefta passage sometimes to a greater and sometimes to a lesser extent than in the corresponding Mishnah text. Where the Mishnah passage has an anonymous ruling, Tosefta may have the same ruling attributed to a named rabbinic master. Where Mishnah presents a ruling as a "saying" of

---

2. While this is my experience, it is a claim that is certainly amenable to empirical testing, which I have not done.

3. Figures established by Neusner in the late 1970s, first in *History of the Mishnaic Law* and confirmed by his many subsequent studies.

a named rabbinic authority, Tosefta may present the same ruling in the name of a different authority. Where the Mishnah passage has no dispute, Tosefta may have one. Where Mishnah presents us with a dispute, Tosefta may present the same dispute followed by a debate. And while Tosefta does this over and over again, it nonetheless uses the same repertoire of literary-rhetorical conventions and constructs as Mishnah, barring just a few exceptions that prove the rule. And still, as we shall discuss later, these subtle differences sustained over many passages of Tosefta constitute "a difference that makes a difference."

For the moment, however, know that over the course of this chapter, I will identify few (in fact, only two) additional, formalized literary-rhetorical structures found in Tosefta that are not characteristic Mishnah. The upshot—having worked through the previous chapter on Mishnah, you possess 90 percent or more of the skills required to master Tosefta's formalized literary-rhetorical conventions—grounds for calm and confidence on your part, as previously remarked. And yet . . . a reader of Tosefta who has a good sense of Mishnah's *modus operandi* would quickly conclude that Tosefta is not Mishnah in the literary-rhetorical equivalent of a blind taste-test. In terms of gaining a sense of the literary-rhetorical constructs and conventions of Tosefta, a chief lesson of this chapter will be how striking similarity begets marked difference.

I have just reassured you that the literary-rhetorical conventions and structures encountered in Mishnah account for almost all of what is found in Tosefta. On this front, you have little totally new to learn in this chapter. So why is this chapter about the same length as the previous one in this volume? The answer is simple; this chapter really focuses on what Tosefta does with these largely Mishnaic-like traits, and, as I shall explain, what it does can only be discerned in comparison with the Mishnah, with which it shares so much. Working through those comparisons with you takes up a great deal of the chapter ahead, and it is somewhat "page intensive." But you have already acquired in chapter 4 the base knowledge to work through the issues and learn the lessons that are to follow.

LESSONS FROM AN EXERCISE IN IMAGINATIVE FORGERY

Let me begin to illustrate my claim about "similarity begetting different" by presenting a "fake" Mishnah passage followed by an "ersatz" Tosefta passage, all based on chapter 4's made-up statute of an imagined highway code. The statute, you will remember, read as follows:

> All vehicles, motorized or not, and pedestrians come to a full stop at intersections with stop signs facing them; the order of priority in which vehicles and/or pedestrians proceed is: vehicles that do not have a stop sign facing them as they approach the intersection, followed by pedestrians, followed by the vehicles in the order that they first came to a full stop, or if two stopped simultaneously, the vehicle that is to the right hand of the driver of the other.

And I further imagined an underlying Supreme Court ruling, based on the constitutional rights of the individual, that, in effect, mandated all states or provinces to pass comprehensive highway-codes:

> It is unconstitutional to not have a highway code, lest the constitutional right to have one's life reasonably protected by government be abrogated by any level of government, federal, state/provincial, or municipal.

On this basis, I provided, in what might be considered in normal, discursive English, a fully articulated, again-made-up rule-sentence about four-way stops.

> If two motor vehicles, or two cyclists, or a motor vehicle and a cyclist approach an intersection with a four-way stop from directions that are at right angles to one another, and no pedestrians are attempting to cross such that the pedestrians would cross in front of the approaching vehicles or cyclists, then the vehicle or cyclist that reaches the intersection first and first comes to a full stop, proceeds first through the intersection, and the other vehicle or cyclist, after also coming to a full stop, proceeds through the intersection only after the first vehicle or cyclist has cleared the intersection.

Having read chapter 4, you now know that a typical Mishnah passage dealing with such matters would not look like this at all. How might such a passage look; what might a typically formulated passage from "Mishnah Tractate Highway Code" look like? Perhaps something like this:

1. Two approach a four-way stop—

2. one from the south, and

3. one from the east—

4. east has priority.

5. From the north, and

6. from the east—

7. north as priority.

8. From the west, and

9. from the east—

10. both proceed.

11. If one signals a left turn,

12. the other has priority.

13. Justice Jones says: The other does not have priority.

14. Three approach a four way stop—

15. from the south, and

16. from the east, and

17. from the north—

18. north and south have priority.

19. Justice Jones says: North has priority

20. From the south, and

21. from the east, and

22. from the west—

23. east and west have priority.

24. Justice Jones says: East has priority.

Let us enumerate the ways in which the foregoing is typically Mishnaic. First, it is highly laconic; think of all the language that would have to be interpolated in square brackets to make it fully intelligible. Minimally, we would need to specify that we are dealing with automobiles (and or cyclists) throughout, and not pedestrians; and we would have to specify that the operators of the vehicles do not know who arrived first at the intersection, or who first came to a full stop. Second, a number of sentences are apocopated; that is, the subject of the sentence switches over its course. Third, one cannot make sense of any of this without antecedent knowledge of the relevant section of the highway code, *or* one would have to induce the relevant general rule that applies to all of these cases from the rulings given in each case, taken together. The principal general rule that would have to be induced from the subsections of this fake Mishnah passage for it to make sense is this: at a four-way stop, if two vehicles approaching at right angles stop simultaneously, the driver who has a vehicle to his or her right must yield right of way to that vehicle. In our made-up statute provided above, that rule is captured in the following language: "the vehicle that is to the right hand of the driver of the other [has right of way, when both vehicles stop simultaneously]." The rulings for the successive, highly laconically phrased cases can only be made sense of if the reader-student can dope out this rule, or if he or she has already learned it. Fourth, there is repetition, balance, and systematic variation and permutation of phrases throughout to generate a series of cases (protases). Fifth, similarly worded, laconically phrased rulings (apodases) appear for each case. Sixth, "sayings" attributed to a "Justice Jones" appear at sections 13, 19 and 24, making these subsections into disputes—Jones vs. the anonymous authority—and the language attributed to Justice Jones in each case matches the phraseology of the anonymous rulings that precede Jones's.

In order to make sense of the whole and its individual subsections, the reader-student of this "spun-out" ("fake") Mishnah passage must engage in an analysis of each case to dope out its inner logic in light of an underlying (but unstated) rule that can be induced only from the series of laconically formulated cases and rulings. That is, reading (and understanding) this passage necessitates a certain type of analytic engagement (a) to discern why in each case the ruling is what it is, and (b) to identify the unstated general rules that underlie all of the rulings. Finally, one would have to address the question, On what basis might Jones rule differently? If the reader is a novice to Mishnah study, the reader will rely on someone who has mastered Mishnah for guidance in such an analytic, interpretive exercise.

Now, what might an equally fake, parallel Tosefta passage look like? Perhaps like this (with language that is identical to our fake Mishnah passage in boldface).

1. **One from the south, and**
2. **one from the east,** and
3. they do not know who arrived first—
4. **east has priority**,

In the Seat of Moses

5. when there are no pedestrians.
6. **From the west, and**
7. **from the east—**
8. **both proceed.**
9. **If one signals a left turn,**
10. Justice Smith says: **The other has priority.**
11. Justice Jones says: **The other does not have priority.**
12. Said to him Justice Jones: No statute gives one priority?
13. Said to him Justice Smith: Avoiding harm is a priority;
14. For if both shall proceed, they may crash,
15. as it is said, "To have one's life."

What do we see in this ersatz Tosefta, viewed in light of its parallel fake Mishnah? First, much of the language is identical to that of our fake Mishnah (as indicated by the boldface type in the ersatz Tosefta). Second, our ersatz Tosefta's opening section lacks an intelligible context. That is, without the fake Mishnah in hand (which begins with "two approach a four-way stop"), it is more difficult to surmise what the ersatz Tosefta is talking about. Third, there is no ersatz Tosefta at all for sections 5–7 and 14–24 of the fake Mishnah. Fourth, at 3 and 5 of the ersatz Tosefta, one finds language that the fake Mishnah lacks, and that *extra* language makes the parallel section of the fake Mishnah more intelligible by supplying essential missing information, *when* one reads the Mishnah passage *in light of* the Tosefta passage. Fifth, the anonymous ruling at line 12 of the fake Mishnah is attributed to Justice Smith at line 10 of the ersatz Tosefta. Sixth, further to the first dispute in the fake Mishnah, in which an opposing ruling is attributed to "Justice Jones," the ersatz Tosefta provides a debate (12–14); the debate provides reasons or counterreasons for the rulings attributed in turn to Justices Jones and Smith, *as if* Smith and Jones were in direct discourse with one another. Seventh, and finally, the reasoning attributed to Smith in the ersatz Tosefta's debate is bolstered by an appeal to a Scripture-like verse—here a snippet of a phrase ("to have one's life") cited from my made-up Supreme Court decision. Where life and limb may be at risk, the inner logic of the application of rules takes second seat to avoiding potential tragedy, which is the real underlying reason for the whole highway code in the first place, is it not? Note that citing only a few words from the Supreme Court's statement suffices "to recall" and invoke the entirety of the Court's language.

In sum, ersatz Tosefta, first, has made fake Mishnah more intelligible by adding language (at 3 and 5 of ersatz Tosefta) that must otherwise be logically interpolated into our fake Mishnah. While this serves to make fake Mishnah easier to understand, clarifying matters, it adds nothing truly *new* to what is already conveyed in fake Mishnah. As far as ersatz Tosefta sections 9 through 15 are concerned, ersatz Tosefta is supplying *additional and new information* directly relevant to the parallel section of fake Mishnah, information that fake Mishnah does not provide and that cannot otherwise be surmised from a close study of fake Mishnah. What is that additional new information? According to ersatz Tosefta, Justice Smith is the authority behind one of the anonymous rulings in fake Mishnah, a ruling disputed by Jones. And ersatz Tosefta further provides some reasoning for the opposing positions of Smith and Jones. Bingo! Ersatz Tosefta is typical of that earlier-mentioned 66 percent to 80 percent of the "real" Tosefta that (1) sometimes seems to cite and gloss "real" Mishnah and thereby to clarify the latter, *or* that (2) serves to provide additional new materials that directly complement or complete what is found in the parallel passages in "real" Mishnah.

Yet, for all of the important *differences* between the two made-up passages, there is not a single literary-rhetorical device or construct used in our ersatz Tosefta passage that is not *typical* of the Mishnah's literary-rhetorical conventions and constructs already encountered in chapter 4 of this book. How Mishnah-like is our ersatz Tosefta in its use of typically Mishnaic literary-rhetorical conventions! And yet, how different is the resulting ersatz Tosefta passage than the fake-Mishnah passage to which the ersatz Tosefta passage is obviously related! It is precisely in this confluence and divergence that the challenges, and principal lessons, of this chapter lie for you. As should be clear from our made-up passages, the focus of this chapter lies in how Toseftan materials use these overwhelmingly Mishnah-like literary-rhetorical formulations in ways that will seem at once both familiar and novel—for similar and yet different ends than Mishnah. And one can readily understand from the lessons of my two forgeries why it is that literary-historical scholars have been drawn to debates about the literary-historical relationship between Mishnah and Tosefta—an issue that is not a focus of this chapter or book, as compelling as it may be.[4]

4. The provision of extensive footnotes in which the scholarly debates about issues

are discussed is not consistent with the aims of this book. But here is one place where an exception will prove the rule, because the literary-historical relationship of Tosefta to Mishnah is important in deciding what Tosefta actually is. While this issue arises several times in the course of this volume, it is only here that I will engage the matter in any detail with reference to the scholarly literature on the topic. Therefore, for those wishing to follow up on these modern-scholarly, literary-historical debates concerning the relationship of Mishnah to Tosefta, permit me to lay out some of the principal lines of controversy, using my made-up Mishnah and Tosefta passages. Any scholar looking at two passages like these two made-up texts will conclude that there is a literary-historical relationship between them. Moreover, if one is talking about a document, Tosefta, 66–80 percent of which comprises passages which parallel, as my ersatz one does, a Mishnah passage, then one is drawn into a debate about not only the literary-historical relationship between parallel passages, but also about the literary-historical relationship between the documents and their authorships. At the level of individual parallel passages, someone is copying from someone, directly or indirectly. At the level of the two documents as a whole, Mishnah and Tosefta, did one document's authors have the other (or some protoversion of the other) as a model. At either level, of individual parallel passages and of whole documents, there are broadly speaking five types of literary-historical options. (1) Mishnah is some sort of epitome and development of Tosefta. (2) Tosefta is composed to elucidate and expand upon Mishnah. (3) Both Mishnah and Tosefta are developments of some antecedent work, either a proto-Mishnah or proto-Tosefta. (4) Both Mishnah and Tosefta draw upon a common body of traditions that were circulating among groups to which their respective authorships belonged, and upon which their authorships each drew independently. (5) Some combination of the foregoing produced Mishnah and Tosefta. Sorting these matters out and choosing the most probable answer or combination of answers would require *systematically comparing a huge proportion of Tosefta passages to their parallel Mishnah passages*, and then looking as well at those passages in Tosefta (roughly 1/3 to 1/5 of Tosefta) that have no real parallel passages in Mishnah at all. The reason for my italics in the preceding sentence is simple. One can readily take a select sample of Tosefta passages, compare them to their closest kin in Mishnah and argue for any one of these solutions. But only one scholar, in my view, has come close to satisfying what I have placed in italics, Jacob Neusner together with some of his doctoral students at the end of the 1970s and early 1980s. He/they have looked at every Mishnah and Tosefta passage. If I were to characterize their findings in terms of the five options given above, and dovetail them with my own, albeit much less comprehensive, experience in comparing Mishnah and Tosefta passages in many different tractates, I would formulate matters as follows. Options 2 and 4 in combination are the dominant forces that have produced Tosefta and its constituent passages, although here and there in some individual instances options 1, 3, and (obviously) 5 explain the evidence before us. That is to say, in my view Tosefta is overwhelmingly the product of an author or authors who set out to create materials and ultimately a document that serves Mishnah-study. In that process, among other things Tosefta's authors drew upon a body of traditions, many or most of which were likely also available to a large extent to Mishnah's authorship, choosing to further Mishnah-study by providing materials that Mishnah authors did not prioritize for their own reasons (or in some instances did not have). I find it difficult to square the weight of the facts on the ground with any other equally or more parsimonious explanation.

For the sake of pedagogy, permit me to relate what you see in my fake Mishnah and ersatz Tosefta to my just-articulated position. Sections 1–4 of fake Mishnah are clarified by sections 1–5 of ersatz Tosefta. I view option 2 as the most likely historical process that produced the text of ersatz Tosefta. Erstaz Tosefta drops fake Mishnah's "two approach a four-way stop," because the intended reader of ersatz Tosefta does not need it, as Mishnah is open before the reader. Then ersatz Tosefta interpolates into fake Mishnah clarifying language. (If the process at this instance were the reverse, that is, fake Mishnah is an epitome of ersatz Tosefta, I see little motivation for fake Mishnah to have dropped language that makes matters clearer when keeping that language would not denature fake-Mishnah's rhetorical-literary conventions in any way. What now of 9–15 of ersatz Tosefta? Its authorship (me) has recourse to some antecedent traditions about Smith vs. Jones that fake Mishnah either does not know, or did not care to use because Smith's position being the dominant view, in fake Mishnah opinion, would be better presented as an anonymous ruling. This is a commonly found technique of Mishnah's authors. Ersatz Tosefta's author (me) does not favor such "information loss" from the bank of circulating traditions and so has added it to fake Tosefta's elaboration of fake Mishnah's version, as often seems to happen in "real" Tosefta. Hence behind sections 9–15 of ersatz Tosefta are literary-historical processes 2 and 4 (and, therefore, 5 as well). Imagine the work required to do just such a literary analysis for the lion's part or all of Mishnah and Tosefta. It would be, and for some, has been, the work of many years.

Jacob Neusner's conclusions about Tosefta, what it does and, therefore, how its passages came to be are best summarized in Neusner, *Tosefta*. See also Neusner, *Bavli that Might*. Neusner's articulation of the relationship of Toseftan to Mishnaic materials is first substantively and coherently articulated in his *History of the Mishnaic, Part 21*.

Hauptman, Friedman, and Kulp have all argued for the historical-literary primacy of many Tosefta passages over their Mishnaic counterparts. See Kulp, "Organizational," 52–78; Hauptman, "Does," 224–40; "Tosefta as a Commentary," 109–132; Friedman, *Tosefta Atiqta*; "Primacy," 99–121; Houtman, *Mishnah*. See also Hauptman, *Rereading*. A similar position on Tosefta may be found in Alexander, *Transmitting Mishnah*.

Two scholars have articulated more nuanced views than Kulp, etc. The two, in effect, give Neusner, with whom in general I concur, his due, while contextualizing and qualifying the positions of Kulp and others. I find the nuanced articulation of Harry Fox on where he stands in this debate helpful. See Fox, "Introducing Tosefta," 1–30. And one may return as well to the more recently published work of Brody, *Mishnah*.

Another type of evidence relevant to the dating of Tosefta and its materials is linguistic; Yaakov Elman, for example, has argued that Toseftan materials are exemplars of "Middle Hebrew I" (like Mishnah), still in use in the Land of Israel through the third century (as a written and spoken language, like Aramaic and Greek) and into (perhaps) the early fourth century (as a written and spoken language, like Aramaic and Greek), when the transition to Middle Hebrew II (a literary, but generally not spoken, version of Hebrew) took place. At the risk of being redundant, Middle Hebrew II is not represented in Toseftan materials. This linguistic evidence (among other evidence that may be adduced) tends to weigh against the views of some few scholars who have argued that Tosefta is a later (e.g, fifth century) compilation of "tannaitic" traditions, since one would be hard-pressed to account for the almost total absence of Middle Hebrew II from its materials. See Elman, *Authority*; "Babylonian Baraitot," 1–29.

In the Seat of Moses

THE CHALLENGE OF DEEP DIFFERENCE EXPRESSED THROUGH SIGNIFICANT SIMILARITY IN TOSEFTA AND MISHNAH

I now turn from the ersatz to the "real," both to consolidate and to extend the lessons just learned. On the one hand, Tosefta is, as already stated, the most Mishnah-like of all the early rabbinic legal documents discussed in this book,[5] not only in its Mishnah-like repertoire of formalized literary-rhetorical conventions, but also in many other substantive respects. So much so that more than four decades ago, when I was pursuing my doctoral studies, my doctoral supervisor, my fellow students, and I routinely referred to "Mishnah-Tosefta," as if the two documents were a single body of second-century and early third-century rabbinic evidence for historical research.

The most simple and straightforward type of Toseftan passage, such as the one already cited in chapter 3 that appears to cite and gloss a passage of Mishnah, illustrates this similarity to a tee. It and its parallel passage in Mishnah are worth repeating here to make the point—first, the Mishnah passage at m. Bekhorot 1:1a, and then its cognate Tosefta passage at t. Bekhorot 1:1a.

I begin with m. Bekhorot 1:1a:

> He who purchases the foetus of an ass of a Gentile, and he who sells to him, even though it is not permitted, and he who forms a partnership with him, and he who receives from him, and he who gives to him in trust is exempt from the law of the firstling, as it is said, "Of an Israelite" (Numbers 3:13), but not of others.

Now, t. Bekhorot 1:1a (with language that equates to Mishnah's in boldface):

> **He who purchases the foetus of an ass of** an idol worshipper, **and he who sells to him, even though it is not permitted, and he who forms a partnership with him**—he who gives to him in partnership—**and he who receives from him, and he who gives to him in trust is exempt from the law of the firstling, as it is said, "Of an Israelite" (Numbers 3:13), but not of others.**

---

5. With the possible exception of the so-called "minor tractates" (*masekhtot qetanot*), which, incidentally have received far less modern scholarly attention than the documents discussed in this book, even though they, or their source materials, date from late antiquity (perhaps from the fifth century CE) and probably from rabbinic circles in the Land of Israel.

The correspondence between the two passages—exhibiting the same literary-rhetorical conventions, as well as almost the same wording—is anything but fortuitous. By some literary-historical process that may be simple or complex (and about which I will not venture an opinion just yet), the one passage has been *made* to almost replicate the other, save for Tosefta's additional language, "he who gives to him in partnership." It is highly unlikely that this is the result of accident.

The foregoing is an example of "extreme likeness and correspondence" between a Toseftan and Mishnaic passage. (It resembles the likeness of sections 1 to 4 of our fake Mishnah to sections 1 to 5 of our ersatz Tosefta.) But overall one may assert a sameness on many fronts, even with regard to passages that do not correspond so exactly as do m. Bekhorot 1:1a and t. Bekhorot 1:1a. Let me list those similarities.

I began this chapter by (1) enumerating the Mishnaic literary-rhetorical conventions and constructs that are also found throughout Tosefta; I will not repeat that list here. At an even more generic level, (2) the same language, "Mishnaic" Hebrew (sometimes designated Middle Hebrew I), is used consistently throughout both documents. Generally, (3) the names of rabbinic masters to whom Mishnah often attributes rulings appear as well in Tosefta's attributed sayings, disputes, debates, and precedent stories. I say "generally" for two reasons. First, because Tosefta sometimes attributes a given ruling to a different master than Mishnah does. Or Tosefta may have an attribution to a named master, where in the cognate Mishnah passage there is an anonymous ruling (just as I did in my ersatz Tosefta at section 10). Second, while the repertoire of named masters in Mishnah also appears in Tosefta, Tosefta's repertoire is somewhat broader than Mishnah's list. That is, Tosefta attributes traditions to some named masters who do *not* appear at all among Mishnah's attributed traditions. Historians of early rabbinic Judaism have always concluded that these exclusively "Toseftan" rabbis are either contemporaries of their "Mishnaic colleagues," or the immediate disciples or younger contemporaries of the last generation of rabbinic masters who figure in Mishnah. They are all assumed to be *tannaim*, rabbinic authorities who lived prior to or near c. 220–230 CE, around the time that Rabbi Judah the Prince, the traditionally identified author of Mishnah, died. (Indeed, in Tosefta some rulings are attributed to "Rebbe" himself, the early rabbinic moniker for Rabbi Judah the Prince.) Why should historians be drawn to such a conclusion at all? For a number of reasons, significant among them the similarity of language and style that entails across Mishnah and Tosefta. Furthermore, Toseftan and Toseftan-like materials are cited in both the Jerusalem and Babylonian Talmuds as *beraitot* ("outside [sources]"), that is, as traditions outside Mishnah the origins of which, in the Talmuds' view, are contemporary with Mishnah's content, and the authority of which is exceeded only by Scripture itself and by Mishnah's passages.[6]

In addition to similarities of language and dialect, of formal literary-rhetorical constructs, and of the cadre of named authorities to which rulings are attributed, other parallels obtain between Mishnah and Tosefta. (4) The thematic and topical agenda of the materials appearing in Tosefta largely accords with Mishnah's. As noted in chapter 3, (5) materials found in our Tosefta are similarly ordered in Mishnah; so much so that the extant Tosefta manuscripts[7] all group, arrange and subdivide its contents in accordance with the same "Orders," tractates, and (for the most part) "chapters" as Mishnah's thematic and topical divisions.

Many of these similarities of Mishnah to Tosefta may be illustrated by appealing, as we did in chapter 3, to the contents of Tosefta Tractate Gittin, chapter 1:1–7. I choose it because, in comparison to t. Bekhorot 1:1a's *near replication* of m. Bekhorot 1:1a, t. Gittin 1:1–7 does not so closely correspond to its Mishnah parallel, m. Gittin 1:1–3. Rather, t. Gittin 1:1–7 relates topically and thematically to the contents of Mishnah Tractate Gittin, chapter 1:1–3, and shares a significant amount of language with it.[8] (In these

---

6. Several passages in the Jerusalem Talmud concern the relative weight in rabbinic study and deliberation of Scripture, Mishnah, and what is called *talmud* and *ha-tosafot* (pl., "the supplemental [materials]") or *ha-tosefet* (sg. "the supplement"); see y. Peah 2:4 and its parallel in y. Haggigah 1:8, and y. Horayot 3:5. The passage in y. Horayot is prefaced by the often-cited statement, "Always pursue [the study of] the Mishnah more than the Talmud."

7. Which, alas, are all medieval, that is, much later than any scholarly dating of the composition of Tosefta; the range of opinions for the latter runs from the last half of the third century to first quarter of the fifth. I favor a date toward the earlier part of the range, at least for the 66 to 80 percent of Tosefta that more directly relates to Mishnah as commentary or complement.

8. Although the subdivision of Tosefta's chapters into individual passages (e.g. 1:1, 1:2, 1:3, etc.) often differs from Mishnah's, as one might expect given how much longer Tosefta is than Mishnah. Moreover, the subdivision of Tosefta's chapters into individual passages also differs from manuscript to manuscript, and the latters' subdivisions often differ from the standard printed Hebrew edition of the Tosefta found in the Vilna edition of the Babylonian Talmud. Of course, all of these subdivisions into individual passages were done by scribal copyists years after Tosefta was first produced. The different subdivisions do not change the fact that, grosso modo, subject matter in Tosefta is ordered in

respects, their resemblance is more akin to that of our ersatz Tosefta's sections 6 to 15 to the corresponding content of our fake Mishnah.) Again, the likeness you are about to see of t. Gittin 1:1–7 to m. Gittin 1:1–3 cannot be fortuitous; it is by design, even though several different literary-historical hypotheses could be fashioned to account for this. Permit me to rehearse first, m. Gittin 1:1–3 and then t. Gittin 1:1–7 (translations my own[9]).

Mishnah Gittin 1:1–3

1:1

He who brings a writ from a Mediterranean province—it is required that he say: In my presence it was written, and in my presence it was signed. R. Gamaliel says: Even so he who brings from Reqem[10] and from Heger.[11] R. Eliezer says: Even so, from Kefar Ludim to Lod. And the sages say: It is not required that he say, In my presence it was written, and in my presence it was signed, except he who brings from a Mediterranean province and he who takes.

And he who brings from province to province in a Mediterranean province—it is required that he say: In my presence it was written, and in my presence it was signed. R. Simeon b. Gamaliel says: Even from hegemony to hegemony.

1:2

R. Judah says: From Reqem to the East, and Reqem is like the East; from Ashqalon to the South and Ashqalon is like the South; from Acco to the North, and Acco is like the North. R. Meir says: Acco is like the Land of Israel for writs.

---

accordance with subject matter in Mishnah.

9. Based on Lightstone, *Mishnah*, 35, 82–83.

10. The Roman-period Nabatean metropolis Raqim/Reqmu = Petra, today in Jordan south and slightly east of the Dead Sea.

11. Another major Roman-period, Nabatean city, Hegra, south and east of Petra in what is today northwestern Saudi Arabia.

1:3

He who brings a writ within the Land of Israel—it is not required that he say: In my presence it was written, and in my presence it was signed. If there are regarding it challengers, it shall be made to stand on its signatures.

He who brings a writ from a Mediterranean province, and he cannot say, In my presence it was written, and in my presence it was signed—if there are on it witnesses, it shall be made to stand on its signatures.

And now, Tosefta (with language that duplicates Mishnah's in boldface).

Tosefta Gittin 1:1–7

1:1

He who brings a writ from Syria **is like** him who brings a writ from outside the Land; **it is required that he say: In my presence it was written, and in my presence it was signed.**

From trans-Jordan—**is like him who brings from the Land of Israel, and it is not required that he say; In my presence it was written, and in my presence it was signed.**

1:2

He who brings a writ from a Mediterranean province, and cannot say: In my presence it was written, and in my presence it was signed—if it is possible to **make it stand on its signatures**, it is fit; and if not, it is unfit.

They used to say, They did not say that **he should say: In my presence it was written, and in my presence it was signed,** in order to be stringent, rather to be lenient upon him.

1:3

He who brings a writ from a Mediterranean province, and it was not **written in his presence**, and it was not **signed in his presence**—Lo, this person returns it to his locale, and he convenes a court, and it **makes it stand upon its signatures**, and **he brings** it and says: An agent of the court am I.

In **the Land of Israel,** an agent appoints an agent. R. Simeon b. Gamaliel says: An agent does not appoint an agent as regards writs.

1:4

In the beginning, they used to say: **From province to province.** They revisited to say: From neighborhood to neighborhood. **R. Simeon b. Gamaliel says: Also from hegemony to hegemony.**

1:5

There is a stringency as regards **the Mediterranean province** that is not so as regards **the Land of Israel**, and with regards **the Land of Israel** that is not so as regards **the Mediterranean province.**

Since **he who brings a writ from a Mediterranean province—it is required that he say: In my presence it was written, and in my presence it was signed; if there are regarding it challengers, it shall be made to stand on its signatures. He who brings a writ from the Land of Israel** cannot say: **In my presence it was written, and in my presence it was signed;** if there are on it [the signatures of] witnesses, **it shall be made to stand on its signatures.**

1:6

How [do they proceed when] they said, **it shall be made to stand on its signatures?** When they said: This is our handwriting—it is fit. But we do not recognize either the man or the woman—it is fit. This is not our handwriting, but others testify that it is their handwriting, or their handwriting was adduced from another place—it is fit.

1:7

R. Meir says, Acco and its hinterland **is like the Land of Israel as regards writs.** And the sages say, **Acco** and its hinterland are like outside the Land as regards writs.

It once happened concerning someone from Kefar Sissi, who brought before R. Ishmael a writ of divorce. He said to him: Even so, you are required **to say, In my presence it was written and in my presence it was signed**, and it does not require witnesses. After he left, said before him R. Illai: Rabbi, Kefar Sissi is the territory of **the Land of Israel**, closer to Sepphoris than to **Acco**. He said to him, Since the matter is settled with a leniency, it is settled.

One can readily see that the correspondence between m. Gittin 1:1–3 and t. Gittin 1:1–7 is nowhere near as stark and exact as that between m. Bekhorot 1:1a and t. Bekhorot 1:1a. In the case of Mishnah and t. Bekhorot 1:1a, we are certainly dealing with *the very same passage*, in one of which an explanatory gloss appears that the other passage lacks. This is clearly not the case for these passages of Mishnah and Tosefta Gittin, chapter 1. Something different is going on than citation with light glossing; as mentioned, what one sees in these two passages is more akin to the relationship between our earlier fake Mishnah passage and its ersatz Tosefta parallel, sections 6–15. Later I shall say more about what that "something different" is. But at this juncture, I wish you simply to take note of the topical/thematic correspondence across the passages presented from Mishnah and Tosefta Gittin. Even though one does *not* see here the almost total replication of one passage by the other, t. Gittin 1:1–7's sections all link in some fashion with content in m. Gittin 1:1–3. Yes, the order in which topics come up in t. Gittin 1:1–7 is not *exactly* the same as their order in the Mishnah passage. For example, the Tosefta's ruling at t. Gittin 1:4 about a writ transported from "province to province" and from "hegemony to hegemony" returns us to the rulings at the end of m. Gittin 1:1, *after* the Tosefta's treatment of matters at t. Gittin 1:2 and 1:3 have effectively *added to* Mishnah's treatment of matters at 1:3. Nevertheless, that there is a close topical/thematic correspondence between m. Gittin 1:1–3 and t. Gittin 1:1–7 is undeniable, and the recurrence of exact phrases in the two documents attests as well to their literary-historical relationship—again, not likely an accident. Moreover, that t. Gittin 1:1 seems to start in *medias res*, without some intelligible referent for its first rulings, *and* that m. Gittin 1:1 would serve well to provide that intelligible referent, should only reinforce the impression that a very deliberate relationship, indeed a dependent relationship of some sort, entails between these Mishnah and Tosefta passages, however one might account for it.

There are other similarities between m. Gittin 1:1–3 and t. Gittin 1:1–7; the similar use of anonymous, tightly formulated, declarative sentences, comprised of statements of circumstances (protases) and rulings (apodases), is evident throughout the Tosefta passage. One finds, as we do routinely in Mishnah, balance and repetition in language used across several individual passages' protases and apodases. Disputes, too, are found in this extended Tosefta passage at 1:2, 1:3, and 1:7. Consequently, attributions to named rabbinic sages appear in both passages. Attributions to Simeon b. Gamaliel and Meir are found in both the Mishnah and Tosefta passages in disputes. In two instances in Tosefta their names are associated with the same rulings assigned to them in Mishnah; an additional ruling is assigned in Tosefta to Simeon b. Gamaliel in a dispute that Mishnah does not have.

Tosefta Gittin 1:7 concludes with a precedent story in which the *dramatis personae* are Ishmael and Ilai; m. Gittin 1:1–3 does not have this precedent story, but the precedent story's relevance to the topic of both Mishnah and Tosefta is obvious. Whatever is going on in this Tosefta passage vis-à-vis its parallel Mishnah passage, it displays typically Mishnah-like literary-rhetorical forms and conventions throughout.

And yet, on the other hand, by the time you have worked through the entirety of this chapter, it will be apparent to you that, notwithstanding the many similarities, Tosefta is also *not* Mishnah-like in very substantial ways. Even this second-time-around glance at just t. Gittin 1:1–7, viewed in light of m. Gittin 1:1–3, may have already raised your antennae in this last regard. For one, Tosefta, that is, the document as a whole, is three and a half to four times the length of Mishnah. Obviously, *prima facie*, it must be doing some things that Mishnah does not do, or be providing materials that Mishnah does not provide. As we shall discuss later, when Tosefta is more expansive in its treatment of a subtopic than its parallel passage in Mishnah, or doing different things, Tosefta often

> (a) provides attributed sayings to named rabbinic authorities where Mishnah has few or none,
>
> (b) gives us disputes where there are none in the corresponding Mishnah texts,
>
> (c) presents "debates," where Mishnah proffers disputes only,
>
> (d) conveys precedent stories that Mishnah lacks, and so on.

And some of what will be seen to fall under "and so on" are more different still than just providing more Mishnah-like literary-rhetorical constructs than Mishnah provides. Our sample passage from t. Gittin 1:1–7 is a harbinger of some of these additional literary-rhetorical formulations. For example, take:

> – "they used to say, . . . in order to be stringent, rather to be lenient upon him" (at t. Gittin 1:2);
>
> – "in the beginning, they used to say. . . . they revisited to say . . . . (at t. Gittin 1:4); and
>
> – "there is a stringency as regards . . . that is not so as regards . . . , and with regards . . . that is not so as regards . . ." (at t. Gittin 1:5).

These are formalized phrases that appear far more frequently in Tosefta (and in Tosefta-like passages cited in the Talmuds, called *beraitot*) than in Mishnah, where they are a rarity. Moreover, such formalized phrases seem intended to preface or invite some sort of editorial, historical, or analytic comment about some rule that is *antecedent* to the ruling at hand, usually presented in the parallel Mishnah chapter as well as in the cognate Tosefta passage. Indeed, for Mishnah to so editorialize or provide a historical analysis of its own rulings is so infrequent, relatively speaking, as to appear un-Mishnaic.[12] Clearly, one sees here a hint that Tosefta does more *than* Mishnah, not simply *more of* what Mishnah does.

At one time, from the late nineteenth century through the first two-thirds of the twentieth century, scholars of Mishnah and Tosefta accounted for this relative "expansiveness" of Tosefta by positing that Tosefta preserves early tannaitic traditions that also underlay Mishnah's composition; however, in these scholars' opinions, the authorship of Mishnah tended to compress these traditions in their decidedly Mishnaic style of composition. Most late twentieth-century and twenty-first-century scholars would not ascribe to such a view *holus-bolus* anymore, but some elements of this view survive (or have been revived) in the work of some academic treatises on Tosefta.[13]

However one accounts for these differences (and similarities) between (now real) Tosefta and (real) Mishnah, Tosefta and Mishnah are examples of how two documents among the early rabbinic legal corpus can use almost all the same literary-rhetorical forms, structures, and conventions, but with noticeably different effects and, apparently, to different ends. Indeed, saying something more at this juncture about Tosefta's overall "ends" will facilitate this chapter's account of Tosefta's particular use of what for the most part are typically Mishnaic literary-rhetorical constructs, augmented by a few more that are more properly Toseftan.

---

12. The isolated cases where Mishnah does something like this is where a Mishnah passage will preface a ruling-statement with the formula, "and/but the first Mishnah" (*ve-mishnah rishonah*), referring in these few instances to some protoversion of the passage in question or the legal teaching at hand.

13. See above, this chapter note 4.

Tosefta

TO WHAT PURPOSE TOSEFTA? INTENDED OR NOT?

Having studied a made-up Tosefta passage and its relation to a forged Mishnah text, and having now rehearsed (from chapter 3) a pair of now-familiar real, parallel Mishnah and Tosefta passages, it is worth, as I have just argued, saying a bit more about Tosefta's *function* before continuing to introduce you to more of Tosefta's dominant literary-rhetorical conventions. From the viewpoint of scholarly research, this certainly seems to put the cart before the horse. Conclusions about function and purpose would normally follow from, rather than precede, an analysis of a document's pervasive literary and rhetorical conventions and traits. But in a book dedicated to helping you learn to read Tosefta with more facility, it makes sense for you to have some *prior* sense of *what the text is doing and why*.

But having said this, I am now faced with a vexing dilemma as a historian and anthropologist who studies the early rabbinic movement and its literature. As intimated earlier, there is a substantial amount of scholarly debate about "what" Tosefta "is doing and why." Replicating that debate here, even in summary form, involves one in a set of literary-historical questions and distinctions that are complex,[14] on the one hand, and, on the other, will

---

14. Let me provide some sense of that complexity. Permit me, then, to phrase matters as a literary-historian would. For historians of early rabbinic literature, the many similarities of Mishnah and Tosefta have long begged obvious questions: When and for what purposes was Tosefta (the document) composed? What are the origins and provenance of its (constituent) materials? What is the historical relationship between Mishnah's and Tosefta's materials and sources? What is the relationship between the production of Mishnah and the production of Tosefta, that is, of the documents as a whole? I previously intimated (in note 4 of this chapter) that these questions are active subjects of scholarly debate and disagreement, especially since the late 1990s, even though the scholars of 50 to 100 years ago thought they had, broadly speaking, furnished definitive answers to them.

To even begin to broach these issues, one must begin by making several subtle but important distinctions. Here they are in the form of a list:

- –the distinction between Tosefta's constituent passages as *currently formulated* and whatever sources lie behind them;
- –the distinction between the composition of Tosefta's currently-formulated *constituent passages* and the composition of Tosefta, *the document* as we have it or some protoversion of the document (if there in fact was one);
- –the distinctions among the purposes *originally* served (a) by Tosefta's currently-formulated, constituent passages, (b) by their sources, (c) by the document Tosefta, and (c) by some proto-Tosefta document (if there was one).

In the Seat of Moses

not serve our immediate purposes—to make the reading of Tosefta more accessible to a novice by providing an introduction to Tosefta's dominant literary-rhetorical conventions, which are at once *very* Mishnah-like, and not entirely Mishnah-like either in important ways.

Faced with that dilemma, here is my solution. I will focus what follows on *what came to be* Tosefta's *ultimate* purpose, and, therefore, came as well to be the purpose of its constituent passages, *at some time* over the course of late antiquity between the mid-third and early fifth centuries. That purpose was *to function as an aid to Mishnah study.* In one of my scholarly articles about early rabbinic-group ethos and identity, I designated this approach viewing "Tosefta *in situ,*" that is, serving in a specific context.[15] And that is how I want you to see Tosefta in this chapter, *in situ* as a support to Mishnah study. I know that this runs roughshod over a slew of literary-historical questions and related research—such as about how Tosefta's constituent passages came to be, about how Tosefta as a document came to be composed, and about how all of this relates to the literary-history of Mishnah and its constituent passages. But I offer several justifications for my approach. It provides the easiest and most effective entrée into reading Tosefta. And it does accord, after all, with what can be shown to have ultimately become the dominant and normative way of reading and understanding Toseftan passages in late antique (and subsequent) rabbinic circles, notwithstanding what may (or may not) have happened earlier in literary-historical terms. Such an approach offers a basis for seeing differences and similarities between parallel Mishnah and Tosefta passages' use of literary-rhetorical conventions and constructs in a manner akin to how

---

All of these distinctions are present (sometimes explicitly, sometimes, alas, only implicitly) in scholarly introductions to, and monographs and journal articles about, Tosefta. And since, as you now know, Tosefta is the most Mishnah-like document in the early rabbinic corpus, both topically and in terms of its use of Mishnah-like literary-rhetorical constructs and structures, but is in some very discernible ways different than Mishnah, all of these distinctions end up being articulated by scholars in terms of literary-historical relations with Mishnah. For example, are Tosefta's *sources* and Mishnah's *sources* one and the same body of traditions? Is a *current* Tosefta *passage* prior to and so may (historically) "explain" a parallel Mishnah-passage, or vice-versa? Is a proto-Tosefta document in fact the proto-Mishnah, of which our extant Mishnah is a secondary development? Need I go on formulating such questions to make the point? Which is this: as important as these issues are, they a rabbit hole not to be gone down, if your purpose in reading this book is to get a toe-hold on reading Tosefta's passages, which are constructed of overwhelmingly Mishnah-like literary forms, and yet come out quite different than Mishnah, notwithstanding the similarities.

15. Lightstone, "Textual Study and Social Formation, Part II" (forthcoming).

ancient students of this literature ultimately came to engage those differences and similarities—that is (to hammer home the point), during focused Mishnah study, for which Tosefta was an aid.

Let me now provide some historical justification for seeing Tosefta and its constituent passages as coming ultimately to have served to aid Mishnah study in late antiquity rabbinic circles sometime in the period specified.[16]

I begin with the name of the document itself. Whoever named it "Tosefta" and those who thereafter accepted the name are telegraphing to us what they understand to be the document's intended purpose. They certainly are communicating the ends for which they use it. How so? *Tosefta* is an Aramaic noun in the singular-emphaticus form meaning "*the*

---

16. Whether this is the so-called original purpose for which Tosefta, the document, or Tosefta's constituent passages, were composed is not at issue in this volume. That said, I do personally subscribe to the scholarly view that (a) views Tosefta, *the document*, as a composition originally intended to aid Mishnah study, that (b) understands some two-thirds to four-fifths of Tosefta's passage *as currently formulated* to be later than and dependent upon their parallel Mishnah passages, and that (c) posits the existence of some earlier body of rabbinic traditions (written and/or oral) upon which the authorship of both Tosefta and Mishnah drew, each in their own fashion. Whether we have much or any of these earlier rabbinic traditions in their original forms and language is questionable. Mishnah's pervasive literary-rhetorical conventions represent a significant steam-roller-like process via which the authorship of Mishnah's tractates significantly shaped the language of its constituent passages and "chapters." It is likely that much of any original language of Mishnah's sources was "crushed" in the process. If language in Tosefta's passages at many junctures is similar, and often identical to, the language in parallel Mishnah passages, then the parsimonious explanation is that it is dependent upon Mishnah's language in some fashion. That Tosefta often proffers content that Mishnah does not have bespeaks of reliance on earlier rabbinic traditions either not known to, or not used by, Mishnah's authors. But as a general rule, these earlier rabbinic traditions have likely been reformulated in the language of the Mishnah passages for which the Tosefta passage is an aid. That Tosefta's authorship reformulated the substance they had in hand, *a-la-*Mishnah's language, rhetoric and literary forms is again the most parsimonious view that accounts for what we see *overall* in Tosefta, exceptions granted. (And, indeed, exceptions have been credibly identified by a number of scholars. See the further discussion and references above in note 4 of this chapter.) But it is not only the more parsimonious account, it is also the most historically reasonable. Why? Once Mishnah was created and promulgated, Mishnah study and mastery was the *ne-plus-ultra* of inner-group activity in third-century rabbinic circles. Even memorization of Mishnah, or of significant proportions of it, was expected. With so much focus on Mishnah and Mishnah mastery, it is reasonable that the formulation of additional rabbinic traditions believed to be *tannaitic* would, where possible, be (re-)caste in Mishnaic language and literary-rhetorical forms, to the point of replicating Mishnah's language verbatim where appropriate. The foregoing, then, represents where I currently stand on this complex and recently-much-debated issue.

supplement." The use of the singular-emphaticus form of the noun is interesting, as it is meant to encompass a/the document as a whole. The same letters could be equally pronounced in Aramaic as *tosefata*, the plural-emphaticus form, meaning "the supplements," which would refer instead to the constituent passages in the document.[17] Both *tosefta* (sg.) and *tosefata* (pl.) imply, moreover, that *the document or its constituent passages* serve to elucidate *something else*. Given the ordering of Tosefta's materials so as to correspond topically and thematically with the "Orders," tractates, and individual "chapters" of Mishnah, it is obvious that whoever so named the document saw Tosefta as a companion-document serving the study and elucidation of Mishnah.

When was the document so named? That is not easy to determine. After all, not all ancient documents bear names given them by their authors at the time of their authorship. Sometimes book titles are bestowed or changed later by those who come to use that document in a certain way. For example, we do not know whether the Gospel of Mark or the Gospel of Matthew bore these names at the time that they were composed. Indeed, it is likely that they did not. Only Luke explicitly identifies himself as the author of the Gospel that bears his name, just as Luke identifies himself as the author of the Acts of the Apostles. As just argued, entitling the Tosefta, "*tosefta*" (or "*tosefata*") is significant, implying the document was authored for the purpose of supplementing the study of something else, namely, the Mishnah. Clearly, then, *by the time* the Tosefta came to bear its current title, it is reasonable to conclude that Tosefta was *perceived to be*, and *was used* as, a companion to Mishnah study. Now, several passages in the Babylonian Talmud, composed c. 600 CE, refer to a *tosefta* (Aramaic, singular-emphaticus), which in context is understood to be a collection of *beraitot* (pl.), a term meaning "outside" traditions—that is, not contained in but related to the Mishnah.[18] Again, both *tosefta* and *beraita* (sg.) or *beraitot* (pl) imply service to a more preeminent document, Mishnah. The

---

17. The document could have been named *tosefata* or *toseftaʾot*, both plural nouns, the first in a strictly Aramaic plural form, the latter in a mixed Aramaic-Hebrew plural morphology not uncommonly used in early-rabbinic and medieval-rabbinic documents. Some late ninteenth- and early twentieth-century scholars believe that the Tosefta's original name was *tosefata*, implying that the document is a collection of "additional materials" (in the plural)—again, additional to those in Mishnah. Since written Hebrew and Aramaic are largely consonantal languages, that is usually written without all vowels being represented, *tosefta* (sg.) and *tosefata* (pl.) would quite properly and commonly be written in exactly the same way.

18. b. Shavuʿot 41b, b. Megilah 28b, b. Kiddushin 49b, b. Sanhedrin 86a.

Jerusalem Talmud, authored c. 400–450 CE, contains references in Hebrew to *ha-tosafot* (plural-emphaticus)[19] and *ha-tosefet*[20] (singular-emphaticus), meaning "the supplements" and "the supplement" respectively. These passages in the Jerusalem Talmud expressly discuss documents or bodies of rabbinic tradition that have an essential place in the early rabbinic curriculum. And again, that to which these materials are "supplemental" is clearly Mishnah. With these terminological usages in the Jerusalem Talmud we are getting close in time to when "our" Tosefta is understood to have been authored, *even if* we cannot know with certainty that "our" Tosefta is the referent of these passages.

There is another basis in evidence for establishing that "our" Tosefta was understood quite early on to serve Mishnah study by proffering a body of supplementary traditions, believed to be of tannaitic origin, that elucidated Mishnah. That basis may be formulated as follows:

> –the earliest compositions that came to be included in the larger, more elaborate composite essays of both the Jerusalem and Babylonian Talmuds used what they designated as extra-Mishnaic, tannaitic sources in their discussions and elaborations of Mishnah; these sources are what are later called *beraitot*;
>
> –many of the passages in "our" Tosefta, *which is certainly understood to be a collection of beraitot*, have direct parallel passages in these extra-Mishnaic, tannaitic sources cited in the two Talmuds as *beraitot*; in fact, it is the 66 percent to 80 percent of Tosefta materials that are most closely related to parallel Mishnah passages in substance and language that most frequently have parallels in the *beraitot* cited by the Talmuds.

If one considers carefully these two claims, then it follows from these evidentiary grounds that "our" Tosefta (the document) and/or its constituent passages would have been understood in late antique rabbinic circles to be materials serving Mishnah study and analysis from a fairly early period, in the decades and several centuries following the promulgation of Mishnah itself.

In conclusion let me summarize what I hope to have conveyed in this section of the chapter. First, that Tosefta ("The Supplement"), that is, the document, would at some point *come to* bear such a name makes eminent sense, and it makes equal sense that its constituent passages would have

---

19. y. Peah 2:4 (13a) and its parallel in y. Hagiggah.1:8 (7b).
20. y. Horayot 3:5 (19b).

been designated in Aramaic or Hebrew or in hybrid Hebrew-Aramaic (in the plural) as *tosefata, ha-tosafot,* or *ha-tosefta' ot* ("the supplements"). To what was it (or were they) supplemental? To Mishnah! And how could it have likely come to be otherwise? Since, as stated in chapters 2, 3, and 4, soon after its production and promulgation, Mishnah, and not any other rabbinic composition or body of rabbinic traditions, became the primary object of study within the early rabbinic group. Mastery of Mishnah (together with mastery of the Hebrew Scriptures) made one a rabbi, and lifelong study of Mishnah, among other things, kept one an ongoing *bona-fide* member of the rabbinic group. When Mishnah assumed such importance, which it did soon after its promulgation near the turn of the third century CE, *any* other similar compilation, like Tosefta, would come *to serve the study of Mishnah*, which was the preeminent, inner-group rabbinic activity.[21]

21. If, then, Tosefta (in the singular), was so named when it was *first* produced, or very soon thereafter, then it is a reasonable hypothesis that the document *was authored* for the purpose of aiding Mishnah-study in some fashion. If, however, Tosefta's name (again in the singular) was given it many decades or more after Tosefta was produced, then its name in itself does not necessarily attest to the purpose that *its production* was meant *originally* to serve. That purpose would have to be established on other evidentiary grounds. (And that is precisely one of the major issues that underlies the renewed scholarly debate that has been taking place since the late 1990s.) If the contents of Tosefta were referred to from an early date in the plural, *tosefata* or *toseftaʾot* or *tosafot,* meaning "the supplements," then, again, we would hypothesize that Tosefta's constituent materials circulated among rabbinic circles to serve in Mishnah study.

There are, no doubt, literary-historical scholars who will view the foregoing arguments as running roughshod over important literary-historical questions. Some may understandably say: Consider that perhaps Tosefta was not produced all at once, but in several stages—one's head begins to spin a bit as one considers what might be the "original" intended purpose(s) of a Tosefta which may have evolved over several stages of composition. Yes, there has been considerable debate in scholarly circles over the last twenty years about how and why Tosefta came to be (see above, note 4), and some have even argued that some of its early stages of development may predate the composition of Mishnah itself, making an early version of Tosefta a kind of proto-Mishnah (a view with which I do not agree). As already noted in the chapter's text and in the preceding footnotes, the literary-historical relationship between the substance and constituent sources of Mishnah and Tosefta is a matter of considerable debate. Remember my view on these matters (as per note 17 above): (1) both Mishnah and Tosefta draw from a common pool of earlier rabbinic traditions, some of which may have circulated in written form and some of which circulated in oral form; (2) none of the items of this pool have survived independently of Mishnah, Tosefta and of other later rabbinic legal compositions; (3) to maintain that *some* Tosefta passages reflect something of this common pool that is older than the formulation in the related passage in Mishnah is certainly reasonable and at times demonstrable; (4) but I am ever more convinced that Tosefta *as a whole* is post-Mishnaic both as regards time of composition as well as substantive agenda; (5)

Tosefta

Second, while scholarly debates about the precise literary-historical relationship between Mishnah and Tosefta may be of *interest* to you, the readers of this volume, my argument is that it need not *matter* to you, in working through *this* book, the *sole* purpose of which is to make early rabbinic legal texts (even in translation) more accessible to you by helping you gain familiarity with their principal repertoire of literary-rhetorical conventions. Why? Because the best way to master Tosefta's use of what are largely Mishnah-like, literary-rhetorical conventions, formulations, and structures is to look at Tosefta passages over against their parallel or correlated Mishnah passages. In any case, at some point in late antique rabbinic circles, this is exactly how Tosefta and/or its constituent passages were read, *in situ*, as an aid and companion in the study and mastery of Mishnah. This is certainly so for the estimated 66 percent to 80 percent of Tosefta for which there are closely correlated Mishnah passages. And

---

moreover, I am convinced that the major constituent bodies of *material* in Tosefta (some 66 percent to 80 percent of the document) that either cite and gloss Mishnah or, to use Neusner's term, complement Mishnah are post-Mishnaic *in formulation*, even if they draw on older content. I am unconvinced of the validity of an hypothesis articulated by Judith Hauptman (see above, this chapter, note 4) that the "core" of Tosefta *is* the *first* Mishnah and that our extant Mishnah is a development of it. One of the reasons for my stance is that even if the *substance* of a number of Tosefta passages can be argued to be pre-Mishnaic and underlying a Mishnah passage, the rhetorical and literary traits—the way things are formulated in language—show over and over again Tosefta's dependence on language that was formulated by our extant Mishnah's authorship.

The hypothesis that Tosefta is post-Mishnaic is the "traditional" one, going back to at least Sherira but was supported in modern scholarly circles by almost all scholars until the last decade of the twentieth century, when Hauptman and others, like Friedman, Houtman, and Kulp, offered their countervailing arguments (for references, see above, this chapter, note 4). Jacob Neusner, among others, including myself, continue to maintain Mishnah's historical primacy to Tosefta, albeit in a very nuanced articulation, as implied above. Neusner's work on Mishnah and correlative Tosefta passages is still unparalleled in terms of its breadth, covering most, and, if one includes the dissertations of his students in the late 1970s, virtually all, of Mishnah and Tosefta. Nor has anyone in modern scholarship so carefully analyzed Mishnah's dominant literary and formal traits. Neusner, therefore, can speak of dominant tendencies over vast swaths of the texts of both Mishnah and Tosefta from an evidentiary base that no else has been able to muster. That in itself does not make him right, but it does make his evidence better. More recently still, Brody, *Mishnah*, has called into question the methods and reasoning of scholars such as Hauptman and Friedman, who have argued for the historical primacy of some proto-Tosefta over Mishnah. Brody's argument is simple: that some Tosefta passages, or their substance, can sometimes be demonstrated to underlie their parallel passages in Mishnah, proves only that this entails in some cases, and does not provide sufficient evidence for a claim that generally or often Tosefta passages are the basis for their correlative Mishnah passages.

by extension the same came to be the case for the one-third to one-fifth of Tosefta's passages with a less direct but merely topical relation to Mishnah. The foregoing is further borne out by that the fact, stated earlier, that "our" Tosefta's materials are organized in accordance with the same tractates and their constituent "chapters" as Mishnah, and that many Tosefta passages read on their own (without Mishnah) lack an intelligible context, as we shall see in subsequent sections of this chapter. But when they are read *with* the correlative Mishnah passage, are rendered (more) intelligible.

Lesson number 1 of this chapter was this: Tosefta and its passages are the most Mishnah-like of all early rabbinic legal literature, but Tosefta's passages differ from Mishnah in important ways—ways to be teased out to a greater extent later. Lesson number 2 is doubled-barreled: Tosefta and its constituent passages at some point in late antiquity came to serve Mishnah study; the easiest and best way to read Tosefta, whether as a novice or an expert, is to read it with the correlative Mishnah chapter open beside it, just as ancient Mishnah students did. One will thereby find Tosefta far more intelligible and, by consequence, accessible.

How, now, will the remainder of this chapter develop? Since, as has been repeated a number of times, Tosefta exhibits all of Mishnah's pervasive literary-rhetorical forms and conventions, some more frequently than Mishnah, some less frequently, but with a "difference that makes a difference," and since, as stated earlier, there are just a few literary-rhetorical structures and conventions found in Tosefta that are not characteristic of Mishnah, then I shall proceed as follows. First, I shall introduce you to those literary-rhetorical structures and conventions found in Tosefta that are *not* characteristic of Mishnah, so that they become part of your existing literary-rhetorical repertoire of structures and forms. Second, I shall present extended passages of Mishnah, in one instance an entire Mishnah "chapter" already familiar to you from chapter 4, followed by the entire parallel sections of Tosefta. You shall then be able both to see what Tosefta "does with Mishnah" and what it is like to "study Mishnah" with Tosefta as an aid, as an ancient rabbinic reader of Mishnah might have done with Tosefta's content in hand. (In the last chapter of this volume, I will return to this matter and ask, What does such a use of Tosefta indirectly tell us about the evolution of the ethos of the early rabbinic movement and of the normative skills expected of a rabbi?)

Tosefta

SOME PARTICULARLY TOSEFTAN LITERARY-RHETORICAL CONSTRUCTS: ELABORATING AND MOVING BEYOND THE MISHNAH'S REPERTOIRE

The Redefined/Redirected Dispute

As remarked, several formal literary-rhetorical constructs appear in Tosefta that are rarely, if ever, encountered in Mishnah. The first that we shall look at is the redefined/redirected dispute. You will remember that the "classic" Mishnaic dispute is built on several standard elements:

(a) an articulation of (hypothetical) circumstances of a case—that is, the protasis of a Mishnaic declarative sentence—followed by

(b) not one, but two tightly formulated, matched, opposing rulings—that is, two apodases of a declarative sentence,

(c) at least one of which apodasis is attributed as a "saying" to a named rabbinic authority.

This simple formula accounts for several versions of the dispute form and their variations.

In chapter 4, I represented these versions in a series of ersatz disputes, as follows:

a A cow which gives birth to a male, and they do not know if she has [previously] borne [offspring]—[the owner] gives nothing to a priest.

Rabbi Judah says: [The owner] gives [the offspring] to a priest.

a' A cow which gives birth to a male, and they do not know if she has [previously] borne [offspring]—

Rabbi Judah says: [The owner] gives [the offspring] to a priest.

And [the] sages say: [The owner] gives nothing to a priest.

b A cow which gives birth to a male, and they do not know if she has [previously] borne [offspring],

Rabbi Yose says, [The owner] gives nothing to a priest.

Rabbi Judah says: [The owner] gives [the offspring] to a priest.

b' A cow which gives birth to a male, and they do not know if she has [previously] borne [offspring], [the owner] gives nothing to a priest, **the words of Rabbi Yose**.

In the Seat of Moses

Rabbi Judah says: [The owner] gives [the offspring] to a priest.

If one were to diagram these types of the dispute form, it might be represented in the following manner:

   a circumstance(s) (i.e., protasis),

      ruling 1 (i.e., apodasis 1),

      Rabbi r says + ruling 2 (i.e., apodasis 2)

   a' circumstance(s) (i.e., protasis)

      Rabbi r says + ruling 2 (i.e., apodasis 2)

      And [the] sages say + ruling 1 (i.e., apodasis 1)

   b circumstance(s) (i.e., protasis)

      Rabbi r says + ruling 1 (i.e., apodasis 1)

      Rabbi r' says + ruling 2 (i.e., apodasis 2)

   b' circumstance(s) (i.e., protasis),

      ruling 1 (i.e., apodasis 1) + the words of Rabbi r

      Rabbi r' says + ruling 2 (i.e., apodasis 2).

How simple and elegant are these! Versions a and a' pit an anonymous, supposedly majority view against an attributed, putatively minority view. Versions b and b' juxtapose two opposing authorities' opinions.

When an analytically inclined ancient student of Mishnah (or a modern one, for that matter) confronts a Mishnaic dispute, one of the questions that may come to the student's mind is, Can one equally justify in Halakha both opposing legal positions concerning this single set of hypothetical circumstances? Or to put matters even more simply, Why do the disputants disagree? In chapter 4, I presented the Mishnaic "debate" as a formalized literary-rhetorical construct that broaches such questions. Debates do appear in Mishnah, but not as frequently as they do in Tosefta. As already stated, Tosefta quite frequently will supply a debate where the corresponding, parallel Mishnah passage presents only a dispute.

But Tosefta will at times do something quite different with a dispute, whether that dispute appears as well in the parallel Mishnah passage, or appears only in Tosefta as Tosefta's supplement *in situ* to the corresponding Mishnah's single anonymous ruling. Instead of providing a debate in order to venture views about the competing logic of the two attributed, opposing rulings, Tosefta does almost the opposite. Tosefta tells us that it is about to redefine the case itself, moves on to present an alternative formulation of the circumstances, and then "transfers" the two disputants' opposing rulings from the original hypothetical circumstances to the new, redefined ones.[22] Does this sound complicated? It really is not, because stock formulaic language is used in every instance *to alert us* to exactly what is about to happen in such a passage.

Let me illustrate such a redefined/redirected dispute by creating one using a now-familiar ersatz Mishnaic dispute. Note the language in boldface. It is the typical formulaic language that effects the redefined/redirected dispute; this formulaic language are your *signposts* in the literary rhetorical structure you are about to see.

1. A cow which gives birth to a male, and they do not know if she has [previously] borne [offspring]—

2. Rabbi Yose says, [The owner] gives nothing to a priest.

3. Rabbi Judah says: [The owner] gives [the offspring] to a priest.

4. **Said Rabbi Nathan: Rabbi Yose and Rabbi Judah did not dispute concerning**:

5. A cow which gives birth to a male, and they do not know if she has [previously] borne [offspring]—

6. [with regard to] **which** [case the owner] gives nothing to a priest.

7. [Rather] **concerning what did they dispute? Concerning:**

8. A cow which gives birth to two males, and she has not [previously] borne [offspring], and they do not know which came out first—

9. [Concerning] **which**

10. Rabbi Yose says, [The owner] gives nothing to a priest.

11. Rabbi Judah says: [The owner] gives [one of the offspring] to a priest.

The entire ersatz passage falls neatly into three sections: lines 1 to 3, lines 4 to 6, and lines 7 to 11. Lines 1 to 3 provide the "original dispute" that

---

22. This presentation and discussion draws heavily from my previously published article on what Tosefta's evidence may tell us about the evolution of the early rabbinic guild's ethos and its cadre's expected professional skills in the century or centuries following the promulgation of Mishnah during which Mishnah study helped define the profile of the bona fide rabbi. See Lightstone, "Textual Study and Social Formation, Part II" (forthcoming). My citations/translations of m. Gittin 1:5 and t. Gittin 1:8–9 also appear in this same article.

includes the opposing rulings attributed to Yose and Judah respectively. Lines 4 to 6 *undo* the dispute:

> –first, by telling us using stock formulaic language at line 4 that Yose and Judah did not have differing views on the case defined in the "original dispute"—"Said Rabbi Nathan: Rabbi Yose and Rabbi Judah did not dispute concerning...";

> –second, by recasting the original dispute as a Mishnaic declarative sentence with a single unattributed ruling (apodasis) preceded by the formulaic pronoun "which" at line 6.

(The introduction at line 4 of a third named authority, here Rabbi Nathan, as the purveyor of what follows is not uncommon, but is not a universal feature of the redefined/redirected dispute either.) In effect, what was Yose's position at line 2 of the original dispute is now given as an anonymous, unchallenged view at line 6, is it not? The last section, lines 7–11, again starts with stock formulaic language—"[Rather] concerning what did they dispute? Concerning..."—that *alerts* the reader to be prepared to see,

> –third, revised circumstances comprising a new case.

Finally, stock language at line 9—"which"—introduces,

> –fourth, the two disputants' original, opposing rulings (lines 10–11), now attached to the new, "redefined" case.

The opposing views attributed Yose and Judah have been reassigned, or "redirected," to these modified hypothetical circumstances. Let me diagram this out for you; again note the boldfaced stock language that conducts one through this particular literary-rhetorical structure.

1. circumstance(s) 1 (i.e., protasis 1)
2. Rabbi r says + ruling 1 (i.e., apodasis 1)
3. Rabbi r' says + ruling 2 (i.e., apodasis 2)
4. **Said Rabbi r": Rabbi r and Rabbi r' did not dispute concerning**:
5. circumstance(s) 1 (i.e., protasis 1)
6. [concerning] **which** + ruling 1 (i.e., apodasis 1)
7. [Rather] **concerning what did they dispute? Concerning:**
8. circumstance(s) 2 (i.e., protasis 2)
9. [Concerning] **which**

10. Rabbi r says + ruling 1 (i.e., apodasis 1)

11. Rabbi r' says + ruling 2 (i.e., apodasis 2)

This schematic of our made-up redefined/redirected dispute clearly shows the inner workings of this literary-rhetorical structure. Circumstances 1 appears at both lines 1 and 5. But at line 1, circumstances 1 is the protasis for a dispute, ruling 1 vs. ruling 2. In contrast, at line 5, circumstance 1 is followed by ruling 1 only at line 6; this makes lines 5 and 6 a normal anonymous, Mishnaic rule-sentence, if one ignores "which" at line 6. Lines 8, 10, and 11 form another, "new" dispute with circumstances 2 defining the case, and lines 10 and 11 completing the dispute by reusing the disputants' rulings 1 and 2 from lines 2 and 3. In all, minus what I have called the "signpost stock language" in boldface, we have:

- a dispute;
- a declarative rule-sentence (using one of the rulings of the preceding dispute); and
- a new dispute (created by assigning the "old" rulings of the first dispute to the "new" circumstances of the redefined case).

One final, and I hope obvious, point—the redefined/redirected dispute relies on the dispute structure and builds upon it, just as the debate structure does. Without Mishnaic disputes, neither formalized debates nor such formalized redefined/redirected disputes in the forms we have them would be possible. Moreover, both the dispute and the redefined/redirected dispute rely upon the typical structure of the declarative rule-sentence.

My fake passages have the virtue of being perfect examples of their literary-rhetorical types. Now let us look at two real passages, one from Mishnah (m. Gittin 1:5) and its correlative passage from Tosefta (t. Gittin 1:8–9). Be prepared! "Real" passages are apt to be a bit more complex and messy than my "ideal" ersatz ones. But remember to look for the stock language that *signals*, and then *conducts us through*, the redefined/redirected dispute. If you attend to this language, you cannot get "lost." That "signpost language" is *not* in boldface this time, because I will now revert back to my earlier practice; boldfaced language in the Tosefta passage highlights verbatim parallels in the corresponding Mishnah passage.[23] But I have put that "signpost language in SMALL CAPS, to make them stand out. First, Mishnah:

---

23. You may be confused, or curious about the use of "idolater" in Tosefta, where Mishnah has "Gentile." The different terminology simply represents different medieval scribes' sensitivities to the predilections of non-Jewish (usually Christian) authorities

In the Seat of Moses

m. Gittin 1:5

a. Any writ that has upon it [the signature of] a Samaritan witness

b. is unfit,

c. except for writs [of divorce] of women and manumission papers of slaves.

d. It once happened that they brought before R. Gamaliel in Kefar Otnai a writ [of divorce] of a woman,

e. and its witnesses were Samaritan witnesses,

f. and he declared [it] fit.

g. Any bonds issuing from [court] bureaus of the Gentiles—

h. even though their signatories are Gentiles—

i. are fit,

j. except for writs [of divorce] of women and manumission papers of slaves.

k. R. Simeon says: Also these are fit.

l. They specified [that the latter were unfit] only when they were done in a nonprofessional tribunal. (translation my own[24])

Let us take a brief look at the structure of this Mishnah passage before preceding to its correlated Tosefta. Lines a–c and lines g–j of Mishnah are formulated to provide reasonably well-matched declarative rule-sentences, in which the articulated rule is followed by expressly stated exceptions to the rule "for writs [of divorce] of women and manumission papers of slaves." Lines d–f of Mishnah provide a standard precedent story to legitimate the "exception" to the rule for writs of divorce. In contrast, Mishnah's line k (the opposing ruling attributed to Simeon) turns g–k into a dispute. And Mishnah's line l, at the very end, can be read in two slightly different ways. One way is to see it as an explanatory gloss of Simeon's ruling, as if it were

---

who were responsible for censoring Judaic texts that contained what they perceived to be language that insulted non-Jews, which could result in the confiscation of the manuscript or a worse fate for the scribe or the owner of the manuscript. Christians (and Muslims), obviously, did not consider themselves idolaters and therefore would not view passages in Judaic manuscripts that referred to "idolaters" as implying anything negative about them or their institutions.

24. Based on Lightstone, *Mishnah*, 36.

Tosefta

the completion of Simeon's legal opinion; that is to say, Simeon agrees with the anonymous ruling: when a Gentile court is staffed by nonprofessionals but disagrees with the anonymous ruling in the case of Gentile tribunals staffed by professional jurists. The other way of reading the Mishnah's last line, line l, is somewhat different, even though the end result is the same; one could read the last line as an attempt to harmonize somewhat the opposing rulings of the dispute, by explicating the view of the anonymous authorities behind i–j. On this reading, the "they" of the last line, line l, refers to these anonymous authorities of i–j, and explains that "they" are not completely at odds with the disputing ruling attributed to Simeon. Rather, "they" agree with Simeon, *if and when* writs of divorce and manumission papers of slaves are enacted by professionally staffed, Gentile tribunals. If a Gentile tribunal were staffed by nonprofessionals, the dispute would still stand. Have you now got the structure and literary-rhetorical structures of m. Gittin 1:5 well in hand?

- a–b –Anonymous ruling;
- c –exception;
- d–f –precedent story.
- g–i –Anonymous ruling;
- j –exception;
- k –disputing opinion (disputing the exception);
- l –gloss mitigating somewhat the gulf between the disputing parties.

In light of this, let us now see how Tosefta (at t. Gittin 1:8–9), read *in situ* as an aid to Mishnah study, would have the Mishnah student understand m. Gittin 1:5. Remember, verbatim Mishnah language appearing in Tosefta is in **boldface**, the signpost language of the redefined/redirected-dispute structure is in SMALL CAPS.

t. Gittin 1:8–9

a. R. Judah says: Even though its two witnesses are Kutim [Samaritans],

b. it **is fit**.

c. Said R. Judah [**the following**] incident occurred: they brought before R. Gamaliel to Kefar Otnai a writ of divorce, and its witnesses were Kutim [i.e., Samaritans],

d. **and he declared it fit** [m. 1:5c–e].
e. **Any bonds issuing from [court] bureaus of idolaters—even though their signatories are Gentiles** [m. 1:5f–g] |—
f. R. Aqiva **declares fit** in the case of all of them,
g. and sages declare [them] unfit in the case of **writs of divorce and** in the case of **manumission papers of slaves** [m. 1:5i].
h. SAID R. ELEAZAR b. R. YOSE: Thus said R. Simeon b. Gamaliel to them, the elders at Sidon: R. AQUIVA AND THE SAGES DID NOT DISPUTE CONCERNING **bonds issuing from [court] bureaus of idolaters,** that **even though their signatories are Gentiles** [m. 1:5f–g]
i. [they] **are fit.**
j. CONCERNING WHAT DID THEY DISPUTE?
k. CONCERNING [those] **that were done in a nonprofessional tribunal** [m. 1:5l] |—
l. [concerning] WHICH R. Aqiva **declares fit** in the case of all of them,
m. and the sages declare [them] unfit in the case of **writs of divorce and** in the case of **manumission papers of slaves.**
n. Rabbi Simeon b. Gamaliel says: Even **writs of divorce and manumission papers of slaves are fit** in the case of a place [in] which an Israelite does not sign. (translation my own[25])

This Tosefta passage, like its correlative Mishnah passage, falls neatly into two sections, a–d, and e–n. Lines a–d relate to the subtopic of the first part of our Mishnah passage, writs upon which Samaritans (aka Kutim) have signed as witnesses; lines e–n parallel the substance of the second half of our Mishnah pericope, writs upon which Gentiles (aka idolaters) have placed their signatures as witnesses. The amount of language in **boldface** indicates the likely literary-historical dependence of one the passages on the other in some fashion. Finally, where the legal *content* of the Mishnah and Tosefta passages are parallel, the legal *outcomes* of the two passages are identical. From a legal perspective, only line n in Tosefta is new; it articulates a hypothetical circumstance not contemplated in Mishnah at all, and ascribes a ruling to Simeon b. Gamaliel. The effect of line n is interesting, as

25. Based on Lightstone, *Mishnah*, 84.

either it turns k–n into a three-party dispute, which is not, strictly speaking, classical dispute-form protocol in Mishnah, *or* it can be read as an attempt to gloss "the sages" ruling at m, reducing even further the grounds for difference between Aqiva and "the sages."

Let me now turn from legal substance and parallels of content and language between t. Gittin 1:8–9 and m. Gittin 1:5 to comments about literary-rhetorical form and structure. I start with Tosefta lines a–d. It in effect presents "the exception" to the rule at Mishnah line c, which is conveyed anonymously in Mishnah, as an independent attributed saying conveyed in Tosefta in the name of R. Judah. And the precedent story involving Gamaliel at Mishnah lines d–f is repeated in Tosefta, now attributed to Judah as well. What is entirely missing in Tosefta is Mishnah's anonymous ruling at Mishnah lines a–b. And without the latter in Tosefta, "Judah's" ruling at Tosefta lines a–b completely lacks an intelligible context. Without the Mishnah passage open beside one, the reader of Tosefta lines a–b cannot know what in the world "Judah's" ruling is talking about. (Although, a clever, analytic mind might reconstruct part of the case at hand from the precedent story that follows in Tosefta.) So, if I were to make out the literary-rhetorical structure of Tosefta lines a–d, it would look like this:

> a–b –independent attributed legal "saying" *without complete legal circumstances (protasis) logically required specified*;
>
> c –attribution + precedent story.

The upshot? (1) Read this Tosefta together with parallel Mishnah. (2) Read that way, Tosefta conveys to the Mishnah student that Judah is the rabbinic authority behind the anonymous ruling in Mishnah; taken *in situ*, this amounts to a kind of early rabbinic tradition-historical explication of Mishnah by Tosefta.

What of the second half of our Tosefta passage, which parallels the second half of its Mishnah parallel? Leaving aside the very last attributed saying at Tosefta line n, I want you to notice four things in particular. (1) The disputing legal opinion, which Mishnah attributes to Simeon, the Tosefta passage attributes to Aqiva (who was a rabbinic master of the generation preceding Simeon). (2) Tosefta lines e–g is structured as a dispute between Aqiva and "the sages," while its parallel in Mishnah is structured as a dispute between an anonymous ruling and Simeon. Furthermore, (3) two different versions of the dispute form are in evidence in the Tosefta and Mishnah respectively, conveying the same content, slightly reordered, using the same language.

Now comes the *piece-de-resistance*. Look at the language in SMALL CAPS at Tosefta's lines h, j, k and l. This is (4) the signpost language indicating that the literary-rhetorical construct at hand in Tosefta lines h–m is a redefined/redirected dispute. The redefined/redirected dispute is conveyed in the name of Eleazar b. R. Yose, and it is conflated, from a literary-rhetorical-structural perspective, with partial or truncated precedent-story language—the standard language "it once happened that" is missing. That is, the redirected dispute was taught by Simeon b. Gamaliel to the "elders of Sidon." I have no basis for pronouncing on the historicity of such stories (or of attributions to named masters in general). Rather what I want you to see is literary-rhetorical constructs and their use (and sometimes abuse), and the manner in which from time to time they are hybridized—as in the case at hand, where what is *primarily* a redefined/redirected dispute in literary-rhetorical form has been melded with a precedent-story structure. The lesson: recognize the literary-rhetorical constructs in the text, and you know what is going on and what to expect. Again, diagraming it will help.

> e–g -dispute (of form: case + rabbi x says + ruling 1 + sages say + ruling 2)
>
> h–m -partial precedent story + redefined/redirected dispute

Permit some further remarks about what is going on in this particular redefined/redirected dispute in Tosefta and to relate the latter to the parallel section of the Mishnah passage, discussed earlier. As already noted, we see names in Tosefta that differ from, or are lacking entirely in, the parallel Mishnah. If one reads Tosefta *in situ*, as if it functions to serve Mishnah study, then once again the reader of Tosefta will conclude something about which rabbinic authorities are the "original" purveyors of which (or whose) legal opinions. Second, read *in* situ, as an aid to understanding Mishnah, Tosefta's redefined/redirected dispute is, in effect, settling any queries the Mishnah student might have had about how precisely to take the last line (line l) of Mishnah, which read, "They specified [that the latter were unfit] only when they were done in a nonprofessional tribunal." Earlier, you and I struggled over how precisely to understand this gloss. Was it mean to be read as if it were the continuation of Simeon's ruling? Or was it intended to be an explication of the anonymous ruling's position? Tosefta has settled the matter altogether and without ambiguity by using the structure of the redefined/redirected dispute. Has it not?! It is *as if* the formulator of this Tosefta passage took the final gloss of m. Gittin 1:5 and used it as a basis for rewriting the hypothetical circumstances (that is, the case) about which the disputants ruled. Simeon/Aqiva and "they"/"the sages" did not rule differently about *this*—because on *this* they all agreed—but disputed about *that* related matter, concerning which one ruled in one direction and the other ruled in the opposite direction. Finished and utterly clear![26]

It is propitious that in m. Gittin 1:5 and t. Gittin 1:8–9, we see how a Tosefta passage, read *in situ* as an aid to Mishnah study, provides a definitive reading of a problematic statement in Mishnah by proffering a redefined/redirected dispute. In truth, however, many/most redefined/redirected disputes that appear in Tosefta have no such overt textual hooks in an antecedent Mishnaic dispute upon which to hang their exercise to redefine the case about which the disputants differ. So, in such cases, what engendered the redefined/redirected dispute? It is hard to definitively say. Perhaps at times those who composed the redefined/redirected dispute genuinely had knowledge of a tradition in which the case disputed differed. It is hard to muster arguments that appeal to the existence of alleged traditions that have not independently survived. Nor is it necessary. Because it is equally possible that the critical analysis of the contents of a Mishnaic-type dispute would invite the analyst to posit a different set of circumstances about which the disputing authorities disagree, particularly when it is difficult to understand why the parties would have disagreed about the case "originally" spelled out in the dispute. All that is necessary is to posit serious analytic engagement with the Mishnah text and early rabbinic traditions generally. And this engagement we know to have occurred in late antique rabbinic circles, as I have previously indicated. The production of redefined/redirected disputes need be nothing more than a reflection of that engagement.

---

26. I have little doubt that someone might argue that the last line (line l) of m. Gittin 1:5 could be a later addition to a protoversion of this Mishnah passage inspired by the redefined/redirected dispute conveyed in the Tosefta passage at hand. While this is possible, we have little basis for knowing that this is what happened. Certainly, to repeat what I say in the body of the text of this chapter, Tosefta presents in many other passages such redefined/redirected disputes where there is nothing like line l of m. Gittin 1:5 to give the Tosefta occasion to do so.

In the Seat of Moses

THE TOSEFTAN HALAKHIC-MIDRASHIC-LIKE CONSTRUCT: A "NEW AND DIFFERENT" LITERARY-RHETORICAL CONSTRUCT FOR ARGUING FROM SCRIPTURE

With this section of the chapter you will be breaking new ground. Or perhaps it is more accurate to say, Tosefta will be taking you into new territory. That territory involves a focus on the legal content of Scripture unlike what we have seen until now. Because we will see in a sample Tosefta passage what might well be classified as "legal midrash" (*midrash Halakha* in Hebrew, a term usually anglicized as "Halakhic Midrash"). In Toseftan passages or Tosefta-like passages (*beraitot*) that might be classified as "legal midrash," the relative weight of the relationship of the passage to Mishnah's content, on the one hand, and to biblical Scripture, on the other, shifts dramatically. Understanding that shift, as it appears in some (although, admittedly, relatively few) Tosefta passages will pay dividends later, because such "legal, midrashically structured" passages make up the bulk of the mini-compositions of the early rabbinic corpus of documents known as the Halakhic Midrashim (mentioned in chapters 2 and 3), and such passages appear liberally among the *beraitot* (the allegedly "tannaitic" materials that do not appear in Mishnah) cited in the two Talmuds. So, once again, some hard work now on your part provides building blocks for later.

Before conducting you into this new territory, let me recap a little. Tosefta is, generally speaking, ordered in accordance with the same thematic, topical, and subtopical organization of the successive "chapters" of Mishnah's tractates. Not exactly so, admittedly. But close enough so that to find Tosefta passages that relate, let us say, to the pericopae of the fifth "chapter" of Mishnah Tractate Bekhorot, one need only look at the fifth "chapter" of Tosefta Bekhorot. And within that fifth "chapter" of Tosefta Bekhorot the ordering of passages will, roughly speaking, follow the order of the subtopics of the parallel "chapter" in Mishnah. What this means is this: Mishnah is (or became) the "base text" of Tosefta (*in situ*), when Mishnah was taken as the core object of study within ancient rabbinic circles, and when Tosefta was understood to be a "supplement" serving Mishnah study. In such a context, one reads a Mishnah passage or several successive Mishnah passages that form a mini-composition, and then one seeks critically to understand it. *In that process*, one looks for help to correlative sections of the Tosefta, conveniently ordered so that the parallel Toseftan materials are easily found that function to "comment upon," to "complement" or "complete," and to "supplement" Mishnah, to use Jacob Neusner's categorization of Tosefta's passages.

Simple! Yes? And useful too beyond reading Tosefta. Because to a significant extent, the constituent compositions and composite "essays" of the Jerusalem and Babylonian Talmuds are organized, roughly speaking, in a manner similar to Tosefta; that is to say, the ordering of these Talmudic compositions and "essays" reflects the ordering of materials in the correlative Mishnah tractates, just as in Tosefta (even though neither the Jerusalem Talmud nor the Babylonian have parallel tractates for all of Mishnah's tractates). For both Talmuds, then, Mishnah functions as the base text, just as it does for Tosefta *in situ*. So, again, Mishnah study was *formally* paramount even as the study of Talmudic compositions gained ascendency in the early rabbinic movement in the latter part of late antiquity.

But wait! The few ancient rabbinic sources that talk about the early rabbinic curriculum readily admit that there is one body of literature that surpasses Mishnah in authority: that is Scripture. Is this mere lip service, just a technicality? Because, after all, to profess otherwise would have been tantamount to placing oneself outside of the fold of Judaism. (Even) early Christianity would not, or could not, disavow the supreme authority of the Judaic Scriptures. Marcion tried to do just that and was decried as a Christian heretic. But mere lip service it was not—neither in the case of early Christianity, nor in the case of the rabbinic authorships of Mishnah and Tosefta. As I have remarked in earlier chapters, the legal content of Scripture constitutes a core, antecedent, substantive context of Mishnah's and Tosefta's passages throughout. And this is the case even though Scripture is, at best, only episodically cited in either Mishnah or Tosefta as proof-texts. Scripture is very frequently there "behind" the substance of Mishnah's and Tosefta's passages, and it is allowed to peek out from time to time and show its face.

That said, in a few passages in Tosefta, Scripture takes a very different role, much more out front and at center stage. And again, this happens via an identifiable formalized literary-rhetorical construct yet to be encountered in either chapters 4 or 5 of this volume. Moreover, as intimated at the outset of this section of the chapter, the Toseftan literary-rhetorical construct I am about to present appears to resemble those that are the core building blocks of passages in those early rabbinic documents collectively known as the Halakhic Midrashim, the books of legal midrash. I have chosen the word "resemble"—that is, similar but not the same—in the foregoing sentence for a particular reason, and I will be better able to explain why in chapter 6, which will focus on the Halakhic Midrashim specifically.

To contextualize my presentation to you of this Halakhic-Midrashic-*like* literary-rhetorical construct sometimes evident in Tosefta, I would like, first, to review and rehearse what you have already seen to be formalized ways in which Mishnah or Tosefta can explicitly adduce Scripture. This will help you consolidate what you have already learned about the role of citing Scripture in the formal literary-rhetorical constructs of Mishnah's (and Tosefta's) passages. In broad terms, I have already presented two such ways in chapter 4 on Mishnah, both of which appear in Tosefta passages.

One such form is what I earlier called (simple) proof-texting, sometimes although not always with a further explanatory gloss. The use of proof-texting is captured in the schematization of Mishnaic (or Toseftan) passages that exhibits the following formal structure:

a. -circumstances of case;

b. -ruling;

c. -"as it is said" + short citation of Scripture;

d. -with or without a short statement of relevance of the scriptural citation to the ruling.

Lines a–b together constitute a declarative rule-sentence. Line c introduces a snippet of a citation of Scripture in support of b; these short citations are prefaced by the formulaic language, "as it is said" (*she-ne'emar*, passive perfect). Line d is a succinct gloss of line c, hinting at how the scriptural citation is to be understood as supporting the antecedent ruling. Such glosses may or may not appear; when they do not, readers must figure out for themselves the relevance to the ruling of the scriptural proof-text.

Mishnah Tractate Bekhorot 1:1a and t. Bekhorot 1:1a, passages that you have already seen, provide apt examples of such simple proof-texting. Here is t. Bekhorot 1:1a, again, with language that equates to Mishnah's in boldface:

a. **He who purchases the foetus of an ass of** an idol worshipper,

b. **and he who sells to him,**

c. **even though it is not permitted,**

d. **and he who forms a partnership with him—**

e. [that is,] he who gives to him in partnership—

> f. and he who receives from him, and he who gives to him in trust—
> g. is exempt from the law of the firstling,
> h. as it is said, "Of an Israelite" (Numbers 3:13),
> i. but not of others.

In this passage, line h provides a proof-text—just a fragment of the relevant language of Numbers 3:13 is cited—followed at line i with a very short explanatory gloss that further telegraphs the relevance of the Scripture cited to the preceding sections of the Mishnah passage. The formulaic language, "as it is said" (*she-ne'emar*), appears as expected, introducing a scriptural citation when proof-texting occurs in either Mishnah or Tosefta. All this should look familiar to you by now.

The second form of explicit appeal to Scripture that you have already encountered in this volume is sometimes seen in "debates" in Mishnah and in Tosefta. Chapter 4 (on Mishnah) introduced you to the "debate" construct. Since, in fact, instances of the use of the Mishnaic-"debate" construct are more commonly found in Tosefta—Tosefta's passages will sometimes supply debates for Mishnah's "disputes" where Mishnah has none—it follows that citations of Scripture *within* "debates" are also more commonly seen in Toseftan materials. Remember the "debate"? "Debates" always rely upon, and are attached to, an antecedent "dispute" between two named rabbinic authorities, or between a named rabbinic personage and "the sages" (or, more rarely, between a named rabbinic figure and an anonymously conveyed rule-sentence). "Disputes"-*cum*-"debates" are typically structured something like this:

> a -circumstances of case;
> b -Rabbi r says + ruling 1;
> c -and the sages say + (opposed) ruling 2.
> d -They said to him + brief rationale for ruling 2 (or brief counterreason to ruling 1);
> e -he said to them + brief rationale for ruling 1 (or brief counterreason to ruling 2).

In the foregoing schematization, lines a–c form the "dispute," and lines d and e constitute the "debate." In disputes the parties "say" things, in the present-participial form, while in debates the disputing parties "said" their rationales, in the third-person perfect tense, "to" the other party.

In the Seat of Moses

Now, you will remember that citations from Scripture sometimes fit into "debates." How? Scripture may be briefly cited within the rationale or counterreasoning. As I remarked about "debates" in chapter 4, such rationales or counterreasons are often brief analogical arguments. In fact, in subsequent chapters of this book on the Jerusalem and Babylonian Talmuds, you shall encounter various types of analogical arguments, because they are by far the preferred mode of argumentation in early rabbinic literature. Analogical arguments work by arguing that

–*a*, which has characteristic *x*,

–is more like *b*, which has characteristic *x'*,

–than it is like *c*, which has characteristic *y*;

–therefore, when making rulings,

–*a* should *be treated* more like *b*, and

–*a* should/need *not be treated* like *c*.

Stew (*a*), which has a lot of liquid and some solids (characteristic *x*), is more like soup (*b*), which also has a lot of liquid and more solids (characteristic x'), than it is like steak (*c*), which is mostly solid and has little liquid (characteristic *y*). Therefore, the table *should be* set with spoons for eating stew (*a*), just as the table is set with spoons for eating soup (*b*). And the table *need not* be set with knives and forks when serving stew (*a*), as it would be when serving steak (*c*).

Sometimes characteristics *x*, *x'*, and *y* in an Mishnaic or Toseftan analogical argument can be scriptural phrases or verses that Scripture itself has linked respectively to circumstances *a*, *b*, and *c*. In such instances, those scriptural phrases will be alluded to or explicitly cited as the determinative characteristics that one is comparing in these brief analogical arguments. Let me rehearse a Mishnah passage, m. Negaʿim 10:2, already presented in chapter 4, that does precisely this.

The overall theme of Tractate Negaʿim, of which m. Negaʿim 10:2 treats a subtopic, is skin diseases that render one "unclean." A focus of both the Tractate and the relevant verses in Scripture is symptomology, helping one accurately to identify these skin diseases. One such disease that is the concern of the biblical book of Leviticus is the "bright spot," a symptom of which is a "bald spot" emerging where normal hair usually grows when the skin is healthy. As the "bright spot" begins to develop, the hairs, which will presumably soon fall out, first appear abnormal, an early symptom of the underlying skin disease. Here then is Mishnah Tractate Negaʿim 10:2, as previously presented in chapter 4.

m. Negaʿim 10:2 (translation my own)

- a. 1. "Thin yellow hair [in the circumference of the bald spot] renders unclean,
    2. [whether the thin yellow hairs] are gathered [together within the spot],
    3. or spread [throughout],
    4. [whether] forming a circle [within in the spot],
    5. or not forming a circle,
    6. [whether] preceding [the bald spot's appearance],
    7. or not preceding [the bald spot's appearance],"

    the words of Rabbi Judah.

- b. **Rabbi Simeon says,** "[The thin yellow hair] renders unclean only [when] preceding [the bald spot's appearance]."

- c. **Said Rabbi Simeon,**
    1. "And [lo] it is reasonable [from an argument *a fortiori*];
    2. if [in the case of the appearance of] white hairs, [with respect to] which [the presence in the affected spot of] other [normal-colored] hair does not forefend from its [ie., the white hair's] power [to render one unclean], [nonetheless, the white hair] renders [one] unclean only [when the bald spot's appearance] has changed,
    3. [then in the case of the appearance of] thin yellow hair, [with respect to] which [the presence in the affected spot of] other [normal-colored] hair does forefend from its [i.e., the thin yellow hair's] power [to render one unclean], is it [then] not [all the more so] reasonable that [thin yellow hair] renders [one] unclean only [when the bald spot's appearance] has changed?"

- d. **Said [to him] Rabbi Judah,**
    1. "[In] every case where one is required to say [i.e, rule, that abnormally colored hair renders one unclean only when the bald spot's appearance] has changed, it [Scripture explicitly] stated [that the appearance] changed (see Leviticus 13:3)

2. But [concerning] the bald spot—as it is said [in Scripture] concerning it, 'and there not be in it yellow hair' (Leviticus 13:32)—

3. [the appearance therein of yellow hair] renders unclean [whether the bald spot's appearance] changed,

4. or has not changed."

Again, I will not immerse you in the legal details of this arcane area of biblical and Mishnaic purity law. Rather, I point out that sections a–b of the passage form a typically structured "dispute," and sections c–d form a well-structured Mishnaic debate. Both rationales presented in the debate portion of the passage—one "said" to be Rabbi Simeon's reasoning, and the other "said" to be Rabbi Judah's—are types of analogical arguments; what we earlier called "characteristic" features of cases are compared in order to determine whether the case at hand should be treated as more or less analogous to some other circumstance where practice is well established. In the argument "said" to be Judah's, those "characteristics" are references to scriptural data. And this is how reference to, or citation of, Scripture can be normatively used in "debates" in Mishnah and Tosefta.

Our review is complete; "now, for something completely different,"[27] a formalized literary-rhetorical construct sometimes (although rarely) found in Tosefta that uses scriptural citation in a manner that begins to resemble what is routinely encountered in Halakhic-Midrashic documents of the early rabbinic legal corpus. In presenting this *Halakhic-Midrashic*-like, formalized structure, I am going to reverse my normal practice of first providing a schematic structure of the literary-rhetorical construct and then presenting an exemplary (real) passage. I think, in this case, the schematization of the structure will be more intelligible to you *after* you have seen an actual exemplar. As I have done throughout this chapter of Toseftan constructs, I will first present the Mishnah passage, of which the Tosefta text is a parallel. We return to what you should now recognize as a very familiar Mishnah passage, Mishnah Tractate Bekhorot 1:1; except this time I shall present 1:1a (presented before), followed immediately by 1:1b (not yet presented). Tosefta Bekhorot 1:1a–1b follows my presentation of the Mishnah.

---

27. To borrow shamelessly the name of one of the original Monte Python TV shows and one of their first movies.

Tosefta

m. Bekhorot 1:1a–1b (translation my own[28])

1:1a

    a. 1. He who purchases the foetus of an ass of a Gentile[, and the foetus when born will be a firstborn, if it is a male],

       2. and he who sells to him [the Gentile, the foetus of an ass],

       3. even though it [such a sale] is not permitted

       4. and he who forms a partnership with him [the Gentile, so that they co-own the foetus],

       5. and he who receives [a pregnant ass] from him [a Gentile],

       6. and he who gives [a pregnant ass] to him [a Gentile] in trust—

    b. is exempt from the law of the firstborn,

    c. as it said, "[Of an Israelite "] (Numbers 3:13),

    d. but not of others.

1:1b

    a. Priests and Levites are exempt [from the law of the firstling of an ass]

    b. from an argument *a fortiori*:

    c. If [the Levites] redeemed that [animal] of an Israelite in the wilderness, it is logical that they should [automatically have] redeem[ed] their own.

By now you should be able to recite m. Bekhorot 1:1a by heart (in your sleep). But look now at 1:1b, which you have not previously seen. Line a of 1:1b is a very laconic Mishnaic rule-sentence. The case at hand is merely "priests and Levites"; the ruling is "are exempt" (one word, a plural present participle). Everything else that would render this rule-sentence intelligible must be interpolated by the reader of Mishnah. The rule-sentence at line a of 1:1b is followed by a rationale for it, signaled formulaically at line b, and given at line c. An argument *a fortiori*, like its opposite, an argument *a miniori*, is a common type of analogical argument. For example, here is an argument *a miniori* that a new teenage driver might unleash on a parent:

    if you let me drive on freeways (on which accidents are more likely to be fatal),

28. Based on Lightstone, *Rhetoric*, 175.

then certainly you should let me drive on city streets (on which accidents are less likely to be fatal and more likely to result in damage to property only).

But at m. Bekhorot 1:1b the analogues being proposed in the argument have to do with a story in Scripture (see Numbers 3:45) in which the Levites become a sacerdotal class by replacing the firstborn Israelite men, who by some more ancient, Middle Eastern or Israelite social-cultural convention should have formed the cadre of priestly-sacerdotal functionaries. In that biblical account, curiously, the Levites' animals redeem the Israelite's animals too. Odd, but so it is in the Scripture's narrative. So, here, restated, is the analogical argument of line c of m. Bekhorot 1:1b:

> if a Levite's animal could effect the redemption of an Israelite's animal in the Wilderness at the time of Moses' leadership, as per God's instructions for the consecration of the Levites, then all the more so, thereafter, should a Levite's animal be able to redeem itself (that is, the Levite's animal does not need to be redeemed by substituting a lamb for it).

Frankly, I find the argument of the teenage driver a more convincing argument. As to line c of m. Bekhorot 1:1b, while a biblical story in Numbers 3 lies behind line c's argument, Scripture is never actually cited as a proof-text in the argument.

Now, t. Bekhorot 1:1a–1b, with language that is the verbatim parallel of Mishnah in boldface, as usual. But this time watch for language in SMALL CAPS, because, as I will remark latter, that language falls into the category of formulaic, "signpost" language that serves to structure Halakhic-Midrashic-like constructs.

t. Bekhorot 1:1a–1b (translation my own[29])

1:1a

    a. 1. **He who purchases the foetus of an ass of a Gentile**[, and the foetus when born will be a firstborn, if it is a male],

       2. **and he who sells to him** [the Gentile, the foetus of an ass],

       3. even though it [such a sale] is not permitted

       4. **and he who forms a partnership with him** [the Gentile, so that they co-own the foetus],

       5. [that is,] he who gives to him within a partnership

---

29. Based on Lightstone, *Rhetoric*, 190–91.

> 6. and he who receives [a pregnant ass] from him [a Gentile],
>
> 7. and he who gives [a pregnant ass] to him [a Gentile] in trust—
>
> b. is exempt from the law of the firstborn,
>
> c. as it said, "Of an Israelite" (Numbers 3:13),
>
> d. but not of others.

1:1b
> a. And so you [must] say in the case of (*ve-khein ata omer b*) priests and in the case of Levites [namely, that they are not liable for the laws of the redemption of the firstling in the case of unclean animals, as per m. Bekhorot 1:1b].
>
> b. Because since (*mi-pnei she*) the priests and the Levites are liable in the case of [the firstling of] a clean animal [as stated in m. Bekhorot 2:1], one might (*yakhol*) [think] them to be liable [also] in the case of [the firstling of] an unclean animal [for which, incidentally, we are explicitly told in m. Bekhorot 1:1b that Levites are not liable].
>
> c. Scripture [however] says (*tilmod lomar*): "Of humankind and of animal-kind" (Exodus 13:2; Numbers 18:15)—
>
> d. that which applies to you in the case of humankind applies to you in the case of animal-kind.
>
> e. That which does not apply to you in the case of humankind does not apply to you in the case of animal-kind.
>
> f. [Thus] they exempted (*yatz'u*) the Levites from the law of the firstling of an unclean beast.
>
> g. But they [Israelites] give the redemption for [an Israelite] firstborn son and the redemption for the firstling of an ass to the priests only [and not to either a priest or a Levite, despite the fact that priests and Levites are similarly exempted by m. Bekhorot 1:1b].

I suspect that you must be asking yourself, What the . . . [supply your choice of expletive] is going on here? It is easy; you just have not seen something like this before. It is just another formula-driven literary-rhetorical construct, structured with stock language that functions as signposts. Signposts tell you where you are and what to expect ahead. The signpost language marks the parts of the structure, as follows:

In the Seat of Moses

a. AND SO YOU [must] SAY IN THE CASE OF + statement of established ruling 1;

b. BECAUSE, SINCE + statement of related ruling 2,

c. ONE MIGHT (*yakhol*) [think] + ruling 1 is not the case;

d. SCRIPTURE [however] SAYS (*tilmod lomar*) + citation of scriptural verse,

e. With or without analogical argument using the data of the verse;

f. [Thus] THEY EXEMPTED (or THEY INCLUDED) + restatement in short form of ruling 1.

The signpost language that I have placed in SMALL CAPS has its variations, and the variations of it may be seen in other similarly structured passages in Tosefta, in the Halakhic Midrashim, and in those *beraitot* cited in the Talmuds that display Halakhic-Midrashic-like form and structure. You will find all of the variations easily recognizable, especially after you have worked through the next chapter. So, do not worry. For now, let us look at the inner structure of the construct just presented, as exemplified by t. Bekhorot 1:1b.

The whole point of the structure is to demonstrate that some (sometimes analogical) argument *from Scripture* is required to establish the appropriate rule—at t. Bekhorot 1:1b, to establish that priests and Levites are exempt from the law of the firstling of an ass, which is an unclean species—(often) because without the that argument from Scripture one might *logically, but mistakenly,* argue (sometimes analogically) that the rule is otherwise. In our passage the appropriate rule is alluded to at the outset, but not fully stated. Why only alluded to? Because it is stated elsewhere, namely, in m. Bekhorot 1:1b. The "logical-but-mistaken" argument for the opposite, inappropriate ruling follows. It is an argument from analogy. And what is the analogous circumstance and ruling that leads one to what will ultimately be shown to be the wrong position? It is a ruling about priests' and Levites' liability for firstlings of *clean* animals. Where does the latter come from? From m. Bekhorot 2:1b—that is, from the very next chapter of Mishnah Bekhorot. Next in our Halakhic-Midrashic-like structure comes the citation of the verse from Scripture that will save the day, by providing a scriptural basis for arguing our way back to the appropriate ruling alluded to (or stated) at the outset of the structure. In Halakhic-Midrashic-like constructs, SCRIPTURE SAYS (*tilmod lomar,* but now often vocalized *talmud lomar*) is often—I cannot say always—the formulaic language used to preface a citation of Scripture, as opposed to what you are used to seeing so far, "as it is said" (*she-ne'enar*). The Scripture cited forms the basis for a different analogical argument that reestablishes the normative and probative status of the ruling with which we began: priests and Levites are exempt from the law of the firstling of an ass, which is an unclean animal.

Before leaving this exemplar of the use of a Halakhic-Midrashic-like construct at t. Bekhorot 1:1b, I would like briefly to turn our attention to the relationship of this Toseftan passage to its parallel(s) in Mishnah. First, I want to recall that the opening line of the Tosefta passage is completely unintelligible on its own. "And *so* you must say" refers to nothing that precedes it Tosefta. But it certainly refers to some rule-statementf, which it does not itself supply. That rule-seentence is found in Mishnah, at m. Bekhorot 1:1b. *In situ*, then, Tosefta relies on Mishnah for an intelligible context,[30] and without Mishnah open beside the Tosefta, the reader would be lost. Second—and we have not yet seen this before in any of our sample Toseftan passages—t. Bekhorot 1:1b expressly refers to another Mishnaic ruling from *elsewhere* in Mishnah (in this case, from m. Bekhorot 2:1b) in composing a passage that *in situ* is intended to illuminate m. Bekhorot 1:1b. Tosefta is "cross-referencing" two Mishnah passages separated by a complete "chapter." Why is this significant? Because *in situ* this Tosefta passage is doing dual duty. On the one hand, t. Bekhorot 1:1b argues that without the argument based on Scripture, logic alone might have driven those who composed m. Bekhorot 1:1b to the opposite and incorrect ruling, namely, that priests and Levites *are liable* for the firstling of an ass (which they are in fact not). So, Tosefta is trying to tell us that those who composed m. Bekhorot 1:1b would have had to rely on scriptural argument to arrive at their ruling, if they knew and agreed with the ruling that appears to m. Bekhorot 2:1b. Else, m. Bekhorot 1:1b would have *reasonably* concluded in the basis of m. Bekhorot 2:1b that priests and Levites are liable for the firstling of an ass. One the other hand, t. Bekhorot 1:1b is also engaged in a kind of Mishnah-text criticism of a certain type. Why do I *need* Mishnah *explicitly* to provide us with the ruling at 1:1b? Because, again, if they had not, one might have reasoned from m. Bekhorot 2:1b to a false conclusion about priests' and Levites' liability for the firstling of an ass. Therefore, m.

---

30. And without Mishnah as that intelligible context, the reader of Tosefta would have necessarily to rely on some other appropriate source for a topically relevant rule-statement. Such an alternative source is not extant.

Bekhorot 1:1b had to be *explicit* that they are *not* liable for the firstling of an ass. Is this not a bit of text criticism of Mishnah on the part of this Tosefta passage? I think so. And similar types of text-critical analyses of Mishnah are found in the Talmuds, especially the Babylonian Talmud, which routinely asks of a Mishnah passage, "Why did Mishnah [explicitly] have to teach us this item?" Tosefta is, then, a harbinger of things to come in a number of respects. And why not, if Tosefta, taken *in situ* as an aid to Mishnah study, is a first step on the way to the Talmuds' sustained analyses of the Mishnah text!? Tosefta's content and literary-rhetorical constructs are building blocks in the development of early rabbinic legal literature from the Mishnah to the Talmuds, just as they are for you in building familiarity with these early rabbinic formalized, literary-rhetorical structures.

PUTTING IT ALL TOGETHER: MISHNAH AND TOSEFTA, SO SIMILAR, BUT SIGNIFICANTLY DIFFERENT

I began this chapter with the claim that virtually all of the literary-rhetorical constructs used in Mishnah are also found in Tosefta, making Tosefta the most Mishnah like of all early rabbinic legal literature. Yes, Tosefta displays perhaps a greater penchant to supply attributions, to provide disputes, where the parallel Mishnah passage has only anonymous rule-sentences, and to provide disputes with debates, where the correlative Mishnah text has only a dispute. But Tosefta's greater penchant to do these things is expressed by using literary-rhetorical forms and structures that are well attested in Mishnah. So, this chapter needed to introduce you to only two "new" literary-rhetorical constructs found in Tosefta (and virtually absent from Mishnah): the redefined/redirected dispute, and the Halakhic-Midrashic-like structure. And I cannot even say that the latter is rampant in Tosefta; only that it is found in Tosefta.

Notwithstanding the foregoing, I have periodically asserted unequivocally that Tosefta differs from Mishnah in literary-rhetorical terms, and I have stated that this is a "difference that makes a difference." Have you sensed that difference in the sample passages already presented in this chapter? Are you yet able to articulate that difference? That difference lies in two related observations, one which you may have already discerned, the other which you will not (yet) have been able to observe, although it is related to the first.

One is that so many—between two-thirds and four-fifths—of Tosefta's passages are not fully intelligible on their own but rely on the content of their correlative Mishnah passages in order to be completely intelligible. You have already seen this aspect of Tosefta's dependence on Mishnah in the exemplar Toseftan passages presented earlier. And related to this dependence is the frequent repetition of phrases, in the exact same language, in Tosefta and in its parallel passage in Mishnah. Someone copied from someone. And while at times the Toseftan passage may preserve the earlier articulation of the rabbinic legal tradition, it is overwhelmingly the case that *in its current formulation* the language of the Tosefta passage has been copied from the parallel Mishnah passage. In short, Tosefta (or minimally the two-thirds to four-fifths of it that more directly relates to Mishnah's content) is in its current formulation a "derivative" and "dependent" document, rather than an "independent," "autonomous" statement. In contrast, Mishnah is formulated as such an independent, autonomous statement, even though, as I spelled out in chapter 4, the reader of Mishnah requires much antecedent knowledge to make sense of it, and even though a great deal of Tosefta serves to aid Mishnah study. Most of Tosefta cannot be intelligibly read without Mishnah open beside the reader. Mishnah can be intelligibly be read on its own, even though much prior knowledge is demanded of the reader and even though most Tosefta passages serve to aid the reader of Mishnah by supplying more attributions to named authorities, precedent stories, disputes and debates, etc.

The other "difference that makes a difference" will, as I said, not yet have been evident to you, although once I describe it, it will make eminent sense in light of difference number 1. The literary unity, coherence, and sense of "flow" of Tosefta's "chapters" are extremely diminished in comparison to Mishnah's "chapters." Tosefta's "chapters" by comparison are just more disjointed. Now, upon reflection, this should make perfect sense. Why? If most of the individual passages of Tosefta depend in significant ways upon their parallel Mishnah passages for intelligible contexts—for their very intelligibility—then it follows that these Tosefta passages are, in literary terms, much less dependent upon the Tosefta passages that precede them for their intelligibility. In other words, Mishnah's "chapters" are chapters in a way that Tosefta's "chapters" are not.

How can I make this important distinction clearer for you? Simply by recalling what makes a good paragraph of English prose, and what gives a section of any well-written essay its unity and coherence. In a good paragraph, each sentence is a complete thought, and each sentence logically follows upon those that preceded it. And paragraphs are similarly ordered logically so that there is logical flow from one to the next, each building upon the thoughts of the former. A Mishnah "chapter," as you saw in chapter 4, is like an extended paragraph or like a mini-essay. But how can a Tosefta "chapter" appear similar, when (a) its units often (even if not universally) logically follow from, and depend upon, some passage in Mishnah, more than they do upon the preceding Tosefta passages, and when (b) many Tosefta passages are not even "complete thoughts" on their own but require in their current formulation content supplied from Mishnah to be made into complete thoughts? All this is to say, strong "chapter-ness" is not a strong feature of Tosefta; and while Tosefta aids Mishnah study, and the document was promulgated for this purpose, it is darn difficult to read Tosefta without Mishnah. So, my advice—as novice readers of early rabbinic literature, do not tax yourselves to try to read Tosefta on its own. It would be frustrating and less rewarding.

A FINAL SELF-GUIDED EXERCISE IN READING TOSEFTA

If you want to explore further the foregoing claims for yourself, the remaining last pages of this chapter on Tosefta offer you the opportunity. Below, I provide a translation of the entire first "chapter" of Tosefta Gittin, t. Gittin 1:1–2:4,[31] about half of which you have already seen, but in piecemeal fashion, as examples of how Tosefta goes about its business, using largely-Mishnaic-like literary rhetorical constructs to do so. I suggest you do three things in three passes through this Tosefta "chapter."

> (1) Identify the literary-rhetorical constructs and conventions used. For example, look for laconic rule-sentences that show economy of language, for repetition of phrases, variation of factors to spin out a series of related hypothetical cases, for cadence, assonance, and alliteration. Search out attributions to named rabbinic authorities and to "the sages." Look at the use

---

31. Remember, "chapters" in Mishnah and Tosefta are topical units that only *roughly* correspond to how the medieval scribes who copied these documents chose to subdivide tractates into chapters and constituent passages. Consequently, the first "chapter" of Tosefta Tractate Gittin, t. Gittin 1:1–2:4 (as per the divisions of the text of Tosefta printed with the standard Vilna edition of the Baylonian Talmud) parallels the content of the first "chapter" of Mishnah Tractate Gittin, m. Gittin 1:1—2:2.

of attributions to named rabbinic authorities in independent attributed sayings, in "disputes," in "debates," in any "redefined/redirected disputes," and in precedent stories. Are there appeals to Scripture in the Tosefta passage, and if so, what literary-rhetorical structure do they take?

(2) Look for the ways in which the constituent passages of Tosefta's "chapter" relate to the passages of the first "chapter" of Mishnah Tractate Gittin, provided in full near the end of chapter 4. (To aid you, I have specified for each passage in Tosefta the Mishnah passage to which the Toseftan unit relates.) Does much of the language of Tosefta equal the language of Mishnah? (Here, again, you have help, as I have placed in boldface phrases and words in Tosefta that exactly parallel language in Mishnah.) Ask yourself, does the Tosefta passage stand on its own as a completely self-contained, intelligible unit, or does having the corresponding Mishnah passage open beside the Tosefta passage provide the latter with valuable context or make the Toseftan parallel more intelligible? If each Tosefta passage were read, *in situ*, as an aid to Mishnah study, as we know they were once Mishnah study became the central document and focus of the "core curriculum" of early rabbinic circles, how does the Toseftan passage relate to its parallel Mishnah passage? *In situ*, does it (a) cite and explicate Mishnah, (b) expand upon, fill out, and extend Mishnah, or (c) stand largely independent of Mishnah's content and just relate generally to the topical agenda of the Mishnah? These three alternatives correspond to Jacob Neusner's classification of Tosefta passages as either commentary, complement (in the sense of "completing"), or supplement to Mishnah passages.

(3) Finally, and perhaps more difficult for a novice reader of Mishnah and Tosefta, consider for yourself whether t. Gittin 1:1–2:4 exhibits stronger or weaker "chapter-ness" than its parallel Mishnah "chapter," cited in full at the end of chapter 4 of this volume. Compare them for the type of unity, coherence, and flow one would seek out in a well-articulated paragraph of English prose and in a section of an essay. Is the Tosefta "chapter" "tight"? At the end of chapter 4, I pointed out that Mishnah "chapters" not only exhibit topical unity but also achieve unity by using the repetition of phrases, words, and even grammatical tenses and morphology to help "mark out" a "chapter." Ask yourself whether Tosefta does the same, or whether "chapter-ness" in

Tosefta is more derivative of the "chapter-ness" of the corresponding Mishnah "chapter."

The first "chapter" of Tosefta Gittin, t. Gittin 1:1—2:4, follows. Again, boldface type equals language found in m. Gittin 1:1–2:2, unless I have explicitly indicated that it has come from elsewhere in Mishnah. Language in italics reflects equivalent language from elsewhere in Tosefta Gittin, as indicated. For each passage of the Tosefta "chapter," I have designated in parentheses the Mishnah passage to which it relates. This will help you keep "an eye on" the relevant passages in m. Gittin's first "chapter" (presented at end of chapter 4), while you read this Tosefta "chapter."

t. Gittin 1:1–2:4 (translation my own[32])

1:1 (relates to m. Gittin 1:1–2)

> **He who brings a writ from** Syria **is like** him who brings a writ from outside the Land; **it is required that he say: In my presence it was written, and in my presence it was signed.**
>
> From trans-Jordan—**is like him who brings from the Land of Israel,** and **it is not required that he say: In my presence it was written, and in my presence it was signed.**

1:2 (relates to m. Gittin 1:3)

> **He who brings a writ from a Mediterranean province, and cannot say: In my presence it was written, and in my presence it was signed**—if it is possible to **make it stand on its signatures, it is fit**; and if not, **it is unfit.**
>
> They used to say, They did not say that **he should say: In my presence it was written, and in my presence it was signed,** in order to be stringent, rather to be lenient upon him.

1:3 (relates to m. Gittin 1:3)

> **He who brings a writ from a Mediterranean province**, and it was not **written in his presence**, and it was not **signed in his presence**—Lo, this person returns it to his locale, and he convenes a court, and it **makes it stand upon its signatures**, and **he brings** it and says: An agent of the court am I.

---

32. Based on Lightstone, *Mishnah*, 82–86, with collaboration of M. Mamfredis.

In **the Land of Israel,** an agent appoints an agent. R. Simeon b. Gamaliel says: An agent does not appoint an agent as regards writs.

1:4 (relates to m. Gittin 1:1)

In the beginning, they used to say: **From province to province.** They revisited to say: From neighbourhood to neighbourhood. **R. Simeon b. Gamaliel says: Also from hegemony to hegemony.**

1:5 (relates to m. Gittin 1:3)

There is a stringency as regards **the Mediterranean province** that is not so as regards **the Land of Israel,** and with regards **the Land of Israel** that is not so as regards **the Mediterranean province.**

Since **he who brings a writ from a Mediterranean province—it is required that he say: In my presence it was written, and in my presence it was signed; if there are regarding it challengers, it shall be made to stand on its signatures.** He who brings a writ from the Land of Israel cannot say: **In my presence it was written, and in my presence it was signed;** if there are on it [the signatures of] witnesses, **it shall be made to stand on its signatures.**

1:6 (relates to m. Gittin 1:3)

How [do they proceed when] they said, **it shall be made to stand on its signatures?** When they said: This is our handwriting—**it is fit**. But we do not recognize either the man or the woman—**it is fit**. This is not our handwriting, but others testify that it is their handwriting, or their handwriting was adduced from another place—**it is fit**.

1:7 (relates to m. Gittin 1:2)

R. Meir says, Acco and its hinterland **is like the Land of Israel as regards writs**. And the sages say, **Acco** and its hinterland are like outside the Land as regards writs.

It once happened concerning someone from Kefar Sissi, who brought before Rabbi Ishmael a writ of divorce. He said to him: Even so, you are required **to say, In my presence it was written and in my presence it was signed**, and it does not require witnesses. After he left, said before him Rabbi Illai: Rabbi, Kefar Sissi is the territory of **the Land of Israel**, closer to Sepphoris than to **Acco**. He said to him, Since the matter is settled with a leniency, it is settled.

In the Seat of Moses

1:8 (relates to m. Gittin 1:4–5a)

> R. Judah says: Even though its two witnesses are Kutim [Samaritans], it **is fit**.
>
> Said R. Judah: [**The following**] **incident occurred: They brought before R. Gamaliel to Kefar Otnai a writ of divorce, and its witnesses were Kutim [i.e., Samaritans], and he declared it fit.**

1:9 (relates to m. Gittin 1:5b)

> **Any bonds issuing from [court] bureaus of idolaters—even though their signatories are idolaters—R. Aqiva declares fit** in the case of all of them, and sages declare [them] unfit in the case of **writs of divorce and** in the case of **manumission papers of slaves.**
>
> Said R. Eleazar b. R. Yose: Thus said R. Simeon b. Gamaliel to them, the elders at Sidon: Rabbi Aqiva and the sages did not dispute **concerning bonds issuing from [court] bureaus of idolaters,** that **even though their signatories are idolaters** [they] **are fit.** Concerning what did they dispute? Concerning [those] **that were done in a nonprofessional tribunal—**[concerning] which R. Aqiva **declares fit** in the case of all of them, and the sages declare [them] unfit in the case of **writs of divorce and** in the case of **manumission papers of slaves.**
>
> Rabbi Simeon b. Gamaliel says: Even **writs of divorce and manumission papers of slaves are fit** in the case of a place [in] which an Israelite does not sign.

1:10 (relates to m. Gittin 1:6a)

> Said Rabbi Eleazer: We said to **R. Meir**: For what [reason do you hold your view that] **They benefit** a slave **when not in his [or her] presence?**
>
> **He said to us**: It is but **a liability [or obligation]** upon him [or her]. For if he [or she] was the slave of a priest, [then] it is the case [that] one **renders** him [or her] **unfit for [eating a] heave-offering** [that is owned by his/her priestly master].
>
> We said to him: And lo, is it not [the case that] **if he [the priest] should wish not to feed** him, and not to support him, the **authority** is his [to decide].
>
> He said to us: And lo, is it not [the case that] **a slave of a priest that fled and a wife of a priest that rebelled—lo, these [persons] eat of [the priest's] heave offering** [see t. Terumah 10:8]!? But [with

Tosefta

respect to] a wife it is not so! Rather they owe her food, and they declare her unfit for (lit., from) [eating] heave-offering.

1:11 (relates to m. Gittin 1:6b, and to content at m. Gittin 6:1, paralleled at t. Gittin 4(=6):1–2)

> **One who says: Give this maneh to so-and-so,** which I owe him, [or] give this **maneh to so-and-so,** [which is] a collateral deposit, which he has [placed] in my possession (lit., hand), [or] take this **maneh to so-and-so,** [which is] a collateral deposit, which he has [placed] in my possession—**If one wishes to retract, one may** not **retract,** and one is liable for it, until [the other] one shall receive what is his [or hers].
>
> [One who says:] **Take** this **maneh to so-and-so,** [or] give this **maneh to so-and-so,** [or take this deed of gift **to so-and-so,** [or] give this deed of gift **to so-and-so,** if one wishes to retract, one may retract.**
>
> [If] one went and found that [the intended beneficiary] **had died, one shall return** [in Hebrew, same as, "one may retract"] it to the one who gave [it]. If [that person too] died [in the interim], one returns it to his [or her] heirs.
>
> [One who says:] *make so-and-so receive* (boldfaced italics = language at m. Gittin 6:1 and its paralleled at t. Gittin 4[=6]:1) this **maneh,** [or] *make so-and-so benefit* (italics = language at t. Gittin 4[=6]:1) from this gift, [or] *make* **so-and-so** *receive* this deed of gift, [or] *make* **so-and-so** *benefit* from this deed of gift, **if one wishes to retract, one may** not **retract.**
>
> [If] one went and found that [the intended beneficiary] had **died,** one shall return [it] to the one who gave it to him [to transport].
>
> And if [one sought to return it] **after** the **death** [of the one who gave it to him to deliver], he shall return [it] to the heirs, since one does not benefit the dead person **after death.**
>
> [One who says:] *carry* (t. Gittin 4[=6]:2b) this **maneh to so-and-so,** [or] *bear* (italics=t. Gittin 4[=6]:2b) *this* **maneh to so-and-so,** [or] *let* this **maneh** *be* (italics=t. Gittin 4[=6]:2b) for **so-and-so** by your [own] hands, and [the intended benefactor] **died,** if the heirs wished to compel him [to return the money], they may not.
>
> And one need not say [i.e., all the more so] as regards **one who says:** *Make* him *benefit* (italics = language at t. Gittin 4[=6]:1), and as regards **one who says: Make** him **receive** (boldface=m. Gittin 6:1).

2:1 (related to m. Gittin 2:1a)

One who brings a writ [of divorce] from a Mediterranean province, and gave it to her [the wife to be divorced], and did not **say: in my presence it was written, and in my presence it was signed**—lo, this one takes it from her, even after three years, returns, and gives it to her, and shall say to her: **In my presence it was written and in my presence it was signed.**

2:2 (relates to m. Gittin 2:1a, supplementing it with matters not taken up in, but relevant to, m. Gittin 1:1:1–2:1's content)

A wife is trusted when she shall say: This writ, which you gave to me, [which] is torn, is fit, [or which] is torn, is unfit (see t. Gittin 7:11 and t. Baba Batra 11:11). [If] there was torn in it a tear of a court, it is unfit. R. Simeon says: [If the wife has stated that the torn writ is fit,] one glues [together] the torn [pieces], and gives [it back] to her, and **says** to her: **In my presence it was written and in my presence it was signed.**

2:3 (relates to m. Gittin 2:1b)

One says: In my presence it was written, and one [i.e., another] **says: In my presence it was signed**—[the writ] is unfit.

Two [bring a writ and] **say: In our presence it was written, and one says: In my presence it was signed**—R. Judah declares [the writ] **fit** in this [instance].

2:4 (relates to m. Gittin 2:2)

R. Simeon says: Even [if] **one wrote it** (Mishnah's language is, "it was written) **today** (Mishnah's language is, "in the daytime'), **and one signed it** (Mishnah's language is, "it was signed") **on the morrow** (Mishnah's language is, "in the night time")—[**the writ**] **is fit.**

[If] one wrote it in this town, one should not sign it in another town, and [i.e., but] if one should [have happened to] sign it in another town, it **is fit.**

[If] one wrote it in the Land [of Israel], and one signed it outside the Land [of Israel], **it is required that he should say: In my presence it was written, and in my presence it was signed.**

[If] one wrote it outside the Land [of Israel], and one signed it inside the Land [of Israel], **it is not required that he should say: In my presence it was written, and in my presence it was signed.**

Tosefta

What have you observed and found? Here is some of what I observe. First, virtually all of the literary-rhetorical constructs and conventions used in this Tosefta "chapter" are Mishnah-like, with one blatant caveat, which I shall articulate a little later. We may observe standard declarative rule-sentences that are very similar to Mishnah's, attributed sayings not in disputes (e.g., Simeon's at t. Gittin 2:2), disputes (e.g., at t. Gittin 1:3, 1:4, 1:7 and 1:9), a debate (e.g., at t. Gittin 1:10), precedent stories (e.g., at t. Gittin 1:7, 1:8). As one often finds in Mishnah, specific phrases are repeated, systematically varied, permuted and concatenated to spin out a series of related cases on which to rule. Tosefta Gittin 1:11 is an excellent example of such a process of spinning out of hypothetical cases by the systematic variation of a few terms. It begins to rival Mishnah's "spun-out" series of cases in Mishnah Tractate Bekhorot 1 (presented in chapters 3 and 4) regarding first one, then two female asses, that have not before borne young, that give birth to combinations of male and female offspring. One finds a "redefined/redirected dispute" in this Tosefta chapter (at t. Gittin 1:9); as you learned earlier, such "redefined/redirected disputes" are found in Tosefta but appear relatively infrequently in Mishnah. Finally, I would point out that not a single appeal to Scripture, using any of the formalized, standard ways of doing so, is found in this Tosefta "chapter." (Nor, admittedly, does any appeal to Scripture appear in the parallel Mishnah "chapter" either.) In all, we have ample indication in t. Gittin 1:1–2:4 of just how Mishnaic-like the literary-rhetorical constructs and structures of Tosefta are. So, the claim with which we commenced chapter 5—mastering Mishnah's literary-rhetorical conventions is a firm foundation for reading Tosefta—is well illustrated in t. Gittin 1:1–2:4.

Second, it is hard to find in our Tosefta "chapter" any passage that does not link to the corresponding "chapter" in Mishnah in some fashion. Undoubtedly, one observes that, *throughout*, the two "chapters" share language in a manner that cannot be fortuitous—a point I made earlier when we examined some sample Tosefta passages. But the links between the "chapters" go beyond shared phrases. They go over the same topical and subtopical ground, and, roughly speaking, take up those topics and subtopics in the same order. The Mishnah "chapter" in question (see the end of chapter 4) takes up the following topics and subtopics in order:

m. Gittin 1:1–3

a) Topic: Required attestations when transporting a writ (of divorce) from outside the Land of Israel;

a.i) Subtopic: the requirement that the writ be written before and signed by witnesses, and that the bearer of the writ have witnessed both these acts, and that the bearer's declaration affirm the same;

a.ii) Subtopic: boundaries of the Land of Israel;

a.iii) Subtopic: the bearer of a writ (of divorce) from one place to another need not have witnessed the writing and signing of the writ before witnesses;

a.iv) Subtopic: the requirement of establishing the validity of the writ on the confirmation of the validity of witnesses' signatures.

m. Gittin 1:4–6

b) Topic: comparisons of writs of divorce and manumission declarations of slaves as regards legal processes;

b.i) Subtopic: the comparison as regards the bearer's capacity to declare having seen the document written and signed before the witnesses whose signatures appear on the document;

b.ii) Subtopic: the comparison as regards the witnesses being Samaritans;

b.iii) Subtopic: the comparison as regards writs issued in non-Jewish tribunals;

b.iv) Subtopic: comparison as regards the conditions under which the one who instructed the preparation of the writs may countermand these instructions and thereby halt the process;

b.v) Subtopic: comparison as regards cases where the one who instructed either the preparation and execution of such writs or the delivery of something of value, and parties to the process die before the process is completed.

m. Gittin 2:1

c) Topic: Cases where one or two bearers of the writ can only attest to having witnessed half of the process of writing and signing the writ before witnesses whose signatures appear on the document;

m. Gittin 2:2

Topic: Cases where the preparation and signing of the writ did not occur on the same day.

Tosefta

Do the successive passages of the Tosefta "chapter," t. Gittin 1:1—2:4, roughly follow the same sequence of topics and subtopics? Yes! On the other hand, the passages of the Tosefta "chapter" expend much more ink on some of Mishnah's topics and subtopics than on others. For example, subtopics b.iv and b.v receive an expansive treatment in t. Gittin 1:11. The few hypothetical cases in Mishnah are significantly spun out in Tosefta by positing, first, different language used by the person ordering the preparation and execution of the process and, second, different points at which one or another party to the process has died before its completion. The possibilities developed for the different language that could be used by the initiator of the process seem to draw on language contained in m. Gittin 6:1 (fully five "chapters" away in Mishnah Gittin), as well as upon language found in the Tosefta passages that parallel m. Gittin 6:1. On the other hand, by contrast, subtopic a.i is not really taken up in Tosefta at all; in fact, because it is not taken up, the very first passage of Tosefta lacks an intelligible context, which the reader can only discern by reading the Mishnah alongside the Tosefta (a point I made earlier).[33] Finally, only t. Gittin 2:2 does not explicate or expand upon one of the topics or subtopics of the parallel Mishnah "chapter," edifying as it may be. Nor, interestingly, does t. Gittin 2:2 share as much language with our Mishnah "chapter" as the other Tosefta passages do. Only the use of the repeated formula, "in my presence ... signed," serves to tie it to either the Mishnah "chapter" or to the rest of Tosefta "chapter" in which it appears. Could this formula have been worked into t. Gittin 2:2 to serve to integrate it into t. Gitten 1:1–2:4? An interesting question, because the necessity for the bearer of the writ to declare "in my presence ... signed" is entirely extraneous to the principal point of t. Gittin 2:2, which is the authority of the wife's declarations about the status and validity of her writ of divorce. Additionally, I would note that t. Gittin 2:3 adds nothing new as far as I can tell to its counterpart in Mishnah, other than providing slightly different wording for the same.

Moreover, at the risk of being repetitious, we witness throughout t. Gittin 1:1–2:4, the appearance of attributions to named authorities where Mishnah has none, or where Tosefta has attributed rulings to a different named authority than the attribution appearing in Mishnah. We also see disputes in this Tosefta "chapter" where Mishnah has declarative

---

33. Some medieval copyists actually place a goodly portion of the language m. Gittin 1:1 at the beginning of t. Gittin 1:1 and thereby provide that intelligible context within the Tosefta passage. See M.S. Zuckermandel's edition of the Erfurt manuscript of Tosefta and the commentary of S. Lieberman in *Tosefet Rishonim* for t. Gittin 1:1.

rule-sentences only, and a precedent story where Mishnah has none. And—lest you have forgotten—Tosefta has provided a redefined/redirected version of one of Mishnah's disputes (at t. Gittin 1:9).

Third, what can one say of the "chapter-ness" of this Toseftan "chapter"? It's complicated! Why? Because one's views are likely to be colored by how one chooses to account for four sustained features of this Toseftan "chapter," which are typical of the vast majority of Tosefta. They are, to repeat earlier assertions:

1) much language is shared by the parallel Mishnaic and Toseftan "chapters;

2) often (although not always) a Tosefta passage is not fully intelligible on its own and is rendered intelligible when read together with the corresponding passage in Mishnah;

3) not only is there significant topical correspondence between the Mishnah "chapters" and their Toseftan parallels, but also

4) the very order of topics and subtopics taken up in turn within a "chapter" of Tosefta usually follows the topical and subtopical order of the corresponding Mishnah "chapter."

How do these observations color *my* view of the "chapter-ness" of a Tosefta "chapter"? I am inclined to view a Tosefta chapter's "chapter-ness," not as a feature it possesses in its own right, that is, because of the work of Tosefta's own authors' attempts to imbue its "chapters" with unity, coherence, and flow. Rather I would tend to view the "chapter-ness" of a Tosefta "chapter" as largely derivative of, and dependent upon, the coherence, unity, and flow of the corresponding Mishnah "chapter."

Now the foregoing paragraph takes both you and me to the very door of exploring serious and compelling literary-historical issues about how Toseftan passages, chapters, and tractates came to be, and about whether these literary-historical processes affected not only the creation of Tosefta's passages but also of Mishnah's. It is not the purpose of this book to take you through that door. Nor is it in your interest that I do so. That said, however, the observations of the foregoing paragraphs do indeed reinforce one of the important lessons stressed repeatedly throughout this chapter, a lesson that will make your life easier whenever you confront a Tosefta passage. It is this: read Tosefta's passages and "chapters" with the corresponding Mishnah passages and "chapters" open before you, always!

In the next chapter, chapter 6, of this volume, you are about to enter the realm of a very different sort of early rabbinic legal literature, one in which, for the first time in this volume, biblical Scriptures, and specifically the books of Exodus, Leviticus, Numbers, and Deuteronomy, take center stage. I refer to the documents collectively known as the Halakhic Midrashim (*midrashei Halakha*). As in the transition from chapter 4 (on Mishnah) to chapter 5 (on Tosefta), your entrée to chapter 6 has already been facilitated by what you have learned so far about how early rabbinic texts periodically use Scripture to justify rulings and launch arguments from analogy. But in the documents of the Halakhic Midrashim, what until now happened episodically becomes ubiquitous, a literary-rhetorical shift that is dramatic indeed.

SUGGESTIONS FOR FURTHER READING

Fox, "Introducing Tosefta," 1–30.

Mandel, "The Tosefta," 316–35.

Neusner, *Tosefta: An Introduction*.

Neusner, "Describing Tosefta: A Systematic Account," 39–72.

6

Halakhic Midrash

THE PRINCIPAL LESSON OF THIS CHAPTER: HOW THE "OLD" AND FAMILIAR IS REFRAMED IN THE "NEW" AND ABOUT-TO-BECOME FAMILIAR

In this chapter on Halakhic midrash, you will encounter a very different type of early rabbinic legal literature than Mishnah and Tosefta. Once again, among the more important factors that give this literature its characteristic qualities are its more commonly used and distinctive, literary-rhetorical conventions. Familiarity, therefore, with these literary-rhetorical conventions provides the novice reader and expert alike with a basic roadmap and associated road-signage for navigating each and every passage of Halakhic midrash. In fact, in chapter 5 you and I have already examined a passage, t. Bekhorot 1:1b, that has taken us down that road a bit. You will remember that I called the formalized structure exhibited by t. Bekhorot 1:1b, Halakhic-Midrashic-*like*—this for reasons that will become apparent over the course of this chapter.

It is, however, not only chapter 5's discussion of the Halakhic-Midrashic-*like*, literary-rhetorical structure of t. Bekhorot 1:1b that paves the road for your reading of the chapter ahead. Most of everything else you have learned in chapters 4 and 5 does as well. In working through this book, one's previous good deeds do get rewarded. How so in this chapter?

Halakhic Midrash

In passage after passage of Halakhic Midrash you will recognize (and I will point out) literary-rhetorical conventions and constructs that liberally appear in Mishnah and Tosefta. But in the passages of the Halakhic Midrashim, you will see those now-familiar conventions and constructs inserted, almost holus-bolus, *within* new ones. It is these "new ones" that define what is Halakhic-Midrashic about the passages. The now-familiar (from Mishnah and Tosefta) is, in effect, "reframed" by their insertion into what is not yet familiar (in Halakhic midrash) but soon will be. And that reframing has to do, specifically, with making a statement or a series of related statements, over and over again in passage after passage, about the place of the study of Scripture in contemplating the Halakha, the life conducted in accordance with Torah-law as taught by the rabbis. By contrast, in Mishnah and Tosefta, Scripture's legal content was often left behind the scenes, and made explicit appearances in front of the curtain only episodically. In passages that are Halakhic-Midrashic in form, Scripture's content is always center stage and in the spotlight.

I have just remarked about the "reframing" in Halakhic-Midrashic passages of antecedent forms of early rabbinic expression. I am, furthermore, inclined also to say that this "reframing" is at the heart of the two more generally applicable lessons that I wish you to learn from this chapter's presentations. The first is that in each successive type of early rabbinic legal oeuvre, from Mishnah through to the Babylonian Talmud, major literary-rhetorical conventions from the "earlier" documents tend to be used in, and adapted to the specific needs of, the "later" documents. The second lesson is closely related to the first: this reuse and adaptation tends to happen precisely by the imposition of "newer" conventional literary-rhetorical "superstructures," into which elements displaying the "older" conventions are placed, and in which they are, as I have characterized matters, "re-framed." Typically, in normal discourse on subjects, when matters are "reframed" our understanding of them shifts. So too, as one looks at one type of early rabbinic legal document after another. As characteristic literary-rhetorical conventions are reused, and integrated into, new overarching constructs, comparable shifts take place in the *intellectual preoccupations and operations* that are engendered in the reader. What is demanded of the engaged reader, whether ancient or modern, shifts accordingly.

I realize that the foregoing comes dangerously close to proffering a literary-historical account of the development of early rabbinic legal literature and of its characteristic literary-rhetorical norms from Mishnah to the

Babylonian Talmud. As I have already said several times before, literary-historical issues are not the focus of this volume; in fact, these are issues I intentionally try to skirt or bracket. Nonetheless, the two lessons just articulated will make it easier for you to learn to decipher these ancient texts. It is, I maintain, much easier to learn to read, let us say, the Babylonian Talmud, once one has already become familiar with the more dominant literary-rhetorical conventions of Mishnah, Tosefta, and the Halakhic Midrashim, because of the way in which materials that look like the latter are included in the distinctively Talmudic compositions of the former.

I am now quite a bit ahead of myself. Let me take several steps back and begin again, first, with some clarification about the designations "Halakhic midrash" and "the Halakhic Midrashim."

IT'S ALL A MATTER OF CLASS: CLASSIFYING "HALAKHIC MIDRASH" AND "*THE* HALAKHIC MIDRASHIM"

By way of rehearsing some of what you have read in chapter 3, "Halakhic midrash" is a moniker for a class of early rabbinic legal *passages* (or "mini-compositions," if you will) that exhibit certain specific, formalized, literary-rhetorical structures. "Halakhic" is an anglicized adjective based on the Hebrew word "Halakha," which means "the way," as in "the way one is to follow and act in accordance with Torah." "Midrash" is the general term used to refer to various formalized rabbinic approaches to the explication of the Hebrew Scriptures for either legal (i.e., "Halakhic") purposes or for homiletical (i.e., "aggadic") ends. "Explication," I admit, is an ambiguous, wishy-washy term, and that ambiguity is quite intentional on my part, since "midrash" comprises a host of approaches to Scripture, many of which appear quite divorced from what would normally be considered exegesis, commentary, or interpretation.

Halakhic-Midrashic passages, then, use a limited number of literary-rhetorical constructs in order to "relate" Halakhic teachings to their "putative" biblical sources, so that Halakha "appears" to be derived from, or the meaning of, the Scripture. Why have scare-quotation marks in such a statement? Because I suspect that a substantial subgroup of this volume's readers will have had an abiding interest in the Jewish biblical texts and will have read commentaries on Scripture. In using terms like "relates," "appears," and "putative" (in quotation marks) I am preparing these readers

Halakhic Midrash

for the unexpected. Be prepared to suspend your expectations of what a biblical commentary does. Why, will be very clear by this chapter's end.

As I have indicated in the previous chapter, some (relatively few) passages in Tosefta exhibit an Halakhic-Midrashic-like, literary-rhetorical structure. In chapter 5, I mapped out one rather typical Halakhic-Midrashic structure and presented an example from t. Bekhorot 1:1b. Futhermore, both Talmuds will not infrequently cite Halakhic-Midrashic-like passages as "tannaitic" sources, that is, as *beraitot* (pl., *baraita*, sg.). *Beraitot*, you will recall, are a class of sources, cited in the two Talmuds, that are extraneous to Mishnah, but the origins of which the Talmuds' authors believe to be roughly contemporaneous with Mishnah's content. (Whether they actually are contemporaneous is another matter altogether and is not a literary-historical issue germane to this volume.) So, Halakhic-Midrashic-like passages are found in Tosefta (rarely), as well as in the Jerusalem Talmud and the Babylonian Talmud. But passages so structured may not be said to *characterize generally* either Tosefta or the Talmuds. Rather Halakhic-Midrashic-structured pericopae are *episodically* found in these early rabbinic, legal documents. Therefore, Halakhic-Midrashic passages, some of which resemble the Halakhic-Midrashic-*like* one you have already seen in Tosefta at t. Bekhorot 1:1b, will be encountered in both Talmuds, but do not define what is characteristic of the content or literary-rhetorical make-up of either the Jerusalem Talmud or the Babylonian Talmud. Not so of the corpus of "the Halakhic Midrashim," to the definition of which I now turn.

I have been using the term "Halakhic midrash" to name a particular type or class of *passages* that exhibit certain formalized literary-rhetorical properties and conventions, and that appear episodically in a number of different early rabbinic legal documents. By contrast, "*the* Halahkic Midrashim" (*midrashim* is the plural of *midrash*) refers, not to a class of *passages*, but to a class of early rabbinic *documents*. These documents are:

- the Mekhilta of R. Ishmael (concerning Exodus);
- the Mekhilta of R. Simeon b. Yokhai (also concerning Exodus);
- Sifra debe Rav (concerning Leviticus);
- Sifre Bamidbar (or Sifre Numbers);
- Sifre Zutta (also concerning Numbers); and
- Sifre Devarim (or Sifre Deuteronomy).

As a corpus of literature, these documents of the Halakhic Midrashim share some specific traits. Each of three of these traits I would specify as necessary, and neither one of the three is sufficient in itself to define this class of texts. The first trait is that passages that exhibit formalized Halakhic-Midrashic-like structures *dominate* in these documents, rather than just episodically appear in them.

The second trait of these documents is that none of them are organized topically and thematically, as are Mishnah, Tosefta, the Jerusalem Talmud, and the Babylonian Talmud. In fact, the Mishnah's subdivisions into thematic tractates, each with a series of topical "chapters," comprised of a relatively coherent and unified number of subtopical passages, provides the overarching organizational map for the tractates of the Tosefta as well as for those of each of the two Talmuds. The latter, it may be said, are all organized "Mishnaically." Those documents that are included in the class of "*the* Halakhic Midrashim" are organized "scripturally," in accordance with the order of the verses of those books of the Hebrew Bible that are the principal scriptural sources for Halakha. These are the books of Exodus, Leviticus, Numbers, and Deuteronomy, four of the five books designated in Judaic tradition as "the Torah of Moses." One of the features of the Hebrew Bible is that its legal/Halakhic content tends to be concentrated in these books. Why? So that the Scriptures' legal content may be primarily associated with the stories about Moses' leadership and his unique stature in the Hebrew Scriptures. Because the order of the Halakhic-legal content of these four biblical books provides the ordering or organizing principle of each of the books of the Halakhic Midrashim, if and when there is some thematic and topical continuity or unity from one passage to the next in the Halakhic Midrashim, that continuity is a derivative reflection (only?) of whatever topical or thematic continuity exists as one moves from one biblical verse to the next. To put matters in another way, the verses in Scripture, one after the other, are the "base texts" for all of the documents of the Halakhic Midrashim (as you would expect of most biblical commentaries). This is wholly different from what ones sees in Mishnah and Tosefta, or in the Jerusalem or Babylonian Talmud.

The third trait of the documents that comprise the class of early rabbinic literature called the Halakhic Midrashim is related to the second; the boundaries of each document are dictated by the boundaries of one or another of the four biblical books just named. So, the beginning and end of each of the two Mekhilta's is bounded by the beginning and end of the book

Halakhic Midrash

of Exodus. Sifra by Leviticus. Sifre Bamidbar and Sifre Zutta by Numbers. And Sifre Devarim by Deuteronomy. So, for example, Sifra, the base text of which is Leviticus, will not topically commence with the explication of verses found somewhere in Exodus or end by treating verses in Numbers. Nor will an individual passage in Sifra ordinarily commence with a citation of a verse in Exodus or Numbers; rather each of Sifra's passages will be "headed" or "prefaced" by a verse or fragment of a verse cited from Leviticus, even though *within* such a passage verses may be adduced from elsewhere in Scripture in the course of its "argument(s) from Scripture" in support of a particular Halakhic position.

Now, having elaborated three defining traits of the documents that comprise the class of the Halalkic Midrashim, I feel compelled to qualify my claims in two important ways. First, none of the documents of the Halakhic Midrashim expounds upon each and every verse of the biblical book that is its base text—not even upon each and every verse that is Halakhic/legal in content. All that I have said is that the verses that are expounded upon are taken in the order in which they appear in the Bible. What do I mean? Simply this: that in any of these documents, a Halakhic-Midrashic passage that expounds upon, let us say, Leviticus 3:1 may be followed by a passage that expounds upon verse 3:20, with verses 3:2 to 3:19 ignored. And as a corollary, a passage expounding verse 3:20 will not ordinarily be followed by a passage expounding 3:1. Why some verses with legal content are ignored, I do not know, and I have no way of knowing; one can only speculate. It is akin to asking why Mishnah treats some subtopics but not others, or why Tosefta does not provide materials that aid in the study of absolutely every passage of Mishnah. All we can say is that it does not and, if we are prone to speculate as to why, to admit that speculation is not worth very much. My second qualification is that while Halakhic-Midrashic passages *dominate* in the documents of the Halakhic Midrashim, not all of the passages of every document of the Halakhic Midrashim is "Halakhic," that is, legal in content. Some passages are "aggadic" midrash, that is, homiletical in nature. This is especially so in each of the two Mekhiltas, which are, for example, enamoured with the story of the exodus, with the biblical narrative of the events at the Red Sea (or Sea of Reeds), and with the biblical poetry embedded in the latter. Since this volume's focus is on *legal* literary-rhetorical constructs in the "legal" literature of the early rabbinic movement, I shall not be dealing with forms of "Aggadic" Midrash at all in this book, notwithstanding that some Aggadic Midrash appears in the Halakhic

In the Seat of Moses

Midrashim (and for that matter, in each of the two Talmuds as well). Aggada (or Haggadah) and Aggadic Midrash are just too different a kettle of fish from Halakhic literature generally and from Halakhic midrash.

When did Halakhic Midrash (as a literary-rhetorical category of *passages*) and the Halakhic Midrashim (as a category of early rabbinic documents) emerge? We have dealt with this in summary fashion in chapter 3. What I will say (and repeat) here is this. Passages that exhibit Halakhic-Midrashic literary-rhetorical conventions have been *deemed* to be "tannaitic" by traditional rabbinic sources from late antiquity on. The latter believed them to stem from the rabbinic authorities active up to and around the production and initial promulgation of Mishnah, let us say, up to 220–230 CE. Most modern academic specialists in early rabbinic literature have viewed these *passages* as stemming from the third to the fourth (or even early fifth) centuries, but some modern scholars have dated the Halakhic-Midrashic-like *form* or construct itself to the period preceding the composition of the Mishnah.[1] In my view, no one has convincingly shown that any meaningful number of Halakhic-Midrashic passages predate Mishnah's production. And, by contrast, there is ample evidence for dating the use of the Halakhic-Midrashic literary-rhetorical construct to the period soon after the promulgation of Mishnah, that is, in third and immediately subsequent century or centuries.

Opinions concerning dating of the *documents* of the Halakhic Midrashim have also varied. One mid-twentieth-century scholar, Saul Lieberman, views Sifre Zutta as one of the earliest, dating it to the early third century. Another, B. Z. Wacholder, considered the Mekhilta deR. Ishmael to be early medieval in date, perhaps from the eighth century. Louis Finkelstein, also a major mid-twentieth-century figure in the field, argued that much of Sifra predated Mishnah, perhaps by as much as a century and a half. And a recent late twentieth-century study by R. Reichman has also argued for a pre-Mishnaic date for some, or a major part, of Sifra.[2] Again, no one in my opinion has convincingly argued the case for either pre-Mishnaic or medieval dates for the composition of these documents. All of the Halakhic

---

1. Halivni is the most prominent scholar who has promoted such a view, articulated, for example, in Halivni, *Midrash*. Halivni's book provides excellent characterizations of the literary types of early rabbinic legal literature. It is just his literary-historical ordering of these types with which I disagree.

2. Reichman, *Mishna*; see the review of this work by Stemberger, Review. Stemberger conveniently reviews the range of modern scholarly views on the dating of the Halakhic Midrashim.

Midrashim were likely composed in the mushy middle ground, after the authorship of Mishnah and before the authorship the Babylonian Talmud, even if "activist" medieval scribes may have further massaged these texts.

"COMMENTARIES" OF A SORT (?)

Earlier this chapter, I suggested that readers familiar with Bible study and biblical commentaries should expect the unexpected, when later in this chapter, I present sample texts from the Halakhic Midrashim in order to illustrate and discuss some of the more dominant literary-rhetorical constructs and conventions that characterize this class of documents. I stated that Halakhic-Midrashic passages throughout the Halakhic Midrashim "relate" specific rabbinic legal rulings to the scriptural verses that are their "putative" sources and from which the rulings "appear" or "are said" to have been derived. I intimated that the words in scare-quotation marks are intended to communicate that matters may be *other* than they are made to appear to be. As you will see throughout this chapter, recognizing that this is so will make life easier for you, when you try to make sense of individual Halakhic-Midrashic passages. Nonetheless, the Halakhic Midrashim are each composed as a "commentary of sorts" on a selection of verses, taken in order, of one of the books of Exodus, Leviticus, Numbers, or Deuteronomy. And even if viewing them in light of what you or I would normally expect a commentary to do will make for an overly frustrating time, it is helpful for you to know in advance the types of relations between rabbinic rulings and Scripture that Halakhic-Midrashic passages "putatively" seek to establish. Why? Because these "intended" relations help guide the structure of each passage, aided and abetted by the use of the appropriate stock literary-rhetorical construct and its associated "signpost" language. Chief among these intended relations between rabbinic teachings and Scripture are the following five types:

1) the rabbinic teaching is portrayed as *the interpretation of* the Scripture at hand, hence the former stands as a commentary on the latter;

2) the Scripture at hand is portrayed as the *origin or ground of* the rabbinic teaching;

3) the Scripture/scriptural verse or phrase at hand is portrayed as *partly the origin* of the rabbinic teaching, but anchored to that partial scriptural origin alone, the rabbinic teaching would be

incomplete or insufficient, and therefore lead the rabbinic legal mind, exercising reason, to an erroneous position; however, *other scriptural verses/phrases necessarily come to bear and avert such error*;

4) from the/a rabbinic teaching alone one could logically draw an erroneous, related legal conclusion in applying the teaching to a specific set of circumstances, were it not the case that *a scriptural phrase proffers the necessary complement/corrective to logical (but erroneous) inferences based on the/a rabbinic teaching alone.*

5) in deciding whether one rabbinic ruling or another (seemingly-equally plausible) ruling is appropriate for a specific set of circumstances, Scripture is portrayed as *providing authoritative evidence for definitively classifying the case at hand* as falling within the purview one, but not the other, legal ruling. Often, this exercise uses scriptural grounds for either asserting or denying that one case is analogous to another; if the analogy is asserted, then the same laws apply to both, and if the analogy is denied, then distinct rulings apply to each.

Throughout this chapter I repeatedly refer to these types and endeavour to associate specific, formalized literary-rhetorical conventions with them. These conventions make sense primarily in light of the various tasks required of them, that is, to denote that Scripture relates to specific Halakhic rulings in one or another of these five ways. Let me briefly explain this last point.

Types 1 and 2 of this list are quite straightforward, served by equally straightforward literary-rhetorical constructs. Types 3, 4 and 5 each necessarily involve some form of "argumentation" and/or "counterargumentation"—you might argue (wrongly) that the appropriate ruling is x, but with the right scriptural verse(s) in view, one must argue/conclude that the appropriate ruling is y. Thus, a passage of Halakhic Midrash that is of type 3, 4, or 5 will exhibit somewhat more elaborated, formalized literary-rhetorical structures. Not to worry! You already have a head start, because one such structure, or one version of it, is that exhibited by t. Bekhorot 1:1b, with which you are already familiar from your work in chapter 5. (Incidentally, of which type is t. Bekhorot 1:1b an example? Of number 4? Or perhaps of type 5?) You should also take heart from the fact that, as you will see in this chapter, the formalized literary-rhetorical constructs that serve types 3, 4, and 5 all share some basic traits. They do so because they are all variations on a larger theme: logic can lead one astray in determining the Halakha, when one is not using all of the appropriate biblical verses as data in the exercise of that logic.

My list of five types of scriptural-Halakhic relations putatively established in Halakhic-Midrashic passages is by no means complete, and they are, moreover, *ideal* types only; "hybrid" passages sometimes blend them. Other passages are truncated or just more-poorly-conceived instances of the type. Moreover, not all documents of the Halakhic Midrashim *equally* evince *all* of the types on my list. Each document has its own idiomatic characteristics and to some extent its own *versions* of the stock literary formularies that are the signposts and structuring elements of its formalized rhetoric. Perhaps, this being the case, each document has as well its own agenda, similar to but slightly different than the other. But despite this range of idiomatic traits and of variations of the rhetorical structures and stock formularies, there is sufficient semblance across all of the (legal sections) of the Halakhic Midrashim that mastering the rhetoric of one document, for example Sifra (on Leviticus), provides a firm basis for easily mastering the rhetoric of another, such as Sifre Bamidbar (on Numbers).

That this is the case has two implications: one analytic, the other practical. First, this fact lends credence to the claim that we are dealing with a true family (*genus*) or class of documents within early rabbinic literature. For that class, our list of five (ideal) types of relations portrayed between Scripture and rabbinic rulings suffices to provide a good sense of the range and nature of what the Halakhic Midrashim and their constituent passages do. Second, more practically, that fact indicates that for our purposes, namely, providing you with a basic introduction to the rhetoric of the Halakhic Midrashim, presenting some exemplary passages from one or several of the documents will suffice to ground you in this literature as a whole.

CHARACTERISTICALLY HALAKHIC-MIDRASHIC CONSTRUSTS MAKE LIBERAL USE OF MANY FORMALIZED LITERARY-RHETORICAL CONVENTIONS FOUND IN MISHNAH AND TOSEFTA FOR SAYING THINGS

Let me now take up one of the principal claims made at the outset of this chapter and discuss it in greater detail. Throughout this book and at the beginning of this chapter, I have repeatedly made the point that what you master in learning the literary-rhetorical conventions of Mishnah and then Tosefta will continue to pay dividends as you proceed to look at other early rabbinic legal literature. Without intending to beg (or, for that matter, answer here) any literary-historical questions about the relations among Mishnah, Tosefta, the Halakhic Midrashim, and the Talmuds, I will explicitly list for you those many formalized literary-rhetorical constructs and "rules" for expressing things found in passages of Mishnah and Tosefta that are found as well in Halakhic-Midrashic passages.

You *will not* encounter in Halakhic-Midrashic passages significantly new forms for articulating declarative rule-sentences' protases (case circumstances) and apodases (rulings). You *will* encounter laconically phrased case circumstances and associated rulings that in form and character resemble those of Mishnah and Tosefta. You *will not* see vastly different ways of attributing a rule-sentence or just its apodasis to a named rabbinic authority than you have already seen in Mishnah and Tosefta. In the Halakhic Midrashim, structured arguments from analogy, including arguments *a fortiori* or *a miniori*, will appear in formalized structures that closely resemble their use in "debates" in Mishnah and Tosefta. The significant difference is that in Halakhic-Midrashic passages the basis for accepting or rejecting a hypothetical analogy will almost always be rooted in the scriptural verses cited, because claiming such roots in Scripture is what the Halakhic Midrashim are all about. In other words, the formulators of Halakhic-Midrashic passages and of the Halakhic Midrashim stand within the same larger "practice" of the use of literary-rhetorical conventions as do the formulators of Mishnah and Tosefta, notwithstanding the entirely idiomatic agenda of the Halakhic Midrashim among the documents produced by the early rabbinic movement.

Let me now be exceedingly specific in presenting those pervasive literary-rhetorical constructs and conventions found in Mishnah and Tosefta that (also) appear within Halakhic-Midrashic passages. Such a presentation also has the merit of providing you with a whirlwind review of what you have already learned in chapters 4 and 5. Following, then, is a catalogue of sorts of literary-rhetorical features of Mishnah and Tosefta that are carried forward into the Halakhic Midrashim and Halakhic-Midrashic passages:

i) the highly laconic *unattributed declarative rule-sentence*, with or without apocopation, of the form,

case/circumstances + ruling;

Halakhic Midrash

ii) the equally laconic *ruling attributed to a named rabbinic master*, of the form,

> *rabbi x says + case/circumstances + ruling,*

and its variations;

iii) *the dispute*, characterized by highly laconic, balanced attributed rulings (apodases) to a common case/circumstances (prodasis), such as,

> *case/circumstances +*
>
> *rabbi x says + ruling (or anonymous ruling) +*
>
> *rabbi y says + opposite ruling.*

and its variations;

iv) to some (but lesser) extent, *the debate*, which builds upon the dispute in this manner—

> *case/circumstances +*
>
> *rabbi x says + ruling (or anonymous ruling) +*
>
> *rabbi y says + opposite ruling +*
>
> *said to him (x) rabbi y (or, he (rabbi y) said to them) + counterargument +*
>
> *said to him (y) rabbi x (or they said to him (rabbi y)) + counterargument.*

While the debate form per se, is less reflected in the Halakhic Midrashim,

v) the *forms of argument used in the debate form* in Mishnah and Tosefta are very much adopted in, and adapted to, the Halakhic Midrashim, often using positive and negative arguments from analogy, such as,

> *if in the case of a, which has characteristic b, you say rule c applies,*
>
> *then in the case of a', which has characteristic b', how can you say rule c applies,*

and their several Mishnaic and Toseftan variations.

But in the Halakhic Midrashim, the "characteristics" b and b' that form the basis for drawing or rejecting an analogy will normally be replaced by scriptural phrase b or b'. Or, very often, the argument from analogy in the Halakhic Midrashim takes the form:

scriptural phrase [indicating b is analogous to b'];

just as/since in the case of a, which has characteristic b, rule c applied,

so too/then in the case of a', which has characteristic b', rule c also applies.

And, as one might expect,

vi) *the adducing of a scriptural proof-text*, using the form,

as it is said (she-ne'emar) + scriptural citation

and its variations,

found episodically in Mishnah and Tosefta, and more frequently in the Halakhic Midrashim. To this, Halakhic-Midrashic passages add their "preferred" scriptural citation formula, "Scripture says" (*tilmod lomar*, now popularly pronounced *talmud lomar*). As we shall see, "Scripture says" is idiomatically Halakhic-Midrashic, signpost language. But more on this later.

Only

vii) the *precedent story*—

it once happened that (*ma'aseh she/be*) + plus place/dramatis personae/case circumstance + ruling

somewhat used in Mishnah, and more liberally so in Tosefta, seems to me infrequently found in the Halakhic Midrashim.[3] But "infrequently" does not mean "never," and later in this chapter you will see an attempt to integrate, however awkwardly, a precedent-story-like tradition into a Halakhic-Midrashic passage.

With so much that is Mishnah-like and Tosefta-like found in the formalized language of the Halakhic Midrashim, how, then, does this idiomatic literature achieve its own ends through distinctive literary-rhetorical constructs, while still operating within a frame of literary-rhetorical norms that (also) characterize Mishnah and Tosefta? It is easy (although that may be easy for me to say)! The conventional and distinctive literary-rhetorical forms and structures of Halakhic Midrash provide, as I have already intimated, the superstructure for Halakhic-Midrashic passages; the language that appears before, in-between, and after the elements of the superstructure

---

3. I hasten to say, however, that I have undertaken no systematic study that would provide strong warrant for this last-mentioned claim. It is simply my impression from years of reading these rabbinic texts.

are routinely Mishnah-like and Tosefta-like language. So, you, the reader, just have to learn some of the dominant literary-rhetorical constructs that typically constitute the superstructures of Halakhic-Midrashic passages. And it is via one or another of these relatively few superstructural literary-rhetorical constructs that any one passage displays Scripture-to-Halakha relations of types 1, 2, 3, 4, or 5 elaborated earlier.

How will you come to recognize such Halakhic-Midrashic superstructural elements for what they are and what they are supposed to achieve? Also easy! Each Halakhic-Midrashic construct has its "signpost" language. Although, as mentioned, this language varies somewhat from document to document, it does not vary so much that you will have difficulty recognizing it and using it to "shepherd" yourself through the intended "logic" of the Halakhic-Midrashic passage. Moreover, as mentioned earlier, you have already encountered one such formalized Halakhic-Midrashic superstructure in the Halakhic-Midrashic-*like* passage at Tosefta-Bekhorot 1:1b, discussed in chapter 5.

To this point, admittedly, this chapter has been remarkably abstract. It is time to get concrete. That is where you will gain purchase on the Halakhic Midrashim. And it is also where the real work for you in digesting the core literary-rhetorical features of this literature will be undertaken. And what better place to begin than by looking at a "fake" passage of Halakhic midrash, into which I am able to "bake" those elements I wish you to see.

FAKING IT AGAIN: A FAKE PASSAGE OF "HALAKHIC MIDRASH"

If one defining characteristic of the Halakhic Midrashim is that within them, *passages* exhibiting halalkic-midrashic literary-rhetorical (superstructural) constructs dominate, then let me preview with you some of the basic features of one of its characteristic literary formulations. How? How else, but back to the highway code and another "fake" passage. The passage that I have "faked" is concocted to display a-type-3-relation between Scripture and the Halakha. That is, a given scriptural phrase is the partial source of a legal teaching/ruling that, without *all* relevant Scripture in hand, can be wrongly construed by erroneous logic. Enter a second, complementary, scriptural phrase that provides the basis for reasoning to the proper legal ruling. Now, do you remember our "ersatz" Tosefta on the theme of vehicles approaching an intersection with a four-way stop? It appeared near the beginning of chapter 5. That ersatz Tosefta looked like this (with the bold-faced parts representing language that is identical to my "fake" Mishnah, to which our "erstz" Tosefta was construed to relate):

1. **One from the south, and**
2. **one from the east,** and
3. they do not know who arrived first—
4. **east has priority,**
5. when there are no pedestrians.
6. **From the west, and**
7. **from the east—**
8. **both proceed.**
9. **If one signals a left turn,**
10. Justice Smith says: **The other has priority.**
11. **Justice Jones says: The other does not have priority**.
12. Said to him Justice Jones: No statute gives one priority?
13. Said to him Justice Smith: Avoiding harm is a priority;
14. For if both shall proceed, they may crash,
15. as it is said, "To have one's life."

If you go back to the beginning of chapter 5, you will see that this "ersatz" Tosefta served to aid the study of the parallel "fake" Mishnah passage, with which it shared considerable language, in several ways. You will remember (or you will see, if you turn back to the beginning of chapter 5), that lines 9 through 15 of our "ersatz" Tosefta do two things. First, lines 9 to 15 turn a dispute in the antecedent "fake" Mishnah between an *anonymous* rule-sentence and a ruling attributed to "Justice Jones" into a dispute between "Smith" and "Jones." Then lines 9 to 15 add a debate to the dispute, where the "fake" Mishnah has only the dispute. At the end of the Toseftan debate, Smith's argument is supported by the citation of a "Scripture-like" proof-text, actually a phrase from our made-up statement from the Supreme Court ordering state and provincial governments to have highway laws in order to protect the constitutional right of citizens to have their governments provide them with reasonable protections. The "Scripture-like" citation of the phrase from the made-up Supreme Court decision was introduced by the formulaic language, "as it is said" (*she-ne'emar*), which in Mishnah and Tosefta introduces a citation of Scripture, where Scripture

Halakhic Midrash

is used as a proof-text for an antecedent position. At this juncture, what I want you to notice is that the logical connection of the cited "Scripture" at line 15 of the ersatz Tosefta passage to the antecedent position of Smith is not fully spelled out. You are left to infer *how* the Scripture logically supports Smith's view, and figuring this out often entails reading more of the Scripture than the few words actually cited as a proof-text. Right? Right!

Now, Halakhic-Midrashic passages typically do something quite different with Scripture than "proof-texting." To show this, permit me to reproduce for you from the beginning of chapter 5 the entire made-up statement from our fictitious Supreme Court; the statement is our complete verse from "Scripture."

> It is unconstitutional to not have a highway code, lest the constitutional right to have one's life reasonably protected by government be abrogated by any level of government, federal, state/provincial, or municipal.

With this *whole* "scriptural" verse in mind—and, after all, early rabbis would likely know Scripture by heart, especially the Five Books of Moses—consider the following "fake" Halakhic-Midrashic passage, noting the "signpost language" in SMALL CAPS, as well as the phrases in **boldface**, which (again) equal language in our earlier-concocted, "fake" Mishnah at the beginning of chapter 5.

1. "It is unconstitutional to not have a highway code"—
2. ON THE BASIS OF THIS THEY SAID (*mikan amru*):
3. **Two approach a four-way stop**—
4. **from the west, and**
5. **from the east**—
6. **if one signals a left turn,**
7. **The other has priority.**
8. DO YOU SAY THAT (*ata omer*)
9. **the other has priority?**
10. OR IS IT NOT [PERHAPS EQUALLY REASONABLE TO CONCLUDE] THAT (*o ayno ela*)
11. **the other does not have priority?**
12. SCRIPTURE SAYS (*tilmod lomar*):
13. "to have one's life"—

In the Seat of Moses

14. [indicating] preserving life takes precedence over putting life at risk,
15. [IMPLYING THAT ONE IS] TO EXCLUDE [THE VIEW THAT] (*le-hotzi*):
16. **the other does not have priority?**

Is your head spinning again? Sorry. But you will soon see that this "fake" Halakhic-Midrashic passage is quite simple, because the signpost language takes one through the logic inherent in this literary-rhetorical construct, which generally accords with one of the common, standardized variations of Halakhic-Midrashic passages. Let me break down the components of this fake passage. First, the passage begins with a "scriptural" citation at line 1, which is a partial citation only of our made-up Supreme Court statement. Later, at line 13, we encounter a second "scriptural citation," again a partial, but different, citation than the one with which the passage begins. The second citation is introduced with the "citation formula" at line 12, which I have translated "SCRIPTURE SAYS." But this is a very loose paraphrase of what the Hebrew formulaic language actually says, which is closer to "learn (*tilmod*) to say (*lomar*, in the infinitive form)." *Tilmod lomar* (now commonly pronounced, *talmud lomar*) always introduces a scriptural citation that will be used *to resolve* in some fashion the problem raised in the lines that precede it. This problem is always one that the *initial* scriptural citation, *taken on its own*, is portrayed as incapable of resolving. In fact, the initial scriptural citation may be portrayed as having invited more than one possible legal position, only one of which can be correct. So, whatever else is going on in a passage such as this, the upshot is that *both* scriptural sources cited must *necessarily* be considered, or else one gets into trouble. And consideration of neither citation on its own, especially not the initial citation, is sufficient to avoid adopting inappropriate legal positions.

"SCRIPTURE SAYS" (*tilmod lomar*), at line 12, is just one part of the "signpost" language that appears throughout this fake passage. The other elements of the "signpost" language appear at lines 2, 8, 10, followed by our now familiar line 12, and finally line 15. Let me reproduce all of this signpost language in small caps. In between this signpost language let me characterize the kind of content that appears in our fake Halakhic-Midrashic passage.

1. scriptural citation 1—
2. ON THE BASIS OF THIS THEY SAID (*mikan amru*):

Halakhic Midrash

    3. statement of legal circumstances +

    4. (correct) legal ruling 1.

5. DO YOU SAY THAT (*ata omer*)

    6. (correct) legal ruling 1?

7. OR IS IT NOT [PERHAPS EQALLY REASONABLE TO CONCLUDE] that (*o ayno ela*)

    8. (incorrect) legal ruling 2?

9. SCRIPTURE SAYS (*tilmod lomar*):

    10. scriptural citation 2;

    11. brief "argument" based on scriptural citation 2,

12. [IMPLYING THAT ONE IS] TO EXCLUDE [THE VIEW THAT] (*le-hotzi*)

    13. (incorrect) legal ruling 2.

It should be clearer, now, from the foregoing that we have a *schematic* for a formalized type of mini composition. Moreover, if what I have called "signpost" language is really "stock" language that *tends* to appear always roughly in the same order, and if what appears before, in between, and after the "stock" bits tends, roughly speaking, to be the type of elements that I have characterized in normal type, then such schematized and formalized mini-compositions will *tend* always to end up doing much the same thing. Will they not? And what is that thing that they will tend to do? To demonstrate that (1) the true blue legal position is based in Scripture, but (2) only once *all* of the relevant bits of Scripture are brought into the argument, because (3) if all the relevant bits of Scripture are not brought to bear, then logic either takes one to an inappropriate legal stance or leaves one with an unresolved dispute between two seemingly-equally possible positions.

Let us now turn our attention to the elements, other than "scriptural" citations, that appear *in between* the signpost language of our "fake" passage of Halakhic midrash. Lines 3–7, 9, 11, and 16 are all in boldface, indicating that they repeat verbatim language in our fake Mishnah. Let me reproduce just those lines.

    3. **Two approach a four-way stop—**

    4. **from the west, and**

    5. **from the east—**

    6. **if one signals a left turn,**

7. the other has priority.

9. the other has priority?

11. the other does not have priority?

16. the other does not have priority?

Lines 3–6 form a typically-formulated, Mishnaic protasis of a declarative rule-sentence, spelling out in laconic fashion a set of circumstances that constitute a case. Line 7 is a characteristically short Mishnah-like apodosis, a ruling, and is simply repeated at line 9, but with a question mark. Line 11 is an opposing ruling, formulated in the same language as the first apodosis, again completely Mishnah-like. What do we have here? A typical Mishnaic dispute, minus any attribution to a named rabbinic authority. Almost all of the language in this "fake" Halakhic-Midrashic passage that is *not* a citation of "Scripture" or signpost language *is* typically Mishnaic in literary-rhetorical formulation. The only remaining language in the whole passage that is neither signpost language nor "scriptural" citation is line 14, a brief explanatory gloss that provides the barest bones of an argument linking the "Scripture" cited at line 13 to the passage's conclusions. And in truth, in literary-rhetorical terms it would fit into any "debate" in Mishnah or Tosefta. Now, you will say, "But you made up this fake Halakhic-Midrashic passage *from* your fake Mishnah passage in chapter 5, and that is why its language is so Mishnaic in character!" That is true. But as you will see, it is also *true to* much of what you will see in passages of the Halakhic Midrashim, and will see in other Halakhic-Midrashic passages encountered among the *beraitot* cited in the Talmuds.

I have pointed to what is Mishnah-like in my "fake" passage of Halakhic-Midrash. Let us return to the distinctively Halakhic-Midrashic language in our "fake" passage, which I have placed in SMALL CAPS, indicating that it functions as "signpost" language.

The stock "signpost" language I have chosen to use in this "fake" passage is one of several closely related variations of its kind. Over the course of this chapter you will see several variations used in a number of "real" sample Halakhic-Midrashic passages taken from documents among the corpus of the Halakhic Midrashim. For example, in some passages the stock language, "ON THE BASIS OF THIS THEY SAID (*mikan amru*)," does not appear, and the opening scriptural citation 1 is just glossed by the "statement of legal circumstances + (correct) legal ruling." Moreover, the nature of the "brief argument based on scriptural citation 2" will determine which

Halakhic Midrash

variation of the stock formula, "[IMPLYING THAT ONE IS] TO EXCLUDE [THE VIEW THAT] (*le-hotzi*)," is used. Indeed, the argument from scriptural citation 2 may at times provide the basis for inferring that one is TO INCLUDE (*le-havih*) a particular circumstance or position rather than TO EXCLUDE (*le-hotzi*) one. In addition, the nature itself of the argument from scriptural citation 2 may be quite different from passage to passage, triggering at times arguments from analogy, *a fortiori* arguments from Scripture, or *a miniori* arguments from Scripture. Remember, you have already seen such arguments from analogy in use in chapters 4 and 5, especially in "debates," and the formalized literary-rhetorical conventions for such arguments will not differ greatly, when they are used within Halakhic-Midrashic-structured passages, usually after scriptural citation 2. By the end of this chapter, I believe that you will have the tools and knowledge that will allow you to spot still other variations that you may encounter. What most of these variations have in common is that they produce mini compositions that exhibit much the same *tendencies* as my fake one does. Which means that taken together such mini-compositions are *tendentious*; they all convey a *similar* message about the necessary place and use of Scripture in legal reasoning about vastly *different* idiomatic content—sometimes about firstlings, sometimes about writs of divorce, and so on. But more of this later.

Before leaving this "fake" passage in favor of some "real" ones, I wish to point out several other contrived characteristics that I have "baked" into my "fake" Halakhic-Midrashic passage. I have already pointed out how I have so contrived the language of our fake passage so as to use verbatim phrases from the "fake" Mishnah passage (and from the "ersatz" Tosefta pericope) appearing near the outset of chapter 5. Do *all* "real" Halakhic-Midrashic passages reproduce language from passages in Mishnah and/or Tosefta (or, for that matter, from Toseftan-like *beraitot* of the Talmuds)? No, they do not. But they do so enough to be noticeable. And even when they do not, the literary-rhetorical features of the language appearing in between the bits that comprise the formalized superstructure and its "signpost" language of an Halakhic-Midrashic passage are often typically Mishnaic-Toseftan in its literary-rhetorical character, and, moreover, halalkic-midrashic passages' legal *content* often parallels the content of Mishnah, or Tosefta (or of Tosefta-like *beraitot*), even if it does not reproduce verbatim Mishnah's or Tosefta's language. So, when such Halakhic-Midrashic mini-compositions go about their tendentious business, and if you have difficulty grasping the legal positions that are being argued about, look to parallel passages in

In the Seat of Moses

Mishnah and Tosefta to fill out your grasp of the legal issues.[4] This will save you needless headaches in determining what is at issue in the content of any one Halakhic-Midrashic passage.

Also baked into my "fake" Halakhic-Midrashic passage is another feature that, in my opinion, one encounters frequently in reading real Halakhic-Midrashic mini-compositions. Frequently one is left scratching one's head about how the *specific* legal ruling that is said to derive from the initial "scriptural citation 1" can be drawn from that citation by any reasonable means. Yes, there may be a strong *topical* link between the scriptural citation and the specific legal position, and in that very "loose" sense the claim "ON THE BASIS OF THIS THEY SAID" makes some sense. But beyond that topical link, one is left wondering *how* the specifics of the rule have been, or could possibly be, derived from the cited Scripture. I wish at this point unequivocally to comfort you; the fault is unlikely to reside in your inability to discern the specific exegetical path from the Scriptural verse to the stated Halakha. Rather, in my view, it is often the case that the *specifics* of the Halakhic teaching have been derived independently of any exegesis of the Scripture in question, even if the latter may be said with some justification to be a biblical warrant in *general* for the former. Therefore, in my "fake" Halakhic-Midrashic passage, one can readily see that the opening phrase of the made-up Supreme court statement (cited as if it were Scripture) is a *general* warrant for establishing rules for the highway. But one cannot see how that opening "scriptural" phrase might lead one to articulate the *specifics* of the rule about two automobiles approaching a four-way stop from opposing directions, when one of the two is signaling its intention to make a left turn at the intersection. That specific rule for the given circumstances has been arrived at independently of any deep exegetical consideration of the meaning of the Supreme Court statement, *even if* it makes sense to *appeal to* the Supreme Court statement to justify one legal view over another. In other words, in many instances, do not expect to find in Halakhic-Midrashic passages historically credible or logically compelling representations of how *specific* Halakhic rulings were derived, or are logically derivable, from the scriptural verses from which they are said to have sprung. In these instances, you would be on a fool's errand to act otherwise. If I am correct in this last "lesson," then what are its implications for understanding what those passages that exhibit variations of

---

4. These parallels in Mishnah and Tosefta will often be noted in footnotes to standard translations of Halakhic-Midrashic documents, where they exist.

the Halakhic-Midrashic literary-rhetorical construct actually achieve? My response must hark back to what I earlier said such passages *tend* to do— to their *tendentious* character. They are an early rabbinic "protest" against the use of logic alone in deriving the Halakha *independently of Scripture*, indeed of *all of the relevant bits and pieces of Scripture* to be found, whether hither or yon, in the biblical text. Whether this protest is credible is another matter altogether. For now, let us turn from the "fake" to the "real."

ATTENDING TO SCRIPTURE "REALLY" MATTERS: SOME DOMINANT LITERARY-RHETORICAL COMPOSITIONAL CONVENTIONS THAT CHARACTERIZE "REAL" PASSAGES FROM THE HALAKHIC MIDRASHIM

Gaining Confidence from What You Already Know: Lessons from Halakhic-Midrashic-like Tosefta Bekhorot 1:1b

In chapter 5 you were introduced to what I called a "Halakhic-Midrashic-like" passage at t. Bekhorot 1:1b. Let us start with another brief look at this Tosefta passage, so that I may subsequently point out what makes it "Halakhic-Midrashic-*like*," rather than "Halakhic-Midrashic." I will place what I have been calling versions of stock "signpost" language, language that shepherds one through the formalized, structured mini-composition in SMALL CAPS, as I have done previously.

t. Bekhorot 1:1b (translation my own[5]):

> a. AND SO YOU [must] SAY IN THE CASE OF (*ve-khein ata omer b*) priests and in the case of Levites [namely, that they are not liable for the laws of the redemption of the firstling in the case of unclean animals, as per m. Bekhorot 1:1b].
>
> b. BECAUSE, SINCE (*mi-pnei she*) the priests and the Levites are liable in the case of [the firstling of] a clean animal [as stated in m. Bekhorot 2:1], ONE MIGHT (*yakhol*) [think] them to be liable [also] in the case of [the firstling of] an unclean animal [for which, incidentally, we are explicitly told in m. Bekhorot 1:1b that Levites are not liable].

---

5. Based on Lightstone, *Rhetoric*, 190–91.

In the Seat of Moses

c. SCRIPTURE [however] SAYS (*tilmod lomar*): "Of humankind and of animal-kind" (Exodus 13:2; Numbers 18:15)—

d. that which applies to you in the case of humankind applies to you in the case of animal-kind.

e. That which does not apply to you in the case of humankind does not apply to you in the case of animal-kind.

f. [Thus] THEY EXEMPTED (*yatz'u*) the Levites from the law of the firstling of an unclean beast.

g. But they [Israelites] give the redemption for [an Israelite] first-born son

h. and the redemption for the firstling of an ass to the priests only [and not to either a priest or a Levite, despite the fact that priests and Levites are similarly exempted by m. Bekhorot 1:1b].

If I were to produce a schematic of t. Bekhorot 1:1b using the signpost language as the skeleton of this mini-composition, it would look like this:

1. AND SO YOU [must] SAY IN THE CASE OF (*ve-khein ata omer b*)

    2. allusion only to a legal ruling 1 (—the actual rule sentence appears in Mishnah)

3. BECAUSE, SINCE (*mi-pnei she*)

    4. paraphrase of a related analogous Mishnah ruling 2

5. ONE MIGHT (*yakhol*) [think]

    6. not legal ruling 1

7. SCRIPTURE SAYS (*tilmod lomar*)

    8. scriptural citation 2

    9. stated analogy supported by scriptural citation 2

10. THEY EXEMPTED (*yatz'u*)

    11. restated legal ruling 1

    12. gloss of foregoing stating legal ruling 3

That the "signpost" structuring language of t. Bekhorot 1:1b (at lines 1, 3, 5, 7, and 10 in the schematic) bears a very close family resemblance to that of my "fake" Halakhic-Midrashic passage is easily discerned. The specific versions of the signpost language seen in t. Bekhorot 1:1b are simply engendered by the specific types of "arguments" used at line 4 and 9, both of which are appeals to analogous factors. Similarly, the "content-sections" of

Halakhic Midrash

this mini-composition, that is, those parts that lie before, in-between, and after the stock "signpost" language, correspond closely to that which you would expect from the previous section of this chapter. The *tendency* of the whole passage looks, at first glance, pretty much like what our "fake" Halakhic-Midrashic passage tended to do. That is, to indicate that without further recourse to all relevant Scripture, logic alone (here based on an analogy) will lead one astray. However, once the full array of the bits of relevant Scripture are considered, the more appropriate analogy is apparent, and we are brought back to the appropriate conclusion (that is, ruling 1). So why is t. Bekhorot 1:1b Halakhic-Midrashic-*like*, rather than Halakhic-Midrashic? Simply put, there is no scriptural citation 1 and there is no actual statement of ruling 1 at the beginning of the mini-composition that is said to have been derived from scriptural citation 1. The former is no-where to be found, and the latter is contained in the parallel passage at m. Bekhorot 1:1b, which our Tosefta passage relies upon for an intelligible context, like so many other Tosefta passages. To put matters glibly, we have in t. Bekhorot 1:1b either a Halakhic-Midrashic passage that has been "tosefta-ized" to serve to explicate a Mishnah passage, on which the Tosefta passage has been (typically) made to depend for its intelligibility, or we have a Tosefta passage that has adapted a conventionally-structured, Halakhic-Midrashic format to build a passage designed to serve to explain why Mishnah's ruling is needed, not why Scripture's statement is necessary. Either way, there is in t. Bekhorot 1:1b some odd mismatch of literary-rhetorical construct, on the one hand, and function, on the other. There are two important lessons for you to be drawn from this rehearsal of what is going on in t. Bekhorot 1:1b. The first is this: not only are there variations to standardized literary-rhetorical forms (and you should not be flummoxed when passages do not stick closely to the standard script), but also it is sometimes the case that literary-rhetorical constructs are "badly" used or used for "inappropriate" purposes (and you should not allow yourselves to be overly frustrated when the resulting passage does not quite make sense). Sometimes a passage does not make good sense, because it does not. The second lesson is closely related to the first: with knowledge of the basic dominant literary-rhetorical constructs in hand, not only is it much easier to know what is going on in a passage, but it is also easier to recognize what should have been going on, even when it is not. I cannot stress enough how internalizing these two lessons will make your lives easier when you encounter early rabbinic legal literature. And our encounter with t. Bekhorot 1:1b is a case in point; it is a passage the formulator of which was slightly "off his (or her) game," or who adapted and extended the use of standard Halakhic-Midrashic protocols beyond its normal use, with less than stunning success.

So, how has rehearsing t. Bekhorot 1:1b been a fitting start to examining samples of "real" Halakhic-Midrashic passages? If you now clearly see what seems "slightly off" in t. Bekhorot 1:1b, then recognizing what is "going on" in the passages presented and discussed in the remainder of this chapter will be easy.

A Selection of Core Halakhic-Midrashic Literary-Rhetorical Constructs

Earlier, I listed five ideal "types" of halalkic-midrashic passages found in the Halakhic Midrashim, corresponding to five types of "relations" such passages *tend* to try to establish between Scripture and specific teachings of the Halakha. This typology provides a useful way of distinguishing various normative Halakhic-Midrashic literary-rhetorical conventions. As I turn to real, sample texts from some of the Halakhic Midrashim, I will try to relate various standard constructs to one or another of the five "types."

Some of the literary-rhetorical constructs of Halakhic Midrash are remarkably simple. Take, for example, the straightforward *claim of the basis of Halakha in Scripture*—

1. scriptural citation
2. ON THE BASIS OF THIS THEY SAID (*mi-kan amru*),
3. statement of circumstances + ruling.

Such a simple construct may comprise a short pericope all by itself, and its intention is clear, and clearly stated. That is, the passage's intent is to state that the Halakhic position is based on the particular Scripture in hand, without further elaboration or argument. In our ideal typology, such a passage falls under the aegis of "type 2."

In other instances, no specific signpost language intervenes between the citation of Scripture and the rabbinic legal teaching; *Scripture and statement of Halakha are* just *juxtaposed*, the latter just glossing the former—

1. scriptural citation
2. statement of circumstances + ruling—

Halakhic Midrash

constituting the entirety of an admittedly brief passage. The reader is left to discern whether the intent is to establish a "type 1" relationship between the two elements—the Halakhic position is the straightforward legal interpretation of Scripture—or a "type 2" relationship—the Scripture is the basis for the Halakhic position.

Passages that fall under types 3, 4, or 5 of our typology all have in common the juxtaposition of an "appropriate" Halakhic teaching with an "inappropriate" one. The latter, such passages *argue*, may be reasonably justified as much as the former, in the absence of considering *all* of the relevant scriptural bits. But when all of the scriptural bits are included in one's logical operations, only the appropriate legal teaching is shown to be supportable. Consequently, in such passages, several elements of a literary-rhetorical construct tend to be present, with additional stock signpost language used given the specific nature of the arguments being made. For example, the bare-bones-elements of such a formalized structure will be something like,

1. scriptural citation 1
2. (correct) legal ruling 1
3. OR/OR IS IT NOT/PERHAPS/I MIGHT (REASONABLY SURMISE)/SINCE ... I MIGHT ...
4. (incorrect) legal ruling 2
5. scriptural citation 1 or 2
6. (correct) legal ruling 1.

Additional elements with further stock signpost language will be added primarily at one or another of three places in this bare-bones version of the structure:

(a) *between element 1 and 2* in order to state explicitly the relationship of the "(correct) legal ruling 1" to Scripture (for example, ON THE BASIS OF THIS THEY SAID);

(b) *somewhere between element 2 and 5*, when the (faulty) logical operations that point to "(incorrect) legal ruling 2" require explicit demonstration (for example, SINCE . . . ONE MIGHT [THINK] ...), and/or

(c) *between elements 5 and 6*, to spell out the logical operations (often an argument from analogy of some sort) that take us from the data provided by the scriptural citation at element 5 back to the (correct) legal ruling 1 (for example, [SCRIPTURE LIKENS . . . TO . . . , TO EXCLUDE/EXEMPT/INCLUDE . . .).

One version of such a more-elaborated Halakhic-Midrashic structure would look a lot like that already seen at t. Bekhorot 1:1b, which, however, lacks the initial scriptural citation (at element 1) and the explicit initial statement of the "(correct) legal ruling 1," because it has been "tosefta-ized" to serve to explicate and depend upon m. Bekhorot 1:1b. If I were to supply the missing elements, that is, if I were to "de-tosefta-ize" t. Bekhorot 1:1b, its formalized structure might look like this (with the "bare-bones" elements in boldface, and signpost language still in SMALL CAPS):

1. **Scriptural citation 1**

2. ON THE BASIS OF THIS THEY SAID (*mikan amru*)

3. **(correct) legal ruling 1**

4. OR, SINCE (*o mi-pnei she*)

5. (correct) legal ruling 2

6. ONE MIGHT (*yakhol*) [think]

7. **not legal ruling 1**

8. SCRIPTURE SAYS (*tilmod lomar*)

9. **scriptural citation 2**

10. stated analogy supported by scriptural citation 2

11. THEY EXEMPTED (*yatz'u*)

12. **(restated correct) legal ruling 1**

If one reads through this schematization of a "de-tosefta-ized" version of t. Bekhorot 1:1b, first attending to only those "bare-bones" elements that are in boldfaced type, and second looking at all the other "additional" elements, it is easy to see how the overall more-elaborated construct draws upon supplementary stock, signpost language to make the whole into one stylized, formalized composition. The schematization you have before you is one exemplary version of the Halakhic-Midrashic constructs that serve in cases where the relationship of Scripture to Halakha is portrayed as either type 3, 4, or 5, or as some hybrid thereof. Moreover, the range of variation of versions of this more elaborated, Halakhic-Midrashic construct is not so great as to be difficult for you to recognize.

How shall I demonstrate this last claim to you? I shall simply present several extended compositions from the Halakhic Midrashim and comment on the formalized structure of their constituent passages. You will see that you already have enough under your belt to perceive what is going on. Some of the passages are very simple, usually because they assert type 1 or type 2 relations with Scripture, as in

- scriptural citation
- ON THE BASIS OF THIS THEY SAID (*mi-kan amru*),
- statement of circumstances + ruling.

Others are more elaborate because they intend to demonstrate type 3, 4, or 5 relations between Halakha and the biblical text. Of the latter type, some are spun-out to considerable length, using various arguments one after another, usually some form of argument from analogy, to establish

- whether case *a* is analogous to case *b*,
- as indicated by scripture *i*,
- and consequently rabbinic rule *x* applies,

or

- whether case *a* is analogous to case *b'*,
- as indicated by scripture *ii*,
- and consequently ruling *x'* applies.

The resulting pericope can continue to be spun out as long as one can identify scriptural phrases that alternatively support one analogy or the other. Proffer yet another possible rabbinic ruling (ruling *x"*) that might apply to case *a*, and the pericope can be spun out even further. Moreover, add attributions to names rabbinic authorities, as in a Mishnaic or Toseftan debate, and one has an elaborated Halakic-Midrashic debate. But no matter how extended and spun out such Halakhic-Midrashic essays become, they are still composed of the relatively limited stock of Halakhic-Midrashic constructs (with related, stock signpost language) married to the literary-rhetorical structures of Mishnah and Tosefta, with which you are already familiar.

In the Seat of Moses

Two Sample, Extended Compositions of Halakhic Midrash Decoded: Mekhitla deR. Simeon, Bo, 13:1–2 and Sifre Numbers, Korah, Pisqa 118a

Over the course of the remainder of this chapter, I will take you through two extended Halakhic-Midrashic compositions, each taken from one of the documents of the Halakhic Midrashim. The first is of moderate length and is cited from the Mekhilta deR. Simeon, Bo 13:1–2.[6] The base-text in Scripture of this passage is Exodus 13:1–2. The second and lengthier composition presented below is Sifre Numbers, Korah 118a,[7] and "expounds" (if one can call it that) upon Numbers 18:15–18. I have chosen these two passages primarily because the Halakhic content, which concerns the priestly gift of the firstborn, is familiar to you, and because you have already seen some passages from Mishnah and Tosefta that deal with this topic. In fact, some of the language in each of these two Halakhic-Midrashic passages parallels verbatim language found in Mishnah and/or Tosefta (as will be indicated).

In the discussion of each of the two sample passages/compositions, I will point out several features that I wish you to note. Obviously, I will remark upon the use of what are formalized Halakhic-Midrashic literary-rhetorical conventions and constructs, often served by stock, signpost language. I will point out examples of the use of standard Mishnaic-Toseftan literary-rhetorical conventions that sit embedded in the distinctively Halakhic-Midrashic elements. And I will ask you to discern with me whether the relationship espoused between Scripture and Halakha is of type 1, 2, 3, 4, and/or 5.[8]

---

6. Epstein edition, 37–38.

7. Horowitz edition, 138–39.

8. So that you will not have to constantly turn back to the earlier part of this chapter where I define these five types, let me redescribe the ideal types here:

1) the rabbinic teaching is portrayed as *the interpretation of* the scripture at hand, hence the former stands as a commentary on the latter;

2) the scripture at hand is portrayed as the *origin or ground of* the rabbinic teaching;

3) the scripture/scriptural verse or phrase at hand is portrayed as *partly the origin* of the rabbinic teaching, but anchored to that partial scriptural origin alone, the rabbinic teaching would be incomplete or insufficient, and therefore lead the rabbinic legal mind, exercising reason, to an erroneous position; however, *other scriptural verses/phrases necessarily come to bear and avert such error*;

4) from the/a rabbinic teaching alone one could logically draw an erroneous, related legal conclusion in applying the teaching to a specific set of circumstances, were it not the case that *a scriptural phrase proffers the necessary complement/corrective to logical (but*

Halakhic Midrash
Mekhitla deR. Simeon, Bo, 13:1–2

As just stated, the scriptural base text for Mekhitla deR. Simeon, Bo, 13:1–2 is Exodus 13:1–2. It reads (translation my own):

> (1) And the Lord spoke to Moses saying: (2) Sanctify for me every firstling that opens every womb among the people of Israel, among humankind and among beast—it is mine.

Following is the related extended passage from the Mekhitla deR. Simeon (translation my own), with verbatim parallels with Mishnah in **boldface**, language that equals Tosefta underscored, and Halakhic-Midrashic signpost language in SMALL CAPS.

Mekhitla deR. Simeon, Bo, 13:1–2 (translation my own):

i

A. "And the Lord spoke to Moses saying: Sanctify for me" (Exodus 13:1–2a)—

B. THERE IS NO (*ain*) [meaning that can be ascribed to] "sanctify for me" OTHER THAN (*ela*) separate for me.

C. IT IS POSSIBLE (*yakhol*) [THAT I MIGHT CONCLUDE THAT] if you separate it, it is sanctified, and if not, it is not sanctified [that is, retains its 'mundane' status].

D. SCRIPTURE SAYS (*tilmod lomar*): "it is mine"—

E. whether you separate it, or whether you do not separate it [it is nonetheless sanctified].

ii

F. "That opens [every] womb"—

G. SINGLES OUT (*prat*) [i.e., EXCLUDES from the category that born by] Caesarian birth.

iii

---

erroneous) inferences based on the/a rabbinic teaching alone;

5) in deciding whether one rabbinic ruling or another (seemingly equally plausible) ruling is appropriate for a specific set of circumstances, Scripture is portrayed as *providing authoritative evidence for definitively classifying the case at hand* as falling within the purview of one, but not the other, legal ruling. Often, this exercise uses scriptural grounds for either asserting or denying that one case is analogous to another; if the analogy is asserted, then the same laws apply to both, and if the analogy is denied, then distinct rulings apply to each.

H. "Among the people of Israel"—

I. I HAVE (*ain li*) [i.e., I understand that the law pertains to] ONLY (*ela*) an Israelite.

J. WHENCE (*minayin*) [do I understand] to include proselytes, slaves, and freedmen?

K. SCRIPTURE SAYS (*tilmod lomar*): "[every] firstling" [my emendation of the text].

iv

L. "Every firstling"—

M. FROM THIS YOU SAY [concerning] a female proselyte whose impregnation was not in a state of sanctification [i.e., before conversion], and her giving birth was in a state of sanctification—

N. **[her son] is a firstling as regards inheritance, and is not a firstling as regards [having to give redemption money to] the priest.**

O. Rabbi Yose the Galilean says: [The son] is a firstling as regards inheritance and as regards the priest,

P. as it is said (*she-ne'emar*): "That opens every womb among the people of Israel"—

Q. [meaning] as long as (*ad she*) they open a womb of an Israelite [= m. Bekhorot 8:1c].

v

R. "Among humankind and among beast"—

S. That [law] which applies to you regarding humankind, [also] applies to you regarding a[n unclean domestic] beast (= t. Bekhorot 1:1b, see also m. Bekhorot 2:1b)—

T. [Thus] THEY EXCLUDED Levites [from the law of the firstling of an unclean domestic animal] (= t. Bekhorot 1:1b),

U. SINCE (*she*) you have not applied to them [the law of the firstling] with regard to humankind [i.e., they do not pay redemption money to the priests for their firstling sons], [THEN] do not apply to them [the law of the firstling] with regard to a beast [i.e., the firstlings of their flock] (see m. Bekhorot 2:1b).

V. "It is mine"—

W. That which is certain[ly a firstling], and not that is in doubt.

X. "It is mine"—

Y. Whether you separate it out, and whether you do not separate it out.

Z. "*It* (singular) is mine"—

AA. There is only one firstling as regards inheritance.

BB. "*It* (singular) is mine"—

CC. it is sacrificed [if it is an animal that is fit for sacrifice], and its substitute is not sacrificed.

We can dispense with section vi of this composition summary. In succession, four briefly-stated Halakhic positions are simply tacked onto the same phrase of the biblical verse that is the base text for the extended passage, with the implication that the latter is the ground for the former. In each of the four we have the "structure."

>   scriptural citation + rabbinic legal teaching.

Of course, "structure" may be a bit of an overstatement. There is nothing joining the two elements in each of the four—no ON THE BASIS OF THIS THEY SAID or any other stock joining language. The language and formulation of the rabbinic legal teachings are such that it could easily be found in Mishnah or Tosefta. The type of relationship of each of the four "exegeses" of "it is mine" is easy to discern; each of the four claims a type 2 relationship between Scripture and the stated Halakha. That is, the former is the ground for the latter. Do any of these four Halakhic "readings" of "it is mine" amount to what one would today deem an exegetical commentary on a biblical verse? Hardly. And that was one of the lessons I conveyed earlier in the chapter; namely, adjust your expectations, and do not be overly concerned if you cannot discern any "reasonable" way that the specifics of the Halakha can be said to be derived from an exegesis of the biblical verse at hand.

Section ii of the extended composition, like the four parts of section vi, seems to have a very simple formal structure, in which the base-verse of Scripture is juxtaposed with a Halakhic teaching said to be derived from the verse. But here stock Halakhic-Midrashic, signpost language (SINGLES

OUT/EXCLUDES) signals how one is to "logically" derive the rabbinic teaching from the verse. The type of relationship between Scripture and Halakha is of type 1. The specificity of Scripture's language ("opening the womb" as opposed to noting, more simply, that the offspring is the first to be born to the dame) provides warrant for surmising that the specificity intends to rule out some other circumstances. That is precisely what the language, SINGLES OUT/EXCLUDES, signals as the way to read the scriptural clause. You see?! That is exactly what formalized signpost language is supposed to do, point to the intellectual operations required of the reader to understand the passage at hand.

Let us next take section iv. It is curious because the last two-thirds of the section (in boldface) are verbatim Mishnah, with characteristically Mishnaic literary-rhetorical traits and constructs. The first one-third of the section is a characteristic opening to a typical Halakhic-Midrashic passage, is it not? Let us take a closer look. We start with a citation from the base-scriptural verse, followed by the midrashic, structural signpost language, FROM THIS YOU CAN SAY, followed by a protasis (i.e., specification of case circumstances) of a typically formulated Mishnah-like or Tosefta-like rule sentence. This gives one something that accords with the following schematization:

> scriptural citation 1,
>
> FROM THIS YOU SAY
>
> protasis (only) for ruling 1.

Then the Mishnah "citation" takes over the section, giving us:

> apodasis for ruling 1,
>
> rabbi x says + ruling 2,
>
> as it it said (*she-ne' emar*) + scriptural citation 2,
>
> interpretive gloss of scriptural citation 2 supporting ruling 2.

What have we got? The last two-thirds is a Mishnaic dispute, in which the second, opposing ruling is supported by the citation of a scriptural proof-text, glossed by a brief explication of the relevance of the proof-text to the last-specified disputant's ruling. Even the formalized language for introducing the proof-text, "as it is said" (*she-ne' emar*), is the standard Mishnaic-Toseftan usage, not the more typically Halakhic-Midrashic SCRIPTURE SAYS (*tilmod lomar*). The formulator of this passage of the Mekhilta has

Halakhic Midrash

integrated a Mishnah passage, with all of its typically Mishnaic/Toseftan literary-rhetorical constructs and conventions, into this extended Halakhic-Midrashic composition by simply providing a standard Halakhic-Midrashic beginning for it. How neat is that?!

Let us turn to the remaining sections of this extended composition, starting with the first at section i. Section i, like the others, commences with a citation of a clause from the base-scriptural verse, and the signpost language that follows indicates that the rabbinic teaching that immediately ensues is the interpretation of scriptural citation 1. In schematized format, what we have is—

> scriptural citation 1,
>
> THERE IS NO . . . OTHER THAN + ruling 1.

So, ruling 1 is said to be the meaning of the biblical clause, making this opening part of section i an example of asserting a type-1 relationship with Scripture; the rabbinic ruling is an interpretation of the meaning of the biblical language cited. The remainder of section i, switches gears, rather elegantly. It argues that if one accepts ruling 1 at face value, without consideration of any other factors, logic might lead one to a(n erroneous) corollary, articulated as ruling 2. Enter the second scriptural phrase, scriptural citation 2. Only with scriptural citation 2 fully considered does one conclude that ruling 2 is not appropriate, and that the complement of ruling 1 is yet another legal teaching, ruling 3. The schematization of the last half of section i looks like this:

> IT IS POSSIBLE [THAT I MIGHT CONCLUDE THAT] . . . + ruling 2,
>
> SCRIPTURE SAYS + scriptural citation 2,
>
> ruling 3.

So, section i, which starts in a manner that looks like a type 1 passage—asserting that a rabbinic Halakha is the interpretation of Scripture—then takes on a type 4 agenda—applying reason alone, that is, without further consideration of language in Scripture, may drive one to an erroneous legal position, for which the corrective is attention to additional biblical language. In effect, section i is stating that Scripture's "it is mine" is not a redundant clause, the presence of which accords with the aesthetics of biblical Hebrew. The apparent redundancy is there for a substantive Halakhic purpose.

In the Seat of Moses

Section iii of the extended mini-essay in Mekhilta deR. Simeon, Bo, 13:1–2 is a classic, but slightly-truncated, example of portraying a type 3 relationship between Halakha and Scripture. That is, the base scripture is the basis for part of the relevant Halakha, but we are left hanging for the origins in Scripture of the ruling's Halakhic complement. Enter a second scriptural citation that is said to provide that basis. Section iii's structure is:

> scriptural citation 1,
>
> I HAVE (*ain li*) ONLY (*ela*) + ruling 1,
>
> WHENCE (*min'ayin*) + ruling 2.
>
> SCRIPTURE SAYS (*tilmod lomar*) + scriptural citation 2.

One would like to have seen the section end with the assertion that scriptural citation 2 supports ruling 2—something like,

> TO INCLUDE + ruling 2.

But it is not unusual for formalized ways of saying things to be selectively used. The intended conclusion of this section has in no way been compromised by its formulator having truncated the section somewhat.

The only part of Mekhilta deR. Simeon, Bo 13:1–2 not yet discussed is section v. And I must admit its structure is peculiar. I am sorely tempted to assign you, the reader, the task of identifying on your own what makes it odd, because you already have in hand all of the tools and knowledge required to dissect section v. Try to do this, before reading on....

So, here is what I make of section v. It starts with a scriptural citation and immediately moves on that basis to state not a ruling understood to be derived from Scripture, but to assert an analogy said to be supported by the verse. An Halakhic position is now presented; we are to gather that the Halakha in question is based upon the analogy, as indicated by typical signpost language. But the actual analogical argument follows at the end of section v. Thus we have:

> scriptural citation 1,
>
> asserted analogy based on citation 1.
>
> [THUS] THEY EXCLUDED + ruling 1,
>
> SINCE (*she*) ... [THEN] ... + restated ruling 1,

264

What happened here? I note three somewhat atypical things. First, the last two elements of the schematized section are in the wrong order. "Normally" one would expect the order to be:

> SINCE (*she*) ... [THEN] ... + restated ruling1,
>
> [THUS] THEY EXCLUDED + ruling 1—

that is, analogical argument followed by the Halakhic conclusion. Second, with my little correction of the order of things at the end, the whole of section v strikes me as something one would expect in the *second half* of a well-structured Halakhic-Midrashic passage asserting a type 3, 4, or 5 relation between the Halakha at hand and the biblical text. That is to say, the entirety of section v is what one would "normally" expect from scriptural citation 2 onward in a well-structured passage. Let me show you, by adding a "front-half" (in *italics*) to the corrected schematization of section v (in normal type)—

> *scriptural citation 1,*
>
> *ruling 1,*
>
> OR *I* MIGHT [THINK] + *ruling 2,*
>
> SCRIPTURE *says* + scriptural citation 1 (emend to 2),
>
> asserted analogy based on citation 1 (emend to 2).
>
> SINCE (*she*) ... [THEN] ... + restated ruling 1 (order corrected),
>
> [THUS] THEY EXCLUDED + ruling 1 (order corrected).

You see, that would make an elegantly structured Halakhic-Midrashic passage, would it not? Third, without the "front-half," section v cannot perform the function of a type 3, 4, or 5 passage. It may only function as a type 1 or 2 pericope of Halakhic midrash; either the ruling is the interpretation of Scripture, or Scripture is portrayed as the ground for the ruling.

What lesson can one learn from scrutiny of section v? It is obvious that familiarity with the "normal" literary-rhetorical conventions of Halakhic Midrash is equally valuable in making sense of what is going on in both well-constructed and "oddly"-constructed passages of the genre. Sometimes, "oddly" constructed passages appear to be creative genius; and sometimes they are just odd. Perhaps sections iv and v demonstrated the challenges these passages' formulators had in integrating block citations of Mishnah and Tosefta into these Halakhic-Midrashic pericopae.

In the Seat of Moses

There is one more extended Halakhic-Midrashic passage I would like to present to you in this chapter, because it shows how Mishnaic and Toseftan constructs and conventions not only can be integrated into elaborate Halakhic-Midrashic mini-essays, but can be used to "spin them out" to greater lengths. I turn then to Sifre Numbers, Korah, 118a.

Sifre Numbers, Korah, 118a

With Sifre Numbers, Korah, 118a we stay with the now-familiar Halakhic theme of the sanctity of the firstling in Scripture and in the Halakha. Sticking with this area of rabbinic (and biblical) law will make it easier for you to focus on the literary-rhetorical features of this extensive mini-essay of Halakhic midrash. The law of the firstling is treated at a number of junctures in "the Torah of Moses." The Mekhilta passage just analyzed treated Exodus 13:1–2 as its base text. The composition in Sifre Numbers, Korah, 118a uses Numbers 18:15–18 as its point of departure.

> Every firstling of all living flesh, which shall be offered to the Lord, both of humankind and of beast, shall be yours [i.e., the priests']; but you shall surely redeem the firstling of humankind, and the firstling of the unclean beast you shall [as well] redeem. And [concerning] its redemption, from the age of one month you shall redeem [it] for your silver measure of five shekels in the shekels of the Sanctuary, that is twenty *gerah*. But the firstling of an ox, or the firstling of a sheep, or the firstling of a goat you shall not redeem; they are holy; their blood you shall splash on the altar; and their fatty parts you shall ignite as a fire-offering of pleasing odour to the Lord. And their flesh shall be yours [i.e., the priests']; like the chest of the waive-offering and the right shoulder, it shall be yours.

Sifre Numbers, Korah, 118a follows, with language that equals Mishnah's in **boldface**, Tosefta's <u>underscored</u>, and Halakhic-Midrashic "signpost" language in SMALL CAPS.
Sifre Numbers, Korah, 118a[9]:

I

A. "Every firstling of all living flesh"—

B. I [MIGHT] SURMISE [THAT] EVEN [of] the wild beast IS IMPLIED!

---

[9]. Translation of Sifre Numbers, Korah 118a (ed. Horowitz, 138, ln. 1–139, ln. 16) is my own, based on an earlier version in Lightstone, *Rhetoric*, 215–22.

Halakhic Midrash

C. SCRIPTURE SAYS: "which shall be offered to the Lord"—

D. TO EXCLUDE the wild beast [which cannot be offered as a sacrifice].

E.1. [PERHAPS, RATHER] THE IMPLICATION IS TO EXCLUDE [both] the wild beast

E.2. AND TO EXCLUDE the blemished [animal, which also cannot be offered as a sacrifice].

F. SCRIPTURE SAYS: "Both of humankind and of beast"—

G. TO INCLUDE the blemished.

IIa

A. "Both of humankind and of beast"—

B. that which applies to you in the case of humankind applies to you in the case of an animal.

C. [Thus] Levites ARE EXCLUDED (= t. Bekkorot 1:1b);[10]

D.1. SINCE [the law of the firstling] of humankind does not apply to you in their case,

D.2. [THEN the law of the firstling] of an [unclean] animal should not apply to you in their case.

IIb

A. "Both of humankind and of beast"—

B. [Scripture] EQUATES the firstling of humankind WITH the firstling of an animal.

C.1. JUST AS [concerning] the firstling of an animal, aborted foeti exempt [subsequent offspring] from the law of the firstling,

C.2. SO TOO [concerning] the firstling of humankind, aborted foeti exempt [subsequent offspring] from the law of the firstling.[11]

---

10. See parallels at Sifre Zutta, Korah, 18:15 (Horowitz, ed., 295); see Mek. deR. Ishmael, Bo, 16 (Horowitz and Rabin, eds., 58), and Mek. deR. Simeon Bo 13:1–2 (Epstein and Melamed, eds., 37–38).

11. See parallel content at m. Bekhorot 8:1; t. Bekhorot 6:1; Mek. deR. Ishmael, Bo, 16 (Horowitz and Rabin, eds., 58).

D.1. Just as [concerning] the firstling of humankind, one is obligated to give [the redemption money] to the priest wherever he shall desire,

D.2. So too [concerning] the firstling of an animal, one is obligated to give [the redemption-lamb, or the firstling itself in the case of a clean animal] to the priest wherever he shall desire.[12]

IIc

A. Because it says: "And there you shall bring your burnt offerings and your holocaust offerings, etc. . . . and the firstlings of your flock" (Deuteronomy 12:6),

B. I [might] surmise [that] even in the case of the place [of the Sanctuary] being distant, it would be incumbent upon one to sustain it and bring it to the Temple.

C. Scripture says: "Both of humankind and of beast" —

D.1. Just as [concerning] the firstling of humankind, one is obligated to give [the redemption money] to the priest wherever he shall desire,

D.2. So too [concerning] the firstling of an animal, one is obligated to give [the redemption-lamb, or the firstling itself in the case of a clean animal] to the priest wherever he shall desire.[13]

E.1. And just as [concerning] the firstling of humankind, one sustains it for thirty days [and then redeems it]

E.2. So too [concerning] the firstling of an animal, one sustains it for thirty days [and then redeems it or gives it to the priest to be sacrificed] (equals content at m. Bekhorot 3:1; t. Bekhorot 3:1).[14]

III

A. "But you shall surely redeem"—

B. This was a question which was asked before the sages in the Vineyard at Yavneh:

C. [Concerning] a firstling [of an ass] which died,

---

12. See parallel content at Mek. deR. Ishmael, Bo, 16, (Horowitz and Rabin, eds., 58).
13. See parallels at Mek. deR. Ishmael, Bo, 16 (Horowitz and Rabin, eds., 58).
14. See parallels at Mek. deR. Ishmael, Bo, 16 (Horowitz and Rabin, eds., 58).

D.1. what of the owners [being permitted] to redeem it

D.2. and to feed it to dogs?

E. EXPOUNDED R. Tarfon:

F. "But you shall surely redeem"—

G.1. you redeem the living,

G.2. and [on the contrary] you do not redeem the dead;

H.1. you redeem the unclean,

H.2. and [on the contrary] you do not redeem the clean.

IV

A. "But you shall surely redeem"—

B. I [MIGHT] SURMISE [THAT] EVEN [redeeming] all other unclean animal[s] IS IMPLIED.

C. SCRIPTURE SAYS: "And the firstling of an ass you shall redeem with a sheep" (Exodus 34:20)—

D.1. you redeem the firstling of an ass,

D.2. and [on the contrary] you do not redeem the firstling of any other unclean animal (see t. Bekhorot 1:2).

E.1. OR [PERHAPS, I MIGHT CONCLUDE] from this verse THAT] the firstling of an ass you redeem with a sheep,

E.2. AND [on the contrary] any other unclean animal with clothing

E.3. AND utensils!?

F. SCRIPTURE SAYS, again, elsewhere: "And any firstling of an ass you shall redeem with a sheep" (Exodus 13:13)[15]—

G.1. with a sheep you redeem,

G.2. AND [on the contrary] you do not redeem with clothing

G.3. AND utensils.

H. IF SO, WHY DOES SCRIPTURE SAY: "But you shall surely redeem?"

---

15. Exodus 13:13 is the only other possible cognate verse that could be used at this juncture, but reads: . . . וכל פטר.

In the Seat of Moses

I.1. IF IT IS IS NOT [CONCERNED WITH] the matter that they redeem an unclean beast,

I.2. [THEN] ASSIGN IT TO the matter that they sanctify an unclean beast for the upkeep of the Temple,

I.3. and they subsequently redeem it from the sanctity of the upkeep of the Temple [and that with which they redeem it is donated for the Temple's upkeep in its stead].[16]

V

A. "Redeem"—

B. [i.e.,] immediately.

C. DO YOU SAY: "Redeem"—[i.e,] immediately?

D. OR IS IT after a time ONLY?

E. SCRIPTURE SAYS: "And [concerning] its redemption, from the age of one month you shall redeem [it] for your [. . .] measure of five shekels"—

F. [i.e., only] the one redeemed with five selahs is redeemed after a time.

G. LO, WHY [THEN] DOES SCRIPTURE SAY: "You shall redeem"?

H. You shall redeem immediately [the firstling of an ass with a sheep].[17]

VI

A. "And [concerning] its redemption, from the age of one month you shall redeem [it]"—

B. [THIS IS] A GENERAL STATEMENT.

C. "For your silver measure of five shekels "—

D. [THIS IS] A SPECIFICATION.

E. A GENERAL STATEMENT AND [subsequently] A SPECIFICATION—

---

16. See parallel to section IV in Mek. deR. Ishmael, Bo, 18 (Horowitz and Rabin, eds., 71, lines 8–14).

17. The conclusions drawn in section V appear to contradict those drawn in section II and parallel legal content at m. Bekhorot 3:1 and t. Bekhorot 3:1.

Halakhic Midrash

INCLUDED IN THE GENERAL STATEMENT IS THAT WHICH IS IN THE SPECIFICATION ONLY, [meaning, one redeems the firstling with five shekels of silver].

F. "And all firstborn sons of humankind you shall redeem" (Exodus 13:13)—

G. [HAS SCRIPTURE] REVERTED TO A GENERAL STATEMENT?

H. OR HAVE YOU [MERELY RE]STATED A GENERAL STATEMENT [INHERENT IN] THE FIRST GENERAL STATEMENT [i.e., the two general statements are to be assimilated to one another and not treated as two independent sources]?

I.1. [NO!] IT [CAN] ONLY [BE TAKEN AS] A GENERAL STATEMENT, AND A SPECIFICATION [FOLLOWING IT], AND [THEN] A [SECOND]GENERAL STATEMENT—

I.2. YOU [MUST] REASON [BY GENERALIZING] ON THE BASIS OF THE SPECIFICATION ONLY.

J.1. [The verses, therefore, intend] TO INFORM YOU [that]

J.2. JUST AS THE SPECIFICATION INDICATES [one redeems with something in the larger category of] movable property

J.3. [against] which there [can be] no liability [that is, it cannot be mortgaged],

J.4. SO TOO THE [SECOND] GENERAL STATEMENT [INDICATES the use of] ONLY movable property

J.5. [against] which there [can be] no liablity [that is, it cannot be mortgaged].

K.1. ON THE BASIS OF THESE THEY SAID:

K.2. With anything they redeem the firstling of humankind,

K.3. except **slaves**

K.4. **and deeds**

K.5. **and immovable property** (see m. Bekhorot 8:8).

L.1. Rabbi [Judah the Patriarch] says:

L.2. Even so with anything they redeem the firstling of humankind,

L.3. except deeds.[18]

VII

A.1. "That is twenty *gerah*"—

A.2. WHY IS IT SAID (i.e, why do I need Scripture to says this)?

B.1. BECAUSE IT SAYS: "And [concerning] its redemption, from the age of one month you shall redeem [it] for your silver measure,"

B.2. I [MIGHT] HAVE [UNDERSTOOD] ONLY silver [is used].

C. WHENCE [DO I LEARN] that equal in value to silver [may be used]?

D. SCRIPTURE SAYS: "That is twenty *gerah*."

VIII

A.1. "But the firstling of an ox"—

A.2. [i.e.,] a genuine ox.

B.1. "Or the firstling of a sheep"—

B.2. [i.e.,] a genuine sheep.

C.1. "Or the firstling of a goat"—

C.2. [i.e,] a genuine goat;

D. [Scripture thereby intends] TO EXCLUDE mixed-kinds (see m. Bekhorot 1:2; t. Bekhorot 1:5 and 1:13).

Admittedly, there seems to be a lot more going on in Sifre Numbers, Korah, 118a than went on in Mekhilta deR. Simeon, Bo, 13:1–2. A number of the constituent passages of the former are longer and more complex by far, with more "back-and-forth" argumentation. But, in fact, the complexity results primarily from the formulators' creativity in "spinning out" matters using the same relatively simple Halakhic-Midrashic superstructural elements, served by standard, stock, signpost language that is identical to or akin to language you have ready encountered. Indeed, by now, even without my use of SMALL CAPS, you should have been able to recognize the conventional, Halakhic-Midrashic, superstructural language evident in this extended passage, notwithstanding its penchant for spinning out matters

---

18. See parallel to section VI in Mek. deR. Ishmael, Bo, 18 (Horowitz and Rabin, eds., 72, lines 1–8).

to an extent beyond what you have seen earlier in this section and this chapter. Moreover, (I hope) you also will have begun to be able to anticipate where each constituent passage of this extended composition is taking you, by reason of the signpost effects of the language conducting you through each pericope—expect a right turn ahead, a left turn after that, a destination point lies just beyond. Even in Sifre Numbers, Korah, 118a, with its more complex constituent passages, relatively few (logical) operations are used—and they are almost all signaled by the superstructural, formalized language—to generate these passages. To show you that this is the case, let me schematically re-present this extended passage, denoting the actual stock, signpost language that is superstructural, and just characterizing the elements that lie before, in between, and after this language. (Actually, you should already be able to do this yourself.)

i

A. scriptural citation 1

B. I [MIGHT] SURMISE [THAT] EVEN + (erroneous) ruling 1 + IS IMPLIED

C. SCRIPTURE SAYS + scriptural citation 2

D. TO EXCLUDE + (erroneous) ruling 1

E.1. [PERHAPS, RATHER] THE IMPLICATION IS TO EXCLUDE + (erroneous) ruling 1

E.2. AND TO EXCLUDE + (correct) ruling 2

F. SCRIPTURE SAYS + scriptural citation 3

G. TO INCLUDE + (correct) ruling 2

iia

A. scriptural citation 1

B. stated analogy

C. + (correct) ruling 1

D.1. SINCE + (analogous) ruling 2

D.2. [THEN] + (correct) ruling 2

iib

In the Seat of Moses

A. scriptural citation 1
B. EQUATES + analogous case 1+ WITH + analogous case 2
C.1. JUST AS + analogous case 1 + (correct) ruling 1
C.2. SO TOO + analogous case 2 + (correct) ruling 1
D.1. JUST AS + analogous case 1 + (correct) ruling 2
D.2. SO TOO + analogous case 2 + (correct) ruling 2

iic

A. BECAUSE IT SAYS + scriptural citation 2
B. I [MIGHT] SURMISE [THAT] EVEN + (erroneous) ruling 3
C. SCRIPTURE SAYS + scriptural citation 1
D.1. JUST AS + analogous case 1 + (correct) ruling 4
D.2. SO TOO + analogous case 2 + (correct) ruling 4
E.1. AND JUST AS + analogous case 1 + (correct) ruling 5
E.2. SO TOO + analogous case 2 + (correct) ruling 5

iii

A. scriptural citation 1
B. place + dramatis personae
C. case circumstances
D.1. question re. ruling 1?
D.2. question re. ruling 2?
E. EXPOUNDED R. x
F. scriptural citation 1
G.1. (correct) ruling 1
G.2. not + (erroneous) ruling 3
H.1. (correct) ruling 2
H.2. not + (erroneous) ruling 4

iv

A. scriptural citation 1
B. I [MIGHT] SURMISE [THAT] EVEN + (erroneous) ruling 1 + IS IMPLIED.
C. SCRIPTURE SAYS: + scriptural citation 2
D.1. (correct) ruling 2
D.2. not + (erroneous) ruling 1
E.1. OR [PERHAPS, I MIGHT CONCLUDE THAT] + (correct) ruling 3
E.2. AND + (erroneous) ruling 4
E.3. AND + (erroneous) ruling 5
F. SCRIPTURE SAYS, + scriptural citation 3
G.1. + (correct) ruling 3
G.2. AND + not (erroneous) ruling 4
G.3. AND + not (erroneous) ruling 5
H. IF SO, WHY DOES SCRIPTURE SAY + scriptural citation 1
I.1. IF IT IS NOT [CONCERNED WITH] + case of (erroneous) ruling 1
I.2. [THEN] ASSIGN IT TO + case of (correct) ruling 6
I.3. + (correct) ruling 6

v

A. scriptural citation 1
B. + (correct) ruling 1
C. DO YOU SAY: + (correct) ruling 1
D. OR IS IT + (erroneous) ruling 2 + ONLY
E. SCRIPTURE SAYS + scriptural citation 2
F. + (correct) ruling 2'
G. LO, WHY THEN DOES SCRITPURE SAY + scriptural citation 1
H. + (correct) ruling 1

vi

A. scriptural citation 1

B. [THIS IS] A GENERAL STATEMENT.

C. scriptural citation 2

D. [THIS IS] A SPECIFICATION.

E. A GENERAL STATEMENT [subsequently] A SPECIFICATION INCLUDED IN THE GENERAL STATEMENT IS THAT WHICH IS IN THE SPECIFICATION ONLY

F. scriptural citation 3

G. [HAS SCRIPTURE] REVERTED TO A GENERAL STATEMENT

H. OR HAVE YOU [MERELY RE]STATED A GENERAL STATEMENT [INHERENT IN] THE FIRST GENERAL STATEMENT?

I.1. [NO!] IT [CAN] ONLY [BE TAKEN AS] A GENERAL STATEMENT, AND SPECIFICATION [FOLLOWING IT], AND [THEN] A [SECOND] GENERAL STATEMENT.

I.2. YOU [MUST] REASON [BY GENERALIZING] ON THE BASIS OF THE SPECIFICATION ONLY.

J.1. TO INFORM YOU

J.2. JUST AS THE SPECIFICATION INDICATES + (correct) circumstances/ruling 1

J.3. + (correct) circumstances/ruling 1'

J.4. SO TOO THE [SECOND] GENERAL STATEMENT [INDICATES the use of] ONLY + (correct) circumstances/ruling 1

J.5. + (correct) circumstances/ruling 1'

K.1. ON THE BASIS OF THIS THEY SAID

K.2. + (correct) ruling 2

K.3. + not ruling 3

K.4. + not ruling 4

K.5. + not ruling 5

L.1. Rabbi x says

L.2. + (correct) ruling 2 [i.e., without exceptions 3 and 5].

L.3. + not ruling 4

vii

A.1.   scriptural citation 1

A.2.   WHY IS IT SAID

B.1.   BECAUSE IT SAYS + scriptural citation 2

B.2.   I [MIGHT] HAVE [UNDERSTOOD] ONLY + (erroneous) ruling 1

C.   WHENCE [DO I LEARN] + (correct) ruling 2

D.   SCRIPTURE SAYS + scriptural citation 1

viii

A.1.   scriptural citation 1

A.2.   + (correct) ruling 1

B.1.   scriptural citation 2

B.2.   + (correct) ruling 2

C.1.   scriptural citation 3

C.2.   + (correct) ruling 3

D.   TO EXCLUDE + (erroneous) ruling 4

The eight individual passages, sections i to viii, making up this extended Halakhic-Midrashic mini-essay each tend to begin with a citation from the "base text" of Scripture, and juxtapose with it a rabbinic legal teaching. Sometimes stock language joins them (as in, FROM THIS THEY SAID), sometimes not. From this point, the formulator of any passage has a delimited number of options from which to choose. The passage may just end, in which case it is a type 1 or type 2 passage—the stated legal rule is the interpretation of the cited Scripture or is grounded in it, period. If the passage does not end here, then several additional things will then happen. (1) Either an inference must be made that the ruling might be (erroneously) surmised to be otherwise, or it is inferred that the ruling is correct but still deficient and must be supplemented with an additional legal teaching to be complete. But the reader is often alerted that this is happening with signpost structural language (such as: I HAVE ONLY … WHENCE …, or DO YOU SAY … OR IS IT … ONLY, or I [MIGHT] SURMISE [THAT] EVEN … IS IMPLIED, etc.). When this happens, served by whatever stock, signpost language, then the reader knows that the passage will be of type 3, 4, or 5.

That is, the base scripture is ground for only a partial, and therefore insufficient articulation of the law, or the base scripture is in itself insufficient either to prevent logic from reasoning to a different, but erroneous, legal position, or to allow one definitively to choose between two possible legal rulings. The issue then becomes this: On what scriptural basis does one rule out the erroneous position (thereby confirming the correct one), or on what scriptural grounds is one able to supplement the correct, but as yet deficient, ruling? Consequently, (2) a second scriptural citation needs to be adduced (SCRIPTURE SAYS . . .), on the basis of which (3) an argument may be articulated by analogical or other reasoning (for example, JUST AS . . . SO TOO, or SINCE . . . THEN . . . , etc.) that (4) leads us back to the correct or to the complete legal position—the erroneous or partial Halakhic stance having been ruled out (TO EXCLUDE/TO INCLUDE . . .). That the reasoning may seem less than reasonable, or that the plain meaning of Scripture may seem to you to be quite other than what is made of it, should not be overly concerning. These passages often are not exegetical commentaries on Scripture, in the normal sense of the word, exegesis. They are not even poor attempts at exegesis, but something else entirely. They read Scripture partly for its straightforward meaning—after all, the rabbinic laws of the firstling are indeed grounded in the plain sense of the scriptural laws concerning the firstling—but also as if Scripture is a "code." In a code, every word and every seeming superfluity of language is there for a reason. Halakhic Midrash attributes meaning, and therefore purpose, to these superfluities and redundancies, and asserts, furthermore, that without attention to all of the relevant code elements of Scripture, legal reasoning on its own might lead one to erroneous conclusions.

The other thing that is noteworthy about the passages of this extended mini-essay is, as previously remarked, their use of the "standard" Halakhic-Midrashic structural elements to "spin out" matters. Many of the passages of Sifre Numbers, Korah, 118a go more than "one round." How is this achieved? Very simply, passages of type 3, 4, and 5, posit *additional* erroneous rulings to which logic, unaided by another scriptural citation, might drive one, and proceed to rule each out on the basis of successive scriptural citation and appropriate (usually analogical) "reasoning." Or, for passage of type 1 or 2, simply concatenate scriptural citations and the rulings said to be derived from them.

Halakhic Midrash

Several constituent passages of Sifre Numbers' mini-essay deserve special mention, because they will, no doubt, have seemed to you to be different.

Take, for example, passage iii. It has integrated many of the formal elements of a precedent story into the pericope; in fact, the precedent-story-like elements have just been tacked on to the citation of the base scriptural verse. To give credence to such a claim, just strip away the initial citation of the base scripture and add in its stead the stock precedent-story prefacing-language, "It once happened that" (*ma'aseh she/be*)—producing something like, "It once happened that this question was asked before the sages in the Vineyard at Yavneh . . ." The exegetical "saying" attributed to R. Tarfon is not introduced with the familiar "R. x says" or "said R. x" formulary, but with one that you have not yet seen, "expounded (*darash*) R. x." *Darash* is the verbal root of the word *midrash*. The use of this attributional formula usually signals that the "saying" that follows will cite Scripture and then proffer an interpretation of it.

The last part of section vi is just a pretty typical Mishnaic/Toseftan dispute, joined to the rest of the passage by "ON THE BASIS OF THIS THEY SAID" (referring back to a previous scriptural citation and its alleged Halakhic meaning).

The first two-thirds of section vi is something different entirely. While replete with stock formalized language (hence the language in SMALL CAPS) none of that language will as yet be familiar to you from discussions so far in this chapter. Here is why the language in SMALL CAPS will have confused you; in the context of section vi, the language refers to standard *rules* for interpreting Scripture for Halakhic purposes rather than signaling "logical" operations, which has been the norm so far. But, of course, you had no way of knowing that section vi refers to several such standardized rules. Where are these rules articulated, and why have I not begun this discussion with a presentation of them? The rules may be found in the opening chapter of the Halakhic-Midrashic document, Sifra (on Levicitus). Why have I not taken you through them? Knowing them is (it may be startling to say) far less helpful in teaching you to read Halakhic-Midrashic passages than the route I have chosen; that is, to introduce you to the standard superstructural elements and associated signpost language that generate most Halakhic-Midrashic passages. I will go so far as to suggest that the "rules" for Halakhic-Midrashic exegesis of Scripture found at the outset of Sifra are more likely a later abstraction of what Halakhic-Midrashic passages tend

In the Seat of Moses

to do. And it is the latter that I wish you to be able to recognize. In short, passages like section vi are *not* the norm. Now if that is true, then could one reformulate passage vi to accord with what is the norm? Absolutely! One need only reformulate it using the following typical structure:

> scriptural citation 1
>
> I might surmise + (erroneous) ruling
>
> scriptural citation 2
>
> just as ... so too ....
>
> on the basis of this they said:
>
> legal ruling/Mishnah citation

As proof of this here is the resulting revised perciope.

1. "And [concerning] its redemption, from the age of one month you shall redeem [it]"—
2. I might surmise that with anything I redeem
3. Scripture says: "For your silver measure of five shekels" (literally, "for your *value* of five shekels"—
4. just as I redeem with five shekels, which are movable property [against] which there [can be] no liability, so too I redeem with anything that is movable property [against] which there [can be] no liability.
5. On the basis of this they said:
6. With anything they redeem the firstling of humankind,
7. except **slaves and deeds and immovable property** (see m. Bekhorot 8:8).

My reformulated pericope far more accords with what one finds in Halakhic-Midrashic documents than the pericope we actually have at section vi. What, then, is one to make of the passage we do have at vi, replete with references to formalized exegetical principles? I really do not know.[19]

    19. As I have stated, the prologue to Sifra articulates the formal exegetical rules (attributed to R. Ishmael) for expounding upon the legal content in Scripture. The prologue, known to traditional Jews as the Baraita deRabbi Ishmael, is also recited near the beginning of the daily rabbinic prayer service. But the prologue's legal rules are rarely cited within pericopae of the Halakhic Midrashim, pericope vi of our passage being one of those rarities. Many scholars believe that the Baraita deRabbi Ishmael is a late (medieval?) addition to Sifra. But, if so, I would dearly love to find manuscript evidence or a

280

Halakhic Midrash

I have escorted you through two elaborated mini-essays of Halakhic Midrash. I cannot leave so much detail without some generally summative remarks about them. The exemplary passages of the Halakhic Midrashim give evidence of a very limited number of formalized rhetorical/literary structures, served by an equally delimited number of stock literary formularies. In the simplest structure the base/opening scriptural citation is glossed by a rabbinic legal teaching/ruling, understood to be either the interpretation of the cited verse or the ruling that has its foundation in the verse. Very commonly, the base scriptural citation/verse is followed by the presentation of an erroneous or deficient rabbinic ruling/teaching, and a complementary verse is cited as the foundation for adducing the appropriate or complete rabbinic ruling on the matter. This is achieved by portraying the second verse as delimiting or extending the ruling, or providing the basis for asserting or denying an analogy. From time to time, simple, stock joining language ("on the basis of this they said") facilitates appending a ruling formulated elsewhere, often in Mishnah or Tosefta, as the concluding/conclusive ruling of the pericope.

As a final point, it is clear from the rhetorical structures in evidence in the two passages of the Halakhic Midrashim analyzed here that scriptural exegesis (in any normal sense of the term) is not what is happening here. Far too often, one would be hard pressed to see that the act of elucidating a scriptural verse would, in and of itself, logically result in the rabbinic teaching attached to it. At the foundation of the rhetoric is the inescapable impression that the authors know the valid rabbinic teaching *before the fact, as it were, and independently of Scripture*. (That is to say, at too many junctures, without knowing the Halakha in advance, one would be hard pressed to "discover" the Halakha though such "exegetical" processes.) Rather, the rhetoric of the Halakhic Midrashim appears to be an *ideological-like* exercise to demonstrate the necessity of grounding rabbinic legal teaching in Scripture, indeed in *all* of the relevant scriptural verses and in every apparent redundancy and stylistic flourish in the verses, in order to mitigate a risk. That risk is portrayed over and over again in the rhetorical structures: that with no scriptural ground, or incomplete scriptural ground, legal reasoning may well drive one to an erroneous or deficient formulation of the rabbinic law at issue. That this, and not the *bona fide* attempt systematically to elucidate Scripture, is the objective of the rhetorical structures is further

---

parallel passage in another early rabbinic document that has formulated vi differently— closer to my own reformulation of it.

supported by what I can only characterize as a relative disinterest in the integrity of scriptural passages themselves taken in their own right. We do not see scriptural phrases interpreted in the context of the sentences, paragraphs, and chapters of which they are a part and which give them meaning in context. Rather we are presented with disjointed, fragmented, and deconstructed bits and pieces of Scripture, notwithstanding the fact that these scriptural words and phrases are taken in order and that the resulting Halakhic-Midrashic passages in the Halakhic Midrashim are seen to follow the chapters and verses of the biblical books in question.

DID THE HALAKHIC-MIDRASHIC "REFRAMING" OF SCRIPTURE'S RELATION TO HALAKHA WORK?

At the outset of this chapter I make a specific claim: that many of the standard literary-rhetorical conventions and constructs already familiar from this volume's discussion of Mishnah and Tosefta are taken up as well into passages that are Halakhic-Midrashic in form. How? By these constructs' insertion into, and "reframing" by, those encompassing formalized structures that are characteristic of Midrash Halakha. In the process, I further stated, in passage after passage of the Halakhic Midrashim, Scripture's relation to the determination of the Halakha is itself "reframed." One may well ask, at this chapter's conclusion, did the "reframing" work? Did these forms of arguing from Scripture to Halakhic ruling become a dominant mode of rabbinic reasoning about the Halakha, such that Halakhic Midrash becomes the lens for understanding Mishnah, which in the third, fourth, and fifth centuries remained at the core of the early rabbinic curriculum? On balance, I would have to say, no. They did not. Yes, "Halakhic-Midrashically structured" passages do appear in the compositions and extended "essays" of both the Jerusalem and Babylonian Talmuds—which is why this chapter is an important step for you, the reader—but they never defined what either Talmud tends to do in their extended essays. Nor did any document of the Halakhic Midrashim ever displace Mishnah as a principal object of early rabbinic study. Only the Babylonian Talmud (eventually) did that, with Mishnah being (eventually) relegated to second place. All other early rabbinic texts, such as the Tosefta, the Halakhic Midrashim, and the Jerusalem Talmud would eventually be relegated to the status of aids to the study of the Babylonian Talmud and Mishnah. It is telling that one of the more comprehensive, publicly available, digital-online sources for early rabbinic legal literature, that of mahon-mamre.org, provides digital versions of the Hebrew Bible, Mishnah, Tosefta, Jerusalem Talmud, and Babylonian Talmud. Mahon-mamre.org, as of the writing of this book, presents not a single text of the Halakhic Midrashim. The latter's reframing was, it seems, largely seen as a dead end for Halakhic reasoning, and largely remains so even today in traditional rabbinic circles. Its value lies primarily in understanding the Halakhic-Midrashically structured passages taken up into the "reframing" literary-rhetorical conventions and constructs of the two Talmuds. In the next chapter, I turn to the earlier of the two Talmuds, called the Jerusalem Talmud.

SUGGESTIONS FOR FURTHER READING

Harris, "Midrash Halachah," 136–68.

Kahana, "Halakhic Midrashim," 3–106.

Neusner and Green, *Writing with Scripture*.

7

The Two Talmuds
The Jerusalem Talmud

There are two Late-Antique rabbinic oeuvres that bear the name, Talmud (also designated by its Aramaic equivalent, Gemara): the Jerusalem Talmud or Yerushalmi (JT/y. and sometimes PT); and the Babyloninan Talmud or Bavli (BT/b.). The term "talmud" derives from the Hebrew verb root, *lmd*, meaning to teach or learn depending upon the verb form; "Gemara" is its exact Aramaic cognate and derives from the verb root *gmr*. As will become apparent in this and in the next chapter, what is being "learned" or "taught" in the Yerushalmi or Bavli is analysis of Mishnah passages *in light of other "relevant" rabbinic traditions in hand* at the time of each Talmud's production. As we shall see, the Talmuds' model(s) for analyzing Mishnah is(are) of a highly specific nature. And this and the following chapter aim to introduce you to the some of the most basic, overarching literary-rhetorical conventions and structures that constitute that "specific nature" of Mishnah study.

An analytic Talmudic "essay," short or long, on a given Mishnah text is often referred to in contemporary rabbinic academies where Talmud is studied as a *sugya* (pl. *sugyot*), an Aramaic word for "lesson."[1] In each

---

1. I have never managed to identify one normative, *analytic* definition and usage of the term *sugya* (*sugyot* in the pl.). So, what I offer here is my own "stipulated" definition, which in my view is useful, and is a useful approximation of how those in the world of the contemporary rabbinic academy use the term. The term is derived from the Aramaic verb *sgy*, "to walk," the cognate of the Hebrew, *hlkh*. If one is being "walked through" a

Talmud, these "lessons," or more accurately stated, the component compositions of these composite lessons, unfold in accordance with fairly consistently applied norms for how they ought to be structured. And these recurrent structures are all served by a stock of formalized terminology that shepherd us through the composite mini-essay that is the *sugya* of Talmud on a given Mishnah passage.[2]

Now, normative literary "structures" served by stock terminology that act as "signposts" that "shepherd" us through these structures—does this not all sound familiar? It should! Because it is no different from what you, the readers, have encountered in the preceding chapters of this book. You are now going to learn how *sugyot* of Talmud in the Yerushalmi and Bavli structure their compositions and signpost (to use an awkward verb) your passage through these structures, just as you have learned to do for passages in Mishnah, Tosefta, and the legal sections of the Halakhic Midrashim. But, as you will shortly see, you come to the deciphering of Yerushalmi and Bavli legal passages with a great deal of "cash in the bank" upon which to draw. Let me explain this last remark.

In the first paragraph of this chapter I characterized legal passages in the two Talmuds as "analysis of Mishnah passages *in light of other 'relevant' rabbinic traditions in hand*." So, citations of Mishnah passages and of other rabbinic traditions that are brought to bear as authoritative sources in *sugyot* constitute a significant percentage of the substance of most Talmud passages. And guess what? On the basis of the preceding chapters of this book, you already have the tools necessary to decipher these cited sources, since they are either no different or not significantly different in style, structure and rhetoric than what you have already encountered and mastered.

---

full perusal of a Mishnah text, then one is undergoing "a lesson." And "lesson" seems to be the best colloquial translation of *sugya*.

2. None of this is to say that either Talmud's *sugyot* should be taken as transcriptions of lessons actually delivered in ancient rabbinic academies or "houses of study" in either Mesopotamia or the Land of Israel. Even if our Talmuds' *sugyot* have been informed by transmissions stemming from the actual activity of Mishnah analysis undertaken in ancient rabbis' study halls, they are imaginative, "literary" reconstitutions by the authorships of the Talmuds of what *might* have happened or *should* happen in such lessons. Why have I placed "literary" in quotation marks? Because I do not intend to take a stand on whether and to what extent the authorships of our extant *sugyot* in the two Talmuds were initially composed in writing or orally. Early rabbinic culture valued orality; this is known. But they also could not avoid writing their compositions down in order to assure their transmission or as study aids. On the subject of the role of orality in the composition of the Talmuds, I find the work of Elman to be balanced and informative, as represented in Elman, "Orality and the Redaction."

In the Seat of Moses

It is only how these sources are *typically* woven together in an analysis of a Mishnah passage that you must now learn. And there is still another bonus. While the Yerushalmi and Bavli are by no means identical, there is certainly enough of a family resemblance between sugyot in the Yerushalmi and in the Bavli that what is learned in the service of reading the former applies almost whole hog in reading the latter. So your work in this chapter, which looks at sample legal passages in the Yershalmi, serves you well in the next chapter, in which I shall review with you several typical legal passages in the Bavli.

But I have gotten ahead of myself in anticipation of what is to come. Let me, then, back up and start from where we need to begin to understand Talmud, or more specifically, the legal parts of the two Talmuds, which constitute by far the majority of their content.[3]

In contemporary traditional rabbinic circles, the Yerushalmi (c. turn of the fifth century CE) is the earlier but less studied of the two Talmuds that bear the designation. In fact, in traditional rabbinic academies today, the Jerusalem Talmud is hardly ever studied in its own right. Rather it is sometimes "consulted," if a passage of the Yerushalmi will elucidate a portion of the Bavli (c. 600 CE). Why? Because throughout the medieval and early modern periods the Babylonian Talmud became the primary object of study within institutions of rabbinic learning.[4] Today, the Bavli still enjoys

---

3. About 80 percent of Bavli (and likely even more of the Yerushalmi) is devoted to the analysis of Mishnah or to topics and materials related to Mishnah analysis, and is, consequently, legal/Halakhic in nature. Neusner is unequivocal when on this point he states, in Neusner, *First Steps*, 44–48, that four-fifths of Bavli's discourse (its composites, compositions, and conglomerates) may be classified as either Mishnah commentary of various sorts (that is, What does Mishnah mean? What is the basis of Mishnah's rulings, including its basis in Scripture? To what circumstances does it apply or not? Who is the rabbinic authority behind which ruling? etc.) or the examination of other legal issues related to but not directly addressed in the analysis of the Mishnah text at hand, sometimes concerning abstract legal principles suggested by analysis of Mishnah. This leaves about 20 percent of Bavli's sugyot, which may be classified as either Scripture commentary or as "other" content. Moreover, in his *Rules of Composition*, 15, Neusner observes that the Bavli tends to consistently order these classes of materials: "Mishnah exegesis nearly always comes first, abstract legal speculation, last." *Rules of Composition* is in some respects a synopsis of aspects of, and in other respects represents the underlying "spreadsheet" of quantified observations for, Neusner, *Bavli's One Voice*.

4. We certainly know that sometime over the course of the seventh through ninth centuries the study of the Babylonian Talmud supplanted the study of Mishnah as the core, inner-group rabbinic activity that marked one as a rabbi—*for those members of the rabbinate who saw the Babylonian rabbinic academies as seats of authority*. The geographical range of those who acknowledged the hegemonic authority of the Babylonian

this primacy of position in the curriculum of all traditional rabbinic academies. Perhaps it is for this reason that no comprehensive English translation of the Yerushalmi was produced until the 1980s, when Jacob Neusner with some of his students undertook the task.[5] However, as a testimony to rabbinic culture and ethos in the Levant in the latter Roman imperial period, when developments of great importance in Christianity and in eastern Mediterranean imperial society were taking place, the Jerusalem Talmud (JT) provides an important body of evidence indeed.

Like the BT, the JT is not entirely Halakhic (that is, legal) in content, even if it is predominantly so. There are many aggadic-homiletical passages in the JT, and proportionally more in the BT.[6] But this volume's focus is early rabbinic, *legal*, literary-rhetorical conventions and constructs. So, as we have done in chapter 6's treatment of the Halakhic Midrashim, I shall set aside any exploration of the literary-rhetorical conventions of aggadic materials in the JT, just as I shall do when in chapter 8, I discuss the BT.

---

academies expanded greatly during the period of Islam's spread in the Middle East and Mediterranean basin. Indeed, before that three-hundred-year period was concluded, precious few, if any, within rabbinic circles would have seen rabbinic leadership of the Land of Israel or their Talmud Yerushalmi in similar light. We cannot really discern the state of affairs around the time when the Bavli came into existence sometime over the course of the sixth century and/or the early seventh century. Even less so in the fifth century in the Land of Israel, just after the Yerushalmi was produced. Indeed, we do not know whether in the Land of Israel the study of the Yerushalmi in rabbinic circles was ever understood to have significantly supplanted the importance of the study of Mishnah, as the Bavli later did. On the evolution of the study and status of the Bavli in the medieval period, I have found the work of Daniel Boyarin particularly helpful; see Boyarin, *Travelling Homeland*.

5. Until Jacob Neusner and company undertook the work to produce an English translation, the only translation of the Yerushalmi into a modern language was Moshe Schwab's French translation. Schwab's French translation is often quite paraphrastic and is heavily influenced by medieval rabbinic commentaries on the Yerushalmi, especially the Pnei Moshe. In this it resembles Herbert Danby's early twentieth-century translation of the Mishnah, a work of monumental scholarship, but which paves over much of the idiomatic literary-rhetorical characteristics of the text.

6. A considerable amount of Bavli's nonlegal content is grouped in rather large conglomerates that are "aggadic" in content. Jacob Neusner has studied these aggadic conglomerates, which he calls "miscellanies," in an effort to discern their organizing principles. See Neusner, *Bavli's Massive Miscellanies*.

In the Seat of Moses

MOVING FROM THE "TANNAITIC" TO "AMORAIC" AND "POSTAMORAIC" LEGAL LITERATURES: YET ANOTHER REFRAMING OF THE FAMILIAR IN THE AS YET UNFAMILIAR

With the Jerusalem Talmud (JT) and the Babylonian Talmud (BT), we ostensibly leave those early rabbinic documents which rabbinic tradition deemed to be "tannaitic" literature, that is, documents said to represent the work and teachings of rabbinic "teachers"—since "tanna" is derived from the Aramaic verb root, *tny*, "to repeat"—who flourished in the Land of Israel, and whose careers were believed to have been undertaken either earlier than, or contemporaneous with, the generation that produced the Mishnah—let us say, c. 220–230 CE and earlier. According to rabbinic tradition, the Jerusalem Talmud (JT) and the (later) Babylonian Talmud (BT) represent the intellectual world of generations of early rabbinic authorities called *amora'im* (pl., *amora*, sg.), meaning "the ones who pronounce" or "who speak." The latter are the named authorities to whom are attributed teachings appearing in the JT and BT, and whose intellectual lives took place, says rabbinic tradition, after c. 230 CE in the Land of Israel and in the Mesopotamian-Babylonian plain.

That said, the simple designation of some rabbinic *literature* (as opposed to certain named authorities) as "tannaitic" and other *literature* as "amoraic" is rather misleading, given the focus of this volume. How so? First, you already know from previous chapters that several "tannaitic" documents (such as Tosefta and the Halakhic Midrashim) were produced after 230 CE; that is, in the "amoraic" period. Their *contents* "are said" to be "tannaitic," as are the *named authorities* mentioned in these documents. Second, and even more important for you at this juncture, "tannaitic" traditions and citations of materials that also appear in "tannaitic" documents are to be found everywhere and throughout both the JT and the BT. So, if with JT and BT one is ostensibly leaving the "tannaitic" period behind, neither the JT nor the BT is leaving "tannaitic" literature or traditions behind at all. Quite the contrary, as we shall see in this chapter and the next, both the JT and the BT portray a sphere of early rabbinic activity focused on the intense study of "tannaitic" tradition, and especially of Mishnah. The JT and the BT, to a large extent, seem attempts somehow to model for members of the rabbinic guild what it means to be fully engaged with the analysis of Mishnah in light of complementary "tannaitic" (and amoraic) traditions.[7]

Significantly for you, and as noted above, this means that the literary-rhetorical conventions and constructs in evidence in the "tannaitic" traditions embedded in the compositions and mini-essays of both the JT and BT are substantially identical to those that you have already seen and, by now (I hope), mastered by working through chapters 4, 5, and 6 of this book. In entering the literary-rhetorical worlds of the JT and BT, the intellectual, literary, and rhetorical territory reflected in Mishnah, in Tosefta and Tosefta-like traditions, and in Halakhic Midrash remains everywhere present, as the latter are adduced regularly in the Talmuds, and are juxtaposed with "amoraic" traditions, the literary-rhetorical conventions and formalized traits of many of which do not stray too far from their "tannaitic" antecedents, even if they are not identical to them.[8] Consequently, if you have come to recognize and to be somewhat comfortable with the ways in which Mishnah, Tosefta and Tosefta-like passages, and Halakhic-Midrashic pericopae cast content, then what is often attributed to "amoraic" rabbinic masters will not seem alien at all—with one blatant caveat.

Many (although by no means all) teachings attributed to amoraic authorities are in Aramaic, not in the "Mishnaic" Hebrew of the "tannaitic" traditions. Why and when Aramaic, rather than Hebrew, is used for "amoraic" traditions in the JT or BT—that is to say, can one identify rule-like norms for the use of one or the other language in the JT and BT?—is a matter of scholarly debate. Jacob Neusner has shown that there appears to have been such rules governing the authorship of the BT, but he also claims that he cannot discern the same for the JT.[9] So the casting of some amoraic traditions in Hebrew and others in Aramaic serves some purpose in the BT that it does not serve in the JT; we shall, consequently, say more about that purpose in chapter 8, not here. And in any case, if you are reading passages of the JT in English or any other translation, you will not be able to discern what is in Hebrew and what is cast in Aramaic, unless the translator has

---

7. In light of this assertion the BT's production leads to a paradox of sorts, since in the early medieval period, the study of the BT came to displace the study of Mishnah as the *summum-bonum* pursuit of the inner-group life of the rabbinic movement, by that time centered on the several large rabbinic academies (*yeshivot*) operating in the Mesopotamian plain. See again Boyarin, *Travelling Homeland*.

8. This is especially likely to be true of the traditions attributed to the earlier *amora'im* of the Land of Israel and Mesopotamia.

9. Neusner, *Language and Taxonomy*.

adopted a method for signaling such changes in language (as I do in the sample texts presented in this and in the next chapter).

There is a third, even more fundamental sense in which the literature and traditions attributed to "tannaitic" rabbis remain front and center in the two Talmuds. The compositions and extended composite mini-essays of both the JT and BT are formulated as "commentaries" (of a sort) on, and analyses of, Mishnah tractates. So, the documents comprising both the JT and BT are also organized as tractates (*masekhta*, sg., *masekhtot*, pl.), taking the very names of the corresponding Mishnah tractates that are the focus of the Talmud's analysis as their own. So Yerushalmi Tractate Shabbat is organized as an analytical-critical "commentary" of sorts on Mishnah Tractate Shabbat. And *within* each tractate of talmud, whether in the BT or JT, passages from the corresponding Mishnah tractate's "chapters" are discussed and analyzed in the order in which they appear in Mishnah. Does this sound familiar? It should, because this means that the compositions and composite mini-essays of both Talmuds are, broadly speaking, organized in accordance with principles reminiscent of how Tosefta's materials have been organized—that is, "Mishnaicly"—and decidedly not in accordance with the norms for ordering of materials in the Halakhic Midrashim. There is a sense in which Tosefta and the two Talmuds stand within the same ethos of rabbinic *paideia* (of organized, institutionalized curricula and learning), a point to which I will return in the last chapter of this book.

As already noted in chapter 3, neither the JT nor the BT has tractates of "talmud" for each and every tractate of Mishnah.[10] But that in no way diminishes the compelling nature of the observations just made in the preceding paragraph: that Mishnah tractates form the "base" text for corresponding tractates of the JT and BT, *just as was the case for Tosefta*. In other words, tractates of the JT and BT are fundamentally documents which are organized to analyze Mishnah. Each and every tractate of the JT goes about this task in more or less the same way, exhibiting more or less the same literary-rhetorical conventions and constructs to do so. And the same may be said of the BT. However, how the JT goes about this business is not entirely the same as how the BT does. Each Talmud dances to its own literary-rhetorical tune, even if there is a significant family resemblance that subtends the two Talmuds. This is why, on the one hand, each Talmud

---

10. As remarked in chapter 3, each of the JT and the BT have tractates for about 60 percent of the tractates of Mishnah, but they are not the same 60 percent. The JT has tractates that the BT does not have, and vice versa.

warrants its own chapter in this volume, even though, on the other hand, 80 percent or more of what you will master in this chapter concerning the JT is applicable to mastering the basic literary-rhetorical conventions and norms of the BT.

There is finally a fourth, quite different and important, sense in which it is overly facile to denote either the JT or the BT as "amoraic" literature, as rabbinic tradition and some modern-period introductions stemming from the social world of contemporary rabbinic academies tend to do. In both the JT and BT, tannaitic and amoraic traditions are embedded in encompassing and pervasive literary-rhetorical structures that are "postamoraic" and anonymous.

Historically speaking, "postamoraic" means different things in the context of the JT and BT. As regards the BT, "postamoraic" means later than the *historically latest* named amoraic authority mentioned in the BT. Ravina II is that person and, according to tradition, he died in Sura in Mesopotamia in the last decade of the fifth century CE. With respect to the JT, the careers of those historically latest, named *amora'im*, whose alleged traditions are cited in Land of Israel's Talmud, flourished in the last half of the fourth century, let us say, approximately 120 years earlier than Ravina II's death.

What makes the BT's overarching and framing literary-rhetorical constructs BT-*specific* stems from the work of anonymous rabbinic authors working in Mesopotamia *after* Ravina II's death—that is, in the sixth century and perhaps into the early seventh century. And those who did the same in fashioning the JT in a characteristically JT-*specific* manner did so in the Galilee sometime near the turn of the fifth century, perhaps (according to some scholars) working into the middle or later decades[11]—let us say, just before, during, or soon after the reign of the Roman emperor Theodosius II.[12] One way or another, before the Babylonian *amora*, Ravina

11. Rabbinic tradition and circles within modern rabbinic academies (*yeshivot*) simply attribute the production of JT to the latest seminal, named *amora'im* active in the Land of Israel, and the production of the BT to the latest Babylonian-Mesopotamian *amora'im* of note. This manner of attributing the authorship of the two Talmuds is reflected in the tenth-century Epistle of Rabbi Sherira Gaon, whose views in this matter have been repeated with only minor adjustments in traditional rabbinic circles ever since. Almost all modern academic scholars on the topic reject this approach and its conclusions and firmly attribute the production of our BT and JT to postamoraic authorships. For example, see Halivni, *Formation*, as well as Halivni, *Midrash*.

12. The period around the reign of Theodosius II in the fifth century CE is a watershed moment in the Roman Empire. Rome was sacked by "barbarians" migrating from

In the Seat of Moses

II, died, the work on the JT was complete in the Land of Israel. What this means, whether one seeks to understand the pervasive literary-rhetorical agenda that makes the JT, JT, or that makes the BT, BT, is this: both tannaitic and amoraic traditions are taken up into the Talmuds and reframed by authors who are *post*amoraic in their respective geographical regions of operation—the Land of Israel and Mesopotamia, respectively—making the resulting compositions, composites and essays characteristically "Talmudic" in distinctively JT-ean or BT-ean ways.

Of course, the foregoing begs at least two important question, given this volume's principal focus. (1) How much do the JT and BT differ and in what ways? And (2) how much do those differences matter to readers like yourselves who are attempting to get a toe-hold on the literary-rhetorical conventions and constructs that will make these Talmuds more accessible to you? The answers to these questions, when considered together, may surprise you. To the first, I must say: The two Talmuds differ in a number

---

Central and Eastern Europe and Western Asia, which signaled the beginning of the concentration of Roman hegemony in the Eastern Empire and its slow withdrawal from the West in favor of Gothic, Ostrogothic, and Visigothic rule in Italy, Spain, southern France, and Western North Africa. Equally important, while Christianity increasingly enjoyed imperial patronage from Constantine's reign on, the real attempt by Roman officials to Christianize the Roman Empire takes place in the fifth century; Theodosius II is a seminal figure in this development. At the end of the first quarter of the fifth century, most of the powers and privileges that the Romans had bestowed on the Jewish Patriarch in the Land of Israel were revoked. Over the course of the fifth century, so-called pagans and Jews were banned from high office in the imperial administration and the military, and from some professions (e.g., the legal profession). Soon after, they were banned from any such offices, high or not. In Justinian's time in the sixth century, these restrictions were reasserted and augmented, perhaps because their implementation had been spotty or half-hearted in the fifth century. The practices of paganism became banned, and restrictions were placed on the practices of Judaism, on synagogue construction and reconstruction. Finally, in the early sixth century, the great schools of philosophy (associated with "pagan," that is, non-Christian, thought and culture) were closed in what remained of the Roman Empire. Some of these schools reopened in the sixth century in Persian-ruled Mesopotamia under the patronage of the Persian emperor, Kurush Noshirwan the Great. If the JT is composed by its anonymous, postamoraic authors just before, during, or soon after the reign of Theodosius II, then its production lies at the very commencement of enhanced efforts to Christianize the Roman Empire. Yet, the "amoraic" traditions themselves, stemming from mid-4th-century and earlier named authorities, show little concern about a rampant-Christianizing campaign by the Roman government. For the "amoraic" elements in the JT, Christians exist and are a problem (as a Jewish heresy perhaps, or as a movement with origins in a Jewish heresy), but the Roman imperial order is still associated with so-called paganism and high literary culture, and high culture and thought outside Jewish circles are associated with that of the pagan philosophical schools.

of quite substantial ways. These differences include, among other things, terminology, rules of composition, and analytic agenda. And quite a lot of detailed modern scholarship has been dedicated to these differences. My answer to the second question, as you might have anticipated from remarks made earlier, runs entirely counter to the direction of my response to the first. I have already stated that a basic grasp of the literary-rhetorical conventions and constructs of the legal sections of one Talmud provides a pretty firm foundation for beginning to read the other Talmud.[13] Given,

---

13. In fact, the differences notwithstanding, the similarities of how compositions in JT and in BT go about their core business at the rhetorical-structural level is such that one may well conclude that a common underlying set of norms for this way of treating Mishnah analysis probably predates and *independently* informs those that produced the JT and BT. I say "independently," because while the authors of the JT and BT shared many sources, the latter did not seem to have the work of the former in front of them; in general, the BT's *sugyot* are not developments of the JT's "parallel" *sugyot*. These observations, therefore, lead one to conclude that some norms of studying Mishnah "Talmudic-ly" existed and had become entrenched before either authorship of the two extant Talmuds undertook their work independently of one another. In the last chapter of this book, I shall have more to say about this.

Of course, all of this begs questions about the literary-historical relationship of the Yerushalmi and Bavli. I have generally skirted matters of literary history in this book. They do not concern its principal purpose, as I have stated many times already. But for those who are interested, here is my perspective on the matter, and I shall say no more about the subject in this or in the next chapter. Of course, there is ample scholarly literature on this topic, and a variety of opinions, and I shall reference some of the more recent scholarship only in the course of my remarks in the remainder of this note and thereafter make no further reference to these scholarly works.

Given the generally accepted conclusion that the JT was formulated between, let us say, 150 to 200 years before the BT, and given that the rabbinic movements of the Land of Israel and Mesopotamia were regularly in contact with one another, it stands to reason that a burning scholarly question will have been whether the JT formed a basis for the authoring of the BT. Their authors certainly shared an overlapping pool of both tannaitic and amoraic traditions, and both authorships similarly organized their work as Mishnah commentary and analysis. Moreover, as I shall point out later in this chapter and the next, the "questions" that both the JT and BT "ask" in their respective enterprises of Mishnah elucidation often resemble one another, as do, in many instances, how these questions are addressed. This cannot be the result of some historical accident. That said, as I state above, it appears to be the case that the vast majority of composites and mini-essays of the BT are *not* developments of their "parallels" in the JT, even when these parallels adduce the very same tannaitic traditions (and sometimes the same amoraic sources) in their respective analyses of Mishnah. More often than not, BT's composite mini-essays are not modeled on their parallels in JT, in my experience.

There are many contemporary scholarly works on this topic, and the matter is undoubtedly one that remains hotly debated. For an example of this debate one may read Hayes, *Between*; countered by Neusner, *Are the Talmuds Interchangeable?* (Neusner's

therefore, the focussed objectives of this book, I shall pay relatively little attention in this chapter and the next to the issues drawn in the wake of the first question about the differences between the JT and BT, and focus on literary-rhetorical literacy that facilitates the reading of either Talmud.[14] I start with the JT only because it is the earlier of the two Talmuds, not because it is necessarily the easier to decipher. But for our particular purposes, I could have gone about matters the other way around. At the risk of repeating myself in service to a good cause, that being to reassure you, the upshot is this: all the lessons about to be learned in what follows about how to read JT-ean legal compositions and composite mini-essays apply almost whole hog to the BT, *mutandis mutandi*.

---

counterargument is to Hayes's dissertation, of which her book *Between* is the published version.) See also Gray, *Talmud in Exile*; Neusner, *Two Talmuds*.

Amid the scholarly debate on this issue, I find elucidating, well balanced, and nuanced Yaakov Elman's view on the role of Palestinian traditions in the work of Babylonian rabbis' formulation of their Talmud. Elman states in "Orality and the Redaction," 87:

> ... [T]he existence of large-scale Palestinian structures within the Bavli may point to some written transmission; we have already seen that the evidence for written texts of the Amoraic period is Palestinian in provenance. Nevertheless, there is little doubt, as modern scholarship has maintained for the last century, that the Bavli's redactors did not have the redacted Yerushalmi before them. Nevertheless, it would seem that some more elaborate Palestinian texts reached them, beyond the relatively short *memrot* that are explicitly attributed to (usually early) Palestinian Amoraim.

Of course, the statements I have just made in the body of the text of this chapter and near the beginning of this note betray my leanings on this question, and the exemplary Yerushalmi and Bavli composite essays discussed and analyzed later in this chapter and the next unequivocally support my leanings. As we shall see in these two chapters regarding two composite essays discussing one and the same Mishnah passage, the authors of the Bavli composite did *not* use the "parallel" Yerushalmi composite *at all* as a model for their own essay. However, let me stress once again that these are issues which are critically important from a literary-historical perspective, but they are not my preoccupation here.

14. I reserve for the last chapter of this volume my musings about some of the most obvious ways in which JT and BT differ and about what significance may be attributed to these more blatant differences.

The Two Talmuds

JT, AN ARCHITECTURAL STRUCTURE INTO WHICH VARIOUS TYPES OF (OFTEN "PREFABRICATED") MATERIALS ARE PLACED

A full mini-essay or even a more modestly-sized composition of the JT (or of the BT) may seem to you like a trip to alien territory—at first glance. But let me assure you that only part of that territory should be alien to you—as of yet—at this juncture. Why? Because once again and as intimated earlier, learning to cope with the literary-rhetorical conventions and constructs of the Jerusalem Talmud involves recognizing the by-now-familiar embedded within a new JT-ean literary-rhetorical framework that by this chapter's end will no longer seem mysterious at all.

The familiar comprises passages and citations of parts of passages that are of three types; they are

(1) Mishnaic;

(2) Toseftan (and Tosefta-like); and

(3) Halakhic-Midrashic in character—

all usually in Hebrew. When cited in JT-ean compositions, Toseftan, Tosefta-like, and Halakhic-Midrashic passages are referred to in traditional rabbinic circles as *beraitot* (pl.; *baraita*, sg.). As stated in chapters 5 and 6, *baraita* designates an authoritative "tannaitic" tradition that is not contained in (literally, is "outside" of) the Mishnah; *beraitot* are second in authority only to Mishnah passages (and, of course, Scripture itself). The literary-rhetorical traits of no Mishnah passage or *baraita*-tradition appearing in either Talmud should appear foreign to you by now. The unfamiliar that is characteristically JT-ean is of an additional three types:

> (4) materials attributed to named *amora'im* and anonymous materials traditionally understood to reflect "amoraic" traditions that in literary-rhetorical terms bear some family resemblance to the types of passages you have already seen in the so-called "tannaitic" documents;
>
> (5) a layer of formalized critical-analysis and argument, sometimes bearing attributions to "amoraic" authorities and sometimes anonymously presented, that is "dialectic," in that arguments will be made and challenged by counterarguments; and
>
> (6) elements that frame and help structure passages by posing critical-analytical questions, or by inviting certain types of

critical-analytical argument and inquiry, about Mishnah (primarily) and (secondarily) about other "tannaitic" and "amoraic" passages and teachings.

Elements of types 4, 5, and 6 are sometimes in Hebrew and sometimes in Aramaic, and, as already mentioned, it is difficult to discern in JT rules that determine the use of one or the other language. Elements of type 4, "amoraic" traditions and sources that to some lesser or greater degree, depending on the individual tradition, resemble "tannaitic" materials, will not present much difficulty for you from the perspective of their literary-rhetorical features. Either they tend to gloss, comment on, complement, or supplement a "tannaitic" source, often Mishnah, resembling somewhat the way Tosefta or Tosefta-like sources do, or they may proffer scriptural grounds for legal teachings in a manner recalling some of the constructs of Halakhic midrash, or they gloss other "amoraic" teachings. This is not to say that this "amoraic" body of traditions in the JT's architecture displays formal traits identical to "tannaitic" traditions; it does not. To note just one difference by way of example, attributions tend to be in the perfect tense (e.g., "said rabbi x"), which in "tannaitic" materials is used almost exclusively for "debates." And "amoraic" attributional formulas often supply naming-chains (e.g., "said rabbi x in the name of rabbi y" or "said rabbi x [that] rabbi y said"). When "amoraic" materials gloss "tannaitic" materials or other "amoraic" sources, they will tend not to be fully articulated sentences and to rely on the antecedent source for an intelligible content. But you have already seen this before, for example, in many Tosefta passages. On the whole, type-4 material, then, does not warrant special attention in this chapter. You will recognize in it the "amoraic" counterparts of literary-rhetorical forms and conventions found in Mishnah, Tosefta and Halakhic Midrash, of which conventions they are likely third- and fourth-century developments. In short, you will "figure it out" yourselves, without an extensive discussion in this volume of their literary-rhetorical traits.

The same cannot be said of elements of type 5 and of type 6 in the architecture of the JT. This is where your challenge as novice readers of Talmud will lie. And this chapter, beginning with the next section, will focus especially on the literary-rhetorical features of these elements.

LET'S ASK QUESTIONS, ANSWER THEM, AND THEN (SOMETIMES) ARGUE ABOUT THE APPROPRIATENESS OF THE ANSWER, SO WE CAN PROPOSE ANOTHER

In the previous section, I characterized a specific layer of the JT's language (type 6) as framing/structuring language, formalized language that poses questions or invites specific forms of analysis of Mishnah (primarily) and of other "tannaitic" and "amoraic" traditions (secondarily). Most compositions, composites, and extended mini-essays appear *as if* they are generated by this type-6 language, which likely comes from the postamoraic authorship of the Yerushalmi. Why do I use the term "*as if,*" in italics, in the previous sentence? Because I wish to highlight this language's literary-rhetorical *function*, without making explicit or implicit claims about the actual literary-historical development of these JT-ean compositions or composites. To say that this is their literary-rhetorical function is to highlight these stock terms' service as the literary-rhetorical architectural superstructure of JT's compositions and composite mini-essays, much as steel girders do in a building. Everything else is (made to appear to be) attached to it and supported by it, or, to mix metaphors, (are made to) appear to be drawn in their wake.

Type-6 language is served by a rich but still-relatively restrained repertoire of highly laconic stock literary-rhetorical formularies that *signal* (a) the posing of specific sorts of questions demanding appropriate answers or (b) the invitation to engage in particular types of critical/analytical discussion. The latter, in turn, often calls for adducing *secondary* authoritative sources in support of such analyses or arguments. These sources may be *beraitot* (type-2 and type-3 elements), or "amoraic" teachings (type-4 elements) that are similar to *beraitot*, or related passages from secondary Mishnah passages (type-1 elements)—that is, Mishnaic passages other than the one that is the primary object of the composition's analysis. To what end? As already stated, to address critical or analytical questions posed about a *primary* authoritative source or issue. First and foremost, those critical and analytical questions are posed about Mishnah; about 60 percent of the Mishnah's tractates and "chapters" provide the "base text," that is to say, the *primary* authoritative sources that are the principal objects of inquiry of the entirety of JT's (as well as the BT's) literary endeavours. That is what makes the JT and the BT documents focused on critical analysis of

In the Seat of Moses

Mishnah. (As to why both JT and BT each have no corresponding tractates for 40 percent or so of Mishnah's tractates—and puzzlingly, a different 40 percent in each case—no one really knows.)

So, to summarize and repeat, type-6 (postamoraic) stock language functions to frame and to (appear to) drive the critical-analytical discussion of JT's compositions about Mishnah passages. And in so doing, other sources will often be adduced in the process, and this is where the "prefabricated" materials of types 1 (other Mishnaic materials), 2 (Toseftan and Tosefta-like passages), 3 (Halakhic-Midrashic pericopae), and 4 ("amoraic" teachings) will be incorporated into the composition's superstructural frame.

How might I better characterize, and prepare you to see, the framing/structural role of type-6 elements, signaled by their stock formularies, in the JT (and BT)? By asking you first to engage with me in an act of creative imagination.

If I were to give you an ancient legal text like Mishnah, with its rule-sentences, disputes, debates, and precedent stories, and if, furthermore, I were to ask you to tell me what critical and analytical questions might occur to you to pose about passages like a Mishnah text, what would you ask? Would it not occur to you to ask questions such as

What does the passage actually mean?

What precise circumstances does the law assume to be present?

Why should the rule be what it is said to be?

Why should the rule be different in some seemingly comparable case, if indeed it is?

What or who is the authoritative source for the ruling that bears no attribution?

In the case of disputes, why do the two "disputants" disagree about what the appropriate ruling ought to be for ostensibly the same posited circumstances?

Is there a basis for deciding which disputant's position is correct?

Can one posit additional circumstances that would render both positions correct?

In the case of debates, do the two "debaters'" arguments make equally good sense?

Why might one of the parties to the "debate" not concede to the reasoning of the other party?

Are the posited circumstances that comprise the case ruled upon clearly or fully articulated?

Why do we need a ruling about these circumstances at all?

Are there different but related circumstances for which a ruling is needed, but not provided?

How would each of the disputing parties rule in the case defined by these different but related circumstances?

You can readily understand from this simple exercise of *imagining* some appropriate critical/analytic questions how a document, the overarching compositional purpose of which is to pose (and answer) such questions of Mishnah, will have a very different literary-rhetorical agenda, and therefore a different repertoire of stock literary-rhetorical formulae, than Mishnah, Tosefta and Tosefta-like passages, and Halakhic-Mdrashic passages. And you might even now be able to imagine how, in posing these questions of a Mishnah passage, the citation of *other* Mishnah passages, of Toseftan and Tosefta-like materials, of Halakhic-Midrashic pericopae, and of teachings of similar ilk attributed to *amora'im* (what I earlier designated materials of types 1, 2, 3, and 4) might come into play in service of contemplating answers to such questions. For instance, Toseftan materials might confirm the meaning of a Mishnah passage, or might be understood to supply the name of an authority behind an anonymous Mishnah ruling by supplying an attributed saying or a dispute where Mishnah has neither. Or Toseftan-like sources might proffer reasons for the disputants' opposing rulings by giving us a debate where Mishnah has only the dispute. Another Mishnah ruling, cognate in some fashion to the Mishnah passage under analysis, may provide an apt legal analogy in order to help justify the Mishnah ruling under review. Or a Halakhic-Midrashic passage may provide the "logic" that grounds the Mishnah rule being analyzed in Scripture.

Our exercise of imagining critical-analytic questions that one might pose while closely studying a Mishnah passage has produced language in standard, complete English sentences. As you probably have come to expect by this point in the volume, early rabbinic literary-rhetorical conventions often evince stock, highly laconic and formulaic language, a linguistic shorthand that functions as a kind of standardized code for what the reader is to expect or to do. For example, the question, "Why should the rule be what it is said to be?" could be formulaically reduced to simply "Why?" "What or who is the authoritative source for the ruling?" could be reduced formulaically to just "Who taught?" or to "Whence?" This now begins to resemble the type of stock, highly laconic signaling formularies that serve to indicate what type of question is being posed or what type of analysis is being requested. And as with so much of the stock, shorthand formulae and signpost terminology that you have seen so far in this book, the reader of JT (or BT) is left to fill in the missing bits of the question so that it is a complete statement about the specific matter at hand: "Who [is the tannaitic authority who] taught [Mishnah's anonymously conveyed ruling that the bearer of a writ of divorce from the Mediterranean provinces must be able to declare that the writ was written and signed in his presence]?" That is a lot to fill in. Where does the reader of JT (or BT) get the substance to make these interpolations? Simply from (a) recognition of what the formulaic shorthand is supposed to signal, and from (b) the contextual language that both precedes and follows the formulaic terminology.

Just by way of introduction to what is to follow later, let me show you at this juncture what some of this formulaic code for posing critical questions and inviting analysis (type-6 elements) *actually* looks like by extracting and organizing a list of formalized terms of this type from just one extended mini-essay of the JT, y. Avodah Zarah 1:6 (which I shall present in full later). Now, I should forewarn you that in creating this list, I have been very conservative in assigning formalized language to this category. That is to say, if I have had any question as to whether formalized terminology "signposts" asking questions, asserting challenges, and inviting analyses *versus* shepherding us through arguments and analyses, I have assigned the terminology to the latter (i.e., type-5 language) rather than the former category (i.e, type-6 language). Later in this chapter, I shall say more about why I have done so, and why, in the next chapter, I will no longer exercise such excessive conservatism. Below, then, is the resulting list of such formularies (in the right-hand column), organized by their "structuring" function (specified in the left-hand column),[15] compiled from y. Avodah Zarah 1:6.[16]

Analytic Function	Formulary in y. AZ 1:6
demanding a reason	why?
challenge inviting further analysis	(none discernable in y. AZ 1:6)
introducing an authoritative source to commence/spark or to resolve argumentation	–there we have taught/learned ... –as/and it has been taught ...
inviting further analysis or argumentation	–what!? –what is the difference among them? –what distinguishes ... ? –but they (might have/should have/would have) responded to him how?
introducing an alternative/hypothesis to spark further analysis	–they should have said ... –in accordance with his approach they (might have/should have/could have) responded to him ...
asking for some authoritative basis	–and whence ... ? –who taught it?
drawing interim or final conclusions to an analytical problem	(none discernable in y. AZ 1:6)

Two things, even at this early stage in this introduction to JT-ean literary-rhetorical conventions, are evident about the catalogue of stock formularies in the right-hand column of this list. Every stock phrase or term serves either *to invite something specific in its wake* and/or *to steer the "conversation" in a certain direction*, does it not? In other words, we have here just another set of formalized, *signpost* language. You have seen formalized, signpost language before in this volume (for example, in chapter 6's treatment of the literary-rhetorical conventions of the Halakhic

---

15. I will use this same classification of types of analytic function again in chapter 8 in presenting BT's literary-rhetorical conventions, and contrasting them with JT's. Formularies extracted from just one composition of JT will not capture the total array of such JT-ean formalized terms of type 6. Hence, in part, the paucity of such formulaic terms in some functional categories. But it is in fact the case that BT displays a comparative richesse of such structuring, critical/analytic formularies, as will be evident in the next chapter, and as I have sought to demonstrate in Lightstone, *Rhetoric*, 49–75.

16. From Lightstone, *Rhetoric*, 72–74.

Midrashim). As already indicated from this list extracted from one JT-ean composite mini-essay, y. Avodah Zarah 1:6, the postamoraic authorship's repertoire of signpost, structuring language is simply richer and invites a correspondingly richer and decidedly more analytic set of "operations" than the "arguments" from Scripture of Halakhic midrash. The analytic "operations" that are drawn in the wake of JT's stock structuring language are, as previously stated, answers and arguments, sometimes attributed to amora'im and sometimes provided anonymously. Above we classified these elements that provide analyses, arguments, and answers as type-5 language. And in the case of signpost language demanding a "superior" authoritative source to resolve an argument or respond to a question, the composition may adduce within those arguments and analyses "tannaitic" material, such as, (another, related) Mishnah passage, a Tosefta pericope or Tosefta-like source, a Halakhic-Midrashic passage, or even an authoritative amoraic teaching.

MAY I HAVE AN ARGUMENT, PLEASE?

To recap what has been articulated so far, in the JT, stock literary-rhetorical terminology signals type-6 elements that provide the "superstructure" of compositions; these elements invite analysis, response, and argument, which earlier in this chapter I characterized as the type-5 elements of a JT-ean composition. The latter I described as a layer of formalized critical-analysis and argument, sometimes attributed to *amora'im*, that is "dialectic." By this I mean that arguments will be challenged by counterarguments—back and forth, until an allegedly compelling response is left to "carry the day" (or not). This literary-rhetorical layer (that is, our type-5 elements) of the JT (and the BT) is also served by a class of stock, formalized language, equally sparse, frugal and laconic in formulation, that provides (let us say) the "substructure" of JT-ean arguments and analyses—the joists and studs, supported by the superstructure, to which the substance of the arguments, and supporting "evidence" are attached. Let me now make some preliminary, orienting remarks about this layer of JT-ean language and provide a foretaste of the stock, formalized terms that serve it.

Those of you who are fans of the early Monty Python movies or who are old enough to remember their original television show, "Monty Python's Flying Circus," may recall their famous "argument scene." A professional "arguer" operates out of a small office. Any person who felt the need to have an argument—who, after all, does feel argumentative at times?—could avail himself or herself of these professional paid services, when feeling grouchy. After all, far better to argue with a professional service and get it out of your system, than to do so at home with one's partner or children. Some hapless individual enters the office, not to have an argument to assuage their grouchiness, but to get street directions, and becomes unintentionally embroiled in the "arguer's" professional *raison d'etre*, for which payment is then requested. In this comedy sketch, every remark of the hapless guest in the "arguer's" office is met with a challenge, objection or question. Entering into the realm of what I have enumerated as type-5 language in the JT (or BT, for that matter), itself attached to a latticework of type-6 terms that pose analytic questions and invite further analysis, is like venturing into this office, because a composition of JT framed by an opening question about a Mishnah passage sometimes proceeds immediately to a definitive answer, but often does not. When it does not, and this is frequently the case, the composition will challenge, test and reject several responses before settling on a final resolution—or, sometimes, no final resolution is endorsed at all, and the last (unopposed) answer is just left there, as if to carry the day. In these many instances, "round one" of a "bout" will not suffice to produce a definitive result, and several more "rounds" will ensue, incorporating an answer, a challenge, a second answer, another challenge, etc. The opening question "sets up" the bout, and invites particular types of responses, argument and/or supporting evidence, which in turn engender challenges and counterarguments that incur another "round."

All of this—answer, challenge, new answer, new challenge—is, as mentioned, structured by its own highly-laconic, stock formulaic terms, providing the "substructure" of individual compositions' analyses that are occasioned by the "superstructural" queries. These substructural formulaic terms "shepherd" one through the arguments and counterarguments. This "substructural," stock terminology of the type-5 layer of the JT is often so laconic, so sparse, in nature that it is hard to see it for what it is, unless someone points it out to you. But when someone does, one immediately perceives the *rhythm-like cadence and flow of the back-and-forth* of the analyses—within "rounds" of the "bout" and between "rounds"—through which this type of signpost language leads one. In fact, in learning to read passages of the JT (or BT), perceiving this sense of rhythm goes a very long way in assuring that the reader does not lose his or her way in the composition, which is why in contemporary traditional rabbinic academies (*yeshivot*), students studying Talmud often read to themselves aloud in a kind of singsong voice. The resulting scene is not the image one normally has of a quiet study hall, where even breathing too loudly may result in hostile looks from others who are trying to concentrate.

Permit me to give you a sense of all of this by extracting the stock formulaic language serving and signaling both type-6 and type-5 elements from just one composition of the larger composite at y. Avodah Zarah 1:6. Attend to the language that is not in square brackets.

[OPENING OF BOUT]

> [reference to Mishnah citation that is the base text of the composition]

Why?

[ROUND ONE]

> [laconically stated assertion 1, functioning as analogy]

but

> [laconically stated assertion 2, functioning as counteranalogy]

but

> [laconically stated assertion 3, functioning as counter-counteranalogy]

[ROUND TWO]

One can say,

there in the former case,

> [laconically stated assertion 4, functioning as an counter-counter-counteranalogy]

verily here

> [laconically stated assertion 5, functioning as an analogy],

since

> [stated circumstances, supporting analogy],

it is not

> [laconic statement]

[ROUND THREE]

>Said R. x in the name of y:
>
>That there
>
>>[in circumstances that seem similar but not legitimately analogous to Mishnah's . . .]
>
>Henceforth [in the case at hand]
>
>>[in circumstances that are stated in Mishnah . . .]
>>
>>[stated conclusive reason for Mishnah's ruling].

As I remarked earlier, I have deliberately been overly conservative and cautious, indeed, probably too cautious, in assigning stock formulaic language to the category of superstructural signpost language (type 6). I will continue to exercise this cautious conservatism in this chapter. I have done this in the belief that for you, the readers, an initial entry into Talmudic compositions will be made easier this way. (In the next chapter, I will be less conservative in this respect, because you will have already gained a footing in Talmudic discourse, after having worked through this chapter.) That said, the "why" at the outset of this composition is undoubtedly a stock term serving a type-6 element function. "Why" is superstructural, highly-laconic, signpost language at the broadest level, and the *entire* composition is drawn in its wake. It is all—just this one word, "why?"—that informs us of the outcome that is expected from what follows, namely, to discern the reason, or reasoning, behind Mishnah's rule in these particular circumstances.

The rest of the language of this composition tries several analogical approaches to answering the opening, one-word question. The whole composition goes three "rounds" before settling on a supposedly compelling conclusion—since the composition just stops after "round" three. The first "round" itself has several internal "rounds." What I wish you to see in particular is this: all "rounds" are *marked-out* by the most laconic of terms used as signpost language with specific functions in conducting the countering, back-and-forth flow (the rhythm) and tenor of the arguments and analyses:

>–"but . . . but . . .";
>
>–"one can say in the former case . . . verily here . . . since . . . it is not . . .";
>
>–"that there . . . henceforth . . ."

In the Seat of Moses

While my archconservative approach to diagramming of things as superstructural has led me to further indent this language, marking this language as substructural, formulaic terms that shepherd us through argumentation, one can readily see that some of these terms (like "one can say" and "but") in fact do a kind of double duty; they also function to alert us that a counter-argument is about the follow. In this respect, some of these terms "also" and "simultaneously" work as type-6 structural formularies. While I stand by my distinction between stock language serving the posing of questions and inviting analyses, on the one hand, and those terms that shepherd us through argumentation (often with supporting evidence adduced), the categories do overlap somewhat.

The only other formulaic language in the composition that is present is the attributional formula, "said R. x in the name of y." Rabbis x and y are, in this instance, *amora'im*. So, the final and (supposedly) definitive "round" of the bout is, in this case, attributed to amoraic authorities. But there is nothing remarkably different in kind about the argument attributed to the amoraic authorities in "round" three, when compared with the anonymously conveyed arguments in "rounds" one and two. And the highly laconic signpost language that signals the back and forth, the give and take, of the argument from analogy is not substantially different in the final argument attributed to named *amora'im* than in the arguments that precede it. If fact, the signpost language of the attributed argument in "round" three seems closely related to that of "round" two: in both instances the back-and-forth analogical argument is "marked" by language that contrasts "there" [in that case] with "here" [in this case]—the rhetorical equivalent of the contemporary English terms, "in the former case . . . in the latter case." As for the "but . . . but . . ." in "round" one, even in colloquial modern English we signal that counterevidence is about to be adduced by using the term "but." That is why in meetings one is supposed to avoid using the word, if one can, in order not to come across as overly argumentative or dismissive of others' views. So why designate "said . . . said" as formulaic language serving/signaling type-5 elements, the elements of a JT-ean composition in which argument, analysis and counterargument proceed? Why not just denote "said . . . said" as a stock formula for attributing what is to follow to named authorities? Because in JT "said . . ." often denotes *more than* an attribution to a named rabbi; it (like "but") can *also* signal that what follows proffers a different argument or a counter-argument to what has preceded it. Do we not do much the same in modern English when we designate an unresolved conflict as a "(s)he-said-(s)he-said situation"? "Said . . . Said," therefore, can serve to create the back-and-forth rhythm that is so helpful in discerning what is happening, or supposed to happen, in the composition. Because of this, "said," like "but," sometimes does double duty, as a term shepherding us through the dialectic-argumentative discourse (type-5 elements) and as a marker that a counterargument in that discourse is about to take place, in which case it functions *as well* as a structural signpost (type–6 element). Where have we seen this before? In "debates" in Mishnah and Tosefta (fully discussed in chapter 4): "said to him . . ., said to him . . ." Debates, when found in Mishnah or Tosefta, follow disputes, in which there are two opposing, matched views. When "said . . ." functions in JT not just to attribute something to a named sage, but to signal a coming counterargument, it functions outside of the "tannaitic" dispute/debate structure. Then, again, "said" can also function in a manner that is like neither type-6 nor type-5 terminology. For example, when "said . . ." functions in JT (or BT) just to attribute a view to an "amoraic" authority, it serves as a type-4 element, the introduction of an "amoraic" source not too different than, even if not of equal authority to, a "tannaitic" source, to which type-4 elements often bear a strong resemblance, as stated earlier. "Said" is certainly a multi-purpose term in Talmudic compositions. But when it helps establish and mark the back-and-forth cadence of part of a JT-ean or BT-ean composition it is certainly more than a term for assigning materials to named rabbinic figures.

What about the language I have not presented from this sample composition, that which is just represented in square brackets? Some of this language are rule-sentences or parts of rule-sentences that will not seem overly alien to you at all, given what you have already seen in Mishnah and Tosefta, even though this composition within y. Avodah Zarah's composite essay cites no tannaitic sources in any of its rounds. The rule-sentences, whole or partial, have protases (case circumstances) and apodases (rulings), specified or understood. And analogical arguments, "marked out" by their sparse signpost terminology, often do nothing more than compare two or more rule-sentences: [if] "there" in those circumstances, the rule is this, [then] "here" in these circumstances, the rule is/is not/should be/should not be . . ." "There" and "here," "but" and "but" signal comparison, sometimes to find that the comparators are similar in ways that are germane, in which case one conclusion follows, and at other times to assert that the comparators are not similar, in which case a different conclusion follows. All this will become increasingly clear when, later in this chapter, sample compositions and composite mini-essays of JT are presented and discussed.

WHAT IS TO BE LEARNED BY "FAKING IT"?

To this juncture, what this chapter has conveyed has been rather abstract in nature, punctuated by some extracted samples of stock formulaic language that either poses questions and invites analysis, or that marshals the reader through the "rounds" of argument/analysis and counterargument that are portrayed as addressing the "bout's" opening query. It is time to get concrete, to show you how a typically JT-ean composition, served by its stock, formalized terminology, poses questions and invites analysis, orders "rounds" of response and counterresponse, and cites authoritative sources, especially "tannaitic" ones, in support of these arguments—all to elucidate a Mishnah passage that is the base-text of the composition. And, once again, I shall commence the process of making it "real" for you by concocting a "fake" JT-ean passage about (what else?) the highway code and an intersection with a four-way stop. In the ersatz JT-ean composition that follows I have used SMALL CAPS to highlight stock formulaic language of types 6 and 5, underscoring the latter to distinguish it from the former.

[Mishnah]

1. From the west, and
2. from the east—
3. both proceed [Mishnah Highway Code 1:1a].

[Gemara]

4. WHO TAUGHT IT?

ROUND 1

5. SAID Rabbi Scott [an *amora*] [THAT] Rabbi Angus [an *amora*] SAID: Justice Smith [a *tanna*, taught it],
6. AS HAS BEEN TAUGHT [in a *baraita*]:

7. From the west, and
8. from the east—
9. both proceed.
10. If one signals a left turn,
11. Justice Smith says: The other has priority.
12. Justice Jones says: The other does not have priority [Tosefta Highway Code 1:1].
13. WHAT [can one seriously maintain that Justice Smith is the tannaitic authority behind the Mishnah]!?
14. THERE [in Tosefta Highway Code 1:1] Justice Smith said [his ruling] regarding one [who] signals a left turn,
15. HERE [in Mishnah Highway Code 1:1, Mishnah teaches] not regarding one [who] signals a left turn.

ROUND 2

16. [THEN] WHO TAUGHT IT [i.e., the ruling in Mishnah Highway Code 1:1a]?
17. SAID Rabbi Robert [an *amora*]: Justice Jones [taught it].
18. AS HAS BEEN TAUGHT [in the same *baraita*]:
19. Justice Jones says: The other does not have priority [Tosefta Highway Code 1:1]
20. THERE [in Tosefta 1:1] Justice Jones does not concern himself with whether one signals a left turn;
21. HERE [in the section of Mishnah 1:1 under analysis] we are not concerned with whether one signals a left turn.
22. WHAT, [how can one maintain that the Mishnah passage under analysis is not concerned about whether one signals a left turn]!?
23. [SINCE] THERE WE HAVE TAUGHT [a little later in Mishnah 1:1b]:
24. If one signals a left turn,
25. the other has priority.
26. Justice Jones says: The other does not have priority [Mishnah Mishnah 1:1b].

In the Seat of Moses

ROUND 3

27. WHO [THEN] TAUGHT IT [i.e., Mishnah Highway Code 1:1a]?
28. [It is] Justice Franklin [a *tanna*], and Smith and Jones [only] concern themselves with one who signals a left turn.
29. AS HAS BEEN TAUGHT [in the a *baraita* that is not found in our Tosefta Highway Code].
30. Justice Franklin says: [Since] drivers often do not signal, both proceed with caution.

The entire "fake" JT-ean composition before you is structured by its penultimate author (myself, in this case) to address one question posed about the made-up snippet of Mishnah (from chapter 5) that is this composition's "base text." In a rabbinic world in which it is known that different "tannaitic" rabbis held different and opposing views, can one identify the anonymous ruling of Mishnah Highway Code 1:1a—the first ruling in this made-up Mishnah passage—with any views attributed to a known "tannaitic" authority? This amounts to a request to engage in source criticism of a type.

The "fake" JT-ean composition explores three possible answers, based on three pieces of evidence: part of the "ersatz" Tosefta passage (from chapter 5) that complements this made-up Mishnah passage; the second half of the very same made-up Mishnah passage (1:1b); and a *baraita*, concocted by me for this occasion, which is a Tosefta-like gloss of our made-up Mishnah passage. The conveyed positions of the *tanna'im*, Smith, Jones, and Franklin are considered in light of Mishnah to see if the first part of the Mishnah (1:1a) "must be" attributed to their authority. In the cases of Smith and Jones, some objection to that attribution may be proffered. But not so for Franklin, because the *baraita* (the "tannaitic" tradition) that conveys Franklin's teaching indicates that we should not pay excessive attention to signaling, when fashioning rules for the Highway Code, since too many drivers fail to signal. It seems to be Franklin's position that if we fashion the rules intended to protect people on the assumption that drivers *always* signal, then we would be placing people in danger's way, which is precisely what the Mishnah Tractate Highway Code is trying to prevent. Therefore, we should just demand that everyone exercise caution in these circumstances. This can be squared with the ruling of the made-up Mishnah at 1:1a, independently of its disputed rulings at 1:1b, which our ersatz Tosefta tells us are the positions of Smith and Jones respectively. Hence, job done and analysis complete for the opening structuring question posed at the outset of the "fake" JT-ean composition!

Now, let us briefly review the formal, structured architecture of this fake JT-ean composition, noting how highly laconic, stock, formalized language (in SMALL CAPS) provides the markers of the composition's superstructure and substructure. WHO TAUGHT IT?/WHAT!? and AS HAS BEEN TAUGHT/THEE WE HAVE TAUGHT repeat to provide the basic superstructure of the tripartite composition; they are examples of type-6 formulaic language. The former terms pose the question to be answered, or signal that a different answer must be sought because a counterargument is about to follow. The latter signal that any legitimate resolution must rest on a "tannaitic" source (a type-1, type-2, or type-3 element). The fake JT-ean passage appeals to two such "tannaitic" sources, a snippet from our ersatz Tosefta from chapter 5 of this volume and a "baraita," a Tosefta-like "tannaitic" traditions, that I have made up on the spot.

THERE/HERE is signpost language of the substructural elements within "rounds." They signal *comparisons* of two (or more) sets of circumstances and rulings, in order to deny (or assert) that the sets are analogous so that the named authority of one may be assigned as the authority behind the other. These stock logico-comparative terms are examples of formulaic language of type 5. SAID . . . / SAID . . . [THAT] . . . SAID introduces teachings attributed to amoraic authorities, whose "sayings" proffer materials that provide putative responses to the analytic questions posed. As formulaic language, they signal type-4 elements. It is worth looking at how the content that "is signaled" by these stock terms is formulated; and for this purpose, I will remove all the interpolations in square brackets. Round one opens with the first attempt at an answer, attributed to two *amora'im*:
SAID Rabbi Scott, Rabbi Angus SAID: Justice Smith.
How laconic a response is that, just "Justice Smith"!? What follows is the citation of our ersatz Tosefta as corroborating evidence. Round one concludes with a counterargument, signaled by the stock, dialectic terms for analogical arguments, THERE . . . HERE. Again, I have eliminated all of my interpolations to highlight the extremely laconic character not only of the signpost terms but also of the content that they engender.

> THERE, Justice Smith said regarding one, signals a left turn;

> HERE, not regarding one, signals a left turn.

THERE . . . HERE compares the operative case circumstances of the two sources, declares them to be different, and we are left to conclude that without a basis for seeing the two sources as analogous, "Justice Smith" is not the answer to the question.

Rounds 2 and 3 of this fake JT-ean passage use no additional stock, literary-rhetorical signpost terms either to pose questions and invite answers (type-6 elements) or to structure arguments and counterarguments in response (type-5 elements). All thirty lines of this fake JT-ean composition are spun out with just those operational terms discussed in the preceding two paragraphs. They provide the superstructure and substructure to which everything else is attached, and they also establish the rhythm and cadence that informs the reader how one moves through the back-and-forth of the arguments and counterarguments, and the adducing of evidence in their support.

As has been the case in previous chapters of this volume, my "fake" passages have been composed to be near-perfect examples of their genre. They are "ideal" formulations. "Real" passages and compositions are rarely perfect. But the fake ideal does prepare you to recognize what is going on in the imperfect "real" texts, to samples of which we turn in the rest of this chapter.

WHAT "REALLY" GOES ON IN JT'S COMPOSITIONS AND EXTENDED COMPOSITE MINI-ESSAYS: SOME SAMPLES

A Short Composition

To begin this chapter's examination of the formalized literary-rhetorical conventions of "real" JT-ean texts, I return first to the snippet that I presented in chapter 3 from JT Tractate Gittin 1:1a. The latter is *Gemara* (aka., *talmud*) in the Yerushalmi to the opening section of Mishnah Tractate Gittin 1:1a, which reads:

Mishnah Gittin 1:1a

> He who brings a writ from a Mediterranean province—it is required that he say: In my presence it was written, and in my presence it was signed.

The Two Talmuds

Now the JT. As I did in chapter 3, language in y. Gittin 1:1a that is in Aramaic is in *italics*. Verbatim language from Mishnah is in **boldface**, and verbatim Tosefta is represented as underscored, small letters. But this time, I shall place the superstructural and substructural, signpost language of JT in SMALL CAPS—underscored for the latter, not underscored for the former—just as I did for the "fake" JT-ean text in the previous section. (By the way, I will henceforth stop further segmenting JT's texts into "rounds" of a "bout," since my point has been made in this respect, and distinguishing "within-round" countering from "between-round" ones is sometimes an arbitrary judgment on my part.)

JT Gittin 1:1a (*italics* = language in Aramaic, **boldface** = Mishnah's language, underscored small letters = Tosefta's language, SMALL CAPS = superstructural signpost language, UNDERSCORED SMALL CAPS = substructural signpost language, translation my own)

[**GEMARA**]

1. AND [they raised an] OBJECTION/DIFFICULTY (*ve-qashya*): Whether **he who brings** a writ of gift **from a Mediterranean province**—TROUBLES (*hash*) to say: **In my presence it was written, and in my presence it was signed**!? [Obviously, he does not. So why should he have to make such a declaration in the case of bringing a writ of divorce from a Mediterranean province?]

2. R. Joshua b. Levi SAID: IT IS DIFFERENT (*shenaya*) *as* they are not expert in the details of writs [of divorce].

3. SAID R. Yohanan: They dealt leniently (see t. Gittin 1:2,5) with her, that she should not remain an abandoned wife.

4. BUT IS IT [not] THE CASE (*ve-haiynu*) [that this] leniency, IS BUT (*aiyno ela*) a stringency (see t. Gittin 1:2,5)!?

5. SINCE (*she*) if he did not say to her: **In my presence it was written, and in my presence it was signed**, EVEN SO (*af*), you do not permit her to be married [again].

6. SAID R. Yose: The stringency that you have imposed upon her at the outset, that **he is required** to say: **In my presence it was written, and in my presence it was signed**, you have made a leniency for her in the end.

7. SINCE (*she*) if one came and challenged (see m. Gittin 1:3) [the writ's validity], his challenge is null and void.

In the Seat of Moses

8. R. Mana IS OF THE VIEW (*savar*): SAY (*maymar*), WHEN (*be*) he challenged [a matter] extraneous to the body [of the writ's text]; RATHER/BUT (*aval*), WHEN (*be*) he challenged [a matter] intrinsic to the body [of the writ's text]!?

9. WHEN (*be*) he challenged [a matter] that is not material. EVEN (*afyloo*)when he challenged a matter that is material!?

10. SAID R. Yose b. R. Bun: BECAUSE (*mykevan*) YOU SAY THAT THE REASON [is] (*detaymar deta'ma*) the stringency that you have imposed upon her at the outset, that **he is required to say: In my presence it was written, and in my presence it was signed,** you have made a leniency for her in the end,

11. SINCE (*she*) if one came and challenged [the writ's validity], his challenge is null and void, [then] IT IS (*havay*) [established that] THERE IS NO DIFFERENCE (*la shnaya*), [whether] he challenged [a matter] extraneous to the body [of the writ's text]; [or] he challenged [a matter] intrinsic to the body [of the writ's text], [or] he challenged [a matter] that is not material, [or] he challenged a matter that is material.

12. AND TROUBLE (*ve-hhash*) [him] to say[, In my presence it was written, and in my presence it was signed], lest they signed [it] with unfit witnesses!?

13. SAID R. Abun: IS IT THE CASE (*ayno*) [that] it is suspect of having an error by the hand of heaven [i.e., do such things just happen by chance]!?

14. [No!] In a court it is suspect of having an error;

15. [consequently] SINCE (*she*) it [the court] knows that if someone comes and challenges it, his challenge [must be] null and void, [so] it has it signed by fit witness.

Let us begin by surveying this passage in order to understand how it should be read—which, typically, is not immediately self-evident. The entirety of the passage is engendered by an implied question, signaled by the stock, signpost formulaic language, "AND [they raised an] OBJECTION/DIFFICULTY." However, the question is only partially posed. Indeed, one might say, it is not really posed at all, as I have had to supply it as an interpolation in square brackets. How typically laconic! Let us look more closely at this "unposed" questioning, which invites all of the analysis, argument and counterargument that follows in this modestly sized composition. Simply put, how have I, the translator, deduced the question at hand, and what do

The Two Talmuds

my thought processes, which I shall presently spell out, tell you about the role that stock, superstructural, question-posing terminology plays in JT-ean (and BT-ean) compositions?

The question from which the entire composition flows arises from adducing a *supposedly analogous* situation to the case at hand in m. Gittin 1:1a, which deals with writs of divorce transported from foreign lands to be enacted in the Land of Israel. Mishnah says that the bearer of such writs of divorce must be able to declare that the writ was written and signed in the bearer's presence. The supposed analogy concerns one bearing not a writ of divorce, but a deed of gift, from a Mediterranean province. Such an agent does not have to attest that one has personally seen the writing and signing of the deed of gift. So, *why* should one rule *differently* in the case of writs of divorce; what is different about writs of divorce; *why* must the bearer of a writ of divorce have to make such a declaration in similar circumstances? That is the question fully articulated in my mind, but nowhere explicitly articulated in this passage of *Gemara*. Consequently, I have had to interpolate that question into line 1.

But how is one to gather all that from the language actually supplied at the opening of the *Gemara*? Several things about the text in front of us provide compelling indicators.

The first is to understand that the stock formulaic language, "AND [they raised an] OBJECTION/DIFFICULTY," coupled with the terminology, "TROUBLES," has led me to place both an exclamation mark and a question mark at the end of the first "sentence" of this composition. In other words, the opening statement is to be read as something troubling or shocking: One who bears a deed of *gift* from abroad *does not* have to make such a declaration!? That is a "shocker," given what the Mishnah-pericope under examination has just taught us about writs of divorce! And the implied question about writs of divorce then follows by implication: If one *does not* have to do so in the case of deeds of gift, should not one *also not* have to do so in the case writs of divorce? So why does Mishnah, which is the highest authority (after Scripture) treat writs of divorce differently?

There also was a second formulaic clue to which my mind twigged that served to confirm my reading of what the fully-articulated question must be. The initial attempt, attributed to the *amora*, Joshua b. Levi, at line 2, to address the question commences with the stock, type-5, signpost language, "IT IS DIFFERENT." What is different, and from what? We are being told that two cases are going to be compared to establish that (or whether) they are different. This helps confirm our initial reading about what the opening question actually is in its entirety. That is, why should Mishnah teach that writs of divorce are to be treated *differently* than line 1's rule about deeds of gift? The formulaic language of line 2, then confirms our reading of line 1's unstated question.

But there is, third, still more help that confirms our reading. The statement at line 3, attributed to another *amora*, Yohanan, further confirms that one of the cases being compared is the case at hand in m. Gittin 1:1a about writs of divorce. And one could continue to survey lines 4 and those following it with the same result. So, the confirmation of our reading of the highly-laconic and incomplete question that opens this JT-ean composition is complete and firmly established.

What is to be learned from the preceding paragraphs about the superstructuring and substructuring, stock terminology of JT-ean compositions and about how a novice learns to make sense of what is going on? I go back to something I said earlier (a) about context and (b) about rhythm and cadence. The stock formulaic language that signals and introduces type-6 and type-5 elements work together to establish a back-and-forth cadence of one statement responding to another. When trying to unpack the meaning of line 1, I read *forward* and I use that "to-ing and fro-ing" of the elements as contextual information to establish, first, what line 1 fully intends to say, and then, using the same technique, to determine more fully what each element in turn is communicating. Read forward a bit, and read back a bit—several times. With each pass, you will be able to "construct" or "re-construct" more of the content of each piece of the composition, just as I did eventually to fully articulate the opening question. I realize that this is not how one normally reads discursive language of a text. Perhaps it is more akin to how one comes fully to grasp the meaning of all of the lines of some difficult poetry. In a JT-ean passage (or a BT-ean one), I am always reading a bit ahead (and sometimes a bit back as well), and then I return to reconsider the meaning of the element directly in front of me.

So, by reading ahead a bit, we have come fully to grasp the opening question to which the rest of the composition offers successive responses. We are now confident that the question is this: Why are writs of divorce different than other legal documents, such that the bearer of the writ from foreign lands must make such a declaration?

Line 2 provides the first attempt, attributed to an *amora*, at providing a reason for treating writs of divorce differently. That is juxtaposed at line 3 with a different reason, attributed to another "amoraic" figure. So, the attribution-language," SAID . . . SAID" additionally serves to juxtapose opposing answers to the question.

"BUT IT IS [not] THE CASE . . . ?" at line 4 signals that an anonymously conveyed counterargument for line 3 is about to follow; that counterargument is then fully articulated at line 5 ("SINCE (*she*) . . ., EVEN SO . . ."). And lines 6 and 7, convey a similarly structured counter-counterargument, attributed to an *amora*. The reasons and reasoning of lines 3 through 7 all seem to recall an aspect of t. Gittin 1:2,5's treatment of m. Gittin 1:1–3. This Tosefta text was presented in chapter 5 of this volume, and, among other things, it introduced the notion that the declaration required of the bearer of the writ of divorce from foreign lands seemed like a "stringency," but was actually a "leniency," since it reduced the incidence of women being left in a difficult limbo-situation, in which they were neither married nor divorced at the same time, and therefore unable to move on with their lives.

With lines 8 and 9, a new type of concern is raised in order to challenge the argument proffered at lines 6 and 7. If the legal teaching attributed to the *amora*, Mana, is correct, then the argument of lines 6–7 does not stand up *in all instances*. The declaration by the bearer is supposed to make the writ of divorce "challenge-proof." This benefits the woman, because one does not want her to be in a legal-limbo, that is, married and not married at one and the same time. Mana is of the view that different types of challenges are of different levels of importance. So one might reasonably think that not all challenges are obviated by the bearer's declaration; only some are.

How do I read all this into the statement of Mana's view? Again, I have partially based my reading of lines 8 and 9 on the "signals" given me by the type-5 formulaic language: "SAY . . . WHEN . . . RATHER/BUT . . . WHEN . . . WHEN . . . EVEN SO . . ." "SAY," in the imperative, conveys a challenge; "WHEN . . . RATHER/BUT . . . WHEN . . . WHEN . . . EVEN SO" signals comparison and contrast. In addition to paying attention to the signals provided by formulaic type-5 language, I have also looked ahead and looked back in the composition to keep the back-and-forth cadence of the composition top of mind, so that I can "place" and read lines 8 and 9 in that context. Consequently, I have placed exclamation and question marks after lines 8 and 9 to covey the notions that Mana's view challenges the response at line 7.

Mana's legal teaching is signaled by the formulaic language, R. x "*IS OF THE VIEW*." And the sum total effect of adducing Mana's legal opinion amounts to a countering of the counter-counterargument.

Now the composition must assess whether Mana's legal stance, with its implied challenge of the answer provided at line 7, should win the assent of others. The first attempt at lines 10–11, attributed to Yose b. Bun, an *amora*, to counter the implications of Mana's view takes the position at line 6, attributed to the *amora*, Yose, as axiomatic, and then reasons from that that Mana's view should not be accepted. The reasoning of lines 10–11 is something like this: if Mishnah's rule is what it is in order to be lenient to the benefit of the woman in question, then Mana's "view" whittles away at Mishnah's alleged motivation for the rule. And so the counterargument attributed to Mana cannot be accepted. Why accept Yose's statement, reminiscent of Tosefta, as axiomatic? I do not know. Perhaps because it too alludes to t. Gittin 1:2,5's content: the apparent stringency is in fact a lenient stance, and one wishes to take the lenient stance in writs of divorce to the benefit of the woman.

The type-5 formulaic terminology of lines 10–11 clearly tells us how these two lines are to be read in context. *SAID* once again does the double duty it so often fulfils in JT: to attribute what follows to a named amora, as well as to signal that what follows is juxtaposed with and counters what preceded it. "*BECAUSE YOU SAY THAT THE REASON* [*is*]" at line 10 further confirms this, since the "you" tells us that the antecedent position is being directly addressed. Line 11 takes the axiomatic notion that Mishnah intends to be lenient and fashions an argument with the aid of signpost language—*SINCE*... [then] *IT IS* [established that] *THERE IS NO DIFFERENCE* ..."—that signals drawing a conclusion from a probative premise.

Mana's objection is now "toast" for this JT-ean composition. So, we are left with two possible, but differing, responses to the opening question at line 1 that are still possibilities: the answer given at line 2 and the one given at line 3, all counters to line 3's response having been put to bed.

Line 12 now proffers a third response to the opening question, and to do so "picks up" the formulaic terminology of line 1, "*TROUBLE*," meaning "demand that" one do something. This response is provided anonymously. Lines 13–15 then do away with the proposal of line 12. "*SAID*" at line 13 again does its double duty to provide an attribution to an *amora* as well as to signal that what follows juxtaposes and challenges what immediately precedes it. "*IS IT THE CASE* ..." then signals a counterfactual statement, which demands I place an exclamation mark and a question mark at the end of line 13. Line 14 completes the challenge begun at line 13. And line 15 draws a conclusion from the premise of the counterfactual statement: "<u>SINCE</u> ... [must be] ...[so] ...." As I have had to do throughout this JT-ean composition, sorting out how to read lines 13–15 required that I attend to context—in this case, by reading backwards and attending to how lines 13–15 fit the back-and-forth cadence of the composition. The response at line 13 has been rejected, and once more we are left with two answers still standing to the opening question at line 1, that attributed at line 2 to the *amora*, Joshua b. Levi, and another attributed at line 3 to the *amora*, Yohanan. And so it stands by the end of line 15.

Before rehearsing or further drawing some lessons from this close reading of y. Gittin 1:1a, permit me to diagram the whole, so you can get a bird's-eye view of what you have seen "close up."

[MISHNAH]
[m. Gittin 1:1a]
[GEMARA]
1. AND *[they raised an]* OBJECTION/DIFFICULTY

    [possibly comparable case to Mishnah's]

  TROUBLES

    [Mishnah's ruling applied to possibly comparable case]!?

    [Implied question arises from foregoing]

2. X <u>SAID</u>

  <u>IT IS DIFFERENT</u>

    [posited response 1]

3. <u>SAID</u> y

    [alternative posited response 2, with allusion to Tosefta]

4. <u>BUT IS IT</u> [not] <u>THE CASE</u> ... <u>IS BUT</u>

    [objection to response 2, positing the opposite]

5. <u>SINCE</u>

    [posited situation]

  <u>EVEN SO</u> (*af*)

    [outcome Mishnah, as per Tosefta, supposedly wishes to prevent]

6. *SAID Z*

   [outcome supposedly desired by Mishnah as per Tosefta]

7. SINCE

   [posited situation]

   [outcome supposedly desired by Mishnah as per Tosefta, counters objection at lines 4–5]

8. XX *IS OF THE VIEW,*

SAY,

WHEN

   [more refined circumstances 1 than posited so far]

RATHER/BUT,

WHEN

   [more refined circumstances 1' than posited so far]!?

9. WHEN

   [more refined circumstances 2 than posited so far]

EVEN WHEN

   [more refined circumstances 2' than posited so far; counters counter to objection at lines 6–7]!?

10. *SAID yy*

BECAUSE

YOU SAY THAT THE REASON [is]

   [as per line 6: outcome supposedly desired by Mishnah as per Tosefta]

11. SINCE

   [circumstances]

[then] *IT IS* [established that]

THERE IS NO DIFFERENCE

   [among posited circumstances 1, 1', 2, or 2', counters counter at lines 8–9]

12. AND TROUBLE

   [Mishnah's ruling]

[because of]

   [posited response 3]

13. <u>SAID</u> ZZ

IS IT THE CASE

[counterfactual statement!?]

14. [No!]

[factual statement]

15. [consequently] <u>SINCE</u>

[posited reasonable situation as premise]

[must be]

[so]

[posited reasonable outcome, countering posited response 3]

Several lessons should be drawn by you from my having taken you through my reading of the JT-ean composition at y. Gittin 1:1a concerning m. Gittin 1:1a. Some of these lessons I have mentioned in passing along the way:

> (a) attend to stock, signpost language that signals superstructural (type-6) and substructural dialectical (type-5) elements of the composition, that is, those formularies that signal the problem to be addressed or the question posed (e.g., WHAT!? WHY? [They raised an] OBJECTION/DIFFICULTY!? WHO TAUGHT IT?), and those that signal arguments or counterarguments and each's form of reasoning (e.g., <u>SAID</u>, <u>SINCE</u> . . . EVEN SO, THERE . . . HERE, BUT IT [not] . . .);
>
> (b) get a sense of the back-and-forth cadence of the composition;
>
> (c) in deciphering any one line, read forward, and review what preceded the line, in order to establish where the line fits in context.

To these strategies, I would add several related ones.

> (d) Go over the entire composition in the manner suggested several times, because with each "pass" you will gain greater clarity about what the passage is communicating and how all the bits and pieces contribute to each element of the composition.

As a corollary to the preceding point,

> (e) do not be overly concerned if you cannot decipher the entire composition on the first pass; if a line remains an enigma the first time through, move on and see if on the second pass it

appears less enigmatic, because you have a better sense of how the composition as a whole develops and flows.

(f) Have not only the "base" Mishnah-text treated by the Gemara at hand and open beside you, but also the relevant "chapter" of Tosefta.

In y. Gittin 1:1a, Tosefta is not actually cited, but some of the arguments/responses made in the JT-ean composition allude to content more fully presented in Tosefta.

A Composite Mini-essay

A composition, of which y. Gittin 1:1a is an apt example, is the basic building block of any *Gemara* in the JT (and in the BT). Yes, the composition is not an indivisible entity. It has its constituent parts: posed questions; individual arguments and counterarguments; cited amoraic sources and tannaitic sources. But unless these are put together in a composition of sorts, with a beginning, middle and end—and the end may be no more conclusive that just being the last response left standing to the opening posed question—then we simply do not have anything that might legitimately be classified as *Gemara*.

Sometimes, a single composition constitutes the entire analysis of the "base" text from Mishnah that is under consideration, and the JT (or BT) then moves on to consider the next "base" text from Mishnah. In contemporary traditional rabbinic circles, such a composition could be considered a complete *sugya*, namely, the sum total of the *Gemara*'s treatment of (or "lesson" on) that single snippet of Mishnah.

More often, in the JT, and especially so in the BT, a *series* of individual compositions are brought together to form a *sugya* that treats a particular Mishnah passage or part thereof. The same rule-sentence or passage of Mishnah will be the object of one question after another—Who taught it? Why does the Mishnah rule this way? What is its source? Is it not contradicted by this other "tannaitic" tradition!? etc.—all addressed to one and the same Mishnah text. Each question will be made to appear to generate its own composition. Sometimes the conclusion of one composition is made to appear to be the inspiration for the next posed question, which commences the next composition. (Of course, this "appearance" of things is often the work of the penultimate, anonymous authorships of each of the Talmuds.) As a result, a series of such compositions, made sometimes to cohere well, and sometimes more loosely, form a "composite" mini-essay about the particular Mishnah text under examination. Now, in such instances, the "composite" mini-essay, not any single composition, is the *sugya*, the "lesson" that one is "walked through" about the Mishnah text at hand.[17]

For you, being confronted with such a composite mini-essay should not be an occasion for panic. It is just a series of (sometimes closely related, sometimes more-loosely related) compositions. All you need to do is to work through each composition in turn, just as we have done together with y. Gittin 1:1a. How (or indeed, whether) the entire composite mini-essay coheres as a unified treatment of things is a matter you can take up as an intellectual exercise, *after* you have deciphered each individual composite, as I have demonstrated, with the aid of the literary-rhetorical "signals" and the strategies that this chapter modeled in the preceding section. That said, let me just show you what a composite mini-essay of the JT is like, the *sugya* of y. Avodah Zarah 1:6. When I deal in the next chapter with the BT, I shall show you this Yerushalmi-composite's BT-ean parallel, so that you can get a sense of the similarities and differences of JT-ean and BT-ean *sugyot*. Indeed, my intention later to show you the corresponding BT-ean *sugya* to y. Avodah Zarah 1:6 is why I am, with apologies, whisking you away from our now-well-hashed topic, the status of a foetus of an ass subject to the law of the firstling, when Gentiles have some economic stake in the animal (m. Bekhorot 1:1). Instead, I conduct you to the more general issue of the sale of domestic animals to Gentiles, m. Avodah Zarah 1:6, which is the base-text of the JT-ean composite mini-essay soon to follow. Why? There is no extant JT-ean tractate for Mishnah Tractate Bekhorot to which we may compare a BT-ean *sugya*.

Following is, first, the entirety of m. Avodah Zarah 1:6, followed by the JT-ean composite mini-essay at y. Avodah Zarah 1:6.

---

17. I have borrowed the terms "composition" and "composite," and (roughly speaking, but not precisely) the distinction between them from Neusner's use of these terms in his analyses of the Talmuds, particularly of the BT. Of this there are many examples in Neunser's publications, I shall point to just several: *Bavli: An Introduction*; *How the Bavli*; *Bavli's One Voice*; *Reader's Guide*.

In the Seat of Moses

Mishnah Avodah Zarah 1:6 (translation my own[18])

A. [In] a locale [in] which they are accustomed to sell small cattle [e.g., sheep or goats] to idolaters,

B. they [are permitted to] sell.

C. [In] a locale [in] which they are not accustomed to sell [small cattle] to them,

D. they do not [permit one to] sell.

E.1. And in any locale, they do not [permit one to] sell to them

E.2. large cattle [e.g., oxen, asses, and horses],

E.3. calves,

E.4. and foals [of asses or of horses]—

F. whether whole, or maimed.

G. R. Judah permits in the case of a maimed [animal],

H. and Ben-Batayra permits in the case of a horse.

The Mishnah pericope opens with a double-barrelled rule about the sale of small domestic animals to non-Jews, A–B and C–D, with well-balanced protases and apodases, with matching language throughout, as one would expect from well-formulated Mishnah. The upshot is that in this case, local custom dictates the rule. E.1–2 provides a third rule-sentence, again using language reflecting that of A–B and C–D, this time about the sale of large domesticated animals. With large domesticated animals, Mishnah proffers a rule that is not predicated on different local practices. The sale of large domestic animals to Gentiles is forbidden. E.3–4 and F elaborate or ramify the rule at E.1–2. "Large" domestic specifies that are not yet fully grown are still "large" animals for the purposes of the law. Nor does it matter what the physical state of the animal is. G, in a ruling attributed to Judah, then disputes F in good Mishnaic dispute form. F, attributed to Ben-Batayra disputes the principal ruling at E.1–2. According to F, horses are not affected by the general rule.

Now the composite mini-essay at y. Avodah Zarah 1:6. As I have done with y. Gittin 1:1a, superstructural formulaic language that poses questions or invites analysis is in SMALL CAPS, and formulaic language that provides the substructure for arguments and analyses is in <u>UNDERSCORED SMALL</u>

---

18. Adpated from Lightstone, *Rhetoric,* 27.

CAPS. Verbatim citations of Mishnah are in **boldface** and language that parallels Tosefta is underscored. Finally, Aramaic is in *italics*.

Yerushalmi Avodah Zarah 1:6 (translation my own[19])

I

1. WHAT!? And is one permitted to rear [small cattle]!?

2. SAID R. Ba: *As is the case* of the Mahir, which is sixteen [Roman] miles by 16 [Roman] miles, [in which district one may rear small cattle].

II

1. THEY SHOULD HAVE SAID (*havvan b'eyy maymar*):

2. THE ONE WHO SAID (*ma'n demar*) it is permitted **to sell** [also maintains] it is permitted to billet (my emendation) [cattle owned by an Israelite with an idolater]

3. AND THE ONE WHO SAID (*ma'n demar*) it is forbidden **to sell** [also maintains] it is forbidden to billet.

4. [Said] R. Yonah: [Said] R. Leazar in the name of Rav: And EVEN THE ONE WHO SAID (*ma'n demar*) *in the case of the one who said* it is permitted **to sell**, it would be [nevertheless] forbidden to billet.

5. AND WHAT DISTINGUISHES [endeavoring] **to sell** from [endeavoring] to billet?

6. From the moment one sells it to him it is the cattle of the idolater.

7. From the moment he billets it with him, it is [still] the cattle of the Israelite,

8. and he [the idolater] is suspect with respect to it[s treatment].

III

1. [In] **a locale [in] which they are not accustomed to sell [small cattle] to them, they do not [permit one to] sell.**

2. WHY?

3. BECAUSE one removes it from the purview [of the laws pertaining to] shearing.

4. [Then] CONSIDER that it was a goat [and not shorn]. [So now why?]

---

19. Adpated from Lightstone, *Rhetoric*, 49–57.

5. BECAUSE one removes it from the purview of the laws of the firstling.

6. [Then] CONSIDER that it was a male [which will, obviously, never give birth to firstling]. [So now why?]

7. BECAUSE one removes it from the purview of the priestly gifts.

8. HENCEFORTH [if this were the reason] one should not sell him wheat,

9. BECAUSE one removes it from [liability for] the dough offering.

10. [And similarly] one should not sell him wine and oil,

11. BECAUSE one removes them from [liability for] the blessing [said before partaking of them].

IV

1. **[In] any locale they do not [permit one to] sell to them large cattle.**

2. WHY [the distinction between large and small cattle]?

3. BECAUSE in the case of] large cattle, there is with respect to it [the matter of] liability for a sin offering [as when one uses them to do labour on the Sabbath, for example, by hitching it to a plow or a wagon].

4. BUT [in the case of] small cattle, there is not with respect to it [the matter of] liability for a sin offering [since one does not do such labour with small cattle].

5. BUT will [the idolater] not milk and will he not shear [small cattle on the Sabbath, acts also incurring a sin offering]?

6. [So now WHY?]

7. ONE [can] SAY:

8. THERE (taman) [in the former case], it [the animal, by its own labour] is liable [that is, makes the owner liable].

9. VERILY, HERE (baram hakha) he [the owner, by reason of an act which is his only] is liable.

10. SINCE [i.e., from the moment] he has sold it to him, is it not considered the non-Jew's animal [i.e., no longer subject to the laws of the Sabbath]?

11. SAID R. Ami the Babylonian in the name of Ravnin (alternative trans.: rabbanin, the rabbis) THAT THERE (de-taman) [in the former case, with respect to large cattle], sometimes one

sells it on trial, and he [the idolater] returns it after three days, and it happens that [on the Sabbath] he [the idolater] works an animal which is an Israelite's.

12. HENCEFORTH [if this were the reason], [selling] on trial [should be] forbidden, [BUT] when not on trial, [selling should be] permitted.

13. THIS[, the latter, was forbidden] ON ACCOUNT OF [fear that the idolater might work the animal on the Sabbath in] THAT[, the former, case, that is to say, one usually leads to the other].

V

1. [If] one transgressed and sold [cattle to an idolater], they fine one.

2. Just as they fine one for [cases in which] the law [forbids such a sale], so [too] they fine one for [cases in which] custom [forbids such a sale].

3. AND WHENCE [do we learn] that they fine one for [cases in which] custom [forbids such a sale]?

4. A certain person sold his camel to an Aramean [alternative reading: Roman].

5. The case came before Resh Laqish [aka Rabbi Simeon b. Laqish],

6. And he fined him double [the value of the animal],

7. so that [the Israelite] will [feel compelled to arrange that the idolater] return the camel to him.

8. SAID R. Yose b. R. Bun:

9. [He must have fined] the agent, [not the Israelite owner],

10. and they accused him, this man [of being] the [Israelite] agent of the Aramean [alternative reading: Roman].

11. [Let us hypothesize that] R. Simeon b. Laqish ACCORDS WITH (ke-) [i.e., is based upon the view of] R. Judah,

12. AS IT IS TAUGHT (de-tny) (in a *baraita* paralleled at t. Bekhorot 2:1) *in the name of R. Judah:*

13. He who buys an animal from a non-Jew and it gave birth [and the offspring was] a firstling—

14. they estimate with him its [the firstling's] worth, and they give half the value to the priest.

15. [If the Israelite] gave it to him in trust,

In the Seat of Moses

16. one estimates with him what its value is worth, and he gives [an amount equal to] all of the value to the priest.

17. And sages say: Since the hand of the non-Jew intervenes,[then] [the animal has ceased [to be subject to] the law of the firstling (cf. m. Bekhorot 1:1).

18. [No, that hypothesis is not substantiated, because] *[Of]* GREATER *[legal weight]* THAN *[the law according to]* R. Simeon b. Laqish IS *[the law according to]* R. Judah.

19. THAT WHICH SAID R. Judah*[was said]* ON ACCOUNT OF the laws of the firstling.

20. THAT WHICH SAID R. Simeon b. Laqish *[was said]* FOR the laws of *[the sale of]* large cattle [, so the view attributed to R. Judah in the "tannaitic"/*beraita* source cannot be considered the authoritative basis for the view of Simeon b. Laqish].

VI

1. **R. Judah permits in the case of a maimed [animal].**

2. R. Judah stated [his view] only **in the case of a maimed [animal] which cannot be healed** (parallels t. Avodah Zarah 2:1).

3. They said to him: and is it not [the case] that (parallels t. Avodah Zarah 2:1) he [the non-Jew] brings over to her [, the maimed animal,] a male, and he mounts her and she gives birth (parallels t. Avodah Zarah 2:1)?

4. He said to them: Moreover, I stated [my view] only in the case of a male horse which cannot be healed.

5. They said to him: And is it not [the case] that [the non-Jew] brings to him a female, and she is mounted by him, and she gives birth?

6. [SAID] R. Abin in the name of Ravnim THAT THERE (*de-taman*) IT IS STATED THAT it is forbidden to sell to them [unborn] foeti.

7. THERE WE HAVE LEARNED (*taman tnynan*) [in m. Bekhorot 1:1]:

8. **He who buys the foetus of an ass of a Gentile [, and the foetus, if male, will be the firstborn offspring of the ass],**

9. **and he who sells to him [the foetus of an ass],**

10. **even though it is not permitted,**

11. **and he who forms a partnership with him [the Gentile],**

12. **and he who receives from him [, the Gentile, such a foetus in trust],**

13. **and he who gives** [such a foetus] **to him** [the Gentile] **in trust—**

14. [the foetus] **is exempt from the law of the firstling.**

15. R. Haggai INQUIRED BEFORE *(ba'a qomay)* R. Yose:

16. DOES THIS NOT STATE *(layt hada amara)* that it is forbidden to sell them [unborn] foeti?

17. He said to him: R. Abin [speaking] in the name of Ravnin has already anticipated you:

18. THAT THERE *(de-taman)* IT IS STATED THAT it is forbidden to sell to them [unborn] foeti.

VII

1. **Ben Betayra permits in the case of a horse.**

2. Ben Betayra STATED [his view] ONLY **in the case of** a male **horse,** WHICH kills its owner in battle.

3. AND THERE ARE THOSE WHO SAY: WHICH pursues females.

4. AND THERE ARE THOSE WHO SAY: WHICH stands and urinates.

5. WHAT [case(s) account for] THE DIFFERENCES BETWEEN THEM *(ma baynaiyhon)*?

6. A gelding.

7. [With respect to] THE ONE WHO SAYS *(man damar)*: WHICH pursues females, [a gelding] does not pursue [females].

8. BUT [with respect to] THE ONE WHO SAYS *(man damar)*: it stands and urinates, EVEN SO this one [i.e., the gelding] stands and urinates.

9. R. Tanhum b. R. Hiyya [said]: When they [i.e., horses] do harm [to people], they [idolaters] hitch it to millstones [and make the horse work on the Sabbath].

10. [Said] R. Yose b. R. Bun in the name of R. Huna: Ben Betayra and R. Nathan have both said [essentially] the same thing.

11. AS IT HAS BEEN TAUGHT *(de-tny)* [in a baraita paralleled at t. Shabbat 8(9):34]:

12. [If on the Sabbath] one removed [from a private to a public domain] cattle, wild beasts, or birds—whether alive or dead—one is liable [on account of transgressing the Sabbath].

13. R. Nathan says: [In the case of] dead [ones], one is liable; [in the case of] live [ones], one is exempt.

14. AND [WHAT OF THE VIEW OF] our Rabbis?

15. THEY ARE [OF THE VIEW THAT] WITH RESPECT TO THEM (*iyt lehon*), one is liable for a sin-offering [in the latter case].

16. AND/BUT HOW [WOULD] THEY [i.e., the anonymous authorities in the Mishnah] HAVE RESPONDED TO HIM [Ben Betayra] (*ve-iynun metivin layh akhan*)?

17. IN ACCORDANCE WITH HIS APPROACH THEY RESPONDED TO HIM—

18. IN ACCORDANCE WITH YOUR APPROACH, WHEN YOU [Ben Betayra] SAY: because of the law of the Sabbath rest [which is not at issue in the sale of a horse to idolaters, since riding a horse on the Sabbath is not prohibited by biblical law],

19. THEN I [WOULD] BE [OF THE VIEW THAT] (*af ana iyt ly*) when they [horses] do harm, they hitch it to millstones [and the horse is made to do work on the Sabbath in a fashion which is prohibited by biblical law].

20. Rabbi [Judah the Patriarch] says: Say I that it is forbidden on account of two things—

21. on account of [the laws pertaining to the sale of] the accoutrements of weaponry [to idolaters],

22. and on account of [the laws pertaining to the sale of] large cattle [to idolaters] (*baraita* parallel to t. Avodah Zarah 2:1).

VIII

1. AND IT HAS BEEN TAUGHT (*u-tny*):

2. so [too] is a large wild beast like small cattle [with respect to the matter of selling to idolaters] (in a *baraita*, only the underscored terms are paralleled at t. Avodah Zarah 2:1).

3. WHO TAUGHT IT (*man tenytah*)?

4. Rabbi [Judah the Patriarch].

5. [However] the words [i.e., view] of the sages [is][as] R. Bisnah [said:] R. Hannan b. Bar [said] in the name of Rav:

6. A large wild beast is like large cattle (again see parallel terms at t. Avodah Zarah 2:1) [with respect to the matter of selling to an idolater].

Admittedly, at first glance the foregoing composite mini-essay from y. Avodah Zarah 1:6 is a lot to take in and to decipher. However, the task is made much easier using the strategies described earlier. Break the whole

The Two Talmuds

composite down into its parts, its compositions. And attend to the signpost, formulaic language that (i) signals superstructuring questions and that (ii) shepherds one, as subsubstructure, through dialectical argument and analysis. Keep reading "forwards" and "backwards" in each composition to do this. After that you only (!?) have to try to make sense of the legal content and reasoning. Believe me, the latter is much easier to make sense of, once you have done the preparatory steps. The following schematization/mapping of the entire composite mini-essay, with formulaic signpost language indicated as usual, should further help you discern what is going on in y. Avodah Zarah 1:6.

I

  –Querying/challenging the accuracy/legitimacy of ruling in Mishnah *ad locum*: WHAT!? + question

   –SAID R. . . . + answer

II

  –Proffering a more differentiated version of Mishnah ruling *ad locum*: THEY SHOULD HAVE SAID . . .

   –Alternative legal opinion: THE ONE WHO SAID . . .

   –Alternative legal opinion: AND THE ONE WHO SAID . . .

   –EVEN THE ONE WHO SAID + attributed saying disputing antecedent legal opinion

  –Questioning the practical purpose of such differentiation: AND WHAT DISTINGUISHES . . . ?

   –Answer

III

  –Mishnah citation *ad locum*

  –Asking for a reason for ruling: WHY?

   –BECAUSE + answer/reason

   –CONSIDER + posited alternative circumstances that undermine answer

   –BECAUSE + alternative reason

   –CONSIDER + alternative posited circumstances that undermine foregoing

   –BECAUSE + alternative reason

331

        –Counterargument in the form of a double *reductio ad absurdum*: HENCEFORTH BECAUSE ... BECAUSE ...

IV

–Mishnah citation *ad locum*

–Asking for a reason for ruling: WHY [the distinction between ...]?

    –[BECAUSE] + reason

    –BUT + challenge to reason

    –BUT + challenge to challenge

–[So now WHY the distinction in law between ...?]

    –New reason for distinction: ONE [can] SAY ... THERE ... VERILY, HERE ... SINCE ...?

    –Alternative reason for last-mentioned distinction (attributed to named rabbi): SAID ... THAT THERE ...

    –Challenge to the last-offered reason: HENCEFORTH ... [BUT] ...

    –Final reason for distinction: THIS ON ACCOUNT OF THAT

V

–Statement of law complementing Mishnah citation *ad locum*

–Extension of law also complementing Mishnah citation *ad locum*

–Request for authoritative source for extension: AND WHENCE [do we learn] ...?

    –Precedent story (in Aramaic) involving ruling by an amoraic authority + reason for the authority's ruling

    –Positing (in Aramaic) of modified circumstances for the precedent story attributed to another amoraic authority: SAID R. ...

–[Implied request for earlier (i.e., tannaitic) authority/source for the extension of the law as per the judgment given in the precedent story]

    –Hypothesized tannitaic authority: R. x ACCORDS WITH (ke-) ... R. y

    –Citation of source citing/paralleling Tosefta (and reflecting a Mishnah passage not *ad locum*): AS IT IS TAUGHT (de-tny) (in a *baraita*) in the name of R. y ...

–[Implied objection to positing antecedent authority/source as basis for judgment in precedent story]

    –Reason for objection (in Aramaic): *[Of]* GREATER *[legal weight]* THAN *[the law according to]* R. x IS *[the law according to]* R. y.

    –Substantiation for the reason for the objection (in Aramaic): THAT WHICH SAID R. y *[was said]* ON ACCOUNT OF . . .; THAT WHICH SAID R. x *[was said]* FOR . . .

VI

–Mishnah citation *ad locum*, [citation of first disputant's ruling contra the Mishnah's anonymous ruling]

    –Explication of disputant's view in Mishnah, by delimiting circumstances of case (parallels correlative Tosefta passage)

    –Debate-counter (parallels same correlative Tosefta passage)

    –Debate-counter to counter (not present in the correlative Tosefta passage)

    –Debate-counter to the immediately preceding debate-counter (not present in the correlative Tosefta passage)

–Attributed reference to/restatement of topically-related Mishnah passage not *ad locum*: [SAID] R. . . . THAT THERE IT IS STATED THAT . . .

–Citation of the Mishnah passage not ad locum: THERE WE HAVE LEARNED . . .

    –Precedent-story-like Q&A exchange between two amoraic authorities: R. a INQUIRED BEFORE R. b: DOES THIS NOT STATE . . .; He said to him: R. . . . THAT THERE IT IS STATED THAT . . . + restatement of attributed reference to/restatement of topically-related Mishnah passage not *ad locum*.

VII

–Mishnah citation *ad locum*, [citation of second disputant's ruling contra the Mishnah's anonymous ruling]

    –Explication of second disputant's view in Mishnah, by delimiting circumstances of case and positing a reason for the disputant's view in those delimited circumstances: x STATED [his view] ONLY in the case of . . . WHICH . . .

333

In the Seat of Moses

- Second alternative explication of second disputant's view in Mishnah, positing a second, different reason: AND THERE ARE THOSE WHO SAY: WHICH ...

- Third alternative explication of second disputant's view in Mishnah, positing a third, different reason: AND THERE ARE THOSE WHO SAY: WHICH ...

  - Query as to the exact delimited circumstances where the second and third alternative reasons become significant: WHAT *[case(s) account for]* THE DIFFERENCES BETWEEN THEM?

    - Answer hypothesizing such a delimited circumstance

    - Explication of possible significance for each of the second and third alternatives given above of the hypothesized circumstance: *[With respect to]* THE ONE WHO SAYS, WHICH ...; BUT *[with respect to]* THE ONE WHO SAYS ..., EVEN SO ...

    - Statement (attributed to amoraic authority) the effect of which is to undermine all the reasons proffered so far for the explication of second disputant's view in Mishnah *ad locum* (this supporting the anonymous ruling in the Mishnah against the second disputant)

- Statement (attributed to amoraic authority) asserting that second disputant's view in Mishnah *ad locum* accords with ruling attributed to another named tannaitic rabbi as per another (tannatic) source

- Citation of *baraita*/Toseftan passage not correlative to Mishnah *ad locum*: AS IT HAS TAUGHT [in a *baraita* paralleled in Tosefta]: ...

- Implied question about the view of the anonymous authority in the baraita/Tosefta just cited: AND [WHAT IS THE VIEW OF] our Rabbis?

  - Reprise and explication the anonymous ruling of "our Rabbis" in the last-cited baraita/Tosefta passage: THEY ARE [OF THE VIEW THAT] WITH RESPECT TO THEM ... + explicated ruling

- Query as to how those authorities represented by anonymous ruling in Mishnah *ad locum* would have countered/challenged the second disputant's ruling under discussion: AND/BUT HOW WOULD THEY HAVE RESPONDED TO HIM?

- –Specification of type of counter-argument, viz., turning the second disputant's own approach against him: IN ACCORDANCE WITH HIS APPROACH THEY RESPONDED TO HIM—
- –Counter-argument based on second disputant's own premises/reason: IN ACCORDANCE WITH YOUR APPROACH, WHEN YOU SAY . . . , THEN I [WOULD] BE [OF THE VIEW THAT] . . .
- –Citation of *baraita*/Tosefta explicating and providing reasons for anonymous view, disputed by the second disputant, in the Mishnah *ad locum*, (without any citation formulary for *beraitot*): Rabbi [Judah the Patriarch] says: Say I that + *baraita*/Tosefta

VIII

- –Citation of *baraita*/Tosefta parallel complementing Mishnah *ad locum*: AND IT HAS TAUGHT . . .
- –Query about which named tannaitic authority's view is represented: WHO TAUGHT IT?
  - –Answer: name of rabbinic authority provided for the anonymous ruling
- –Query about what the "majority" view would be contra the now-named, single tannaitic authority's view: the words of the sages . . . ?
  - –Fashioning/reconstruction of the "majority" view, attributed to named amoraic rabbis, achieved by varying the language of the *baraita*/Tosefta parallel

There you have it, my schematization of the entire composite mini-essay at y. Avodah Zarah 1:6 and all of its constituent compositions. That said, I now have an admission to make. As I look at my own segmentation of this composite mini-essay and of its composites—a text which I have read many times over by now—I am still not certain that I have properly segmented all of its elements. Indeed, every time I have gone over this text, I have changed somewhat either my translation or my schematization of it. To admit this is tantamount to saying that I am not, even now, *completely* confident that I have *fully and accurately* deciphered this text of the Yerushalmi. I say this not (just) to express humility when faced with understanding these JT-ean composite mini-essays, but to make a pedagogical point. One, because of the state of these texts—all scholars of the Yerushalmi bemoan the state of the text in comparison to the BT's—and, two, because of the arcane nature of their content, and, three, because of their laconic modes of expression, and, four, because of the "inside-baseball" character of their reasoning, centuries of traditional rabbinic scholars have debated the meaning of various lines of each composite of the JT (and of the BT) as well. Consequently, my hesitation to declare total victory in deciphering y. Avodah Zarah 1:6 stands within a longstanding tradition of such hesitancy. Yet it does not stop me from "making a go of it." And neither should it stop you, using the strategies elaborated earlier, and demonstrated in this chapter's discussion of sample texts of the Yerushalmi.

WHAT HAS JT ACCOMPLISHED FROM A LITERARY-RHETORICAL PERSPECTIVE?

There is an implicit, unstated historical-like claim encoded in the literary-rhetorical nature of the JT (and of the BT, as well). It is this: that its compositions and composite mini-essays (a) have resulted from, and (b) reflect something of the actual nature of, the *amora'im*'s own critical-analytical engagement in Mishnah study, undertaken *in light of* the other "tannaitic" materials in their possession, and in light of amoraic teachings that complemented these tannaitic materials. I wish we could be reasonably confident that such a historical-*like* claim is actually historical in some significant sense. And it is certainly the case that many modern scholars' literary-historical studies of the JT (and of the BT) deal directly or indirectly with just this issue, even though the consensus view is that both the JT and the BT are the work of postamoraic authorships who are responsible for considerable framing of the materials in their possession. I have consistently steered away from such literary-historical matters throughout this book and will not change my course now. But I will say this: Whatever the literary-historical reality may be, the result is to produce a text which models a consistent mode of critical-engagement with Mishnah study, in light of complementary sources believed to be contemporary with Mishnah as well as sources ear-marked as post-Mishnaic. The Talmuds' *post*amoriac-period authors "stage" that representation of critical engagement with Mishnah in the amoraic period. When you read and decipher JT-ean (or BT-ean) passages, as I have done with you in this chapter (and will do again in the next) for some sample texts, you are participating in these authors' "play" about Mishnah study in late antiquity. (I shall return to these issues in the last chapter of the book, when I shall have you reflect on what will have been your experience encountering these texts' dominant literary-rhetorical conventions and structures and attempt to relate that experience to what might have been core aspects of what it meant to be a member of the rabbinic group in late antiquity.)

When, now, we turn to the Bavli, the BT, we shall see a play that is more polished, more elaborated and more sophisticated, *but certainly of the same genre*. But being part of the same over-arching genre does not make them the same or imply necessarily that their goals are entirely identical.

SUGGESTIONS FOR FURTHER READING

Goldberg, "The Palestinian Talmud," 302–22.

Neusner, *Judaism in Society*.

Neusner, *Yerushalmi*.

Zelcer, *Guide to the Jerusalem Talmud*.

8

The Two Talmuds
The Babylonian Talmud

HOW THE BABYLONIAN TALMUD MARKS THE BEGINNING OF AN HISTORICAL SEA-CHANGE WORTH NOTING

The advent of the Babylonian Talmud (BT/b. or "Bavli") marks the beginning of significant developments within both the rabbinic group and "rabbinic" Judaism, and I will expend some ink telling you why. But I must first reassure you that the Bavli's (eventual) historical significance in no ways makes the challenges you face in gaining a handle on the Bavli's literary-rhetorical conventions and constructs any more difficult. In fact, the opposite will prove to be the case. What you have learned about reading the Yerushalmi, the Jerusalem Talmud (JT/y.), is *entirely* portable to the reading of the legal passages of the BT, with very little more to master to bridge the gap.

That said, understanding something of the BT's place in a sea change within rabbinism and rabbinic Judaism—terms I have little used in this volume to this point—should help you appreciate the advantage you gain from what will be your enhanced access to the BT's text by this chapter's end. So, having stated numerous times that literary history or the history of Judaism is not this book's focus, I will, nonetheless, offer some remarks at

The Two Talmuds

the outset of this second-last chapter about the rise of the Bavli to preeminence in rabbinic Judaism, before introducing you to the BT's basic literary and rhetorical conventions and constructs.

As intimated already in chapters 2 and 3, for about four hundred years, that is, from the turn of the third century CE to perhaps as late as the turn of the seventh century, Mishnah was the most important text within early rabbinic circles (second in authority only to Biblical Scriptures themselves), and the study of Mishnah was among the most important activities within rabbinic circles.[1] Mishnah study was the foremost pursuit that *made* a rabbi a rabbi, and that *marked* a rabbi as a rabbi. Toseftan materials,[2] Halakhic midrashim, other *beraitot*, and the Jerusalem Talmud all came to play a role in serving Mishnah study in some fashion.

In the beginning (or perhaps more accurately stated, on the face of it), the Bavli, produced over the mid-sixth and early seventh centuries CE, seemed intended to serve the same ends as other earlier rabbinic legal texts and traditions, that is, to serve Mishnah study as the quintessential rabbinic within-group activity.[3] But sometime over the course of the seventh to ninth centuries, mastery of the BT displaced mastery of Mishnah as the hallmark of rabbinic *bona fides* and credentials. Perhaps this sea change may say something about the Bavli itself and how it differs from these earlier rabbinic texts, including, perhaps, the earlier Talmud, the Yerushalmi. I do not doubt that such an argument can be made, and some have made it, implicitly or explicitly.[4] But it is easy for such arguments to become after-

---

1. While this assertion is neither novel nor controversial, I have written extensively about its implications for the fashioning of the early rabbinic guild and its social identity. See, for example, Lightstone, "Textual Study and Social Formation."

2. In a follow-up study to that mentioned in the preceding note, I have also described the social meaning and significance of Tosefta's dominant literary-rhetorical features for a group for whom Mishnah study as a socially formative activity. See Lightstone, "Textual Study and Social Formation, Part II" (forthcoming).

3. I say "in-group" pursuit, because I make no claims here about the hierarchy of rabbis' activities or duties outside of their rabbinic circles or institutions in the Jewish communities at large in which the rabbis lived and came to exercise various functions.

4. For example, I believe that some elements of just this are evident in Neusner, *Judaism, the Classical Statement*. Neusner and others sometimes describe the Bavli as "encyclopaedic" in its inclusion of legal, homiletical, narrative, folkloric, "scientific," medical and other content representing the range of intellectual and cultural heritage preserved and developed within the rabbinic groups of late antiquity. To say this is to make a comparative claim—comparing the Bavli to other early rabbinic documents, and especially, by implication, to compare the Bavli to that other Talmud, the Yerushalmi. For example, Boyarin's spellbinding book about the dissemination of rabbinic-Talmudic learning from

In the Seat of Moses

the-fact Bavli apologetics or Bavli panegyrics—as if those things that are intrinsically different about the Bavli account for its "success"—eclipsing other important factors at play.[5] Equally (or perhaps more) compelling reasons may be found in the political history of early medieval Judaism, as it emerges from the social world of late antiquity. Thus the following, very brief account.

The rabbinic academies (*yeshivot*) founded in late-Persian-era Mesopotamia became the focal points for the mastery of rabbinic tradition and literature. These academies displaced the centrality and authority of rabbinic circles in the Land of Israel, as the latter began to decline and their power and prestige to become circumscribed in the increasingly anti-Judaic climate of the fifth- and especially sixth-century, now-Christianized, Byzantine-Roman Empire. And while the Babylonian rabbinic movement had inherited, preserved, and vociferously studied the substantial literary heritage of their counterparts in the Land of Israel—indeed, in the end, it is partly (or largely) through the work of Babylonian rabbinic centers that this literary heritage survived—it was *their* talmud, the Babylonian Talmud, that they privileged, quite understandably, over the Jerusalem Talmud. What is novel, and perhaps surprising, is that the study of the Babylonian Talmud, which, after all, is organized as an analysis of about 60 percent of Mishnah's tractates (just like the Yerushalmi),[6] should come to supplant the study of

---

Mesopotamia, *Traveling Homeland*, during the medieval period approvingly cites (on page 48) the following remarks of Kalman, *Jewish Babylonia*, ix:

> Much more so than Palestinian rabbinic compilations, the Bavli is encyclopedic in character, meaning that it contains more varieties of rabbinic literature than roughly contemporaneous Palestinian compilations. The Bavli, for example, is much richer in nonlegal scriptural commentary (aggadic midrash) than is the Yerushalmi, which is more narrowly focused on law and Mishnah commentary.

The term "encyclopedic" is chosen as a modifier, and what in this citation begins as a comparison of the wider-ranging content of the Bavli with "Palestinian rabbinic compilations" (in the plural) is immediately illustrated by what for Kalman is the most obvious comparator, the Yerushalmi.

5. At the risk of overly emphasizing this point—it is too easy to follow the path of argument that something about the nature of the Bavli itself is the cause of its historical success and triumph in becoming the most important and authoritative rabbinic text. But I think it is a methodologically fraught path of argument. Politics and history are much more dominant factors, to of which appeals may be made that do not result in circular reasoning so often underlying arguments that the Bavli's (allegedly) superior intellectual substance and encyclopaedic range explain its triumph.

6. But not the same 60 percent, as noted in chapter 3.

Mishnah itself as the core curriculum of the would-be rabbi. Thereafter, the Bavli comes to be at the heart of the lifelong continuing education of rabbis. Not only did students (and faculty) at these Mesopotamian academies study *the* Talmud (that is, their *Babylonian* Talmud), but also study conventions were organized (allegedly twice yearly) by these academies and attended by a local, regional, and international rabbinic clientele until at least the tenth century. To these gatherings (called *kallot*, pl., *kallah*, sg.) came alumni and other rabbinic scholars to study the Bavli. Indeed, the standard administrative structure of the Babylonian rabbinic academies included persons designated by the title *rashei kallah*. *Rosh* means "head" or "director," and *kallah* is the designation for these Bavli study conventions.[7] It might not be inappropriate to liken the *kallot* to pilgrimage. Except the holy sites tended to be one of the several large Babylonian *yeshivot*, the pilgrims were rabbinic scholars from near and far, and the principal activity of the pilgrims was the study of designated tractates of the Bavli.[8]

So, Bavli study became and remained the central, most authoritative activity in rabbinic circles, displacing Mishnah study, *wherever* rabbinic Judaism and rabbis were to be found, not just in the territory between the Tigris and Euphrates Rivers. And it remained thus well after the hegemony of the Babylonian academies gave way to the decentralization of rabbinic-Talmudic learning and expertise and its dissemination from the Middle East to various centers across the Mediterranean, central Europe and, still later, Eastern Europe, until well into the nineteenth century (and thereafter, in twentieth-century, to North and South America and to the modern State of Israel). How this decentralization happened is, of course, also not germane to the main purposes of this volume. But "in for a penny, in for a pound"—it is also worth a brief telling. To make a long story very short, permit me to mention just two parts in this historical process.[9]

---

7. In fact, an early medieval prayer (in Aramaic), still recited in traditional synagogue liturgies today, asks that good fortune, health, and sustenance be provided to the personnel of the *yeshivot*, mentioning by title the officials of the academy.

8. Likening the *kallot* to religious pilgrimage is an idea that came to me from reading Boyarin, *Traveling Homeland*, 9–32.

9. In a recent book that argues that the Bavli became a textual-homeland for medieval rabbinic Diaspora Jews, Boyarin compellingly describes the dissemination in the tenth and immediately subsequent centuries of the capacity to independently interpret the Bavli in Jewish communities of the Mediterranean world and Rhineland. See Boyarin, *Traveling Homeland*, 9–32.

In the Seat of Moses

The first is the Babylonian rabbinic academies' assertion of their authority over the legal and religious systems of Jewish communities of the Middle East and Mediterranean lands. Without this projection of their authority in the first place, the conditions for the second part of the process would not have arisen. The success of the extension of the hegemony of the Babylonian *yeshivot* has much to do with the successes of the early Muslim Caliphate in Baghdad throughout the Near East and Mediterranean lands, coupled with the geographical, and ultimately political, proximity of the Babylonian *yeshivot* to the Baghdad Caliphate.[10] When the Caliphate looked to leaders in the nearby Jewish communities with whom to parlay, the heads of the *yeshivot* pressed their claim (sometimes in the face of competing claimants) to represent Jews and Judaism in the Caliphate's growing geographical range of control and influence.[11] Consequently, in this stage, Judaic legal and religious practice throughout this vast geography came to be arbitrated for significant numbers of Jews by the heads of the Babylonian *yeshivot*, based on their knowledge and understanding of, as one might expect, their Talmud, the Babylonian Talmud. This first stage occurred over the latter seventh and especially the eighth and ninth centuries and into the tenth century.

Now stage two. Beginning in the tenth century, the expertise independently—that is, independently of the Babylonian *yeshivot*—to interpret the Babylonian Talmud emerges in several centers in the Mediterranean world, and over the tenth through twelfth centuries further expands into central Europe's Rhine Valley.[12] Prominent rabbinic figures in North Africa, Spain, France, and the Rhineland, to name a few locales, begin writing

---

10. In conversation with me in the Fall of 2017, Professor Lee I. Levine of the Hebrew University emphasized this point.

11. By this date, the heads of the Babylonian rabbinic academies had largely coopted the office of the Resh Galuta, the Exilarch, who had for centuries been recognized and endorsed by the Persian Imperial government as the head of the Jewish communities in Mesopotamia and in Persian-controlled lands to the east and north. But by the end of the sixth century many of the powers of the Exilarch had been whittled down by the Persian government during a major reorganization of the latter's governing model in favor of a more centralized system. Concurrently, the rabbinic movement in Mesopotamia, now, itself just becoming "centralized" in large rabbinic academies, increasingly exerted their influence over the Exilarch, who was expected to have undergone a substantial rabbinic education as a one qualification for the office.

12. One might say that over the centuries the Babylonian *yeshivot*'s success in educating a cadre of rabbinic-Talmudic scholars who settled in a number of centers around the Mediterranean ultimately "did in" the Babylonian *yeshivot*'s exclusive authority.

commentaries on the Bavli and epistles on legal matters to which Bavli's content had to be applied. These commentaries and epistles are still read in twenty-first-century rabbinic academies and seminaries. And by the late eighteenth and nineteenth centuries, the rabbinic *yeshivot* of Eastern Europe enjoyed a prestige that, perhaps aptly, recalled that of the Babylonian *yeshivot* about a millennium earlier. So prestigious was Talmudic, yeshiva-based learning in Eastern Europe in the nineteenth century that wealthy Jewish merchants sought out promising Talmudic scholars as marriage partners for their daughters and then financially supported the couple and their children. This allowed the scholar son-in-law to continue to devote time (that would otherwise have to be spent on making a living) to Talmudic learning. Of course, the institutions of Talmudic learning were male bastions (and have remained so until recently, when notable exceptions have arisen). It is this Eastern European culture of reverence for the study of the Bavli inside and outside the study halls of the *yeshivot* that underlies the plot of the 1983 movie *Yentl*, starring Barbara Streisand.[13] Yentl, a young Jewish woman living in Eastern Europe, disguises herself as a boy in order to enter a rabbinic academy to study *the* Talmud, that is Bavli.

BT AND JT: FUNDAMENTALLY SIMILAR, AND DISTINCTIVELY DIFFERENT

These Animals Seem to Be One Species

As remarked earlier, to say that the Bavli came to mark an historical sea change in rabbinic Judaism does *not* mean that it is a sea change for you. How so? With this chapter, you are truly on the home stretch. The challenges you have yet to face, those being to master enough core rhetorical and literary conventions to allow a first entry into the *legal* passages of the text of the Babylonian Talmud (the Bavli, or BT), are minimal in comparison to what you have already mastered in having worked through chapters 4 through 7 of this book. Why? Because everything that you have learned in those preceding chapters is relevant to reading the BT. And, more specifically, what you have learned about reading and deciphering the Yerushalmi is especially apt and is fully portable to tackling the Bavli.[14] By way of

---

13. The movie was based both on a short story by I. B. Singer titled, "Yentl the Yeshiva Boy," and on a stage play cowritten by L. Napolin and I. B. Singer.

14. In saying this I must register a caveat. The statement of the high relevance of what

In the Seat of Moses

reassurance and as an entry to what follows, let me repeat what I wrote in chapter 7 (pages 292–94).

> (1) How much do the JT and BT differ and in what ways? And (2) how much do those differences matter to readers like yourselves who are attempting to get a toe-hold on the literary-rhetorical conventions and constructs that will make these Talmuds more accessible to you? The answers to these questions, when considered together, may surprise you. To the first, I must say: The two Talmuds differ in a number of quite substantial ways. These differences include, among other things, terminology, rules of composition and analytic agenda. . . . . . My answer to the second question . . . runs entirely counter to the direction of the first. I have already stated that a basic grasp of the literary-rhetorical conventions and constructs of the legal sections of one Talmud provides a pretty firm foundation for beginning to read the other Talmud . . . I start with the JT only because it is the earlier of the two Talmuds, not because it is necessarily the easier to decipher. But for our particular purposes, I could have gone about matters the other way around . . . [T]he upshot is this: all the lessons . . . learned . . . about how to read JT-ean legal compositions and composite mini-essays apply almost whole hog to the BT, *mutandis mutandi*.

Let me rehearse some of the salient similarities of the JT and BT. Of course, at the most fundamental level, both BT and JT are organized in tractates that take their names from corresponding Mishnah's tractates. And within BT's and JT's tractates, Mishnah's passages are taken in order as objects of commentary and analysis, using other tannaitic and amoraic traditions in hand to accomplish the task. Both BT and JT contain aggadic materials. In fact, Bavli contains not only aggadic traditions, but also, on occasion, massive miscellanies of the them,[15] as well as other cultural knowledge and folklore of its time and place. Yet BT, like JT, is fundamentally still a legal text, concerned with the analysis of Halakhic materials.[16]

---

you have learned in the preceding chapter about reading the Yerushalmi is not intended to imply anything about the literary-historical relationship of the JT to the BT. That is a complex matter about which there remains a great deal of scholarly debate that is not terribly germane to this book's purpose or yours in reading it.

15. Neusner, *Bavli's Massive Miscellanies*.

16. In other words, it would be inaccurate or an exaggeration to say that Bavli's "encyclopaedic" tendencies and its penchant, in comparison to the JT, for including aggadic material overwhelms its focus on legal matters generally or Mishnah commentary and analysis specifically. Neusner is unequivocal when on this point he states, in Neusner,

The Two Talmuds

Indeed, everything you have learned in chapter 7 about deciphering legal compositions and extended composite mini-essays of the Yerushalmi (the JT) applies equally to the BT. Specifically, the accounts in the previous chapter about how the JT uses

- –type-1 elements: Mishnah passages,
- –type-2 elements: Tosefta passages and Tosefta-like passages (*beraitot*),
- –type-3 elements: Halakhic-Midrashic passages (also understood to be *beraitot*), and
- –type-4 elements: "amoraic" sources usually attributed to named authorities that bear a family resemblance to "tannaitic" sources,

and incorporates these into compositions and composite mini-essays using

- –type-5 elements: a layer of formalized critical-analytical arguments, sometimes attributed to *amora'im* and sometimes not, often creating back-and-forth, rhythm-like, dialectical "discussions" (all served by fairly standardized "substructural," highly-laconic stock terminology of argumentation), and
- –type-6 elements: a top-most, "superstructuring" layer of language that poses questions, makes challenges, and invites types of analysis of specific sorts (also served by an array of stock "superstructuring" formularies)—

all of this is *entirely* portable to deciphering what is going on in the BT and to acquiring a basic level of accessibility to the *sugyot*, the compositions and the composite legal mini-essays, of the Bavli.[17] Therefore, none of the

---

First Steps, 44–48, that four-fifths of Bavli's discourse (its composites, compositions and conglomerates) may be classified as either Mishnah commentary of various sorts (that is, What does Mishnah mean? What is the basis of Mishnah's rulings, including its basis in Scripture? To what circumstances does it apply or not, Who is the rabbinic authority behind which ruling? etc.) or the examination of other legal issues related to but not directly addressed in the analysis of the Mishnah text at hand, sometimes concerning abstract legal principles suggested by analysis of Mishnah. This leaves about 20 percent of Bavli's *sugyot* which may be classified as either Scripture commentary or as "other" content. Moreover, in his *Rules of Composition*, 15, Neusner observes that the Bavli tends to consistently order these classes of materials: "Mishnah exegesis nearly always comes first, abstract legal speculation, last." *Rules of Composition* is in some respect a synopsis of aspects of, and in other respects represents the underlying "spreadsheet" of quantified observations for, Neusner, *Bavli's One Voice*.

17. When looking at my six-element classification of the building blocks of the BT (or JT) I am struck by how many of them end up as chapter headings in an "older" classic,

In the Seat of Moses

foregoing bears repeating and elaboration here. And as is the case in the JT, the type-6 language of the BT and a good deal of the type-5 language of BT derives from the *post*amoraic authorship of the Bavli, who, in Bavli's case, undertook their work in the sixth into perhaps the early seventh century CE in Persian-ruled Mesopotamia. In other words, Bavli's postamoraic authorship undertook their massive project some 150 to two hundred years after the authors of the Yerushami had completed their own. Bavli's authors had at their disposal not only the tannaitic and amoraic traditions from the Land of Israel and Babylonia-Mesopotamia that circulated in about 400 CE, when the production of the JT was mounted, but also the traditions of the Babylonian *amora'im*, whose careers spanned the fifth century up until the death of Ravina II near that century's end.

Now, having made the assertions of the preceding paragraph, which unequivocally state that all of the rhetorical-literary lessons of the previous chapter about the Yerushalmi apply whole-hog in the current chapter about the Bavli, I have perhaps placed myself in a somewhat precarious position among my academic colleagues. A significant amount of scholarship has been done, and is still being done, that compares the JT and BT from many angles. The latter, the BT, is by no means (just?) the Mesopotamian rabbis' version of the former, the JT. There are many differences between the two Talmuds, and the literary-historical relationship between them is complex (and still debated). There is not even an iron-clad scholarly consensus around whether the BT's *sugyot* tend to be developments of the earlier parallel compositions in the JT. Some have argued convincingly one way, and others have proffered meritorious arguments in the opposite direction. And while I have my own views on the subject, it would be a considerable digression to air and to defend them here[18] in a volume the purpose of

---

literary-historical introduction to the talmuds by Albeck, in his *Mavo LeTalmudim*. One of the major differences between my own portrayal (and for that matter, of Neunser's) of the issues is the degree to which Albeck gives weight to the historical value of the attribution of materials in the Talmuds to named tannaitic and amoraic authorities. Viewed through this lens, that is, the prima facie historical validity of the attributions to named rabbis, the resulting scholarship produces a very different viewpoint. My own approach simply bypasses the question of the validity of the attributions to focus on structural relations in the documents and how materials are made to fit in the structure by the documents' penultimate authorships.

18. It is not centrally germane to this book to discuss the literary-historical relationship of the Yerushalmi (JT) and Bavli (BT), especially the question of whether the Bavli's authors tended to have before them the extant Yerushalmi's compositions or composite essays when composing their own. As stated, there is ample scholarly literature on this

which is quite delimited and focused, namely, to provide you with the basic tools required to begin to commence reading these documents without getting lost in an alien world. How? By outlining for you the basic features of their literary-rhetorical structures and conventions, familiarity with which

---

topic, and a variety of opinions, and I shall reference in this note some of the more recent scholarship only.

Given the generally accepted conclusion that the JT was formulated between, let us say, 150 to 200 years before the BT, and given that the rabbinic movements of the Land of Israel and Mesopotamia were regularly in contact with one another, it stands to reason that a burning scholarly question will have been whether the JT formed a basis for the authoring of the BT. Their authors certainly shared an overlapping pool of both tannaitic and amoraic traditions, and both authorships similarly organized their work as Mishnah commentary and analysis. Moreover, as I shall point out later, the "questions" that both the JT and BT "ask" in their respective enterprises of Mishnah elucidation often resemble one another, as do, in many instances, how these questions are addressed. This cannot be the result of some historical accident. That said, it appears to be the case that the vast majority of composites and mini-essays of the BT are *not* developments of their putative "parallels" in the JT, even when these parallels adduce the same tannaitic traditions (and sometimes the same amoraic sources) in their respective analyses of Mishnah. More often than not BT's composite mini-essays are not modelled on their parallels in JT, in my experience.

That said, there are many contemporary scholarly works on this topic, and the matter is undoubtedly one that remains hotly debated. For an example of this debate one may read, Hayes, *Between*, countered by Neusner, *Are the Talmuds*. (Neusner's counterargument is to Hayes's dissertation, of which her book by Oxford University Press is the published version.) See also, Gray, *Talmud*; and Neusner, *Two Talmuds*.

Amid the scholarly debate on this issue, I find elucidating, well balanced, and nuanced Yaakov Elman's view on the role of Palestinian traditions in the work of Babylonian rabbis' formulation of their Talmud. Elman, in "Orality and the Redaction," 87, states:

> ... [T]he existence of large-scale Palestinian structures within the Bavli may point to some written transmission; we have already seen that the evidence for written texts of the Amoraic period is Palestinian in provenance. Nevertheless, there is little doubt, as modern scholarship has maintained for the last century, that the Bavli's redactors did not have the redacted Yerushalmi before them. Nevertheless, it would seem that some more elaborate Palestinian texts reached them, beyond the relatively short *memrot* that are explicitly attributed to (usually early) Palestinian Amoraim.

While the JT and BT passages reviewed in chapters 7 and 8 of this book are insufficient grounds upon which to build a probative account of the BT's dependence, or lack thereof, on the JT, I will say this. As we shall see, it is clear that b. Avodah Zarah 14b–16a (discussed in this chapter) is certainly not literarily dependent upon its "parallel" in the JT at y. Avodah Zarah 1:6 (analyzed in the preceding chapter). The authors of the Bavli composite did not use the "parallel" Yerushalmi composite *at all* as a model for their own essay. However, let me stress once again that these are issues that are critically important from a literary-historical perspective, but they are not my preoccupation here.

make these documents more accessible to a novice student of them. And in these respects, I stand by the assertions of the opening of this chapter and of this very paragraph.

The practical upshot of the lessons of chapter 7 carrying over to this chapter are these. First, I will not repeat here what would essentially be a rehearsal of almost half of the preceding chapter. Second, and in a related vein, you do not need me to present a fake BT composition to orient you to what is to come. My fake JT passage in chapter 7 (pages 308–12) suffices. Reread it to get in the mood, if you are so inclined. Third, I, nonetheless, owe you, the readers, some prior warning and a very basic, brief account of what you will encounter in BT compositions that differs from your encounter with the JT texts presented in the previous chapter. And it is to the latter that I now turn.

These Animals Are Distinctive Subspecies, Adapted, Perhaps, to Different Ends

One of the privileges of my academic career is to talk with, and learn from, people in my academic field who are smarter and more learned than I am. I am grateful for my encounters with all of them. One such person with whom I spoke before undertaking to write this chapter was Professor Daniel Boyarin of the University of California, Berkeley. Over coffee,[19] I commenced our conversation by asking him this leading question: How do you account for the differences between the Bavli and Yerushalmi? Professor Boyarin displayed a sparkling and mischievous sense of humor. His initial answer was meant to be humorous and "tongue-in-cheek." The Bavli's authors had nearly two centuries more to "*patchky* around," he said. *Patchky* is a Yiddish word that I would best translate into colloquial English as "tinker with." There is likely a great deal of truth hidden behind his humorous formulation. He knew it and I recognized it. But that truth needs very nuanced articulation.

Without asserting that the authors of BT's composite mini-essays depended upon the earlier-formulated, parallel passages found in the JT— and from what I personally have seen, I am not confident that I would make such an assertion as a common or general rule—there is certainly a strong family resemblance between what the BT tends to do and what the JT tends

---

19. In Berkeley, California, in April 2018.

to do. The preceding subsection of this chapter went to some lengths to assert the semblance. That said,[20] by way of comparison and contrast:

- compositions and composite essays in the BT seem much more highly "developed" (even if they are not always longer, although very often they are);
- the Bavli's compositions and composites display a far greater commitment to dialectical analysis and argument undertaken for their own sake;
- BT has a far richer and more consistently used set of "structural" and "substructural" formalized terminology (which all still fit into my type-5-element and type-6-element categories); and
- BT's compositions and composites are couched in "clearer" language, which makes deciphering a BT passage (comparatively) easier.

Even the use of Aramaic and Hebrew in the BT seems more consistent and rule-bound, according to Jacob Neusner. Neusner remarks that in the BT, Hebrew tends to be used for authoritative sources (whether "tannaitic" or "amoraic"), and Aramaic is used for posing questions, for inviting analysis, and for making arguments (in which authoritative sources, in Hebrew, are often adduced as evidence).[21] Neusner's claims about the use of Hebrew vs. Aramaic in the BT may be easily "translated" into our categorization of elements of the JT's and BT's compositions and composite mini-essays. More consistently in the BT, Hebrew is used for type-1 through type-4 elements, and Aramaic for type-5 and type-6 elements; language helps demarcate literary function in the Bavli in a manner or to a degree that does not occur in the JT. So, use of Aramaic in BT is an additional literary-rhetorical signpost of what is about to happen.

The foregoing list of differences is merely technical. More important is to ask: To what ends are these different features of the BT used? This takes me back to my coffee conversation with Professor Boyarin. To paraphrase him, the Yerushalmi ultimately *seeks answers* to the questions it poses, questions largely about Mishnah's meaning and rulings, about their application, and about their relationship to other tannaitic and amoraic

---

20. My own, highly technical analyses of the similarities and differences of the literary features of the Bavli and the Yerushalmi may be found in Lightstone, *Rhetoric*, 49–76, 235–45. For a sample of other scholarly works comparing BT and JT see above, chapter 7, note 13.

21. Neusner, *Two Talmuds*.

teachings. The Bavli, by comparison, very often does not, and its authorship is quite content *to prove or to disprove* all of the posited alternative answers to a problem. If matters are left unresolved, so be it. Moreover, according to Neusner, the Bavli will often raise abstract legal issues arising from, but not directly relevant to its analysis of Mishnah's issues, and then proceed to engage in dialectical back-and-forth "discussion" of these abstract principles, again sometimes to no conclusive end.[22] And to this I would add the following distinguishing observation: a significant number of Bavli's compositions take as their *point of departure*, not a Mishnah rule-sentence, or even a Tosefta or Tosefta-like passage, but an amoraic legal position (a type-4 element, in my classification of things), having only a general topical relation to the Mishnah passage at hand, and then subject these amoraic teachings to the same questioning and analysis it would normally devote to a Mishnah rule-statement.

How may I characterize these more distinctively BT-ean traits? I join most other academic students of the Bavli in seeing in BT an ethos of valuing analysis for its own sake, whether or not one arrives at (or minimally, in addition to arriving at) a probative solution to a question about the meaning, significance, application of, or authoritative basis for a Mishnah passage.[23] And if analysis and dialectical (back-and-forth) argument—or rather modeling this activity for the Bavli's devoted students—is the (or a) desideratum for its own sake, then *speedily* and *concisely* reaching a probative end to a particular *sugya* does not necessarily serve the text's purposes. Rather, keeping the argument, challenges, and counterarguments going does. Hence, comparatively speaking, many of Bavli's composite miniessays are much longer than would be the norm for the JT, as I intimated earlier.[24]

Neusner articulates this distinctive "end" or "goal" in the BT in different language, but I believe he is trying to put words to similar observations, when he writes,

---

22. Neusner calls this "abstract legal speculation" in the Bavli: see Neusner, *Rules of Composition*, 15.

23. Again, this characterization of the Bavli's "goal" corresponds closely with my own formulation of more than twenty years ago in Lightstone, *Rhetoric*, 247–81.

24. This is reflected in the observation that the Bavli, which has tractates for 37 (or 36 1/2 if you will) of Mishnah's tractates is between 65 percent to 70 percent longer than the Yerushalmi, which has tractates for 39 of Mishnah's tractates. Some of these basic distinguishing observations about the JT vs. BT, are catalogued in Zelcer, *Guide*, 56–57.

> The difference [between the Yerushalmi's and the Bavli's treatment of matters consistently] is intellectual and, appropriately, comes to the surface in hermeneutics; the *Bavli's composites' framers consistently treat as a question to be investigated the exegetical hypotheses that the Yerushalmi's compositions' authors happily accept as conclusive*. All the secondary devices of testing an allegation . . . serve the primary goal [of the Bavli]. The second recurrent difference is that the *Bavli's framers find themselves constantly drawn toward questions of generalization and abstraction . . . , moving from case to principle to new case to new principle, then asking whether the substrate of principles forms a single, tight fabric*. The Yerushalmi's authors rarely, if ever, produce that chimera. [interpolations my own]²⁵

Two and a half decades ago, I too sought to capture in language what I had found in the Bavli's pervasive literary-rhetorical conventions, so similar as they are to the Yerushalmi's, that distinguished the BT from the JT. I wrote the following.

> . . . [M]eaning, order and purpose in the Bavli derive only in part from Mishnah, and rarely if ever from other authoritative data. In large measure order and purpose emanate from Bavli's structural and dialectical formularies [comment: which in this volume I have called type-6 and type-5 elements]. What the Talmud undertakes with its argument-statements [i.e., type-5 elements], elaborated composites (*sugyot*) and larger composite essays is more open-ended analysis, seemingly for its own sake. The dialectical, scholastic-like process of analysis to no particular end is a central purpose of the Bavli. Just as the Bavli may be said not to be exclusively (or even primarily) interested in Mishnah's meaning—a trait highlighted by our comparative examination of Toseftan and Yerushalmi passages—so too it is not particularly interested in legal adjudication based upon Mishnah alone, or in combination with any other data. The Bavli deconstructs in order to create its own characteristic structures of open ended questioning based upon diverse and discrete snippets of holy-text materials [i.e., what this volume in chapters 7 and 8 I call type-1, type-2, type-3 and type-4 elements].²⁶

Clearly, Boyarin, Neusner and I are trying to put words to what seems different about the BT, *given its similarities to the JT*. Neusner's formulation of

---

25. Neusner, *Two Talmuds*, xxxiv (italics added).
26. Lightstone, *Rhetoric*, 252.

the meaning of those differences goes somewhat further in making claims about the BT's authors' intellectual program than I (or perhaps Boyarin) seem prepared to go. But we are all on the same track, nonetheless, even if we have not all chosen to have gone the same distance along it.

How, then, would I sum up the importance of these distinctions between the JT and BT for you, the reader of this volume with its focused purpose. I would say this: (1) the BT is more "polished" than the JT; (2) with a somewhat wider array of stock type-5 and type-6 rhetorical formularies and constructs; (3) that are nonetheless very similar in function to JT's stock formularies and constructs; and (4) BT's compositions and composites often take back-and-forth "bouts" and "rounds" much further than JT does, and (5) to no particular end than to model that this can (and should) be done without the necessity of arriving at a final, probative answer to the question with which the composition or composite essay started. Perhaps one can say that BT differs from JT in the degree to which it pushes matters, and this difference in degree is so significant that it amounts to a difference in kind and purpose. For you, at this stage of first encounters with the Bavli, the upshot is very simple indeed and little cause for concern: just be prepared for a difference in degree, that is all. And with this, we may plunge into some exemplars of Bavli's compositions and their integration into larger composite essays, using the same methods of presentation as we used in chapter 7 for passages of the Yerushalmi.

LET'S ASK QUESTIONS, ANSWER THEM, CHALLENGE THE ANSWERS IN ORDER TO PROFFER ALTERNATIVE RESPONSES, AND THEN CHALLENGE EACH OF THESE IN TURN— THEN (OFTEN) REPEAT THE PROCESS

The subtitle of this section is a deliberate play on words of the corresponding subtitle in chapter 7. What is new here follows the subtitle's dash: "then (often) repeat the process." I mean to convey generally what I have written earlier in this chapter about both the likenesses and differences one encounters when first grappling with legal compositions and composites in the BT, having been exposed, as you have been, to their counterparts in the JT. The BT has a decided penchant for spinning out the posing of questions, the positing of responses, and the challenging or testing of those responses. Bavli does this to a degree that the extended engagement in dialectical argument, using tannaitic (Palestinian) and amoraic (Palestinian and Babylonian) sources in the process, often takes priority over coming to a definitive answer, whether that is a definitive answer about a question posed about the Mishnah text that occasioned the *sugya*, or about some question posed or challenge made to some secondary tannatic or amoraic teaching. Indeed, if the dialectical-analytic "journey" has for the Bavli's authorship such intrinsic value, why speedily bring that journey to its "conclusion," or indeed to any conclusion at all?

Perhaps this especial culture of the Bavli's authorship accounts for the fact that the Bavli has a more developed and more consistently used stock of terminological formulae for posing questions and launching challenges (type-6 elements' stock terminology) and for engaging in subsequent analysis and argument (type-5 elements' stock language) than does Bavli's counterpart talmud, the Yerushalmi.[27] In chapter 7 I produced a list of type-6 stock terms used in y. Avodah Zarah 1:6 and categorized this list by function. The list could not be understood as an exhaustive one of JT's structural formulaic language for posing questions and inviting analyses of specific sorts, as it represents only those formularies that appear in y. Avodah Zarah 1:6's extended composite mini-essay on Mishnah Avodah Zarah 1:6. But that list is certainly indicative and exemplary of such stock terminology in the Yerushalmi. What if I were to do exactly the same for comparable, type-6-element stock terminology that is used in the Bavli's composite that is the exact counterpart of y. Avodah Zarah 1:6's treatment of Mishnah Avodah 1:6. That extended, "parallel" composite essay is found in b. Avodah Zarah 14b–16a. (Note that page references in the Bavli are different than the Yerushalmi. In referencing BT one uses the tractate name, the folio number of the standard printed [Vilna] edition—i.e., a page with two sides—and the side of the folio, "a" for the first side, "b" for the second side). Both extended composites bring together compositions that comment upon and analyze the very same Mishnah passage (m. Avodah Zarah 1:6). In the list that presently follows I will do two things differently: I will list the stock type-6 element-serving formularies for *both* y. Avodah Zarah 1:6 *and* b. Avodah Zarah 14b–16a; and I shall place in parentheses

---

27. The scholarly consensus is that, in part, the consistency and uniformity in the use of formal terminology in the BT results from early medieval rabbinic scholars' continuing attempts to harmonize terminological usage in the Bavli. This reflects the elevated place of the Bavli in the core curriculum of early medieval rabbinic circles. It is the text that is vociferously studied that is more likely to be increasingly polished in the process by scribes who copy it.

after each the number of times each formulary is used in their respective parallel composites. For the sake of comparability, I am still exercising in this listing the arch-conservatism applied in the previous chapter when assigning language to this category of formalized terminology. (Thereafter, I will abandon that conservatism for the remainder of this chapter, for that approach will have served its initial pedagogical purposes.) Here, then, is the new dual list, with frequency of use indicated.

Type-6 Formularies[28]	in b. AZ 14b–16a	in y. AZ 1:6
demanding a reason	–why? (1) –what is [the reason]? (1) –what is the reason? (9) –the reason that . . . ? (1) –but according to your reasoning . . . what is the reason? (1)	–why? (2)
challenge inviting further analysis	–but is it alright!? (1) –but is it!? (1) –is that to say!? (1) –x challenged it . . .!? (3) –and they rebuffed it . . .!? (1)	

28. Lightstone, *Rhetoric*, 72–74.

introducing an authoritative source to commence/spark or to resolve argumentation	–and so we have taught/learned (2) –as it has been taught (1) –for lo it is taught (1) –our rabbis taught (2) –as we have taught/learned (1) –but moreover it is taught (1) –and/but we have taught/learned (1) –come and hear (1) –lo, you have said (1) –said [x + citation that opens an elaborated structure] (2) –said [x + rhetorical questioning or alternative view] (9)	–there we have taught/learned ... (1) –as/and it has taught ... (3)
inviting further analysis or argumentation	–[but] it differs (1) –what is similar? (1) –how are they similar? (1) –and here, with what are we dealing? The case of ... (1) –well and good ... but. . .? (1) –it was asked of them ...what? (1) –ask of x, ask of y [as introduction to an elaborated structure] (1) –ask of x [as introduction to substructure within an elaborated structure] (1)	–what!? (1) –what is the difference among them? (1) –what distinguishes . . .? (1) –but they (might have/should have/would have) responded to him how? (1)

introducing an alternative/hypothesis to spark further analysis	–or perhaps (1) –and if you say . . . then, lo . . . (1) –rather (5) –and now that you have said (1) –and if it should occur to you (2)	–they should have said . . . (1) –in accordance with his approach they (might have/should have) responded to him . . . (1)
asking for some authoritative basis	–and whence will you say that we have said . . .? (1)	–and whence . . .? (1) –who taught it? (1)
drawing conclusions to an analytical problem (as a launching pad for renewed questioning), or final conclusions	–therefore. . . (1) –always . . . (1) –learn from this (1) –but x must have reversed [position] (1)	(none discernable in y. AZ 1:6)

Later we shall look at the entirety of b. Avodah Zarah 14b–16a in the same manner as we examined and deciphered the principal parts of y. Avodah Zarah 1:6 in chapter 7. But at this juncture, what stands out about our parallel lists that helps prepare you for what you will later see in this composite essay of the Bavli?

The first observation is that the list for b. Avodah Zarah 14b–16a is considerably longer than for its counterpart, composite essay in y. Avodah Zarah 1:6. Thirty-nine (39) distinct formularies are used in b. Avodah Zarah 14b–16a; only eleven appear in y. Avodah Zarah 1:6. The second observation reinforces the impression gained from the first: b. Avodah Zarah 14b–16a's thirty-nine stock formularies are used sixty-five times in the Bavli composite essay, when I add up the numbers in the parentheses. In contrast, y. Avodah Zarah 1:6's eleven stock type-6-element terms are used fourteen times in the Yerushalmi's.

What do these numbers indicate? Foremost, that the Bavli's treatment of Mishnah Avodah Zarah 1:6 launches sixty-five separate analyses using its richer array of stock language for introducing questions and inviting analyses. The Yerushalmi's treatment of the same base Mishnah passage launches only fourteen inquiries with its comparatively restrained set of terminology for introducing or signaling such criticism. If this is representative of how Bavli, as distinct from the Yerushalmi, approaches its mandate—and I assure you that it is representative[29]—then you are forewarned and prepared

29. In my more technical-scholarly work on Bavli's rhetoric, I took pains to provide

for what you will see in the Bavli. The Bavli has a far greater commitment than is evident in the Yerushalmi to analysis and criticism. As intimated earlier, this amounts to a difference in kind (and therefore, in agenda), when compared to the other Talmud. What one sees clearly reflected in these numbers is what, in the previous section of this chapter, I reported about how Boyarin, Neusner, and others have characterized what makes Bavli so different from the Yerushalmi, their many similarities notwithstanding. But this difference in both degree and mandate, does *not* necessarily make the processes of deciphering a Bavli composition or extended composite essay all that different than deciphering a Yerushalmi one. It just takes more time and more stick-to-it-ness—what in Yiddish is humorously referred to as "sitz-fleisch," the capacity to sit longer to work through things. In chapter 7, I prepared you for reading a Yerushalmi composition and composite essay by using the metaphor of boxing bouts and rounds. Bavli compositions and composite essays often have more bouts and rounds, and the contest is more frequently left unresolved—as if the skill shown in the bouts and rounds is the point, not declaring a winner.

I would be remiss were I not to voice a caveat, before concluding this section. The list of Bavli's formularies just catalogued and discussed is not exhaustive of all of Bavli's stock structural terminology for posing questions and inviting analyses in BT's legal compositions and composite essays. There are others. But this list in highly indicative, and after mastering the remainder of this chapter, you will be able to identify these others on your own, because they function similarly to the terminological signpost language for launching analysis and inquiry that is found in the sample Bavli texts that follow. Consistency in terminological usage is a strength of the Bavli. Perhaps this is a result of the importance of Bavli study in rabbinic circles after its promulgation in the late sixth or early seventh century, since after its creation its text continued to be "polished" by copyist/editors. And if you master enough Hebrew and Aramaic and should decide to spend considerably more time and effort studying Bavli passages than is involved in mastering this volume, you will no doubt find useful the several medieval and modern lexicons (both long and short) dedicated specifically

---

evidence for just this assertion and to indicate that the kind and use of stock, question-posing/analysis-inviting formularies examined in detail in my sample Bavli passages likely represented the state of affairs for the Bavli as a whole. For the evidence and analyses that underlie these claims, see Lightstone, *Rhetoric*, 283–85, 19, notes 5–7.

to Bavli's technical terms and formularies. These lexicons are in daily use in modern rabbinic academies.[30]

WHAT "REALLY" GOES ON IN BT'S COMPOSITIONS AND EXTENDED COMPOSITE MINI-ESSAYS: SOME SAMPLES

We have reached the juncture in this chapter where I will take you through two sample Bavli texts. If on proceeding, you should feel a bit unprepared, and this may well be the case if you have read chapter 7 quite a while ago, then I have an easy fix. Simply reread pages 288–312 of the preceding chapter, and then return to *this spot* in chapter 8. You will be right as rain, I assure you.

Our first sample Bavli text is the one you and I together have already briefly reviewed in chapter 3, b. Gittin 2a–4a. It takes as its point of departure and object of analysis the first rule-sentence of m. Gittin 1:1 about the transport by emissary of a writ of divorce from "Mediterranean lands" to the Land of Israel for execution. Remember that Mishnah passage's first rule-sentence?

> He who brings a writ from a Mediterranean province—it is required that he say: In my presence it was written, and in my presence it was signed.

What I wish you to attend to in the Bavli passage that "treats" this first sentence of Mishnah Gittin is BT's ebb and flow, back and forth, of (i) posing questions and inviting analysis (type-6 elements), (ii) arguing positions in response or juxtaposing more than one argument in response (type-5 elements), (iii) signaling challenges to such responses with further questions and invitations for further analyses (type-6 elements again), (iv) followed by yet more arguments, analyses, and counter-arguments (type-5 elements again).

Arguments need "data," and that data will be seen to be introduced in arguments and analyses by adducing "authoritative" sources of various ilks. In Bavli generally, these data may be from Mishnah (type 1) itself, Tosefta and other Tosefta-like traditions (type 2), Halakhic-Midrashic passages

---

30. Talmudic legal literature also has penchant for the use of Hebrew and Aramaic abbreviations, a reflection of the labor and material costs of reproduction, first by scribes and later by printers. There are several dictionaries of these too.

(type 3), and amoraic teachings (type 4). Not all of these types of authoritative sources are adduced in our first sample passage, b. Gittin 2a–4a.

At the risk of harping repeatedly on one point—it is even more essential in reading Bavli than in reading Yerushalmi to *catch the rhythm*—the ebb-and-flow, back-and-forth cadence—within the individual compositions that are brought together to make up the composite mini-essay. Perceiving this prevents you from getting lost. And I have made generous use of interpolations to help you better see that rhythm and flow. Again, as I did in the previous chapter(s), I will also format the fonts to help you perceive what is going on. Stock formularies serving type-6 elements will be in SMALL CAPS, and those serving type-5 elements will appear in underscored SMALL CAPS; these are the "codes" alerting you to what is about to happen. Mishnah citations will be in **boldface**; Tosefta is underscored regular type. Aramaic is *italics*; whatever is not in italics is in Hebrew (although it may be boldfaced, or underscored, and perhaps on occasion in SMALL CAPS). Having abandoned my previously adopted conservatism in assigning language to the structural (type-6) category, you will now see me on occasion assigning terms such as "said" or "but" to this category, when they *also* serve on their own to "signpost" an impending counterargument, without the more explicit language for doing so, such as "they objected to/challenged it." Also in service of helping you discern the structure of the sample composite, I have subdivided the passage using Roman numerals to designate individual compositions, and I have numbered the subparts in each subdivision using Arabic numerals, just I did for Yerushalmi passages presented in chapter 7. Whether someone else would demarcate the beginning and end of individual compositions in this extended composite as I have is beside the point for your/my purposes.

As you read this sample text of BT, first read it through to discern its structure and flow; then reread it for its content. And read it a third time, again for its structure and flow. The key exercise and challenge in reading the BT, as it was with the Yerushalmi texts examined in chapter 7, lie in deciphering each individual composition, because the composite essay (whatever its larger goals and analytic agenda may be) is more or less a "stacking" of individual compositions.

m. Gittin 1:1a (translation my own):

> He who brings a writ from a Mediterranean province—it is required that he say: In my presence it was written, and in my presence it was signed.

In the Seat of Moses

b. Gittin 2a–4a (i.e., BT to m. Gittin 1:1a, translation my own):

[GEMARA]

I

1. WHAT IS THE REASON?

2. Rabbah SAID: BECAUSE they are not expert [in the Mediterranean provinces] with regard to [executing the writ of divorce] in her name [see m. Gittin 3:1].

3. Rava SAID: BECAUSE witnesses are not present to make it stand [see m. Gittin 1:3 and t. Gittin 1:3,5–6].

II

1. WHAT DIFFERENTIATES THEM [i.e., Rabbah's and Rava's answers, in practical terms]?

2. WHAT DIFFERENTIATES THEM IS: -[A STATE OF AFFAIRS IN] WHICH two [emissaries together] have brought it, [IN WHICH CASE Rabbah only would require the declaration, as two witnesses are present];

3. IF SO, [ALSO] from province to province in the Land of Israel [IN WHICH CASE Rava only would require the declaration, as within the land of Israel those who execute such writs know and observe the requirement to execute it in the wife's name];

4. IF SO, [ALSO] within the same province in a Mediterranean province [IN WHICH CASE Rabbah only would require the declaration, since the witnesses are nearby if the writ's witnesses must be authenticated].

III

1. AND AS REGARDS Rabbah, WHO SAID: BECAUSE they are not expert with regard to [executing the writ of divorce] in her name,

2. LET HIM [ie., why does he too not] require [that] two [bring the writ], so that it accords with all [cases requiring] witnesses in [the laws of] the Torah!?

3. [PERHAPS, Rabbah is OF THE VIEW THAT] one witness is trustworthy regarding prohibitions.

4. [WELL, ONE MIGHT COUNTER such a position hypothetically attributed to Rabbah on these grounds:]

5. LET US SAY THAT WE SAY [that] one witness is trustworthy, WHEN [we are dealing with a case], SUCH AS, [WHEN] we do not know whether [at hand is] a piece of fat [forbidden for

consumption] or fat [permitted for consumption], IN WHICH INSTANCE *it is not known* [for certain whether one is dealing with a matter that is] *a prohibition.*

6. BUT HERE [in the case at hand] IN WHICH IT IS known [for certain that one deals with a potential instance of] *the prohibition* of adultery, IT IS *a matter of forbidden sexual relations,* AND *a matter of forbidden sexual relations is not* [dealt with by] *less than two* [witnesses].

7. MOST [in fact] are expert [with regard to executing the writ of divorce in her name].

8. AND EVEN AS REGARDS R. Meir, WHO *is concerned about exceptions,* [NONETHELESS] *the ordinary judicial scribe* [who would be preparing the document] *has learned the teaching* [that the writ of divorce must be executed in her name].

9. AND IT IS *the rabbis* WHO *have required* [the declaration by the bearer of the writ coming from the Mediterranean provinces]. AND IN THIS [CASE], ON ACCOUNT OF [their concern that the woman not become] *an abandoned wife, our rabbis dealt leniently with her* [by allowing a single emissary bringing a writ of divorce from a Mediterranean province to the Land of Israel to validate the document by testifying that the writ was written and signed in his presence].

10. THIS IS *a leniency* [for her]!?[RATHER] IT IS *a stringency* [for her]!

11. SINCE IF *you required two* [emissaries], [THEN] *the husband* [can]*not come and challenge* [the writ's validity] *and invalidate it.* [BUT IF] *one* [brings the writ], [THEN] *the husband* [can] *come and challenge* [the writ's validity] *and invalidate it.*

12. [NOT AT ALL!] BECAUSE OF WHAT Mar HAS SAID: Before how many [witnesses] do they give it [the writ of divorce] to her?

13. R. Yohanan [is of one view], AND R. Hanina [is of another view]. ONE SAID: Before two [witnesses]. AND ONE [i.e., the other] SAID: Before three [witnesses]. [THEREFORE,] AB INITIO, [the emissary, knowing that the writ must be presented before witnesses] *is scrupulous* [about the process and all requisites], AND *he will not come* [bearing an invalid writ], AND [allow] *himself to be denigrated* [before two or three witnesses].

14. AND AS REGARDS Rava, WHO SAID: BECAUSE witnesses are not present to make it stand,

15. LET HIM [ie., why does he too not] require [that] two [bring the writ], SO THAT it accords with all [cases requiring] deeds?

16. [PERHAPS, Rava IS OF THE VIEW THAT] one witness is trustworthy regarding prohibitions.

17. [WELL, ONE MIGHT COUNTER such a position hypothetically attributed to Rava on these grounds:]

18. LET US SAY THAT WE SAY [that] one witness is trustworthy, WHEN [we are dealing with a case] SUCH AS, [WHEN] we do not know whether [at hand is] a piece of fat [forbidden for consumption] or fat [permitted for consumption], IN WHICH INSTANCE IT IS not known [for certain whether one is dealing with a matter that is] *a prohibition.*

19. BUT HERE [in the case at hand] IN WHICH IT IS known [for certain that one deals with a potential instance of] *the prohibition* of adultery, IT IS a matter of forbidden sexual relations, AND a matter of forbidden sexual relations is not [dealt with by] less than two [witnesses].

20. IN TRUTH, [IT IS THE CASE] THAT IN *the execution of deeds we do not even need* [witnesses' signatures]—

21. [THIS] *in accordance with* [the view of] Resh Laqish, AS SAID Resh Laqish: the [legal force of names of] witnesses inscribed on the deed are like those whose testimonies are examined by a court. [That is, the witnesses' signatures have true value only on appeal, but ab initio are not needed to execute the deed].

22. AND IT IS *the rabbis* WHO *have required* [the declaration by the bearer of the writ coming from the Mediterranean provinces]. AND IN THIS [case], ON ACCOUNT OF [their concern that the woman not become] *an abandoned wife, our rabbis dealt leniently with her* [by allowing a single emissary bringing a writ of divorce from a Mediterranean province to the Land of Israel to validate the document by testifying that the writ was written and signed in his presence].

23. THIS IS *a leniency* [for her]!?[RATHER] IT IS *a stringency* [for her]!

24. SINCE IF *you required two* [emissaries], [THEN] *the husband* [can]*not come and challenge* [the writ's validity] *and invalidate it.* [BUT IF] *one* [brings the writ], [THEN] *the husband* [can] *come and challenge* [the writ's validity] *and invalidate it.*

25. [NOT AT ALL!] BECAUSE OF WHAT Mar HAS SAID: Before how many [witnesses] do they give it [the writ of divorce] to her?

26. R. Yohanan [is of one view], AND R. Hanina [is of another view]. ONE SAID: Before two [witnesses]. AND ONE [i.e., the other] SAID: Before three [witnesses]. [THEREFORE,] AB INITIO, [the emissary, knowing that the writ must be presented before witnesses] *is scrupulous* [about the process and all requisites], AND *he will not come* [bearing an invalid writ], AND [allow] *himself to be denigrated* [before two or three witnesses].

IV

1. AND [as regards] Rava, WHAT IS THE REASON HE DID NOT SAY AS Rabbah did?

2. [Rava WOULD SAY:] WHO HAS TAUGHT [in Mishnah that the bearer of the writ of divorce must say:] **In my presence it was written** in her name, **and in my presence it was signed** in her name!? [No one! Because Mishnah makes no such stipulation.]

3. AND Rabbah [WOULD RESPOND HOW to this argument]?

4. IN TRUTH, LET [Mishnah] TEACH THUSLY [i.e., that is what Mishnah really means to convey]. BUT IF *you increase what one* [must] *say*, [THEN] *he will truncate* [what he must say]. HERE TOO, he will come and truncate one [word] in three; one in two he will not truncate.

5. AND [as regards] *Rabbah*, WHAT IS THE REASON HE DID NOT SAY AS *Rava did* [i.e., share Rava's view]?

6. HE [Rabbah] WOULD SAY TO YOU: IF SO, LET the Mishnah TEACH, **In my presence it was signed**, and no more. **In my presence it was written**—WHY DO I REQUIRE IT [BE TAUGHT by Mishnah]!? LEARN FROM THIS, THAT IT CONCERNS THE MATTER [of writing the writ of divorce] in her name [see m. Gittin 3:1: "in the woman's name"].

7. AND [as regards] *Rava*, [HOW WOULD HE RESPOND to this argument]?

8. IN TRUTH, LET the Mishnah TEACH THUSLY. BUT IF SO, [THEN] he will come and substitute [this process for the one that] *validates ordinary deeds*, [namely] with one witness.

9. AND [HOW WOULD] Rabbah [RESPOND to Rava's preceding response]?

10. [Rabbah WOULD SAY:] HOW ARE [THE CASES] SIMILAR!?

In the Seat of Moses

11. *THERE* [as regards ordinary deeds], [the bearer must declare], "We know . . ." *HERE* [as regards writs of divorce], [the bearer must declare], "In my presence . . . ."

12. *THERE* a woman is not [considered a] *trustworthy* [witness]. *HERE* a woman is [considered a] *trustworthy* [witness].

13. *THERE* the person directly concerned in the matter is not [considered a] *trustworthy* [witness]. *HERE* the person directly concerned is [considered a] *trustworthy* [witness].

14. *AND* [HOW WOULD] *Rava* [RESPOND to Rabbah response to him]?

15. *HE WOULD SAY TO YOU: IT IS BECAUSE HERE* [too, in the case of the bearer of writs of divorce], *IF* they should say, "I know . . ." [rather than, "In my presence . . ."], [THEN] *who will not deem* [the bearer] *trustworthy? AND SINCE* should he say, "I know . . .," [AND] *they deem* [him] *trustworthy,* [THEN] *he will come and substitute* [this process for the one that] *validates ordinary deeds,* [namely] *with one witness.*

V

1. *AND* [AS REGARDS] *Rabbah, WHO SAID, BECAUSE* they are not expert [in the Mediterranean provinces] with regard to [executing the writ of divorce] in her name [see m. Gittin 3:1: "in the woman's name"], *WHO IS THE TANNAITIC AUTHORITY who requires that* [the writ of divorce] *be written in her name, and requires that* [the writ] *be signed in her name?*

2. *IF* [ONE HYPOTHESIZES THAT] *IT IS* R. Meir [WHO IS THE TANNAITIC AUTHORITY], [THEN] signing [a writ of divorce]—*he requires* [being in her name], [BUT] writing [a writ of divorce]—*he does not require* [being in her name]. [So, one cannot adduce R. Meir as the tannaitic authority for these requirements.]

3. *AS WE HAVE TAUGHT* [in m. Gittin 2:4]: **They do not write [a writ of divorce] on something affixed to the ground. If they wrote it on something affixed to the ground, and uprooted it, and gave it to her—it [the writ] is fit.** [And, as a rule of thumb, the BT assumes that anonymous legal views in Mishnah follow R. Meir's views, unless there is a tannaitic source that implies otherwise.]

4. *IF* [ONE HYPOTHESIZES THAT] *IT IS* R. Eleazar [WHO IS THE TANNAITIC AUTHORITY], *THEN* writing [a writ of divorce]—*he requires* [being in her name], [BUT] signing [a writ of

divorce]—*he does not require* [being in her name]. [So, one cannot adduce R. Eleazar as the tannaitic authority for these requirements.]

5. AND IF YOU SHOULD SAY [THAT NONETHELESS] IT IS INVARA-IBLY R. Eleazar [WHO IS THE TANNAITIC AUTHORITY], SINCE R. Eleazar *does not require* signing [the writ in her name, by reason of an injunction] *from the Torah*, [BUT] *does require* [signing the writ in her name, by reason of an injunction] from the rabbis—BUT LO, three [types of] writs are declared invalid by [decree of] the rabbis, AND R. Eleazer [IN CONTRAST] *does not require* signing [the writ] in her name [for the writ to be valid].

6. AS WE HAVE TAUGHT [in m. Gittin 9:4]: **Three** [types of] **writs** [of divorce] **are unfit, and if** [the wife re]**married** [on the assumption that the writ was indeed valid], **the offspring** [resulting from the remarriage] **is** [nonetheless] **fit:** [i] **He** [the husband] **wrote** [the writ] **in his handwriting, and there are no witnesses[' signatures] on it;** [ii] **there are witnesses['s signatures] on it, and there is no date** [specified] **in it;** [iii] **there is a date** [specified] **in it, and there is only one witness'[s name specified] in it**—**lo, these three** [types of] **writs** [of divorce] **are unfit, and if** [the wife re]**married** [on the assumption that the writ was indeed valid], **the offspring** [resulting from the remarriage] **is** [nonetheless] **fit. R. Eleazar says: Even if there are no witnesses'** [names or signatures] **on it, but it** [the writ of divorce] **was given to her before witnesses,** [the writ] **is fit, and she claims** [the settlement specified in her marriage contract even] **from mortgaged assets** [of her former husband]**, since witnesses sign the** [writ of divorce] **only due to** [the aspiration to effect] **social justice in the world** (*tiqun 'olam*) [that is, by further protecting the woman].

7. BUT [RATHER] IT IS [INDEED] R. Meir [WHO IS THE TANNAITIC AUTHORITY], SINCE R. Meir *does not require* signing [the writ in her name, by reason of an injunction] *from the Torah*, [BUT] *does require* [signing the writ in her name, by reason of an injunction] from the rabbis—

8. AND LO, SAID R. *Nahman:* R. Meir USED TO SAY: Even if he found it [a writ of divorce] in the garbage, and he signed it, and he gave it to her—[the writ] is fit.

9. AND IF YOU SHOULD SAY: WE TEACH THUSLY [namely, that in R. Meir's view, such a writ is valid by reason of the requirements] *from the Torah* [only, but we do not teach that the writ is

valid when the further requirements set by the rabbis are taken into account]—*IF SO, HE* [R. Nahman] WOULD HAVE TO [HAVE SAID THAT] R. Meir USED TO SAY: [the writ is fit by reason of] a dictum of the Torah.

10. RATHER, IT IS INVARIABLY R. Eleazar [WHO IS THE TANNAITIC AUTHORITY], *SINCE* R. Eleazar *does not require* signing [the writ in her name].

11. [BUT PERHAPS THIS IS Eleazar's view] *WHEN* there are no witnesses[' signatures on the writ of divorce] at all [see above citation of Eleazar's view in m. Gittin 9:4], [BUT] *WHEN* there are witnesses[' signatures on the writ of divorce], [PERHAPS] he [Eleazar] does require [that the writ be signed in her name],

12 *As* R. Abba SAID: R. Eleazar acknowledges that in the case of [a writ of divorce with] an error in [the body of] it[s text], it [the writ] is unfit.

13. R. Ashi SAID: WHO IS THIS [WHO IS THE TANNAITIC AUTHORITY]?

14. *IT IS* R. Judah.

15. *AS WE HAVE TAUGHT* [in m. Gittin 2:4]: (**They do not write [a writ of divorce] on something affixed to the ground. If they wrote it on something affixed to the ground, and uprooted it, and gave it to her—it [the writ] is fit.) R. Judah declares [it] unfit, until its writing and its signing is on something uprooted.**

16. *AND AB INITIO, WHAT IS THE REASON THAT WE HAVE NOT ESTABLISHED* [AT THE OUTSET THAT] R. Judah [IS THE TANNAITIC AUTHORITY]?

17. *WE* [FIRST] *HAVE* [ATTEMPTED] *TO RETURN TO* R. Meir [AS THE POSSIBLE TANNAITIC AUTHORITY], *SINCE* anonymous Mishnah [law] *is* [generally based on the views of] R. Meir.

18. *WE* [THEN] *RETURNED TO* [CONSIDER] R. Eleazar [AS THE POSSIBLE TANNAITIC AUTHORITY], *SINCE* we have established [that generally] *the Halakha accords with him in cases of writs* [of divorce].

By the third time through reading the foregoing BT passage, attending to each of its constituent compositions as integral units, the skills you will have acquired in working through chapter 7 should have begun to kick in. By attending to the type-6 signpost language (language helping to pose questions or inviting analysis) and to type-5 signpost language (language providing the skeletal frame of answers/arguments/analyses)—all in SMALL CAPS in my translation—you will have begun to pick up the back-and-forth flow of the principal parts of this composite essay.

Do you remember that in chapter 7 I suggested that in deciphering Talmud passages, it often helps to read subsections of compositions both forwards and backwards? Figuring out the exact question posed or invitations for analysis is sometimes aided by reading backwards from the answers and analyses that follow, indeed, just as often as reading forward to discern the nature of the argument or analysis from the question, invitation for analysis, or challenge to the antecedent answer. This kind of bidirectional approach helps in deciphering the passage. Why does this help? It has to do with the laconic nature of the text, whether Bavli or Yerushalmi (which is why I have inserted so many interpolations for you). Each time you read forward in a subsection and then backward, your mind fills in more of the "missing" bits that are *logically required* to figure out what is going on—again, always attending to the rhythm and cadence of the back-and-forth of the answers, arguments, and analyses, because this too helps overcome the laconic nature of Talmudic use of language. One analysis is followed by its counteranalysis, which is followed by *its* counteranalysis. So, each analysis should have similarities and correspondences, or they will not speak to one another as they are meant to do in an individual composition. And these necessary similarities and correspondences make each of the analyses mutually illuminating and mutually interpretive for the reader. So, the extreme dialectic nature of Bavli discourse, in comparison to the Yerushalmi, can become an invaluable aid in deciphering a BT passage.

Let us look at the structure and flow of this passage in light of the foregoing. I have already designated the "big" structural compositional components of this composite for you using Roman numerals. But I will proceed to take you through this composite Bavli passage (at times) in even smaller, digestible chunks, from beginning to end.

Section I is the departure point for the entirety of the composite. The point of departure, as already noted, is a straightforward question about the first rule-sentence of the first Mishnah passage in Mishnah Tractate Gittin. Mishnah Gittin 1:1 offers no reasons for its ruling, an all too common feature of Mishnah, as you already know. So, section I of the Bavli passage asks, simply, what Mishnah's reason is—WHAT IS THE REASON? And the section proceeds to provide two matched, but differing, answers, each attributed to a different amoraic authority, one to Rava and the other to Rabbah. Note that here, as in the Yerushalmi, SAID ... SAID can function as structural signpost language, not just a way of assigning content to a named rabbi. SAID + BECAUSE ... SAID + BECAUSE ... alerts us that two differing answers to the initial question are present. This differs from the use of "said" (rabbi x) in debates in Mishnah and Tosefta, where what we expect is that each of two named figures in an antecedent dispute will have attributed to them a very brief argument for their respective ruling or against their disputant's ruling on a specific (hypothetical) case. But it is easy to see how SAID ... SAID ... as Talmudic structural signpost language for two differing reasons or analyses addressing a common question will have developed from the Mishnaic and Toseftan uses of "said" in debates.

There is, at this juncture in the BT passage, no attempt to assert which of the two posited reasons, Rava's or Rabbah's, is the correct one. Rather faced with two competing reasons for Mishnah's ruling, the Bavli passage takes a quite different direction, which is a fairly standard affair for BT. Section II asks whether the reasons proffered in the names of Rava and Rabbah make a practical difference in the application of the Mishnah's rulings about properly enacting and executing writs of divorce—WHAT DIFFERENTIATES THEM? That is to say, are there practical circumstances in which Rava's reason would have us rule in one direction in light of Mishnah's supposed underlying intent, and Rabbah's reason would have us rule in another direction in light of Mishnah's supposed underlying intent. Section II then posits *three* such hypothetical circumstances, clearly demarcated by using signpost language—[A STATE OF AFFAIRS] WHICH ... IF SO [ALSO] ... IF SO [ALSO]. So, accepting either Rava's or Rabbah's reason is demonstrated to have practical and divergent consequences in a least three possible states of affairs.

Now I admit that Section II does not expressly state how adopting Rava's or Rabbah's position would matter in practice in each of these three posited circumstances, but only specifies three case in which it would make a difference. I have chosen to spell out for you in my interpolations what practical difference would result. And I have chosen to do so for several reasons. One is so that you really understand that there is a different outcome depending on which reason, Rava's or Rabbah's, one adopts. The other reason, in a similar vein, is to show better how Sections I and II cohere. A third motivation is because, as we shall see later, the issue of how many witnesses need to be present for what types of cases is taken up in subsequent compositions of the composite essay. That is to say, the upshot of the practical difference between adopting Rava's or Rabbah's alleged reason for Mishnah's rule is germane to what follows in Sections III, IV and V of this extended Bavli passage. So, how did I arrive at the content of my interpolations? I did what I have advised you to do. I read Section II *several times over, backwards and forward, in light of Section I*. It took logical mental work to fill in the content of my interpolations, to be sure, but it is not rocket science either.

So, what have we so far in b. Gittin 2a–4a? A question (a type-6 element) in Section I, followed by a amoraic tradition proffering two different answers (a type-4 element). As of yet there is no argument or analysis demanded. That begins in Section II, which opens with a question that demands an analysis (a type-6 element), followed by three posited cases, with respect to each of which one can *argue* (type-5 elements) that the two different answers would matter. Let me, then, just map out the structure of the composite to this point at the end of Section II.

I

  1. WHAT IS THE REASON?

  2. X SAID:

    BECAUSE

      [+ reason 1]

  3. Y SAID:

    BECAUSE

      [+ reason 2]

II

  1. WHAT DIFFERENTIATES THEM [i.e., x's and y's reasons, in practical terms]?

  2. WHAT DIFFERENTIATES THEM IS:

    [A STATE OF AFFAIRS IN] WHICH

      [+ posited circumstances 1]

  3. IF SO,

    [ALSO]

      [+ posited circumstances 2]

  4. IF SO,

    [ALSO]

      [+ posited circumstances 3]

In the Seat of Moses

Let us now proceed to Section III of this composite, in which the focus begins to veer (further?) away from analysis of the first rule-sentence of m. Gittin 1:1 in order now to undertake critical analysis of Rava's and Rabbah's purported views. Using structuring language (AND AS REGARDS X, WHO SAID . . ., LET HIM . . .!?), Section III begins by asking why Rabbah does/did not *additionally* require that two emissaries bring the writ of divorce from foreign lands, so that now we have two valid witnesses presenting the document at its destination point. This would, it seems, obviate all problems regarding authentication of the writ, because the two emissaries would constitute a valid pair of corroborating witnesses under rabbinic law. Since we have been told that Rabbah's concern is limited to the writing of the writ "in her name," that is, for the named wife in particular, we must hypothesize that his views about required numbers of witnesses leads him *not* to make this additional stipulation. And so (at III.3.) such a view is *hypothetically* attributed to him, and III.4, 5, and 6 argue that attributing such a hypothetical view to Rabbah is not reasonable, for the reasons given. The substructuring formalized language of argument and analysis clearly takes one through the reasoning, which is based on *disproving an analogy*, a common form of early rabbinic analysis, as we have seen many times in this volume. Now, I must admit that my translation has facilitated the perceived flow of the passage's analysis with my interpolations at III.3 and 4. How did I manage this? I read "backwards" through this section, as well as forwards. Section III.1–6, then, is structured as follows with the aid of formalized structuring and substructuring language, which you should by now more easily recognize when you encounter it:

III.1–6

1. AND AS REGARDS X, WHO SAID:

    BECAUSE

    [+reason 1]

2. LET HIM . . .!?

    [proposed ruling 1]

3. [PERHAPS, X IS OF THE VIEW THAT]

    [posited ruling 2]

4. [WELL, ONE MIGHT COUNTER . . .]

5. LET US SAY THAT WE SAY

    [posited ruling 2],

  WHEN, SUCH AS, [WHEN]

    [hypothetical case a]

  IN WHICH INSTANCE

    [circumstances a']

6. BUT HERE [in the case at hand]

  IN WHICH IT IS

    [circumstances b]

  IT IS

    [circumstances b']

  AND

    [ruling 1].

Section III.7 now challenges Rabbah's posited reason for m. Gittin 1:1's ruling: namely, that outside the Land of Israel those bodies issuing writs of divorce are not experts in appropriately drafting and executing such documents "in the particular woman's name." III.7 uses stock terminology to assert the opposite (MOST ..., that is, it is generally the case that ...). But "mostly" is not "always," a preoccupation the passage here associates with the tannaitic authority, R. Meir. Still, as III.7–9 argues, when writs of divorce are concerned, the consensus view (not questioned, even by Meir) is that those who prepare such writs know that the writ must be written in the particular woman's name, *pace* Rabbah (who, at the beginning of this composite essay is alleged to assert that that expertise is lacking). So, now, why Mishnah's ruling? To be lenient in cases of such writs for the woman's sake, by allowing just one emissary to deliver the writ and make the appropriate attestations, without requiring that a second emissary be present so that the two can constitute a valid pair of witnesses. The concern for the woman is that she not end up in limbo, abandoned by her husband (who has acted to divorce her) but unable to remarry without a writ of divorce that is recognized as valid. This reason, that is, leniency, is on the face of it different than both Rabbah's and Rava's, and is somewhat reminiscent of the rationale given in t. Gittin 1:2 (a passage that we looked at back in chapter 4). Now, III.7–9 proffers less argument, and more straightforwardly

In the Seat of Moses

makes assertions about rabbinic authorities' views that its adduces to make its overall point. And that point is this: Rabbah's posited reason for Mishnah's ruling does not seem to stand up under scrutiny. Here is how this subsection is structured.

III.7–9

    7. MOST

        [opposite of reason 1]

    8. AND EVEN AS REGARDS R. X,

        <u>WHO</u>

        [stated position of x]

        [<u>NONETHELESS</u>]

        [stated facts indicating opposite of reason 1]

    9. AND IT IS *the rabbis*

        <u>WHO</u>

        [allusion to m. Gittin 1:1's ruling]

        AND IN THIS [CASE],

        <u>ON ACCOUNT OF</u>

        [reason 3]

Section III.10–11 continues the back-and-forth analysis by immediately challenging the newly-presented, third reason (adduced on behalf of the anonymous majority of "the rabbis") for Mishnah's ruling. It poses a rhetorical question and then answers it in the contrary. This is signaled using simple, contrastive, formulaic terms (THIS IS ...!? [RATHER] IT IS ...!). Does this really benefit the woman!? The challenge is supported by an argument that contrasts two hypothetical circumstances, aided by language typically serving type–5 elements (SINCE IF ...). If one emissary only is present to bear witness to the preparation of the writ of divorce, the husband (having a change of heart much later) may in the future launch a legal objection. Now, how does that benefit the woman, who may end up in a very difficult legal status!? III.12–13 then "challenges the challenge," proffering as evidence the *amora*, Mar's, attestation of the teachings of two other authorities, Yohanan and Hanina. In Section III.12–13, we encounter again what you have seen already elsewhere, the "structural" use of "said ...

said" to juxtapose countering or just different views. The upshot of Mar's argument is that according to whichever position, Yohanan's or Hanina's, the emissary must bear witness before witnesses at the point of delivery of the writ. And knowing this from the outset, that is, when the writ is first written and signed, the emissary will be scrupulous in meeting all legal obligations, according to Mar's alleged argument. Here, then, is our charting of III.10–13.

III.10–13

  10. THIS IS

      [reason 3]!?

  [RATHER] IT IS

      [opposite of reason 3]!

  11. SINCE IF

      [circumstances a],

  [THEN]

      [result not a].

  [BUT IF]

      [circumstances a']

  [THEN]

      [result a]

  12. [NOT AT ALL!] BECAUSE OF WHAT X HAS SAID:

      [question about what law is]?

  13. R. y, AND R. z.

ONE SAID:

      [ruling b]

AND ONE SAID:

      [ruling b']

  [THEREFORE,] AB INITIO,

    ..., AND ..., AND ...

      [argument in support of challenge at III.12].

In the Seat of Moses

From Section III.14 to the end of Section III at III.26, the composite will now reengage with the posited reason of Rava (given in Section I.3) for Mishnah's ruling. Rava's reported view is that an emissary must be able to declare that the writ of divorce was written and signed by witnesses in the emissary's presence, because these witnesses will not be present at the point of delivery. The passage will now critique and analyse Rava's posited reasons in much the same way it did for Rabbah's. Indeed, much of the language and structure of III.14–26 parallels what we have observed already in III.1–13. From the perspective of having to decipher the passage as a whole, this parallelism helps one immensely, since the logic of the first half can be used to decipher the second half, and vice-versa. Again, reading "backwards" often helps as much as reading "forwards."

Section III.14–26 commences by repeating for Rava's posited reason for Mishnah's ruling the very same analysis that the composition presented in III.1–6 for Rabbah's. So, I need not take you through the logic of the analysis again; it has not changed. Nor has how it is structured with stock formulaic type-5 and type-6 language, as documented in the following.

III.14–19

> 14. AND AS REGARDS X, WHO SAID:
>
>   <u>BECAUSE</u>
>
>   [+reason 2]
>
> 15. LET HIM . . .!?
>
>   [proposed ruling 1]
>
> 16. [PERHAPS, X IS OF THE VIEW THAT]
>
>   [posited ruling 2]
>
> 17. [WELL, ONE MIGHT COUNTER . . .]
>
> 18. LET US SAY THAT WE SAY
>
>   [posited ruling 2],
>
>   <u>WHEN, SUCH AS, [WHEN]</u>
>
>   [hypothetical case a]
>
>   <u>IN WHICH INSTANCE</u>
>
>   [circumstances a']

19. BUT HERE [in the case at hand]

　IN WHICH IT IS

　　[circumstances b]

　IT IS

　　[circumstances b']

　AND

　　[ruling 1].

At this juncture, from III.20, the treatment of Rava's posited reason must differ somewhat from that to which Rabbah's was subjected. Why? Because Rava's alleged reason concerns the absence of the witnesses at the point of delivery of the writ of divorce. Rava's reason is challenged by adducing a view, supported by an amoraic tradition at III.21 attributed to Resh Laqish: witnesses' signatures are not, strictly speaking, necessary on any deeds. This signaling of a counterposition, which raises an objection to Rava's reason, is "signposted" by IN TRUTH, [IT IS THE CASE]. This formulary is the parallel of MOST, the signpost language that prefaced what was earlier conveyed in Meir's name to challenge Rabbah's rationale for Mishnah's ruling. Now, at this juncture, the supporting amoraic counterevidence is signaled with the language, [THIS] *in accordance with* [the view of] . . ., AS SAID. The upshot of the countering of Rava's position is this, according to the composition's use of what is attributed to Resh Laqish: Rava's posited reason for Mishnah's ruling, namely, because the witnesses to the writ of divorce are not present to attest to their signatures, does not stand scrutiny, because strictly speaking we do not need witnesses' signatures on *any* deeds.

Having now raised an objection that specifically addresses Rava's posited reason, this subsection of the composition now returns at III.22 to the parallel track laid down in III.1–13 at III.9. Indeed, III.22–26 repeats III.9–13; it is the anonymous plurality of authorities, "the rabbis," who have placed additional (even if, strictly speaking, unnecessary) demands on persons executing writs of divorce at a distance, so that the women not be left in limbo (or worse yet, be accused of adultery after having remarried), should someone subsequently challenge the validity of the writ. And this (strictly unnecessary) novelty that the rabbis have introduced to protect the woman, is characterized as a "leniency" (language recalling t. Gittin 1:2). Now the remainder of the Section until its conclusion at III.26 can repeat

In the Seat of Moses

the very same challenges and responses, and adduce the same supporting evidence, as its parallel in III.1–13, as this charting shows.

III.20–22

20. IN TRUTH, [IT IS THE CASE] THAT IN

   [opposite of reason 2]

21. [THIS] ... X, AS SAID X

22. AND IT IS *the rabbis*

   <u>WHO</u>

   [allusion to m. Gittin 1:1's ruling]

   AND IN THIS [CASE],

   <u>ON ACCOUNT OF</u>

   [reason 3]

III.23–26

23. THIS IS

   [reason 3]!?

   [RATHER] IT IS

   [opposite of reason 3]!

24. <u>SINCE IF</u>

   [circumstances a],

   [<u>THEN</u>]

   [result not a].

   [<u>BUT IF</u>]

   [circumstances a']

   [<u>THEN</u>]

   [result a]

25. [NOT AT ALL!] BECAUSE OF WHAT X HAS SAID:

   [question about what law is]?

26. R. y, and R. z.

   ONE SAID:

   [ruling b]

   AND ONE SAID:

   [ruling b']

   [THEREFORE,] *AB INITIO*,

   . . ., AND . . ., AND . . .

   [argument in support of challenge at III.25].

It is indeed tempting to ponder why the composition at Section III essentially goes over the same *entire* ground twice, and virtually identically, for Rabbah's and then Rava's posited reasons. What is the point? No doubt, one may propose tradition-history and text-history responses to such a question. And while such responses many well offer an explanation, pondering the effect upon, or the purpose served for, the engaged student of the Talmud might suggest an additional claim. Namely, to show and model the value of *complete* critical engagement with the legal sources. Why should Rava's or Rabbah's position not get the full critical treatment, even if they end up being the same treatment?

Section IV of the composite undertakes another "dual" round of parallel analyses of first Rava's and then Rabbah's posited reasons (given at I.2–3). This Section subdivides structurally into at least two subsections, IV.1–8 and IV.9–15.

Subsection IV.1–8 asks for each of the two *amora'im* in turn, Why did he not adopt the other's reason? This is one of the stock questions Bavli typically poses in type-6 elements, when the text conveys two alternative viewpoints attributed to named authorities. The language, AND [as regards] X, WHAT IS THE REASON HE DID NOT SAY AS Y? is formulaic and structural. It will often, as it does in this composition, drag in its wake, a hypothetical response that one might posit for x—[X WOULD SAY] WHO HAS LEARNED [in Mishnah]. . .—followed by a posited hypothetical rebuttal for y—AND y, [HOW WOULD Y RESPOND to this argument]? *IN TRUTH LET* [Mishnah] TEACH THUSLY . . .). LEARNED and LET TEACH are coded, signpost terms alerting the reader that a Mishnah text is about to be adduced and its precise choice of words considered carefully. Then the whole structure is repeated for authority y's position, followed by a hypothetical rebuttal by x. As has been the case throughout this composite, the symmetry in Section

In the Seat of Moses

IV of the literary-rhetorical structures, served by stock structural language, establishes clear cadence and rhythm—back-and-forth, then repeat. This helps the reader decipher the composition and to fill in the lacunae with interpolations (as I have done) to make the text fully intelligible. Here is Section IV.1–8's schematic outline.

IV.1–8.

   1. AND [as regards] x,

      WHAT IS THE REASON HE DID NOT SAY AS *y*?

   2. [X WOULD SAY:]

      <u>WHO HAS LEARNED</u> [in Mishnah]

         [+ hypothetical modified text of Mishnah]...!?

   3. AND y [HOW WOULD y RESPOND]?

   4. IN TRUTH,

      LET [Mishnah] TEACH THUSLY.

      BUT

      <u>IF</u>

         [revised circumstances as per emended Mishnah],

      [<u>THEN</u>]

         [possible undesired outcome].

      <u>HERE TOO</u>

         [possible undesired outcome].

   5. AND [as regards] *y*,

      WHAT IS THE REASON HE DID NOT SAY AS *x*?

   6. HE [y] WOULD SAY TO YOU:

      IF SO,

      <u>LET</u> the Mishnah <u>TEACH</u>,

         [+ hypothetical modified text of Mishnah]!

         [Mishnah text as is]

      WHY DO I REQUIRE IT [BE TAUGHT] by Mishnah]!?

      LEARN FROM THIS,

THAT IT CONCERNS THE MATTER

[y posited reason 1].

7. AND [as regards] *x*, [HOW WOULD HE RESPOND]?

8. IN TRUTH, LET the Mishnah TEACH THUSLY.

BUT

IF SO, [THEN]

[possible undesired outcome].

The remaining subsection of IV, that is, IV.9–15, simply spins out two more hypothetical rebuttals for Rabbah and Rava. First, the author imagines what Rabbah's rebuttal to Rava's rebuttal of Rabbah might look like. Second, in line with Bavli's penchant for symmetry and cadence, the composition's creators imagine what Rava might say to rebut what was just presented as Rabbah's last rebuttal of Rava's previous rebuttal of Rabbah. Now, in the preceding two sentences, I have been deliberately playful, have I not? It may not be good prose, but I am attempting to drive home the point that I have repeatedly made in this chapter about deciphering Bavli's compositions. Attend to the back-and-forth cadence of these compositions, and use it and the resulting parallelism to perceive the composition's structure. This is an invaluable strategy in coming to terms with the meaning of many Bavli passages.

Before diagramming IV.9–15 with formulaic language serving type-6 and type-5 elements, let me say something about the nature of the arguments hypothetically assigned to Rava and Rabbah in IV.1–9. As is characteristic of so much of early rabbinic legal argument seen to this point in this volume, what is put in the mouth of Rabbah are arguments from analogy. Two things are alike in this compelling way, and so are to be treated similarly. Or two things are unlike one another in this compelling way, and therefore should not be treated similarly. Rabbah's rebuttal of Rava's rebuttal asserts that ordinary deeds and writs of divorce are compellingly unlike one another, because (a) the formulaic language the bearer is supposed to use differs, (b) the status of women as valid witnesses differs in the two type of cases, and (c) "interested" parties' status as witnesses differs in the two classes of documents. Rava's counter rebuttal at IV.14–15 reverts to an argument that appeals to unintended, undesirable consequences. Here is the mapping of IV.9–15, with its structural and substructural language

In the Seat of Moses

for posing questions and challenges, and for fashioning arguments using authoritative data.

IV.9–15

9. AND [HOW WOULD] *y* [RESPOND to x]?
10. [y WOULD SAY:]

    HOW ARE [THE CASES] SIMILAR!?
11. *THERE*

    [in one case + compelling trait];

    HERE

    [in the other case + compelling distinguishing trait].
12. *THERE*

    [in one case + compelling trait];

    HERE

    [in the other case + compelling distinguishing trait].
13. *THERE*

    [in one case + compelling trait];

    HERE

    [in the other case + compelling distinguishing trait].
14. AND [HOW WOULD] *x* [RESPOND to y's response to him]?
15. HE WOULD SAY TO YOU:

    IT IS BECAUSE HERE, IF

    [hypothetical circumstances]

    [THEN]

    [possible result]!?

    AND SINCE

    [possible result],

    [THEN]

    [undesirable outcome].

We now come to the final section (or composition) of our first sample composite mini-essay. Section V, despite its to-and-fro-ing, is less complicated than it might appear at first glance. Section V undertakes a speculative exploration to identify a tannaitic authority, *by name*, who is the source underlying Rabbah's posited reason (at I.2) for Mishnah's rule-sentence at m. Gittin 1:1. Rabbah, according to Section I.2, holds that Mishnah is concerned that outside of the Land of Israel, persons or judicial bodies that prepare writs of divorce do not know that every writ of divorce drafted must be written for a specific named woman. This means, in effect, that the emissary who bears the writ to its destination is attesting that the writ was written "in her [the wife's] name" and signed by the witnesses "in her [the wife's] name." And indeed, earlier in this Bavli composite mini-essay (at IV.1–4), we saw that just such an interpretation of m. Gittin 1:1a is offered in association with Rabbah's view, even though the actual wording of m. Gittin 1:1a does not specify this. Remember the following?

IV

> 1. AND [as regards] Rava, WHAT IS THE REASON HE DID NOT SAY AS Rabbah did?
>
> 2. [Rava WOULD SAY:] WHO HAS LEARNED [in Mishnah that the bearer of the writ of divorce must say:] **In my presence it was written** in her name, **and in my presence it was signed** in her name!? [No one! Because Mishnah makes no such stipulation.]
>
> 3. AND Rabbah [HOW WOULD YOU RESPOND to this argument]?
>
> 4. IN TRUTH, LET [Mishnah] TEACH THUSLY [i.e., that is what Mishnah really means to convey]. BUT IF you increase what one [must] say, [THEN] he will truncate [what he must say]. HERE TOO, he will come and truncate one [word] in three; one in two he will not truncate.

Now, m. Gittin 3:1a explicitly rules that a writ of divorce that is *not* written in a specific woman's name is invalid.

> Any writ [of divorce] that was not written in the name of the woman [who is to receive it] is unfit (m. Gittin 3:1a).

But that rule-sentence at m. Gittin 3:1a does not bear an attribution to a named rabbi. Moreover, m. Gittin 3:1a does not say, for that matter, that persons or judicial bodies outside the Land of Israel that prepare writs of divorce are ignorant of the requirement to compose a specific writ of divorce using the name of the woman who is to be its recipient. So, who might be the *named* tannaitic rabbinic authority who teaches that a writ of divorce must be written in the specific woman's name, and/or that an emissary who bears such a writ from a "Mediterranean province" to its destination in the Land of Israel is effectively declaring upon arrival that the writ written and signed in the emissary's presence was written expressly for the woman who is to receive the writ? The type-6, stock language at Section V.1 used to launch this search for a named source is typical and ubiquitous in the Bavli.

> AND [AS REGARDS] *Rabbah*, WHO SAID, BECAUSE they are not expert [in the Mediterranean provinces] with regard to [executing the writ of divorce] in her name [see m. Gittin 3:1: "in the woman's name"], WHO IS THE TANNATIC AUTHORITY *who requires that* [the writ of divorce] be written in her name, *and requires tha*t [the writ] be signed in her name?

Of course, if there were some tannaitic source known to the Bavli's authorship, whether from elsewhere in Mishnah, or in Tosefta, or in a Tosefta-like *baraita*, in which a named rabbi is said to have expressly taught this, then the Bavli authorship would certainly have cited it somewhere in Section V of this composition (if not earlier). But, apparently, there is no such source known to the Bavli. Therefore, as is typical for the Bavli in compositions of this nature, the hunt is on for sources bearing attributions to named tannaitic authorities that say something akin to, or related to, the topic at hand. The Bavli explores such sources, each in turn, to consider whether one can logically *extrapolate* from these sources what the named authority in question *would*, to be consistent, *logically have had to have taught* about our case. Would such a named authority, given what one knows of the views attributed to that person, have to have *also* ruled that the bearer of a writ to the Land of Israel from elsewhere must be able, in effect, to attest "*that* [the writ of divorce was] . . . written in her name, *and* . . . signed in her name," since, according to Rabbah, one cannot assume that outside the Land of Israel, those preparing writs of divorce know that writs of divorce that are *not* written in the specific woman's name are invalid (as per m. Gittin 3:1)?

What is the signpost language that "takes us through" this search? Stock formulaic language, such as, IF IT IS R. x or . . . AND IF YOU SHOULD SAY IT IS INVARIABLY R. x, posits a named tannaitic rabbi as the authority in question. THEN or SINCE, or sometimes BUT, precedes the articulation of R. x's known position on a related point of law, which either dovetails by logical necessity with the position articulated by Rabbah or does not.

The Two Talmuds

If it does, our question is answered, if it does not, Bavli must proceed to hypothesize that it is some other *tanna* that we seek, and the process repeats itself. Along the way, the composition may, at times, adduce citations of tannaitic sources that confirm R. x's position on the related point of law, e.g., AS WE HAVE TAUGHT, plus citation of the source.

The final part of Section V, the last in this composite mini-essay, concludes with what I find a remarkable subsection at V.16–18. It starts at V.13–15 with an attribution to R. Ashi, a fifth-century *amora*, of the supposedly definitive answer to our quest: WHO IS THIS [WHO IS THE TANNAITIC AUTHORITY] [that underpins Rabbah's stated rationale for m. Gittin 1:1]? V.13–15 repeats much of the patterned language and exploratory process of what we have seen in the subsections that precede it: IT IS R. Judah, AS WE HAVE TAUGHT [in m. Gittin 2:4]... But what follows at the very end of this composition is a bit of "text criticism" of Section V as a whole, by asking, in effect, Why did the composition consider other possibilities, when it was known *ab initio* that R. Judah is the underlying tannaitic authority whose identity we have been seeking? The answer is a rationale based on a rule-of-thumb hierarchy of early rabbinic masters' traditions in certain areas of law. But it seems to me that it is also an answer that can be read as flying in the face of a defining literary-rhetorical feature of Bavli as a whole, namely to raise questions, posit answers, challenge the answers, try new answers, challenge these too, then repeat—all for its own sake. Here, then, to conclude our treatment of b. Gittin 2a–4a is my charting of Section V.

V

1. AND [AS REGARDS] X, WHO SAID,

    BECAUSE

    [posited reason 1]

    WHO IS THE TANNAITIC AUTHORITY

    [re-statement of m. Gittin 1:1a's content with reason 1 integrated into it]?

2. IF [ONE HYPOTHESIZES THAT]

    IT IS

    [R. a]

    [WHO IS THE TANNAITIC AUTHORITY],

In the Seat of Moses

[THEN]

  [statement of R. a's position on related legal matter]

[BUT]

  [statement of R. a's position on related legal matter]

3. AS WE HAVE TAUGHT

  [Mishnah citation assumed to reflect R. a's position]

4. IF [ONE HYPOTHESIZES THAT]

  IT IS

  [R. b]

  [WHO IS THE TANNAITIC AUTHORITY],

  [THEN]

    [statement of R. b's position on related legal matter]

  [BUT]

    [statement of R. b's position on related legal matter]

5. AND

  IF YOU SHOULD SAY [THAT NONETHELESS]

  IT IS INVARIABLY

  [R. b]

  [WHO IS THE TANNAITIC AUTHORITY],

  SINCE

    [statement of R. b's position on related legal matter]

  [BUT]

    [statement of R. b's position on related legal matter]

  BUT LO

    [reference to statement of case]

  AND

    [statement of R. b's position on this related legal matter]

6. AS WE HAVE BEEN TAUGHT

[Mishnah citation regarding statement of case, in which a ruling attributed to R. b appears]

7. BUT [RATHER] IT IS [INDEED]

[R. a]

[WHO IS THE TANNAITIC AUTHORITY],

SINCE

[statement of R. a's position on related legal matter]

[BUT]

[statement of R. a's position on related legal matter]

8. AND LO, SAID

[R. c, R. a]

USED TO SAY

[statement of R. a's position on related legal matter]

9. AND

IF YOU SHOULD SAY:

WE TEACH THUSLY

[modified statement of R. a's position on related legal matter]

IF SO, HE

[R. c]

WOULD HAVE TO [HAVE SAID THAT]

[R. a]

USED TO SAY

[further modified statement of R. a's position on related legal matter]

10. RATHER,

INVARIABLY IT IS

[R. b]

[WHO IS THE TANNAITIC AUTHORITY],

SINCE

[R. b]

[statement of R. b's position on related legal matter]

11. [BUT PERHAPS THIS IS R. b's VIEW]

    <u>WHEN</u>

    [modified case circumstances]

    [BUT]

    <u>WHEN</u>

    [case circumstances at hand]

    [<u>PERHAPS</u>]

    [posited statement of R. b's position on circumstances at hand]

12. *As*

    [R. d]

    SAID:

    [R. b]

    [statement of R. b's position on related circumstances]

13. [R. e]

    SAID:

    WHO IS THIS [WHO IS THE TANNAITIC AUTHORITY]?

14. *IT IS*

    [R. f].

15. *AS WE HAVE TAUGHT*

    [citation of Mishnah including ruling attributed to R. f]

16. *AND AB INITIO, WHAT IS THE REASON THAT WE HAVE NOT ESTABLISHED* [AT THE OUTSET THAT]

    [R. f]

    [IS THE TANNAITIC AUTHORITY]?

17. *WE* [FIRST] *HAVE* [ATTEMPTED] *TO RETURN TO*

    [R. a]

    <u>SINCE</u>

    [general statement about R. a's authority in Mishnah law]

18. WE [THEN] RETURNED TO [CONSIDER]

    [R. b]

    <u>SINCE</u>

        [general statement about R. b's authority in Mishnah law concerning writs of divorce specifically]

There you have it, we have worked through the entire composite essay taking each constituent composition of it in turn and applying the same deciphering techniques used earlier in chapter 7 with a noticeably shorter JT-ean composite. The difference in the length (and, therefore, in complexity) of the two passages both matters and does not matter. It does not matter in terms of the techniques that I have taught you to use to decipher them, which include, as you will remember, to take matters composition by composition. Longer compositions, comprised of more units of challenges, questions, answers, rebuttals, etc., require a higher degree of intellectual stamina and focus to keep all the twists and turns and "to-ing and fro-ing" straight in one's head. But longer composite essays, comprised of more compositions, just take more time to work through; they are not more serious intellectual exercises for you per se. The JT-ean passage that is the "parallel" to the BT-ean passage just examined was comprised of just one composition of fourteen subunits in length. Our "corresponding" BT passage is comprised of five compositions, but one of them is twenty-six subunits in length. Another is eighteen subunits long. A third is fifteen subunits long. Some are as short as three subunits long, although this is unusual.

We have now come to our final sample text of this volume, your second encounter with an exemplary composite essay from the Bavli. You have all of the tools and techniques in hand to decipher this second passage, b. Avodah Zarah 14b–16a, which is the BT-ean counterpart to y. Avodah Zarah 1:6, which you read and deciphered in chapter 7. And because you have all of the tools required to cope with this Bavli composite, I will leave most of the deciphering to you this time, rather than do it for you. Consider this something of a final, take-home exam, to do (mostly) on your own. Here is what I have done, as I have for all passages we have looked at in chapter 7 and in chapter 8 to this point. The composite essay at b. Avodah Zarah 14b–16a is subdivided by me into its constituent compositions (or as nearly so as my current understanding of this passage allows) as indicated by Roman numerals. And I have subdivided each composition into its basic substantive subunits. Font type is used to distinguish different types of elements and language, exactly as it has been used above. That means that stock formularies serving type-6 elements will be in SMALL CAPS, and those serving type-5 elements will appear in underscored SMALL CAPS; these are the "codes" alerting you to what is about to happen. Mishnah citations will be in **boldface**; Tosefta is underscored regular type. Aramaic is *italics*; whatever is not in italics is in Hebrew (although it may be boldfaced or underscored, and perhaps on occasion in SMALL CAPS). I would remind you again that I have abandoned my previously adopted conservatism in assigning language to the structural-service (type-6) category; so you will now see me on occasion assigning terms such as "said" or "but" to this category, when they *also* serve on their own to "signpost" an impending counterargument, without the more explicit language for doing so, such as "they objected to/challenged it."

It is a long passage, to be sure. Some of its constituent compositions are about two-dozen subunits long, and there are 11 compositions in the composite. This time, both to aid you and as a reflection of my wishing you, the reader, to confront this exercise more on your own, I have presented the entire passage twice. It appears the first time as nonschematized text, with my coding of elements by font, as before. Then I *immediately* present my schematization of it, much as I have done for previous Talmudic passages, but I have left all of the idiomatic content intact (such as, "an idolater worries his animal will become infertile"), rather than just characterizing it in square brackets (such as, [reason 1]). You may, if you choose, read each composition in turn both in its nonschematized and schematized format, as you go about your work. Remember, my previous advice. Attend to signpost language serving type-5 and type-6 elements. Get into the back-and-forth flow of each composition. Fill in your deciphering by reading both forwards and backwards several times over within each composition. Note the use of type-1 elements (Mishnah citations), type-2 elements (Toseftan materials and tosefta-like traditions), type-3 elements (Halakhic-Midrashic passages), and type-4 elements (traditions like one or another of the former types, but attributed to *amora'im*), and their integration into the composition by type-5 and type-6 formulaic-service language. Do all this and you will be fine. It is your deciphering project now, not mine to do for you.

The legal topic of the BT composite is now familiar to you, the sale of animals by a Jew to an idolater. The BT composite takes m. Avodah Zarah (AZ) 1:6 as its point of departure and (nominally) as its principal object of analysis, just as did y. Avodah Zarah 1:6. Here is that Mishnah passage once again.

m. Avodah Zarah 1:6 (translation my own[31])

A. [In] a locale [in] which they are accustomed to sell a small cattle [e.g., sheep or goats] to idolaters

B. they [are permited to] sell

C. [In] a locale [in] which they are not accustomed to sell [small cattle] to them

D. they do not [permit one to] sell

E.1. And in any locale, they do not [permit one to] sell to them

2. large cattle [e.g., oxen]

3. calves

4. and foals [of asses or of horses]—

F. whether whole, or maimed.

G. R. Judah permits in the case of a maimed [animal],

H. and Ben-Batayra permits in the case of a horse.

And now the Bavli passage, which commences by challenging the two paired rule-sentences with which the Mishnah passage begins.

b. Avodah Zarah 14b–16a (translation my own[32])

I

1. Is that to say that There is no prohibition, [and] There is [i.e., it is a matter of] custom [only]?

2. [No] Where it is the custom [to have] a prohibition, it is [so] accustomed; Where it is the custom [to have] a dispensation, it is [so] accustomed.

3. And they rebuffed it [by citing the following from m. AZ 2:1]:

4. **One does not stable a cattle at the inns of idolaters, because they are suspect with respect to bestiality.**

---

31. Based upon and adapted from Lightstone, *Rhetoric*, 27.
32. Based upon and adapted from Lightstone, *Rhetoric*, 28–44.

In the Seat of Moses

5. SAID Rav: **In a locale where** they permitted **to sell,** they permitted to billet; [in] **a locale where** they forbade to billet, they forbade **to sell.**

6. But R. Eliezer SAYS: <u>EVEN</u> **in a locale where** they forbade to billet, it is permitted **to sell.**

7. WHAT IS THE REASON?

8. An idolater worries that his [own] animal will become infertile.

9. *But even so* [MUST] Rav [HAVE] REVERSED [HIS VIEW].

10. FOR *Rav* SAID THE OPPOSITE [AS WELL].

11. SAID *R. Shila b. Abimi* IN THE NAME OF *Rav*: An idolater worries that his [own] animal will become infertile.

II

1. **And in any locale they do** [not permit one to] **sell to them large cattle,** etc.

2. WHAT IS THE REASON?

3. <u>LET IT BE [ASSUMED]</u> THAT *we do not fear* **bestiality** (m. AZ 2:1) [will take place];

4. [RATHER, NOW] *we fear that [the idolater] does work with it [on the Sabbath].*

5. BUT <u>LET</u> it [the animal] be worked [on the Sabbath]!

6. <u>SINCE</u> [IT IS THE CASE] THAT [the Israelite] sold it, [THEN] [the idolater] has acquired it[, and the animal is no longer subject to the laws of the Sabbath].

7. [RATHER], [they instituted] a decree [against the sale of large cattle] <u>ON ACCOUNT OF</u> [cases of idolaters] borrowing [the animal and working it on the Sabbath], <u>AND ON ACCOUNT OF</u> [cases of idolaters] leasing [the animal and working it on the Sabbath, in which two cases the animal is still owned by the Israelite.]

8. [BUT] [also in the case of] borrowing *he acquires [possession of] it,* [and so too in the case of] leasing he acquires [possession of] it.

9. RATHER SAID *Rami b. R. Yiva*: <u>ON ACCOUNT OF</u> *[cases of selling animals on a] trial [basis];* <u>SINCE</u> *at times when one sells it oneself close to the*

setting of the sun on the onset of the Sabbath, AND he himself said to him come try it, AND he listens to him, AND he goes on account of him.

10. BUT IT IS ALRIGHT THAT he goes, [is it not?]

11. BUT he is driving his animal on the Sabbath.

12. AND he who drives his animal on the Sabbath is liable for a sin offering [if the act was done in error] (see b. Shabbat 153b).

13. R. Shisha b. R. Idi CHALLENGED IT:

14. BUT [in the case of] leasing, WHO [HOLDS THAT] he acquired possession of it [in the first place]!?

15. AND SO WE HAVE TAUGHT [in m. AZ 1:9]: **Even in the locale where they say [that it is permitted] to lease [a house to an idolater], they did not say [thus if the house will be used] as a dwelling, because [the idolater] will bring into it an idol [and the Israelite will thereby be participating indirectly in idolatry.**

16. AND IF IT SHOULD OCCUR TO YOU [THAT in] leasing, [the lessee] acquired [possession], [THEN IN] THIS [CASE JUST CITED] whatever he wishes to bring into his house, let him bring in.

17. Idolatry DIFFERS IN THAT it is [a more] severe [case].

18. AS IT IS WRITTEN [in Deuteronomy 7 and cited in m. AZ 1:9], **"You shall not bring an abomination [i.e., an idol] into your house."**

19. R. Isaac b. R. Mesharsheya CHALLENGED IT:

20. BUT [in the case of] leasing, WHO [HOLDS THAT] he acquired possession of it [in the first place]!?

21. AND SO WE HAVE TAUGHT [in m. Terumot 11:9]: **An Israelite who leased a cow from a priest, may feed it beans that are heave offering; but a priest who leased a cow from an Israelite—even though its feeding is his obligation, he may not feed her beans that are heave offering** [i.e., the cow's status as regards being able to be fed sanctified produce does not change as a result of being leased].

22. AND IF IT SHOULD OCCUR TO YOU [that in] leasing, [the lessee] acquired [possession], [THEN] WHY [IN CASE JUST CITED] should he not feed it [heave offering], [since] the cow [presumably] is his!?

23. RATHER LEARN FROM THIS [i.e., from the immediately preceding] [that in] leasing, [the lessee] has not acquired [possession].

In the Seat of Moses

24. AND NOW THAT YOU HAVE SAID *[that in]* leasing, *[the lessee]* has not acquired *[possession]*,

25. [WE CONCLUDE THAT]

   25.1. [they instituted] a decree [against the sale of large cattle] on account of [cases of idolaters] leasing [the animal and working it on the Sabbath],

   25.2. [and they instituted] a decree [against the sale of large cattle] on account of [cases of idolaters] borrowing [the animal and working it on the Sabbath],

   25.3. [and they instituted] a decree [against the sale of large cattle] on account of [cases of idolaters buying an animal on a] *trial* [basis and, with the complicity of the Israelite, working it on the Sabbath].

III

1. *Rav Ada permitted the sale of an ass by the agency of a broker.*

2. *[WHY COULD HE HAVE PERMITTED IT IN THIS CASE?]* IF [as we have deduced above,] they instituted a decree [against the sale of large cattle] ON ACCOUNT OF [cases of idolaters buying an animal on a] *trial* [basis and, with the complicity of the Israelite, working it on the Sabbath], [THEN] THIS ONE [i.e, the Israelite owner who uses the services of a broker] does not [even] know [the buyer, such that he can] listen to him and go on account of him [and be complicit in driving the animal on the Sabbath].

3. AND IF [as we also have deduced above,] they instituted a decree [against the sale of large cattle] ON ACCOUNT OF [cases of idolaters] borrowing and leasing [an animal and working the Israelite's animal on the Sabbath], SINCE [the animal] is not his [i.e., the broker's, to lend or lease], [THEN] he does not lend or lease [the animal].

4. AND FURTHERMORE [we may conclude in this last case that the broker will neither lend nor lease the animal] ON ACCOUNT OF [the fact] that he does not [wish to] reveal [to the prospective buyer] any blemish in it.

IV

1. *Rav Huna sold a certain cow to an idolater.*

2. Said to him Rav Hisda: WHAT IS THE REASON the master did thus [in apparent violation of m. AZ 1:6]?

3. He [Huna] said to him: SAY [THAT] [the idolater] bought it for slaughter.

4. And whence will you say that we have [so] said [i.e., taught] as in this manner [i.e. in such a case]?

5. As we have taught [in m. Shevi'it. 5:8]:

   5.1. The House of Shammai say: one may not sell to him [a non-Jew] a threshing cow on the sabbatical year;

   5.2. but the House of Hillel permit [such a sale], because he [the non-Jew] might [intend to] slaughter it.

6. Said Rabbah:

7. What is similar [about the cases]!?

8. There [in the case just cited] a person is not commanded with respect to causing his animal to rest on the Sabbatical Year;

   Here [in the case of Huna's sale of his animal] a person is commanded with respect to causing his animal to rest on the Sabbath.

9. Said to him Abbaye: And [is it the case that] everywhere that a person is commanded [with respect to it] it is forbidden?

10. But, lo, [consider] [the case of] a field—for which a person is commanded with respect to its rest on the Sabbatical Year—

11. But we have been taught (marginal note Vilna ed. emends: As it has been taught) [see t. Shevi'it 4:5]:

    11.1. The House of Shammai say: A person may not sell a ploughed field [to a non-Jew] during the Sabbatical Year (t. missing: ploughed).

    11.2. But The House of Hillel permit [such a sale], because he may leave it fallow (t. missing: because . . . fallow).

12. R. Ashi challenged it:

13. And [is it the case that] everywhere that a person is not commanded [with respect to it], it is permitted?

14. But, lo [consider] [agricultural] tools—for which a person is not commanded with respect to causing [agricultural] tools to rest on the Sabbatical Year.

In the Seat of Moses

15. BUT WE HAVE TAUGHT [in m. Shevi'it 5:6]: **These are the tools which a person** (some m. texts read: **an artisan**) **is not permitted to sell to them** [i.e., to non-Jews] **on the sabbatical year: a plow and its accoutrements; a harness; a seeder; and a hoe.**

16. RATHER SAID R. Ashi: <u>WHENEVER IT IS POSSIBLE</u> to posit (lit.: hang it on) [some extenuating circumstance], we [so] posit, <u>AND</u> [<u>THIS</u>] <u>EVEN THOUGH</u> one is commanded [explicitly with respect to the matter]; <u>AND WHENEVER IT IS NOT POSSIBLE</u> to [so] posit, we do not [so] posit, <u>EVEN THOUGH</u> one is not commanded [explicitly with respect to the matter].

V

1. *Rabbah sold a certain ass to an Israelite suspected of selling [large cattle] to idolaters.*

2. SAID TO HIM Abbaye: WHAT IS THE REASON *the master did thus [in apparent violation of m. AZ 1:6]?*

3. HE [Rabbah] SAID TO HIM: *I sold it to an Israelite.*

4. HE [Abbaye] SAID TO HIM: BUT, LO, [CONSIDER THAT][33] *He goes and sells it to an idolater!*

5. [Rabbah responded: *Does it make sense that*] *to an idolater they sell [when one can posit extenuating circumstances], [BUT] to an Israelite they do not sell [lest he in turn sell it to an idolater]!?*

6. HE [Abbaye] RESPONDED TO HIM [by, seemingly, citing a tannaitic source that substitutes "Sammaritans" for m. AZ 1:6's "idolaters"]:

    6.1. **In a locale in which they are accustomed to sell small cattle** to Samaritans, **they [are permitted to] sell;**

    6.2. **[where they are accustomed] not to sell, they do not sell.**

7. WHAT IS THE REASON?

8. IF ONE SAYS ON ACCOUNT OF *their being suspect with respect to* **bestiality**, [THEN IN THE VIEW OF] WHOM *are they suspect?*

9. AND (i.e., for), LO, IT IS TAUGHT [in a tannaitic source that parallels t. AZ 3:2 and 3:1]:

---

[33]. This line is missing in the digitized text of the standard Vilna edition found on www.mechon-mamre.org, but the line appears in the digitized text of the Vilna edition on the CDs of *Otzar HaTorah HaMemuhshevet* (Bnai Brak, Israel)

9.1 **they do not billet cattle at the stables of idolaters** (m. AZ 2:1)—

9.2. [neither] male [cattle] with male [idolaters],

9.3. and [not] female [cattle] with female [idolaters],

9.4. and one need not mention [the obvious cases of]

9.5. female [cattle] with male [idolaters],

9.6. and male [cattle] with female [idolaters].

9.7. And they do not entrust cattle to their shepherds.

9.8. And they do not leave themselves alone with them,

9.9. And they do not entrust a minor child with them so that he will instruct him in the study of books,

9.10 and to instruct him crafts.

9.11. But **they do billet cattle at the stables of** Samaritans (m. AZ 2:1)—

9.12. [whether] male [cattle] with female [Samaritans],

9.13. and female [cattle] with male [Samaritans],

9.14. and one need not mention [the obvious cases of]

9.15. male [cattle] with male [Samaritans],

9.16. and female [cattle] with female [Samaritans].

9.17. And they do entrust cattle to their shepherds.

9.18. And they do leave themselves alone with them

9.19. And they do entrust a minor child with them so that he will instruct him in the study of books,

9.20. and to instruct him [in] crafts.

10. THEREFORE [it would appear that], they [Samaritans] are not suspect.

11. BUT, MOREOVER, IT IS [ALSO] TAUGHT [in another tannaitic source, that has parallels at t. AZ 2:4]:

   11.1. They sell to them

   11.2. neither weapons,

   11.3. nor the accoutrements of weapons,

   11.4. And they sell to them

11.5. neither a block [for placing on prisoners' feet],

11.6. nor collars [for placing on prisoners' necks],

11.7. nor leg-irons,

11.8. nor iron chains—

11.9. the same [holds for] an idolater, as [for] a Samaritan.

12. WHAT IS THE REASON?

13. IF WE SAY THAT they are suspect with respect to shedding of [innocent] blood, [THEN IN THE VIEW OF] WHOM are they suspect?

14. LO, YOU HAVE [ALREADY] SAID [as cited above in a tannaitic source that has a parallel at t. AZ 3:1]: And they do leave themselves alone with them [i.e., Samaritans].

15. RATHER [one does not sell them weapons, etc.] ON ACCOUNT OF [THE FACT] THAT [the Samaritan] will go and sell it to an idolater.

16. AND IF YOU SAY: [Is there not a distinction to be made between an Israelite and a Samaritan because] a Samaritan does not do repentance but an Israelite does do repentance?

17. BUT, LO, SAID R. Nahman: Rabbah b. Abuhah: JUST AS they said it is forbidden to sell to an idolater, SO TOO it is forbidden to sell to an Israelite suspected of selling to an idolater.

18. He [Rabbah, upon learning of the just-cited tradition,] hurried after him [the Israelite to whom he had sold the ass] for a distance of three Persian miles [in order to buy back the animal]—

19. AND THERE ARE THOSE WHO SAY [THAT IT WAS]one Persian mile in the badlands—

20. and he did not meet him.

VI

1. SAID R. Dimi b. Abba: JUST AS it is forbidden to sell [arms] to an idolater, [SO TOO] it is forbidden to sell [arms] to bandits.

2. HOW ARE [THE TWO CASES] COMPARABLE [i.e., So, why do we need both articulated]?

3. IF he [the bandit] is suspected of killing, [THEN] IT IS SELF-EVIDENT THAT THESE ARE [i.e., we are dealing with] idolaters [and the second part of the above-cited tradition is not required].

4. AND IF [IT IS THE CASE] THAT he does not kill [and he is an Israelite], WHY [should one] not sell arms to him [in which case the second part of the above-cited tradition is again not required]?

5. [INDEED, WE MUST] ALWAYS [i.e., NORMALLY, ASSUME IN THIS CASE] THAT he does not kill [and he is an Israelite],

6. AND HERE [IN THIS CASE] with what are we dealing?

7. [IT IS] THE CASE OF a hold-up, [during which] sometimes he acts to save himself [and may kill or injure his pursuers].

VII

1. OUR RABBIS TAUGHT [this in a tannaitic source, without parallel in either m. or t.]:

   1.1. They do not sell them [i.e., idolaters] shields;

   1.2. and there are those who say: They sell them shields.

2. WHAT IS THE REASON [that they forbid such a sale according to the former opinion]?

3. IF [YOU WERE] TO SAY [THAT IT IS] ON ACCOUNT OF [THE FACT] THAT they defend themselves,

4. [THEN] IF SO, EVEN wheat and barley ALSO [should] not [be sold to idolaters, since they use them as well to sustain themselves; but one may sell wheat and barley idolaters. So why not shields?].

5. SAID Rav (Rosh reads or emends to: R. Pappa): IT IS NOT POSSIBLE [THAT] HERE TOO [regarding shields one can say the same, namely, they sustain their lives only with them]!

6. [RATHER] THERE ARE THOSE THAT SAY [REGARDING] shields [THAT] THE REASON IS THIS THAT it is not [permitted to sell shields to them]—

7. THAT BECAUSE [WHEN] their weapons are complete[ly used up], [THEN] they kill with them [i.e., with their shields].

8. [BUT AS REGARDS] [the second part of the tannaitic source, i.e.,] and there are those who say: They sell them shields—[WHAT IS THE REASON]? [THEIR REASON IS]

In the Seat of Moses

9. THAT BECAUSE [WHEN] their weapons are complete[ly used up], [THEN] they surely flee.

10. SAID R. Nahman: SAID Rabbah b. Avuha: The law is in accordance with [the view of] those who say [that they do sell shields to them].

VIII

1. SAID R. Adda b. Ahavah: They do not sell them iron bars.

2. WHAT IS THE REASON?

3. [IT IS] ON ACCOUNT OF [THE FACT] THAT they forge from them weapons.

4. [BUT] IF SO EVEN hoes and pick-axes ALSO [should not be sold to them, as they may be reforged as weapons]!

5. SAID R. Zavid: [INDEED, EVEN SO] WITH REGARD TO Hindu tools [which presumably are made of metal of a type that can also be made into weapons].

6. BUT [REGARDING] our current era, IN WHICH we sell [such things to them]—SAID R. Ashi [we sell] to Persians,

7. SINCE they defend us.

IX

1. **calves and foals**, [etc.] (= m. AZ 1:6, sections E.3–E.4)—

2. IT WAS TAUGHT (in a tannaitic source that parallels t. AZ 2:1):

   2.1. **R. Judah permits in the case of a maimed [animal]** (= m. 1:6, sec. G),

   2.2. which cannot be healed

   2.3. and live (sec. 2.1. missing in t.).

   2.4. They said to him: But do they not have her mounted [by a male], and she gives birth?

3. AND SINCE they have her mounted, and she gives birth, they [the rabbis] came to [the opinion of] delaying it[s transfer of ownership to the idolater].

4. [AND] HE [WOULD HAVE] SAID TO THEM [IN RESPONSE]: When will she [indeed] give birth!?

5. Why [does R. Judah believe she will not give birth]?

6. She [once maimed] will not receive a male [attempting to mount her].

X

1. **Ben Betayra permits in the case of a horse** (m. AZ 1:6)

2. It was taught [in a tannaitic source that parallels t. AZ 2:1]:

   2.1. **Ben Betayra permits in the case of a horse** (m. AZ 1:6),

   2.2. because he does work [on the Sabbath], for which one is not liable for a sin-offering.

   2.3. And Rabbi [Judah the Patriarch] (t. reads: the Sages forbid) forbids

   2.4. on account of two things:

   2.5. one, on account of the teaching regarding the accoutrements of weapons,

   2.6. and the other, on account of the teaching regarding large cattle.

3. Well and good [the reason stated, namely,]

4. [on account of] the teaching regarding the accoutrements of weapons (t. AZ 2:1),

5. [as] there are those that are killed by its kick.

6. But [with regard to the other reason stated, namely,] the teaching regarding large cattle (t. AZ 2:1),

7. What is [the reasoning of R. Judah the Patriarch]?

8. Said R. Yohanan: When it grows old they [hitch it to a mill and] they grind with it [grain] in millstones on the Sabbath.

9. Said R. Yohanan: The law accords with [the view of] Ben Betayra.

XI

1. It was asked of them:

2. [In the case] of a fattened ox,

3. What is [the law regarding] it?

4. Ask of

In the Seat of Moses

5. R. Judah [i.e., how Judah would rule, and you would reason to one response].

6. ASK OF

7. Our Rabbis [i.e., how Our Rabbis would rule, and you would reason to another response].

8. ASK OF

9. R. Judah [i.e., how Judah would rule, and you would reason to this response]?

10. THUS FAR R. Judah permitted

11. ONLY IN THE CASE OF **a maimed [animal]** (m. AZ 1:6),

12. WHICH does not fall within the category of [the prohibition with respect to] work [on the Sabbath, because the animal is unfit for work].

13. BUT THIS ONE [the fattened ox]—

14. SINCE he [the idolater who has purchased it] leaves it [to lose sufficient weight to work, and then] it does fall within the category of [the prohibition with respect to] work [on the Sabbath],

15. [THEN] it [would be] forbidden[, in R. Judah's view, to sell it to an idolater].

16. OR PERHAPS:

17. EVEN Our Rabbis forbade [sale to an idolater]

18. IN THAT CASE [i.e., of a maimed animal] ONLY

19. [those maimed animals] WHOSE normal course is other than for slaughter.

20. BUT,

21. THIS ONE [i.e., the fattened ox],

22. WHOSE normal course is for slaughter—

23. EVEN Our Rabbis [would have] permitted.

24. COME AND HEAR [what a relevant tannaitic source has to say that may shed light on the matter at hand, namely,]

25. THAT WHICH SAID Rav Judah: SAID Samuel:

26.1. Those of the House of Rabbi [Judah the Patriarch] used to sacrifice a fattened ox on [i.e., in honor of] their [the Romans'] festival day.

26.2. [Rabbi Judah] deducted [from his revenues] forty thousand [in coin as a bribe] so that they did not sacrifice it on the self-same day, but on the morrow.

26.3. [Later, Rabbi Judah] deducted [from his revenues an additional] forty thousand [in coin as a bribe] so that they did not sacrifice it [i.e., they did not hand it over] alive, but [already] slaughtered.

26.4. [Still later, Rabbi Judah] deducted [from his revenues an additional] forty thousand [in coin as a bribe] so that they did not sacrifice it at all.

27. WHAT IS THE REASON [for Rabbi Judah the Patriarch's actions]?

28. IT IS [CERTAINLY] NOT ON ACCOUNT OF [CONCERN THAT] PERHAPS he [the idolator] will leave it [until it loses sufficient weight to be used as a work-animal and be worked on the Sabbath]!

29. AND [SO] ACCORDING TO YOUR REASONING

30. [when it states explicitly: so] that they did not sacrifice it on the self-same day, but on the morrow—

31. WHAT IS THE REASON [for such an action taken by Rabbi Judah the Patriarch]!?

32. RATHER Rabbi [Judah the Patriarch] wished to do away with the thing [altogether], and he thought about how to do away [with it], and came [to the view that the best strategy was to have it done away with] little by little.

33. BUT IS IT [i.e., the reason we sought earlier for why it might be forbidden to sell a fattened ox to idolaters,] THAT one leaves it [the fattened ox to lose weight and] to get strong and one does work [with it on the Sabbath]?

34. SAID R. Ashi: SAID TO ME Zavida: [With respect to] a [fattened] ox—we leave it [to slim down], and [then] one does the work of two [normal oxen].

Now, my charted schematization of the same composition, b. Avodah Zarah 14b–16a, follows.

In the Seat of Moses

I

1. Is that to say that

    There is no

    prohibition,

    [and] There is

    [i.e., it is a matter of] custom [only]?

2. [No]

    Where

    it is the custom [to have] a prohibition, it is [so] accustomed;

    Where

    it is the custom [to have] a dispensation, it is [so] accustomed.

3. And they rebuffed it [by citing the following from m. AZ 2:1]

    4. one does not stable a cattle at the inns of idolaters, because they are suspect with respect to bestiality.

5. Said

    Rav:

    in a locale where they permitted **to sell**, they permitted to billet [in] **a locale where** they forbade to billet, they forbade **to sell**.

6. But

    R. Eliezer

says:

    even

    in a locale where they forbade to billet, it is permitted **to sell**.

7. What is the reason?

    8. An idolater worries that his [own] animal will become infertile.

9. But even so [must]

    Rav

[have] reversed [his view].

10. For

> Rav

SAID THE OPPOSITE [AS WELL].

11. SAID

> R. Shila b. Abimi

IN THE NAME OF

> Rav:
>
> An idolater worries that his [own] animal will become infertile.

II

1. **And in any locale they do [not permit one to] sell to them large cattle**, etc.

2. WHAT IS THE REASON?

   3. *LET IT BE [ASSUMED]* THAT

   > we do not fear **bestiality** (m. AZ 2:1) [*will take place*];

   4. [*RATHER, NOW*]

   > we fear that [the idolater] does work with it [on the Sabbath].

5. BUT

   LET

   > it [the animal] be worked [on the Sabbath]!

6. SINCE [*IT IS THE CASE*] THAT

   > [the Israelite] sold it,

   [THEN]

   > [the idolater] has acquired it[, and the animal is no longer subject to the laws of the Sabbath].

7. [RATHER],

   > [they instituted] a decree [against the sale of large cattle]

   ON ACCOUNT OF

   > [cases of idolaters] borrowing [the animal and working it on the Sabbath],

   AND ON ACCOUNT OF

[cases of idolaters] leasing [the animal and working it on the Sabbath, in which two cases the animal is still owned by the Israelite.]

8. [BUT]

[also in the case of] borrowing *he acquires [possession of] it, [and so too in the case of] leasing he acquires [possession of] it.*

9. RATHER

SAID

Rami b. R. Yiva

<u>ON ACCOUNT OF</u>

[cases of selling animals on a] trial [basis];

<u>SINCE</u>

at times when one sells it oneself close to the setting of the sun on the onset of the Sabbath,

<u>AND</u>

he himself said to him come try it,

<u>AND</u>

he listens to him,

<u>AND</u>

he goes on account of him.

10. BUT IT IS ALRIGHT THAT

he goes, [is it not?]

11. BUT

he is driving his animal on the Sabbath.

12. <u>AND</u>

he who drives his animal on the Sabbath is liable for a sin-offering [if the act was done in error] (see b. Shabbat 153b).

13. *R. Shisha b. R. Idi*

CHALLENGED IT:

14. BUT

>[in the case of] leasing,

WHO [HOLDS THAT]

>he acquired possession of it [in the first place]!?

15. AND SO WE HAVE TAUGHT [in m. AZ 1:9]:

>**Even in the locale where they say [that it is permitted] to lease [a house to an idolater], they did not say [thus if the house will be used] as a dwelling, because [the idolater] will bring into it an idol [and the Israelite will thereby be participating indirectly in idolatry.**

16. AND IF IT SHOULD OCCUR TO YOU

>[THAT in]

>leasing, [the lessee] *acquired* [*possession*],

[THEN IN] THIS [CASE JUST CITED]

>whatever he wishes to bring into his house, let him bring in.

>17. Idolatry

DIFFERS

>IN THAT

>it is [a more] severe [case].

18. AS IT IS WRITTEN [in Deuteronomy 7 and cited in m. AZ 1:9],

>**"You shall not bring an abomination [i.e., an idol] into your house."**

>19. R. Isaac b. R. Mesharsheya

CHALLENGED IT:

20. BUT

>[in the case of] leasing,

WHO [HOLDS THAT]

>he acquired possession of it [in the first place]!?

21. AND SO WE HAVE TAUGHT [in m. Terumot 11:9]:

An Israelite who leased a cow from a priest, may feed it beans that are heave offering; but a priest who leased a cow from an Israelite—even though its feeding is his obligation, he may not feed her beans that are heave offering [i.e., the cow's status as regards being able to be fed sanctified produce does not change as a result of being leased].

22. AND IF IT SHOULD OCCUR TO YOU

>[that in] leasing, [the lessee] acquired [possession],

>[THEN] WHY [IN CASE JUST CITED]

>should he not feed it [heave offering], [since] the cow [presumably] is his!?

23. RATHER

LEARN FROM THIS [i.e., from the immediately preceding]

>[that in] leasing, [the lessee] has not acquired [possession].

24. AND NOW

THAT YOU HAVE SAID

>[that in] leasing, [the lessee] has not acquired [possession],

25. [WE CONCLUDE THAT]

>>25.1. [they instituted] a decree [against the sale of large cattle] on account of [cases of idolaters] leasing [the animal and working it on the Sabbath],

>>25.2. [and they instituted] a decree [against the sale of large cattle] on account of [cases of idolaters] borrowing [the animal and working it on the Sabbath],

>>25.3. [and they instituted] a decree [against the sale of large cattle] on account of [cases of idolaters buying an animal on a] *trial* [basis and, with the complicity of the Israelite, working it on the Sabbath].

III

1. *Rav Ada permitted the sale of an ass by the agency of a broker.*
2. [WHY COULD HE HAVE PERMITTED IT IN THIS CASE?]

IF

> [as we have deduced above,] they instituted a decree [against the sale of large cattle]

ON ACCOUNT OF

> [cases of idolaters buying an animal on a] *trial* [basis and, with the complicity of the Israelite, working it on the Sabbath],

[THEN] THIS ONE

> [*i.e, the Israelite owner who uses the services of a broker*] *does not* [even] *know* [*the buyer, such that he can*] *listen to him and go on account of him* [*and be complicit in driving the animal on the Sabbath*].

3. AND

IF

> [as we also have deduced above,] they instituted a decree [against the sale of large cattle]

ON ACCOUNT OF

> [cases of idolaters] borrowing and leasing [an animal and working the Israelite's animal on the Sabbath],

SINCE

> [*the animal*] *is not his* [*i.e., the broker's, to lend or lease*],

[THEN]

> *he does not lend or lease* [*the animal*].

4. AND FURTHERMORE

> [we may conclude in this last case that the broker will neither lend nor lease the animal]

ON ACCOUNT OF

> [the fact] that *he does not* [*wish to*] *reveal* [*to the prospective buyer*] *any blemish in it*.

IV

1. *Rav Huna sold a certain cow to an idolater.*

2. SAID TO HIM

In the Seat of Moses

> *Rav Hisda:*

WHAT IS THE REASON

> the master did thus [in apparent violation of m. AZ 1:6]?

3. HE [Huna] SAID TO HIM:

> <u>SAY [THAT]</u>
>
> > [the idolater] bought it for slaughter.

4. AND WHENCE WILL YOU SAY THAT

WE HAVE [SO] SAID [I.E. TAUGHT]

AS IN THE MANNER OF [I.E. SUCH A CASE]?

5. AS WE HAVE TAUGHT [in m. Shevi'it 5:8]:

> > **The House of Shammai say:**
> >
> > **one may not sell to him [a non-Jew] a threshing cow on the sabbatical year;**
> >
> > **but the House of Hillel**
> >
> > **permit [such a sale], because he [the non-Jew] might [intend to] slaughter it.**

6. SAID

> *Rabbah:*

7. WHAT IS SIMILAR [about the cases]!?

> 8. <u>THERE</u>
>
> > [in the case just cited] a person is not commanded with respect to causing his animal to rest on the Sabbatical Year;
>
> <u>HERE</u>
>
> > [in the case of Huna's sale of his animal] a person is commanded with respect to causing his animal to rest on the Sabbath.

9. SAID TO HIM

> *Abbaye:*

AND [IS IT THE CASE THAT] EVERYWHERE THAT

> a person is commanded [with respect to it] it is forbidden?

10. BUT, LO, [CONSIDER]

[the case of] a field—

FOR WHICH

a person is commanded with respect to its rest on the Sabbatical Year—

11. BUT WE HAVE TAUGHT (marginal note Vilna ed. emends: AS IT HAS BEEN TAUGHT) [see t. Shevi'it 4:5]:

11.1. The House of Shammai say:

A person may not sell a ploughed field [to a non-Jew] during the Sabbatical Year (t. missing: ploughed).

11.2. But The House of Hillel

permit [such a sale], because he may leave it fallow (t. missing: because . . . fallow).

12. R. Ashi

CHALLENGED IT:

13. AND [IS IT THE CASE THAT] EVERYWHERE THAT

a person is not commanded [with respect to it], *it is permitted*?

14. BUT, LO, [CONSIDER]

[agricultural] tools—

FOR WHICH

a person is not commanded with respect to causing [agricultural] tools to rest on the Sabbatical Year.

15. BUT WE HAVE TAUGHT [in m. Shevi'it 5:6]:

these are the tools which a person (some m. texts read: **an artisan**) **is not permitted to sell to them [i.e., to non-Jews] on the sabbatical year: a plow and its accoutrements; a harness; a seeder; and a hoe.**

16. RATHER

SAID

R. Ashi:

WHENEVER IT IS POSSIBLE

> to posit (lit.: hang it on) [some extenuating circumstance], we [so] posit,

AND [THIS] EVEN THOUGH

> one is commanded [explicitly with respect to the matter];

AND WHENEVER IT IS NOT POSSIBLE

> to [so] posit, we do not [so] posit,

EVEN THOUGH

> one is not commanded [explicitly with respect to the matter].

V

1. Rabbah sold a certain ass to an Israelite suspected of selling [large cattle] to idolaters.

    2. SAID TO HIM

    > Abbaye:

    WHAT IS THE REASON

    > the master did thus [in apparent violation of m. AZ 1:6]?

    3. HE [Rabbah] SAID TO HIM:

    > I sold it to an Israelite.

    4. HE [Abbaye] SAID TO HIM:

    BUT, LO, [CONSIDER THAT][34]

    > He goes and sells it to an idolater!

    5. [Rabbah responded: Does it make sense that]

    > to an idolater they sell [when one can posit extenuating circumstances],

    [BUT]

    > to an Israelite they do not sell [lest he in turn sell it to an idolater]!?

    6. HE [Abbaye] RESPONDED TO HIM:

    > **6.1. in a locale in which they are accustomed to sell small cattle** to Samaritans, **they [are permitted to] sell;**

---

34. This line is missing in the digitized text of the standard Vilna edition found on www.mechon-mamre.org, but appears in the digitized text of the Vilna edition on the CDs of *Otzar HaTorah HaMemuhshevet* (Bnai Brak, Israel)

6.2. [where they are accustomed] not to sell, they do not sell.

7. WHAT IS THE REASON?

8. IF ONE SAYS

IT IS ON ACCOUNT OF

their being suspect with respect to **bestiality**,

[THEN IN THE VIEW OF] WHOM

are they suspect?

9. AND (i.e., for), LO, IT IS TAUGHT [in a tannaitic source that significantly parallels t. AZ 3:2 and 3:1]:

9.1 **they do not billet cattle at the stables of idolaters** (m. AZ 2:1)—

9.2. [neither] male [cattle] with male [idolaters],

9.3. and [not] female [cattle] with female [idolaters],

9.4. and one need not mention [the obvious cases of]

9.5. female [cattle] with male [idolaters],

9.6. and male [cattle] with female [idolaters].

9.7. And they do not entrust cattle to their shepherds.

9.8. And they do not leave themselves alone with them,

9.9. And they do not entrust a minor child with them so that he will instruct him in the study of books,

9.10 and to instruct him crafts.

9.11. But **they do billet cattle at the stables of** Samaritans (m. AZ 2:1)—

9.12. [whether] male [cattle] with female [Samaritans],

9.13. and female [cattle] with male [Samaritans],

9.14. and one need not mention [the obvious cases of]

9.15. male [cattle] with male [Samaritans],

9.16. and female [cattle] with female [Samaritans].

9.17. And they do entrust cattle to their shepherds.

9.18. And they do leave themselves alone with them

> 9.19. And they do entrust a minor child with them so that he will instruct him in the study of books,
>
> 9.20. and to instruct him [in] crafts.

10. THEREFORE [it would appear that],

> they [Samaritans] are not suspect.

11. BUT, MOREOVER,

IT IS [ALSO] TAUGHT [in another tannaitic source, that has parallels at t. AZ 2:4]:

> 11.1. They sell to them
>
> 11.2. neither weapons,
>
> 11.3. nor the accoutrements of weapons,
>
> 11.4. And they sell to them
>
> 11.5. neither a block [for placing on prisoners' feet],
>
> 11.6. nor collars [for placing on prisoners' necks],
>
> 11.7. nor leg-irons,
>
> 11.8. nor iron chains—
>
> 11.9. the same [holds for] an idolater, as [for] a Samaritan.

12. WHAT IS THE REASON?

13. IF WE SAY

THAT

> they are suspect with respect to shedding of [innocent] blood,

[THEN IN THE VIEW OF] WHOM

> are they suspect?

14. LO, YOU HAVE [ALREADY] SAID [as cited above in a tannaitic source that has a parallel at t. AZ 3:1]:

> And they do leave themselves alone with them [i.e., Samaritans].

15. RATHER

> [one does not sell them weapons, etc.]
>
> ON ACCOUNT OF [THE FACT] THAT
>
> [the Samaritan] will go and sell it to an idolater.

16. AND IF YOU SAY

    [is there not a distinction to be made between an Israelite and a Samaritan because] a Samaritan does not do repentance but an Israelite does do repentance?

17. BUT, LO, SAID

    R. Nahman:

    Rabbah b. Abuhah:

JUST AS

    they said it is forbidden to sell to an idolater,

SO TOO

    it is forbidden to sell to an Israelite suspected of selling to an idolater.

18. He [Rabbah, upon learning of the just-cited tradition,] hurried after him [the Israelite to whom he had sold the ass] for a distance of three Persian miles—

19. AND THERE ARE THOSE WHO SAY [THAT IT WAS]

    one Persian mile in the badlands—

20. and he did not meet him.

VI

1. SAID

    R. Dimi b. Abba:

JUST AS

    it is forbidden to sell [arms] to an idolater,

[SO TOO]

    it is forbidden to sell [arms] to bandits.

2. HOW ARE [THE TWO CASES] COMPARABLE [i.e., So, why do we need both articulated]?

    3. IF

    he [the bandit] is suspected of killing,

[THEN]

IT IS SELF-EVIDENT THAT

    THESE ARE [i.e., we are dealing with]

        idolaters [and the second part of the above-cited tradition is not required].

    4. *AND IF* [*IT IS THE CASE*] *THAT*

        he does not kill [and he is an Israelite],

WHY

        [should one] not sell arms to him [in which case the second part of the above-cited tradition is again not required]?

    5. [*INDEED, WE MUST*] *ALWAYS* [I.E., NORMALLY, ASSUME IN THIS CASE] *THAT*

        he does not kill [and he is an Israelite],

    6. *AND HERE* [IN THIS CASE] *with what are we dealing?*

    7. [*It is*] *THE CASE OF*

        a hold-up, [during which] sometimes he acts to save himself [and may kill or injure his pursuers].

VII

1. *OUR RABBIS TAUGHT* [this in a tannaitic source]:

    1.1. They do not sell them [i.e., idolaters] shields;

    1.2. and there are those who say: They sell them shields.

2. *WHAT IS THE REASON* [that they forbid such a sale according to the former opinion]?

3. *IF* [*YOU WERE*] *TO SAY*

[*THAT IT IS*] *ON ACCOUNT OF* [*THE FACT*] *THAT*

    they defend themselves,

4. [*THEN*] *IF SO,*

    EVEN

        wheat and barley

    ALSO

[should] not [be sold to idolaters, since they use them as well to sustain themselves; but one may sell wheat and barley idolaters. So why not shields?].

5. SAID

Rav (Rosh reads or emends to: R. Pappa):

IT IS NOT POSSIBLE

[THAT] HERE TOO

[regarding shields one can say the same, namely, they sustain their lives only with them]!

6. [RATHER]

THERE ARE THOSE THAT SAY [REGARDING]

shields

[THAT] THE REASON IS THAT

It is not [permitted to sell shields to them]—

7. THAT BECAUSE

[WHEN]

their weapons are complete[ly used up],

[THEN]

they kill with them [i.e., with their shields].

8. [BUT AS REGARDS]

[the second part of the tannaitic source, i.e.,

and there are those who say: They sell them shields—

[THEIR REASON IS]

9. THAT BECAUSE

[WHEN]

their weapons are complete[ly used up],

[THEN]

they surely flee.

10. SAID

R. Nahman:

<u>SAID</u>

>Rabbah b. Avuha:
>
>the law is in accordance with [the view of]
>
>those who say [that they do sell shields to them].

VIII

1. *SAID*

   >R. Adda b. Ahavah:
   >
   >They do not sell them iron bars.

2. *WHAT IS THE REASON?*

   3. [*IT IS*] <u>ON ACCOUNT OF</u> [*THE FACT*] <u>THAT</u>

      >they forge from them weapons.

4. [*BUT*] *IF SO*

   <u>EVEN</u>

   >hoes and pick-axes

   <u>ALSO</u>

   >[should not be sold to them, as they may be reforged as weapons]!

5. *SAID*

   >R. Zavid:

   <u>[INDEED, EVEN SO] WITH REGARD TO</u>

   >Hindu tools.

6. *BUT* [*REGARDING*]

   >our current era,

   <u>IN WHICH</u>

   >we sell [such things to them]—

SAID

>R. Ashi
>
>[we sell] to Persians,

7. SINCE

>they defend us.

IX

1. **calves and foals**, [etc.] (= m. AZ 1:6, sections E.3–E.4)—

2. It was taught (in a tannaitic source that parallels t. AZ 2:1):

> 2.1. <u>R. Judah permits in the case of a maimed [animal]</u> (= m. 1:6, sec. G),
>
> 2.2. <u>which cannot be healed</u>
>
> 2.3. <u>and live (sec. 2.1. missing in t.).</u>
>
> 2.4. <u>They said to him: But do they not have her mounted [by a male], and she gives birth?</u>

3. AND SINCE

> they have her mounted, and she gives birth,
>
> they [the rabbis] came to [opinion of]
>
> delaying it[s transfer of ownership to the idolater].

4. [AND] HE [WOULD HAVE] SAID TO THEM [IN RESPONSE]:

> When will she [indeed] give birth!?

5. WHY

> [does R. Judah believe she will not give birth]?
>
> 6. She [once maimed] will not receive a male [attempting to mount her].

X

1. **Ben Betayra permits in the case of a horse** (m. AZ 1:6)

2. IT WAS TAUGHT [in a tannaitic source that parallels t. AZ 2:1]:

> 2.1. **<u>Ben Betayra permits in the case of a horse</u>** (m. AZ 1:6),
>
> 2.2. <u>because he does work [on the Sabbath], for which one is not liable for a sin-offering.</u>
>
> 2.3. <u>And Rabbi [Judah the Patriarch] (t. reads: the Sages forbid) forbids</u>
>
> 2.4. <u>on account of two things:</u>

2.5. <u>one, on account of the teaching regarding the accoutrements of weapons,</u>

2.6. <u>and the other, on account of the teaching regarding large cattle.</u>

3. WELL AND GOOD [THE REASON, NAMELY,]

    4. <u>[on account of] the teaching regarding the accoutrements of weapons (t. AZ 2:1),</u>

    5. [AS] THERE ARE THOSE THAT

are killed by its kick.

6. BUT [WITH REGARD TO THE OTHER REASON STATED, NAMELY,]

<u>the teaching regarding large cattle (t. AZ 2:1),</u>

7. WHAT IS THE REASONING OF R. *Judah the Patriarch*]?

8. SAID

    R. Yohanan:

When it grows old they [hitch it to a mill and] they grind with it [grain] in millstones on the Sabbath.

9. SAID

    R. Yohanan:

The law accords with [the view of]

Ben Betayra.

XI

1. IT WAS ASKED OF THEM:

    2. [In the case] of a fattened ox,

3. WHAT IS [THE LAW REGARDING] IT?

4. ASK OF

    5. R. Judah [i.e., how Judah would rule, and you would reason to one response].

6. ASK OF

    7. Our Rabbis [i.e., how Our Rabbis would rule, and you would reason to another response].

8. ASK OF

> 9. R. Judah [i.e., how Judah would rule, and you would reason to this response].

10. THUS FAR

> R. Judah permitted

11. ONLY IN THE CASE OF

> **a maimed [animal]** (m. AZ 1:6),

12. WHICH

> does not fall within the category of [the prohibition with respect to] work [on the Sabbath, because the animal is unfit for work].

13. BUT

> THIS ONE
>
> [the fattened ox]—

14. SINCE

> he [the idolater who has purchased it] leaves it [to lose sufficient weight to work, and then] it does fall within the category of [the prohibition with respect to] work [on the Sabbath],

15. [THEN]

> it [would be] forbidden[, in R. Judah's view, to sell it to an idolater].

16. OR PERHAPS:

> 17. EVEN
>
> Our Rabbis *forbade [sale to an idolater]*

18. IN THAT CASE

> [i.e., of a maimed animal]

ONLY,

> 19. [those maimed animals]

WHOSE

> normal course is other than for slaughter.

20. BUT,

> 21. THIS ONE

In the Seat of Moses

[i.e., the fattened ox],

22. WHOSE

normal course is for slaughter—

23. EVEN

Our Rabbis [would have] permitted.

24. COME AND HEAR [what a relevant tannaitic source has to say that may shed light on the matter at hand, namely,]

25. THAT WHICH SAID

Rav Judah:

SAID

Samuel:

26.1. Those of the House of Rabbi [Judah the Patriarch] used to sacrifice a fattened ox on [i.e., in honor of] their [the Romans'] festival day.

26.2. [Rabbi Judah] deducted [from his revenues] forty thousand [in coin as a bribe] so that they did not sacrifice it on the self-same day, but on the morrow.

26.3. [Later, Rabbi Judah] deducted [from his revenues an additional] forty thousand [in coin as a bribe] so that they did not sacrifice it [i.e., they did not hand it over] alive, but [already] slaughtered.

26.4. [Still later, Rabbi Judah] deducted [from his revenues an additional] forty thousand [in coin as a bribe] so that they did not sacrifice it at all.

27. WHAT IS THE REASON

[for Rabbi Judah the Patriarch's actions]?

28. IT IS [CERTAINLY] NOT ON ACCOUNT OF [CONCERN THAT] PERHAPS

he [the idolater] will leave it [until it loses sufficient weight to be used as a work-animal and be worked on the Sabbath]!

29. AND [SO] ACCORDING TO YOUR REASONING

30. [when it states explicitly: so] that they did not sacrifice it on the self-same day, but on the morrow—

31. WHAT IS THE REASON

[for such an action taken by Rabbi Judah the Patriarch]!?

32. RATHER

Rabbi [Judah the Patriarch] wished to do away with the thing [altogether], and he thought about how to do away [with it], and came [to the view that the best strategy was to have it done away with] little by little.

33. BUT IS IT [i.e., the reason we sought earlier for why it might be forbidden to sell a fattened ox to idolaters,] THAT

one leaves it [the fattened ox to lose weight and] to get strong and one does work [with it on the Sabbath]?

34. SAID

R. Ashi:

SAID TO ME

Zavida:

[With respect to] a [fattened] ox—we leave it [to slim down], and [then] one does the work of two [normal oxen].

Well, I must assume that you have worked through b. Avodah Zarah 14b–16a, a complete and probably mid-sized Bavli composite legal essay. I have no doubt that you will have needed to read each constituent composition several times over, before you intellectually mastered the back-and-forth analyses. As stated, I shall not go over that ground with you, as I have done before. You should be beyond that by now. But I will make some second-order observations about this Bavli passage, in the expectation that you will find them edifying, and perhaps useful, now that you have done the work of deciphering it with the skills you have acquired in working through chapter 7 and to this point in chapter 8.

One interesting feature of the compositions of this Bavli composite essay is that not every composition deals with the interpretation, analysis, or criticism of our Mishnah passage. Sections/compositions I and II do. And so do sections/compositions IX and X. But that leaves seven of the eleven compositions of this passage that do not "originate" with the analysis of m. Avodah Zarah 1:6. What are these seven compositions actually up to?

Five of the seven (at III, IV, V, VI, VIII) take as their points of departure legal positions attributed in one fashion or another to an *amora*. One (VII) is a composition that opens with the citation of a *baraita* (here an extra-Mishnaic tannaitic tradition that does *not* have a parallel in Tosefta). And one (XI), the final composition of the passage, simply starts with a question: IT WAS ASKED OF THEM, in the case of a fattened ox, WHAT IS [THE LAW REGARDING] IT? That is to say, Can a Jew sell such an animal to an idolater? In all of these seven compositions, the back-and-forth analysis and hypothetical questioning then ensues, just as if the composition were a treatment of an aspect of the base Mishnah text that is the starting point of the composite essay.

Are these seven compositions all off-topic, in the sense that they do not deal with "our" Mishnah? Yes and no. The "no" is obvious; in each case no part of Mishnah has been portrayed as the starting point of the composition. The "yes" is more complex; in each case there is *either* a substantive "overlap" of concern with the Mishnah passage, just not with anything explicitly stated in the Mishnah text, *or* a substantive "overlap" of concern with the discussion and analysis of an antecedent composition in the composite essay. So, for example, the question at IX about the "fattened ox" could be taken as a specific case related to but not raised in Mishnah. And the composition then goes about its analysis and dialectics, much as it would if the "fattened ox" were a case in Mishnah. Similarly, Section V's composition emerges from a precedent story involving an *amora*, Rabbah, in which a situation has arisen that (like the "fattened ox") is a case related to but not dealt with at all in Mishnah. Section IV's composition also concerns an action of an *amora*, which is taken as legal precedent, but which appears to contradict Mishnah's rulings. In contrast, Sections/compositions VI and VII commence with amoraic legal positions about selling arms to idolaters and/or bandits. Where is the substantive overlap with our Mishnah's content? There is none really. Rather the topical "overlap" is with a tannaitic source (that parallels t. Avodah Zarah 2:4) cited in Section/composition V and with that composition's subsequent arguments, which revolve in large part around the topic of selling weapons to idolaters.

Does all of this say something that is representative of Bavli, that makes it distinctively Bavli? Again the answer is both "no" and "yes." It would be inappropriate for me to maintain that this never happens in the

Yerushalmi. That is the "no." As to the "yes"—it is my impression that such a "ramification" beyond Mishnah's subject matter of the very *generative* topics of the compositions that together comprise the composite essay that ostensibly treats a given Mishnah passage is *not* a rarity in Bavli. Rather it falls well within Bavli's composites' *modus operandi*. And it demonstrates, among other things, how within a composite essay compositions may be generated by, or at least depend upon for topical coherence and intelligibility, antecedent compositions, as is the case of Sections VI's and VII's topical relationship with Section V, for example. It is as if part of Section V constituted the "Mishnah" for Sections VI and VII. Moreover, the phenomena we are seeing in b. Avodah Zarah 14b–16a is also an attestation to the perceived status of amoraic legal teachings as equal (!?) to tanniatic ones, and so (equally!?) worthy of a Talmudic composition, but not a composite essay, which still begins with Mishnah analysis and commentary.

I raise these second- and third-order issues in the reading of the Bavli passage that you have now deciphered on your own, with the tools and techniques you will have already acquired, for several reasons. First, I believe it will help you decipher other Bavli passages when you are forewarned that not all compositions of an extended composite essay will actually deal with the Mishnah passage at hand as their point of departure. Second, I believe that sensitizing you to this feature of Bavli passages is a good segue to the remarks I wish to make in the final chapter of this book. These remarks concern the "reader experience" and type of "reader engagement" demanded by two very different sets of "students" of Mishnah, Toseftan and Tosefta-like passages, of Halakhic-Midrashic traditions, and of compositions and composite essays of the Bavli and Yerushalmi. One set are you, my readers, who have now worked through eight chapters of this book. The other set comprises ancient rabbis and ancient novice would-be rabbis of the early third century through early seventh century, initially in the Land of Israel under Roman rule, and soon thereafter in Mesopotamia largely under Persian rule. They devoted themselves to the study of these texts as a core within group activity in rabbinic circles—especially to Mishnah study for about four hundred years, and thereafter to Bavli study. As I help you reflect on your experience, I offer you a unique vantage point to reflect on how some core aspects of their shared "professional-guild" identity and associated intellectual skills are likely to have been shaped and reinforced by studying such texts with one another, as we know they did. Consider chapter 9, then, as a bonus check that you may cash because of the particular experience you have had, having worked through this book.

SUGGESTIONS FOR FURTHER READING

Goldberg, "The Babylonian Talmud," 323–66.

Greenbaum, "Talmudic Rhetoric," 151–69.

Jacobs, *The Talmudic Argument*.

Kraemer, *The Mind of the Talmud*.

Neusner, *Judaism, the Classical Statement*.

Neusner, *How the Bavli Is Constructed*.

Neusner, *First Steps in the Talmud*.

Moscovitz, *Talmudic Reasoning*.

Rubenstein, *The Culture of the Babylonian Talmud*.

9

Final Thoughts
You and Early Rabbinic *Paideia*

THE END IS AT HAND, BUT TO WHAT ENDS MAY IT BE PUT?

The preceding chapter marks the culmination of your work to assimilate the lessons of this book. You will have acquired an introductory-level familiarity with the most pervasive, basic, literary-rhetorical traits and conventions that characterize the major genres of early rabbinic legal literature in Mishnah, Tosefta, the Halakhic Midrashim, the Jerusalem Talmud, and the Babylonian Talmud. This literature spans nearly half a millennium of early rabbinic, literary output in the Land of Israel under Roman and Byzantine-Roman rule and in Persian-ruled Mesopotamia.

The purpose of this volume has been to help you acquire basic, core tools that would permit you access to this literature, the production of which parallels about 400 years of development of the early rabbinic group from c. 200 CE to just after c. 600 CE. It is a literature, particularly in its latest formulation, the Babylonian Talmud, which came to assume a place of extraordinary authority in the history of Judaism in the medieval into modern periods. This happened, as stated in chapter 8, as a result of the "rabbinization" of almost all Jewish communities in Near Eastern,

Mediterranean, and Southern and Central European lands between the seventh and eleventh centuries.

What you now do with your newly acquired or enhanced access is yours to decide in light of your interests and disciplinary focus. Whether you consult this body of legal literature in translation only or choose to undertake the work also to read these documents in their original Hebrew and Aramaic is your decision. To borrow just part of the teaching in a folkloric (aggadic) passage attributed to the protorabbinic, Pharisaic master, Hillel, "[Now] go learn" (*zil gmor*).

There is an ocean of evidence to be plumbed in this literature to advance many types of inquiry on an array of possible subjects—ancient medicine, law, early Judaism(s), administration and governance in late antiquity, religion and society in the Roman period, to name just a few. By way of providing an example of such inquiries, what this concluding chapter attempts to do is have you glimpse one aspect of the early rabbinic group's culture—that is, to do a bit of social/cultural history of the early rabbinic group itself—by capitalizing precisely on your acquired experiences and skills in working through chapters 4 through 8. It is a particularly apt topic with which to conclude this volume, because, as I shall show, the actual data I shall adduce to address aspects of this subject are the very same basic literary-rhetorical traits and conventions described in this volume and now familiar to you. My social-historical claim is this: that these very same core and basic literary-rhetorical traits of the early rabbis' legal texts and traditions will have played a significant (even if not exclusive) role in representing and shaping important aspects of their shared, group identity over a four-centuries-long period, and, therefore, we may describe and characterize those aspects. Let me explain the bases for my claim.

You have acquired specific *skills* in working through this volume. But in the process you have also acquired important *knowledge about some key early rabbinic (legal) texts*. What is that knowledge? *You understand their more pervasive basic literary-rhetorical traits, constructs, and conventions.* Now, these traits and conventions also *fundamentally condition and construct the reader experience and reader engagement*[1] *of every and any student* of Mishnah, of Toseftan materials, of Halakhic-Midrashic passages, and of compositions and composite essays in the Yerushalmi and the Bavli. Whom

---

1. I use the term "reader" here as a matter of convenience. I do not intend to beg, nor do I need to beg, any questions about whether ancient students of these texts engaged with them in written form, or in oral form, or in some combination of both. For my purposes in this chapter, it does not matter.

do I include in the rubric of "every and any student"? Of course, you are now among them, as am I. *But so are the ancient rabbis themselves and their disciples, novice would-be rabbis*, who studied this literature when it was initially produced and promulgated by and within the early rabbinic movement of which they were a part.

As I stated in chapter 1, no one is born with knowledge of these basic literary-rhetorical traits and conventions; not you or I, and not ancient, would-be rabbis. These traits and conventions must have been learned and mastered by them (just as we have had to do), or these ancient texts' passages would have remained opaque even to ancient students. It follows that social institutions existed in antiquity to instil this mastery, as they do today. Moreover, we may reasonably assert that the acquisition of this knowledge was not part and parcel of some universal curriculum taught to all Jews of Roman/Byzantine Palestine or Persian-ruled Babylonia. While there has been much scholarly debate about basic, general and advanced literacy among Roman-period Jews in the Land of Israel or Mesopotamia,[2] it is likely that only a few—that is, members of a cultural elite—would have acquired the high-level literacy in Hebrew and/or Aramaic to tackle these early rabbinic legal texts.[3] But the study of these texts, like their production, was certainly a rabbinic enterprise, an enterprise that set the rabbis, all rabbis, apart as a distinct group (no doubt among other, competing, highly educated elites) within ancient Jewish society. And the same must be said of the acquisition of the skills and knowledge to cope with this literature's pervasive literary-rhetorical conventions. Acquiring these skills and knowledge will have been part of the curriculum of novices of the rabbinic movement in antiquity as part and parcel (explicitly or indirectly) of their instruction in, and study of, these texts. That is why specifically rabbinic, social institutions of one form or another will have necessarily

---

2. See Hezser, *Jewish Literacy*, and its assessment in Bar-Ilan, "Literacy among the Jews," 217–22, as well as Hezser, "Jewish Literacy," 149–196. See also Bar-Ilan, "Illiteracy as Reflected, 1–12; Bar-Ilan, "Illiteracy in the Land," 46–61. See Wise, "Language." In this interesting study, Wise concludes that (discounting professional scribes) about 25 percent of males among *the property owner class* of second-century Judean families had a reasonable level of literacy, allowing them to read and write business-related daily correspondence, and this primarily in Aramaic, as opposed to Greek or Hebrew.

3. Some, like Hezser, *Jewish Literacy*, have proposed that literacy among the early rabbis was not at the level that one might otherwise suppose, because of their valuing of oral transmission of their texts. Without denying their ideological commitment to orality, I see the evidence as overwhelmingly supporting the notion of high-level literacy among the early rabbis. See Lapin, "Origins."

existed in antiquity to inculcate these skills and to master these texts—the master-disciple circle, and/or the House of Study, and (later) the large-scale protouniversity-like *yeshivot* academies.[4]

Let me go further still. The fullest comprehension of what the passages of each of these documents, or genres and subgenres, of rabbinic legal literature mean is conditioned by the *demands* their characteristic literary-rhetorical traits and conventions place on the reader. Now comes the critical claim; *if* the study of *any* of these texts was a core, highly valued, near-universal activity within early rabbinic circles, then identifying those *demands* is tantamount to identifying some of the principal common traits that characterized the shared identity of members of the early rabbinic group. So, does reliable historical evidence allow us reasonably to remove the conditional "if-clause" of the preceding conditional sentence? The answer is an unequivocal "yes," as I shall presently explain.

MISHNAH STUDY AS EARLY RABBINIC *PAIDEIA*

One may assert with confidence that Mishnah study was such an activity, definitively supplanted only centuries later by the study of the Bavli. And until the ascendancy of the Bavli to the apex of the rabbinic learning, Toseftan materials, other Toseftan-like traditions, midrashic-halahkic materials, amoraic traditions, the Yerushalmi's and even initially the Bavli's *sugyot* were either conceived to serve Mishnah-study or subsequently pressed into the service of Mishnah-study.

As already intimated in chapters 2 and 3, we know that with Mishnah's production and promulgation by and within early rabbinic circles in Roman-ruled Palestine c. 200 CE, Mishnah study and mastery of its content became the central within-group activity within these circles. The rabbinic novices/disciples studied Mishnah with their masters/teachers, this, in part, to become rabbis. Rabbinic masters studied Mishnah with one another as a life-long activity, even while they taught the next generation of novices/disciples. The mastery of Mishnah was, arguably, the most important hallmark of being a rabbi from the perspective of those within the early rabbinic group.

The evidence in support of the foregoing assertions is nothing short of overwhelming, as I have already indicated in chapters 2 and 3. In chapter 3 I cited, and cite again here, a passage from the early rabbinic document, Avot

---

4. See Goodblatt, *Rabbinic Institutions*; Rubenstein, "Social and Institutional," 58–74.

de Rabbi Nathan, version a (AVRNa). AVRNa is text containing materials that may be characterized as Tosefta-like commentary and supplements to Tractate Avot, itself a (likely)mid-third-century addition to Mishnah that extols the values of Torah study and rabbinic discipleship. Quoting verbatim and elaborating upon a passage of Avot (the part in boldface), AVRNa 8:1[5] proceeds to remark upon the core early rabbinic curriculum.

AVRNa 8:1:

> F. Joshua b. Perahiah and Nithai the Arbelite received [the transmitted Torah] from them.
>
> G. Joshua b. Perahiah says,
>
>> 1. "Appoint for yourself a rabbinic master [as a teacher] (*rav*);
>> 2. "and acquire for yourself an associate [with whom to study];
>> 3. "and judge every person as meritorious [on balance, that is, give everyone the benefit of the doubt]."
>
> H. "Appoint for yourself a rabbinic master." How so?
>
> I. This teaches that one should appoint for oneself a rabbinic master [that is, one should not flit from one rabbinic master to another] [with whom to study on a] regular basis.
>
> J. And one should learn from him scripture, and mishnah, and legal midrash, and aggadot [that latter being edifying tales about/from the rabbis].[6]

---

5. The translation of AVRNa 8:1 is my own, taken from Lightstone, "Textual Study and Social Formation: The Case," 26.

6. The dating of Avot de Rabbi Nathan (AVRN) has been much disputed by modern scholarship. A century ago, the scholarly consensus was that the AVRN was compiled sometime in the seventh to ninth centuries CE. In the early 1970s, Anthony J. Saldarini undertook a careful comparison of the two recensions of AVRN and Avot. He concluded that in all probability early versions of AVRN, likely circulating in oral form, were almost contemporaneous with early versions of Avot, dating from near (or perhaps just prior to) the time of Mishnah's authoritative composition at the turn of the third century CE. Saldarini also points out that all recensions of AVRN take pains to attribute traditions to rabbinic authorities contemporaneous with Mishnaic sages (tannaim), save for three exceptions that prove the rule. One must be cautious in drawing conclusions from the latter observation, because of a penchant for anachronistic attribution to earlier authorities in rabbinic literature. My own view is that in its earliest version(s) AVRN likely predates the authoring of the Palestinian Talmud sometime in the early fifth century, and so sits in the period bounded by Avot in the mid-third century and the Palestinian Talmud. See Saldarini, *Fathers*, 1–16.

In the Seat of Moses

For AVRNa 8:1, only the study of Scripture itself ranks higher than Mishnah study, followed by legal (i.e., Halakhic) midrash, which, as you know, attempts to (re)establish the link between Mishnah-like legal dicta and Scripture. Similar in ethos to AVRNa 8:1 is an (alleged) *baraita* passage (without any parallel in Tosefta) in the Bavli, at b. Baba Metzia 33a, that I also cited in chapter 3.

b. B.M. 33a:

> Our Rabbis taught: Those who occupy themselves [just] with [the study of] Scripture are of limited value; with [the study of] Mishnah [but not of subsequent rabbinic teachings] are certainly of value and will be recompensed [for their study]; with [the study of] Talmud, nothing is of greater value. But always pursue the [study of the] Mishnah more than the [study of] Talmud.[7]

Reflected in this allegedly tannaitic tradition cited in a Bavli composition is an increasingly dominant mode of rabbinic study focused on "Talmud" and, in a gloss of the former sentiment, the (re)assertion that Mishnah study is primary. Clearly, the early rabbinic core curriculum has now expanded, but Mishnah study remains (or in the eyes of the framer, or glossator, of this supposed *Talmud*, should remain) its quintessence. Moreover, several compositions in the Yerushalmi[8] concern the relative positioning in the early rabbinic core curriculum of Scripture, Mishnah, *Talmud*, *ha-tosafot* ("the supplemental" materials) or *ha-tosefet* ("the supplement"). In all instances, Scripture's primacy aside, these latter-mentioned genres of early rabbinic sources seem clearly placed in a context in which they are aids to, modes of, or developments in, Mishnah-study.

Furthermore, the very organization of constituent materials in Tosefta, the Yerushalmi and Bavli, whatever the origins of these materials, attests to their normative use as aids to Mishnah study. Why else organize these substantial *opera* in accordance with the grouping and ordering of Mishnah's

---

7. This is my own translation, taken from Lightstone, "Textual Study and Social Formation: The Case," 27. My translation is influenced by Zaiman, "Traditional Study," 3. Similar views of the place of Mishnah in the early rabbinic core curriculum are expressed in Avot 5:21; but Avot 5:21 together with Avot 6 are generally agreed to be later additions to Avot. In this last regard, see Albeck's commentary in *Shishah*, Seder Neziqim, 380, note 20.

8. See y. Peah 2:4 and its parallel y. Haggigah 1:8, as well as y. Horayot 3:5, which glosses the statement, "Always pursue [the study of] the Mishnah more than the Talmud," the same statement with which the previously-cited, alleged baraita in b. Baba Metzia 33a has been itself glossed.

Final Thoughts

tractates, intermediate "chapters" and individual passages? Moreover, as we have seen in chapters 5, 7, and 8, a significant proportion of these constituent materials, so ordered, are themselves cast as Mishnah commentary, Mishnah complement, or Mishnah analysis. About two-thirds to four-fifths of Tosefta's individual passages either cite and gloss a Mishnah passage or rule-sentence, or substantively extend or topically complete a Mishnah passage. A great many of the Yerushalmi's and Bavli's legal compositions (the literary units woven into these Talmuds' extended composite essays) pose questions concerning Mishnah passages and proceed to address these questions. What is all of this, if not an indication of an evolving, highly valued practice of Mishnah study over a four-hudred-year period?

Finally, as noted in chapters 2 and 3, the production of Mishnah was attributed early on to "Rabbi" Judah the Patriarch, the Roman-supported authority over the administration of Jewish communal affairs in the Land of Israel (and nearby, adjacent territories) in the latter decades of the second century and the first decades of the third. Identifying Judah as Mishnah's architect speaks volumes for the rabbis' regard for Mishnah as their (first) *magnum opus*, notwithstanding that it is not clear what role Judah played in Mishnah's production or promulgation. It seems appropriate to say that Mishnah study was to the nascent rabbinic group what the concept and content of *paideia*, the ideal of learning and the model curriculum, was to the socioeconomic and administrative governing elite of Greco-Roman society. That is, in both cases, such study was meant to bestow upon its practitioners the social status and social authority to lead and to rule, or at least bolster claims to fulfil such roles.[9] To repeat what I stated in chapter 2, "Mishnah . . . imagine[s] rabbis to be *a group of specifically schooled individuals regarded as authoritative consultants to, and agents of, the ruling civil, administrative, judicial and sacerdotal authorities.*"[10]

So now we may reflect on what Mishnah study *demanded* of its devoted students in (antecedent) *knowledge* and *intellectual skills* immediately after Mishnah's promulgation within rabbinic circles as their principal object of study. And we may further inquire about *what types of analyses and questions* were begged when, in the latter third and fourth centuries, Toseftan, Tosefta-like, Halakhic-Midrashic, and other traditions were preserved, collected, and laid beside those specific Mishnah passages for which they came to function as "study aids." And, finally, we may divine

---

9. See, for example, See Goodman, "Texts"; Davies, *Scribes*, 15–36; Bar-Ilan, "Scribes."
10 See page 52 above.

what intellectual skills and traits were modeled and inculcated when, by the turn of the fifth century the basic elements and procedures of what it meant to examine Mishnah "Talmudic-ly" or "Gemar-ic-ly" began to be dominant, as is suggested by the fact that these basic elements and procedures are common to and underpin the compositions of both Talmuds, the Yerushalmi and Bavli—remember, the extant *sugyot* of the JT and BT were produced more or less in their current form largely independently of one another, and some 150 to two hundred years apart, in the Land of Israel and in Mesopotamia respectively. To undertake this inquiry is, as I have intimated, to begin to make claims about some core, shared traits that characterized (at least in part) normative, early rabbinic expertise and, therefore, constituted important elements of rabbis' shared identity and their "profile" as a distinctive group, class, or guild in their social milieu. And the core evidence for such an inquiry is precisely that which you have now acquired by diligently working through chapters 4 through 8 of this book.

And, at the risk of being repetitious, what is the evidence for such an inquiry as the one proposed in the foregoing paragraph? It is no more or less than the basic, most pervasive literary-rhetorical traits of the rabbis' principal legal documents, viewed in light of the *demands* these traits placed on the devoted students who seek fully to understand these texts— that is to understand Mishah in its own right, to understand Mishnah in light of other traditions, such as Tosefta's, rallied to aid in Mishnah's study, and to analyze Mishnah "Talmudic-ly or "Gemara-ic-ly." So, the evidence is closely related to what you, the readers of this volume, have mastered. It is the evidence to which you now have had some initial, introductory exposure, coupled with your "reader experience" of tackling the sample passages presented in the antecedent chapters of this book. In the remainder of this chapter, I shall briefly review those experiences and link them to scholarship that I have undertaken,[11] independently of, but in parallel with, the writing of this volume, on the topic of core components of the shared, group identity and "professional" profile of members of the early rabbinic

---

11. That independent but "parallel" research appears in a trio of essays: (i) Lightstone, "Study as a Socially Formative," a slightly revised version of my "Textual Study and Social Formation." (ii) Lightstone, "When Tosefta," a lightly revised version of Lightstone, "Textual Study and Social Formation: Part II"; (iii) Lightstone, "Studying Mishnah 'Talmudic-ly." This trio of articles, in earlier versions, were written for and presented at the annual meetings of the European Association of Biblical Studies (EABS), which for four years (2015–18) hosted the Research Group called Sociological and Anthropological Approaches to the Study of the Evidence of the Mishnah.

Final Thoughts

"guild." In my bringing together these "parallel" streams, you are about to engage in one example of sociorhetorical approaches to social-historical and sociocultural inquiry, that is, analysis that draws social-historical and social-cultural conclusions from the evidence of pervasive, normative literary-rhetorical patterns and conventions linked to specific groups.

MODES OF MISHNAH-*PAIDEIA* AND THE SHAPING OF EARLY RABBINIC GROUP IDENTITY

As an heuristic division, I provisionally distinguish three different modes—I will not (yet) say "stages"—of Mishnah study.

(1) The devoted, ancient student of Mishnah, together with fellow students and (initially) with their masters, will have had to comprehend Mishnah's text *in its own right*, or to use a metaphor from golf, "play the ball as it lies."

(2) (Perhaps very soon or immediately after its promulgation,) Mishnah studies were furthered or facilitated by the "laying alongside" of Mishnah's passages of other illuminating early rabbinic traditions, so that the former may be contemplated in light of the latter. Tosefta represents such a collection—even if its passages did not constitute the totality of such traditions available as aides to Mishnah study. That Tosefta came to serve Mishnah-study is by far the most parsimonious of propositions about Tosefta's *use* (and perhaps even its intended purpose, given how Tosefta's framers have formulated and organized their materials, that is, "Mishnaic-ly").[12]

Finally, (3) a shared norm evolved about what it meant to study Mishnah "Talmudic-ly" or "Gemara-ic-ly." As we have seen in exemplary passages of the Yerushalmi and Bavli discussed in chapters 7 and 8, this norm proffered particular ways in which "other" topically-related traditions attributed to *tannaim* and *amoraim* were to be brought to bear to address and answer analytic and critical questions about Mishnah, and to "pressure test" those answers by attempting to disprove them. These endeavours to "prove" and "disprove" frequently involved analogical arguments of various types, in many of which the appeal to these other tannaitic and amoraic traditions, or to newly posited circumstances, or to the wording of relevant verses in Scripture were proffered as probative evidence. The resulting

---

12. As I have conveyed in chapters 2, 3, and 5 (see esp. notes 4, 14, 16, and 21 in chapter 5).

compositions, therefore, exhibit the "back-and-forth" rhythm and cadence that is so characteristic of the JT and (even more so) the BT, so much so that perceiving this "back-and-forth" rhythm and cadence becomes an important strategy in the readers' work to decipher Talmudic/Gemaraic compositions. As intimated above, and as seen in working through chapters 7 and 8, the basic structural elements that constituted this normative, "Gemara-ic" approach to Mishnah-analysis are common to both Talmuds, and, therefore, seem to have predated and substantially informed the work of the authorships of the Bavli and Yerushalmi; these norms are evident in a vast majority of the Yerushalmi's and Bavli's compositions.

I cannot, nor need I, assert that these three modes of Mishnah study may historically be so neatly sequenced as my enumeration of them might simplistically be understood to imply. It is clear that mode 3 existed by the time the authorship of the Yerushalmi began their work near the turn of the fifth century in the Land of Israel. And it is equally clear that mode 3 had migrated to Mesopotamian rabbinic circles, apart from (and probably before) the transmission of the Yerushalmi itself to the eastern contingent of the rabbinic movement. In Mesopotamia, mode 3 was further refined and developed by the authorship of the Bavli, working in the sixth and perhaps into the early seventh century. That mode 2 predates mode 3 is a reasonable hypothesis to put forward. As my teacher, Professor Jacob Neusner, has put it, the Tosefta, in a sense, is the Talmud that "might have been,"[13] namely, a gathering, collation, and ordering of "other" early rabbinic, "tannaitic" traditions that came to be placed alongside Mishnah to aid in the latter's study. To what degree modes 1 and 2 represent distinct sequenced stages in Mishnah study is difficult to say. About two-thirds to four-fifths of Tosefta's passages are not fully comprehensible without the corresponding Mishnah passage open beside it to provide an intelligible context. This suggests that these Tosefta passages, *in their current form*,[14] postdate and depend upon their parallel Mishnah passages. In other words, for two-thirds of Tosefta's passages, mode 2 is likely a development of mode 1. So, it is hard to support a claim that mode 2 itself represents the very beginnings of Mishnah study, or that there was no time in the evolution of early-rabbinic *paideia* that the

---

13. Neusner, *Bavli that Might*.

14. I emphasize "in their current form," because I wish to distinguish this claim from the assertion that the content of Toseftan passages is always post-Mishnaic, which may or may not always be the case. That some or many Tosefta passages preserve content that is contemporary with, or even earlier than, their Mishnah parallels is likely, and in a number of instances demonstrable. See above, chapter 5, notes 4, 14, 16, and 21.

Final Thoughts

Mishnah text *as is*, with its specific, characteristic literary-rhetorical traits, had to be confronted and deciphered in devoted Mishnah-study.

The readers of this volume will notice a stark lacuna in the preceding paragraphs. Where in the foregoing are *the* Halakhic Midrashim, the subject of chapter 6. You will remember that in chapter 6 I made the distinction between Halakhic-Midrashic-type passages, with their distinct literary-rhetorical conventions, and a genre of rabbinic literature called *the* Halakhic Midrashim. In the latter, Halakhic-Midrashic passages (some of which appear, as we have seen in chapter 5, among materials in the Tosefta) were collected and ordered "scripturally," that is, in accordance with the order of sections and verses of the books of Exodus through Deuteronomy, to which these passages are topically related. The authorships of the Halakhic Midrashim seem, therefore, to have proffered a corrective element in the developing norms of early-rabbinic, legal *paideia*. For them, the systemic roots of rabbinic Halakha in Scripture must (also?) be systematically explored (or demonstrated) as a sustained exercise attached to the ordered study of Scripture itself. Clearly, the rabbinic circles that developed the "Talmudic/Gemara-ic" approach to early rabbinic, legal *paideia* did not adopt the perspective reflected in *the* Halakhic Midrashim, even while they incorporated individual Halakhic-Midrashic materials into Talmudic/Gemara-ic compositions among the "other," related, early rabbinic traditions routinely brought to bear in Mishnah analysis. The dominant trend reflected in Talmud/Gemara, no doubt, was to continue to focus on Mishnah study, albeit in accordance with the mode-3 norms for its pursuit. In this respect, mode-3-norms resemble the choices made by the authorship of Tosefta to include some Halakhic-Midrashic traditions within their oeuvre ordered in accordance with the organization of subject matter in Mishnah.

Now to the heart of this chapter's topic—What specific shared core competencies seem reflected in, and demanded by, each of mode-1, mode-2, and mode-3 approaches to sustained engagement with the Mishnah text? As I have argued above, answering this question says something significant about the development of a shared, group identity within the early rabbinic movement over an approximately four-hundred-year period, because we know that Mishnah study was among the rabbinic movement's principal, identity-forming activities. And as you will shortly see, answering this question relates to what you will have experienced in working through chapters 4 through 8 of this book.

In the Seat of Moses

Mode-1-Type Skills and Traits: Engagement with Mishnah "As the Ball Lies"[15]

Cast your minds back to the challenges of working through chapter 4, where you confronted core, pervasive literary-rhetorical traits of Mishnah. Remember, for example, the first sample Mishnah passage presented there, m. Bekhorot 1:1a, the opening passage of the Mishnah tractate concerning "firstlings," males born to Israelite women or to the dames of domestic animals that have never before given birth to offspring. Below, again, are two versions of that Mishnah passage.[16] The first is my translation without any interpolations to fill in the missing information that makes this passage intelligible. The second includes such interpolations.

m. Bekhorot 1:1a (as is, without interpolations)

1. He who purchases the foetus of an ass of a Gentile,
2. And he who sell to him,
3. Even though it is not permitted.
4. And he who forms a partnership with him,
5. And he who receives from him,
6. And he who gives to him in trust—
7. is exempt from the law of the firstling,
8. as it is said, "Of an Israelite" (Numbers 3:13),
9. but not of others.

m. Bek. 1:1a (with my interpolations)

1. He [an Israelite] who purchases the foetus of an ass of a Gentile [, and the foetus, when born, if it turns out to be male, will be a firstborn of the ass owned by the Gentile],
2. And he [an Israelite] who sells to him [, the Gentile, the foetus of an ass of the Israelite, and the foetus, when born, if it turns out to be male, will be the firstborn of the ass owned by the Israelite],
3. Even though it is not permitted [for an Israelite to contract such a sale to a Gentile].

---

15. The content of the section that follows stems from my research and analyses in Lightstone "Textual Study and Social Formation."
16. Cited from Lightstone, "Textual Study and Social Formation," 31–32.

Final Thoughts

4. And he [an Israelite] who forms a partnership with him [the Gentile, so that they co-own the foetus of an ass owned by either the Gentile or the Israelite, and, subsequently, when the foetus is born, it is both male and a firstborn of the ass],

5. And he [an Israelite] who receives [a pregnant ass] from him [a Gentile, and, subsequently, when the foetus is born, it is both male and a firstborn of the ass],

6. And he [an Israelite] who gives [a pregnant ass] to him [a Gentile,] in trust [and, subsequently, when the foetus is born, it is both male and a firstborn of the ass]—

7. [in all of the foregoing cases, the foetus, when born] is exempt from the law of the firstling [of unclean species as enjoined in the biblical Scriptures].

8. as it is said, "Of an Israelite" (Numbers 3:13),

9. but not of others.

Permit me three observations about this passage, all of which are characteristic of Mishnah's basic, pervasive literary-rhetorical traits and conventions, and all of which should be familiar to you from your having worked through chapter 4.

First, the contrast between my two versions highlights how much information is typically missing from Mishnaic rule-sentences. This missing information is essential to understand what precise circumstances constitute the cases for which Mishnah provides rulings. The autonomous reader of Mishnah must be able to supply that missing content. As a corollary, the logic of the ruling(s) cannot be understood, unless the circumstances of the case(s) in question can be fully articulated. And, surely, discerning and contemplating that logic must be part and parcel of devoted engagement in Mishnah study, else why study Mishnah at all?

Second, the citation at the end of m. Bekhorot 1:1a of the snippet of Scripture (at Numbers 3:13) as a "proof-text" for the ruling does little or nothing to mitigate another essential lacuna that must be addressed to understand this Mishnah passage, which, after all, is the very opening passage of the first "chapter" of Tractate Bekhorot (concerning the sanctity of first-born males). That lacuna is this: that a substantial body of scriptural, sacerdotal law stands behind the opening passage of this Mishnah tractate.[17]

---

17. Scriptural law concerning the firstling appears in Exodus 12:2, 11–13; 22:28–19;

That law is never rehearsed or summarized in the Mishnah. But m. Bekhorot 1:1a cannot be understood without knowledge of that scriptural law. The fact is that Scripture's laws stand behind much of Mishnah's tractates, but, similarly, is rarely rehearsed, summarized, or even referenced. Nevertheless, thorough knowledge of that scriptural law is essential to understanding Mishnah at very many junctures.

Third, at many junctures in Mishnah, other unstated and unspecified, legal principles, appearing neither in Mishnah nor in Scripture, logically underlie Mishnah passages. In the case of m. Bekhorot 1:1a, it is assumed, but not stated, that the law of the gift of the firstling of "unclean species" of domestic beasts applies to donkeys only, and to no other unclean domestic species.

To summarize so far, as illustrated by the example provided at m. Bekhorot 1:1a—Mishnah's highly laconic literary-rhetorical style demands of its devoted student (i) the rational-logical intellectual engagement to fill in the facts of the case in light of the rulings given, so that (ii) the rulings and circumstances ruled upon make sense in light of one another, (iii) all within some more encompassing system of rabbinic legal principles and antecedent law, much of which is in Scripture and much of which is unstated, and little or nothing of which is actually provided in Mishnah. These are demands placed on the Mishnah student that require a certain array of intellectual skills, on the one hand, and the acquisition of antecedent knowledge, on the other. And so we may posit that the acquisition of this knowledge and the honing of these intellectual skills (a) formed an important part of early rabbinic *paideia* and, therefore, (b) constituted some significant part of early rabbinic group identity, because of the privileged place of devoted Mishnah study in the within-group "life" of the early-rabbinic movement.

Two other closely related literary-rhetorical traits of Mishnah's passages further ramify the claims of the preceding paragraph. These traits too were illustrated and discussed in chapter 4. First, you will remember our observation that many Mishnah passages have a decided penchant for spinning out lists of hypothetical cases by systematically varying two or more circumstances that together comprise the cases to be ruled upon. The following schematization illustrates this.

Circumstance a + circumstance b + circumstance c + ruling x;

Circumstance not a + circumstance b + circumstance c; or

34: 19–20; Leviticus 27:26; Numbers 3:13; 18:15–18; Deuteronomy 14:23; 15:19–23.

Final Thoughts

Circumstance not *a* + circumstance not *b* + circumstance *c* + ruling not *x*;

Circumstance not *a* + circumstance not *b* + circumstance not *c* + ruling *x*.

A Mishnah passage so structured could go on to permute all possible combinations of circumstances *a*, *b*, and *c*, each permuted combination comprising a different case for which a ruling *x* or not *x* is provided. For each such case, the engaged student of the passage must contemplate why each variation of the constituent circumstances matters, such that one rule or its opposite is appropriate.

An example of such a Mishnah passage is m. Bekhorot 1:3–4a, also presented in chapter 4's discussions of Mishnah's pervasive literary-rhetorical norms. Here, once more, is that chapter's presentation of the passage, without interpolations, so that its full rhythm and cadence are evident as hypothetical circumstances are varied and permuted. In the translation, "which"(*she*), "and"(*ve*) and "or"(*o*) are **boldfaced**, to highlight their concatenating-permutative function; these terms join the circumstances that comprise each case or category of cases.

m. Bekhorot 1:3–4a (without interpolations)[18]

1:3

    1. An ass **which** had not given birth **and** bore two males—

    2. one gives a single lamb to the priest.

    3. Male **and** female—

    4. one separates a single lamb for himself.

    5. Two asses **which** had not given birth **and** bore two males—

    6. one gives two lambs to the priest.

    7. A male **and** a female **or** two males **and** a female—

    8. one gives a single lamb to the priest.

    9. Two females **and** one male, **or** two males **and** two females—

    10. there is nothing here for the priest.

1:4a

    11. One gave birth, **and** one **which** had not given birth, **and** they bore two males—

---

18. Translation my own, based on Lightstone, *Rhetoric*, 178–80; and Lightstone, "Textual Study and Social Formation," 33–34.

In the Seat of Moses

12. one gives a single lamb to the priest.

13. A male **and** female—

14. one separates a single lamb for himself.

I draw a particular conclusion from the many Mishnah passages, like this one, that spin out cases by systematically varying the concatenated circumstances. Namely, that Mishnah at these many junctures demonstrates that its purpose is not to preserve case law, or to proffer a law code, but to provide an intellectual, legal exercise of sorts, driven by the contemplation of closely related, but yet distinctively different, hypothetical cases. The Mishnah student will necessarily have to consider why the ruling given is appropriate in each case. For some of these cases the "why" is, frankly, entirely self-evident and pedestrian, for others more careful analysis of the "why" is demanded. Passages such as these reinforce, in my mind, the claims I made above that Mishnah demands of its students a type of rational-logical, intellectual engagement to discern how the rulings and the circumstances ruled upon make sense in light of one another—now as regards a series of related cases of varied circumstances. Turn the kaleidoscope of circumstances a quarter turn. Does the same rule still apply or not, and why?

The second frequently-encountered, literary-rhetorical construct in Mishnah that further reinforces the foregoing claims is the Mishnaic "dispute." Again, in chapter 4 you have seen several versions of the dispute form. I need refer here to only one of these variations to make my point. However, any of the dispute form's variations would equally have done the job for my purposes in this discussion. Here is my schematization of one type of typically structured dispute in Mishnah:

–circumstances comprising case + ruling;

–rabbi *x* says + opposite ruling.

Such disputes are unlikely to be minutes of discussions among rabbinic masters who disagreed about a case. They are simply too contrived and stylized to be so.[19] The circumstances and rulings in disputes are all couched in the same type of laconic language in accordance with the same literary-rhetorical conventions as are evident in other rule-sentences and passages in Mishnah. *Even if* some historical tradition of some particular rabbi's dissenting view might, in some fashion, lie behind disputes, that

---

19. I have discussed and referenced the scholarship on this point in Lightstone, "Naming Names."

historical tradition is unlikely to have been cast in the language reflected in Mishnah, and neither will the language of that part of any antecedent, alleged historical tradition that articulates the case upon which the rabbinic authority is "remembered" to have ruled in such-and-such a way.

So, what is the effect for the intellectually-engaged Mishnah student of providing these rhetorically-constituted disputes? What they effect in the process of Mishnah-study is the contemplation of how and why each of the two opposing rulings for the same posited case may be apt. How is it the case that the posited circumstances may be so classified in law such that one of the rulings is appropriate, and then reclassified in law so that the opposite ruling is appropriate? Again devoted engagement with the Mishnah is all about examining the basis for classifying hypothetical cases defined by the collation of posited circumstances. Is the case to be classified in this way, so that one rule applies, or is it to be classified in that way, so that the opposite ruling applies? And what are the rationales for such classifications?[20]

To conclude, engagement with the Mishnah text as it is—"as the ball lies"—invites, demands, and inculcates rational analysis of complex circumstances precisely in order *to then classify* them in law. The engaged Mishnah student is invited to discern whether and why cases, each defined by a set of circumstances, are to be placed in one pigeon-hole, to which law *x* applied, or in a different pigeon-hole, in which case law *x* does not apply or law *y* does. This analytic skill of discerning the reason for classifying cases one way or the other is made all the more intellectually engaging by having to "fill in" Mishnah's often laconic presentation of the circumstances of cases—the missing bits that I have interpolated into my translations of sample Mishnah passages. This acumen for the classification of closely related cases would seem to have been a core professional skill and preoccupation of the members of the early rabbinic guild, a skill reflected in, and modelled and inculcated by, Mishnah study. To this one may add, the acquisition of a comprehensive knowledge of Scriptural law and of a body of legal principles and legal teachings that function as the premises of Mishnah's treatment of matters, but are infrequently, and in some cases never, explicitly or fully articulated.

None of these skills and none of this knowledge is acquired *in utero*, although some persons may be more naturally endowed with the intellectual

---

20. I have more fully discussed this effect of disputes on engagement with the Mishnah text in Lightstone, "Naming Names."

capacity to acquire and to hone them than others. So the evidence of Mishnah's most pervasive literary rhetorical traits bespeaks a social formation, a group, in which these traits and knowledge are particularly valued and nurtured by some organized, institutionalized means. Welcome to glimpsing the institutionalized, early rabbinic circles among whom Mishnah was first produced, promulgated, and studied—in mode-1 of devoted engagement in Mishnah-*paideia*.

Mode-2-Type Skills and Traits: Engagement with Mishnah "Tosefta-ic-ly"[21]

You will remember that in working through chapter 5 on Tosefta, almost everything that you learned about Mishnah's literary-rhetorical traits and constructs could be applied to the deciphering of Tosefta's passages. Tosefta's passages were quite Mishnah-like. In Toseftan materials, rule-sentences, disputes, debates and precedent stories all appeared to be little different than similar literary-rhetorical constructs in Mishnah. But Tosefta passages do, nonetheless, evince important differences when compared to Mishnah. Tosefta seems to have a greater penchant than Mishnah for attributing rulings to named rabbinic masters. Tosefta makes greater use of the dispute form, in which of course, the names of rabbinic authorities must appear. Or Tosefta will supply the name of one of the disputing parties where Mishnah has anonymous "sages" disputing an individual named master's ruling. Tosefta will often proffer a "debate" for a Mishnaic dispute, where Mishnah has only a dispute. There are more precedent stories in Tosefta than Mishnah. In a number of passages, Tosefta will "redirect" a Mishnaic dispute: rabbi x and rabbi y did not dispute case a (as they appear to do in Mishnah), concerning which they agree that the law is z, but rather they disputed case a', concerning which rabbi x rules that the law is z, and rabbi y rules that the law is not z.

Many Tosefta passages appear either to cite and expand upon the corresponding passages in Mishnah, or "complete" and "complement" the parallel passage in Mishnah. As noted earlier, these latter two types of Toseftan materials amount to about two-thirds to four-fifths of Tosefta's content. And such passages often cannot be *fully* understood on their own, because they rely to a greater or lesser degree upon the corresponding Mishnah

---

21. The content of the section that follows stems from my research and analyses in Lightstone, "When Tosefta."

passages for context. The other third (or less) of Tosefta's passages topically supplement Mishnah 's treatment of subjects.

If one takes these observations and adds to them that "our" Tosefta has organized and ordered its materials in accordance with the order of corresponding topics and passages in Mishnah's tractates and "chapters," then it is evident both *that and why* Tosefta's materials (and other Toseftan-like materials) *came to be used* in late antiquity as an aid to Mishnah study.[22] This is further confirmed in mode-3 Mishnah study, that is, the "Talmudic"/"Gemara-ic" study of Mishnah. How so? In chapters 8 and 9, we saw that the underlying literary-rhetorical norms for both Yerushalmi's and Bavli's compositions analyzing Mishnah passages involved, among other things, the collating of "other" relevant, authoritative sources, including Toseftan and Tosefta-like materials, within a framework of posing questions and addressing them. In this sense, mode-3 engagement with Mishnah "Talmudic-ly/Gemara-ic-ly" seems to have assimilated and transformed mode-2 engagement with Mishnah "tosefta-ic-ly," to coin yet another neologism.

How, then, will mode-2 engagement with Mishnah "tosefta-ic-ly" have differed from mode-1 engagement of Mishnah "as the ball lies"? Will the former have simply further reinforced those skills and the evident need for prerequisite knowledge demanded by the latter? Or will engagement with Mishnah "tosefta-ic-ly" have induced in the engaged Mishnah-student other alternative or additional demands and skills? My response to these questions is a bit complex, and comes in three parts.

First, because much of Tosefta's materials are so Mishnah-like in terms of their literary-rhetorical traits and conventions, the study of Mishnah together with the study of correlative Tosefta passages involves similar intellectual engagement, skills and background knowledge. However, second, when a Tosefta passage in effect serves to comment upon, interpret, or supplies additional information for understanding its corresponding Mishnah passage, Tosefta is "doing some of the work" that would otherwise

---

22. I make this assertion without necessarily intending to beg the question of where Tosefta's materials, or the content for Tosefta's materials, came from. See above, chapter 5, notes 4, 14, 16, and 21, for my views in this topic and for a sampling of the more recent published scholarship on these matters. Furthermore, as stated earlier, passages in the Yerushalmi that remark upon normative rabbinic curriculum of study prescribe along with the study of Mishnah the examination of *ha-tosefet* or *ha-tosafot*; see y. Peah 2:4 and its parallel y. Haggigah 1:8, as well as y. Horayot 3:5. *Ha-tosefet*, which Neusner chooses to translate as "the Supplement," is the exact Hebrew lexical and morphological equivalent of the Aramaic title of "our" document, *Tosefta*: See Neusner, *Yerushalmi*, 130.

be required when engaging Mishnah in mode-1 study, that is, on Mishnah's own terms. One might say that in such instances of viewing Tosefta's use as an aid to Mishnah study, Tosefta is "showing the way" one might proceed, and is easing the burden somewhat in the process. That is why, many years ago, my doctoral dissertation supervisor, Professor Jacob Neusner, counseled me, rightly or wrongly, to always read Mishnah with the corresponding chapter of Tosefta in hand. I say "rightly," because it helped to do so, and "wrongly," because it prejudiced my reading and analysis of Mishnah the way any "commentary" might.[23] Commentaries often have agendas of their own that they impose upon the text commented upon. And so, at times, does Tosefta.[24]

The third part of my response is more subtle. Juxtaposing topically (and often literarily) related passages from Tosefta and Mishnah will, in a number of instances, have facilitated the posing and answering of very different types of analytic questions about Mishnah passages than might otherwise have been the case. One may say that with such juxtaposition of passages, specific types of questions are routinely begged. Such analytic questions are about the text of the Mishnah and its underlying tradition history, which is not always the same as pondering the logic of its classification of hypothetical cases. For example, when Tosefta presents a rule-sentence and attributes it to a named master, where Mishnah's "parallel" rule-sentence is presented anonymously, the question is begged: Is/was the rabbinic master in Tosefta the authority behind Mishnah's rule? In other words, one is induced by the Tosefta passage to engage in a sort of "historical" source-criticism of the Mishnah passage. Again, this is a very different exercise and preoccupation than pondering the logic of the classification of things effected by the Mishnaic ruling being what it is said to be. If one, consequently, posits that Tosefta's named authority is the source of Mishnah's rule, then a further question might be begged: Does Mishnah's ruling here in this case cohere with rulings attributed to this rabbinic master that appear elsewhere in Mishnah on other cases? Now we are beginning to *test* in some fashion the hypothesis, based on Tosefta's additional information, about the origins of Mishnah's ruling. Once more, the ground of the

23. In this vein, Neusner followed his own counsel when he undertook his monumental twenty-two-volume opus, *History of Mishnaic Law*. Each Mishnah passage of each tractate of the Order of Purities is discussed by Neusner together with its correlative Tosefta passages.

24. A point that Professor Fishbane of Touro College and University Systems in New York has often made in conversation with me.

Final Thoughts

skills demanded by the engaged Mishnah student is shifting or expanding beyond those inherent in mode-1 engagement with Mishnah. And, again, when Tosefta "redirects" a dispute in Mishnah—rabbi x and rabbi y did not dispute case a (as they appear to do in Mishnah), concerning which they agree that the law is z, but rather they disputed case a', concerning which rabbi x rules that the law is z, and rabbi y rules that the law is not z—another analytic question about Mishnah is begged and answered by Tosefta's passage at one and the same time. How so? On what basis can case a be classified first to make rabbi x's ruling appropriate and then be reclassified to make rabbi y's opposing ruling appropriate? According to the "redirected" Toseftan dispute, it cannot, so the opposing rulings are transferred to a slightly different set of circumstances, case a'. This, of course, begs for the question to be reposed about case a'.

Let me go further still in this vein by having us together engage in a little "thought experiment." This "thought experiment"[25] will look astonishingly familiar from your having worked through chapters 8 and 9 of this volume. Here it goes!

Let us imagine a Tosefta passage used as an aid in the study of an imagined Mishnah passage. Our imaginary Mishnah passage states:

> Circumstances comprising case a;
>
> rabbi x permits;
>
> and rabbi y forbids.

And the correlative, imagined Tosefta passage reads:

> Circumstances comprising case a;
>
> rabbi x permits;
>
> and rabbi y forbids,
>
> because of z.

Viewed as an aid to Mishnah study, imaginary Tosefta cites and glosses imaginary Mishnah, adding reason z to y's ruling. Several questions might now be begged in the engaged student's mind. For example, the Tosefta is seen to answer the unstated question,

> *What is the reason that rabbi y forbids in our Mishnah passage?*

---

25. This "thought experiment" in the next several paragraphs is almost unchanged from my essay, Lightstone, "Studying Mishnah 'Talmudic-ly.'"

But that is not the end of the matter. A second obvious question begged is,

So, what is the reason that rabbi x permits?

And two more questions are drawn in the wake of these two.

Why would rabbi x not see the validity of rabbi y's reason?
And why would rabbi y not see the validity of rabbi x's reason?

If, furthermore, our imagined Tosefta passage were to have continued with a typical Mishnaic-Toseftan "debate"—

He [y] said to him [x] + reason/argument countering *x*'s ruling,

He [x] said to him [y] + reason/argument countering *y*'s ruling—

then the "debate" would not only beg the questions at hand as articulated above, but also will have supplied partial answers.

What both our "thought experiment" and the paragraphs that preceded it show is that given the tendency of Tosefta at various junctures to supply (relatively speaking) more information, more names, more disputes, more debates, and more precedent stories where the correlative Mishnah passages have few or none of these, the use of Tosefta as an aid to Mishnah study induces and steers towards certain types of questions and analyses that may not otherwise readily arise within mode-1 study. Mode-1 study, as I suggested earlier, consistently induces the examination of Mishnah's systems of classification of things through the contemplation of hypothetical cases. Mode-2, "Tosefta-ic" study of Mishnah does so too, and *additionally* permits and therefore, promotes, a type of source-analysis and critical-tradition-history of "parallel" Mishnah passages.

Mode-3-Type Skills and Traits: Engagement with Mishnah "Talmudic-ly/Gemara-ic-ly"[26]

The foregoing thought experiment also suggests how mode-2 study of Mishnah "tosefta-ic-ly" may have morphed into mode-3, "Talmudic/Gemara-ic" engagement with Mishnah sometime before the turn of the fifth century, when the production of the Yerushalmi was probably underway or complete in the Land of Israel. For anyone familiar with Yerushalmi's or Bavli's legal compositions, as you have become from reading chapters 7 and

---

26. The content of the section that follows stems from my research and analyses in Lightstone, "Studying Mishnah 'Talmudic-ly."

8, it is easy to see how our thought experiment would lead one to generate a typical, albeit short, Talmudic composition concerning the Mishnah passage at hand, *if one made explicit* the queries begged by the juxtaposition of our imagined Mishnaic and Toseftan passages, and then cited the latter in support of the responses to those queries about the former. One need only add some "pressure testing" of some answers and supporting arguments (by attempting to prove some of the answers to be wrong, and then trying to disprove the disproof, etc.), and one would have an immediately recognizable exemplar of its literary genre, *Gemara*. All one would need to do to create such a typically Gemara-ic composition is to use the appropriate, stock-formulaic language for Bavli's or Yerushalmi's articulation of questions, objections, analyses and arguments, answers, and for citing authoritative sources in the process. In other words, there is a line of continuity joining the use of Tosefta and/or Tosefta-like passages as aids to Mishnah study, on the one hand, and, on the other, the structuring of Talmudic compositions in the Yerushalmi or Bavli, where formalized questions about, and invitations for analysis of, Mishnah engender arguments in support of which other tannaitic and amoraic traditions are adduced. As stressed numerous times, and rightly so, the Talmudic/Gemara-ic-mode-3 composition will then often proceed to try to disprove the answer proffered to its questions, repose the question, and proffer alternative answers—themselves to be "pressure tested" by attempted disproof.[27] Where Bavli and Yerushalmi will frequently differ is in the former's tendency to disprove, if it can, all posited solutions, leaving no answer standing. Moreover, as we have seen in chapter 8, a Bavli *sugya* brings together in its extended composite essays, compositions treating the Mishnah passage at hand or part thereof, as well as compositions treating other topically relevant tannaitic or amoraic teachings, which a Bavli composition will then analyze just as it would have a Mishnah text. In so doing, Bavli demonstrates that mode-3 analyses may also be extended to traditions, subjects, and legal principles beyond those arising within the Mishnah passage proper. Within each composition of the extended composite *sugya*, the "back and forth cadence"—argument and counterargument, the adducing of evidence and counterevidence from cited tannaitic and amoraic traditions, and proof, disproof, disproof of the disproof—will often be signposted with stock formulaic indicators, but

---

27. I am grateful here for Daniel Boyarin's characterization of what I have called "pressure testing." He gracefully spent time in conversation with me concerning the distinguishing traits of Bavli *vs.* Yerushalmi when we sat down together in Berkeley, California, in April 2018.

sometimes not fully signposted. The latter instances especially demand of the engaged reader *the capacity to construct for oneself* the "back-and-forth" of the arguments and counterarguments by reading forwards and backwards, and forwards again, using the emerging and deepening perception of the logic of the arguments and counterarguments to discern an emerging structure of the composition in its posing of questions, its proffering of answers and its "pressure testing" of the latter.

Have we come in mode-3-type study of Mishnah a long way from mode-1? In some senses no, and in other senses yes indeed. The analytic and critical contemplation in mode-1 Mishnah-study of how complex sets of circumstances are to be classified, such that one rule and not another applies, still preoccupies a significant portion of many compositions of the BT and JT. But so many more preoccupations also are brought to bear in the Gemara-ic/Talmudic study of Mishnah. So many other questions are asked and addressed, and, therefore, so are many more types of arguments and counterarguments, beyond those that try to establish whether this case to which one rule applies is significantly similar to, or different than, that case. Earlier in this chapter, I argued that because of the enduring place of Mishnah study as perhaps *the* quintessential inner-group activity in early rabbinic circles from c. 200 CE to c. 600 CE, the demands and skills required in Mishnah study will have significantly modeled and shaped core traits of the rabbis as individuals and as a group. In other words, Mishnah study helped shape important aspects of their shared identity. Let me try, then, in the last section of this final chapter to characterize how change in, and development of, some key, requisite rabbinic-professional skills in the transition from mode-1, through mode-2, to mode-3 Mishnah study may have helped shape and reshape early rabbinic, group identity. We will start with the end-point, the Gemara-ic/Talmudic study of Mishnah and consider it in light of the study of Mishnah "as is" or "as the ball lies" or the study of Mishnah "tosefta-ic-ly."

Final Thoughts

BRINGING IT ALL TOGETHER: FROM MISHNAH TO THE BAVLI—THE TRANSFORMATION OF EARLY RABBINIC *PAIDEIA* AND THE EVOLUTION OF EARLY-RABBINIC, CORE, IDENTITY-INFORMING TRAITS AND SKILLS, C. 200 CE TO C. 600 CE[28]

What do the basic, core overarching traits of the two Talmuds, articulated and illustrated in chapters 7 and 8, and framed again in this chapter as mode-3 Mishnah study, suggest about the evolving meaning and impact of Mishnah study in forming core, shared identity traits in the early rabbinic guild centuries after Mishnah's initial promulgation within rabbinic circles as an authoritative text? First, that both Talmuds were organized "Mishnaic-ly" attests to the continuing status of Mishnah study centuries after Mishnah's promulgation, an argument I made earlier in this chapter.

Second, in both Talmuds, the study of Tosefta and Tosefta-like passages, and Halakhic Midrashim is presented as having little significant value in their own right. All are, formally speaking, adduced in the process of Mishnah analysis, together with similar traditions attributed to *amora'im*. This claim must be qualified for the Bavli, a point to which I will return. On the other hand, third, all of these extra-Mishnaic, legal traditions warranted preservation and consideration, and their content must be, in some sense, harmonized with Mishnah's in a process exploring their significance for Mishnah's meaning and their intersection with one another and with Mishnah.

The aforementioned points, singly and together, are important. Why? Because it could well have been different. There is no historical inevitability within rabbinic culture that all other tannaitic and amoraic sources should be marshalled *Gemara*-ic-ly in the effort to discuss Mishnah. The Halakhic midrashists, for example, with their very different conception of the place of Scripture in Halakhic discourse, could have won the day, and one or both "Talmuds" might have been organized "scripturally" rather than "Mishnaic-ly." Or turn-of-the-fifth-century rabbis in the Galilee and turn-of-the-seventh-century rabbis of Babylonia might have anticipated Maimonides' Mishneh Torah. In the twelfth century, Maimonides produced a "new Mishnah" that was a true law code that in effect arbitrated among Mishnah,

---

28. This final section largely reproduces, with some alterations, the final section Lightstone, "Studying Mishnah 'Talmudic-ly.'"

In the Seat of Moses

all tannaitic and amoraic legal traditions, and early medieval interpretations of these to produce a unitary, intended-to-be-comprehensive, legal system and law code. If early rabbis in late antiquity had done something similar, then they may then have made such a code the primary object of rabbinic study and its mastery the hallmark of being a rabbi.[29] But none of this happened, and the most likely reason that it did not is that Mishnah study continued (formally) to occupy the place of privilege in rabbinic inner-group pursuits.

Fourth, as suggested in chapters 7 and 8 (and stated outright earlier in this chapter), the authors of both Talmuds, working largely independently with many common sources, nonetheless seemed to have worked within a prior (necessarily late fourth-century) normative definition of what counted as *Gemara*.[30] Mishnah study, as *the* central core activity, was to be undertaken within this "*Gemara*-ic" template.[31] The basic recipe is straightforward:

(i) one organizes matters around Mishnah texts, taken in order, by tractate, "chapter" and Mishnah passage;

(ii) one musters tannaitic and amoraic traditions that complement, comment upon, or topically supplement the Mishnah passage at hand;

(iii) *on their basis*, one formulates questions about, and identifies issues seemingly begging for critical analysis in, the Mishnah passage;

---

29. Maimonides, in his introduction to the Mishneh Torah, indelicately and injudiciously suggested that his Mishneh Torah should largely supplant study of the Bavli, in order to free up rabbis' time to study philosophy, which for Maimonides was a higher calling. The Maimonidean controversy took about a century to dissipate.

30. The notion that a "*Gemara*-ic" norm developed for studying Mishnah prior to that norm informing the production of the Talmuds is strongly suggested by (a) this book's demonstration that both Talmuds reflect the very same basic structural template for creating Talmud-compositions, and (b) the view of some scholars that these two Talmuds' compositions were created largely independently of one another, even though their authorships shared a common pool of sources. This notion also finds some echo in rabbinic traditions that talk about Talmudic study that patently predate the production of "our" Talmuds. Take again, for example, the alleged *baraita* (without any parallel to my knowledge in Tosefta) at b. BM 33a, cited earlier in this chapter.

31. Among modern scholars, I would credit David Weiss Halivni as the first clearly to state that Talmudic compositions are a literary genre. See Halivni, *Midrash*. By the early 1990s, Jacob Neusner's significant research on Bavli compositions and composites began to appear.

and (iv) one proceeds to create answers and arguments, together with "pressure-testing" challenges and counterarguments (i.e., attempted "dis-proofs") that address these questions using the ancillary sources at hand.

To repeat my earlier question—Are the core, identity-forming, skills and knowledge entailed in devoted, mode-3 Mishnah study (done "*Gemara*-ic-ly") the same, similar, or quite different from those demanded by devoted, mode-1 Mishnah study undertaken with just or primarily the traits of the Mishnah text before one? I have already suggested that the answer to this question was both yes and no. By this I meant that some requisite skills carry forward to the *Gemara*-ic study of Mishnah, some do but are mitigated by what *Gemara* does, and some are new, augmented or modified. Now, let me say more by briefly cataloguing these skills and requisites.

Knowledge of scriptural law and of postscriptural but pre-Mishnaic law largely remains as a requisite. But when other relevant tannaitic and amoraic sources are amassed in accordance with the *Gemara*-ic recipe, some of this knowledge gap may be filled in for one, just as many Tosefta passages do when used as aids to Mishnah study. But by the same token, since we now suspect that the core model for treating Mishnah *Gemara*-ic-ly predates both the Yerushalmi and the Bavli, the student of Mishnah processing Mishnah *Gemara*-ic-ly before our Talmudic compositions were produced must already have become conversant with these other sources, or have had recourse to a master who does. One requisite is made easier; but another, perhaps equally demanding one is demanded of the Mishnah student. So more must be learned, not less, by way of antecedent knowledge of a rich legal tradition.

As we argued, Mishnah study, done "straight up" (a) requires one to fill in the circumstances of the hypothetical cases so that they are complete, and so that the ruling or rulings which follow them, make sense. In a closely related vein, (b) when Mishnah varies circumstances, producing a string of closely related cases, followed by, or punctuated along the way with, rulings, the Mishnah student understands the question that begs exploration to be: Why should these changes in the circumstances matter and how? When (c) there are opposing rulings in Mishnah to the same set of posited circumstances, as in a Mishnaic dispute, the Mishnah student is implicitly invited to ask: Why might the two disputants rule differently? This triad of required skills is part and parcel of what I call advanced abilities to classify closely related things; such taxonomic thinking is demanded by Mishnah study in order to understand why one rule is appropriate in one instance, but not in another seemingly closely related instance.

All three of these intellectual enterprises, regularly demanded *implicitly* when contemplating Mishnah passages, are among the questions routinely and often *explicitly* posed in a *Gemara* composition. Except that the collected, relevant tannaitic, Halakhic-Midrashic, and amoraic sources that are the raw materials for *Gemara*-ic examination of a Mishnah passage may be read as some ready-made answers to such questions. This is, to my mind, a significant shift in the identity-forming skill-set for members of the rabbinic group. Because now the Mishnah student is not necessarily reasoning from the direct confrontation with the Mishnah text, but *"reading backwards"* from the collected, relevant "secondary" sources. This is a different skill, because it involves at its core the "harmonization" of collated sources brought into relation with one another and with Mishnah. It is a skill-set that may have had a preparatory transitional phase, as we have argued earlier, when Toseftan materials were place alongside their "parallel" Mishnah passages to aid in the latters' study. Implicitly, this placing things alongside one another begged certain new questions, such as whether the named authority in a Tosefta passage is the source of the anonymous ruling in the Mishnah. But studying Mishnah "Gemara-ic-ly," among other things, makes *explicit, normalizes, further develops and routinizes* such source-criticism. Both Yerushalmi and Bavli regularly deploy their respective stock terminology to solicit options for "who taught it [i.e., this Mishnah ruling]" or "whence [this Mishnah ruling]." This is now a fully articulated "source-relating" exercise, rather than (or in addition to) the exercise of taxonomic, high-grid-defining skills engendered by Mishnah study.

As we have seen, an important element of the *Gemara*-template is "pressure testing" the validity of answers and arguments by attempting to disprove them. This process of "testing" creates much of the back-and-forth cadence of a *Gemara* composition. As I have remarked several times, the Bavli often takes this much further than the Yerushalmi and without necessarily needing a probative conclusion, since the Bavli does not hestitate in many instances to disprove all possible solutions to its queries. For Bavli, it is as though the process of spinning out counterarguments was understood to be a "good" in and of itself. Again, this represents the modelling of a different (or additional) skill-requisite, quite unrelated to the goal of rendering Mishnah more intelligible.

Final Thoughts

As shown by our translations of Yerushalmi and Bavli composites in chapters 7 and 8, the (extant) *Gemara* compositions are highly laconic. Their back-and-forth flow of question, answer, argument, challenge, counterargument, counter answer, etc. is often not fully discernable or intelligible without extensive interpolation. The reading of Mishnah texts also requires the capacity to interpolate additional information, usually the "filling in" of the missing bits that are essential factors of the hypothetical case for which Mishnah provides a ruling. That is, *the Mishnah student is completing the taxonomic exercise in which Mishnah is engaged.* These two demands to "in-fill" before a text is intelligible—in the case of Mishnah, on one hand, and in the two Talmuds, on the other—do not really appeal to the same intellectual skills at all. For the Mishnah it is the skill of the taxonomic expert (classifying "objects"), as just mentioned; for the Talmuds, it is the skill of the dialectical expert, that is, the discernment and reconstruction of the back-and-forth, point-and-counterpoint flow of argument. Both are transferable, complementary skills, likely (or intended to be?) transferable to activities and duties outside of the inner-group activities of Mishnah study, whether done "straight up" (mode-1) or now "*Gemara*-ic-ly" (mode-3); but, to repeat myself, they are not at all the same. Moreover, the dialectical expert is one for whom "pressure testing" is also a normative skill and a consummate requirement, again a transferable professional asset to a Jewish-communal world outside that of rabbinic circles or institutions, to whom we know the rabbis sought/hoped "to market" their professional skills.

As I stated in chapters 3 and 8, sometime after the rise of Islam, the study of the Bavli effectively *supplanted* the study of Mishnah as a core, identity-forming activity within rabbinic circles. The skills entailed in Bavli-study then became the valued traits of being a rabbi, and therefore informed shared rabbinic identity and defined valued professional "rabbinic" expertise. The rabbinic identity forged in Mishnah study (*á la* mode 1) slipped away (or was subsumed), and Mishnah study never again occupied a place as the quintessentially rabbinic activity within rabbinic circles. And so, as recounted in chapter 8, many centuries later, we get wealthy Jewish merchants in late eighteenth- and early nineteenth-century Eastern Europe proudly subsidizing the lives of their scholastically gifted sons-in-law and their families so that the sons-in-law may devote their time to the lifelong study of Talmud (that is, Bavli study). And we get a work of fiction, made into a movie, depicting the yearning of an Eastern European

Jewish girl, Yentl, to study Talmud in a still exclusively male *yeshiva* (a Talmudic academy); in order to do so, she disguises herself as a boy. And I remember to this day a short story that I read over forty years ago,[32] in which an anonymous narrator recounts the psychology and thoughts of a recently deceased, long-serving American rabbi of a liberal synagogue-congregation. Among those thoughts were feelings of gross inadequacy. Why? Because among other self-recriminations about his career, the rabbi believed that he did not sufficiently devote himself to the life-long study of the Bavli and to its medieval commentaries. And so he felt himself to be a sham—this despite the honor and respect he had earned from his congregants. Bavli study was the ideal still of the quintessential rabbi even in the twentieth century. The skills it required and instilled continued to define the *ideal* profile of "a rabbi" in the now-deceased rabbi's mind. Even as his congregants had valued him for many other worthy traits, or board members sometimes criticized him for his inadequacies or lapses as a spiritual leader and pastor, only he, the rabbi, knew that he had not truly lived up to the ideal of the Talmud scholar.[33]

---

32. Rubenstein's "Rabbi Dies."

33. I cannot end this chapter without qualifying it in the following sense. I do not intend to convey that Mishnah-*paideia* in its three modes spanning about four hundred years was the sole building block of early rabbinic group or professional identity in late antiquity, either in the Land of Israel or Babylonia. I do assert that Mishnah-*paideia* was a major normative force. The early rabbinic "profile" was clearly more than this, if the rabbinic disciple of the sages was to "compete" with other Jewish elites for position, influence or power in Jewish society. For example, I am increasingly convinced that rabbis' professional skills in legal interpretation and arbitration bear comparison with many of the skills expected of Roman jurists in the second century BCE through the second century CE. Moreover, rabbis were seen, or sought to be seen, as holy men too, and needed to be seen to do what other Jewish (or non-Jewish) holy men could do, including healing both physical and emotional ailments and warding off demonic attacks. When rabbis displayed these talents, they were doing so, in their ideological perspective, through the agency gained by Torah learning. But this is a whole other book about early rabbinic group and professional identity, not this one. See Kalmin, "Holy Men"; Cohn, *Memory*, 17–38; and Cohn, "Rabbis as Jurists."

Bibliography

Akenson, Donald H. *Surpassing Wonder: The Invention of the Bible and the Talmuds.* Montreal: McGill-Queens University Press, 1998.
Albeck, Hanokh. *Mavo LeTalmudim (Introduction to the Talmuds).* Tel Aviv: Dvir, 1987.
———. *Shishah Sidre Mishnah.* Jerusalem and Tel Aviv: Mossad Bialik and Dvir, 1951–58.
Alexander, Elizabeth Shanks. *Transmitting Mishnah: The Shaping Influence of Oral Tradition.* Cambridge: Cambridge University Press, 2009.
Alexander, Philip. "Using Rabbinic Literature as a Source for the History of Late-Roman Palestine: Problems and Issues." In *Rabbinic Texts and the History of Late-Roman Palestine,* edited by Martin Goodman and Philip Alexander, 7–24. Proceedings of the British Academy 165. Oxford: The British Academy and Oxford University Press, 2010.
Alon, Gedalyahu. *Jews, Judaism and the Classical World.* Jerusalem: Magnes, 1977.
Avi-Yonah, Michael. *BeYemai Roma UBizantium* (Hebrew). Jerusalem: Mosad Bialik, 1970.
———. *The Jews under Roman and Byzantine Rule: A Political History of Palestine from the Bar Kokhba War to the Arab Conquest.* 1976. Reprint, Jerusalem: Magnes, 1984.
———. "A List of Priestly Courses from Caesarea." *Israel Exploration Journal* 12 (1962) 137–39.
Bar-Ilan, Meir. "Illiteracy as Reflected in the Halakhot concerning the Reading of the Scroll of Esther and the Hallel" (in Hebrew). *Proceedings of the American Academy of Jewish Research* 54 (1987) 1–12.
———. "Illiteracy in the Land of Israel in the First Centuries CE." In *Essays in the Social Scientific Study of Judaism and Jewish Society,* edited by Simcha Fishbane et al., 2:46–61. Hoboken, NJ: Ktav, 1992.
———. "Literacy among the Jews in Antiquity." *Hebrew Studies* 44 (2003) 217–22.
———. "Scribes and Books in the Late Second Commonwealth and Rabbinic Period." In *Compendia Rerum Iudaicarum ad Novum Testamentum,* Section 2, vol. 1, *Mikra,* edited by Martin J. Mulder, 21–38. Assen-Maastricht: Van Gorcum, 1988.
Belayche, Nicole. *Iudaea-Palaestina: The Pagan Cults in Roman Palestine (Second to Fourth Century).* Religion in the Roman Provinces 1. Tübingen: Mohr/Siebeck, 2001.
Blumenthal, David. *Understanding Jewish Mysticism: A Source Reader.* Vol. 1, *The Merkabah Tradition and the Zoharic Tradition.* 2 vols. The Library of Judaic Learning 2. New York: Ktav, 1978.
Boyarin, Daniel. *Border Lines: The Partition of Judaeo-Christianity.* Divinations. Philadelphia: University of Pennsylvania Press, 2004.

Bibliography

———. "The Diadoche of the Rabbis; or Judah the Patriarch at Yavneh." In *Jewish Culture and Society under the Christian Roman Empire*, edited by Richard Kalmin and Seth Schwartz, 285–318. Interdisciplinary Studies in Ancient Culture and Religion 3. Leuven: Peeters, 2003.

———. *A Traveling Homeland: The Babylonian Talmud as Diaspora*. Divinations. Philadelphia: University of Pennsylvania Press, 2015.

Bregman, Marc. "Pseudepigraphy in Rabbinic Literature." In *Papers of the Symposium on Pseudepigraphic Perspectives: The Apocrypha and Pseudepigrapha in Light of the Dead Sea Scrolls, Orion Center for the Study of the Dead Sea Scrolls, Hebrew University of Jerusalem*. Jerusalem: Orion Centre, 1997. http://orion.mscc.huji.ac.il/symposiums/2nd/papers/Bregman97.html.

Brody, Robert. "The Epistle of Sherira Gaon." In *Rabbinic Texts and the History of Late-Roman Palestine*, edited by Martin Goodman and Philip Alexander, 253–64. Proceedings of the British Academy 165. Oxford: The British Academy and Oxford University Press, 2010.

———. *Mishnah and Tosefta Studies*. Jerusalem: Magnes, 2014.

Choi, Jungwha. *Jewish Leadership in Roman Palestine from 70CE to 135CE*. Ancient Judaism and Early Christianity 83. Leiden: Brill, 2013.

Cohen, Shaye J. D. "Epigraphical Rabbis." *Jewish Quarterly Review* 72 (1981) 1–17.

Cohn, Naftali S. *The Memory of the Temple and the Making of the Rabbis*. Divinations. Philadelphia: University of Pennsylvania Press, 2012.

———. "Rabbis as Jurists: On the Representation of Past and Present Legal Institutions in the Mishnah." *Journal of Jewish Studies* 60 (2009) 245–63.

Davies, Philip R. *Scribes and Schools: The Canonization of the Hebrew Scriptures*. Library of Ancient Israel. Louisville: Westminster John Knox, 1998.

Davies, W. D., et al., eds. *The Cambridge History of Judaism*. 4 vols. Cambridge: Cambridge University Press, 1984–2006.

Dolgopolski, Sergey. *What Is Talmud?* New York: Fordham University Press, 2009.

Eisenstadt, David. "Aelia Capitolina: Jerusalem as a Roman Pagan City." In *Jerusalem: Life throughout the Ages in a Holy City*, chapter 5. Ingeborg Rennert Center for Jerusalem Studies of Bar-Ilan University. Ramat-Gan: Bar Ilan University, 1997. http://www.biu.ac.il/JS/rennert/history_5.html.

Eliav, Yaron Z. "The Urban Layout of Aelia Capitolina: A New View from the Perspective of the Temple Mount." In *The Bar Kokhba War Reconsidered: New Perspectives on the Second Jewish Revolt against Rome*, edited by Peter Schäfer, 241–79. Texts and Studies in Ancient Judaism 100. Tübingen: Mohr/Siebeck, 2003.

Elman, Yaakov. *Authority and Tradition: Toseftan Baraitot in Talmudic Babylonia*. New York: Yeshiva University Press, 1994.

———. "Babylonian Baraitot in Tosefta and the 'Dialectology' of Middle Hebrew." *Association for Jewish Studies Review* 16 (1991) 1–29.

———. "Orality and the Redaction of the Babylonian Talmud." *Oral Tradition* 14 (1999) 52–99.

———. "Orality and the Transmission of Tosefta Pisha in Talmudic Literature." In *Introducing Tosefta: Textual, Intratextual and Intertextual Studies*, edited by Harry Fox and Tirzah Meacham, 123–80. New York: Ktav, 1999.

Epstein, Yaakov N., and Ezra Z. Melamed. *Mekhilta de R. Simeon bar Yohai*. Jerusalem: Mekize Nirdamim, 1955.

Bibliography

Eshel, Hanan. "The Bar Kochba Revolt, 132–135 CE." In *The Cambridge History of Judaism*. Vol. 4, *The Late Roman-Rabbinic Period*, edited by Steven T. Katz, 105–27. 4 vols. Cambridge: Cambridge University Press, 2006.

Fox, Harry. "Introducing Tosefta." In *Introducing Tosefta: Textual, Intratextual and Intertextual Studies*, edited by Harry Fox and Tirzah Meacham, 1–30. New York: Ktav, 1999.

Frey, Joerg. "From Text to Community: Methodological Problems Reconstructing Communities behind Texts." In *Jewish and Christian Communal Identities in the Roman World*, edited by Yair Furstenberg, 167–84. Ancient Judaism and Early Christianity 84. Leiden: Brill, 2016.

Friedman, Shamma. "The Primacy of Tosefta to Mishnah in Synoptic Parallels." In *Introducing Tosefta: Textual, Intratextual and Intertextual Studies*, edited by Harry Fox and Tirzah Meacham, 99–121. New York: Ktav, 1999.

——. *Tosefta Atiqta, Pesah Rishon: Synoptic Parallels of Mishna and Tosefta Analysed with a Methodological Introduction*. Ramat Gan: Bar Ilan University Press, 2002.

Fox, Harry, and Tirzah Meacham, eds. *Introducing Tosefta: Textual, Intratextual and Intertextual Studies*. New York: Ktav, 1999

Furstenberg, Yair. "Introduction: Shared Dimensions of Jewish and Christian Communal Identity." In *Jewish and Christian Communal Identities in the Roman World*, edited by Yair Furstenberg, 1–21. Ancient Judaism and Early Christianity 84. Leiden: Brill, 2016.

Gafni, Isaiah M. "How Babylonia Became 'Zion': Shifting Identities in Late Antiquity." In *Jewish Identities in Antiquity: Studies in Memory of Menahem Stern*, edited by Lee I. Levine and Daniel R. Schwartz, 333–48. Texts and Studies in Ancient Judaism 130. Tübingen: Mohr/Siebeck, 2009.

——. *The Jews of Babylonia in the Talmudic Era* (Hebrew). Jerusalem: Zalman Shazar Center for Jewish History, 1990.

Goldberg, Abraham. "The Babylonian Talmud." In *The Literature of the Jewish People in the Period of the Second Temple and the Talmud*. Vol. 3, *The Literature of the Sages: First Part: Oral Tora, Halakha, Mishna, Tosefta, Talmud, External Tractates*, edited by Shmuel Safrai, 323–66. Assen: Van Gorcum, 1987.

——. "The Palestinian Talmud." In *The Literature of the Jewish People in the Period of the Second Temple and the Talmud*. Vol. 3, *The Literature of the Sages, First Part: Oral Tora, Halakha, Mishna, Tosefta, Talmud, External Tractates*, edited by Shmuel Safrai, 303–22. Assen: Van Gorcum, 1987.

Goldenberg, Robert. *The Origins of Judaism: From Canaan to the Rise of Islam*. New York: Cambridge University Press, 2007.

——. "The Destruction of the Jerusalem Temple: Its Meaning and Its Consequences." In *The Cambridge History of Judaism*. Vol. 4, *The Late Roman-Rabbinic Period*, edited by Steven T. Katz, 191–205. 4 vols. Cambridge: Cambridge University Press, 2006.

Goodblatt, David M. *The Monarchic Principle: Studies in Jewish Self-Government in Antiquity*. Texts and Studies in Ancient Judaism 38. Tübingen: Mohr/Siebeck, 1994.

——. *Rabbinic Institutions in Sasanian Babylonia*. Studies in Judaism in Late Antiquity 9. Leiden: Brill, 1975.

Goodman, Martin. *Rome and Jerusalem: The Clash of Ancient Civilizations*. New York: Knopf, 2007.

———. "The Roman State and Jewish Diaspora Communities in the Antonine Age." In *Jewish and Christian Communal Identities in the Roman World*, edited by Yair Furstenberg, 75–86. Ancient Judaism and Early Christianity 94. Leiden: Brill, 2016.

———. "The Roman State and the Jewish Patriarch." In *The Galilee in Late Antiquity*, edited by Lee I. Levine, 127–39. New York: Jewish Theological Seminary, 1992.

———. *State and Society in Roman Galilee, AD 132-212*. Totowa, NJ: Rowman & Allanheld, 1983.

———. "Texts, Scribes and Power in Roman Judea." In *Literacy and Power in the Ancient World*, edited by Alan K. Bowman and Greg Woolf, 99–108. Cambridge: Cambridge University Press, 1994.

———. "Trajan and the Origins of the Bar Kokhba War." In *The Bar Kokhba War Reconsidered: New Perspectives on the Second Jewish Revolt against Rome*, edited by Peter Schäfer, 23–30. Texts and Studies in Ancient Judaism 100. Tübingen: Mohr/Siebeck, 2003.

Goodman, Martin, and Philip Alexander, eds. *Rabbinic Texts and the History of Late-Roman Palestine*. Proceedings of the British Academy 165. Oxford: The British Academy and Oxford University Press, 2010.

Gray, Alyssa M. *A Talmud in Exile: The Influence of Yerushalmi Avodah Zarah on the Formation of Bavli Avodah Zarah*. Brown Judaic Studies 342. Providence: Program in Judaic Studies, Brown University, 2005.

Green, William Scott. "What's in a Name? The Problematic of Rabbinic Biography." In *Approaches to Ancient Judaism: Theory and Practice*, edited by William Scott Green, 1:77–96. 5 vols. Brown Judaic Studies 1. Missoula, MT: Scholars, 1978.

Greenbaum, Andrea. "Talmudic Rhetoric: Explorations for Writing, Reading, and Teaching." In *Judaic Perspectives in Rhetoric and Composition Studies*, edited by Andrea Greenbaum and Deborah Holdstein, 151–69. Research and Teaching in Rhetoric and Composition. Cresskill, NJ: Hampton, 2009.

Gruen, Erich S. *The Construct of Identity in Hellenistic Judaism: Essays on Early Jewish Literature and History*. Deuterocanonical and Cognate Literature Studies 29. Berlin: de Gruyter, 2016.

Halivni, David Weiss. *The Formation of the Babylonian Talmud*. Translated, introduced and annotated by Jeffrey L. Rubenstein. Oxford: Oxford University Press, 2013.

———. *Midrash, Mishnah and Gemara: The Jewish Predilection for Justified Law*. Cambridge: Harvard University Press, 1986.

Harland, Philip A. *Associations, Synagogues and Congregations: Claiming a Place in Ancient Mediterranean Society*. Minneapolis: Fortress, 2003.

———. *Dynamics of Identity in the World of the Early Christians: Associations, Judeans and Cultural Identities*. New York: T. & T. Clark, 2009.

Harris, Jay M. "Midrash Halachah." In *The Cambridge History of Judaism*. Vol. 4, *The Late Roman-Rabbinic Period*, edited by Steven T. Katz, 136–68. 4 vols. Cambridge: Cambridge University Press, 2006.

Hauptman, Judith. "Does the Tosefta Precede the Mishnah? Halakhah, Aggada, and Narrative Coherence." *Judaism* 50 (2001) 224–40.

———. *Rereading the Mishnah: A New Approach to Ancient Jewish Texts*. Texts and Studies in Ancient Judaism 109. Tübingen: Mohr/Siebeck, 2005.

———. "The Tosefta as a Commentary on an Early Mishnah." *Jewish Studies, Internet Journal* 4 (2005) 109–132. https://jewish-faculty.biu.ac.il/files/jewish-faculty/shared/JSIJ4/hauptman.pdf/.

Bibliography

Hayes, Christine Elizabeth. *Between the Babylonian and Palestinian Talmuds: Accounting for the Halakhic Difference in Selected Sugyot from Tractate Avodah Zarah*. New York: Oxford University Press, 1997.

Herman, Geoffrey. "The Talmud in its Babylonian Context: Rava and Bar-Sheshakh: Mani and Mihrshah." In *Between Babylonia and the Land of Israel: Studies in Honour of Isaiah M. Gafni* (in Hebrew), edited by Geoffrey Herman et al., 65–78. Jerusalem: Zalman Shazar Center for Jewish History, 2016.

Herr, Moshe David. "The Identity of the Jewish People before and after the Destruction of the Second Temple: Continuity or Change?" In *Jewish Identities in Antiquity: Studies in Memory of Menahem Stern*, edited by Lee I. Levine and Daniel R. Schwartz, 211–36. Texts and Studies in Ancient Judaism 130. Tübingen: Mohr/Siebeck, 2009.

———. "A Zoroastrian-Sasanian and a Babylonian Talmudic 'Renaissance' at the Beginning of the Third Century: Could this be a Mere Coincidence" (in Hebrew). In *Between Babylonia and the Land of Israel: Studies in Honour of Isaiah M. Gafni* (in Hebrew), edited by Geoffrey Herman et al., 51–64. Jerusalem: Zalman Shazar Center for Jewish History, 2016.

Hezser, Catherine. *Jewish Literacy in Roman Palestine*. Texts and Studies in Ancient Judaism 81. Tübingen: Mohr/Siebeck, 2001.

———. "Jewish Literacy and the Use of Writing in Late Roman Palestine." In *Jewish Culture and Society under the Christian Roman Empire*, edited by Richard Kalmin and Seth Schwartz, 149–96. Interdisciplinary Studies in Ancient Culture and Religion 3. Leuven: Peeters, 2003.

———. *Oxford Handbook of Jewish Daily Life in Roman Palestine*. Oxford Handbooks in Classics and Ancient History. Oxford: Oxford University Press, 2010.

———. *The Social Structure of the Rabbinic Movement in Roman Palestine*. Texts and Studies in Ancient Judaism 66. Tübingen: Mohr/Siebeck, 1997.

Hidary, Richard. "Classical Rhetorical Arrangement and Reasoning in the Talmud: The Case of Yerushalmi Berakhot 1:1." *Association of Jewish Studies Review* 34 (2010) 33–36.

Horbury, Richard. "Rabbinic Perceptions of Christianity and the History of Roman Palestine." In *Rabbinic Texts and the History of Late-Roman Palestine*, edited by Martin Goodman and Philip Alexander, 353–76. Proceedings of the British Academy 165. Oxford: The British Academy and Oxford University Press, 2010).

Horowitz, Haim S. *Sifre Numbers and Sifre Zutta*. Corpus Tannaiticum., sectio 3, pars 3, fasc. 1. Schriften der Gesellschaft zur Förderung der Wissenschaft des Judentums. Jerusalem: Wahrmann, 1966.

Houtman, Alberdina. *Mishnah and Tosefta: A Synoptic Comparison of Tractates Berakhot and Shebiit*. 2 vols. Texts and Studies in Ancient Judaism 59. Tübingen: Mohr/Siebeck, 1997.

Isaac, Benjamin. "Roman Religious Policy and the Bar Kokhba War." In *The Bar Kokhba War Reconsidered: New Perspectives on the Second Jewish Revolt against Rome*, edited by Peter Schäfer, 37–54. Texts and Studies in Ancient Judaism 100. Tübingen: Mohr/Siebeck, 2003.

Jacobs, Louis. *The Talmudic Argument: A Study in Talmudic Reasoning and Methodology*. Cambridge: Cambridge University Press, 1984.

Kahana, Menahem I. "The Halakhic Midrashim." In *The Literature of the Jewish People in the Period of the Second Temple and the Talmud*. Vol. 3, *The Literature of the Sages, Second Part: Midrash and Targum; Liturgy, Poetry, Mysticism; Contracts, Inscriptions,*

Ancient Science; and the Languages of Rabbinic Literature, edited by Shmuel Safrai et al., 3–106. Assen: Van Gorcum, 2006.

Kalmin, Richard. "Holy Men, Rabbis, and Demonic Sages in Late Antiquity." In *Jewish Culture and Society under the Christian Roman Empire*, edited by Richard Kalmin and Seth Schwartz, 211–53. Interdisciplinary Studies in Ancient Culture and Religion 3. Leuven: Peeters, 2003.

———. *Jewish Babylonia between Persia and Roman Palestine*. Oxford: Oxford University Press, 2006.

———. "Problems in the Use of the Babylonian Talmud for the History of Late-Roman Palestine: The Example of Astrology." In *Rabbinic Texts and the History of Late-Roman Palestine*, edited by Martin Goodman and Philip Alexander, 165–84. Proceedings of the British Academy 165. Oxford: The British Academy and Oxford University Press, 2010.

Kalmin, Richard, and Seth Schwartz, eds. *Jewish Culture and Society under the Christian Roman Empire*. Interdisciplinary Studies in Ancient Culture and Religion 3. Leuven: Peeters, 2003.

Katz, Steven T., ed. *The Cambridge History of Judaism*. Vol. 4, *The Late Roman-Rabbinic Period*. 4 vols. Cambridge: Cambridge University Press, 2006.

Kraemer, David C. *The Mind of the Talmud: An Intellectual History of the Bavli*. New York: Oxford University Press, 1990.

———. "The Mishnah." In *The Cambridge History of Judaism*. Vol. 4, *The Late Roman-Rabbinic Period*, edited by Steven T. Katz, 299–315. 4 vols. Cambridge: Cambridge University Press, 2006.

Kulp, Joshua. "Organizational Patterns in the Mishnah in Light of their Toseftan Parallels." *Journal of Jewish Studies* 58 (2007) 52–78.

Lapin, Hayim. "Economy and Society." In *Rabbinic Texts and the History of Late-Roman Palestine*, edited by Martin Goodman and Philip Alexander, 389–402. Proceedings of the British Academy 165. Oxford: The British Academy and Oxford University Press, 2010.

———. "Hegemony and Its Discontents: Rabbis as a Late Antique Provincial Population." In *Jewish Culture and Society under the Christian Roman Empire*, edited by Richard Kalmin and Seth Schwartz, 319–48. Interdisciplinary Studies in Ancient Culture and Religion 3. Leuven: Peeters, 2003.

———. "The Origins and Development of the Rabbinic Movement in the Land of Israel." In *The Cambridge History of Judaism*. Vol. 4, *The Late Roman-Rabbinic Period*, edited by Steven T. Katz, 206–29. 4 vols. Cambridge: Cambridge University Press, 2006.

———. *Rabbis as Romans: The Rabbinic Movement in Palestine, 100–400 CE*. Oxford: Oxford University Press, 2012.

Lavee, Moshe. "Rabbinic Literature and the History of Judaism in Late Antiquity: Challenges, Methodologies and New Approaches." In *Rabbinic Texts and the History of Late-Roman Palestine*, edited by Martin Goodman and Philip Alexander, 319–52. Proceedings of the British Academy 165. Oxford: The British Academy and Oxford University Press, 2010.

Leibner, Uzi. "The Settlement Crisis in the Eastern Galilee during the Late Roman and Early Byzantine Periods: Response to Jodi Magness." In *Jewish Identities in Antiquity: Studies in Memory of Menahem Stern*, edited by Lee I. Levine and Daniel R. Schwartz, 314–20. Texts and Studies in Ancient Judaism 130. Tübingen: Mohr/Siebeck, 2009.

Bibliography

———. "Settlement Patterns in the Eastern Galilee: Implications Regarding the Transformation of Rabbinic Culture in Late Antiquity." In *Jewish Identities in Antiquity: Studies in Memory of Menahem Stern*, edited by Lee I. Levine and Daniel R. Schwartz, 269–95. Texts and Studies in Ancient Judaism 130. Tübingen: Mohr/Siebeck, 2009.

Levine, David. "Between Leadership and Marginality: Models for Evaluating the Role of the Rabbis in the Early Centuries CE." In *Jewish Identities in Antiquity: Studies in Memory of Menahem Stern*, edited by Lee I. Levine and Daniel R. Schwartz, 195–210. Texts and Studies in Ancient Judaism 130. Tübingen: Mohr/Siebeck, 2009.

Levine, Lee I. *The Ancient Synagogue: The First Thousand Years*. New Haven: Yale University Press, 2000.

———. "Introduction: Was There a Crisis in Jewish Settlement in the Eastern Galilee of Late Antiquity." In *Jewish Identities in Antiquity: Studies in Memory of Menahem Stern*, edited by Lee I. Levine and Daniel R. Schwartz, 267–68. Texts and Studies in Ancient Judaism 130. Tübingen: Mohr/Siebeck, 2009.

———. "Jewish Identities in Antiquity: An Introductory Essay." In *Jewish Identities in Antiquity: Studies in Memory of Menahem Stern*, edited by Lee I. Levine and Daniel R. Schwartz, 12–40. Texts and Studies in Ancient Judaism 130. Tübingen: Mohr/Siebeck, 2009.

———. "The Jewish Patriarch (Nasi) in Third Century Palestine." In *Aufstieg und Niedergang der römischen Welt*, II.19.2, edited by Hildegard Temporini and Wolfgang Haase, 649–88. Berlin: de Gruyter, 1979.

———. *The Rabbinic Class of Roman Palestine in Late Antiquity*. Jerusalem and New York: Yad Yitzhaq Ben-Zvi, and Jewish Theological Seminary of America, 1989.

———. "The Status of the Patriarchate in the Third and Fourth Centuries: Sources and Methodology." *Journal of Jewish Studies* 47 (1996) 1–32.

Levine, Lee I., and Daniel R. Schwartz, eds. *Jewish Identities in Antiquity: Studies in Memory of Menahem Stern*. Texts and Studies in Ancient Judaism 130. Tübingen: Mohr/Siebeck, 2009.

Lieberman, Saul. *Tosefet Rishonim*. New York: Jewish Theological Seminary of America, 1999.

Lightstone, Jack N. "Challenges and Opportunities in the Social Scientific Study of the Evidence of the Mishnah." In *Exploring Mishnah's World(s): Social Scientific Approaches*, Simcha Fishbane, Calvin Goldscheider and Jack N. Lightstone. London and New York: Palgrave-Macmillan, forthcoming.

———. *The Commerce of the Sacred: Mediation of the Divine among the Jews in the Greco-Roman Diaspora*. 2nd ed. With a foreword by Willi Braun and updated bibliography by Herbert Basser. New York: Columbia University Press, 2006.

———. *Mishnah and Social Formation of the Early Rabbinic Guild: A Socio-Rhetorical Study*. Waterloo, ON: Wilfrid Laurier University Press, 2002.

———. "Names without 'Lives': Why No 'Lives of the Rabbis' in Early Rabbinic Judaism." *Studies in Religion* 19 (1990) 43–57.

———. "Naming Names: The Meaning and Significance of Disputes and the Use of Attributions to Named Authorities in Mishnah." In *To Fix Torah in Their Hearts: Essays in Biblical Interpretation and Jewish Studies in Honor of B. Barry Levy*, edited by Jacqueline S. du Toit et al., 86–117. Cincinnati: Hebrew Union College Press, 2019.

———. *The Rhetoric of the Babylonian Talmud, Its Social Meaning and Context*. Studies in Christianity and Judaism 6. Waterloo, ON: Wilfrid Laurier University Press, 1994.

———. "Roman Diaspora Judaism." In *A Companion to Roman Religion*, edited by Jörg Rüpke, 345–77. Blackwell Companions to the Ancient World 9. Oxford: Blackwell, 2007.

———. "Sociological and Anthropological Approaches to the Study of the Evidence of the Mishnah: A Call to Scholarly Action and a Programmatic Introduction." *Studies in Judaism, Humanities and the Social Sciences*, forthcoming.

———. "Study as a Socially Formative Activity: The Case of Mishnah Study in the Early Rabbinic Group." In *Exploring Mishnah's World(s): Social Scientific Approaches*, Simcha Fishbane, Calvin Goldscheider and Jack N. Lightstone. London and New York: Palgrave-Macmillan, forthcoming.

———. "Studying Mishnah 'Talmudic-ly': What the Basic Literary-Rhetorical Features of the Talmuds' Legal Compositions and Composite 'essays' Tell Us about Mishnah Study as an Identity-Informing Activity within Rabbinic Groups at the End of Late Antiquity." In *Exploring Mishnah's World(s): Social Scientific Approaches*, Simcha Fishbane, Calvin Goldscheider and Jack N. Lightstone. London and New York: Palgrave-Macmillan, forthcoming.

———. "Textual Study and Social Formation: The Case of Mishnah." *Studies in Judaism, Humanities and the Social Sciences*. 1/1 (2017) 23–44.

———. "Textual Study and Social Formation, Part II: Does the Evidence of Tosefta Confirm that of Mishnah?" *Studies in Judaism, Humanities and the Social Sciences*, forthcoming.

———. "When Speech Is No Speech: The Problem of Early Rabbinic Rhetoric as Discourse." *Semeia* 34 (1985) 53–58.

———. "When Tosefta Was Read in Service of Mishnah-Study: What Pervasive Literary-Rhetorical Traits of Toseftan Materials Divulge about the Evolution of Early Rabbinic Group Identity on the Heels of Mishnah's Promulgation." In *Exploring Mishnah's World(s): Social Scientific Approaches*, Simcha Fishbane, Calvin Goldscheider and Jack N. Lightstone. London and New York: Palgrave-Macmillan, forthcoming.

Linder, Amnon. *The Jews in Imperial Roman Legislation*. Detroit: Wayne State University Press, 1995.

———. "The Legal Status of the Jews in the Roman Empire." In *The Cambridge History of Judaism*. Vol. 4. *The Late Roman-Rabbinic Period*, edited by Steven Katz, 128–73. 4 vols. Cambridge: Cambridge University Press, 2006.

Mack, Burton L., and Vernon K. Robbins. *Patterns of Persuasion in the Gospels*. Foundations & Facets: Literary Facets. 1989. Reprint, Eugene, OR: Wipf & Stock, 2008.

Mandel, Paul. "The Tosefta." In *The Cambridge History of Judaism*, Vol. 4, *The Late Roman-Rabbinic Period*, edited by Steven T. Katz, 316–35. 4 vols. Cambridge: Cambridge University Press, 2006.

Meacham, Tirzah. "Tosefta as Template: Yerushalmi Niddah." In *Introducing Tosefta: Textual, Intratextual and Intertextual Studies*, edited by Harry Fox and Tirzah Meacham, 181–220. New York: Ktav, 1999.

Milikowsky, Chaim. "The *Status Quaestionis* of Research in Rabbinic Literature." In *Rabbinic Texts and the History of Late-Roman Palestine*, edited by Martin Goodman and Philip Alexander, 67–78. Proceedings of the British Academy 165. Oxford: The British Academy and Oxford University Press, 2010.

Bibliography

Millar, Fergus. "The Palestinian Context of Rabbinic Literature." In *Rabbinic Texts and the History of Late-Roman Palestine*, edited by Martin Goodman and Philip Alexander, 25–50. Proceedings of the British Academy 165. Oxford: The British Academy and Oxford University Press, 2010.

Miller, Stuart S. *Sages and Commoners in Late Antique 'Erez Israel': A Philological Inquiry into Local Traditions in Talmud Yerushalmi.* Texts and Studies in Ancient Judaism 111. Tübingen: Mohr/Siebeck, 2006.

———. "Stepped Pools, Stone Vessels, and other Identity Markers of "Complex Common Judaism." *Journal for the Study of Judaism* 41 (2010) 214–43.

Mor, Menahem. "The Geographical Scope of the Bar Kokhba Revolt." In *The Bar Kokhba War Reconsidered: New Perspectives on the Second Jewish Revolt against Rome*, edited by Peter Schäfer, 107–32. Texts and Studies in Ancient Judaism 100. Tübingen: Mohr/Siebeck, 2003.

Moore, George Foote. *Judaism in the First Centuries of the Christian Era.* 3 vols. Cambridge: Harvard University Press, 1954.

Moscovitz, Leib. *Talmudic Reasoning.* Texts and Studies in Ancient Judaism 89. Tübingen: Mohr/Siebeck, 2002.

Neusner, Jacob. *Are the Talmuds Interchangeable? Christine Hayes's Blunder.* South Florida Studies in the History of Judaism 122. Atlanta: Scholars, 1995.

———. *The Bavli: An Introduction.* South Florida Studies in the History of Judaism 42. Atlanta: Scholars, 1992.

———. *The Bavli That Might Have Been: Tosefta's Theory of Mishnah Commentary Compared with the Bavli's.* South Florida Studies in the History of Judaism 18. Atlanta: Scholars, 1991.

———. *Bavli's Massive Miscellanies: The Problem of Agglutinative Discourse in the Talmud of Babylonia.* South Florida Studies in the History of Judaism 43. Atlanta: Scholars, 1992.

———. *The Bavli's One Voice: Types and Forms of Analytical Discourse and Their Fixed Order of Appearance.* South Florida Studies in the History of Judaism 24. Atlanta: Scholars, 1991.

———. "Describing Tosefta: A Systematic Account." In *Introducing Tosefta: Textual, Intratextual and Intertextual Studies*, edited by Harry Fox and Tirzah Meacham, 39–72. New York: Ktav, 1999.

———. *First Steps in the Talmud: A Guide to the Confused.* Studies in Judaism. Lanham, MD: University Press of America, 2011.

———. *A History of the Jews in Babylonia.* 5 vols. Studia Post-biblica 9, 11, 12, 14, 15. Leiden: Brill, 1965–1970.

———. *A History of the Mishnaic Law of Purities, Part 21.* Studies in Judaism in Late Antiquity, 6/21. Leiden: Brill, 1977.

———. *How the Bavli Is Constructed: Identifying the Forests Comprised by the Talmud's Trees.* Studies in Judaism. Lanham, MD: Rowman & Littlefield, 2009.

———. *Introduction to Rabbinic Literature.* New Haven: Yale University Press, 1999.

———. *Judaism in Society: The Evidence of the Yerushalmi; Toward the Natural History of a Religion.* Chicago: University of Chicago Press, 1983.

———. *Judaism, the Classical Statement: The Evidence of the Bavli.* Chicago Studies in the History of Judaism. Reprint, Eugene, OR: Wipf & Stock, 2003.

———. *Language as Taxonomy: The Rules for Using Hebrew and Aramaic in the Babylonian Talmud.* South Florida Studies in the History of Judaism 12. Atlanta: Scholars, 1990.

———. *Mishnah: Introduction and Reader*. 1992. Reprint, Eugene, OR: Wipf & Stock, 2004.

———. *The Place of the Tosefta in the Halakhah of Formative Judaism: What Alberdina Houtman Didn't Notice*. South Florida Studies in the History of Judaism 156. Atlanta: Scholars, 1998.

———. *Rabbinic Traditions about the Pharisees before 70*. Vol. 3, *Conclusions*. 1971. Reprint, Dove Studies in Bible, Language, and History. Eugene, OR: Wipf & Stock, 2003.

———. *The Reader's Guide to the Talmud*. Brill Reference Library of Ancient Judaism 5. Leiden: Brill, 2001.

———. *Reading and Believing: Ancient Judaism and Contemporary Gullibility*. Brown Judaic Studies 113. Atlanta: Scholars, 1986.

———. *The Rules of Composition of the Talmud of Babylonia*. South Florida Studies in the History of Judaism 13. Atlanta: Scholars, 1991.

———. *Tosefta: An Introduction*. South Florida Studies in the History of Judaism 47. Atlanta: Scholars, 1992.

———. *The Two Talmuds Compared*. South Florida Studies in the History of Judaism 53. Atlanta: Scholars, 1996.

———. *The Yerushalmi: The Talmud of the Land of Israel: An Introduction*. Library of Classical Judaism. Northvale, NJ: Aronson, 1993.

Neusner, Jacob, and William Scott Green. *Writing with Scripture: The Authority and Uses of the Hebrew Bible in the Torah of Formative Judaism*. 1989. Reprint, Eugene, OR: Wipf & Stock, 2003.

Newman, Hillel J. "The Normativity of Rabbinic Judaism: Obstacles on the Path to a New Consensus." In *Jewish Identities in Antiquity: Studies in Memory of Menahem Stern*, edited by Lee I. Levine and Daniel R. Schwartz, 165–71. Texts and Studies in Ancient Judaism 130. Tübingen: Mohr/Siebeck, 2009.

Oppenheimer, Aaron. *Between Rome and Babylon*. Texts and Studies in Ancient Judaism 108. Tübingen: Mohr/Siebeck, 2005.

———. *By the Rivers of Babylon: Perspectives on the History of Talmudic Babylonia* (Hebrew). Tel Aviv and Jerusalem: Tel Aviv University and Zalman Shazar Center for Jewish History, 2017.

———. "Politics and Administration." In *Rabbinic Texts and the History of Late-Roman Palestine*, edited by Martin Goodman and Philip Alexander, 377–88. Proceedings of the British Academy 165. Oxford: The British Academy and Oxford University Press, 2010.

Rajak, Tessa. "Synagogue and Community in the Graeco-Roman Diaspora." In *Jews in the Hellenistic and Roman Cities*, edited by John R. Bartlett, 22–38. London: Routledge, 2002.

———. "The Synagogue within the Greco-Roman City." In *Jews, Christians, and Polytheists in the Ancient Synagogue: Cultural Interactions during the Greco-Roman Period*, edited by Steven Fine, 161–73. Baltimore Studies in the History of Judaism. London: Routledge, 1999.

Reichman, Ronen. *Mishna und Sifra: Ein literarkritischer Vergleich paralleler Überlieferungen*. Texts and Studies in Ancient Judaism 68. Tübingen: Mohr/Siebeck, 1998.

———. "The Tosefta and Its Value for Historical Research: Questioning the Historical Reliability of Case Stories." In *Rabbinic Texts and the History of Late-Roman Palestine*,

Bibliography

edited by Martin Goodman and Philip Alexander, 117–28. Proceedings of the British Academy 165. Oxford: The British Academy and Oxford University Press, 2010.

Rubenstein, Jeffrey L. *The Culture of the Babylonian Talmud*. Baltimore: Johns Hopkins University Press, 2003.

———. "Social and Institutional Settings of Rabbinic Literature." In *The Cambridge Companion to the Talmud and Rabbinic Literature*, edited by Charlotte Elisheva Fonrobert and Martin S. Jaffee, 58–74. Cambridge Companions to Religion. Cambridge: Cambridge University Press, 2007.

Rubenstein, Richard L. "A Rabbi Dies" (1971). Originally unpublished until cited in full in Jacob Neusner. *American Judaism: Adventure in Modernity*, 48–58. New York: Ktav, 1978.

Safrai, Zeev. *The Economy of Roman Palestine*. London: Routledge, 1994.

Safrai, Zeev, and Chana Safrai. "To What Extent Did the Rabbis Determine Public Norms?" In *Jewish Identities in Antiquity: Studies in Memory of Menahem Stern*, edited by Lee I. Levine and Daniel R. Schwartz, 172–94. Texts and Studies in Ancient Judaism 130. Tübingen: Mohr/Siebeck, 2009.

Saldarini, Anthony J. *The Fathers according to Rabbi Nathan (Avot de Rabbi Nathan) Version B: Translation and Commentary*. Studies in Judaism in Late Antiquity 11. Leiden: Brill, 1975.

Samely, Alexander. *Forms of Rabbinic Literature and Thought: An Introduction*. Oxford: Oxford University Press, 2007.

Schäfer, Peter. "Bar Kokhba and the Rabbis." In *The Bar Kokhba War Reconsidered: New Perspectives on the Second Jewish Revolt against Rome*, edited by Peter Schäfer, 1–22. Texts and Studies in Ancient Judaism 100. Tübingen: Mohr/Siebeck, 2003.

———, ed. *The Bar Kokhba War Reconsidered: New Perspectives on the Second Jewish Revolt against Rome*. Texts and Studies in Ancient Judaism 100. Tübingen: Mohr/Siebeck, 2003.

———. "Research into Rabbinic Literature: An Attempt to Define the *Status Quaestionis*." In *Rabbinic Texts and the History of Late-Roman Palestine*, edited by Martin Goodman and Philip Alexander, 51–66. Proceedings of the British Academy 165. Oxford: The British Academy and Oxford University Press, 2010.

Schäfer, Peter, and Chaim Milikowsky. "Current Views on the Editing of the Rabbinic Texts of Late Antiquity: Reflections on a Debate after Twenty Years." In *Rabbinic Texts and the History of Late-Roman Palestine*, edited by Martin Goodman and Philip Alexander, 79–89. Proceedings of the British Academy 165. Oxford: The British Academy and Oxford University Press, 2010.

Scholem, Gershom. *Jewish Gnosticism, Merkavah Mysticism and the Talmudic Tradition*. New York: Jewish Theological Seminary, 2015.

Schwartz, Daniel R., and Zeev Weiss. *Was 70 CE a Watershed in Jewish History?* Ancient Judaism and Early Christianity 78. Leiden: Brill, 2012.

Schwartz, Seth. *The Ancient Jews: From Alexander to Muhammad*. Key Themes in Ancient History. Cambridge: Cambridge University Press, 2014.

———. *Imperialism and Jewish Society, 200 B.C.E. to 640 C.E.* Jews, Christians, and Muslims from the Ancient to the Modern World Princeton: Princeton University Press, 2001.

———. "The Political Geography of Rabbinic Texts." In *The Cambridge Companion to the Talmud and Rabbinic Literature*, edited by Charlotte Elisheva Fonrobert and

Martin S. Jaffee, 75–97. Cambridge Companions to Religion. New York: Cambridge University Press, 2007.

———. "'Rabbinic Culture' and Roman Culture." In *Rabbinic Texts and the History of Late-Roman Palestine*, edited by Martin Goodman and Philip Alexander, 283–300. Proceedings of the British Academy 165. Oxford: The British Academy and Oxford University Press, 2010.

———. *Were the Jews a Mediterranean Society? Reciprocity and Solidarity in Ancient Judaism*. Princeton: Princeton University Press, 2010.

Simon-Shoshan, Moshe. *Stories of the Law: Narrative Discourse and the Construction of Authority in the Mishnah*. Oxford: Oxford University Press, 2012.

Stemberger, Gunter, "Halakhic Midrashim as Historical Sources." In *Rabbinic Texts and the History of Late-Roman Palestine*, edited by Martin Goodman and Philip Alexander, 129–42. Proceedings of the British Academy 165. Oxford: The British Academy and Oxford University Press, 2010.

———. Review of Ronen Reichman, *Mishna und Sifra* in *The Annual of Rabbinic Judaism* 3 (2000) 207–10.

Stern, Sacha. "The Talmud Yerushalmi." In *Rabbinic Texts and the History of Late-Roman Palestine*, edited by Martin Goodman and Philip Alexander, 143–64. Proceedings of the British Academy 165. Oxford: The British Academy and Oxford University Press, 2010.

Strack, Herman L. et al. *Introduction to the Talmud and Midrash*. 2nd ed. Minneapolis: Fortress, 1996.

Tennenblat, M. A. *Peraqim Hadashim leToldot Eretz-Yisrael ve-Bavel beTequfat HaTalmud*. Tel-Aviv: Dvir, 1966.

Tropper, Amram. "The State of Mishnah Studies." In *Rabbinic Texts and the History of Late-Roman Palestine*, edited by Martin Goodman and Philip Alexander, 91–116. Proceedings of the British Academy 165. Oxford: The British Academy and Oxford University Press, 2010.

Urbach, Ephraim E. *The Sages: Their Concepts and Beliefs*. Jerusalem: Magnes, 1977.

Wilson, Stephen. *Related Strangers: Jews and Christians, 70 to 170 CE*. Minneapolis: Fortress, 1995.

Wise, Michael Owen. "Language and Literacy in Roman Judaea: A Study of the Bar Kokhba Documents." PhD diss., University of Minnesota, 2012.

Zaiman, Joel. "The Traditional Study of the Mishnah." In *The Modern Study of the Mishnah*, edited by Jacob Neusner, 1–10. Studia Post-biblica 23. Leiden: Brill, 1973.

Zelcer, Hershey. *A Guide to the Jerusalem Talmud*. Boca Raton, FL: Universal Publishers, 2002.

Zuckermandel, M. S., ed. *Tosefta: Based in the Erfurt and Vienna Codices*. Jerusalem: Wahrmann, 1970.

"Jack Lightstone is at the top of his form as he guides the nonspecialized reader to a grasp of rabbinic literature in its multiple guises. Lightstone utilizes his considerable academic and pedagogical talent to create a lucid and cogent introduction to the complex and often daunting literary creations of the rabbis of late antiquity. In doing so, he contributes to a better, more nuanced comprehension of a crucial era in the history of Judaism."

—**Ira Robinson**
Concordia Institute for Canadian Jewish Studies, Concordia University, Montréal

"Jack Lightstone has written an eminently readable—and successful—teaching book for non-specialists introducing how to read early rabbinic literature: Mishnah, Tosefta, the halakic midrashim, and the two Talmuds. His thesis is that the key to understanding this literature, in each of its genres, is to master the highly formulaic rhetorical patterns that serve as signposts and structure the entire discourse. Specialists, too, will benefit from this book and can profitably use it in their teaching."

—**Richard S. Sarason**
Pines School of Graduate Studies, Hebrew Union College-Jewish Institute of Religion, Cincinnati

"Jack Lightstone writes now as the experienced teacher to a diverse audience just beginning to be exposed to the early literary legal classics of rabbinic Judaism, the Mishnah, Tosefta, legal midrash, the Jerusalem Talmud, and the Babylonian Talmud. . . . With skill and sometimes even humor, *In the Seat of Moses* carefully, systematically, and engagingly breaks down the barriers by building the reader's basic knowledge and familiarity with this literature's most pervasive, core literary and rhetorical forms. In so doing, the book opens up a world of evidence from the early rabbis to the non-expert interested in early Judaism, early Christianity, the foundations of rabbinic Judaism, Greco-Roman culture and literature, or ancient law."

—**Simcha Fishbane**
Graduate School of Jewish Studies, Touro College

"I wish this book had been available when I was a graduate student, but I'm grateful to have it even now. With the skill of a master teacher, Lightstone guides his readers into the arcane world of rabbinic legal discourse—from the Mishnah to the Babylonian Talmud—by identifying the literary patterns and rhetorical structures that undergird it. An invaluable *vade mecum*, for novice students and seasoned non-specialists alike."

—**Terence L. Donaldson**
Wycliffe College, University of Toronto

"Drawing upon his own scholarship and years of teaching rabbinic literature to students, laypeople, and scholars in fields related to early rabbinic Judaism, such as early Christianity, emergent Islam, and Greco-Roman culture, Lightstone lays out with pedagogic skill the stylistic conventions of rabbinic literature, document by document. These analyses also enable readers to grasp the competencies and traits of mind nurtured by these works thereby also disclosing key features of the relational and institutional structures of the rabbis between the second and seventh centuries that fostered those developments."

—**Joel Gereboff**
Arizona State University

www.ingramcontent.com/pod-product-compliance
Lightning Source LLC
Chambersburg PA
CBHW021231300426
44111CB00007B/499